# The Structure of Sociological Theory

Advising Editor in Sociology

**CHARLES M. BONJEAN**
*The University of Texas at Austin*

# The Structure of Sociological Theory

**Jonathan H. Turner**
*University of California, Riverside*

Fourth Edition    1986

The Dorsey Press
Chicago, Illinois 60604

ISBN 0-256-03408-7

Library of Congress Catalog Card No. 85-72471

*Printed in the United States of America*

1 2 3 4 5 6 7 8 9 0 MR 3 2 1 0 9 8 7 6

*To my wife: Sandy, Alexandra, Alex,*
*A. R. or whatever you are calling*
*yourself these days*

# Preface

In 1971, I began the first edition of *The Structure of Sociological Theory*. In these 15 years, theoretical sociology has changed. The most important of these changes is the gradual breakdown of intellectual barriers among theoretical perspectives, or "paradigms" as some like to label them. In 1971, it made sense to have separate sections on functional, conflict, exchange, and interactionist theory. It still makes sense, but less so. And I hope that, in the future, these barriers will be a thing of the past. For the present, however, I have retained these four schools of thought and added one more; structural theorizing. But there are some major changes in the way that I treated these five perspectives. Let me enumerate.

First, I have added more European theory. Certainly one big change in the 1980s is the prominence of such German theorists as Jurgen Habermas and Niklas Luhmann and the rise of the British theorist Anthony Giddens. Theory today is truly international, and Americans no longer dominate as they once did when functional theorizing reigned supreme.

Second, I have sought to emphasize the convergence of various theorists and perspectives. There has been considerable borrowing, which, 15 years ago, scholars were less inclined to do. Today, theory is more eclectic, and this is all to the good.

Third, I have completely rewritten every chapter. I had no intention of doing so, but I got involved. In a real sense, this is a new book, but I have retained the old title. Moreover, I have tried to write in a more informal style, which, I hope, is appreciated.

Fourth, I have provided in Chapter 1 a much more extensive review of theory building in sociology. I am no longer content to crudely group theorists into perspectives without exploring the underlying philosophical positions of various theoretical strategies.

Fifth, my own biases are more evident than in previous editions, although I still try to be balanced and fair. Let me summarize my position simply: sociology can be a "natural science"; it can develop abstract theoretical principles and models about generic properties of the universe. Many disagree with me, and I try very hard to let these critics of my position have their say in the chapters to follow. At the same time, I am out to demonstrate the viability of my position.

Certain features of the book remain the same, however. The most important is that analysis is *detailed*. I do not water down the theories. I have sought to simplify and clarify, but not to trivialize. In my view, too many theory books oversimplify to the point of making theories vacuous. In contrast, this is a book about *the structure* of sociological theory, not the surface contours. Moreover, even though I offer my opinion, I try to analyze theoretical perspectives in their own terms. I have not distorted for my own rhetorical purposes; indeed, I have gone out of my way to present theories in their best light.

Finally, I should indicate that this is a much more complete book than its predecessors. I have worked very hard to make it both comprehensive and detailed. Indeed, I spent more time on this project than I ever envisioned. I hope that readers find my effort worthwhile.

**Jonathan H. Turner**

## ACKNOWLEDGMENTS

I wish to thank the Academic Senate of the University of California, Riverside, for providing support for this and all my previous research. Also, I must thank my typist of 15 years, Clara Dean, who corrects my spelling, catches all my referencing mistakes, and reads my horrible handwriting.

J.H.T.

# Contents

**Part Four
Interactionist Theory**

# List of Figures

# List of Tables

| | | |
|---|---|---|
| 2-1 | Requisites of System Levels | 51 |
| 6-1 | Marx's Key Propositions | 136 |
| 6-2 | Simmel's Propositions on Conflict Intensity | 141 |
| 6-3 | Simmel's Propositions on the Functions of Conflict for the Respective Parties | 142 |
| 6-4 | Simmel's Propositions on the Functions of Conflict for the Systemic Whole | 143 |
| 6-5 | Weber's Propositions on Inequality and Conflict | 148 |
| 7-1 | Dahrendorf's Abstract Propositions | 159 |
| 8-1 | Coser's Propositions on the Causes of Conflict | 169 |
| 8-2 | Coser's Propositions on the Violence of Conflict | 171 |
| 8-3 | Coser's Propositions on the Duration of Conflict | 172 |
| 8-4 | Coser's Propositions on the Functions of Conflict for the Respective Parties | 174 |
| 8-5 | Coser's Propositions on the Functions of Conflict for the Social Whole | 175 |
| 10-1 | Georg Simmel's Exchange Principles | 232 |
| 11-1 | Homans's Exchange Principles | 246 |
| 12-1 | Blau's Implicit Exchange Principles | 264 |
| 12-2 | Blau's Conditions for the Differentiation of Power in Social Exchange | 268 |
| 12-3 | Blau's Principles of Exchange Conflict | 273 |
| 13-1 | The Operant Propositions and Initial Corollaries | 295 |
| 13-2 | The Initial Theorems | 296 |
| 15-1 | Convergence and Divergence in the Chicago and Iowa Schools of Symbolic Interactionism | 350 |
| 17-1 | Others and Role Merger in One Situation | 381 |
| 17-2 | Others, Person, and Role in Multiple Settings | 382 |
| 17-3 | Individual Efforts at Role Merger | 383 |
| 20-1 | A Revised List of Blau's "Axioms" | 431 |
| 20-2 | A Revised List of Blau's Basic Theorems | 431 |
| 21-1 | Key Propositions on the Conditions Producing Talk and Conversation | 443 |
| 21-2 | Key Propositions on the Conditions Producing Ritual Activity | 445 |
| 21-3 | Key Propositions on Deference and Demeanor | 447 |
| 21-4 | Key Propositions on Class Cultures | 448 |
| 21-5 | Key Propositions on Sex Stratification | 449 |
| 21-6 | Key Propositions on Age Stratification | 450 |
| 21-7 | Key Propositions on Organizations | 452 |
| 21-8 | Key Propositions on the State, Economy, and Ideology | 453 |
| 22-1 | The Typology of Institutions | 465 |

# CHAPTER 1

# The Nature of Sociological Theorizing

## IS A SCIENCE OF SOCIETY POSSIBLE?

The goal of sociology is to gain knowledge about the nature of human organization. With such knowledge, it is possible to interpret social events in ways that allow for an understanding of how and why these events occur. Yet, I must caution at the very outset that there is widespread disagreement in sociology about the proper way to develop knowledge about the human universe. More than any other social science, sociologists disagree on such fundamental issues as what kind of knowledge is possible, what procedures should be followed in developing this knowledge, what it is we should try to develop knowledge about, and what uses should be made of the knowledge that we generate.

In the last few hundred years, a set of procedures called *science* has gained ascendance in many disciplines as the best way to accumulate knowledge of all phenomena in the universe. But such has not always been the case, and even today, when science pervades every aspect of our lives and our ways of looking at the world, there is still disagreement in sociology over just *what kind* of science, if any, sociology can be. The titular founder of sociology, Auguste Comte, recognized in the early 1800s that the status of a "science of society" was precarious.[1] To defend sociology from its many critics and to legitimate his claims that the emergence of

---

[1]Auguste Comte, *System of Positive Philosophy*, vol. 1 (Paris: Bachelier, 1830). Subsequent portions were published between 1831–42. For a more detailed analysis of Comte's thought, see my and Leonard Beeghley's, *The Emergence of Sociological Theory* (Homewood, Ill.: Dorsey Press, 1981), Chapter 2.

**FIGURE 1–1**   Different Ways of Creating Knowledge

|  | | Is knowledge to be empirical? | |
|---|---|---|---|
| | | Yes | No |
| Is knowledge to be evaluative? | Yes | *Ideologies;* or beliefs that state the way the world should be | *Religions;* or beliefs that state the dictates of supernatural forces |
| | No | *Science;* or the belief that all knowledge is to reflect the actual operation of the empirical world | *Logics;* or the various systems of reasoning that employ rules of calculation |

sociology as a science was now possible, he posited a "law of the three stages." In the religious stage, interpretations of events are initially provided by religious beliefs or by reference to the activities of sacred and supernatural forces. Out of religion comes a metaphysical stage in which logic, mathematics, and other formal systems of reason came to dominate how events were interpreted. And out of these gains in formal reasoning in the metaphysical stage emerges the possibility for "positivism" or a scientific stage, where formal statements are critically examined against carefully collected facts. Comte argued that the accumulation of knowledge about each domain of the universe—the physical, chemical, biological, and finally, the social—passed successively through these three stages. Patterns of human organization were to be the last such domain to move into the positive stage; and in 1830, he trumpeted the call for the use of science to develop knowledge about human affairs.

I mention Comte's advocacy because the issues that he raised still haunt sociology today. More than 150 years after Comte pronounced sociology as in the positive phase, he is denounced in many quarters as naive and just plain wrong. True, his point of view has many supporters, including me, but his faith that there could be a "natural science of society"[2] is hardly shared by all.

One way to gain some perspective on the question of sociology as a science is to examine Figure 1-1, where I have summarized the kinds of belief systems that have been used to interpret events and to generate

---

[2]I have taken this phrase from A. R. Radcliffe-Brown's, *A Natural Science of Society* (Glencoe, Ill.: Free Press, 1948).

knowledge about human affairs.[3] The typology asks two basic questions: (1) is the search for knowledge to be evaluative or neutral? and (2) is the knowledge developed to pertain to actual empirical events and processes or is it to be about nonempirical realities? In other words, should knowledge tell us what *should be* or *what is?* and should it make reference to the observable world or to other, less observable realms? If knowledge is to tell us what should exist (and by implication, what should not occur) in the empirical world, then it is ideological knowledge. If it informs us about what should be but does not pertain to observable events, then the knowledge is religious or about forces and beings in another realm of existence. If knowledge is neither empirical nor evaluative, then it is a formal system of logic, such as mathematics. And if it is about empirical events and nonevaluative, then it is science.

I concede that this typology is crude, but it makes the essential point: There are different ways to look at, interpret, and develop knowledge about the world. Science is only one way. It is based upon the presumption that knowledge can be value free, that it can explain the actual workings of the empirical world, and that it can be revised on the basis of careful observations of empirical events. These characteristics distinguish science from other beliefs about how we should generate understanding and insight.[4] However, even this portrayal of science is questioned by many who would regard it as rather idealized. For these critics, values always figure into what we study. The empirical world is not "just there"; rather it is filtered through concepts and presuppositions. And rarely are facts dispassionately collected to test theories.

And so, I must caution again. Many people, including a large number of philosophers of science and professional sociologists, would question my portrayal of scientific activity. For example, some would argue that science is highly ideological because in depicting what is, it implicitly says

---

[3] I am borrowing the general idea from Talcott Parsons', *The Social System* (New York: Free Press, 1951). For another version of this typology, see my *The Science of Human Organization* (Chicago: Nelson-Hall Publishers, 1985), Chapter 2.

[4] Among several fine introductory works on the nature of scientific theory, the discussion in this chapter draws heavily upon Paul Davidson Reynolds' excellent *A Primer in Theory Construction* (Indianapolis: Bobbs-Merrill, 1971). For excellent introductory works, see Arthur L. Stinchcombe, *Constructing Social Theories* (New York: Harcourt, Brace & World, 1968), pp. 3–56; Karl R. Popper, *The Logic of Scientific Discovery* (New York: Harper & Row, 1959); David Willer and Murray Webster, Jr., "Theoretical Concepts and Observables," *American Sociological Review* 35 (August 1970), pp. 748–57; Hans Zetterberg, *On Theory and Verification in Sociology,* 3d ed. (Totowa, N.J.: Bedminister Press, 1965); Jerald Hage, *Techniques and Problems of Theory Construction in Sociology* (New York: John Wiley & Sons, 1972); Walter L. Wallace, *The Logic of Science in Sociology* (Chicago: Aldine Publishing, 1971); Robert Dubin, *Theory Building* (New York: Free Press, 1969); Jack Gibbs, *Sociological Theory Construction* (Hinsdale, Ill.: Dryden Press, 1972); Herbert M. Blalock, Jr., *Theory Construction: From Verbal to Mathematical Formulations* (Englewood Cliffs, N.J.: Prentice-Hall, 1969); Nicholas C. Mullins, *The Art of Theory: Construction and Use* (New York: Harper & Row, 1971).

that present conditions in society must always be the way things are. In so doing, science is an ideology supporting the status quo.[5] It makes the present seem invariant and lawlike, thereby arresting our imagination about other possibilities for the organization of humans in society. But these kinds of criticisms anticipate what will come in later chapters. For the present, I simply want to emphasize that if we follow Comte's "law of the three stages" or the simple typology in Figure 1-1, others will disagree with the conclusion that sociology can be a science that is easily distinguished from other forms of knowledge.[6]

The fact that there is disagreement over sociology's status as a science makes a review of sociological theory highly problematic, for the vehicle for developing scientific knowledge *is* theory. Scientific theory provides an interpretation of events, but this interpretation must be constantly checked and rechecked against the empirical facts. Yet, if the whole enterprise of science is questioned, then sociological theories that tell us how and why events occur will be very diverse. Depending upon what kind of science, if any, that sociology is considered to be, our theories will vary. Some theories will look like those that Auguste Comte envisioned—that is, very much like those in the natural sciences. Other theoretical approaches will be very different because they are formulated by those who have serious reservations about a social science that fits neatly into the lower left box in Figure 1-1.

These considerations present me with very real problems in defining theory in sociology, but undaunted, let me try to present a minimal portrayal of what I think all sociological theories have in common. Then, we can return to the controversial issues that divide theorists and that make for different kinds of theoretical activity in sociology.

## THE ELEMENTS OF THEORY

Theory is a mental activity. As I have already indicated, it is a process of developing ideas that can allow us to explain how and why events occur.

---

[5]See Chapter 9 on critical theory for the details of this argument.

[6]For example, there is a growing conviction among some sociologists that science is much like any other thought system in that it is devoted to sustaining a particular vision, among a community of individuals called scientists, of what is "really real." Science simply provides one interesting way of constructing and maintaining a vision of reality, but there are other, equally valid views among different communities of individuals. Obviously, I do not accept this argument, but I will explore it in more detail in various chapters. For some interesting explorations of the issues, see Edward A. Tiryakian, "Existential Phenomenology and the Sociological Tradition," *American Sociological Review* 30 (October 1965), pp. 674–88; J. C. McKinney, "Typification, Typologies, and Sociological Theory," *Social Forces* 48 (September 1969), pp. 1–11; Alfred Schutz, "Concept and Theory Formation in the Social Sciences," *Journal of Philosophy* 51 (April 1954), pp. 257–73; Harold Garfinkel, *Studies in Ethnomethodology* (Englewood Cliffs, N.J.: Prentice-Hall, 1967); George Psathas, "Ethnomethods and Phenomenology," *Social Research* 35 (September 1968), pp. 500–520; Don H. Zimmerman and Melvin Pollner, "The Everyday World as a Phenomenon," in *Understanding Everyday Life*, ed. J. D. Douglas (Chicago: Aldine Publishing, 1970), pp. 80–103; and Don H. Zimmerman and D. Lawrence Wieder, "Ethnomethodology and the Problem of Order," in *Understanding Everyday Life*, ed. J. D. Douglas, pp. 285–95.

Theory is constructed with several basic elements or building blocks: (1) concepts, (2) variables, (3) statements, and (4) formats. Although there are many divergent claims about what theory is or should be, these four elements are common to all of them. Let me examine each of these elements in more detail.

## Concepts: The Basic Building Blocks of Theory

Theories are built from concepts. Most generally, concepts denote phenomena; in so doing, they isolate features of the world that are considered, for the moment at hand, important. For example, notions of atoms, protons, neutrons, and the like are concepts, pointing to and isolating phenomena for certain analytical purposes. Familiar sociological concepts would include group, formal organization, power, stratification, interaction, norm, role, status, and socialization. Each term is a concept that embraces aspects of the social world that are considered essential for a particular purpose.

Concepts are constructed from definitions. A definition is a system of terms, such as the sentences of a language, the symbols of logic, or the notation of mathematics, that inform investigators as to the phenomenon denoted by a concept. For example, the concept *conflict* only has meaning when it is defined. One possible definition might be: *Conflict is interaction among social units in which one unit seeks to prevent the other from realizing its goals.* Such a definition allows us to visualize the phenomenon that is denoted by the concept. It enables all investigators to "see the same thing" and to understand what it is that is being studied.

Thus, concepts that are useful in building theory have a special characteristic: they strive to communicate a uniform meaning to all those who use them. However, since concepts are frequently expressed with the words of everyday language, it is difficult to avoid words that connote varied meanings—and hence point to different phenomena—for varying groups of scientists. It is for this reason that many concepts in science are expressed in technical or more "neutral" languages, such as the symbols of mathematics. In sociology, expression of concepts in such special languages is sometimes not only impossible but also undesirable. Hence, the verbal symbols used to develop a concept must be defined as precisely as possible in order that they point to the same phenomena for all investigators.[7] Although perfect consensus may never be attained with conventional language, a body of theory rests on the premise that scholars will do their best to define concepts unambiguously.

I should stress that the concepts of theory reveal a special characteristic: *abstractness*.[8] Some concepts pertain to concrete phenomena at

---

[7]For more detailed work on concept formation, see Carl G. Hempel, *Fundamentals of Concept Formation in Empirical Science* (Chicago: University of Chicago Press, 1952).

[8]For a useful and insightful critique of sociology's inability to generate abstract concepts and theory, see David and Judith Willer, *Systematic Empiricism: Critique of a Pseudoscience* (Englewood Cliffs, N.J.: Prentice-Hall, 1973).

specific times and locations. Other more abstract concepts point to phenomena that are not related to concrete times or locations. For example,
in the context of small-group research, *concrete concepts* would refer to
the persistent interactions of particular individuals, whereas an *abstract*
conceptualization of such phenomena would refer to those general properties of face-to-face groups, which are not tied to particular individuals
interacting at a specified time and location. Whereas abstract concepts
are not tied to a specific context, concrete concepts are. In building theory,
abstract concepts are crucial, although we will see shortly that theorists
disagree considerably on this issue.

Abstractness poses a problem: how do we attach abstract concepts to
the ongoing, everyday world of events? While it is essential that some of
the concepts of theory transcend specific times and places, it is equally
critical that there be procedures for making these abstract concepts relevant to observable situations and occurrences. After all, the utility of an
abstract concept can only be demonstrated when the concept is brought
to bear on some specific empirical problem encountered by investigators;
otherwise, concepts remain detached from the very processes they are
supposed to help investigators understand. Just how to attach concepts
to empirical processes, or the workings of the real world, is an area of
great controversy in sociology. Some argue for very formal procedures for
attaching concepts to empirical events. Those of this persuasion argue
that abstract concepts should be accompanied by a series of statements
known as *operational definitions*, which are sets of procedural instructions
telling investigators how to go about discerning phenomena in the real
world that are denoted by an abstract concept. Others argue that the
nature of our concepts in sociology precludes such formalistic exercises.
At best, concepts can be only sensitizing devices that must change with
alterations of social reality; and so, we can only intuitively and provi-
sionally apply abstract concepts to the actual flow of events. To emulate
the natural sciences in an effort to develop formal operations for attaching
concepts to reality is to ignore the fact that social reality is changeable;
it does not reveal invariant properties like the other domains of the universe.[9] And thus, to think that abstract concepts denote enduring and
invariant properties of the social universe and to presume, therefore, that
the concept itself will never need to be changed is, at best, naive.[10]

---

[9]For examples of this line of argument see Herbert Blumer, *Symbolic Interaction: Perspective and Method* (Englewood Cliffs, N.J.: Prentice-Hall, 1969); or Anthony Giddens,
*New Rules of Sociological Method* (New York: Basic Books, 1977).

[10]For the counterargument, see Jonathan H. Turner, "Toward a Social Physics: Reducing
Sociology's Theoretical Inhibitions," *Humboldt Journal of Social Relations* 7 (Fall/Winter
1979–80), pp. 140–55; "Returning to Social Physics," *Perspectives in Social Theory*, vol. 2,
(1981); "Some Problematic Trends in Sociological Theorizing," *The Wisconsin Sociologist*
15 (Spring/Summer 1978), pp. 80–88; and *Societal Stratification: A Theoretical Analysis*
(New York: Columbia University Press, 1984).

And so the debate rages, taking many different turns. I need not go into detail here, since these issues will be brought out again and again as I move into the substance of sociological theory in subsequent chapters. For the present, I only want to draw the approximate lines of battle.

## Variables as an Important Type of Concept

When used to build theory, two general types of concepts can be distinguished: (1) those that simply label phenomena and (2) those that refer to phenomena that differ in degree.[11] Concepts that merely label phenomena would include such commonly employed abstractions as *dog, cat, group, social class, and star.* When stated in this way, none of these concepts reveal the ways in which the phenomena they denote vary in terms of properties such as size, weight, density, velocity, cohesiveness, or any of the many criteria used to inform investigators about differences in degree among phenomena.

Those who believe, as I do, that sociology can be like other sciences prefer concepts that are translated into variables—that is, into states that vary. We want to know the variable properties—size, degree, intensity, amount, and so forth—of events denoted by a concept. For example, to note that an aggregate of people is a group does not indicate what type of group it is or how it compares with other groups in terms of such criteria as size, differentiation, and cohesiveness. And so for some, the concepts of scientific theory should denote the *variable* features of the world. To understand events requires that we visualize how variation in one phenomenon is related to variation in another. Others, who are less enamored by efforts to make sociology a natural science, are less compulsive about translating concepts into variables. They are far more interested in whether or not concepts sensitize and alert investigators to important processes than they are in converting each concept into a metric that varies in some measurable way. They are not, of course, against the conversion of ideas into variables, but they are cautious about efforts to translate each and every concept into a metric.

## Theoretical Statements and Formats

To be useful, the concepts of theory must be connected to each other. Such connections among concepts constitute theoretical statements. These statements specify the way in which events denoted by concepts are

---

[11]Reynolds, *Primer in Theory Construction*, p. 57; see also Stinchcombe, *Constructing Social Theories*, pp. 38–47 for a discussion of how concepts not only point to variable properties of phenomena but also to the interaction effects of interrelated phenomena. For an interesting discussion of the importance of variable concepts and for guidelines on how to use them, see Hage, *Techniques and Problems of Theory Construction*.

**FIGURE 1-2**   The Elements of Theory in Sociology

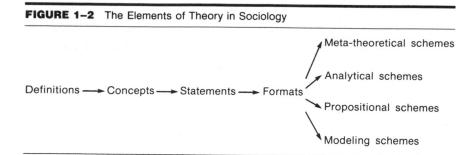

interrelated, and at the same time, they provide an interpretation of how and why events should be connected to each other. When these theoretical statements are grouped together, they constitute what I term a *theoretical format.* I use the word *format* because it is general and can describe many different ways to organize theoretical statements. Indeed, in sociological theory, there is relatively little consensus over just how to organize theoretical statements into a format. And in fact, much of the theoretical controversy in sociology revolves around differences over the best way to develop theoretical statements and to group them together into a format. Depending on one's views about what kind of science, if any, sociology can be, the structure of theoretical statements and their organization into formats differs dramatically. Let me review the range of opinion on the matter.

I think that there are four basic approaches in sociological theory for generating theoretical statements and formats: (1) meta-theoretical schemes, (2) analytical schemes, (3) propositional schemes, and (4) modeling schemes. Figure 1-2 summarizes the relations among these schemes and the basic elements of theory. Concepts are constructed from definitions; theoretical statements link concepts together; and statements are organized into four basic types of formats. However, these four formats can be executed in a variety of ways, and so in reality, there are more than just four strategies for developing theoretical statements and formats. Moreover, these various strategies are not always mutually exclusive, for in executing one of them, we are often led to another as a kind of "next step" in building theory. Yet—and this is a point that I think is crucial—these various approaches are often viewed as antagonistic; and the proponents of each strategy have spilled a great deal of ink sustaining the antagonism. Moreover, even within a particular type of format there is constant battle over the best way to develop theory. For me, this acrimony represents a great tragedy because in a mature science—which, sad to say, sociology is not—these approaches are viewed as highly compatible. Before pursuing this point further, I will delineate in more detail each of these approaches.

**Meta-theoretical schemes.**    This kind of theoretical activity is more comprehensive than ordinary theory. Meta-theoretical schemes are not, by themselves, theories that explain specific classes of events; rather, they explicate the basic issues that a theory must address. In many sociological circles, meta-theory is considered an essential prerequisite to adequate theory building,[12] even though the dictionary definition of "meta" emphasizes "occurring later" and "in succession" to previous activities.[13] Furthermore, in most other sciences, meta-theoretical reflection has occurred *after* a body of formal theoretical statements has been developed. It is typically after a science has used a number of theoretical statements and formats successfully that scholars begin to ask: What are the underlying assumptions about the universe contained in these statements? What strategies are demanded by, or precluded from, these statements and their organization into formats? What kind of knowledge is generated by these statements and formats, and conversely, what is ignored? In sociological theory, however, advocates of meta-theory usually emphasize that we cannot develop theory until we have resolved these more fundamental epistemological and metaphysical questions.

My opinion is that such meta-theorizing has put the cart before the horse, but I emphasize that my opinion is probably in the minority among social theorists. For those who emphasize meta-theory, several preliminary issues must be resolved. These include: (1) What is the basic nature of human activity about which we must develop theory? For example, what is the basic nature of human beings? What is the fundamental nature of society? What is the fundamental nature of the bonds that connect people to each other and to society? (2) What is the appropriate way to develop theory, and what kind of theory is possible? For instance, can we build highly formal systems of abstract laws, as in physics, or must we be content with general concepts that simply sensitize and orient us to important processes? Can we rigorously test theories with precise measurement procedures, or must we use theories as interpretative frameworks that cannot be tested by the same procedures, as in the natural sciences? (3) What is the critical problem on which social theory should concentrate? For instance, should we examine the processes of social integration, or must we concentrate on social conflict? Should we focus on the nature of social action among individuals, or is the major question one of structures of organization? Should we stress the power of ideas, like values and beliefs, or must we focus on the material conditions of people's existence?

A great deal of what is defined as sociological theory involves trying to answer these questions. The old philosophical debates—idealism versus

---

[12]For a forceful and scholarly advocacy of this point, see Jeffrey C. Alexander, *Theoretical Logic in Sociology,* 4 vols. (Berkeley, Calif.: University of California Press, 1982–1984).

[13]Webster's *New Collegiate Dictionary* (Springfield, Mass.: G & C Merriman, 1976).

materialism, induction versus deduction, causation versus association, subjectivism versus objectivism, and so on—are reevoked and analyzed with respect to social reality. At times, meta-theorizing has been true to the meaning of meta and has involved a reanalysis of previous scholars' ideas in light of these philosophical issues.[14] The favorite targets of such analyses are Karl Marx, Max Weber, and Émile Durkheim, and in recent decades, Talcott Parsons (the subject of Chapter 3). The idea behind reanalysis is to summarize the metaphysical and epistemological assumptions of the scholars' work and to show where the schemes went wrong and where they still have utility. Furthermore, on the basis of this assessment, there are some recommendations in reanalyses as to how we should go about building theory and about what this theory should be.

In my view, such reanalysis can be useful when it stimulates actual theory—that is, efforts to explain social events. However, my sense is that meta-theorizing often gets bogged down in weighty philosophical matters and immobilizes theory building. The enduring philosophical questions persist, I would imagine, because they are not resolvable. My feeling is that one just must take a stand on the issues and see what kinds of insights can be generated. But meta-theory often stymies as much as stimulates theoretical activity because it embroils theorists in inherently unresolvable and always debatable controversies. Of course, my opinion is not shared by others, and for our present purposes, the more important conclusion is that a great deal of sociological theory is, in fact, meta-theoretical activity.

**Analytical schemes.**    Much theoretical activity in sociology consists of concepts organized into a typology or classification scheme. Each concept denotes a basic property of the social universe; and then the concepts themselves are organized in a typology.[15] For example, an analytical scheme might assert that "action" is a critical property of the universe; then, it would classify action as one of four types. In turn, social structures might be classified in terms of the prevailing type of action among its participants. To take another example from functional analysis, which I will turn to in the next chapter, a social system might be visualized as having to meet four basic needs to persist (the number of needs could be one, two, three, or a dozen, depending upon the theorist). Structures and processes are then classified in terms of which needs they meet.

There are many different varieties of analytical schemes, but they share an emphasis on typologizing. The concepts of the scheme chop up

---

[14]Alexander's work is more in this tradition. See also Richard Münch, *Theory of Action: Reconstructing the Contributions of Talcott Parsons, Émile Durkheim, and Max Weber* (Frankfurt: Suhrkamp, 1982). I have translated the German title and emphasized this work because it will soon be out in an English translation.

[15]Talcott Parsons' work is of this nature, as we will see in the next chapter. See also Münch.

THE ELEMENTS OF THEORY

the universe; then, the ordering of the concepts into a typology gives the social world a sense of order. Explanation of an empirical event comes whenever a place in the classificatory scheme can be found for the empirical event. For example, if one is using an "action theoretical framework" with four types of action, explanation occurs when behavior can be classified as one of these four types. I have oversimplified here, but the general point is, I think, correct: analytical schemes explain empirical events by finding their niche in a typology.

There are, however, wide variations in the nature of the typologies in analytical schemes. I think that there are two basic types: *naturalistic/positivistic schemes,* which try to develop a tightly woven system of categories that is presumed to capture the way in which the invariant properties of the universe are ordered[16]; and *descriptive/sensitizing schemes,* which are more loosely assembled congeries of concepts intended only to sensitize and orient researchers to certain critical processes.[17] Figure 1–3 summarizes these two types of analytical approaches. Naturalistic/positivistic schemes assume that there are timeless and universal processes in the social universe, much as there are in the physical and biological realms. The goal is to create an abstract conceptual typology that is isomorphic with these timeless processes. In contrast, descriptive/sensitizing schemes are typically more skeptical about the timeless quality of social affairs. Instead, they argue that concepts and their linkages must always be provisional and sensitizing because the nature of human activity is to change those very arrangements denoted by the organization of concepts into theoretical statements. Hence, except for certain very general conceptual categories, the scheme must be flexible and capable of being revised as circumstances in the empirical world change. At best, then, explanation is simply rendering an interpretation of events by seeing them as an instance or example of the provisional and sensitizing concepts in the scheme.

Often it is argued that analytical schemes are a necessary prerequisite for developing other forms of theory. Until one has a scheme that organizes the properties of the universe, it is difficult to develop propositions and models about specific events. For without the general analytical framework, it is asked by proponents of this view, how can a theorist or researcher know what to examine?

**Propositional schemes.**   A proposition is a theoretical statement that specifies the connection between two or more variables. It tells us how variation in one concept is accounted for by variation in another. For example, the propositional statement, "group solidarity is a positive

---

[16] Parsons' and Münch's work represent this approach.

[16] Parsons' and Münch's work represent this approach.

[17] Anthony Giddens' work represents this alternative. See his *The Construction of Society* (Berkeley, Calif.: University of California Press, 1984). See also Chapter 22.

**FIGURE 1–3**    Types of Analytical Schemes

Naturalistic/Positivistic:

Abstract category 1 — Abstract category 2 — Abstract category 3

Abstract category 4 — Abstract category 5 — Abstract category n

Explanation = finding the place in the typology of an empirical event

⟷ : Specify with concepts processes that link clearly defined conceptual categories

Sensitizing/Descriptive

Abstract category 1 — Abstract category 2

Abstract category n — Abstract category 3

Abstract category 4

Explanation = interpreting events by invoking various combinations of categories

⟵ – – ► : Loose and flexible linkages among sensitizing conceptual categories

function of external conflict with other groups," says that as group conflict increases so does the internal sense of solidarity among members of the respective groups involved in the conflict. Thus, two properties of the social universe denoted by variable concepts, "group solidarity" and "conflict," are connected by the proposition that as one increases in value, so does the other.

Propositional schemes vary perhaps the most of all theoretical approaches. They vary primarily along two dimensions: (1) the level of abstraction and (2) the way propositions are organized into formats. Some are highly abstract and contain concepts that do not denote any particular case but all cases of a type (for example, group solidarity and conflict are abstract because no particular empirical instance of conflict and solidarity is addressed). In contrast, other propositional systems are tied to empirical facts and simply summarize relations among events in a particular case (for example, as World War II progressed, nationalism in America increased). Not only do propositional schemes vary in terms of abstractness but also by virtue of how propositions are laced together into a format. Some are woven together by very explicit rules; others are merely loose bunches or congeries of propositions.

I think that by using these two dimensions, several different types of propositional schemes can be isolated: (*a*) axiomatic formats, (*b*) formal formats, and (*c*) various empirical formats. The first two –(*a*) and (*b*)– are clearly theoretical formats, whereas some types of (*c*) are simply research findings that test theories. But I emphasize, these more empirical types of propositional schemes are often considered theory by practicing sociologists, and so, I have included them for our discussion here.

(*a*) An axiomatic organization of theoretical statements involves the following elements. First, it contains a set of concepts. Some of the concepts are highly abstract; others, more concrete. Second, there is always a set of existence statements that describe those types and classes of situations in which the concepts and the propositions that incorporate them apply. These existence statements make up what is usually called the *scope conditions* of the theory. Third, and most nearly unique to the axiomatic format, propositional statements are stated in a hierarchical order. At the top of the hierarchy are *axioms*, or highly abstract statements, from which *all* other theoretical statements are logically derived. These latter statements are usually called *theorems* and are logically derived in accordance with varying rules from the more abstract axioms. The selection of axioms is, in reality, a somewhat arbitrary matter, but usually they are selected with several criteria in mind. The axioms should be consistent with one another, although they do not have to be logically interrelated. The axioms should be highly abstract; they should state relationships among abstract concepts. These relationships should be lawlike in that the more concrete theorems derived from them have not been disproved by empirical investigation. And the axioms should have an intuitive plausibility in that their truth appears to be self-evident.

The end result of tight conformity to axiomatic principles is an inventory or set of interrelated propositions, each derivable from at least one axiom and usually more abstract theorems. There are several advantages to this form of theory construction. First, highly abstract concepts, encompassing a broad range of related phenomena, can be employed. These abstract concepts do not have to be directly measurable since they are logically tied to more specific and measurable propositions that, when empirically tested, can indirectly subject the more abstract propositions and the axioms to empirical tests. Thus, by virtue of this logical interrelatedness of the propositions and axioms, research can be more efficient since the failure to refute a particular proposition lends credence to other propositions and to the axioms. Second, the use of a logical system to derive propositions from abstract axioms can also generate additional propositions that point to previously unknown or unanticipated relationships among social phenomena.

But I emphasize that there are some fatal limitations on the use of axiomatic theory in sociology. In terms of strict adherence to the rules of deduction (the details of which are not critical for my purposes here), most interesting concepts and propositions in sociology cannot be legitimately employed because the concepts are not stated with sufficient precision and because they cannot be incorporated into propositions that state unambiguously the relationship between concepts. Axiomatic theory also requires controls on all potential extraneous variables so that the tight logical system of deduction from axiom to empirical reality is not contaminated by extraneous factors. Sociologists can rarely create such controls.[18] Thus, axiomatic theory can be used only when very precise definitions of concepts exist, when concepts are organized into propositions using a precise calculus that specifies relations unambiguously, and when the contaminating effects of extraneous variables are eliminated.

These limitations are often ignored in propositional theory building, and the language of axiomatic theory is employed (axioms, theorems, corollaries, and the like); but these efforts are, at best, pseudoaxiomatic schemes.[19] In fact, I think it is best to call them formal propositional schemes[20]—the second type of proposition strategy listed earlier.

(b) Formal theories are, in essence, watered down versions of axiomatic schemes. The idea is to develop highly abstract propositions that are used to explain some empirical event. The propositions are usually grouped together and seen as higher order laws; and the goal of explanation is to see empirical events as an instance or example of this "covering law." Deductions from the law are made, but they are much looser, rarely conforming to the strict rules of axiomatic theory. Moreover, there is a recognition that extraneous variables can not always be excluded, and so, the propositions usually have the disclaimer, "other things being equal." That is, if other forces do not impinge, then the relationship among concepts in the proposition should hold true. For example, my earlier example of the relationship between conflict and solidarity might be one abstract proposition in a formal system. Thus, a formal scheme might say, "Other things being equal, group solidarity is a positive function of conflict." Then, we would use this law to explain some empirical event, say, for instance, World War II (the conflict variable) and nationalism in America (the solidarity variable). And we might find an exception to

---

[18]For more details of this argument, see Lee Freese, "Formal Theorizing," *Annual Review of Sociology* 6 (1980), pp. 187–212 and Herbert L. Costner and Robert K. Leik, "Deductions from Axiomatic Theory," *American Sociological Review* 29 (December 1964), pp. 19–35.

[19]See, for example, Peter Blau's excellent *Inequality and Heterogeneity: A Primitive Theory of Social Structure* (New York: Free Press, 1977).

[20]See Freese.

our rule or law, such as America's involvement in the Vietnam War, that contradicts the principle, forcing its revision or the recognition that "all things were not equal." In this case, we might revise the principle by stating a condition under which it holds true: when parties to a conflict perceive the conflict as a threat to their welfare, then the level of solidarity of groups is a positive function of their degree of conflict. Thus, the Vietnam War did not produce internal solidarity in America because it was not defined as a threat to the general welfare (whereas for the North Vietnamese, it was a threat and produced solidarity).

The essential idea here is that in formal theory, an effort is made to create abstract principles. These principles are often clustered together to form a group of laws from which we make rather loose deductions to explain empirical events. Much like axiomatic systems, formal systems are hierarchical, but the restrictions of axiomatic theory are relaxed considerably. Most propositional schemes in sociological theorizing are, therefore, of this formal type.

(c) Yet, much of what is defined as theory in sociology is more empirical. These empirical formats consist of generalizations from specific events in particular empirical contexts. For example, Golden's Law states that "as industrialization increases, the level of literacy in the population increases." Such a proposition is not very abstract; it is filled with empirical content—industrialization and literacy. Moreover, it is not about a timeless process, since industrialization is only a few hundred years old and literacy emerged, at best, only 15,000 years ago. There are many such generalizations in sociology that are considered theoretical. They represent statements of empirical regularities that scholars think are important to understand. Indeed, most substantive areas and subfields of sociology are filled with these kinds of propositions.

Strictly speaking, however, these are not theoretical. They are too tied to empirical contexts. In fact, they are generalizations that are in need of a theory to explain them. Yet, I caution that my opinion about such empirical generalizations is not shared by all. And if we ask scholars working in substantive areas if their generalizations are theory, a good many would answer affirmatively.

There are other kinds of empirical generalizations, however, that raise fewer suspicions about their theoretical merits. These are often termed *middle-range theories,* as we will see in Chapter 4, because they are more abstract than a research finding and because their empirical content pertains to variables that are also found in other domains of social reality.[21] For example, a series of middle-range propositions from the complex organization's literature might be stated: "Increasing size of a bureaucratic

---

[21]See Chapter 4 on Robert K. Merton's work. In particular, consult his *Social Theory and Social Structure* (New York: Free Press, 1975).

organization is positively related to (*a*) increases in the complexity (differentiation) of its structure, (*b*) increases in the reliance on formal rules and regulations, (*c*) increases in the decentralization of authority, and (*d*) increases in span of control for each center of authority."[22] These principles (the truth of which is not at issue here) are more abstract than Golden's Law because they denote a whole class of phenomena—organizations. They also deal with more generic variables—size, differentiation, centralization of power, spans of control, rules, and regulations—that have existed in all times and all places. Moreover, these variables could be stated more abstractly to apply to all organized social systems, not just bureaucratic organizations. For instance, I can visualize a more abstract law that states: "Increasing size of a social system is positively related to (*a*) increases in levels of system differentiation, (*b*) increases in the codification of norms, (*c*) increases in the decentralization of power, and (*d*) increases in the spans of control for each center of power." Now, I am not asserting that these propositions are true, but I see them as interesting laws that can be tested out in many diverse empirical contexts, not just bureaucratic organizations. The central point here is that some empirical generalizations have more theoretical potential than others. If their variables are relatively abstract and if they pertain to basic and fundamental properties of the social universe that exist in other substantive areas of inquiry, then it is more reasonable, I believe, to consider them theoretical.

In sum, then, there are three basic kinds of propositional schemes: axiomatic, formal, and various types of empirical generalizations. These propositional schemes are summarized in Figure 1-4. Although axiomatic formats are elegant and powerful, sociological variables and research typically cannot conform to their restrictions. Instead, we must rely upon formal formats that generate propositions stating abstract relations among variables and then make loosely structured "deductions" to specific empirical cases. Finally, there are empirical formats that consist of generalizations from particular substantive areas; and these are often considered theories of that area. Some of these theories are little more than summaries of research findings that require a theory to explain them. Others are more middle range and have more potential as theory because they are more abstract and pertain to more generic classes of variables.

**Modeling schemes.**    At times, it is useful to draw a picture of social events. Some models are drawn with neutral languages, such as mathematics in which the equation is presumed to map and represent empirical

---

[22]I have borrowed this example from Peter M. Blau's "Applications of a Macrosociological Theory" in *Mathmatizche Analyse von Organisationsstrukktaren und Prozessen* (Internationale Wissenschaftliche Fachkonferenz, vol. 5, March 1981).

**FIGURE 1–4**   Types of Propositional Schemes

Axiomatic:

Formal:

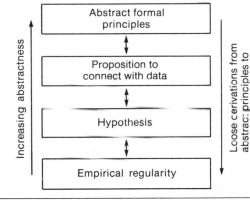

processes.[23] I prefer to visualize such equations as propositions (formal statements of relations among variables) *unless* they can be used to generate a picture or some form of graphic representation of processes. There is no clear consensus on what a model is, but in sociological theory, there is a range of activity that involves representing concepts and their relations as a "picture" that models what are considered the important elements

---

[23]Actually, these are typically "regression equations" and would not constitute modeling as I think it should be defined. A series of differential equations, especially as they are simulated or otherwise graphically represented, would constitute a model.

**FIGURE 1–4** *(concluded)*

Middle-range:

Empirical generalization:

of a social process. Perhaps I am being too restrictive here, but my purpose is to distinguish an important type of theoretical activity.

A model, then, is a diagrammatic representation of social events. The diagrammatic elements of any model include: (1) concepts that denote and highlight certain features of the universe; (2) the arrangement of these concepts in visual space so as to reflect the ordering of events in the universe; and (3) symbols that mark the connections among concepts, such as lines, arrows, vectors, and other ways that represent connections among variables. The elements of a model may be weighted in some way or they may be sequentially organized to express events over time or they may represent complex patterns of relations, such as lag effects, threshold effects, feedback loops, mutual interactions, cycles, and other potential ways that properties of the universe affect each other.[24]

In sociology, I think that most diagrammatic models are constructed to emphasize the causal connections among properties of the universe.

---

[24]A good example of such models is in my *Societal Stratification*. For examples of more empirical, yet still analytical, models, see Gerhard and Jean Lenski, *Human Societies* (New York: McGraw-Hill, 1982).

That is, they are designed to show how changes in the values of one set of variables are related to changes in the values of other variables. Models are typically constructed when there are numerous variables whose causal interrelations an investigator wants to highlight.

With the issue far from clear, my sense is that sociologists generally construct two different types of models, which I will term *analytical* models and *causal* models. This distinction is, I admit, somewhat arbitrary, but I think that it is a necessary one if we are to appreciate the kinds of models that are constructed in sociology. The basis for making this distinction is twofold: First, some models are more abstract than others in that the concepts in them are not tied to any particular case, whereas other models reveal concepts that simply summarize statistically relations among variables in a particular data set. Secondly, more abstract models almost always reveal more complexity in their representation of causal connections among variables. That is, one will find feedback loops, cycles, mutual effects, and other connective representations that complicate the causal connections among the variables in the model and make them difficult to summarize with simple statistics. In contrast, the less abstract models typically depict a clear causal sequence among empirical variables.[25] They typically reveal independent variables that effect variation in some dependent variable; and if the model is more complex, it might also highlight intervening variables and perhaps even some interaction effects among the variables.

Thus, analytical models are more abstract; they highlight more generic properties of the universe; and they portray a complex set of connections among variables. In contrast, causal models are more empirically grounded; they are more likely to devote particular properties of a specific empirical case; and they are likely to present a simple lineal view of causality. These modeling strategies are summarized in Figure 1-5.

Causal models are typically drawn in order to provide a more detailed interpretation of an empirical generalization. They are designed to sort out the respective influences of variables, usually in some temporal sequence, as they operate on some dependent variable of interest. At times, a causal model becomes a way of representing the elements of a middle-range theory so as to connect these elements to the particulars of a specific empirical context. For example, if we wanted to know why the size of a bureaucratic organization is related to its complexity of structure in a particular empirical case of a growing organization, we might translate the more abstract variables of size and complexity into specific empirical indicators and perhaps try to introduce other variables that also influence the relationship between size and complexity in this empirical case. The

---

[25]The "path analysis" that was so popular in American sociology in the 1970s is a good example of such modeling techniques.

**FIGURE 1-5**  Types of Modeling Schemes

Analytical models:

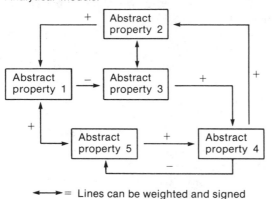

Explanation = ability to map crucial connections (perhaps weighted) among basic properties of a specific class of process or phenomenon

←——➤ = Lines can be weighted and signed

Causal models:

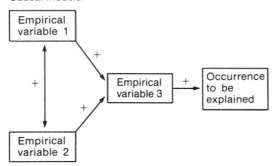

Explanation = tracing of causal connections among measured variables accounting for variation in the occurrence of interest

←——➤ = Lines usually state a statistical association among variables

causal model thus becomes a way to represent with more clarity the empirical association between size and complexity in a specific context.[26]

Analytical models are usually drawn to specify the relations among more abstract and generic processes. Often they are used to delineate the processes that operate to connect the concepts of an axiomatic, or more likely, a formal theory.[27] For example, we might construct a model that tells us more about the processes that operate to generate the relationship between conflict and solidarity or between size and differentiation in

---

[26]For an example of a model for these variables, see Peter M. Blau's "A Formal Theory of Differentiation in Organizations," *American Sociological Review* 35 (April 1970), pp. 201–218. See also Chapter 12.

[27]Ibid. is a good example.

social systems. Additional concepts would be introduced and their weighted, direct, indirect, feedback, cyclical, lagged, and other patterns of effect on each other would be diagramed. In this way, the analytical model tells us more about how and why properties of the universe are connected. In addition to specifying processes among formal propositions, analytical models can be used to describe processes that connect variables in the propositions of a middle-range theory. For example, we might use a model to map out how organization size and complexity are connected by virtue of other processes operating in an organization.

Of course, we can construct analytical models or causal models for their own sake, without reference to an empirical generalization, a middle-range theory, or a formal/axiomatic theory. We may simply prefer modeling to propositional formats. One of the great advantages of modeling is that it allows representation of complex relations among many variables in a reasonably parsimonious fashion. To say the same thing as a model, a propositional format might have to write complex equations or use many words. Thus, by itself, modeling represents a tool that many theorists find preferable to alternative theoretical schemes.

In sum, then, I have isolated four general and a number of more specific ways that sociologists organize concepts and theoretical statements into formats. I believe that this description summarizes the range of approaches, although we could, no doubt, quibble over the various distinctions that I have drawn. But my purpose is not to draw finely tuned distinctions nor enter a dialogue with philosophers of science. Rather, I only want to provide a general perspective for understanding the diversity of activities that sociologists call "theory." We cannot understand the structure of sociological theory without some sense for the underlying, and typically unarticulated, theoretical schemes employed by individual theorists.

As I have mentioned frequently in this description of the elements of theory, these various schemes are often interrelated. Moreover, I have expressed, at least implicitly, personal biases in favor of some schemes. Before closing this opening chapter and moving on to the actual substance of sociological theory, therefore, I would like to explore the relative merits of these theoretical approaches.

## AN ASSESSMENT OF THEORETICAL APPROACHES

### Abstractness and Scope of Various Theoretical Schemes

In Figure 1-6, I have arrayed the major types of approaches to building theory along two dimensions: (1) their level of abstraction and (2) their degree of scope. That is, how abstract are the concepts and statements and how broad a range of phenomena do they encompass? The more the concepts of a theoretical strategy are free of reference to any specific

**FIGURE 1-6**   Variations in Types of Theoretical Formats

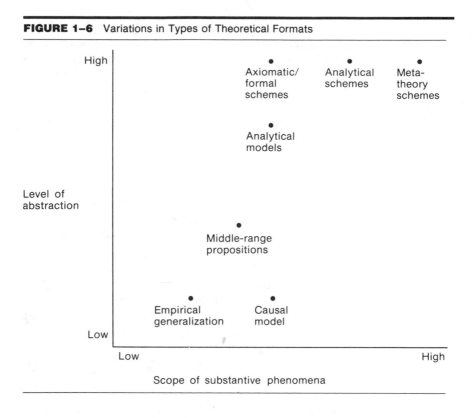

Scope of substantive phenomena

empirical case, the higher is its level of abstraction; and the greater the range of substantive phenomena encompassed by the concepts and statements of an approach, the greater is its scope. Naturally, these are not mutually exclusive, since the process of abstraction by its very nature leads to the inclusion of more cases and, hence, increases the scope of phenomena denoted by concepts. I can certainly be criticized for plotting along nonexclusive dimensions, but my point in Figure 1-6 is not to create an elegant typology. Rather, I simply want to communicate that abstract schemes encompass more substantive phenomena in the social universe. But I also want to emphasize that abstraction, per se, does not always lead to the breadth of coverage. A theoretical format can be highly abstract in that it contains no direct empirical referents, but it can denote only a delimited range of phenomena. Thus, I think that axiomatic and formal propositions tend to be highly abstract, but they typically pertain to a limited range of phenomena. In contrast, analytical schemes and meta-theory are no more abstract than formal or axiomatic theories, but they usually contain more concepts and statements denoting a broader range of social phenomena. And so, while I admit to an overlap in the dimensions of Figure 1-6, the figure communicates my essential point: theoretical schemes vary primarily in terms of two interrelated dimensions, abstraction and scope. Some address a wide range of phenomena with abstract concepts, others only a limited range with equally abstract concepts. Still others are not abstract at all and are thereby limited in scope. And some are more abstract and cover varying ranges of events.

My sense that, in terms of abstraction alone, the various approaches cluster at four diverse levels. Empirical generalizations and causal models are tied to specific empirical contexts. A generalization summarizes a particular set of research findings, whereas a simple causal model typically involves correlational statements linking empirically measured variables. Middle-range propositions are more abstract because they seek to explain events for a whole class of phenomena. Yet, the concepts of middle-range theory reveal empirical content that limits their abstractness. An analytical model is generally more abstract than a middle-range theory because it introduces generic properties of the social universe to explain some general class of empirical events. Axiomatic/formal propositional schemes, analytical schemes, and meta-theory are even more abstract in that they reveal no empirical content about specific times, places, and contexts. They are usually about the basic and universal properties of social organization, human action, or social interaction, without reference to any particular pattern of organization, form of action, or context of interaction.

Of course, this is only a rough grouping. I am well aware that there is variation, but I would submit that the relative position of these three groupings in regard to their respective levels of abstraction is roughly captured in Figure 1-6. For example, an axiomatic scheme may be somewhat less abstract than a meta-theory, but it is not likely to become less abstract than an analytical model or a middle-range theory. What distinguishes theoretical approaches at any given level of abstraction is their scope, or the range of phenomena covered by theoretical statements. The scope of empirical generalizations tends to be limited since they emanate from research findings that, by their nature, focus on a limited range of phenomena (since, after all, there are only so many things that can be studied in even the largest research project). Causal models often add extra variables in an effort to explain more variance, and so they frequently expand the scope somewhat of an empirical generalization. Middle-range theories try to explain a whole class of phenomena—for example, delinquency, revolutions, ethnic antagonism, and urbanization. They are, therefore, broader in scope than empirical generalizations and causal models, but the very goal of middle-range theory is to limit scope by trying to explain only one class of events. Analytical models are usually broader than middle-range theories, but they tend to be limited because they too are about a specific range of phenomena—industrialization, ethnic relations, political centralization, differentiation in organizations, and similar topics. They are somewhat broader in scope because it is easier to include more variables in a model than in a series of middle-range propositions.

Axiomatic/formal propositional schemes tend to be limited in range because they focus on certain generic processes and ignore others. For example, a formal theory might be about differentiation, consensus formation, conflict, exchange, behavior, action, interaction, and similar basic processes in the social universe. Although the proponents of these schemes often claim that their propositions explain much more of reality, it is more reasonable to see these abstract propositions as pertaining to only a limited range of phenomena. Analytical schemes in sociological theory tend to be all-encompassing, seeking to explain human action, interaction, and organization in one grand scheme. They are rarely immodest efforts; and although they differ rather dramatically in their content, they are all similar in their presumption that they encompass all of the social universe that needs to be explained. Meta-theories are very broad but diffuse and imprecise. They explicate all that needs to be explained and present a philosophical justification for developing a particular form of explanation. But they tend to be rather grandiose; and this fact makes them so broad as to be somewhat vacuous.

## Relative Merits of Diverse Theoretical Approaches

My belief is that theory should be abstract. That is, the less substantive content in the concepts, the better they are. For if theories are filled with empirical referents, they are tied to specific contexts and, hence, are not as useful as those that view specific empirical contexts as instances or examples of a more basic underlying process. Most theorists in sociology, however, would disagree with me on this score; and I will return to this point of contention shortly.

I also believe that theory should be such that it can be proven wrong by empirical tests. As a general platitude, few would disagree with this statement. But as a more practical matter of how we should construct theories to be proven wrong, there is enormous disagreement. My sense is that theories must be sufficiently precise in the definitions of concepts and in the organization of concepts into statements that they can be, in principle, measured and tested. It is only through the generation of precise theoretical statements and efforts at their refutation that scientific knowledge can be generated. For me, then, what distinguishes good theoretical statements from the bad ones is that they are *created to be proven wrong*. A theory that, in principle, cannot be proven wrong is not very useful. It becomes a self-sustaining dogma that is accepted on faith. A theory must allow for understanding of events, and hence, it must be tested against the facts of the world. If a theoretical statement is proven wrong by empirical tests, science has advanced. When a theory is rejected, then one less possible line of inquiry will be required in search of an answer to the question, Why? By successively eliminating incorrect statements, those that survive attempts at refutation offer, for the present at least, the most accurate picture of the real world. Although having one's theory refuted may cause professional stigma, refutations are crucial to theory building. It is somewhat disheartening, therefore, that some scientists appear to live in fear of such refutation. For in the ideal scientific process, just the opposite should be the case, as Karl Popper has emphasized:

> Refutations have often been regarded as establishing the failure of a scientist, or at least of his theory. It should be stressed that this is an inductive error. Every refutation should be regarded as a great success; not merely as a success of the scientist who refuted the theory, but also of the scientist who created the refuted theory and who thus in the first instance suggested, if only indirectly, the refuting experiment.[28]

Even statements that survive refutation and hence bring professional prestige to their framers are never fully proven. It is always possible that the next empirical test could disprove them. Yet, if statements consistently survive empirical tests, they have high credibility and are likely to be at the core of a theoretical body of knowledge. But as I have now phrased the issue, many sociological theorists would disagree.

Thus, in my view, the best theoretical statements are those that are highly abstract and, at the same time, are sufficiently precise so as to be testable. Again, as I will document in the chapters to come, a majority of social theorists disagree with me on this score. I have injected my personal views because it is important to understand the biases with which I approach the review and analyses of social theory. Moreover, these biases are the central issue around which the debate over the best approach to developing theory and knowledge rages. Since I have presented my biases, let me elaborate on them by assessing the merits of various approaches in terms of my prejudices.

From my point of view, empirical generalizations and causal models of empirically operationalized variables are not theory at all. They are useful summaries of data that need a theory to explain them. Some would argue that theory can be built *from* such summaries of empirical regularities. That is, we can induce from the facts the more general properties that these facts illustrate. I doubt this, but many disagree. I grant that familiarity with empirical regularities is crucial to developing more abstract and comprehensive theoretical statements, but I doubt if this process of mechanically raising the level of abstraction from empirical findings will produce interesting theory. A much more creative leap of insight is necessary, and so, I would not suggest that theory building begin with a total immersion in the empirical facts. I suspect that once buried in the facts, one rarely rises above them.

---

[28]Karl R. Popper, *Conjectures and Refutations* (New York: Basic Books, 1962), p. 243.

At the other extreme, meta-theory is like empirical facts: interesting but counterproductive. Many scholars feel just the opposite, however. They argue that we must have meta-theory before we try to develop more precise theoretical statements. My opinion is that this has rarely been the case in science, primarily because meta-theory gets bogged down in enduring philosophical issues. The result is that proponents of various philosophical camps become so preoccupied with their debate (which by its nature can never end) that they never get around to developing theory.

Analytical schemes often suffer from the same problems as meta-theory. Naturalistic/positivistic schemes have, I am convinced, a tendency to become overly concerned with their architectural majesty. In an effort to construct an orderly scheme that mirrors at an abstract level the empirical world in all its dimensions, naturalistic/positivistic schemes get ever more complex; and as new elements are added to the scheme, efforts to reconcile new portions with the old take precedence over making the scheme testable. Moreover, the scheme as a whole is impossible to test because relations among its elements cover such a broad range of phenomena and are rarely stated with great precision. And when imprecision is compounded by the abstractness, then empirical tests are infrequent because it is not clear how to test any portion of the scheme. Yet, despite these problems, creators of analytical schemes view them as a necessary prerequisite for developing testable theoretical statements. In their view, one needs to know what is important to tests; and only through an ordered scheme is this possible.

In contrast, sensitizing/descriptive schemes are typically constructed by those who reject a natural science or positivistic perspective on how to accumulate knowledge. One can never have definitive tests of theoretical statements because all statements will eventually be wrong since the social universe is constantly changing its fundamental nature. Thus, one can only use a loose framework of concepts to interpret events and to see if they yield greater understanding of how and why these events occur. Obviously, I do not agree with this kind of argument, although I have found many of these sensitizing schemes very insightful. Yet, much like naturalistic approaches, sensitizing schemes also become self-reinforcing because they are so loosely structured and so often vague (albeit suggestive and insightful) that the facts can always be bent to fit the scheme. Hence, the scheme can never be refuted or, I suspect, revised on the basis of actual empirical events.

This leaves us with axiomatic/formal propositional formats, analytical models, and middle-range propositions. As I have already indicated, axiomatic theorizing is, for the most part, impractical in sociology. In my view, formal theorizing is the most useful approach because it contains abstract concepts that are linked with sufficient precision so as to be testable. Analytical models can be highly insightful, but they are hard to test as a whole. They contain too many concepts, and their linkages are too diverse to be directly tested. And so, it is reasonable to ask: in what sense can they be useful for sociological theorizing? My view is that an analytical model can best be used to specify the processes by which concepts in a formal proposition are connected.[29] For example, if a proposition states that the "degree of differentiation" is a function of "system size," the model can tell us why and how size and differentiation are connected. That is, we can get a better sense for the underlying processes by which size increases differentiation (and perhaps vice versa). Alternatively, analytical models can also be a starting point for formal theorizing. By isolating basic processes and mapping their interconnections, we can get a sense for the important social processes about which we need to develop formal propositions. And although the model as a whole cannot be easily tested (because it is too complex to be subject to a definitive test), we can decompose it into abstract propositional statements that are amenable to definitive tests.

Middle-range propositions are, I feel, less useful as places to begin theory building. They tend to be too filled with empirical content, much of which does not pertain to the more basic, enduring, and generic features of the social universe.[30] For example, a "theory of ethnic antagonism" is often difficult to translate into a more general proposition or model on conflict. Moreover, scholars working at this middle range tend to become increasingly empirical as they seek to devise ways to test their theories. Their propositions become, I have found, ever more like empirical generalizations as more and more research content is added. There is no logical reason why substantive and empirical referents cannot be taken out of middle-range theories and the level of abstraction raised, but such has infrequently occurred. The reason for this is that, because the generalizations are content filled and stated propositionally, they are readily tested; and so, there is a bias to test the propositions as opposed to extract their more generic content and create more abstract propositions.

In Figure 1-7, I have summarized these conclusions in the right column. Meta-theory, naturalistic analytical schemes, and sensitizing schemes are interesting philosophy, but poor theory. Formal propositional statements and analytical models offer the best place to begin theorizing, especially if interplay between them is possible. Middle-range theories have rarely realized their theoretical potential, tending to move toward empirical generalizations as opposed to formal propositions. Causal models and empirical generalizations are useful in that they give theorists some sense of empirical regularities, but by themselves and without creative leaps in scope and abstraction, they are not theoretical. They are usually data in need of a theory.

---

[29] I have tried to illustrate this strategy in my *Societal Stratification*.

[30] I doubt if this was Merton's intent when he formulated this idea, but my sense is that his advocacy became a legitimation for asserting that empirical generalizations were "theory."

**FIGURE 1–7**   Relations among Theoretical Approaches and Potential for Building
Theory

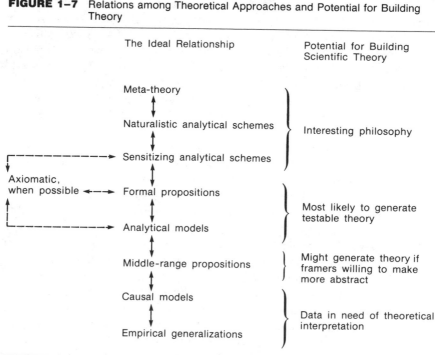

In the left column, I have presented my idealized view of the proper place of each theoretical approach for generating knowledge.[31] If we begin to accumulate bodies of formal laws, then it is desirable to extract out the key concepts and look at these as the basic sensitizing and orienting concepts of sociology (much as magnetism, gravity, relativity, and the like were for early 20th-century physics). We may even want to construct a formal analytical scheme and ponder on the meta-theoretical implications of these. In turn, such pondering can help reformulate or clarify analytical schemes, which can perhaps help construct new, or reverse old, formal propositions. But without a body of formal laws to pull meta-theory and analytical schemes back into the domain of the testable, they become hopelessly self-sustaining and detached from the very reality they are supposed to help clarify.

For building theory, the most crucial interchange is, I believe, between formal propositions and analytical models. There is a creative synergy between translating propositions into models and vice versa. This is the

---

[31]I should emphasize that this is not how things actually work; the diagram represents my *wish* for how sociological theory should be developed.

level at which most theory should be couched. But as I will document in the following chapters, a good many theorists clearly disagree.

Middle-range propositions can inspire analytical models that, in turn, encourage the development of more abstract propositions. Such will be the case, however, only if there already exists a body of useful abstract propositions that can serve as an inducement to middle-range theorists to raise the level of abstraction of their empirically laden statements. Conversely, middle-range theories could potentially be one vehicle by which more abstract propositions—such as on conflict processes—are attached to specific empirical problems—such as ethnic conflict. Thus, middle-range theories become part of the deductive calculus of a formal theoretical system. And finally, the techniques of research generalizations and causal modeling of empirical variables can help test the implication of formal theories. They become the lowest order generalizations in the deductive system of formal theory. They might also stimulate inductive efforts to develop more abstract propositions of greater scope, but as I indicated earlier, I have my doubts if this will occur.

Thus, in my view, there is no necessary conflict among these various approaches to accumulating knowledge. But in actual fact, there is enormous conflict among those, including me and almost all other theorists, who claim that one of these activities is the most essential for developing social theory. Much of the theoretical literature in sociology is consumed with the debates among scholars working with one or the other of these strategies. Indeed, I would imagine that my comments in this section are just more fuel for a fire that shows little potential for extinguishing itself.

## THE STATE OF SOCIOLOGICAL THEORY

### Prevailing Theoretical Schemes in Sociology

The comments above express my opinions, but they have also summarized the state of sociological theorizing. Most theory in sociology is of two basic types: analytical schemes and loose systems of formal propositions. There is some analytical modeling at a general theoretical level; but it is usually part of a system of propositions or general analytical scheme. In specific substantive subfields, there is considerable modeling and middle-range theorizing. Yet, I cannot cover in this volume all of these theories of various subfields. Moreover, much of this work is insufficiently abstract to be true theory; rather, most of it represents a series of summaries of the empirical generalizations that need theoretical explanation. At the other extreme, I will not analyze any of the meta-theoretical schemes that can be found in the theoretical literature. I find these too philosophical to constitute interesting theory. However, if meta-theoretical considerations are part of a general analytical scheme or system of formal propositions, then I will explore these considerations in light of their implications for the theoretical scheme.

Thus, in the pages to follow, the core structure of sociological theory revolves around analytical schemes and formal propositional systems. At times, analytical models and meta-theoretical issues are part of these analytical and propositional schemes, but the essence of sociological theory today is a series of naturalistic analytical schemes, sensitizing analytical schemes, and variously structured systems of abstract formal propositions.

## Enduring Controversies in Sociological Theorizing

In addition to this diversity of schemes employed by various theorists, there is enormous controversy over a number of substantive and strategic issues. Some of this controversy reflects the implicit assumptions of the schemes, per se, but even more if it is the result of different preferences among individual theorists. Let me review some of these controversies, because they will surface again and again in subsequent chapters.

**Can sociology be a science?**    This issue will always confront us in a review of sociological theories. The basic line of argument is: Can sociology be like the other natural sciences, or is there something unique about human affairs?[32] If the social universe is considered to be like other realms, such as that analyzed by physics or biology, then theory tends toward propositional and naturalistic analytical schemes. If human action, interaction, and organization are seen as fundamentally different and as not amenable to analysis with the procedures of natural science, then sensitizing analytical schemes are most likely to be used.

This issue is probably the most divisive in sociological theorizing. At present, I would guess that sociological theorists are about equally split, although I suspect that the natural science advocates have lost ground in recent years to those who do not feel that the theoretical procedures of the other sciences are relevant to human beings. I consider this trend unfortunate, but obviously my feelings are not shared by a growing majority of theorists.

**Should sociological theory be micro or macro?**    This question addresses the issue of whether sociological theory should be about the micro actions and interactions of individuals or the macro social structures that such actions and interactions create.[33] Should we study and

---

[32]See notes 9 and 10 for examples of the two sides on this issue.

[33]This has reemerged as a major issue in sociological theory. For some recent commentaries on it, see K. Knorr-Cetina and A. V. Cicourel, eds., *Advances in Social Theory and Methodology: Toward an Integration of Micro- and Macro-sociologies* (Boston: Routledge & Kegan Paul, 1981); Jonathan H. Turner, "Theoretical Strategies for Linking Micro and Macro Processes: An Evaluation of Seven Approaches," *Western Sociological Review* 14, no. 1 (1983), pp. 4–15.

theorize about people in concrete settings, or should we stand back and look at the institutional complexes of society? Micro theorists typically accuse macro theorists of reifying social structure—that is, of making a reality out of a concept. They see social structure as nothing more than the micro processes of action and interaction among individuals. In their defense, macro theorists see micro theorists as never seeing the forest through the trees. Micro theorists, they argue, are so busy studying interaction, they fail to see that such interaction is constrained by the structures of society.

There have been many conceptual efforts to resolve this debate by developing approaches that address both micro and macro processes.[34] But these efforts typically generate further controversy, as the synthesizing scheme is seen by its critics as having a micro or macro bias. Proponents of micro, macro, or synthetic efforts tend to employ all the approaches outlined earlier. Yet, I sense that those with a micro bias tend to use sensitizing analytical schemes, whereas those theorists who focus on macro structural processes tend to employ formal propositional schemes and naturalistic analytical schemes. Yet, there are so many exceptions to this generalization that I hesitate to make it. But there is at least a slight tendency along these lines.

**Is sociology a paradigmatic science?**    This issue is less burning than the other two that I have mentioned above. But it is an issue when organizing a discussion of various theoretical approaches. Some argue that sociological theory can be divided into several paradigms that hold different views of reality and advocate varying theoretical as well as research strategies.[35]

My feeling is that the concept of paradigm is too strong. As employed by its most visible exponent, Thomas Kuhn,[36] I suspect that no theoretical approach is sufficiently coherent, precise, and established as to constitute a paradigm of abstract concepts and laws as well as verified research findings. If anything, sociology is pre-paradigmatic.

Moreover, I think that the concept of paradigm has been so overused that it has lost any meaning, at least for me. Rather, I think that, at best, sociology has a series of perspectives or orientations that guide theoretical activity, but these perspectives do not constitute, in my view, paradigms in the same sense as this term has been employed in the natural sciences.

---

[34]For examples, see Giddens, *The Constitution of Society,* and Randall Collins, *Conflict Sociology* (New York: Academic Press, 1975). As we will see shortly, many specific perspectives besides these two examples try to provide a reconciliation of micro- and macroprocesses.

[35]The best of these arguments is George Ritzer's *Sociology: A Multiple Paradigm Science* (Boston: Allyn & Bacon, 1975).

[36]Thomas Kuhn, *The Structure of Scientific Revolutions* (Chicago: University of Chicago Press, 1962, 1970).

# THEORETICAL PERSPECTIVES IN SOCIOLOGY

In my view, much of what is labeled sociological theory is, in reality, only a loose clustering of implicit assumptions, some basic concepts, and various kinds of theoretical statements and formats. But none of these is dominant or sufficiently precise to constitute a paradigm. Sometimes assumptions are stated explicitly and serve to inspire abstract theoretical statements containing well-defined concepts, but most sociological theory constitutes a verbal "image of society" rather than a rigorously constructed set of theoretical statements organized into a logically coherent format. Thus, a great deal of "theory" is really a general perspective or orientation for looking at various features of the social world.

The fact that there are many such perspectives in sociology presents me with a problem of exposition. This is compounded when we recognize that the perspectives blend into one another, sometimes rendering it difficult to analyze them separately. My solution to this dilemma is to limit arbitrarily the number of perspectives covered and, at the same time, to act as if they were separable. Accordingly, in the sections to follow, I will analyze five general sociological perspectives or orientations: (1) functional theorizing, (2) conflict theorizing, (3) exchange theorizing, (4) interactionist theorizing, and (5) structuralist theorizing. These general perspectives do not constitute paradigms because the various theorists working within these traditions often disagree over the best strategy, over whether sociology can be a science, and over whether or not the micro, macro, or some combination of the two should be emphasized. Indeed, the debates *within* orientations are frequently far more acrimonious than those between orientations.

I will focus on these perspectives for a number of reasons: (1) They are the most general perspectives in sociology and underlie most specific perspectives in the field. (2) These perspectives are also the most widespread and influential—the subjects of much analytical elaboration and, of course, criticism. (3) Each of these perspectives, at various times, has been proclaimed by its more exuberant proponents as the only one that could take sociology out of its theoretical difficulties. Therefore, each must be considered in a book attempting to assess the structure of sociological theorizing.

For each of these perspectives, I will examine its emergence and then its dominant contemporary practitioners. In so doing, I will emphasize a number of key topics: (1) the assumptions about the nature of the social world that a perspective, and its advocates, hold; (2) the theory-building strategy typically advocated by those working with a perspective; (3) the image of social processes that a perspective reveals; (4) the key concepts and propositions developed within the perspective; and (5) the types of theoretical statements generated within a perspective.

In sum, I think that it is safe to say that sociological theorizing is in its intellectual infancy. Yet, my review of its major orientations will demonstrate that theory in sociology has great potential for developing useful knowledge about the social universe.

# Functional Theorizing

# CHAPTER 2

# The Emergence
# of Functionalism

Even today, I think it is fair to conclude that classical economic ideas dominate sociological theory and social thought in general.[1] From this economic perspective, humans are seen as rational beings who try to maximize their gains and minimize their losses. And I suspect that many still view social life as a kind of marketplace where people buy and sell their qualities in hopes of making a psychic profit. Indeed, social life is a competitive game of people rationally pursuing their interests, with social order somehow emerging out of these clashes of self-interest.

This view of humans is frequently termed *utilitarianism* because there is the assumption that actors are rational and that they try to maximize their "utilities" or rewards and gratifications. Adam Smith is most commonly associated with this perspective because he was the first to conceptualize analytically the dynamics of competitive markets and because he postulated an "invisible hand of order" as emerging from open competition in free markets.[2] Although utilitarianism pervades much of our thinking today, it was even more dominant in the last century. And just as sociology today must overcome the limitations of this narrow view of humans and social organization, so it had to confront utilitarianism in the last century. In fact, I do not think it an exaggeration to say that

---

[1] As I will outline later, exchange theory typically begins with these assumptions. But it also penetrates other perspectives, as we will come to see.

[2] Adam Smith, *An Inquiry into the Nature and Causes of the Wealth of Nations* (London: Davis, 1805; originally published in 1776). Only volume 1 contains these extreme statements. Subsequent portions of the book are quite sociological in nature.

sociology's first theoretical perspective—functionalism—emerged as a re-action against utilitarianism. In questioning utilitarianism, sociology pur-sued an alternative, organicism.

## FUNCTIONALISM AND THE ORGANISMIC ANALOGY

In early 19th-century sociology, humans no longer were viewed as rational and calculating entrepreneurs in a free, open, unregulated, and competitive marketplace. Nor was the doctrine of the "invisible hand of order" con-sidered a very adequate explanation of how social organization could emerge out of free and unbridled competition among individuals. Although util-itarianism remained a prominent social doctrine for the entire 19th cen-tury, the first generation of French sociologists had ceased to accept the assumption that social order would automatically be forthcoming if only free competition among individuals was left intact.

The disenchantment with utilitarianism was aided in France, and to a lesser extent in all of continental Europe, by the disruptive social changes wrought by industrialization and urbanization. Coupled with the political instability of the late 18th century, as revealed most dramatically by the violent French Revolution, early 19th-century social thinkers in France displayed a profound concern with the problems of maintaining the social order. Although each phrased the question somewhat differently, I think it fair to conclude that all social thinkers asked similar questions: Why and how is society possible? What holds society together? What makes societies change?[3]

Whether in France or elsewhere in Europe, the answers to these fun-damental questions were shaped by events occurring in the biological sciences. It was in the 19th century that biological discoveries were to alter significantly the social and intellectual climate of the times. For example, as many of the mysteries of the human body were being dis-covered, the last vestiges of mysticism surrounding the body's functioning were being laid to rest. The diversity of the animal species was finally being systematically recorded under the long-standing classification pro-cedures outlined by the Swedish biologist Carolus Linnaeus. And most importantly, conceptions of evolution, culminating in the theories of Wal-lace and Darwin, were stimulating great intellectual and social contro-versy. Since it was in this social and intellectual milieu that sociology as a self-conscious discipline was born, it is not surprising that conceptions of social order were influenced by a preoccupation with biology.

---

[3]In fact, Adam Smith, had originally posed the question that all French thinkers were to ask: as societies become more complex and differentiated, and as actors live in different worlds, what "force" can hold the social fabric together?

## The Organicism of Auguste Comte (1798–1857)

Auguste Comte is usually credited as being the founder of sociology. Philosophizing about humans and society had, of course, long been a preoccupation of lay people and scholars alike, but it was Comte who advocated a "science of society" and coined the term *sociology*. And although Comte's work was soon to fall into neglect and obscurity and he was to live out his later years in frustration and bitterness, his work profoundly influenced social thought. I think it regrettable that few recognize this influence, even today. Yet, despite Comte's current obscurity, I mark the emergence of the functionalist perspective with his work.[4]

Like most French thinkers of his time, Comte was preoccupied with propagating order and harmony out of the chaos created by the French Revolution. He attacked the individualism of utilitarian doctrines so prominent in England and carried forward Rousseau's and Saint-Simon's desire to develop a "collective philosophy"—one that would provide the principles for creating social consensus. In so doing, however, he articulated the principles of science as they should be applied to society.

Comte felt that human evolution in the 19th century had reached the "positive stage" in which empirical knowledge could be used to understand the social world and to create a better society. Comte thus became an advocate of the application of the scientific method to the study of society—a strategy that, in deference to Comte, is still termed *positivism* in the social sciences. This application of the scientific method was to give birth to a new science, sociology.

Comte's entire intellectual life represented an attempt to legitimate sociology. His efforts on this score went so far as to construct a "hierarchy of the sciences," with sociology as the "queen" of the sciences. Although this hierarchy allowed Comte to assert the importance of sociology and thereby separate it from social philosophy, his most important tactic for legitimating sociology was to borrow terms and concepts from the highly respected biological sciences. Sociology was thus initiated and justified by appeals to the biological sciences—a fact that will help explain why functionalism was sociology's first and, until the 1970s, most dominant theoretical orientation.

Comte saw the affinity between sociology and biology to reside in their common concern with organic bodies. This affinity led him to divide sociology into social "statics," or morphology, and "dynamics," or social growth and progress. But Comte was convinced that although "Biology has hitherto been the guide and preparation for Sociology . . . Sociology will in the future . . . (provide) the ultimate systematization of Biology."

---

[4]Auguste Comte, *The Course of Positive Philosophy* (1830–1842). References are to the more commonly used edition that Harriet Martineau condensed and translated, *The Positive Philosophy of Auguste Comte*, vols. 1, 2, and 3 (London: Bell & Sons, 1898, originally published in 1854).

Comte visualized that with initial borrowing of concepts from biology, and later with the development of positivism in the social sciences, the principles of sociology would inform biology. Thus, sociology must first recognize the correspondence between the individual organism in biology and the social organism in sociology:

> We have thus established a true correspondence between the Statistical Analysis of the Social Organism in Sociology, and that of the Individual Organism in Biology ... If we take the best ascertained points in Biology, we may decompose structure anatomically into *elements*, *tissues*, and *organs*. We have the same things in the Social Organism; and may even use the same names.[5]

Comte then began to make clear analogies between specific types of social structures and the biological concepts:

> I shall treat the Social Organism as definitely composed of the Families which are the true elements or cells, next the Classes or Castes which are its proper tissues, and lastly, of the cities and Communes which are in real organs.[6]

Most of Comte's organismic analogies came in his later works, which were highly flawed.[7] And so, I would be remiss if I left Comte at this point, for he was much more than a simple-minded organicist. My main concern is, of course, with functionalism, but let me pause for a closer look at Comte's positivism, which contains the basic tenets of the abstract propositional approach that I outlined in the last chapter as well as a critique of both causal and functional analysis. Comte preferred the name *social physics* over the current name of our discipline—sociology.[8] He wanted to mold sociology after Newtonian physics in which abstract theoretical principles are used to interpret empirical events. Contrary to many contemporary critics of positivism, who use the term *positivism* as an epithet for *raw empiricism,* Comte argued:

> The next great hindrance to the use of observation is empiricism which is introduced into it by those who, in the name of impartiality, would interdict the use of any theory whatever ... No real observation of any kind of phenomena is possible, except as far as it is first directed, and finally interpreted, by some theory.[9]

---

[5]Auguste Comte, *System of Positive Polity* or *Treatise on Sociology* (London: Burt Franklin, 1875, originally published 1851), pp. 239–40.

[6]Ibid., pp. 241–42.

[7]By the time he wrote *Positive Polity* in 1851, Comte was, in a very real sense, a broken intellectual. Far more important, I feel, is the first work on *Positive Philosophy.*

[8]He was forced to abandon his preferred name because the Belgian statistician, Adolphe Quetelet, had already usurped the label for his statistical analyses.

[9]*Positive Philosophy*, vol. 1, p. 2.

What was such theory to look like? His answer is, I think, very important because he warned against the very functional analysis that he helped initiate in his later works, while he cautioned against excessive concern with the causal modeling so prominent in contemporary sociology. As he stressed:

> The first characteristic of Positive Philosophy is that it regards all phenomena as subject to invariable natural *laws*. Our business is,—seeing how vain any research into what are called *causes*, whether first or final,—to pursue an accurate discovery of these laws, with a view to reducing them to the smallest possible number.[10]

In this passage, "final causes" is Comte's term for functions. We should not, he argued, analyze processes in terms of their consequences, nor should we search for their origins, as "first causes." Rather,

> Our real business is to analyze accurately the circumstances of phenomena, and to connect them by the natural relations of succession and resemblance. The best illustration of this is the case of the doctrine of Gravitation.[11]

Thus, I think it fair to say that Comte's view of positivism rejected the functionalism and the more extreme organicism that was to emerge in the later decades of the 19th century. Indeed, Émile Durkheim was to "turn Comte on his head" and stress that the very essence of adequate scientific explanation was causal and functional analysis.[12] I can only imagine how Comte would turn over in his grave if he had known what Durkheim did to his views. Yet, despite his eloquent advocacy for a social physics modeled after the natural sciences, Comte did reintroduce organic analogies into sociological inquiry, and he did see sociology as closely allied with the biological sciences.[13] And so, we must conclude that it was with Comte that functional theory begins.

In the period between Comte's decline and Durkheim's ascendance as the most forceful advocate of functionalism, Herbert Spencer was to codify functional analysis into a more explicit theoretical strategy. Let me now turn to a brief review of Spencer's contribution.

## The Analytical Functionalism of Herbert Spencer (1820–1903)

Herbert Spencer is a stigmatized figure in contemporary sociology. I think that this is a great tragedy because much contemporary theorizing owes

---

[10]Ibid., p. 5.

[11]Ibid., p. 6.

[12]Émile Durkheim, *The Rules of the Sociological Method* (New York: Free Press, 1938; originally published in 1895).

[13]Organicism was not original with Comte, of course. Plato and other more distant thinkers had also made organismic analogies; Comte simply reintroduced this idea.

an unacknowledged debt to Spencer.[14] Moreover, analyses of Spencer's work tend to focus on the weakest portion of his sociology, its functionalism. But unlike Durkheim two decades later, the anthropological functionalists of the early decades of this century, or the modern functionalists of the contemporary era, Spencer's functional analysis was comparatively recessive. Yet, in what may seem like a contradiction, Spencer anticipated in those few pages devoted to functional analysis all of the main features of modern functionalism.

Like many contemporary functionalists, Spencer saw the universe as divided into realms or domains. For Spencer, these basic realms are the inorganic (physical, chemical), the organic (biological, psychological), and superorganic (sociological).[15] His great philosophical project was to generate a series of abstract principles or laws—what he termed *the first or cardinal principles*—that could explain all of these realms.[16] Needless to say, he was a bit over-ambitious on this score, but the general idea was to explain social processes with abstract laws or principles. The content of these principles borrows from the physics of his time, not the biology. Yet, it is his biological analogizing for which we most remember Spencer; and when making these analogies, he introduced analytical functionalism. But I emphasize again that Spencer saw both the organic and superorganic realms as obeying the same abstract laws, or first principles. Indeed, his organicism is secondary to his effort at making deductions from his abstract first principles.[17]

Spencer published his monumental *Principles of Biology* before his first sociological works.[18] As a consequence, I think, he wanted to demonstrate that both organic and superorganic bodies reveal "parallels in principles of organization" that could be deduced from the first principles. And so, it is not surprising that he compared societies and organisms in terms of their similarity and dissimilarity. Among the points of similarity he emphasized:[19]

[14]See my *Herbert Spencer: Toward a Renewed Appreciation* (Beverly Hills, Calif.: Sage Publications, 1985) for a more detailed presentation of this line of argument.

[15]Herbert Spencer, *The Principles of Sociology* (1874-1896). This work has been reissued in varying volume numbers. References in this chapter are to the three-volume edition (the third edition) issued by D. Appleton and Company, New York, in 1898. In reading this long work, it is much more critical to note the parts (numbered I through VII) than the volumes, since pagination can vary with editions.

[16]These are contained in his *First Principles* (New York: A. C. Burt, 1880, originally published in 1862).

[17]For a more detailed analyses of these, see my and Leonard Beeghley's *Emergence of Sociological Theory* (Homewood, Ill.: Dorsey Press, 1981), pp. 67-76; 106-7.

[18]Herbert Spencer, *The Principles of Biology* (New York: D. Appleton, 1864-1867).

[19]See my *Herbert Spencer: Toward a Renewed Appreciation*, Chapter 4. See also his *Principles of Sociology*, vol. I, part II, pp. 449-57. The bulk of Spencer's organicism is on these few pages of a work that spans more than 2,000 pages, and yet, this is what we most remember about Spencer.

1. As organic and superorganic bodies increase in size, they increase in structure. That is, they become more complex and differentiated.
2. Such differentiation of structures is accompanied by differentiation of functions. Each differentiated structure comes to serve distinctive functions for sustaining the "life" of the systemic whole.
3. Differentiated structures and functions require in both organic and superorganic bodies integration through mutual dependence. Each structure can be sustained only through its dependence upon others for vital substances.
4. Each differentiated structure in both organic and super-organic bodies is, to a degree, a systemic whole by itself (i.e., organs are composed of cells and societies of groupings of individuals), and thus, the larger whole is always influenced by the systemic processes of its constituent parts.
5. The structures of organic and superorganic bodies can "live on" for a while after the destruction of the systemic whole.

These points of similarity between organism and society, Spencer argued, must be qualified for their points of "extreme unlikeness.":[20]

1. There are great differences in the degree of connectedness of the parts, or structures, in organic and social wholes. In superorganic wholes, there is less direct and continuous physical contact and more dispersion of parts than in organic bodies.
2. There are differences in the modes of contact between organic and superorganic systems. In the superorganic, there is much more reliance upon symbols than in the organic.[21]
3. There are differences in the levels of consciousness and voluntarism of parts in organic and superorganic bodies. All units in society are conscious, goal seeking, and reflective, whereas only one unit can potentially be so in organic bodies.

As Spencer continued to analogize the points of similarity between organicism and societies, he began to develop what I call *requisite functionalism*. That is, organic and superorganic bodies reveal certain universal requisites that must be fulfilled in order for them to adapt to an environment. Moreover, these same requisites exist for all organic and superorganic systems. Let me quote Spencer on this point:

> Close study of the facts shows us another striking parallelism. Organs in animals and organs in societies have internal arrangements framed on the same principle.

---

[20]*Principles of Sociology*, part II, pp. 451–62.

[21]Spencer's theory of symbolism is commonly ignored by contemporary sociologists who simply accept Durkheim's critique. Part I of *Principles* contains a very sophisticated analysis of symbols.

> Differing from one another as the viscera of a living creature do in many respects, they have several traits in common. Each viscus contains appliances for conveying nutriment to its parts, for bringing it materials on which to operate, for carrying away the product, for draining off waste matters; as also for regulating its activity.[22]

It is not hard to see the seeds of an argument for universal functional requisites in this passage. Indeed, on the next page from this quote, Spencer argued that "it is the same for society" and proceeded to list the basic functional requisites of societies. For example, each superorganic body

> has a set of agencies which bring the raw material . . .; it has an apparatus of major and minor channels through which the necessities of life are drafted out of the general stocks circulating through the kingdom . . .; it has appliances . . . for bringing those impulses by which the industry of the place is excited or checked; it has local controlling powers, political and ecclesiastical, by which order is maintained and healthful action furthered.

Even though these universal requisites are not as clearly separated as they were to become in modern functional approaches, the logic of the analysis is clear. First, there are certain universal needs or requisites that structures function to meet. These revolve around (a) securing and circulating resources, (b) producing usable substances, and (c) regulating and integrating internal activities through power and symbols. Second, each system level—group, community, region, or whole society—reveals a similar set of needs. Third, the important dynamics of any empirical system revolve around processes that function to meet these universal requisites. Fourth, the level of adaptation of a social unit to its environment is determined by the extent to which it meets these functional requisites.

Thus, by recognizing that certain basic or universal needs must be met, analysis of organic and superorganic systems is simplified. One examines processes with respect to needs for integrating differentiated parts, needs for sustaining the parts of the system, needs for producing and distributing information and substances, and needs for political regulation and control. In simple systems, these needs are met by each element of the system; but when structures begin to grow and become more complex, they are met by distinctive types of structures that specialize in meeting one of these general classes of functions. And as societies become highly complex, then structures become even more specialized and meet only specific subclasses of these general functional needs.

The logic behind this form of requisite functionalism guided much of Spencer's substantive analysis. And it is the essence of functional analysis today. The list of basic needs to be met varies among theorists, but the mode of the analysis remains the same: examine specific types of social

---

[22]*Principles of Sociology*, p. 477.

processes and structures in terms of the needs or requisites that they meet.

## FUNCTIONALISM AND ÉMILE DURKHEIM (1858–1917)

As the inheritor of a long French tradition of social thought, especially Comte's organicism, we should not be surprised that Émile Durkheim's early works were heavily infused with organismic terminology. Although his major work, *The Division of Labor in Society*, was sharply critical of Herbert Spencer, many of Durkheim's formulations were clearly influenced by the 19th-century intellectual preoccupation with biology.[23] Aside from the extensive use of biologically inspired terms, Durkheim's basic assumptions reflected those of the organicists: (1) Society was to be viewed as an entity in itself that could be distinguished from and was not reducible to its constituent parts. In conceiving of society as a reality, *sui generis*, Durkheim in effect gave analytical priority to the social whole. (2) Although such an emphasis by itself did not necessarily reflect organismic inclinations, Durkheim, in giving causal priority to the whole, viewed system parts as fulfilling basic functions, needs, or requisites of that whole. (3) The frequent use of the notion "functional needs" is buttressed by Durkheim's conceptualization of social systems in terms of "normal" and "pathological" states. Such formulations, at the very least, connote the view that social systems have needs that must be fulfilled if "abnormal" states are to be avoided. (4) In viewing systems as normal and pathological, as well as in terms of functions, there is the additional implication that systems have equilibrium points around which normal functioning occurs.

Durkheim recognized all of these dangers and explicitly tried to deal with several of them. First, he was clearly aware of the dangers of teleological analysis—of implying that some future consequence of an event causes that very event to occur. Thus, he warned that the causes of a phenomenon must be distinguished from the ends it serves:

> When, then, the explanation of a social phenomenon is undertaken, we must seek separately the efficient cause which produces it and the function it fulfills. We use the word "function" in preference to "end" or "purpose," precisely because social phenomena do not generally exist for the useful results they produce.[24]

---

[23]Émile Durkheim, *The Division of Labor in Society* (New York: Macmillan, 1933, originally published in 1893). Durkheim tended to ignore the fact that Spencer wore several intellectual hats. He reacted to Spencer's advocacy of utilitarianism, seemingly ignoring the similarity between Spencer's organismic analogy and his own organic formulations as well as the close correspondence between their theories of symbols.

[24]Émile Durkheim, *The Rules of the Sociological Method*, p. 96.

Thus, despite giving analytical priority to the whole and viewing parts as having consequences for certain normal states and hence meeting system requisites, Durkheim remained aware of the dangers of asserting that all systems have "purpose" and that the need to maintain the whole causes the existence of its constituent parts. Yet, Durkheim's insistence that the function of a part for the social whole always be examined sometimes led him, and certainly many of his followers, into questionable teleological reasoning. For example, even when distinguishing *cause* and *function* in his major methodological statement, he leaves room for an illegitimate teleological interpretation: "Consequently, to explain a social fact it is not enough to show the cause on which it depends; we must also, at least in most cases, show its function in the establishment of social order."[25] In this summary phrase, I think that the words "in the establishment of" could connote that the existence of system parts can be explained only by the whole, or social order, that they function to maintain. From this view, it is only a short step to outright teleology: the social fact in question is caused by the needs of the social order that the fact fulfills. Such theoretical statements do not necessarily have to be illegitimate, for it is conceivable that a social system could be programmed to meet certain needs or designated ends and thereby have the capacity to cause variations in cultural items or "social facts" in order to meet these needs or ends. But if such a system is being described by an analyst, it is necessary to document how the system is programmed and how it operates to cause variations in social facts to meet needs or ends. As the above quotation illustrates, Durkheim did not have this kind of system in mind when he formulated his particular brand of functional analysis; thus, he did not wish to state his arguments teleologically.

Despite his warnings to the contrary, Durkheim appears to have taken this short step into teleological reasoning in his substantive works. In his first major work on the division of labor, Durkheim went to great lengths to distinguish between cause (increased population and moral density) and function (integration of society).

However, the causal statements often become fused with functional statements. The argument is, generally, like this: population density increases moral density (rates of contact and interaction); moral density leads to competition, which threatens the social order; in turn, competition for resources results in the specialization of tasks; and specialization creates pressures for mutual interdependence and increased willingness to accept the morality of mutual obligation. This transition to a new social order is not made consciously, or by "unconscious wisdom"; yet, the division of labor is necessary to restore the order that "unbridled

---

[25]Ibid., p. 97.

competition might otherwise destroy."[26] Hence, the impression is left that the threat or the need for social order causes the division of labor. Such reasoning can be construed as an illegitimate teleology, since the consequence or result of the division of labor—social order—is the implied cause of it. At the very least, then, cause and function are not kept as analytically separate as Durkheim so often insisted.

In sum, then, despite Durkheim's warnings about illegitimate teleology, he often appears to waver on the brink of the very traps he wished to avoid. I suspect that the reason for this failing can probably be traced to the organismic assumptions built into his form of sociological analysis. In taking a strong sociologistic position on the question of emergent properties—that is, on the irreducibility of the whole to its individual parts—Durkheim separated sociology from the utilitarianism as well as naive psychology and anthropology of his day.[27] However, in supplementing this emphasis on the social whole with organismic assumptions of function, requisite, need, and normality/pathology, Durkheim helped weld organismic principles to sociological theory for nearly three quarters of a century. The brilliance of his analysis of substantive topics, as well as the suggestive features of his analytical work, made a functional mode of analysis highly appealing to subsequent generations of sociologists and anthropologists.

## FUNCTIONALISM AND THE ANTHROPOLOGICAL TRADITION

I think that functionalism might have died with Durkheim except for the fact that anthropologists began to find it an appealing way to analyze simple societies. Indeed, functionalism as a well-articulated conceptual perspective was perpetuated in the first half of the 20th century by the writings of two anthropologists, Bronislaw Malinowski and A. R. Radcliffe-Brown[28]. Each of these thinkers was heavily influenced by the organicism of Durkheim, as well as by their own field studies among primitive societies. Despite the similarities in their intellectual backgrounds,

[26]Ibid., p. 35. For a more detailed analysis, see my and Alexandra Maryanski's *Functionalism* (Menlo Park, Calif.: Benjamin-Cummings, 1978). See also Percy S. Cohen, *Modern Social Theory* (New York: Basic Books, 1968), pp. 35–37.

[27]Robert A. Nisbet, *Émile Durkheim* (Englewood Cliffs, N.J.: Prentice-Hall, 1965), pp. 9–102.

[28]For basic references on Malinowski's functionalism, see his "Anthropology," *Encyclopedia Britannica*, supplementary vol. 1 (London and New York, 1936); *A Scientific Theory of Culture* (Chapel Hill: University of North Carolina Press, 1944); and *Magic, Science, and Religion and Other Essays* (Glencoe, Ill.: Free Press, 1948). For basic references on A. R. Radcliffe-Brown's functionalism, see his "Structure and Function in Primitive Society," *American Anthropologist* 37 (July-September 1935), pp. 58–72; *Structure and Function in Primitive Society* (Glencoe, Ill.: Free Press, 1952); and *The Andaman Islanders* (Glencoe, Ill.: Free Press, 1948). See also Turner and Maryanski, *Functionalism*.

however, the conceptual perspectives developed by Malinowski and Radcliffe-Brown reveal a considerable number of dissimilarities.

## The Functionalism of A. R. Radcliffe-Brown (1881–1955)

Recognizing that "the concept of function applied to human societies is based on an analogy between social life and organic life" and that "the first systematic formulation of the concept as applying to the strictly scientific study of society was performed by Durkheim," Radcliffe-Brown tried to indicate how some of the problems of organismic analogizing might be overcome.[29] For him, the most serious problem with functionalism was the tendency for analysis to appear teleological. Noting that Durkheim's definition of function pertained to the way in which a part fulfills system needs, Radcliffe-Brown emphasized that, in order to avoid the teleological implications of such analysis, it would be necessary to "substitute for the term 'needs' the term 'necessary condition of existence.' " In doing so, he felt that no universal human or societal needs would be postulated; rather, the question of which conditions were necessary for survival would be an empirical one, an issue that would have to be discovered for each given social system. Furthermore, in recognizing the diversity of conditions necessary for the survival of different systems, analysis would avoid asserting that every item of a culture must have a function and that items in different cultures must have the same function.

Once the dangers of illegitimate teleology were recognized, functional or, to use his term, structural analysis could legitimately proceed from several assumptions: (1) One necessary condition for survival of a society is minimal integration of its parts; (2) The term *function* refers to those processes that maintain this necessary integration or solidarity; (3) Thus, in each society structural features can be shown to contribute to the maintenance of necessary solidarity. In such an analytical approach, social structure and the conditions necessary for its survival are irreducible. In a vein similar to that of Durkheim, Radcliffe-Brown saw society as a reality in and of itself. For this reason he was usually led to visualize cultural items, such as kinship rules and religious rituals, as explicable in terms of social structure—particularly its need for solidarity and integration. For example, in analyzing a lineage system, Radcliffe-Brown would first assume that some minimal degree of solidarity must exist in the system. Processes associated with lineage systems would then be assessed in terms of their consequences for maintaining this solidarity. The conclusion was that lineage systems provided a systematic way of adjudicating

---

[29]Radcliffe-Brown, "Structure and Function in Primitive Society," p. 68. This statement is, of course, incorrect, since the organismic analogy was far more developed in Spencer's work.

conflict in societies where families owned land, because such a system specified who had the right to land and through which side of the family it would always pass. In doing so, the integration of the economic system—landed estates owned by families—is explained.[30]

I believe that this form of analysis poses a number of problems that continue to haunt functional theorists. Although Radcliffe-Brown admitted that "functional unity [integration] of a social system is, of course, a hypothesis," he failed to specify the analytical criteria for assessing just how much or how little functional unity is necessary for system survival, to say nothing of specifying the operations necessary for testing this hypothesis. As subsequent commentators were to discover, without some analytical criteria for determining what is and what is not minimal functional integration and societal survival, the hypothesis cannot be tested, even in principle. Thus, what is typically done is to assume that the existing system is minimally integrated and surviving because it exists and persists. Without carefully documenting how various cultural items promote instances both of integration and malintegration of the social whole, such a strategy can reduce the hypothesis of functional unity to a tautology: if one can find a system to study, then it must be minimally integrated; therefore, lineages that are a part of that system must promote this integration. To discover the contrary would be difficult, since the system, by virtue of being a system, is already composed of integrated parts, such as a lineage system. I see a non sequitur in such reasoning, since it is quite possible to view a cultural item like a lineage system as having both integrative and malintegrative (and other) consequences for the social whole. In his actual ethnographic descriptions, Radcliffe-Brown often slips inadvertently into a pattern of circular reasoning: the fact of a system's existence requires that its existing parts, such as a lineage system, be viewed as contributing to the system's existence. Assuming integration and then assessing the contribution of individual parts to the integrated whole leads to an additional analytical problem. Such a mode of analysis implies that the causes of a particular structure—for example, lineages—lie in the system's needs for integration, which is, I think, most likely an illegitimate teleology.

Radcliffe-Brown would, of course, have denied my conclusions. His awareness of the dangers of illegitimate teleology would have seemingly eliminated the implication that the needs of a system cause the emergence of its parts. And his repeated assertions that the notion of function "does not require the dogmatic assertion that everything in the life of every community has a function" should have led to a rejection of tautological

---

[30]Radcliffe-Brown, *Structure and Function in Primitive Society*, pp. 31–50. For a secondary analysis of this example, see Arthur L. Stinchcombe, "Specious Generality and Functional Theory," *American Sociological Review* 26 (December 1961), pp. 929–30.

reasoning.[31] However, I think that much like Durkheim, what Radcliffe-Brown asserted analytically was frequently not practiced in the concrete empirical analysis of societies. Such lapses were not intended but appeared to be difficult to avoid when functional needs, functional integration, and equilibrium are operating assumptions.[32]

Thus, while Radcliffe-Brown displayed an admirable awareness of the dangers of organicism—especially of the problem of illegitimate teleology and the hypothetical nature of notions of solidarity—he all too often slipped into a pattern of questionable teleological reasoning. Forgetting that integration was only a working hypothesis, he opened his analysis to problems of tautology. Such problems were persistent in Durkheim's analysis; and despite his attempts to the contrary, their spectre haunted even Radcliffe-Brown's insightful essays and ethnographies.

## The Functionalism of Bronislaw Malinowski (1884–1942)

I think that functionalism would have ended with Radcliffe-Brown because it had very little to offer sociologists attempting to study complex societies. Both Durkheim and Radcliffe-Brown posited one basic societal need—integration—and then analyzed system parts in terms of how they meet this need. For sociologists who are concerned with differentiated societies, this is likely to become a rather mechanical task. Moreover, it does not allow for analysis of those aspects of a system part that are not involved in meeting the need for integration.

It was Bronislaw Malinowski's functionalism that was to remove these restrictions; by reintroducing Spencer's approach, it offered a way for modern sociologists to employ functional analysis.[33] Malinowski's scheme reintroduced two important ideas from Spencer: (1) the notion of system levels and (2) the concept of different and multiple system needs at each level. In making these two additions, Malinowski made functional analysis more appealing to 20th-century sociological theorists.

In Malinowski's scheme, there are three system levels: the biological, the social structural, and the symbolic.[34] At each of these levels, one can

---

[31]See for example, Radcliffe-Brown, *Structure and Function in Primitive Society*.

[32]A perceptive critic of an early draft of this manuscript provided an interesting way to visualize the problems of tautology:

When do you have a surviving social system?
When certain survival requisites are met.
How do you know when certain survival requisites are met?
When you have a surviving social system.

[33]Don Martindale, *The Nature and Types of Sociological Theory* (Boston: Houghton Mifflin, 1960), p. 459.

[34]Bronislaw Malinowski, *A Scientific Theory of Culture and Other Essays* (London: Oxford University Press, 1964), pp. 71–125; see also Turner and Maryanski, *Functionalism*, pp. 44–57.

---

**TABLE 2-1**  Requisites of System Levels

---

*Cultural (Symbolic) System Level*

1. Requisites for systems of symbols that provide information necessary to adjust to the environment.
2. Requisites for systems of symbols that provide a sense of control over people's destiny and over chance events.
3. Requisites for systems of symbols that provide members of a society with a sense of a "communal rhythm" in their daily lives and activities.

*Structural (Instrumental) System Level*

1. The requisite for production and distribution of consumer goods.
2. The requisite for social control of behavior and its regulation.
3. The requisite for education of people in traditions and skills.
4. The requisite for organization and execution of authority relations.

---

discern basic needs or survival requisites that must be met if biological health, social-structural integrity, and cultural unity are to exist. Moreover, these system levels constitute a hierarchy, with biological systems at the bottom, social structural arrangements next, and symbolic systems at the highest level. Malinowski stressed that the way in which needs are met at one system level sets constraints on how they are met at the next level in the hierarchy. Yet, he did not advocate a reductionism of any sort; indeed, he thought that each system level reveals its own distinctive requisites and processes meeting these needs. Additionally, he argued that the important system levels for sociological or anthropological analysis are the structural and symbolic. And in this actual discussion, it is the social-structural level that receives the most attention. In Table 2-1, the requisites or needs of the two most sociologically relevant system levels are listed.

In analyzing the structural system level, Malinowski stressed that institutional analysis is necessary. For Malinowski, institutions are the general and relatively stable ways in which activities are organized to meet critical requisites. All institutions, he felt, have certain universal properties or "elements" that can be listed and then used as dimensions for comparing different institutions. These universal elements are:

1. *Personnel:* Who and how many people participate in the institution?
2. *Charter:* What is the purpose of the institution; what are its avowed goals?
3. *Norms:* What are the key norms that regulate and organize conduct?
4. *Material apparatus:* What is the nature of tools and facilities used to organize and regulate conduct in pursuit of goals?
5. *Activity:* How are tasks and activities divided? Who does what?
6. *Function:* What requisite does a pattern of institutional activity meet?

By describing each institution along these six dimensions, Malinowski believed that he had provided a common analytical yardstick for comparing patterns of social organization within and between societies. He even went so far as to construct a list of universal institutions as they resolve not just structural but also biological and symbolic requisites.

In sum, I think that Malinowski's functional approach opened new possibilities for sociologists who had long forgotten Spencer's similar arguments. He suggested to sociologists that attention to system levels is critical in analyzing requisites; he argued that there are universal requisites for each system level; he forcefully emphasized that the structural level is the essence of sociological analysis; and much like Spencer before him and Talcott Parsons a decade later (see next chapter), he posited four universal functional needs at this level—economic adaptation, political authority, educational socialization, and social control—which were to be prominent in subsequent functional schemes. Moreover, he provided a clear method for analyzing institutions as they operate to meet functional requisites. It is fair to say, therefore, that Malinowski drew the rough contours for modern sociological functionalism.

## FUNCTIONALISM AND THE GHOST OF MAX WEBER

I would be remiss if I did not address the impact of Max Weber on sociological theory. During the latter 19th century and into the early part of this century, Weber developed a particular approach for sociological analysis. His approach in a wide range of substantive areas—economic sociology, stratification, complex organizations, sociology of religion, authority and social change, for example—still guides modern research and theory in these areas. In the development of general theoretical orientations, however, Weber's influence has been less direct. Although his impact on some perspectives is clear, I think that his influence on functionalism is less evident. And yet, because several contemporary functionalists were so important in initially exposing American scholars to Weber's thought, I consider it unlikely that these functionalists' theorizing was not influenced by the power of his approach.

What, then, has been Weber's impact on the emergence of functionalism? Generally, I see two aspects of Weber's work as having had an important influence: (1) his substantive vision of "social action" and (2) his strategy for analyzing social structures. Weber argued that sociology must understand social phenomena on two levels, at the "level of meaning" of the actors themselves and at the level of collective action among groupings of actors. Weber's substantive view of the world and his strategy for analyzing its features were thus influenced by these dual concerns. In many ways, Weber viewed two realities—that of the subjective meanings of actions and that of the emergent regularities of social institutions.[35] Much functionalism similarly addresses this dualism: How do the subjective states of actors influence emergent patterns of social organization and vice versa?

As I will discuss shortly, Talcott Parsons, in particular, labeled his functionalism *action theory,* and his early theoretical scheme was devoted to analyzing the basic components and processes of the subjective processes of individual actors. But, much like Weber, Parsons and other functionalists were to move to a more macroscopic concern with emergent patterns of collective action.

This shift from the micro to macro represents only part of the Weberian analytical strategy. One of the most enduring analytical legacies of Weber is his strategy for constructing "ideal types." For Weber, an ideal type represented a category system for "analytically accentuating" the important features of social phenomena. Ideal types are abstractions from empirical reality, and their purpose is to highlight certain common features among similar processes and structures. Moreover, they can be used to compare and contrast empirical events in different contexts by providing a common analytical yardstick. By noting the respective deviations of two or more concrete, empirical situations from the ideal type, it is possible to compare these two situations and thus better understand them. And thus, for virtually all phenomena studied by Weber—religion, organizations, power, and the like—he constructed an ideal type in order to visualize its structure and functioning. In many ways, I think that the ideal-type strategy corresponds to taxonomic procedures for categorizing species and for describing somatic structures and processes in the biological science. I see it as encouraging a concern with conceptual schemes and categories rather than propositions and laws. And so, although Weber's work is devoid of the extensive organismic imagery of Durkheim's or Spencer's, the concern with categorization of different social structures is, I believe, highly compatible with the organismic reasoning of early functionalism. Thus, it is not surprising that contemporary functionalists borrowed the substantive vision of the world implied by the concepts of structure and function as well as Weber's use of the taxonomic approach for studying structures and processes.

For functionalists in general and Talcott Parsons in particular, the construction of conceptual schemes remains an important activity. Functionalists elaborately categorize the social world in order to emphasize the importance of some structures and processes for maintaining the social system. For example, much like Weber before him, Parsons first developed

---

[35]For basic references on Weber, see his *The Theory of Social and Economic Organization* (New York: Free Press, 1947); "Social Action and its Types" in *Theories of Society,* ed. Talcott Parsons et al. (New York: Free Press, 1961); Hans Gerth and C. Wright Mills, eds., *From Max Weber: Essays in Sociology* (New York: Oxford University Press, 1958).

a category system for individual social action and then elaborated this initial system of categories into an incredibly complex, analytical edifice of concepts. What is important to recognize is that this strategy of developing category systems first and then propositions about the relationships among categorized phenomena lies at the heart of contemporary functionalism. This emphasis on category systems is, no doubt, one of the subtle ways that Weber's ideal-type strategy continues to influence functional theorizing in sociology.

## THE EMERGENCE OF FUNCTIONALISM: AN OVERVIEW

With its roots in the organicism of the early 19th century, functionalism is the oldest and, until recent decades, the dominant conceptual perspective in sociology. The organicism of Comte and later that of Spencer and Durkheim clearly influenced the first functional anthropologists—Malinowski and Radcliffe-Brown—who, in turn, with Durkheim's timeless analysis, helped shape the more modern functional perspectives. Coupled with Weber's emphasis on social taxonomies, or ideal types, of both subjective meaning and social structure, a strategy for studying the properties of the "social organism" similarly began to shape contemporary functionalism.

In emphasizing the contribution of sociocultural items to the maintenance of a more inclusive systemic whole, early functional theorists often conceptualized social needs or requisites. The most extensive formulations of this position were of Malinowski, in which institutional arrangements meet one of various levels of needs or requisites: biological, structural, and symbolic. For Émile Durkheim and A. R. Radcliffe-Brown, it was important to analyze separately the causes and functions of a sociocultural item, since the causes of an item could be unrelated to its function in the systemic whole. In their analyses of actual phenomena, however, both Durkheim and Radcliffe-Brown lapsed into assertions that the need for integration caused a particular event—for example, the emergence of a particular type of lineage system or the division of labor.

I see their tendency to blur the distinction between cause and function as generating two related problems in the analyses of Durkheim and Radcliffe-Brown: (1) tautology and (2) illegitimate teleology. To say that a structural item, such as the division of labor, emerges because of the need for social integration is a teleological assertion, for an end state (social integration) is presumed to cause the event (the division of labor), which brings about this very end state. Such a statement is not necessarily illegitimate, since indeed, the social world is rife with systemic wholes that initiate and regulate the very structures and processes maintaining them. However, to assert that the need for integration is the cause of the division of labor is probably an illegitimate teleology: To make the teleology legitimate would require some documentation of the causal chain of events through which needs for integration operate to produce a division of labor. Without such documentation, the statement is vague and theoretically vacuous. Assumptions about and taxonomies of system needs and requisites also create problems of tautology. For unless clear-cut and independent criteria can be established to determine when a system requisite is fulfilled or not fulfilled theoretical statements become circular: a surviving system is meeting its survival needs; the system under study is surviving; a sociocultural item is a part of this system; therefore, it is likely that this item is meeting the system's needs. Such statements are true by definition, since no independent criteria exist for assessing when a requisite is met and whether a given item meets these criteria. To stretch Durkheim's analysis for purposes of illustration, without clear criteria for determining what constitutes integration and what levels of it denote a surviving system, the statement that the division of labor meets an existing system's needs for integration must be true by definition, since the system exists and is therefore surviving and the division of labor is its most conspicuous integrative structure.

In looking back on the theoretical efforts of early functionalists, then, I would see the legacy of their work as follows:

1. The social world was viewed in systemic terms. For the most part, such systems were considered to have needs and requisites that had to be met to assure survival.
2. Despite their concern with evolution, thinkers tended to view systems with needs and requisites as having normal and pathological states—thus connoting system equilibrium and homeostasis.
3. When viewed as a system, the social world was seen as composed of mutually interrelated parts; the analysis of these interrelated parts focused on how they fulfilled requisites of systemic wholes and, hence, maintained system normality or equilibrium.
4. By typically viewing interrelated parts in relation to the maintenance of a systemic whole, causal analysis frequently became vague, lapsing into tautologies and illegitimate teleologies.

Much of contemporary functionalism has attempted to incorporate the suggestiveness of early functional analysis—especially the conception of *system* as composed of interrelated parts.[36] At the same time, current forms of functional theorizing have tried to cope with the analytical problem of teleology and tautology, which Durkheim and Radcliffe-Brown so

---

[36]For a more thorough analysis of the historical legacy of functionalism, see Don Martindale's *The Nature and Types of Sociological Theory* and his "Limits of and Alternatives to Functionalism in Sociology," in *Functionalism in the Social Sciences*, American Academy of Political and Social Science Monograph, no. 5 (Philadelphia, 1965), pp. 144–62; see also in this monograph, Ivan Whitaker, "The Nature and Value of Functionalism in Sociology," pp. 127–43.

unsuccessfully tried to avoid. In borrowing the 19th-century organicism and in exploiting conceptually the utility of viewing system parts as having implications for the operation of systemic wholes, modern functionalism provided early sociological theorizing with a unified conceptual perspective.

Moreover, in developing a concern with conceptual schemes as opposed to systems of propositions, functional theory often appeared to order the complexities of social structures and processes. Yet, the adequacy of this perspective has increasingly been called into question in recent decades. For, as I will emphasize throughout this book, this questioning has often led to excessively polemical and counterproductive debates in sociology. On the positive side, however, the controversy over functional theorizing has also stimulated attempts to expand upon old conceptual perspectives and to develop new perspectives as alternatives to what are perceived to be the inadequacies of functionalism. But for the present, let me concentrate on a detailed overview of contemporary functional theorizing.

# CHAPTER 3

# The Analytical Functionalism of Talcott Parsons

Talcott Parsons was probably the most dominant theorist of his time. It is unlikely, I suspect, that any one theoretical approach will so dominate sociological theory again. For in the years between 1950 and the late 1970s, Parsonian functionalism was clearly the focal point around which theoretical controversy raged. Even those who despised Parsons' functional approach could not ignore it; and even now, several years after his death and well over a decade since its period of dominance, Parsonian functionalism is still the subject of controversy.[1] To appreciate Parsons' achievement, I think it best to start at the beginning in 1937 when he published his first major work, *The Structure of Social Action*,[2] and then, I will trace the continuity of the scheme as it evolved over the next four decades.[3]

---

[1]Although few appear to agree with all aspects of Parsonian theory, rarely has anyone quarreled with the assertion that he has been the dominant sociological figure of this century. For documentation of Parsons' influence, see Robert W. Friedrichs, *A Sociology of Sociology* (New York: Free Press, 1970); and Alvin W. Gouldner, *The Coming Crisis of Western Sociology* (New York: Basic Books, 1970).

[2]Talcott Parsons, *The Structure of Social Action* (New York: McGraw-Hill, 1937); the most recent paperback edition (New York: Free Press, 1968) will be used in subsequent footnotes.

[3]It has been emphasized again and again that such continuity does not exist in Parsons' work. For the most often quoted source of this position, see Joseph F. Scott, "The Changing Foundations of the Parsonian Action Scheme," *American Sociological Review* 28 (October 1969), pp. 716–35. This position is held to be incorrect in the analysis to follow. In addition to the present discussion, see also Jonathan H. Turner and Leonard Beeghley, "Current Folklore in the Criticisms of Parsonian Action Theory," *Sociological Inquiry* 44 (Winter 1974). See also Parsons' reply and comments on this article, ibid. For more recent comments

# THE STRUCTURE OF SOCIAL ACTION

In *The Structure of Social Action,* Parsons advocated an "analytical realism" in building sociological theory. Theory in sociology must utilize a limited number of important concepts that "adequately 'grasp' aspects of the external world ... These concepts do not correspond to concrete phenomena, but to elements in them which are analytically separable from other elements."[4] Thus, first of all, theory must involve the development of concepts that abstract from empirical reality, in all its diversity and confusion, common analytical elements. In this way, concepts will isolate phenomena from their embeddedness in the complex relations that go to make up social reality.

The unique feature of Parsons' analytical realism is the insistence on how these abstract concepts are to be employed in sociological analysis. Parsons did not advocate the immediate incorporation of these concepts into theoretical statements but rather their use to develop a "generalized system of concepts." This use of abstract concepts would involve their ordering into a coherent whole that would reflect the important features of the "real world." What is sought is an organization of concepts into analytical systems that grasp the salient and systemic features of the universe without being overwhelmed by empirical details. This emphasis upon systems of categories represents Parsons' application of Max Weber's ideal-type strategy for analytically accentuating salient features of the world. Thus, much like Weber's work, Parsons believed that theory should initially resemble an elaborate classification and categorization of social phenomena that reflects significant features in the organization of these social phenomena. In the terms of my discussion in Chapter 1, Parsons sought to develop a naturalistic/positivistic conceptual scheme. For in Parsons' view, the empirical world does reveal fundamental properties that can be isolated and studied by a classificatory conceptual scheme.

My sense is that Parsons had more than classification in mind. However, he was advocating the priority of developing systems of concepts over systems of abstract propositions. Concepts in theory should not be incorporated into propositions prematurely. They must first be ordered into analytical systems that are isomorphic with the systemic coherence of reality; then, if one is so inclined, operational definitions can be devised and the concepts can be incorporated into true theoretical statements.

Thus, only after systemic coherence among abstract concepts has been achieved is it fruitful to begin the job of constructing true theory. Parsons'

---

on this issue, see Dean Robert Gerstein, "A Note on the Continuity of Parsonian Action Theory," *Sociological Inquiry* 46 (Winter 1976); Richard Münch, "Talcott Parsons and the Theory of Action I: The Structure of the Kantian Lore" and "Talcott Parsons and the Theory of Action II: The Continuity of the Development," both in *American Journal of Sociology* 86 (December 1981) and 87 (February 1982), respectively, pp. 709–739, 771–826.
    [4]Parsons, *Structure of Social Action*, p. 730.

subsequent theoretical and substantive work makes sense, I feel, only after this classificatory strategy is comprehended. For indeed, throughout his intellectual career—from *The Structure of Social Action* to his recent death—Parsons adhered to this strategy for building sociological theory.[5]

Parsons' strategy for theory building maintains a clear-cut ontological position: the social universe displays systemic features that must be captured by a parallel ordering of abstract concepts. Curiously, the substantive implications of this strategy for viewing the world as composed of systems were recessive in *The Structure of Social Action*. Much more conspicuous were assumptions about the "voluntaristic" nature of the social world.

The "voluntaristic theory of action" represented for Parsons a synthesis of the useful assumptions and concepts of utilitarianism, positivism, and idealism.[6] In reviewing the thought of classical economists, Parsons noted the excessiveness of their utilitarianism: unregulated and atomistic actors in a free and competitive marketplace rationally attempting to choose those behaviors that will maximize their profits in their transactions with others. Such a formulation of the social order presented for Parsons a number of critical problems: Do humans always behave rationally? Are they indeed free and unregulated? How is order possible in an unregulated and competitive system? Yet, Parsons saw as fruitful several features of utilitarian thought, especially the concern with actors as seeking goals and the emphasis on the choice-making capacities of human beings who weigh alternative lines of action. Stated in this minimal form, Parsons felt that the utilitarian heritage could indeed continue to inform sociological theorizing. In a similar critical stance, Parsons rejected the extreme formulations of radical positivists, who tended to view the social world in terms of observable cause-and-effect relationships among physical phenomena. In so doing, he felt, they ignored the complex symbolic functionings of the human mind. Furthermore, Parsons saw the emphasis on observable cause-and-effect relationships as too easily encouraging a sequence of infinite reductionism: groups were reduced to the causal relationships of their individual members; individuals were reducible to the cause-and-effect relationships of their physiological processes; these were reducible to physicochemical relationships, and so on, down to the most

---

[5]See ibid., especially pp. 3–43, 727–76. For an excellent secondary analysis of Parsons' position and why it does not appeal to the critics, see Enno Schwanenberg, "The Two Problems of Order in Parsons' Theory: An Analysis from Within," *Social Forces* 49 (June 1971), pp. 569–81.

[6]For a more recent analysis of Parsons' work in relation to the issues he raised in *The Structure of Social Action*, see Leon Mayhew, "In Defense of Modernity: Talcott Parsons and the Utilitarian Tradition," *American Journal of Sociology* 89 (May 1984), pp. 1273–1306; and Jeffrey C. Alexander, "Formal and Substantive Voluntarism in the Work of Talcott Parsons: A Theoretical Reinterpretation," *American Sociological Review* 43 (Winter 1978), pp. 177–98.

basic cause-and-effect connections among particles of physical matter. Nevertheless, despite these extremes, radical positivism draws attention to the physical parameters of social life and to the deterministic impact of these parameters on much—but, of course, not all—social organization. Finally, in assessing idealism, Parsons saw as useful their conceptions of "ideas" as circumscribing both individual and social processes, although all too frequently these ideas are seen as detached from the ongoing social life they were supposed to regulate.

I cannot possibly communicate the depth of scholarship in Parsons' analysis of these traditions. More important than the details of his analysis is the weaving of selected concepts from each of these traditions into a voluntaristic theory of action.[7] For it is at this starting point that, in accordance with his theory-building strategy, Parsons began to construct a functional theory of social organization. In this initial formulation, he conceptualizes voluntarism as the subjective decision-making processes of individual actors, but he views such decisions as the partial outcome of certain kinds of constraints, both normative and situational. Voluntaristic action therefore involves these basic elements: (1) Actors who, at this point in Parsons' thinking, are individual persons. (2) Actors are viewed as goal seeking. (3) Actors are also in possession of alternative means to achieve the goals. (4) Actors are confronted with a variety of situational conditions, such as their own biological makeup and heredity as well as various external ecological constraints, that influence the selection of goals and means. (5) Actors are seen to be governed by values, norms, and other ideas in that these ideas influence what is considered a goal and what means are selected to achieve it. (6) Action involves actors making subjective decisions about the means to achieve goals, all of which are constrained by ideas and situational conditions.

Figure 3-1 represents this conceptualization of voluntarism. The processes diagramed are often termed the *unit act*, with social action involving a succession of such unit acts by one or more actors. I believe that Parsons chose to focus on such basic units of action for at least two reasons. First, he felt it necessary to synthesize the historical legacy of social thought about the most basic social process and to dissect it into

---

[7]Recently, there has been considerable debate and acrimony over "de-Parsonizing" Weber and Durkheim. The presumption is that Parsons gave a distorted portrayal of these and other figures and it is necessary to reexamine their works in an effort to remove Parsons' interpretation from them. This plea ignores two facts: (1) Parsons never maintained that he was summarizing works; instead he was using works and selectively borrowing concepts to build a theory of action. (2) All sociologists can read these classic thinkers for themselves and derive their own interpretations; there is no reason that they should be overly influenced by Parsons. For the relevant articles, see Jere Cohen, Lawrence E. Hazelrigg, and Whitney Pope, "De-Parsonizing Weber: A Critique of Parsons' Interpretation of Weber's Sociology," *American Sociological Review* 40 (April 1975), pp. 229–41; and Whitney Pope, Jere Cohen, and Lawrence Hazelrigg, "On the Divergence of Weber and Durkheim: A Critique of Parsons' Convergence Thesis," *American Sociological Review* 40 (August 1975), pp. 417–27.

**FIGURE 3-1**   The Units of Voluntaristic Action

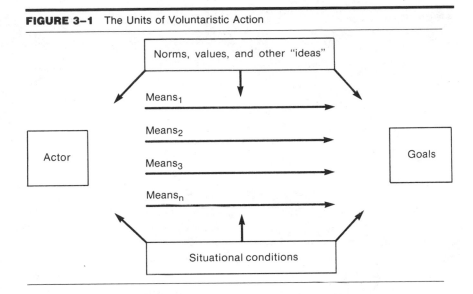

its most elementary components. Second, given his position on what theory should be, the first analytical task in the development of sociological theory is to isolate conceptually the systemic features of the most basic unit from which more complex processes and structures are built.

Once these basic tasks were completed, I think Parsons began to ask: how are unit acts connected to each other, and how can this connectedness be conceptually represented? Indeed, near the end of *The Structure of Social Action*, he recognized that "any atomistic system that deals only with properties identifiable in the unit act ... will of necessity fail to treat these latter elements adequately and be indeterminate as applied to complex systems"[8] However, only the barest hints of what was to come were evident in those closing pages.

Yet, perhaps only through the wisdom of hindsight, Parsons did offer several clues about the features of these more complex systems. Most notable, near the close of this first work, he emphasized that "the concept of action points again to the *organic* property of action systems" [emphasis added].[9] Buttressed by his strategy for building theory—that is, the development of systems of concepts that mirror reality—it is clear that he intended to develop a conceptual scheme that would capture the systemic essence of social reality.

By 1945, eight years after he published *The Structure of Social Action*, Parsons became more explicit about the form this analysis should take:

---

[8]Parsons, *Structure of Social Action*, pp. 748–49.
[9]Ibid, p. 745.

**FIGURE 3–2** Parsons' Conception of Action, Interaction, and Institutionalization

"The structure of social systems cannot be derived directly from the actor-situation frame of reference. It requires functional analysis of the complications introduced by the interaction of a plurality of actors."[10] More significantly, this functional analysis should allow notions of needs to enter: "The functional needs of social integration and the conditions necessary for the functioning of a plurality of actors as a 'unit' system sufficiently well integrated to exist as such impose others."[11] Starting from these assumptions, which bear a close resemblance to those of Spencer, Durkheim, Radcliffe-Brown, and Malinowski, Parsons began to develop a complex functional scheme. Let me now attempt to reconstruct this transition from voluntaristic unit acts to a functional scheme emphasizing the systemic properties of action.

## THE SOCIAL SYSTEM

In Figure 3–2, I have summarized the transition from unit acts to social system.[12] This transition occupies the early parts of Parsons' next significant work, *The Social System*.[13] Drawing inspiration from Max Weber's typological approach to this same topic,[14] Parsons views actors as "oriented" to situations in terms of motives (needs and readiness to mobilize energy) and values (conceptions about what is appropriate). There are three types of motives: (1) cognitive (need for information), (2) cathectic (need for emotional attachment), and (3) evaluative (need for assessment). And, there are three corresponding types of values: (1) cognitive (evaluation in terms of objective standards), (2) appreciative

[10]Talcott Parsons, "The Present Position and Prospect of Systemic Theory in Sociology," *Essays in Sociological Theory* (New York: Free Press, 1949), p. 229.

[11]Ibid.

[12]See also my "The Concept of 'Action' in Sociological Analysis" in *Analytical and Sociological Theories of Action,* ed., G. Seebaβ and Raimo Toumea (Dordrecht, Holland: Reidel, 1985).

[13]Talcott Parsons, *The Social System* (New York: Free Press, 1951).

[14]Max Weber, *Economy and Society*, vol. I (Totowa, N.J.: Bedminister Press, 1968), pp. 1–95.

(evaluation in terms of aesthetic standards), and (3) moral (evaluation in terms of absolute rightness and wrongness). Parsons called these *modes of orientation*. Although I often find this discussion vague, the general idea seems to be that the relative salience of these motives and values for any actor creates a composite type of action, which can be one of three types: (1) instrumental (action oriented to realize explicit goals efficiently), (2) expressive (action directed at realizing emotional satisfactions), and (3) moral (action concerned with realizing standards of right and wrong). That is, depending upon which modes of motivational and value orientation are strongest, an actor will act in one of these basic ways. For example, if cognitive motives are strong and cognitive values most salient, their action will be primarily instrumental, although it will also have expressive and moral content. Thus, the various combinations and permutations of the modes of orientation—that is, motives and values—produce action geared in one of these general directions.

Thus, "unit acts" involve motivational and value orientations and have a general direction as a consequence of what combination of values and motives prevails for an actor. Thus far, Parsons only elaborated upon his conceptualization of the unit act. Here is the critical next step, which, as I mentioned earlier, was only hinted at in the closing pages of *The Structure of Social Action*.

As variously oriented actors (in terms of their configuration of motivational and value orientations) interact, they come to develop agreements and sustain patterns of interaction, which become "institutionalized." Such institutionalized patterns can be, in Parsons' view, conceptualized as a social system. Such a system represents an emergent phenomenon that requires its own conceptual edifice. The normative organization of status-roles becomes Parsons' key to this conceptualization; that is, the subject matter of sociology is the organization of status, roles, and norms. Yet, Parsons recognizes that the actors who are incumbent in such status-roles are motivationally and value oriented; and thus, as he does for patterns of interaction, the task now becomes one of conceptualizing these dimensions of action in systemic terms. The result is the conceptualization of action as composed of three "interpenetrating action systems": the cultural, the social, and the personality. That is, the organization of unit acts into social systems requires a parallel conceptualization of motives and values that become, respectively, the personality and cultural systems. The goal of action theory now becomes understanding how institutionalized patterns of interaction (the social system) are circumscribed by complexes of values, beliefs, norms, and other ideas (the cultural system) and by configurations of motives and role-playing skills (the personality system). Later, Parsons adds the organismic (subsequently called behavioral) system, but let me not get ahead of the story. For at this stage of conceptualization, analyzing social systems involves developing a system of concepts that, first of all, captures the systemic features of society at all its diverse levels and, second, points to the modes of articulation among personality systems, social systems, and cultural patterns.

To capture conceptually the systemic features of culture, social system, and personality, Parsons wastes little time in introducing notions of functional requisites for each of these basic components of action. Such requisites pertain not only to the internal problems of the action components but also to their articulation with one another. Following both Durkheim's and Radcliffe-Brown's lead, he views integration within and among the action systems as a basic survival requisite. Since the social system is his major topic, Parsons is concerned with the integration within the social system itself and between the social system and the cultural patterns, on the one hand, and between the social system and the personality system, on the other. In order for such integration to occur, at least two functional requisites must be met:

1. A social system must have "a sufficient proportion of its component actors adequately motivated to act in accordance with the requirements of its role system"[15]
2. Social systems must avoid "commitment to cultural patterns which either fail to define a minimum of order or which place impossible demands on people and thereby generate deviance and conflict."[16]

Parsons made explicit the incorporation of requisites, which in later works are expanded and made even more prominent. He then attempts to develop a conceptual scheme that reflects the systemic interconnectedness of social systems, although he later returns to the integrative problems posed by the articulation of culture and personality with the social system. Crucial to this conceptualization of the social system is the concept of institutionalization, which refers to relatively stable patterns of interaction among actors in statuses. Such patterns are normatively regulated and infused with cultural patterns. This infusing of values can occur in two ways. First, norms regulating role behaviors can reflect the general values and beliefs of culture. Second, cultural values and other patterns can become internalized in the personality system and, hence, affect that system's need structure, which in turn determines an actor's willingness to enact roles in the social system.

Parsons views institutionalization as both a process and a structure. It is significant that he initially discusses the process of institutionalization and only then refers to it as a structure—a fact that is often ignored by critics who contend that action theory is overly structural. Let me emphasize the point again by reference to Figure 3-2. As a process, in-

---

[15]Talcott Parsons, *The Social System*, p. 27.
[16]Ibid., pp. 27–28.

stitutionalization can be portrayed in the following terms: (1) Actors who are variously oriented enter into situations where they must interact. (2) The way actors are oriented is a reflection of their need structure and how this need structure has been altered by the internalization of cultural patterns. (3) Through specific interaction processes—which are not clearly indicated, but which by implication include role taking, role bargaining, and exchange—norms emerge while actors adjust their orientations to each other. (4) Such norms emerge as a way of adjusting the orientations of actors to each other, but at the same time, they are circumscribed by general cultural patterns. (5) In turn, these norms regulate subsequent interaction, giving it stability. It is through such a process that institutionalized patterns are created, maintained, or altered.

As interactions become institutionalized, a social system can be said to exist, as I have indicated in Figure 3–2. Parsons has typically been concerned with whole societies, but a social system is not necessarily a whole society. Indeed, any organized pattern of interaction, whether a micro or macro form, is termed a social system. When focusing on total societies or large parts of them, Parsons frequently refers to the constituent social systems as subsystems of these larger systemic wholes.

In sum, then, institutionalization is the process through which social structure is built up and maintained. Institutionalized clusters of roles—or, to phrase it differently, stabilized patterns of interaction—comprise a social system. When the given social system is large and is composed of many interrelated institutions, these institutions are typically viewed as subsystems. A total society may be defined as one large system composed of interrelated institutions. At all times, for analytical purposes, it is necessary to remember that a social system is circumscribed by cultural patterns and infused with personality systems.

In his commitment to the development of concepts that reflected the properties of all action systems, Parsons was led to a set of concepts denoting some of the variable properties of these systems. Termed *pattern variables*, they allow for the categorization of the modes of orientation in personality systems, the value patterns of culture, and the normative requirements in social systems. The variables are phrased in terms of polar dichotomies that, depending upon the system under analysis, allow for a rough categorization of decisions by actors, the value orientations of culture, or the normative demands on status roles.

1. *Affectivity-affective neutrality* concerns the amount of emotion or affect that is appropriate in a given interaction situation. Should a great deal or little affect be expressed?
2. *Diffuseness-specificity* denotes the issue of how far-reaching obligations in an interaction situation are to be. Should the obligations be narrow and specific, or should they be extensive and diffuse?
3. *Universalism-particularism* points to the problem of whether evaluation and judgment of others in an interaction situation is to

apply to all actors or should all actors be assessed in terms of the same standards?

4. *Achievement-ascription* deals with the issue of how to assess an actor, whether in terms of performance or on the basis of inborn qualities, such as sex, age, race, and family status. Should an actor treat another on the basis of achievements or ascriptive qualities that are unrelated to performance?

5. *Self-collectivity* denotes the extent to which action is to be oriented to self-interest and individual goals or to group interests and goals. Should actors consider their personal or self-related goals over those of the group or large collectivity in which they are involved?[17]

Some of these concepts, such as self-collectivity, have been dropped from the action scheme, but others, such as universalism-particularism, have assumed greater importance. But I believe that the intent of the pattern variables has remained the same: to categorize dichotomies of decisions, normative demands, and value orientations. However, in *The Social System*, Parsons is inclined to view them as value orientations that circumscribe the norms of the social system and the decisions of the personality system. Thus, the structure of the personality and social systems is a reflection of the dominant patterns of value orientations in culture. This implicit emphasis on the impact of cultural patterns on regulating and controlling other systems of action was to become more explicit in later work, as I will discuss shortly.

For the present, however, it is evident that by 1951, Parsons had already woven a complex conceptual system that emphasizes the process of institutionalization of interaction into stabilized patterns called social systems, which are penetrated by personality and circumscribed by culture. The profile of institutionalized norms, of decisions by actors in roles, and of cultural value orientations can be typified in terms of concepts—the pattern variables—that capture the variable properties in each of these components of action.

Having built this analytical edifice, Parsons returns to a question first raised in *The Structure of Social Action*, which guided all his subsequent theoretical formulations: How do social systems survive? More specifically, why do institutionalized patterns of interaction persist? I think that it is clear now such questions raise the issue of system imperatives or requisites. For Parsons is asking how systems resolve their integrative problems. The answer to this question is provided by the elaboration of additional concepts that point to the ways that personality systems and

[17]These pattern variables were developed in collaboration with Edward Shils and were elaborated upon in *Toward a General Theory of Action* (New York: Harper & Row, 1951), pp. 76–98, 203–4, 183–89. Again, Parsons' debt to Max Weber's concern with constructing ideal types can be seen in his presentation of the pattern variables.

**FIGURE 3–3** Parsons' Early Conception of Integration among Systems of Action

culture are integrated into the social system, thereby providing assurance of some degree of normative coherence and a minimal amount of commitment by actors to conform to norms and play roles. In developing concepts of this kind, Parsons begins to stress the equilibrating tendencies of social systems, which, I believe, was a fatal mistake. For as I will discuss shortly, Parsons left himself open here to severe criticism. But for the moment, let me concentrate on his argument. I have diagrammatically represented his reasoning in Figure 3–3. Now, I will fill in the details.

Just how are personality systems integrated into the social system, thereby promoting equilibrium? At the most abstract level, Parsons conceptualizes two mechanisms that integrate the personality into the social system: (1) mechanisms of socialization and (2) mechanisms of social control. It is through the operation of these mechanisms that personality systems become structured such that they are compatible with the structure of social systems. Let me elaborate on each of these mechanisms.

1. In abstract terms, *mechanisms of socialization* are seen by Parsons as the means through which cultural patterns—values, beliefs, language, and other symbols—are internalized into the personality system, thereby circumscribing its need structure. It is through this process that actors are made willing to deposit motivational energy in roles (thereby willing to conform to norms) and are given the interpersonal and other skills necessary for playing roles. Another function of socialization mechanisms is to provide stable and secure interpersonal ties that alleviate much of the strain, anxiety, and tension associated with acquiring proper motives and skills.

2. *Mechanisms of social control* involve those ways in which status-roles are organized in social systems to reduce strain and deviance. There are numerous specific control mechanisms, including (*a*)

institutionalization, which makes role expectations clear and unambiguous while segregating in time and space contradictory expectations; (b) interpersonal sanctions and gestures, which actors subtly employ to mutually sanction conformity; (c) ritual activities, in which actors act out symbolically sources of strain that could prove disruptive while they reinforce dominant cultural patterns; (d) safety-valve structures, in which pervasive deviant propensities are segregated in time and space from normal institutional patterns; (e) reintegration structures, which are specifically charged with coping with the bringing back into line deviant tendencies; and, finally, (f) the institutionalization into some sectors of a system the capacity to use force and coercion.

These two mechanisms are thus viewed as resolving one of the most persistent integrative problems facing social systems. The other major integrative problem facing social systems concerns how cultural patterns contribute to the maintenance of social order and equilibrium. Again at the most abstract level, Parsons visualizes two ways in which this occurs. (1) Some components of culture, such as language, are basic resources necessary for interaction to occur. Without symbolic resources, communication and hence interaction would not be possible. Thus, by providing common resources for all actors, interaction is made possible by culture. (2) A related but still separable influence of culture on interaction is exerted through the substance of ideas contained in cultural patterns (values, beliefs, ideology, and so forth). These ideas can provide actors with common viewpoints, personal ontologies, or, to borrow from W. I. Thomas, a common "definition of the situation." These common meanings allow interaction to proceed smoothly with minimal disruption.

Naturally, Parsons acknowledges that the mechanisms of socialization and social control are not always successful, hence allowing deviance and social change to occur. But it is clear that the concepts developed in *The Social System* weigh analysis in the direction of looking for processes that maintain the integration and, by implication, the equilibrium of social systems. In Figure 3–4, I have summarized the logic of Parsons' functionalism at this stage in the elaboration of his conceptual scheme.

I see subsequent developments in Parsons' action theory as an attempt to expand upon the basic analytical scheme of *The Social System* that is summarized in Figures 3–2, 3–3, and 3–4 while trying to accommodate some of the critics' charges of a static and conservative conceptual bias (see later section). I do not imagine that the many critics of Parsons will ever be silenced, but some interesting elaborations of the scheme occurred in the quarter century following Parsons' first explicitly functional work. Let me now turn to these.

## THE TRANSITION TO FUNCTIONAL IMPERATIVISM

In collaboration with Robert Bales and Edward Shils, Parsons published *Working Papers in the Theory of Action* shortly after *The Social System*.

**FIGURE 3–4**   Parsons' Mechanism-Equilibrium Functional Analysis

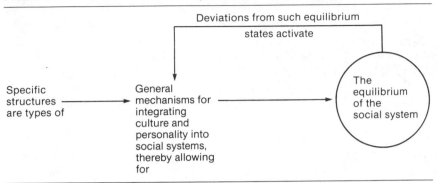

It was in this work that conceptions of functional imperatives came to dominate the general theory of action;[18] and by 1956, with Parsons' and Neil Smelser's publication of *Economy and Society*, the functions of structures for meeting system requisites were well institutionalized into action theory.[19]

During this period, systems of action were conceptualized to have four survival problems, or requisites: adaptation, goal attainment, integration, and latency. *Adaptation* involves the problem of securing from the environment sufficient facilities and then distributing these facilities throughout the system. *Goal attainment* refers to the problem of establishing priorities among system goals and mobilizing system resources for their attainment. *Integration* denotes the problem of coordinating and maintaining viable interrelationships among system units. *Latency* embraces two related problems: pattern maintenance and tension management. Pattern maintenance pertains to the problem of how to insure that actors in the social system display the appropriate characteristics (motives, needs, role-playing skills, and so forth). Tension management concerns the problem of dealing with the internal tensions and strains of actors in the social system.

All of these requisites were, I think, implicit in *The Social System*, but they tended to be viewed under the general problem of integration. In Parson's discussion of integration within and between action systems, problems of securing facilities (adaptation), allocation and goal seeking (goal attainment), socialization and social control (latency) were

---

[18]Talcott Parsons, Robert F. Bales, and Edward A. Shils, *Working Papers in the Theory of Action* (Glencoe, Ill.: Free Press, 1953).

[19]Talcott Parsons and Neil J. Smelser, *Economy and Society* (New York: Free Press, 1956). These requisites are the same as those enumerated by Malinowski. See previous chapter, Table 2–1.

**FIGURE 3–5**   Parsons' Functional Imperativism or Requisite Functionalism

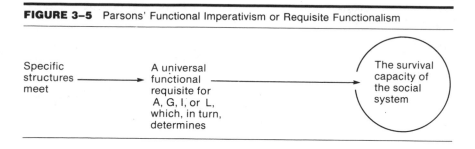

conspicuous. Thus, in my opinion, the development of the four functional requisites—abbreviated A, G, I, and L—is not so much a radical departure from earlier works but an elaboration of concepts implicit in *The Social System.*

With the introduction of A, G, I, L, however, I see a subtle shift away from the analysis of structures to the analysis of functions. Structures are now viewed explicitly in terms of their functional consequences for meeting the four requisites. Interrelationships among specific structures are now analyzed in terms of how their interchanges affect the requisites that each must meet. This shift can be seen in Figure 3–5, especially if compared to Figure 3–4.

As Parsons' conceptual scheme became increasingly oriented to function, social systems are divided into sectors, each corresponding to a functional requisite—that is, A, G, I, or L. In turn, any subsystem can be divided into these four functional sectors. And then, each of these subsystems can be divided into four functional sectors, and so on. This process of "functional sectorization," if I can invent a word to describe it, is illustrated for the adaptive requisite in Figure 3–6.

Of critical analytical importance in this scheme are the interchanges among systems and subsystems. It is difficult to comprehend the functioning of a designated social system without examining the interchanges among its A, G, I, and L sectors, especially since these interchanges are affected by exchanges among constituent subsystems and other systems in the environment. In turn, the functioning of a designated subsystem cannot be understood without examining internal interchanges among its adaptive, goal attainment, integrative, and latency sectors, especially since these interchanges are influenced by exchanges with other subsystems and the more inclusive system of which it is a subsystem. Thus, at this juncture, as important interchanges among the functional sectors of systems and subsystems are outlined, the Parsonian scheme now begins to resemble an elaborate mapping operation.

## THE INFORMATIONAL HIERARCHY OF CONTROL

Toward the end of the 1950s, Parsons turned attention toward interrelationships *among* (rather than within) what were then four distinct ac-

**FIGURE 3–6**  Parsons' Functional Imperativist View of Social Systems

Adaptation                                                    Goal attainment

Latency                                                              Integration

tion systems: culture, social structure, personality, and organism. In many ways, I think this concern represented an odyssey back to the analysis of the basic components of the unit act outlined in *The Structure of Social Action*. But now, each element of the unit act is a full-fledged action system, each confronting four functional problems to resolve: adaptation, goal attainment, integration, and latency. Furthermore, although individual decision making is still a part of action as personalities adjust to the normative demands of status-roles in the social system, the analytical emphasis has shifted to the input-output connections among the four action systems.

It is at this juncture that Parsons begins to visualize an overall action system, with culture, social structure, personality, and organism comprising its constituent subsystems.[20] Each of these subsystems is seen as fulfilling

---

[20]Talcott Parsons, "An Approach to Psychological Theory in Terms of the Theory of

one of the four system requisites—A, G, I, L—of the overall action system. The organism is considered to be the subsystem having the most consequences for resolving adaptive problems since it is ultimately through this system that environmental resources are made available to the other action subsystems. As the goal-seeking and decision-making system, personality is considered to have primary consequences for resolving goal-attainment problems. As an organized network of status-norms integrating the patterns of the cultural system and the needs of personality systems, the social system is viewed as the major integrative subsystem of the general action system. As the repository of symbolic content of interaction, the cultural system is considered to have primary consequences for managing tensions of actors and assuring that the proper symbolic resources are available to assure the maintenance of institutional patterns (latency).

After viewing each action system as a subsystem of a more inclusive, overall one, Parsons begins to explore the interrelations among the four subsystems. What emerges is a hierarchy of informational controls, with culture informationally circumscribing the social system, social structure informationally regulating the personality system, and personality informationally regulating the organismic system. For example, cultural value orientations would be seen as circumscribing or limiting the range of variation in the norms of the social system; in turn, these norms, as translated into expectations for actors playing roles, would be viewed as limiting the kinds of motives and decision-making processes in personality systems; these features of the personality system would then be seen as circumscribing biochemical processes in the organism. Conversely, each system in the hierarchy is also viewed as providing the "energic conditions" necessary for action at the next higher system. That is, the organism provides the energy necessary for the personality system, the personality system provides the energic conditions for the social system, and the organization of personality systems into a social system provides the conditions necessary for a cultural system. Thus, the input-output relations among action systems are reciprocal, with systems exchanging information and energy. Systems high in information circumscribe the utilization of energy at the next lower system level, while each lower system provides the conditions and facilities necessary for action in the next higher system. This scheme has been termed a *cybernetic hierarchy* of control. I have diagramed it in Figure 3–7.

---

Action," in *Psychology: A Science*, ed. S. Koch, vol. 3 (New York: McGraw-Hill, 1958), pp. 612–711. By 1961, these ideas were even more clearly formulated; see Talcott Parsons, "An Outline of the Social System," in *Theories of Society*, ed. T. Parsons, E. Shils, K. D. Naegele, and J. R. Pitts (New York: Free Press, 1961), pp. 30–38. See also Jackson Toby, "Parsons' Theory of Social Evolution," *Contemporary Sociology* 1 (September 1972), pp. 395–401.

**FIGURE 3–7**    Parsons' Cybernetic Hierarchy of Control

| Overall function | System level | Interrelations among system levels | |
|---|---|---|---|
| Latency | Cultural system | Informational controls | ↑ |
| Integration | Social system | | |
| Goal attainment | Personality system | | |
| Adaptation | Organismic system | ↓ | Energic conditions |

# GENERALIZED MEDIA OF EXCHANGE

Until his death, Parsons maintained his interest in the intra- and inter-systemic relationships of the four action systems. Although he was never to develop the concepts fully, he had begun to view these relationships in terms of *generalized symbolic media of exchange.*[21] In any interchange, generalized media are employed—for example, money is used in the economy to facilitate the buying and selling of goods. What typifies these generalized media, such as money, is that they are really symbolic modes of communication. The money is not worth much by itself; its value is evident only in terms of what it says symbolically in an exchange relationship.

Thus, what Parsons proposes is that the links among action components are ultimately informational. This means that transactions are mediated by symbols. Parsons' emphasis on information is consistent with the development of the idea of a cybernetic hierarchy of control. Informational exchanges, or cybernetic controls, are seen as operating in at least three ways. First, the interchanges or exchanges *among* the four subsystems of the overall action system are carried out by means of different types of symbolic media; that is, money, power, influence, or commitments. Second, the interchanges *within* any of the four action systems are also carried out by means of distinctive symbolic media. Finally, the system requisites of adaptation (A), goal attainment (G), integration (I), and latency (L) determine the type of generalized symbolic media used in an inter- or intrasystemic exchange.

---

[21]Parsons' writings on this topic are incomplete, but see his "On the Concept of Political Power," *Proceedings of the American Philosophical Society* 107 (June 1963), pp. 232–62; Talcott Parsons, "On the Concept of Influence," *Public Opinion Quarterly* 27 (Spring 1963), pp. 37–62; and Talcott Parsons, "Some Problems of General Theory," in *Theoretical Sociology: Perspectives and Developments*, ed. J. C. McKinney and E. A. Tiryakian (New York: Appleton-Century-Crofts, 1970), pp. 28–68. See also Talcott Parsons and Gerald M. Platt, *The American University* (Cambridge, Mass.: Harvard Univ. Press, 1975).

Within the social system, the adaptive sector utilizes money as the medium of exchange with the other three sectors; the goal-attainment sector employs power—the capacity to induce conformity—as its principal medium of exchange; the integrative sector of a social system relies upon influence—the capacity to persuade; and the latency sector uses commitments—especially the capacity to be loyal. The analysis of interchanges of specific structures within social systems should thus focus on the input-output exchanges utilizing different symbolic media.

Among the subsystems of the overall action system, a similar analysis of the symbolic media used in exchanges should be undertaken, but Parsons never clearly described the nature of these media.[22] What he appeared to be approaching was a conceptual scheme for analyzing the basic types of symbolic media, or information, linking systems in the cybernetic hierarchy of control.[23]

## PARSONS ON SOCIAL CHANGE

In the last decade of his career, Parsons became increasingly concerned with social change. Built into the cybernetic hierarchy of control is a conceptual scheme for classifying the locus of such social change. What Parsons visualized was that the information-energic interchanges among action systems provide the potential for change within or between the action systems. One source of change may be excesses in either information or energy in the exchange among action systems. In turn, these excesses alter the informational or energic outputs across systems and within any system. For example, excesses of motivation (energy) would have consequences for the enactment of roles and perhaps ultimately for the reorganization of these roles of the normative structure and eventually of cultural value orientations.[24] Another source of change comes from an insufficient supply of either energy or information, again causing external and internal readjustments in the structure of action systems. For example, value (informational) conflict would cause normative conflict (or anomie), which, in turn, would have consequences for the personality and organismic systems. Thus, inherent in the cybernetic hierarchy of control are concepts that point to the sources of both stasis and change.[25]

---

[22]For his first attempt at a statement, see Parsons, "Some Problems of General Theory," pp. 61–68.

[23]For a more readable discussion of these generalized media, see T. S. Turner, "Parsons' Concept of Generalized Media of Social Interaction and its Relevance for Social Anthropology," *Sociological Inquiry* 38 (Spring 1968), pp. 121–34.

[24]There are several bodies of empirical literature that bear on this example. McClelland's work on the achievement motive as initiating economic development in modernizing societies is perhaps the most conspicuous example; see David C. McClelland, *The Achieving Society* (New York: Free Press, 1961).

[25]For a fuller discussion, see Alvin L. Jacobson, "Talcott Parsons: A Theoretical and

To augment this new macro emphasis on change, Parsons utilized the action scheme to analyze social evolution in historical societies. In this context, I think that the first line of *The Structure of Social Action* is of interest: "Who now reads Spencer?" Parsons then answered the question by delineating some of the reasons why Spencer's evolutionary doctrine had been so thoroughly rejected by 1937. Yet, after some 40 years, Parsons chose to reexamine the issue of societal evolution that he had so easily dismissed in the beginning. And in so doing, he reintroduced Spencer's and Durkheim's evolutionary models back into functional theory.

In drawing heavily from Spencer's and Durkheim's insights into societal development,[26] Parsons proposed that the processes of evolution display the following elements:

1. Increasing differentiation of system units into patterns of functional interdependence.
2. Establishment of new principles and mechanisms of integration in differentiating systems.
3. Increasing adaptive capacity of differentiated systems in their environments.

From the perspective of action theory, then, evolution involves: (*a*) increasing differentiation of the personality, social, cultural, and organismic systems from one another; (*b*) increasing differentiation within each of these four action subsystems; (*c*) escalating problems of integration and the emergence of new integrative structures; and (*d*) the upgrading of the survival capacity of each action subsystem, as well as of the overall action system, to its environment.

Parsons then embarked on an ambitious effort in two short volumes to outline the pattern of evolution in historical systems through primitive, intermediate, and modern stages.[27] In contrast with *The Social System*, where he stressed the problem of integration between social systems and personality, Parsons draws attention in his evolutionary model to the inter- and intradifferentiation of the cultural and social systems and to the resulting integrative problems. In fact, each stage of evolution is seen as reflecting a new set of integrative problems between society and culture as each of these systems has become more internally differentiated as well as differentiated from the other. Thus, the concern with the issues of

---

Empirical Analysis of Social Change and Conflict," in *Institutions and Social Exchange: The Sociologies of Talcott Parsons and George C. Homans*, ed. H. Turk and R. L. Simpson (Indianapolis, Ind.: Bobbs-Merrill, 1970).

[26]See last chapter for references.

[27]Talcott Parsons, *Societies: Evolutionary and Comparative Perspectives* and *The System of Modern Societies* (Englewood Cliffs, N.J.: Prentice-Hall, 1966, 1971, respectively). The general stages of development were first outlined in Talcott Parsons, "Evolutionary Universals in Society," *American Sociological Review* 29 (June 1964), pp. 339–57.

integration within and among action systems, so evident in earlier works, was not abandoned but applied to the analysis of specific historical processes.

Even though I think Parsons is vague about the causes of evolutionary change, he sees evolution as guided by the cybernetic hierarchy of controls, especially the informational component. In his documenting how integrative problems of the differentiating social and cultural systems have been resolved in the evolution of historical systems, the informational hierarchy is regarded as crucial because the regulation of societal processes of differentiation must be accompanied by legitimation from cultural patterns (information). Without such informational control, movement to the next stage of development in an evolutionary sequence will be inhibited.

Thus, I see the analysis of social change as an attempt to use the analytical tools of the general theory of action to examine a specific process, the historical development of human societies. What is of interest in this effort is that Parsons developed many propositions about the sequences of change and the processes that will inhibit or accelerate the unfolding of these evolutionary sequences. It is of more than passing interest that preliminary tests of these propositions indicate that, on the whole, they have a great deal of empirical support.[28] But I must concede that in many respects, Parsons' discussion does not improve greatly upon Spencer's. In a sense, Parsons simply recapitulates Spencer's analysis.

## PARSONS ON "THE HUMAN CONDITION"

Again, in a way reminiscent of Spencer's grand theory, Parsons attempted to extend his analytical scheme to all aspects of the universe.[29] In this last conceptual addition, I find it ironic that as it came to a close, Parsons' work increasingly resembled Spencer's. Except for the opening line in *The Structure of Social Action*—"who now reads Spencer?"—Parsons ignored him. Indeed, I am not sure that he even realized how closely his analyses of societal evolution and his conceptualization of the "human condition" resembled Spencer's effort 100 years earlier. At any rate, I see this last effort as more philosophy than sociology. Yet, it represents the culmination of Parsons' thought. Parsons began in 1937 with an analysis of the smallest and most elementary social unit, the act. He then developed a requisite functionalism that embraced four action systems: the social, cultural, personality, and what he called the behavioral in later years (he

---

[28]See Gary L. Buck and Alvin L. Jacobson, "Social Evolution and Structural-Functional Analysis: An Empirical Test," *American Sociological Review* 33 (June 1968), pp. 343–55; A. L. Jacobson, "Talcott Parsons: Theoretical and Empirical Analysis."

[29]Talcott Parsons, *Action Theory and The Human Condition* (New York: Free Press, 1978). See the last chapter and my analysis in "Parsons on the Human Condition," *Contemporary Sociology* 9 (May 1980), pp. 380–83.

**FIGURE 3–8** The Subsystems of the Human Condition

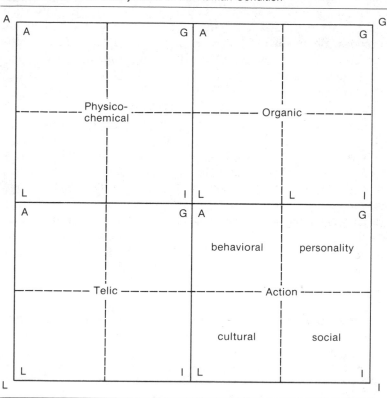

had earlier called this the organismic). And finally, in this desire to understand basic parameters of the human condition, he viewed these four action systems as only one subsystem within the larger system of the universe. This vision is portrayed in Figure 3–8.

As can be seen in Figure 3–8, the universe is divided into four subsystems, each meeting one of the four requisites—that is, A, G, I, or L. The four action systems resolve integrative problems; the organic system handles goal-attainment problems; the physicochemical copes with adaptation problems; and the telic ("ultimate" problems of meaning and cognition) deals with latency problems.

Each of these subsystems employs its own media for intra- and intersubsystem activity. For the action subsystem, the distinctive medium is symbolic meanings; for the telic, it is transcendental ordering; for the organic, it is health; and for the physicochemical, it is empirical ordering (lawlike relations of matter, energy, etc.). There are double interchanges of these media among the four A, G, I, L sectors, with "products" and "factors" being reciprocally exchanged. That is, each subsystem of the universe transmits a product to the others, while it also provides a factor necessary for the operation of other subsystems. Let me illustrate with the L (telic) and I (action) interchange. At the product level, the telic system provides "definitions of human responsibility" to the action subsystems and receives "sentiments of justification" from the action subsystem. At the factor level, the telic provides "categorical imperatives" and receives "acceptance of moral obligations." These double interchanges are, of course, carried out with the distinctive media of the I and A subsystems—that is, transcendental ordering and symbolic meaning, respectively.

The end result of this analysis, is, I feel, a grand metaphysical vision of the universe as it impinges upon human existence. It represents an effort to categorize the universe in terms of systems, subsystems, system requisites, generalized media, and exchanges involving these media. As such, it is no longer sociology but philosophy, or at best, a grand metatheoretical vision. Parsons had indeed come a long way since the humble unit act made its entrance in 1937.

## CRITICISMS OF PARSONIAN FUNCTIONALISM

I cannot imagine a social theorist enduring more criticism than Talcott Parsons received. With each step in the scheme's elaboration, criticism mounted and reached a peak in the late 1960s. And by the early 1970s, these critiques had dislodged Parsonian theory from its once dominant place. Many critiques were unfair, but there was also an element of truth in each. Let me now extract this element with respect to (1) the substantive image of social organization and (2) the logic of his requisite functionalism.

### Criticisms of Parsons' Substantive Image of Society

By the early 1960s, a number of critics had begun to question whether Parsons' emerging "system of concepts" corresponded to events in the real world. I view such a line of criticism as significant because the Parsonian strategy assumes that it is necessary to elaborate a system of concepts that adequately grasp salient features of the social world. Assertions that the maturing system of concepts inadequately mirrors features of actual social systems represent a fundamental challenge to the naturalistic and positivistic assumptions behind Parsons' conceptual scheme.

Ralf Dahrendorf, who is the subject of Chapter 7, codified this growing body of criticism when he likened functionalism to a utopia.[30] Much like

---

[30]Ralf Dahrendorf, "Out of Utopia: Toward a Reorientation of Sociological Analysis,"

prominent portrayals of social utopias of the past, Dahrendorf asserted, Parsons' concepts point to a world that (a) reveals no developmental history, (b) evidences only consensus over values and norms, (c) displays a high degree of integration among its components, and (d) reveals only mechanisms that preserve the status quo. Such an image of society is utopian because there appears little possibility that ubiquitous phenomena like deviance, conflict, and change could ever occur.

The evidence marshaled by Dahrendorf to support these assertions is, I feel, rather minimal and flimsy. Yet, I do not think it difficult to visualize the source of the critics' dismay. With the publication of *The Social System*, the critics charge, Parsons becomes overly concerned with the integration of social systems. In a vein similar to Radcliffe-Brown and Durkheim, Parsons' emphasis on integration involves a disproportionate concern with those processes in social systems that meet this need for integration. In *The Social System*, this concern with integration is evidenced by the tendency to assume, for analytical purposes, a system that is in equilibrium. From this starting point, analysis must then focus on the elaboration of concepts promoting integration and equilibrium. For example, the extended discussion of institutionalization describes the processes whereby structure is built up, with relatively scant mention of concepts denoting the breakdown and change of institutionalized patterns. To compound this omission, a discussion of how institutionalized patterns are maintained by the mechanisms of socialization and social control is launched. For the critics, too much emphasis is placed upon how socialization assures the internalization of values and the alleviation of strains among actors and how mechanisms of social control reduce the potential for malintegration and deviance. When deviance and change are discussed, the critics contend, they are viewed as residual or, in a way reminiscent of Durkheim, as pathological. In fact, deviance, conflict, and change are so alien to the scheme that the social equilibrium is considered to constitute, in Parsons' words, a "first law of social inertia."

The subsequent expansion of concepts denoting four system requisites—adaptation, goal attainment, integration, and latency—has further horrified the critics. For now system processes become almost exclusively viewed in terms of their consequences for meeting an extended list of system needs. In all this concern for the consequences of processes for meeting needs, how is it, the critics ask, that deviance, conflict, and change are to be conceptualized?[31] Are they merely pathological events that occur

---

*American Journal of Sociology* 64 (September 1958), pp. 115–27. This polemic echoed the earlier assessments by others, including David Lockwood, "Some Remarks on 'The Social System,'" *British Journal of Sociology* 7 (June 1950), pp. 134–46; C. Wright Mills, *The Sociological Imagination* (New York: Oxford University Press, 1959), pp. 44–49; and Lewis Coser, *The Functions of Social Conflict* (New York: Free Press, 1956), pp. 1–10.

[31]Leslie Sklair, "The Fate of the Functional Requisites in Parsonian Sociology," *British Journal of Sociology* 21 (March 1970), pp. 30–42.

on those rare occasions when system needs are not met? Or, in reality, are not these phenomena pervasive features of social systems, which are inadequately grasped by the proliferating system of concepts?

The elaboration of the informational hierarchy of control among the overall systems of action and its use to analyze social change did not silence the critics because the only type of change that is conceptualized is evolution, as opposed to revolution and other forms of violent disruption to social systems. Much like Durkheim and Spencer, Parsons' views change as a "progressive" differentiation and integration, with the inexorable progress of societal development delayed from time to time by a failure to integrate the differentiating cultural and social systems.[32]

## The Logical Criticisms of Requisite Functionalism

The problems of illegitimate teleology and tautology have consumed a considerable amount of the literature on functionalism.[33] For the most part, this literature holds that since assumptions of needs and requisites are so prominent in functional theorizing, theoretical statements will too frequently lapse into illegitimate teleologies and tautologies. Typically, conspicuous examples of the functional works of Durkheim, Radcliffe-Brown, and Malinowski are cited to confirm the truth of this assertion, but by implication, the efforts of contemporary functionalists are similarly

[32]Perhaps the most recent and scholarly attempt to document the reasons behind these problems in Parsonian action theory is provided by Alvin Gouldner, *The Coming Crisis of Western Sociology* (New York: Basic Books, 1970). However, John K. Rhoads, "On Gouldner's Crisis of Western Sociology," *American Journal of Sociology* 78 (July 1972), pp. 136–54, emphasizes that Gouldner has perceived what he wants to perceive in Parsons' work, ignoring those passages that would connote just the opposite of stasis, control, consensus, and order. See also Rhoads, "Reply to Gouldner," *American Journal of Sociology* 78 (May 1973), pp. 1493–96, which was written in response to Gouldner's defense of his position (Alvin Gouldner, "For Sociology: 'Varieties of Political Expression' Revisited," *American Journal of Sociology* 78 [March 1973], pp. 1063–93, particularly pp. 1083–93).

[33]For analyses of the logic of functionalist inquiry, see R. B. Braithwaite, *Scientific Explanation* (New York: Harper & Row, 1953), Chapters 9 and 10; Carl G. Hempel, "The Logic of Functional Analysis" in *Symposium on Sociological Theory*, ed. L. Gross (New York: Harper & Row, 1959), pp. 271–307; Percy S. Cohen, *Modern Social Theory* (New York: Basic Books, 1968), pp. 58–64; Francesca Cancian, "Functional Analysis of Change," *American Sociological Review* 25 (December 1960), pp. 818–27; S. F. Nadel, *Foundations of Social Anthropology* (Glencoe, Ill.: The Free Press, 1951), pp. 373–78; Ernest Nagel, "Teleological Explanation and Teleological Systems," in *Readings in the Philosophy of Science*, ed. H. Feigl and M. Brodbeck (New York: Harper & Row, 1953), pp. 537–58; Phillip Ronald Dore, "Function and Cause," *American Sociological Review* 26 (December 1961), pp. 843–53; Charles J. Erasmus, "Obviating the Functions of Functionalism," *Social Forces* 45 (March 1967), pp. 319–28; Harry C. Bredemeier, "The Methodology of Functionalism," *American Sociological Review* 20 (April 1955), pp. 173–80; Bernard Barber, "Structural-Functional Analysis: Some Problems and Misunderstandings," *American Sociological Review* 21 (April 1956), pp. 129–35; Robert K. Merton, *Social Theory and Social Structure* (Glencoe, Ill.: Free Press, 1957), pp. 44–61; Arthur L. Stinchcombe, *Constructing Social Theories* (New York: Harcourt, Brace & World, 1968), pp. 80–116; Hans Zetterberg, *On Theory and Verification in Sociology* (Totowa, N.J.: Bedminister Press, 1965), pp. 74–79.

indicted—otherwise, the criticisms would not be worth the considerable efforts devoted to making them. To the extent that this indirect indictment of Parsons' requisite functionalism can be sustained, I see it as a serious criticism. For Parsons' strategy for theory building has revolved around the assumption that his system of concepts can generate testable propositions that account for events in the empirical world. But if such a conceptual system inspires illegitimate teleologies and tautologous propositions, then its utility as a strategy for building sociological theory can be called into question.

**The issue of teleology.**   Parsons always considered action to be goal directed—whether it is a single unit act or the complex informational and energic interchanges among the organismic, personality, social, and cultural systems. Thus, Parsons' conceptualization of goal attainment as a basic system requisite would make inevitable teleological propositions, since for Parsons much social action can only be understood in terms of the ends it is designed to serve. I think that such propositions are often vague, however, because assessing goal-attainment consequences frequently is a way to obscure the specific causal chains whereby goal-attainment sectors in a system activate processes to meet specified end states. Yet, when looking closely at the Parsonian legacy, it is clear that his many essays are vitally concerned with just how, and through what processes, system processes are activated to meet goal states. For example, Parsons' various works on how political systems strive to legitimate themselves are filled with both analytical and descriptive accounts of how the processes—such as patterns of socialization in educational and kinship institutions—are activated to meet goal-attainment requisites.[34] While the empirical adequacy of this discussion can be questioned, Parsons' analysis does not present illegitimate teleologies, for his work reveals a clear concern for documenting the causal chains involved in activating processes designed to meet various end states.

I think that it is the other three requisites—adaptation, integration, and latency—that would seemingly pose a more serious problem of illegitimate teleology. Critics would argue that to analyze structures and processes in terms of their functions for these three system needs compels analysts to state their propositions teleologically although the processes so described may not be goal directed or teleological. Logically, as several commentators have pointed out, teleological phrasing of propositions in

---

[34]For example, see Talcott Parsons, "Authority, Legitimation and Political Action" in *Authority,* ed. C. J. Friedrich (Cambridge, Mass.: Harvard Univ. Press, 1958); Parsons, "On the Concept of Power"; and Talcott Parsons, "The Political Aspect of Structure and Process," in *Varieties of Political Theory,* ed. David Easton (Englewood Cliffs, N.J.: Prentice-Hall, 1966).

the absence of clear-cut goal-attainment processes does not necessarily make the proposition illegitimate, for at least two reasons.[35]

1. Nagel has argued that phrasing statements in a teleological fashion is merely a shorthand way of stating the same causal relationship nonteleologically.[36] For example, to argue that the relief of anxiety (an end state) is the "latency function" of religion (a present phenomenon) can be rephrased nonteleologically without loss of asserted content: under conditions $C_1$, $C_2$, $C_3$, ... , $C_n$, religion (concept $x$) causes reduction of group anxiety (concept $y$). Such a form is quite acceptable in that it involves existence and relational statements: under $C_1$, $C_2$, ... , $C_n$, variations in $x$ cause variations in $y$. However, other authors have contended that such transposition is not always possible because the existence statements so necessary to such conversion are absent from the statements of functionalists such as Parsons. Without necessary existence statements, the assertion that the function of religion is to reduce group anxiety really means: "The latency needs of the group for low levels of anxiety cause the emergence of religion." I see such statements as illegitimate teleologies since little information is provided about the nature of the "latency purposes" of a given system and the specific causal chains involved in keeping the system in pursuit of its latency goals. Or, if teleology is not intended, then I think that the statement is simply vague, offering none of the necessary information that would allow its conversion to a nonteleological form. As Nadel was led to conclude: "To pronounce at once upon the ultimate functions subserved by social fact is to short-circuit explanation and reduce it to generalities which, so prematurely stated, have little significance."[37]

2. Perhaps the most significant defense of Parsons' tendency to phrase propositions teleologically comes from the fact that such prop-

---

[35]For basic references on the issue, consult G. Bergman, "Purpose, Function and Scientific Explanation," *Acta Sociologica* 5 (1962), pp. 225–28; J. Canfield, "Teleological Explanation in Biology," *The British Journal for the Philosophy of Science*, 14 (1964), pp. 285–95; K. Deutsch, "Mechanism, Teleology and Mind," *Philosophy and Phenomenological Research* 12 (1951), pp. 185–223; C. J. Ducasse, "Explanation, Mechanism, and Teleology," in *Readings in Philosophical Analysis*, ed. H. Feigl and W. Sellars (New York: D. Appleton, 1949); D. Emmet, *Function, Purpose and Powers* (London: Routledge-Kegan, 1958); L. S. Fever, "Causality in the Social Sciences," *Journal of Philosophy* 51 (1954), pp. 191–208; W. W. Isajiw, *Causation and Functionalism in Sociology* (New York: Shocken Books, 1968); A. Kaplan, "Noncausal Explanation," in *Cause and Effect*, ed. D. Lerner (New York: Free Press, 1965); C. A. Mace, "Mechanical and Teleological Causation"; I. Scheffler, "Thoughts on Teleology," *The British Journal for the Philosophy of Science* 9 (1958), pp. 265–84; P. Sztompka, "Teleological Language in Sociology," *The Polish Sociological Bulletin* (1969), pp. 56–69 and *System and Function: Toward a Theory of Society* (New York: Academic Press, 1974).

[36]Nagel, "Teleological Explanation and Teleological Systems."

[37]Nadel, *Foundations of Social Anthropology*, p. 375.

ositions point to reverse causal chains that are typical of many social phenomena.[38] By emphasizing that the function served by a structure in maintaining the needs of the whole could cause the emergence of that structure, Parsons' functional imperativism forces analysis to be attuned to those causal processes involved in the initial selection, from the infinite variety of possible social structures, of only certain types of structures. The persistence over time of these selected structures can also be explained by the needs and/or equilibrium states of the whole: those structures having consequences for meeting needs and/or maintaining an equilibrium have a "selective advantage" over those that do not. I do not think that such statements are illegitimate teleologies, for it is quite possible for the systemic whole to exist prior in time to the structures that emerge and persist to maintain that whole. Furthermore, I do not think it necessary to impute purpose to the systemic whole. Just as in the biophysical world, where ecological and population balances are maintained by nonpurposive selective processes (for example, predators increase until they eat themselves out of food and then decrease until the food supply regenerates itself), so social wholes can maintain themselves in a state of equilibrium or meet the imperatives necessary for survival.

This line of argument has led Stinchcombe to summarize:

> Functional explanations are thus complex forms of causal theories. They involve causal connections among . . . variables as with a special causal priority of the consequences of activity in total explanation. There has been a good deal of philosophical confusion about such explanations, mainly due to the theorist's lack of imagination in realizing the variety of reverse causal processes which can select behavior or structures according to their consequences.[39]

I see the above considerations leading to several tentative conclusions about Parsons' scheme and the issue of teleology: (1) The scheme has always been teleological, from the initial conceptualization of unit acts to the four-function paradigm embracing the concept of goal attainment. (2) Contrary to the opinion of his detractors, most of Parsons' theoretical statements can be converted into nonteleological form, such that relevant statements about the conditions under which $x$ varies with $y$ can be discerned. (3) Parsons' work is replete with reverse causal chains in which a systemic whole existing prior in time to the emergence of subsystems causes the perpetuation of a subsystem because of its selective advantages in meeting problems faced by the systemic whole.

Most of the criticisms outlining the dangers of illegitimate teleology in functional theorizing have drawn examples from early functional

---

[38]Stinchcombe, *Constructing Social Theories*, pp. 87–93.
[39]Ibid., p. 100.

anthropology, where I think that it is relatively easy to expose question-able teleologies. But I do not see how Parsons' notion of system requisites has led him to this same trap, thus allowing the defenders of the action-theoretic strategy to challenge the critics to find conspicuous instances in Parsons' work where there is an illegitimate teleology.

**The issue of tautology.**    Parsons' conceptualization of four system requisites—adaptation, goal attainment, integration, and latency—is based on the assumption that if these requisites are not met, the system's sur-vival is threatened. When employing this assumption, however, it is nec-essary to know what level of failure in meeting each of these requisites is necessary to pronounce a crisis of survival. How does one determine when adaptive needs are not being met? Goal attainment needs? Inte-grative requisites? And latency needs? Unless there is some way to de-termine what constitutes the survival and nonsurvival of a system, I be-lieve that propositions documenting the contribution of items for meeting survival requisites become tautologous: the items meet survival needs of the system because it exists and, therefore, must be surviving. Thus, to phrase propositions with regard to system requisites of adaptation, goal attainment, integration, and latency, Parsons must provide either of two types of information: (1) evidence on a nonsurviving system where a particular item did not exist; or (2) specific criteria as to what constitutes survival and nonsurvival in various types and classes of social systems. Without this kind of information, my sense is that propositions employing notions of requisites are likely to be untestable, even in principle. There-fore, I would not consider them very useful in building sociological theory. And if Parsons' scheme cannot be readily converted into nontautologous propositions that can be tested, his conceptual approach can be ques-tioned. Parsons argued that systems of concepts must precede systems of propositions, but if the system of concepts is likely to generate tautologous propositions, then what is its theoretical utility?

**The theoretical utility of survival imperatives.**    Considering the problems of tautology created by using the concept of requisites, I see it reasonable to ask: what do requisites add to Parsons' theoretical scheme and to the analysis of specific events? For it seems to me that it is possible to document the conditions under which events influence each other in systemic wholes without dragging in notions of survival requisites. In fact, my sense is that Parsons often appears to abandon reference to system requisites when discussing concrete empirical events, causing me to won-der why the requisites are retained in his more formal conceptual edifice.

My answer is that Parsons retained the requisites for strategic rea-sons: to provide crude and rough criteria for distinguishing important from unimportant social processes. Parsons' entire intellectual career was spent elaborating the complex systems of interrelationships among the basic unit acts he first described in *The Structure of Social Action.* The more the system of concepts was brought to bear on increasingly complex patterns or organization among unit acts, the more Parsons relied upon the requisites to sort out what processes in these complex patterns will help explain the most variance. Thus, Parsons' imperatives constitute not so much a metaphysical entity, but a methodological yardstick for distinguishing what is crucial from not crucial among the vast number of potential processes in social systems. Despite the fact that Parsons was unable to specify exact criteria for assessing whether adaptive, goal-attainment, integrative, and latency needs are being met, he used these somewhat vaguely conceptualized requisites to assess the theoretical significance of concrete social phenomena. I am sure that Parsons implicitly employed the requisites this way in his many essays, which even the critics must admit are insightful. And perhaps this fact alone can justify use of the requisites to assess social phenomena.

Furthermore, I can see that the requisites are particularly useful in studying complex empirical systems, because in empirical systems it may be possible to specify more precisely criteria necessary for their survival. With these empirically based requisites as criteria, it may then be possible to distinguish significant from less significant social processes in these systems, thereby assuring more insightful explanations. It appears, then, that despite some of the logical problems created by their retention, Parsons felt that the strategic value of the requisites in explaining social processes more than compensates for the logical difficulties so frequently stressed by the critics. Other functionalists agree, but I think that we should maintain some skepticism here until functional analyses of empirical events prove superior to less problematic alternatives.

## TALCOTT PARSONS: AN OVERVIEW

As it has unfolded over the last decades, the theory of action reveals an enormous amount of continuity—starting with the basic unit act and proliferating into the cybernetic hierarchy of control among the systems of action. Such continuity is the outgrowth of Parsons' particular view of how theory in sociology should be constructed, for he consistently advocated the priority of systems of concepts over systems of propositions. The latter can only be useful when the former task is sufficiently completed. This view, I emphasize, is shared by many, functionalists and nonfunctionalists alike.

Yet the substantive vision of the world connoted by Parsons' concepts and the logical problems imputed to the scheme have stimulated widespread criticism of his functional perspective. In fact, other forms of sociological theorizing cannot be understood unless the revulsion to the perspective is appreciated. As I will emphasize in subsequent chapters, many other theoretical perspectives in sociology typically begin with a rejection of Parsonian functionalism and then proceed to build what is considered a more desirable alternative. In fact, Parsons appears to have become "the straw man" of sociological theorizing. No theory in sociology is considered adequate unless it has performed at least some portions of a ritual rejection of Parsons' analytical functionalism.

# CHAPTER 4

# The Empirical Functionalism of Robert K. Merton

## THEORIES OF THE MIDDLE RANGE

Just as Talcott Parsons was beginning to embrace a form of requisite functionalism,[1] Robert K. Merton launched a critique of Parsons' functional strategy for building sociological theory.[2] At the heart of this criticism was Merton's contention that Parsons' concern for developing an all encompassing system of concepts would prove both futile and sterile. To him, Parsons searched for "a total system of sociological theory, in which observations about every aspect of social behavior, organization, and change promptly find their preordained place, has the same exhilarating challenge and the same small promise as those many all-encompassing philosophical systems which have fallen into deserved disuse."[3]

---

[1]As will be recalled, Parsons in 1945 began to conceptualize unit acts in systemic terms and began to visualize such systems in terms of requisites. See Talcott Parsons, "The Present Position and Prospects of Systemic Theory in Sociology," in *Essays in Sociological Theory* (Glencoe, Ill.: Free Press, 1949). Moreover, Merton may have introduced Parsons to functional analysis, since Merton conducted a seminar at Harvard, where Parsons was a young instructor, on functional theorists such as Malinowski. In fact, I suspect that Merton was a functional theorist several years before Parsons made the conversion. Yet, from the beginning Merton was a critic of the Parsonian approach.

[2]Robert K. Merton, "Discussion of Parsons' 'The Position of Sociological Theory'," *American Sociological Review* 13 (April 1948), pp. 164–68.

[3]Ibid. Most of Merton's significant essays on functionalism have been included, and frequently expanded upon, in Robert K. Merton, *Social Theory and Social Structure* (Glencoe, Ill.: Free Press, 1949). Quotation taken from page 45 of the 1968 edition of this classic work. Most subsequent references will be made to the articles incorporated into this book. For more recent essays on Merton's work, see Lewis A. Coser, ed., *The Idea of Social Structure* (New York: Free Press, 1975).

For Merton, such grand theoretical schemes are premature since the theoretical and empirical groundwork necessary for their completion has not been performed. Just as Einsteinian theory did not emerge without a long cumulative research foundation and theoretical legacy, so sociological theory will have to wait for its Einstein, primarily because "it has not yet found its Kepler—to say nothing of its Newton, Laplace, Gibbs, Maxwell or Planck."[4]

In the absence of this foundation, what passes for sociological theory, in Merton's critical eye, consists of "general orientations toward data, suggesting types of variables which theorists must somehow take into account, rather than clearly formulated, verifiable statements of relationships between specified variables."[5] Strategies advocated by those such as Parsons are not really theory, but philosophical systems, with "their varied suggestiveness, their architectonic splendor, and their sterility."[6] However, to pursue the opposite strategy of constructing inventories of low-level empirical propositions will prove equally sterile, thus suggesting to Merton the need for "theories of the middle range" in sociology. As I emphasized in Chapter 1 (see Figure 1–1), such theories are not highly abstract nor broad. And I am not as optimistic as Merton that they will yield much theoretical payoff. Yet, despite my reservations, Merton's advocacy has developed a wide following, and so, let me try to indicate what made Merton's middle-range strategy so appealing.

In Merton's view, theories of the middle range offer more theoretical promise than Parsons' grand theory. They are couched at a lower level of abstraction and reveal clearly defined and operationalized concepts that are incorporated into statements of covariance for a limited range of phenomena. Although middle-range theories are abstract, they are also connected to the empirical world, thus encouraging the research so necessary for the clarification of concepts and reformulation of theoretical generalizations. Without this interplay between theory and research, Merton contended, theoretical schemes will remain suggestive congeries of concepts, which are incapable of being refuted, while, on the other hand, empirical research will remain unsystematic, disjointed, and of little utility in expanding a body of sociological knowledge. Thus, by following a middle-range strategy, the concepts and propositions of sociological theory will become more tightly organized as theoretically focused empirical research forces clarification, elaboration, and reformulation of the concepts and propositions of each middle-range theory.

From this growing clarity in theories directed at a limited range of phenomena and supported by empirical research can eventually come the

---

[4] Merton, *Social Theory and Social Structure*, p. 47.
[5] Ibid., p. 42.
[6] Ibid., p. 51.

more encompassing theoretical schemes. In fact, for Merton, although it is necessary to concentrate energies on the construction of limited theories that inspire research, theorists must also be concerned with "consolidating the special theories into a more general set of concepts and mutually consistent propositions."[7] The special theories of sociology must therefore be formulated with an eye toward what they can offer more general sociological theorizing. However, just how these middle-range theories should be formulated to facilitate their eventual consolidation into a more general theory poses a difficult analytical problem, for which Merton has a ready solution: a form of functionalism should be utilized in formulating the theories of the middle range. Such functional theorizing is to take the form of a paradigm that would allow for both the easy specification and elaboration of relevant concepts, while encouraging systematic revision and reformulation as empirical findings would dictate. Conceived in this way, functionalism became for Merton a method for building not only theories of the middle range but also the grand theoretical schemes that would someday subsume such theories of the middle range. Thus, in a vein similar to Parsons, functionalism for Merton represents a strategy for ordering concepts and for sorting out significant from insignificant social processes. But, unlike Parsons' strategy, Merton's functional strategy requires first the formulation of a body of middle-range theories. Only when this groundwork has been laid should a functional protocol be used to construct more abstract theoretical systems.

Merton's functionalism has never become as dominant as did Parsons'. Yet, the middle-range strategy is currently the legitimating credo for much theoretical activity. Indeed, as I have argued many times, Merton's middle-range strategy encouraged the proliferation of what I have called "theories of _____" (fill in the blank with any empirical topic).[8] That is, empirical generalizations have been defended as theory, despite the fact that they are not sufficiently abstract. Thus, sociology has spawned a large number of theories about such specific empirical processes as juvenile delinquency, family conflict, race relations, social mobility in America, urbanization, and other empirical events. I am not sure if Merton intended theories of the middle range to be so empirically grounded, but this was the outcome of his advocacy. Virtually none of these theories has been consolidated into more general and abstract propositions because they are too empirical and, therefore, too tied to specific times, places, and contexts. Thus, whereas Merton's functionalism did not catch on,

---

[7]Merton, *Social Theory and Social Structure* (1957), p. 10.

[8]See for examples my *Societal Stratification: A Theoretical Analysis* (New York: Columbia University Press, 1984), Chapter 1; "Returning to Social Physics," *Current Perspectives in Social Theory*, vol. 2 (1981), pp. 187–208; "Toward a Social Physics," *Humboldt Journal of Social Relations* 7 (Spring, 1980), pp. 140–55; "Sociology as a Theory Building Enterprise," *Pacific Sociological Review* 22 (October, 1979), pp. 427–56; "In Defense of Positivism," *Sociological Theory* 3 (2, 1985).

his advocacy for middle-range theory did. I have my doubts as to whether this was for the good of sociological theory, but most sociologists do not share my reservations. Indeed, they see the grounding of theory in research as a great virtue, whereas for me, these "theories of" are little more than statements of empirical regularity that need a more abstract set of propositions to explain them. And so the debate over the best strategy for developing theory rages. My concern here, however, is with Merton's functionalism. And so, let me now turn to his paradigm for functional analysis.

## MERTON'S PARADIGM FOR FUNCTIONAL ANALYSIS

As with most commentators on functional analysis, Merton begins his discussion with a review of the mistakes of early functionalists, particularly the anthropologists Malinowski and Radcliffe-Brown.[9] Generally, Merton saw functional theorizing as potentially embracing three questionable postulates: (1) the functional unity of social systems, (2) the functional universality of social items, and (3) the indispensability of functional items for social systems.[10]

**The functional unity postulate.**    As we can recall from Chapter 2, Radcliffe-Brown, in following Durkheim's lead, frequently transformed the hypothesis that social systems reveal social integration into a necessary requisite or need for social survival. Although it is difficult to argue that human societies do not possess some degree of integration—otherwise they would not be systems—Merton views the degree of integration in a system as an issue to be empirically determined. To assume, however subtly, that a high degree of functional unity must exist in a social system is to define away the important theoretical and empirical questions: What levels of integration exist for different systems? What various types of integration can be discerned? Are varying degrees of integration evident for different segments of a system? And, most importantly, what variety of processes lead to different levels, forms, and types of integration for different spheres of social systems? For Merton, to begin analysis with the postulate of "functional unity" or integration of the social whole can divert attention away from not only these questions but also from the varied and "disparate consequences of a given social or cultural item (usage, belief, behavior pattern, institutions) for diverse social groups and for individual members of these groups."[11]

---

[9]Robert K. Merton, "Manifest and Latent Functions," in *Social Theory and Social Structure* (1968), pp. 74–91.

[10]See Robert K. Merton, *Social Theory and Social Structure*, pp. 45–61.

[11]Merton, *Social Theory and Social Structure* (1968), pp. 81–82.

I am sure that underlying this discussion of the functional unity is an implicit criticism of Parsons' early concern with social integration. As I stressed in Chapter 3, Parsons first postulated only one requisite in his early functional work: the need for integration.[12] Later, this postulate was to be expanded into three additional functional requisites for adaptation, goal attainment, and latency. But Parsons' functionalism appears to have begun with the same concerns evident in Durkheim's and Radcliffe-Brown's work, leading Merton to question the "heuristic value" of an assumption that can divert attention away from important theoretical and empirical questions. Thus, instead of the postulate of functional unity there should be an emphasis on varying types, forms, levels, and spheres of social integration and the varying consequences of the existence of items for specified segments of social systems. In this way, Merton begins to direct functional analysis away from concern with total systems toward an emphasis on how different patterns of social organization within more inclusive social systems are created, maintained, and changed not only by the requisites of the total system but also by interaction among sociocultural items within systemic wholes.

**The issue of functional universality.**    One result of an emphasis on functional unity was that some early anthropologists assumed that if a social item existed in an ongoing system, it must therefore have positive consequences for the integration of the social system. This assumption tended to result in tautologous statements: a system exists; an item is a part of the system; therefore, the item is positively functional for the maintenance of the system.

For Merton, if an examination of empirical systems is undertaken, it is clear that there is a wider range of empirical possibilities. First, items may be not only positively functional for a system or another system item but also dysfunctional for either particular items or the systemic whole. Second, some consequences, whether functional or dysfunctional, are intended and recognized by system incumbents and are thus manifest, whereas other consequences are not intended or recognized and are therefore latent. Thus, in contrast with the assertions of Malinowski and Radcliffe-Brown, Merton proposes the analysis of diverse consequences or functions of sociocultural items—whether positive or negative, manifest or latent—"for individuals, for subgroups, and for the more inclusive social structure and culture."[13] In turn, the analysis of varied consequences requires the calculation of a "net balance of consequences" of items for each other and more inclusive systems. In this way, Merton visualizes contemporary functional thought as compensating for the excesses of

---

[12]See Parsons, "Present Position and Prospects of Systemic Theory" and Talcott Parsons, *The Social System* (Glencoe, Ill.: Free Press, 1951).

[13]Merton, *Social Theory and Social Structure* (1968), p. 84.

earlier forms of analysis by focusing on the crucial types of consequences of sociocultural items for each other and, if the facts dictate, for the social whole.

**The issue of indispensability.**    Somewhat out of context and unfairly, I feel, Merton quotes Malinowski's assertion that every cultural item "fulfills some vital function, has some task to accomplish, represents an indispensable part within a working whole"[14] as simply an extreme statement of two interrelated issues in functional analysis: (1) Do social systems have functional requisites or needs that must be fulfilled? (2) Are there certain crucial structures that are indispensable for fulfilling these functions?

In response to the first question, Merton provides a tentative yes, but with an important qualification: the functional requisites must be established empirically for specific systems. For actual groups or whole societies it is possible to ascertain the "conditions necessary for their survival," and it is of theoretical importance to determine which structures, through what specific processes, have consequences for these conditions. But to assume a system of universal requisites—as Parsons does—adds little to theoretical analysis, since to stress that certain functions must be met in all systems simply leads observers to describe processes in social systems that meet these requisites. Such descriptions, Merton contends, can be done without the excess baggage of system requisites. It is more desirable to describe cultural patterns and then assess their various consequences in meeting the specific needs of different segments of concrete empirical systems.

Merton's answer to the second question is emphatic: empirical evidence makes the assertion that only certain structures can fulfill system requisites obviously false. Examination of the empirical world reveals quite clearly that alternative structures can exist to fulfill basically the same requisites in both similar and diverse systems. This fact leads Merton to postulate the importance in functional analysis of concern with various types of "functional alternatives," or "functional equivalents," and "functional substitutes" within social systems. In this way, functional analysis would not view as indispensable the social items of a system and thereby would avoid the tautologous trap of assuming that items must exist to assure the continued existence of a system. Furthermore, in looking for functional alternatives, analytical attention would be drawn to questions about the range of items that could serve as functional equivalents. If these questions are to be answered adequately, analysts should then determine why a particular item was selected from a range of possible

---

[14] This quote is from an encyclopaedia article where Malinowski was arguing against ethnocentrism. His more scholarly work (see Chapter 2) is much less extreme. See also my and Alexandra Maryanski's *Functionalism* (Menlo Park Calif.: Benjamin-Cummings, 1978).

alternatives, leading to questions about the "structural context" and "structural limits" that might circumscribe the range of alternatives and account for the emergence of one item over another. For Merton, examination of these interrelated questions would thus facilitate the separate analysis of the causes and consequences of structural items. By asking why one particular structure instead of various alternatives had emerged, analysts would not forget to document the specific processes leading to an item's emergence as separate from its functional consequences. In this way, the danger of assuming that items must exist to fulfill system needs would be avoided.

In looking back at Merton's criticisms of traditional anthropological reasoning and at some contemporary functionalists' implications, I think that much of his assessment of these three functional postulates involves the destruction of "straw men." Yet, in destroying these assumptions, Merton was led to formulate alternative postulates that advocated a concern for the multiple consequences of sociocultural items for each other and for more inclusive social wholes, without a priori assumptions of functional needs or imperatives. Rather, functional analysis must specify (1) the social patterns under consideration, whether a systemic whole or some subpart; (2) the various types of consequences of these patterns for empirically established survival requisites; and (3) the processes whereby some patterns rather than others come to exist and have the various consequences for each other and for systemic wholes.

With this form of functional analysis, Merton has sought to provide "the minimum set of concepts with which the sociologist must operate in order to carry through an adequate functional analysis."[15] In doing so, Merton hopes that this strategy will allow sociological analysis to avoid some of the mistaken postulates and assumptions of previous attempts using a functional strategy. Although the functional imperativism of Parsons is only briefly assessed in Merton's proposals, it appears that he is stressing the need for an alternative form of functional analysis in which there is less concern with total systems and abstract statements of system requisites. Instead, to build theories of the middle range, it is necessary to focus attention on the mutual and varied consequences of specified system parts for each other and for systemic wholes. Although these parts and systemic wholes have conditions necessary for their survival, these conditions must be empirically established. For only through a clear understanding of the actual requisites of a concrete system can the needs of social structures provide a useful set of criteria for assessing the consequences, or functions, of social items. Furthermore, although the analysis of consequences of items is the unique feature of functional analysis, it is also necessary to discover the causal processes that have resulted in

---

[15]Merton, *Social Theory and Social Structure* (1968), p. 109.

a particular item having a specified set of consequences for other items and systemic wholes. To assure adherence to this form of structural analysis, Merton went so far as to outline a set of procedures for executing the general guidelines of his functional orientation.

## A PROTOCOL FOR EXECUTING FUNCTIONAL ANALYSIS

To ascertain the causes and consequences of particular structures and processes, Merton insists that functional analysis begins with "sheer description" of individual and group activities. In describing the patterns of interaction and activity among units under investigation, it will be possible to discern clearly the social items to be subjected to functional analysis. Such descriptions can also provide a major clue to the functions performed by such patterned activity. In order for these functions to become more evident, however, additional steps are necessary.

The first of these steps is for investigators to indicate the principal alternatives that are excluded by the dominance of a particular pattern. Such description of the excluded alternatives provides an indication of the structural context from which an observed pattern first emerged and is now maintained—thereby offering further clues about the functions or consequences the item might have for other items and perhaps for the systemic whole. The second analytical step beyond sheer description involves an assessment of the meaning, or mental and emotional significance, of the activity for group members. Description of these meanings may offer some indication of the motives behind the activities of the individuals involved and thereby shed some tentative light on the manifest functions of an activity. These descriptions require a third analytical step of discerning some array of motives for conformity or for deviation among participants, but these motives must not be confused with either the objective description of the pattern or the subsequent assessment of the functions served by the pattern. Yet, by understanding the configuration of motives for conformity and deviation among actors, an assessment of the psychological needs served (or not served) by a pattern can be understood—offering an additional clue to the various functions of the pattern under investigation.

But focusing on the meanings and motives of those involved in an activity can skew analysis away from unintended or latent consequences of the activity. Thus, a final analytical step involves the description of how the patterns under investigation reveal regularities not recognized by participants but appear to have consequences for both the individuals involved and other central patterns or regularities in the system. In this way, analysis will be attuned to the latent functions of an item.

By following each of these steps, Merton assumes that it will be possible to assess the net balance of consequences of the pattern under

**FIGURE 4–1**   Merton's Net Functional Balance Analysis

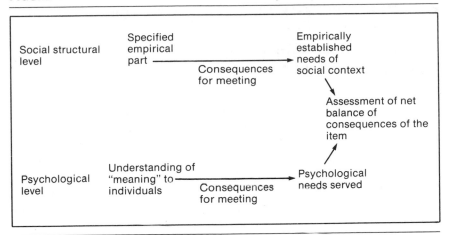

investigation, as well as to determine some of the independent causes of the item. These steps assure that a proper functional inquiry will ensue, because postulates of functional unity, assumptions of survival requisites, and convictions about indispensable parts do not precede the analysis of social structures and processes. On the contrary, attention is drawn only to observable patterns of activity, the structural context in which the focal pattern emerged and persists in the face of potential alternatives, the meaning of these patterns for actors involved, the actors' motives for conformity and deviation, and the implications of the particular pattern for unrecognized needs of individuals and other items in the social system. Thus, with this kind of preliminary work, functional analysis will avoid the logical and empirical problems of previous forms of functionalism. And, in this way, it can provide an understanding of the causes and consequences of system parts for each other and for more inclusive system units.[16] I have diagramed the basic logic of this approach in Figure 4–1.

Looking at Figure 4–1, let me recapitulate the essential elements of Merton's strategy. First of all, only empirical units are to be analyzed, and the part and the social context of the part must be clearly specified. Then, the task is to establish the particular survival requisites of the empirical system—that is, what is necessary for this particular empirical system to survive. By assessing the functions or consequences of an item meeting or not meeting these needs, insight into the nature of a part and its social contexts can be achieved. In addition to this structural analysis must come an analysis of the meaning for participants, particularly since it reveals the psychological needs served or not served by participation

---

[16]Ibid., p. 136.

in a structure. In this way, the net balance of consequences of an item at diverse levels of social organization can be assessed.

## ILLUSTRATING MERTON'S FUNCTIONAL STRATEGY

Merton's paradigm and protocol for constructing functional theories of the middle range are remarkably free of statements about individual and system needs or requisites. In his protocol statements, Merton approaches the question of the needs and requisites fulfilled by a particular item only after description of (1) the item in question, (2) the structural context in which the item survives, and (3) its meaning for the individuals involved. With this information, it is then possible to establish both the manifest and latent functions of an item, as well as the net balance of functions and dysfunctions of the item for varied segments of a social system. Unfortunately, the implied sequencing of functional analysis is not always performed by Merton, presumably for at least two reasons. First, in selecting an established structure in a system for analysis, the investigator usually assumes that the item persists because it is fulfilling some need. As I will make evident, Merton begins (as opposed to concludes) with this assumption in his analysis of political machines—thus leaving him to conclude that "structure affects function and function affects structure." When description of items begins with an implicit assumption of their functions for fulfilling needs, then I think that the descriptions will be performed in ways assuring confirmation of this implicit assumption. Second, in analyzing the structural context of an item and assessing why it emerges and persists over alternative items, I believe it inevitable that there will be preconceptions of the functions served by an item in order to know why it fulfills a set of needs better than would various alternatives. Otherwise, I do not see how it is possible to determine what potential alternatives could exist to substitute for the present item.

For at least these two reasons, then, execution of Merton's strategy is difficult. Let me indicate how this is so by examining Merton's illustration of it. This illustration involves an analysis of American political machines. Much like that of his anthropological straw men, such as Radcliffe-Brown and Malinowski, Merton's need to analyze separately the causes and functions of structural items is not as evident in his actual account of empirical events.

Merton begins his analysis of American political machines with the simple question: "How do they manage to continue in operation?"[17] Following this interesting question is an assumption reminiscent of Malinowski's functional analysis:

---

[17]Ibid., p. 125.

> Preceding from the functional view, therefore, that we should *ordinarily* (not invariably) expect persistent social patterns and social structures to perform positive functions *which are at the time not fulfilled by other patterns and structures*, the thought occurs that perhaps this publicly maligned organization is, *under present conditions*, satisfying basic latent functions. [Merton's emphasis].[18]

The fact that the word *ordinarily* is qualified by the parenthetical phrase *not invariably* is perhaps enough for Merton to escape the change of tautology: if an item persists in a surviving system, it must therefore have positive functions. Yet, my sense is that Merton implicitly argues that if an enduring item does not fulfill manifest functions, then it fulfills latent functions. This leads me to recall Merton's portrayal of Malinowski's dictum that "every custom, material object, idea and belief fulfills some vital function, has some task to accomplish." For Merton, this assumption becomes translated into the dictum that social items that do not fulfill manifest functions must, therefore, fulfill latent ones; and, as is added in a footnote, if the item has dysfunctions for some segments of the population, its persistence implies that it ordinarily must have positive functions for meeting the needs of other segments.

In fairness to Merton's suggestive analysis of political machines, I emphasize that he offered it only as an illustration of the usefulness of the distinction between manifest and latent functions. It was not intended as a full explication of his functional paradigm or protocol, but only as an example of how attention to latent functions can provide new insights into the operation of political machines. However, it appears that Merton's commitment to a clear protocol is not enough to preclude an inadvertent lapse—so typical of earlier functionalists—into the postulates of "universality of functions" and "functional indispensability." Thus, Merton appears to begin his concrete analysis with a set of postulates that he earlier had gone to great lengths to discredit, resulting in this central assumption:

> The key structural function of the Boss is to organize, centralize and maintain in good working condition "the scattered fragments of power" which are at present dispersed through our political organization. By this centralization of political power, *the boss can satisfy the needs of diverse subgroups in the larger community which are not adequately satisfied by legally devised and culturally approved social structures.*[19]

For Merton, political machines emerge in the structural context of a system in which power is decentralized to the extent that it cannot be mobilized to meet the needs of significant population segments. The causal processes by which machines arise in this power vacuum to pick up the

---

[18]Ibid., pp. 125–26.
[19]Ibid., p. 126.

"scattered fragments of power" involve a sequence of events in which political machines are seen as able to satisfy the needs of diverse groups more effectively than "legally devised and culturally approved social structures." Logically, this form of analysis is not necessarily tautologous or an illegitimate teleology—as some critics might charge—because Merton appears to be asserting that political machines at one time had a selective advantage over alternative structures in meeting needs of certain segments in a system. This kind of *reverse causal chain,* to use Stinchcombe's term,[20] is a legitimate form of causal analysis, since system needs are seen as existing prior in time to the events they cause—in this instance, the emergence of political machines in the American social structure. Furthermore, I do not think it necessary to impute purposes—although at times purpose is certainly involved—to the segments of the system affected by the machines. A political machine may be seen as a chance event that had a selective advantage over alternatives in a spiraling process similar to expansions and contradictions of predator populations that grow rapidly until they eat themselves out of prey. Clearly, the emergence of a political machine is both a purposive and nonpurposive process in which the machine meets the prior needs of a population, which has signaled to the machine leaders or bosses the efficacy of their expanded pursuits (purpose) in meeting its needs. Eventually, in a spiraling process of this nature, the original needs of the population, which caused the emergence and expansion of political machines and big-city bosses, may recede in causal significance, while the needs of the well-established political machine cause certain activities that have little consequence (or perhaps a dysfunctional consequence) for the needs of the population.

This kind of causal argument appears to be Merton's intent. Unfortunately, I think that his overriding concern is with discerning the functions of the political machines; consequently, he obscures the causal analysis, for, as he is prone to remark, "Whatever its specific historical origins, the political machine persists as an apparatus for satisfying unfulfilled needs of diverse groups in the population."[21] By bypassing these specific causal chains involved in the emergence of American political machines, Merton is left with the relatively simple and ad hoc task of cross-tabulating the needs of a population and the activities of the political machine that fulfill them.

For example, the political machine fulfills the needs of deprived classes by providing vital services through the local neighborhood ward heeler, including "food baskets and jobs, legal and extralegal advice, setting to rights minor scrapes with the law, helping the bright poor boy to a political scholarship in a local college, looking after the bereaved," and so on. The

---

[20]Arthur L. Stinchcombe, *Constructing Social Theories* (New York: Harcourt, Brace & World, 1968), p. 100.

[21]Merton, *Social Theory and Social Structure* (1968), p. 127.

political machine, according to Merton, can provide these services more effectively than various alternatives, such as welfare agencies, settlement houses, and legal aid clinics, because it offers these services in a personal way through the neighborhood ward heeler with a minimum of questions, red tape, and abuse to people's self-respect. For other populations, such as the business community, the political machines provide another set of needed services—namely, political regulation and control of unbridled competition among corporations and businesses without undue governmental interference in the specific operations of economic enterprises. By virtue of controlling various public agencies and bureaus, the big-city boss can rationalize and organize relations among economic organizations while preventing too much governmental scrutiny into their various illegal activities. The political machine can perform this function more effectively than legal governmental alternatives because it recognizes the need of economic organizations for both regulation and noninterference in certain activities. In contrast, legally constituted government agencies would recognize only the former need—thus giving the political machine a selective advantage over legally constituted government. Similarly, the machine can organize and rationalize illegal economic enterprises concerned with providing illicit services, including gambling, drugs, and prostitution, whereas legally constituted governmental agencies cannot condone, to say nothing of organizing, this kind of prevalent activity. Thus, for both legal and illegal businesses, the political machine provides protection by assuring a stable marketplace, high profits, and selective governmental regulation. Finally, for another population—notably, the deprived—the political machine provides opportunities for social mobility in a society where monetary success is a strong cultural value but where actual opportunities for such success are closed to many deprived groups. Thus, by opening the doors to social mobility for members of deprived groups who do not have "legitimate" opportunities, the political machine meets the needs of the deprived, while assuring itself of loyal, committed, and grateful personnel.

I think that Merton's functional explanation of the persistence of political machines has considerable plausibility. For indeed, the existence of political machines in America was correlated with a relatively ineffective federal establishment, deprived urban masses, high demand for illegal services, and high degrees of economic competition. But I see most of Merton's account as statements of correlation, dressed in functional assumptions about how the needs of diverse subgroups led to the emergence and persistence of political machines. Statements of correlation are obviously not causal statements. To the extent that it simply notes the correlation between social needs and political machines, Merton's analysis will be of little utility in building theoretical statements of the form: under $C_1, C_2, C_3, \ldots, C_n$, $x$ causes variation in $y$. There are many *implied* causal chains in Merton's analysis, but his failure to make them explicit detracts from his analysis. As was emphasized in Chapter 2, Durkheim's concrete analysis of the division of labor lapsed into statements implying, at the very least, that the "need for social order" caused the division of labor.[22] Without explicit statements or analytical models on how the need for order caused the division of labor, the analysis constituted an illegitimate teleology.

The difficulties that the founders of functionalism had in separating cause and function are clearly recognized by Merton and, presumably, was the impetus to his explicating a paradigm and protocol for functional analysis. Yet, much like his predecessors, I see Merton as abandoning the very protocol that would keep cause and function separated. Merton indicates that the emergence and persistence of political machines occur in response to needs, without documenting very precisely the causal chains through which needs cause the emergence and persistence of an event.

I think that Merton also falls into the problem of tautology that he imputed—incorrectly, I emphasize—to Malinowski's functional analysis. By assuming that "ordinarily" persistent structures serve positive functions for meeting the needs of some population segment, Merton indicates that if an item persists in an existing system, then it is functional (perhaps only latently) for some groups. I find it is surprising that Merton falls back onto this postulate, since he went to such great lengths to sound the warning against it. Yet, Merton's analysis of political machines does not start with a description of the phenomenon, nor does he initially address the structural context in which it exists. Rather, Merton begins with the assumption that political machines exist to fulfill a function—if not a manifest function, then a latent one.

This criticism of Merton's analysis of a concrete phenomenon does not mean that, with more specification of causal processes, charges of tautology and illegitimate teleology could be avoided. Indeed, with more specification of the historical origins of the political machines and of the feedback processes between machines and the population segments they serve, Merton's account could be rephrased in less suspicious causal terms. This fact leads to an important question: why did Merton fail to specify the causal chains that would make less suspicious his propositions? One answer is that Merton offered this account of political machines only as an illustration of the utility in the concept of *latent* functions. As an illustration, the account would naturally be brief and not involve a thorough explication of the emergence of political machines in America. Merton's awareness of the problems inherent in previous functional analysis would lend credence to this argument, for how could he fall into the very traps that he sought to avoid?

---

[22]Émile Durkheim, *The Rules of the Sociological Method* (Glencoe, Ill.: Free Press, 1938), p. 96.

However, Durkheim's and Radcliffe-Brown's similar failure to avoid completely the logical problems they clearly understood raises the more fundamental question: is there something about functional analysis that encourages theorists to short-circuit causal explanation? I think that there is something seductive about functional analysis that leads us consistently into these problems. And thus, I would not recommend it as a mode of theoretical explanation. Even as Merton tried to make functionalism more empirical, he fell into the logical problems of illegitimate teleology and tautology. Yet, even with these problems, there has been a revival of functional analysis in recent years, and so despite my misgivings, many theorists continue to use a functional approach. Let me now turn to the most prominent of these "neofunctionalisms."

# CHAPTER 5

# The Systems Functionalism of Niklas Luhmann

As I have stressed in the preceding chapters, functionalism is a mode of analysis that examines how structures and processes meet the needs of a more inclusive social system. Talcott Parsons' requisite functionalism, or "action theory" as he preferred to call it, revolved around the elaboration of an abstract system of categories. In contrast, Robert Merton's more empirically based strategy advocated a situation-specific assessment of functional needs and the structures that meet these needs in a particular empirical context. While all forms of functional analysis, whether Parsons' or Merton's, have become recessive in American theoretical circles,[1] functionalism has, to my surprise, enjoyed a revival in Europe over the last decade, especially in Germany.

There are several prominent European functional theorists,[2] but perhaps the most prominent is the German social theorist Niklas Luhmann.[3] It is not surprising that, as a former student of Parsons' in America, Luhmann is highly analytical and abstract. Yet, he is very critical of

---

[1] There are some notable exceptions, for one still finds elements of Parsons in the work of such scholars as Neil J. Smelser, Jeffrey Alexander, Dean Gerstein, Victor Lidz, Bernard Barber, Adrian Hayes, and other Americans. Most of this work, however, is more empirical and only selectively borrows from Parsons's great conceptual edifice.

[2] For example, the work of Richard Münch is very prominent in both Europe and America. For a recently translated sample, see his *Theory of Action: Reconstructing the Contributions of Talcott Parsons, Émile Durkheim and Max Weber* (Frankfurt: Suhrkamp, 1986).

[3] Luhmann has published extensively, but unfortunately most of his work is in German. The only comprehensive sample of his work in English is his *The Differentiation of Society*, trans. S. Holmes and C. Larmore (New York: Columbia University Press, 1982). The bulk of this chapter borrows from chapters in this book.

Parsonian action theory because it increasingly became "overly concerned with its own architecture." That is, Parsons kept elaborating categories and thereby created a complex analytical edifice that became ever more divorced from empirical reality. But (in contrast to Merton,) Luhmann does not retreat into a wholly empirical functionalism, where each system's varying needs must be empirically established in all their particulars. (Rather,) his alternative is to construct an abstract conceptual scheme that is "relatively simple" but that, at the same time, can be used in "highly complex research programs" and guide the analysis of a wide diversity of empirical events.[4]

As I will discuss, Luhmann has used his conceptual scheme to analyze a variety of empirical processes, and although its architecture is not as complex as Parsonian action theory, it nonetheless tends to bend empirical reality to its purposes. Even so, I find it an intriguing approach that documents the staying power of functional analysis in sociological theory. In this chapter, therefore, my goal is to summarize the basic elements of Luhmann's functionalism and to ascertain the extent to which it offers a viable alternative to earlier forms of functional analysis.

## LUHMANN'S 'GENERAL SYSTEMS' APPROACH

### System and Environment

Luhmann employs what he terms a *general systems* approach.[5] Such an approach stresses the fact that human action becomes organized and structured into systems. When the actions of several people become interrelated, a social system can be said to exist.[6] The basic mechanism by which actions become interrelated so as to create social systems is communication via symbolic codes, (such as words and,) as I will describe shortly, other media. All social systems exist in multidimensional environments, which pose potentially endless complexity with which a system must deal. To exist in a complex environment, therefore, a social system must develop mechanisms for reducing complexity, lest the system simply merge with its environment. These mechanisms involve selecting ways and means for reducing complexity. Such selection creates a boundary between a system and its environment, (thereby allowing it to sustain patterns of interrelated actions. Selection involves a process of choosing how to reduce the complexity of the environment.

The basic functional requisite in Luhmann's analysis is thus "the need to reduce the complexity of the environment in relation to a system

---

[4] Ibid., p. 88.

[5] I should stress this is not an approach that most scholars, who view themselves as general systems theorists, would recognize.

[6] This definition, it should be noted, is the same as Talcott Parsons's. See Chapter 3.

of interrelated actions." I suspect that Luhmann would not accept this translation of his ideas into the metaphor of traditional functionalism, but in fact, this requisite pervades his analysis. All social processes are analyzed with respect to their functions for reducing complexity vis-à-vis an environment. Processes that function in this way are typically defined as *mechanisms* in a manner reminiscent of Talcott Parsons's early discussion in *The Social System*[7] (see Chapter 3). Indeed, as I will document, the bulk of Luhmann's sociology revolves around discussions of such mechanisms—differentiation, ideology, law, symbolic media, and other critical elements of his scheme.

## Dimensions of the Environment

There are three basic dimensions along which the complexity of the environment is reduced by these mechanisms: (1) a temporal dimension, (2) a material dimension, and (3) a symbolic dimension. More than most social theorists, Luhmann is concerned with time as a dimension of the social universe. Time always presents a system with complexity because it reaches into the past, because it embodies complex configurations of acts in the present, and because it involves the vast horizons of the future. Thus, a social system must develop mechanisms for reducing the complexity of time. It must find a way to order this dimension by developing procedures to orient actions to the past, present, and future.[8]

Luhmann is also concerned with the material dimension of the environment—that is, with all of the possible relations among actions in potentially limitless physical space. Luhmann always asks: What mechanisms are developed to order interrelated actions in physical space? What is the structure and form of such ordering of relations?

Luhmann visualizes the third dimension of human systems as the symbolic. Of all the complex symbols and their combinations that humans can conceivably generate, what mechanisms operate to select some symbols over others and to organize them in some ways as opposed to the vast number of potential alternatives? What kinds of symbolic media are selected and used by a social system to organize social actions?

Thus, the mechanisms of a social system that operate to reduce complexity and thereby maintain a boundary between the system and the environment function along three dimensions, the temporal, material, and symbolic. The nature of a social system—its size, form, and differentiation—will be reflected in the mechanisms that it uses to reduce complexity along these dimensions.

---

[7]Talcott Parsons, *The Social System* (New York: Free Press, 1951).
[8]Luhmann, *The Differentiation*, Chapter 12.

## Types of Social Systems

ω + D

A social system exists any time the actions of individuals are "meaningfully interrelated and interconnected," thereby setting them off from the temporal, material, and symbolic environment by virtue of the selection of functional mechanisms. Out of such processes come three basic types of social systems: (1) interaction systems, (2) organization systems, and (3) societal systems.[9]

**Interaction systems.** An interaction system emerges when individuals are co-present and perceive each other. The very act of perception is a selection mechanism that sorts from a much more complex environment, creating a boundary and setting people off as a system. Such systems are elaborated by the use of language in face-to-face communication, thereby reducing complexity even further along the temporal, material, and symbolic dimensions. For example, Luhmann would ask: how does the language and its organization into codes shape people's perceptions of time?; who is included in the conversation?; and what codes and agreements guide conversation and other actions?

Interaction systems reveal certain inherent limitations and vulnerabilities, however. First, only one topic can be discussed at a time, lest the system collapse as everyone tries to talk at once (which, of course, frequently occurs). Second, the varying conversational resources of participants often lead to competition over who is to talk, creating inequalities and tensions that can potentially lead to conflict and system disintegration. Third, talk and conversation are time-consuming because they are sequential; and as a result, an interaction system can never be very complex.

Thus, interaction systems are simple because they involve only those who can be co-present, perceived, and talked to; they are vulnerable to conflict and tension; and they consume a great deal of time. In order for a social system to be larger and more complex, additional organizing principles beyond perceptions of co-presence and sequential talk are essential.

**Organization systems.** These systems coordinate the actions of individuals with respect to specific conditions, such as work on a specific task in exchange for a specific amount of money. They typically have entry and exit rules (for example, come to work for this period of time and leave with this much money); and their main function is to "stabilize highly 'artificial' modes of behavior over a long stretch of time." They resolve the basic problem of reconciling the motivations and dispositions of individuals and the need to get certain tasks done. An organization is not dependent upon the moral commitment of individuals, nor does it

---

[9]Ibid., pp. 71–89.

require normative consensus. Rather, the entrance/exit rules specify tasks in ways that allow individuals to do what is required without wholly identifying with the organization.

Organization systems are thus essential to a complex social order. They reduce environmental complexity by organizing people (1) *in time* by generating entrance and exit rules and by ordering activities in the present and future; (2) *in space* by creating a division of labor, which authority coordinates; and (3) *in symbolic terms* by indicating what is appropriate, what rules apply, and what media, such as money or pay, are to guide action. In his delineation of organization systems, Luhmann stresses that complex social orders do not require consensus over values, beliefs, or norms to be sustained; they can operate quite effectively without motivational commitments of actors. And in fact, their very strength—flexibility and adaptability to changing environmental conditions—depends upon delimited and situational commitments of actors, along with neutral media of communication, such as money.[10]

**Societal systems.**    These systems cut across interaction and organization systems. A societal system is a "comprehensive system of all reciprocally accessible communication actions."[11] Historically, societal systems have been limited by geopolitical considerations, but today Luhmann sees a trend toward one world society. I find Luhmann's discussion on the societal system rather vague, but the general idea can be inferred from his analysis of more specific topics. Let me summarize: Societal systems use highly generalized communication codes, such as money and power, to reduce the complexity of the environment. In so doing, they set broad limits on how and where actions are to be interrelated into interaction and organization systems. They also organize the way time is perceived and how actions are oriented to the past, present, and future.

## System Differentiation, Integration, and Conflict

These three systems—interaction, organization, and societal—cannot be totally separated, since "all social action obviously takes place in society and is ultimately possible only in the form of interaction."[12] Indeed, in very simple societies, they are fused together; but as societies become larger and more complex, these systems become clearly differentiated from each other and irreducible to one another. Organizations become distinctive with respect to (1) their functional domains (government, law,

---

[10]In making this assertion, Luhmann directly attacks Parsons. See Luhmann, *The Differentiation*, Chapter 3.

[11]Ibid., p. 73.

[12]Ibid., p. 79.

education, economy, religion, science), (2) their entrance/exit rules, and (3) their reliance upon distinctive media of communication (money, truth, power, love, etc.). As a consequence, they cannot be reduced to a societal system. Interaction systems follow their own laws, for rarely do people in their conversations strictly follow the guidelines of organizations and society.

In fact, the differentiation of these systems poses a number of problems for the more inclusive system. First, there is the problem of what Luhmann calls "bottlenecks." Interaction systems are slow, sequentially organized patterns of talk, and they follow their own dynamics as people use their resources in conversations. As a result, they often prevent organizations from operating at high levels of efficiency. As people interact, they develop informal agreements and take their time, with the specific tasks of the organization going un- or underperformed. Similarly, as organization systems develop their own structure and programs, their interests often collide, and they become "bottlenecks" to action requirements at the societal level. Second, there is the problem of conflict in differentiated systems. Interactants may disagree on topics; they may become jealous or envious of those with conversational resources. And since interaction systems are small, they cannot become sufficiently complex "to consign marginals to their borders or to otherwise segregate them." At the organizational level, diverse organizations can pursue their interests in ways that are disruptive to both the organization and the more inclusive societal system.

Yet, countervailing these disruptive tendencies are processes that function to maintain social integration. One critical set of processes is the "nesting" of system levels inside each other. Actions within an interactive system are often nested within an organization system; and organizational actions are conducted within a societal system. Hence, the broader, more inclusive system can operate to promote integration in two ways: (1) it provides the temporal, material, and social premises for the selection of actions; and (2) it imposes an order or structure on the proximate environment around any of its subsystems. For example, an organizational system distributes people in space and in an authority hierarchy; it orients them to time; it specifies the relevant communication codes; and it orders the proximate environment (other people, groupings, offices, etc.) of any interaction system. Similarly, the functional division of a society into politics, education, law, economy, family, religion, and science determines the substance of an organization's action, while it orders the proximate environment of any particular organization. For example, societal differentiation of a distinctive economy delimits what any economic organization can do. Thus, a corporation in a capitalist economy will use money as its distinctive communications media; it will articulate with other organizations in terms of market relations; it will organize its workers into bureaucratic organizations with distinctive entrance and exit rules ("work for money"); and it will be oriented to the future, with the past as only a collapsed framework to guide present activity in the pursuit of future outcomes (such as profits and promotions).

In addition to these nesting processes, integration is promoted by the deflection of people's activities across different organizations in diverse functional domains. When there are many organizations in a society, none consumes an individual's sense of identity and self since people's energies are dispersed across several organization systems. As a consequence of their piecemeal involvement, members are unlikely to be emotionally drawn into conflict among organization systems; and when individual members cannot be pulled emotionally into a conflict, its intensity and potential for social disruption is lessened. Moreover, because interaction systems are distinct from the more inclusive organization, any conflict between organizations is often seen by the rank and file as distant and remote to their interests and concerns; it is something "out there" in the environment of their interaction systems, and hence, it is not very involving.

Yet another source of conflict mitigation is the entrance/exit rules of an organization. As these become elaborated into hierarchies, offices, established procedures, salary scales, and the like, they reduce the relevance of members' conflicts outside the organization—for example, their race and religion. Such outside conflicts are separated from those within the organization, and as a result, their salience in the broader societal system is reduced.

And finally, once differentiation of organizations is an established mechanism in a society, then specific social control organizations—law, police, courts—can be easily created to mitigate and resolve conflicts. That is, the generation of distinct organizations that are functionally specific represents a new "social technology"; and once this technology has been used in one context, it can be applied to additional contexts. Thus, the integrative problems created by the differentiation and proliferation of organizations creates the very conditions that can resolve these problems—the capacity to create organizations to mediate among organizations.

And so, while differentiation of three system levels creates problems of integration and conditions conducive to conflict, it also produces countervailing forces for integration. In making this argument, Luhmann emphasizes that in complex systems, order is not sustained by consensus on common values, beliefs, and norms. On the contrary, there is likely to be considerable disagreement over these, except perhaps at the most abstract level. I think that this is an important contribution of Luhmann's sociology, for it distinguishes his theoretical approach from Talcott Parsons, who, I think, overstressed the need for value consensus in complex social systems. Additionally, Luhmann stresses that individuals' moral and emotional attachment to the social fabric is not essential for social integration. To seek a romantic return to a cohesive community, as Émile Durkheim,

Marx, and others have, is impossible in most spheres of a complex society.[13] And rather than viewing this fact as a pathological state—as concepts like alienation, egoism, and anomie connote—the impersonality and neutrality of many encounters in complex systems can be seen as normal and analyzed less evaluatively. Moreover, people's lack of emotional embeddedness in complex systems gives them more freedom, more options, and more flexibility.[14] It also liberates them from the constraints of tradition, the restrictions of dependency on others, and the indignities of surveillance by the powerful that are so typical of less complex societies.

## Communications Media, Reflexivity, and Self-Thematization

Luhmann's system theory stresses the relation of a system to its environment and the mechanisms used to reduce the complexity of it. All social systems are based upon communication among actors as they align their respective modes of conduct. Because action systems are built from communication, Luhmann devotes considerable attention to *communications theory,* as he defines it.[15] In this discussion, he stresses that human communications become reflexive and that this reflexiveness leads to self-thematization. Luhmann thus develops a communications theory revolving around communication codes and media as well as reflexiveness and self-thematization. Below, I briefly explore each of these elements in his theory.

**Communication and codes.**    Luhmann waxes philosophically and metaphorically about these concepts, but in the end he concludes that communication occurs in terms of symbols that signal actors' lines of behavior; and such symbols constitute a code with several properties.[16] First, the organization of symbols into a code guides the selection of alternatives that reduce the complexity of the environment. For example, when someone in an interaction system says that they want to talk about a particular topic, these symbols operate as a code that reduces the complexity of the system in an environment (its members will now discuss this topic and not all the potential alternatives). Secondly, codes are binary and dialectical in that their symbols imply their opposite. For example, the linguistic code, "be a good boy," also implicitly signals its opposite—that is, what is not good and what is not male. As Luhmann

---

[13]See Chapter 2 on Durkheim and Chapter 6 on Marx.

[14]Here, Luhmann takes a page from Georg Simmel's *The Philosophy of Money,* trans. T. Bottomore and D. Frisby (Boston: Routledge & Kegan Paul, 1978).

[15]This theory, like his general systems theory, is not very much like what most communications theorists actually do.

[16]See Luhmann, *The Differentiation,* p. 169.

notes, "language makes negative copies available" by its very nature. Third, in implying their opposite, codes create the potential for the opposite action—for instance, "to be a bad boy." In human codes, then, the very process of selecting lines of action and in reducing complexity with a code also expands potential options (to do just the opposite or some variant of the opposite). This fact makes the human system highly flexible, because the communications codes used to organize the system and reduce complexity also contain implicit messages about alternatives.

**Communications media.**    Communication codes function to stabilize system responses to the environment (while implying alternative responses). Codes can organize communication into distinctive media that further orders system responses. As a society differentiates into functional domains, distinctive media are used to organize the resources of systems in each domain.[17] For example, the economy uses money as its media of communication, which guides interactions within and among economic organizations. And so, in an economy, relations among organizations are conducted in terms of money (buying and selling in markets), and intraorganizational relations among workers are guided by entrance/exit rules structured by money (pay for work at specified times and places). Similarly, power is the distinctive communications media of the political domain; love is the media of the family; truth, the media of science; and so on for other functional domains.[18]

There are several critical generalizations implicit in Luhmann's analysis of communications media. First, the differentiation of social systems into functional domains cannot occur without the development of a distinctive media of communication for that domain. Second, media reduce complexity because they limit the range of action in a system. (For example, love as a medium limits the kinds of relations that are possible in a family system.)[19] Third, even in reducing complexity, media imply their opposite and thus expand potential options, giving systems flexibility (for instance, money for work implies its opposite, work without pay; and the use of power implies its opposite, lack of compliance to political decisions).

**Reflexivity and self-thematization.**    The use of media allows for *reflexivity,* or the capacity to examine the process of action as a part of the action itself. With communications media structuring action, it becomes possible to use these media to think about or reflect upon action. Social units can use money to make money; they employ power to decide

---

[17]Obviously, Luhmann is borrowing Parsons' idea about generalized media. See Chapter 3.

[18]Much like Parsons, this analysis of communications media is never fully explicated or systematically discussed for all functional domains.

[19]We will see shortly, however, that money is the sole exception here.

how power is to be exercised; they can analyze love to decide what is true love; they can use truth to specify the procedures to get at truth; and so on. Luhmann sees this reflexivity as a mechanism that facilitates adaptation of a system to its environment. It does so by ordering responses and reducing complexity, on the one hand, while it provides a system with the capacity to think about new options for action, on the other. For example, it becomes possible to mobilize power to think about new and more adaptive ways to exercise power in political decisions, as is the case when a society's political elite create a constitutional system based on a separation of powers.

As communications media are used reflexively, they allow for what Luhmann terms *self-thematization.* Using media, a system can come to conceptualize itself and relations with the environment in terms of a "perspective" or "theme." Such self-thematization reduces complexity by providing guidelines about how to deal with the temporal, material, and symbolic dimensions of the environment. It becomes possible to have a guiding perspective on how to orient to time, to organize people in space, and to order symbols into codes. For example, money and its reflexive use for self-thematization in a capitalist economy create a concern with the future, an emphasis on rational organization of people, and a set of codes emphasizing impersonal exchanges of services and commodities. The consequence of these self-thematizations is for economic organizations to reduce the complexity of their environments and, thereby, to coordinate social action more effectively.

## Luhmann's Basic Approach

In sum, Luhmann's general systems approach revolves around the system-environment distinction. Systems need to reduce the complexity of their environments in terms of their perceptions about time, their organization of actors in space, and their use of symbols. Processes that reduce complexity are conceptualized as functional mechanisms. There are three types of systems: interaction, organization, and societal. All system processes occur through communications that can develop into distinctive media and allow for reflexivity and self-thematization in a system.

This is, I feel, a fair summary of Luhmann's general systems approach. He uses these concepts as a kind of metaphor for the analysis of specific empirical topics. Yet, as a metaphor, I find his analysis rather vague and imprecise. Seemingly, in reacting against the restrictive architecture of Parsonian action theory, Luhmann has created an imprecise set of concepts with which to analyze social phenomena. Much of this vagueness remains even as Luhmann addresses particular empirical phenomena. But still he is able to develop stimulating insights.

I will now turn to Luhmann's actual analysis of social processes in order to illustrate how he employs this general systems scheme. Virtually all of his work with this scheme has been on the related processes of social evolution and societal differentiation, especially of organization systems in the political, legal, and economic domains of a society.

## LUHMANN'S CONCEPTION OF SOCIAL EVOLUTION

Since Luhmann's substantive discussions are cast into an evolutionary framework, I think it wise to begin by extracting from his diverse writings the key elements of this evolutionary approach. Like other evolutionary theorists, Luhmann views evolution as the process of increasing differentiation of a system in relation to its environment.[20] Such increased differentiation allows a system to develop more flexible relations to its environment and, as a result, to increase its level of adaptation. As systems differentiate, however, there is the problem of integrating diverse subsystems; and as a consequence, new kinds of mechanisms emerge to sustain the integration of the overall system. But unlike most evolutionary theorists, Luhmann uses this general image of evolution in a way that adds several new twists to previous evolutionary approaches.

### The Underlying Mechanisms of Evolution

Luhmann is highly critical of the way traditional theory has analyzed the process of social differentiation.[21] First, traditional theories—from Marx and Durkheim to Parsons—all imply that there are limits as to how divided a system can be, and so, they all postulate an end to the process, which, in Luhmann's view, is little more than an evaluative utopia. Second, traditional theories overstress the importance of value consensus as an integrating mechanism in differentiated systems. Third, these theories see many processes, such as crime, conflict, dissensus over values, and impersonality, as deviant or pathological; however, they are, in fact, inevitable in differentiated systems. Fourth, previous theories have great difficulty handling the persistence of social stratification, viewing it as a source of evil or as a perpetual conflict-producing mechanism.

Luhmann's alternative to these evolutionary models is to use his systems theory to redirect the analysis of social differentiation. Like most functionalists, he analogizes to biology, but not to the physiology of an organism; rather, his analogies are to the processes delineated in the theory of evolution. Thus, he argues for an emphasis of those processes that produce (1) variation, (2) selection, and (3) stabilization of traits in societal

---

[20]This is essentially Parsons' definition (see Chapter 3). It was Spencer's and Durkheim's as well (see Chapter 2).

[21]Luhmann, *The Differentiation*, pp. 255–57.

systems.[22] The reasoning here is that sociocultural evolution is like other forms of biological evolution. Social systems have mechanisms that are the functional equivalents of those in biological evolution. These mechanisms generate variation in the structure of social systems, select those variations that facilitate adaptation of a system, and stabilize these adaptive structures.[23]

Luhmann argues that the "mechanism for variation" inheres in the process of communication and in the formation of codes and media. Since all symbols imply their opposite, there is always the opportunity to act in new ways (a kind of "symbolic mutation"). The very nature of communication permits alternatives, and at times, people act in terms of these alternatives, thereby producing new variations. Indeed, compared to the process of biological mutation, the capacity of human systems for variation is much greater than in biological systems.

The "mechanism for selection" can be found in what Luhmann vaguely terms *communicative success*. I find his discussion here rather imprecise, to say the least, but the general idea is that certain new forms of communication facilitate increased adjustment to an environment by reducing its complexity while allowing for more flexible responses to the environment. For example, the creation of money as a media greatly facilitated adaptation of systems and subsystems to the environment, as did the development of centralized power to coordinate activity in systems. And, because they facilitated survival and adaptation, they were retained in the structure of the social organism.

The "stabilization mechanism" resides in the very process of system formation. That is, new communication codes and media are used to order social actions among subsystems, and in so doing, they create structures, such as political systems and economic orders, that regularize for a time the use of the new communications media. For example, once money is used, it creates an economic order revolving around markets and exchange that, in turn, feeds back and encourages the extension of money as a media of communication. It is out of this reciprocity that some degree of continuity and stability in the economic system ensues.

## Evolution and Social Differentiation

For Luhmann, sociocultural evolution involves differentiation in seven senses.

---

[22]Luhmann's interpretation of the synthetic theory of evolution in biology is, at best, loose and inexact. Again, it is more metaphorical than precise.

[23]Luhmann, *The Differentiation*, p. 265. Luhmann seems completely unaware that Herbert Spencer in his *The Principles of Sociology* (New York: D. Appleton, 1885; originally published in 1874) performed a similar, and more detailed, analysis 100 years ago.

1. Evolution is the increasing differentiation of interaction, organization, and societal systems from each other. That is, interaction systems increasingly become distinct from organization systems, which, in turn, are more clearly separated from societal systems. Although these system levels are nested in each other, they also operate in terms of their unique dynamics.

2. Evolution involves the internal differentiation of these three types of systems. Diverse interaction systems multiply and become different from each other (for example, compare conversations at work, a party, home, and a funeral). Organization systems increase in number and specialize in different activities (compare economic with political organizations; or contrast different types of economic organizations, such as manufacturing and retail organizations). And the societal system becomes differentiated from the organization and interaction systems that comprise it. Moreover, there is an evolutionary trend, Luhmann claims, toward only one world society.

3. Evolution involves the increasing differentiation of societal systems into functional domains, such as economy, polity, law, religion, family, science, and education. Organization subsystems within these domains are specialized to deal with a limited range of environmental contingencies, and in being specialized, they can better deal with them. The overall result for a societal system is increased adaptability and flexibility in its environment.

4. Functional differentiation is accompanied by (and is the result of) the increasing use of distinctive media of communication. For example, organization systems in the economy employ money; those in the polity or government exercise power; those in science depend upon truth; and those in the family domain use love.

5. There is a clear differentiation during evolution among the person, roles, programs, and values. The individual is an entity separated from any roles and organizations in which to participate. One plays many roles, and each involves only a segment or part of a person's personality and sense of self; and in fact, many roles are played with little or no investment of oneself in them. Moreover, most roles persist whether or not any one individual plays them, thereby emphasizing their separation from the person. Such roles are increasingly grouped together into an ever-increasing diversity of what Luhmann calls programs (work, family, play, politics, consumption, etc.) that typically exist inside different kinds of organization systems operating in a distinctive functional domain. Additionally, these roles can be shuffled around into new programs, emphasizing the separation of roles and programs. Finally, societal values become increasingly abstract and general, with the result that they do not pertain to any one functional domain, program, role, or individual.[24] They exist as

---

[24]Luhmann is borrowing here from Émile Durkheim's analysis in *The Division of Labor*

very general criteria that can be selectively invoked to help organize roles into programs or to mobilize individuals to play roles; however, their application to roles and programs is made possible by additional mechanisms such as ideologies, laws, technologies, and norms. For by themselves, societal values are too general and abstract for individuals to use in concrete situations. Indeed, one of the most conspicuous features of highly differentiated systems is the evolution of mechanisms to attach abstract values to concrete roles and programs.

6. Evolution involves the movement through three distinctive forms of differentiation: (1) segmentation, (2) stratification, and (3) functional differentiation.[25] That is, the five processes outlined above have operated historically to create, Luhmann believes, only three distinctive forms of differentiation. When the simplest societies initially differentiate, they do so segmentally in that they create like and equal subsystems that operate very much like the ones from which they emerged. For example, as it initially differentiates, a traditional society will create new lineages, or new villages, that duplicate previous lineages and villages. But segmentation limits a society's complexity and, hence, its capacity to adapt to its environment. And so, alternative forms of differentiation are selected for during sociocultural evolution. Further differentiation creates stratified systems where subsystems vary in terms of their power, wealth, and other resources. These subsystems are ordered hierarchically, and this new form of structure allows for more complex relations with an environment but imposes limitations on how complex the system can become. For as long as the hierarchical order must be maintained, the options of any subsystem are limited by its place in the hierarchy.[26] Thus, pressures build for a third form of differentiation, the functional. Here, communication processes are organized around the specific function to be performed for the societal system. Such a system creates inequalities because some functions have more priority for the system (e.g., economics over religion). This inequality is, however, fundamentally different from that in hierarchically ordered or stratified systems. In a functionally differentiated society, the other subsystems are part of the environment of any given subsystem—for example, organizations in the polity, law, education, religions, science, and family domains are part of the environment of the economy. And although the economy may have functional priority in the society, it treats and responds to the other subsystems in its environment as equals. Thus, inequality in functionally differentiated societies does not create a rigid hierarchy

---

*in Society* (New York: Free Press, 1949; originally published in 1893) as well as Talcott Parsons' discussion of "value generalization." See Chapter 3.

[25]Luhmann, *The Differentiation*, pp. 229-54.

[26]Ibid., p. 235.

of subsystems; and as a consequence, it allows for more autonomy of each subsystem, which, in turn, gives them more flexibility in dealing with their respective environments.[27] The overall consequence of such subsystem autonomy is increased flexibility of the societal system to adjust and adapt to its environment.

7. Evolutionary differentiation increases the complexity of a system and its relationship with the environment. In so doing, it escalates the risks, as Luhmann terms the matter, of making incorrect and maladaptive decisions about how to relate to an environment. For with increased complexity, there is an expanded set of options for a system, but there is a corresponding chance that the selection of options will be dysfunctional for a system's relationship to an environment. For example, any organization in the economy must make decisions about its actions, but there are increased alternatives and escalated unknowns, resulting in expanded risks. In Luhmann's view, the ever-increasing risk level that accompanies evolutionary differentiation must be accompanied by mechanisms to reduce risk, or at least by the perception or sense that risk has been reduced. Thus, evolution always involves an increase in the number and complexity of risk-reducing mechanisms. Such mechanisms also decrease the complexity of a system's environment because they select some options over others. For example, a conservative political ideology is a risk-reducing mechanism because it selects some options from more general values and ignores others. In essence, an ideology assures decision makers that the risks are reduced by accepting the goals of the ideology.[28]

Before proceeding further, let me now summarize these elements of Luhmann's view of evolution in terms of how they change a society's and its constituent subsystem's relation to the temporal, material, and symbolic dimensions of the environment. Temporally, Luhmann argues that social evolution and differentiation lead to efforts at developing a chronological metric, or a standardized way to measure time (clocks, for example). Equally fundamental is a shift in people's perspective from the past to the future. The past becomes highly generalized and lacks specific dictates of what should be done in the present and the future. For as systems become more complex, the past cannot serve as a guide to the present or future because there are too many potentially new contingencies and options. The present sees time as ever more scarce and in short supply; and thus, people become more oriented to the future and the consequences of their present actions. Materially, social differentiation involves: (1) the increasing separation of interaction, organization, and societal systems;

---

[27]I am not asserting, of course, that this assertion by Luhmann is true.
[28]Luhmann, *The Differentiation*, p. 151.

(2) the compartmentalization of organization systems into functional domains; (3) the growing separation of person, role, program, and values; and (4) the movement toward functional differentiation away from segmentation and stratification. And symbolically, communication codes become more complex and organized as distinctive media for a particular functional domain. Moreover, they increasingly function as risk-reducing mechanisms for a universe filled with contingency and uncertainty.

It is with this overall view of sociocultural evolution and differentiation that Luhmann has approached the study of specific organizational systems. As he has consistently argued, an analytical framework is only as good as the insights into empirical processes that it can generate. I find Luhmann's framework much more complex than he contends such a framework should be, and I see it as more metaphorical than analytical.[29] However, it has allowed him to analyze political, legal, and economic processes in functionally differentiated societies in a very intriguing way.

(ie modern society).

# THE FUNCTIONAL DIFFERENTIATION OF SOCIETY

## Politics as a Social System

As societies grow more complex, new structures for reducing complexity emerge. Old processes such as appeals to traditional truths, mutual sympathy, exchange, and barter become ever more inadequate. A system, Luhmann argues, that reaches this point of differentiation must develop the "capacity to make binding decisions." Such capacity is generated out of the problems of increased complexity, but it also becomes an important condition for further differentiation.

In order to make binding decisions, a distinctive media of communication must be used: power.[30] Power is defined by Luhmann as "the possibility of having one's own decisions select alternatives or reduce complexity for others." Thus, whenever one social unit selects alternatives of action for other units, power is being employed as the media of communication.

The use of power to make binding decisions functions to resolve conflicts, to mitigate tensions, and to coordinate activities in complex systems. Societies that can develop political systems capable of performing these functions are better able to deal with their environments. Several conditions, Luhmann believes, facilitate the development of this functional capacity. First, there must be time to make decisions; and the less time an emerging political system is allowed, the more difficulty it will have in becoming autonomous. Second, the emerging political system

---

[29]Indeed, my discussion has simplified it considerably.
[30]Luhmann, *The Differentiation*, p. 151.

must not confront a single power block in its environment, such as a powerful church. Rather, it requires an environment of multiple subsystems whose power is more equally balanced. And so, the more the power in the political subsystem's environment is concentrated, the more difficult is its emergence as an autonomous subsystem. Third, the political system must stabilize its relations with other subsystems in the environment in two distinctive ways: (1) at the level of diffuse legitimacy so that its decisions are accepted as its proper function; and (2) at the level of daily transactions among individuals and subsystems.[31] That is, the greater the problems of a political system in gaining diffuse support for its right to make decisions for other subsystems and the less salient the decisions of the political system for the day-to-day activities, transactions, and routines of system units, then the greater will be its problems in developing into an autonomous subsystem.

Thus, to the extent that a political system has time to develop procedures for making decisions, confront multiple sources of mitigated power, and achieve diffuse legitimacy as well as relevance for specific transactions, then the more it can develop into an autonomous system and the greater will be a society's capacity to adjust to its environment. In so developing, the political system must achieve what Luhmann calls *structural abstraction,* or the capacity to (1) absorb multiple problems, dilemmas, and issues from a wide range of system units and (2) make binding decisions for each of these. Luhmann sees the political system as "absorbing" the problems of its environment and making them internal to the political system. Several variables, he argues, determine the extent to which the political system can perform this function: (1) the degree to which conflicts are defined as political (instead of moral, personal, etc.) and therefore in need of a binding decision, (2) the degree of administrative capacity of the political system to coordinate activities of system units, and (3) the degree of structural differentiation within the political system itself.

This last variable is the most crucial in Luhmann's view. In response to environmental complexity and the need to absorb and deal with problems in this environment, the political system must differentiate along three lines: (1) the creation of a stable bureaucratic administration that executes decisions, (2) the evolution of a separate arena for politics and the emergence of political parties, and (3) the designation of the public as a relevant concern in making binding decisions. Such internal differentiation increases the capacity of the political system to absorb and deal with a wide variety of problems; and as a consequence, it allows for greater complexity in the societal system.

This increased complexity of the political and societal systems also increases the risks of making binding decisions that are maladaptive. For

---

[31]Ibid., pp. 143–44.

as complexity increases, there are always unknown contingencies. Therefore, political systems not only develop mechanisms such as internal differentiation for dealing with complexity, but they also develop mechanisms for reducing risk or the perception of risk. One mechanism is the growing reflexiveness of the political process—that is, its increased reflection upon itself. Such reflection is built into the nature of party politics where the manner and substance of political decisions are analyzed and debated. Another mechanism is what Luhmann calls the *positivation of law,* or the creation of a separate legal system that makes "laws about how to make laws" (more on this shortly in the next section). Yet another mechanism is ideology or symbolic codes that select which values are relevant for a particular set of decisions. A related mechanism is the development of a political code that typifies and categorizes political decisions into a simple typology.[32] For example, the distinction between progressive and conservative politics is, Luhmann argues, an important political code in differentiated societies. Such a code is obviously very general, but this is its virtue because it allows very diverse political acts and decisions to be categorized and interpreted with a simple dichotomy, thereby giving political action a sense of order and reducing perceptions of risk. Luhmann goes so far as to indicate that it is a system's capacity to develop a political code more than consensus of values that leads to social order. For in interpreting actions in terms of the code, a common perspective is maintained, but it is a perspective based upon differences—progressive versus conservative—rather than commonality and consensus. Thus, complex social orders are sustained by their very capacity to create generalized and binary categories for interpreting events rather than by value consensus.

Still another mechanism for reducing risks is arbitrary decision making by elites. However, although such a solution achieves order, it undermines the legitimacy of the political system in the long run because system units come to resent and to resist arbitrary decision making. And a final mechanism is invocation of a traditional moral code (for example, fundamentalistic religious values) that, in Luhmann's terms, "remoralizes" the political process. But when such remoralization occurs, the political system must dedifferentiate because strict adherence to a simple moral code precludes the capacity to deal with complexity (an example of this process would be Iran's return to a theocracy from its previously more complex political system).

In sum, then, I think it fair to say that Luhmann uses his conceptual metaphor to analyze insightfully specific institutional processes, such as government. Yet, he does not use his scheme in a rigorous deductive sense, but much like Parsons before him, he employs the framework as a means

---

[32]Ibid., pp. 168–89.

for denoting and highlighting particular social phenomena. Although I think that much of his analysis of political system differentiation is "old wine in new bottles," there is a shift in emphasis and, as a result, some intriguing but imprecise insights. In a similar vein, Luhmann analyzes the differentiation of the legal system and the economy.

## The Autonomy of the Legal System

As I discussed earlier, Luhmann visualizes social evolution as involving a separation of persons, roles, programs, and values. For him, differentiation of structure occurs at the level of roles and programs. Consequently, there is the problem of how to integrate values and persons into roles organized into programs within organization systems. The functional mechanism for mobilizing and coordinating individuals to play roles is law, whereas the mechanism for making values relevant to programs is ideology.[33] Thus, because law regulates and coordinates people's participation in roles and programs and because social differentiation must always occur at the roles level, it becomes a critical subsystem if a society is to differentiate and evolve. That is, a society cannot become complex without the emergence of an autonomous legal system to specify rights, duties, and obligations of people playing roles.[34]

A certain degree of political differentiation must precede legal differentiation, since there must be a set of structures to make decisions and enforce them. But political processes often impede legal autonomy, as is the case when political elites have used the law for their own narrow purposes. For legal autonomy to emerge, therefore, political development is not enough. Two additional conditions are necessary: (1) "the invocation of sovereignty," or references by system units to legal codes that justify their communications and actions; and (2) "lawmaking sovereignty," or the capacity of organizations in the legal system to decide just what the law will be.

If these two conditions are met, then the legal system can become increasingly reflexive. It can become a topic to itself, creating bodies of procedural and administrative law to regulate the enactment and enforcement of law. In turn, such procedural laws can themselves be the subject of scrutiny. Without this reflexive quality, the legal system cannot be sufficiently flexible to change in accordance with shifting events in its environment. Such flexibility is essential because only through the law can people's actions be tied to the roles that are being differentiated. For example, without what Luhmann calls the "positivization of law" or its

---

[33]Ibid., pp. 90–137.

[34]This is essentially the same conclusion Parsons reached in his description of evolution in *Societies: Evolutionary and Comparative Perspectives* and *The System of Modern Societies* (Englewood Cliffs, N.J.: Prentice-Hall, 1966 and 1971, respectively).

capacity to change itself in response to altered circumstances, new laws and agencies (e.g., workers' compensation, binding arbitration of labor-management disputes, minimum wages, health and safety) could not be created to regulate people's involvement in roles (in this case, work roles in a differentiating economy).

Thus, positivization of the law is a critical condition for societal differentiation. It reduces complexity by specifying relations of actors to roles and relegating cooperation among social system units. But it reduces complexity in a manner that presents options for change under new circumstances; and thus, it becomes a condition for the further differentiation of other functional domains, such as the economic.

## The Economy as a Social System

I think that Luhmann defines the economy in a needlessly elliptical way. For Luhmann, the economy has the function of "deferring a decision about the satisfaction of needs while providing a guarantee that they will be satisfied and so utilizing the time thus acquired."[35] The general idea seems to be that economic activity—production and distribution of goods and services—functions to satisfy basic or primary needs for food, clothing, and shelter as well as derived or secondary needs for less basic goods and services. But it does so in a way not fully appreciated in economic analysis: it restructures humans' orientation to time because economic action is oriented to the satisfaction of future needs. Present economic activity is typically directed at future consumption; and so when a person works and a corporation acts in a market, they are doing so to guarantee that their future will be unproblematic.

I think that Luhmann's definition of the economic subsystem is less critical than his analysis of the processes leading to the creation of an autonomous economic system in society. In traditional and undifferentiated societies, Luhmann argues, only small-scale solutions are possible with respect to doing something in the present to satisfy future needs. One solution is stockpiling of goods, with provisions for the redistribution of stocks to societal members or trade with other societies.[36] Another solution is mutual assistance agreements among individuals, kin groups, or villages. But such patterns of economic organization are very limited because they merge familial, political, religious, and community activity. Only with the differentiation of distinctly economic roles can more complexity and flexibility be structured into economic action. The first key differentiation along these lines is the development of markets with distinctive roles for buyers and sellers.

---

[35]Luhmann, *The Differentiation*, p. 194.
[36]Ibid., p. 197.

A market performs several crucial functions. First, it sets equivalences or the respective values of goods and services. Second, it neutralizes the relevance of other roles—for instance, the familial, religious, and political roles of parties in an exchange. Value is established in terms of the qualities of respective goods, not the positions or characteristics of the buyers and sellers.[37] Third, markets inevitably generate pressures for a new media of communication that is not tied to other functional subsystems. This media is money, and it allows for quick assessments of equivalences and value in terms of an agreed-upon metric. In sum, then, markets create the conditions for the differentiation of distinctly economic roles, for their separation and insulation from other societal roles, and for the creation of a uniquely economic media of communication.

Money is a very unusual media, Luhmann believes, because it "transfers complexity." Unlike other media, money is distinctive because it does not reduce complexity in the environment. For example, the media of power is used to make decisions that direct activity, thereby reducing the complexity of the environment. The media of truth in science is designed to simplify the understanding of a complex universe. And the media of love in the family circumscribes the actions and types of relations among kindred, and in so doing, it reduces complexity. In contrast, money is a neutral vehicle that can always be used to buy and sell many different things. It does not limit; in fact, it opens options and creates new opportunities. For example, to accept money for a good or for one's work does not reduce the seller's or worker's options. The money can be used in many different ways, thereby preserving and even increasing the complexity of the environment. Money thus sets the stage—indeed it encourages—further internal differentiation in the economic subsystem of a society.

In addition to transferring complexity, Luhmann sees money as dramatically altering the time dimension of the environment. Money is a liquid resource that is always "usable in the future." When we have money, it can be used at some future date—whether the next minute or the following year. Money thus collapses time, since it is to be used in the future, hence making the past irrelevant; and the present is defined in terms of what will be done with money in the future. However, this collapsing of time can only come about if (1) money does not inflate over time and (2) it is universally used as the media of exchange (that is, barter, mutual assistance, and other traditional forms of exchange do not still prevail).[38]

Like all media of communication, money is reflexive. It becomes a goal of reflection, debate, and action itself. We can buy and sell money in markets; we can invest money to make more money; or we can condemn

---

[37]Luhmann fails to cite the earlier work of Georg Simmel on these matters. See Simmel's *The Philosophy of Money.*

[38]Luhmann, *The Differentiation*, p. 207.

money as the root of evil or praise it as a goal that is worth pursuing; we can hoard it in banks or we can spread it around in consumptive activity. This reflexive quality of money, coupled with its capacity to transfer complexity and reorient actors to time, is what allows money to become an ever more dominant media of communication in complex societies. Indeed, the economy becomes the primary subsystem of complex societies because its media encourages constant increases in complexity and growth in the economic system. As a consequence, the economy becomes a prominent subsystem in the environment of other functional subsystems—that is, science, polity, family, religion, and education. In fact, it becomes something that must always be dealt with by these other subsystems.

This growing complexity of the economic subsystem increases the risks in human conduct. The potential for making a mistake in providing for a person's future needs or a corporation's profits increases because the number of unknown contingencies dramatically multiplies. Such escalated risks generate pressures, Luhmann argues, for their reduction through the emergence of specific mechanisms. The most important of these mechanisms is the tripart internal differentiation of the economy around (1) households, (2) firms, and (3) markets.[39] There is a "structural selection" for this division, Luhmann believes, because these are structurally and functionally different. Households are segmental systems (structurally the same) and are the primary consumption units. Firms are structurally diverse and the primary productive units. And markets are not so much a unit as a set of processes for distributing goods and services. Luhmann is a bit vague on this point, but it seems that there is strength in this correspondence of basically different structures with major economic functions. Households are segmented structurally and are functionally oriented to consumption; firms are highly differentiated structurally and are functionally geared to production; and markets are processually differentiated in terms of their function to distribute different types of goods and services. Such differentiation reduces complexity, but at the same time, it also allows for flexibility: households can change consumption patterns, firms can alter production, and markets can expand or contract. And since they are separated from each other, each has the capacity to change and redirect its actions, independent of the other. It is this flexibility that allows the economic system to become so prominent in modern industrial societies.

Yet, Luhmann warns, the very complexity of the economy and its importance for other subsystems create pressures for other risk-reducing mechanisms. One of these is intervention by government so that power is used to make binding decisions on production, consumption, and distribution as well as on the availability of money as a media of

---

[39]Ibid., p. 216.

communication. The extensive use of this mechanism, Luhmann believes, reduces risk and complexity in the economy at the expense of its capacity to meet needs in the future and to make flexible adjustments to the environment.

## SYSTEMS FUNCTIONALISM: AN ASSESSMENT OF LUHMANN'S ALTERNATIVE

I think the critical questions in assessing Luhmann's functionalism are: Does it avoid the problems of functional analysis that I have outlined in previous chapters? And does it add any new insights into the dynamics of social systems? Let me begin with the first question.

It seems to me that Luhmann simply ignores the problems of functional analysis. He assumes functional needs and imperatives for reducing complexity and for adaptation to the environment. Then, he simply asserts that mechanisms emerge to meet these needs. I feel there is much here that is illegitimately teleological; system needs miraculously produce the structures to meet these needs; or in other words, effects produce causes. Luhmann does invoke a "social selection" argument in that pressures for adaptation and for reducing complexity create "selection pressures" for some of those system mechanisms that will reduce complexity and increase adaptation. But for any given mechanism, these selection processes are rarely articulated. For example, if "positive law" has selective advantages, then what exactly were the selection pressures for its emergence?; what happened historically to societies that did and did not develop positive law?; and what are the reasons why they did or did not? Without answers to such questions, the theoretical explanation of an event is an illegitimate teleology. Effects produce the things that cause these effects.

More problematic, I think, is the view of explanation in Luhmann's approach: develop a conceptual scheme of categories and use these categories to describe social events. For me, Luhmann ends up simply describing with new words what has occurred historically without really explaining how and why these events occurred (except to state that they met system needs or requisites). For example, to assert that ideologies meet the need to attach values to roles and programs in complex societies simply says that ideologies become prominent in complex societies. But it does not explain how and why this occurs.

Additionally, in an effort to avoid the complex architecture of Parsons' analytical scheme, Luhmann constructs a very loose, metaphorical, and frequently vague alternative. Even more than is the case with Parsons, I suspect, one must internalize the scheme and use it as a general and sensitizing metaphor for interpreting events. As a result, one does not explain by deduction, but by intuition. One senses that this or that process is a "mechanism" that "serves this or that function." Explanation becomes a matter of negotiating the right intuition among communities of Luhmann scholars who have internalized and who accept his concepts, categories, and metaphors.

Moreover, how would one ever refute Luhmann's scheme? When categories are vague and imprecise, when they are often metaphorical, and when explanation is by intuitive use of the scheme, could one ever construct a "test" of the scheme that might throw its utility into doubt? I sense that any such effort would be rejected by adherents to Luhmann's approach as "an incorrect interpretation of what he really meant." Thus, the scheme will always remain intact, and all assaults on its virtue will be defined away.

In light of these problems, what does the scheme offer to sociological theorizing? I think that as explanation of events it has little to offer cumulative theory, but much like Parsons' scheme, it is often used to produce rich and robust substantive insights. Probably the most useful portions of the scheme are (1) the implicit attack on the evaluative substance of much evolutionary thinking, (2) the recognition that complex social systems are integrated in ways other than value consensus, and (3) the emphasis that social processes operate along temporal, material, and symbolic dimensions. In these areas, there are many interesting generalizations to be developed. None of them needs the systems and functional trappings of Luhmann's scheme. One can, for example, analyze entrance/ exit rules independently of viewing them as mechanisms for reducing complexity in organization systems. Or one can examine the effects of money on cognitive orientations to time without all of the jargon about system adaptation.

Thus, the scheme does produce insights that alternative theoretical approaches have not generated. And so, if one finds Luhmann's functional metaphors useful, I see little wrong in using them to isolate interesting social processes. But once this is done, the system's jargon and its functional trappings *should be abandoned*. Then, the process can be examined in ways that can yield testable propositions. Unfortunately, once committed to a system's functional scheme, it is typically difficult to abandon it. As a result, the scheme becomes a grand, self-reinforcing world view; and explanation becomes the intuitive use of the scheme to interpret and describe events.

Thus, Luhmann's systems functionalism is very much like other functionalisms. It is intriguing and seductive. But it can only explain by categorizing events as an instance of this or that element in the scheme. However, the scheme itself can never be tested against the facts of the empirical world. And so, it is interesting metaphysics but poor theory.

# PART TWO

## Conflict Theory

# CHAPTER 6

# The Origins of Conflict and Critical Theorizing

## THE CONFLICT ALTERNATIVE

During the 1950s, as the essentials of the Parsonian scheme were unfolding, one body of criticism was taking on a clear focus. Functional theory in sociology, especially the Parsonian variety, was seen as underemphasizing the conflictual nature of social reality. Soon, attacks along these lines became ceremonial rituals for sociologists who sought theoretical redemption for past sins and who now held that conflict theory was to carry sociology out of its theoretical morass.

David Lockwood argued as early as 1956 that in continually assuming for analytical purposes a system in equilibrium, Parsons had created a fictionalized conception of the social world.[1] From this world of fantasy, as Lockwood phrased the matter, it was inevitable that analysis would emphasize mechanisms that maintained social order rather than those that systematically generated disorder and change. Furthermore, by assuming order and equilibrium, the ubiquitous phenomena of instability, disorder, and conflict too easily became viewed as deviant, abnormal, and pathological. For, in reality, Lockwood insisted, there are mechanisms in societies that make conflict inevitable and inexorable. For example, power differentials assure that some groups will exploit others and constitute a built-in source of tension and conflict in social systems. Additionally, the existence of scarce resources in societies will inevitably generate fights

---

[1]David Lockwood, "Some Remarks on 'The Social System,'" *British Journal of Sociology* 7 (June 1956), pp. 134–46.

over the distribution of these resources. And finally, the fact that different interest groups pursue different goals and hence vie with one another assures that conflict will erupt. These forces, Lockwood contended, represent mechanisms of social disorder that should be as analytically significant to the understanding of social systems as Parsons's mechanisms of socialization and social control.

As I noted in Chapter 3, Ralf Dahrendorf crystallized this line of argument toward the end of the decade by comparing functional theory to a utopia.[2] Utopias usually have few historical antecedents—much like Parsons's hypothesized equilibrium, utopias display universal consensus on prevailing values and institutional arrangements—in a vein remarkably similar to Parsons's concept of institutionalization; and utopias always display processes that operate to maintain existing arrangements—much like the mechanisms of Parsons's social system. Hence, utopias and the social world when viewed from a functional perspective do not change very much, since they do not concern themselves with history, dissension over values, and conflict in institutional arrangements.

At the same time, another body of conflict criticism was emerging. This criticism was mounted against all positivistic social science, especially the functional variety but also any system of theory that proclaimed itself as objective and neutral.[3] All theory that seeks to understand the social world without also exposing the patterns of oppression and domination is, in effect, an ideology supporting the status quo. For in studying the world "as it is," there is an implicit assumption that this is how the social order *must be*. Theoretical knowledge cannot, therefore, merely describe events. It must expose exploitive social arrangements and, at the same time, suggest alternative ways to organize humans in less oppressive ways. Social theory cannot be neutral; rather, it must be emancipatory.

To some extent, the critiques of Parsonian functionalism and positivism owe their inspiration to what I see as contradictory strains in the work of Karl Marx. Those who were to criticize Parsons for his failure to examine conflict tended to accept the positivistic strains in Marx and to propose a conflict sociology that tried to develop abstract propositions explaining the conflictual nature of social reality.[4] In contrast, those who

[2]Ralf Dahrendorf, "Out of Utopia: Toward a Reorientation of Sociological Analysis," *American Journal of Sociology* 744 (September 1958), pp. 115–27.

[3]Herbert Marcuse, *Reason and Revolution* (Boston: Beacon Press, 1960) and *Negations* (Boston: Beacon Press, 1969; originally published 1965); Theodore Adorno, *Negative Dialectics* (New York: Seaburg Press, 1973); Max Horkheimer, *Critical Theory* (New York: Herder and Herder, 1972); Trent Schroyer, "Toward a Critical Theory for Advanced Industrial Society," in *Recent Sociology,* ed. H. P. Dreitzer (New York: Macmillan, 1970); and *The Critique of Domination: The Origins and Development of Critical Theory* (New York: George Braziller Inc., 1973); Jurgen Habermas, *Knowledge and Human Interest* (Boston: Beacon Press, 1971).

[4]For a diverse sampling of these efforts, see William Gamson, *The Strategy of Social Protest* (Homewood, Ill.: Dorsey Press, 1975); Louis Kriesberg, *The Sociology of Social*

criticized positivism in general drew inspiration from the more moralistic and antiscience portions in Marx and, surprisingly, have not been so hostile to Parsons or functionalism in general.

But I hasten to add that Marx was not the only source of inspiration for this emerging range of alternatives. The other prominent German sociologists of the late 19th and early 20th centuries—Max Weber and Georg Simmel—were also decisive in the development of the various conflict sociologies. Simmel was to inspire a more positivistic and functional view of conflict processes than Marx; and his criticisms of Marx's analysis of capitalism have influenced critical theorists who dislike positivism and who emphasize that social theory must be emancipatory. Similarly, Max Weber was to stimulate both the positivistic and critical versions of conflict theorizing. For positivistically inclined theorists, his analysis of stratification has provided a crucial corrective for errors in Marx's analysis of class conflict. And for critical theorists, his historical and evolutionary account of the rise of capitalism and his pessimistic assessment of the process of rationalization in the modern world have forced a reassessment of Marx's naive faith in the coming emancipation of humans.

Thus, out of this ferment among the three great German sociologists—Marx, Weber, and Simmel—emerged a variety of approaches that share little else in common than their use of the works of Marx, Simmel, and

---

*Conflict* (Englewood Cliffs, N.J.: Prentice-Hall, 1973); Anthony Oberschall, *Social Conflict and Social Movements* (Englewood Cliffs, N.J.: Prentice-Hall, 1973); Robin M. Williams, Jr., *Mutual Accommodation: Ethnic Conflict and Cooperation* (Minneapolis, Minn.: University of Minnesota Press, 1977); Randall Collins, *Conflict Sociology* (New York: Academic Press, 1975); Ted Gurr, "Sources of Rebellion in Western Societies: Some Quantitative Evidence," *The Annals* 391 (September 1970), pp. 128–44, A. L. Jacobson, "Intrasocietal Conflict: A Preliminary Test of a Structural Level Theory," *Comparative Political Studies* 6 (1973), pp. 62–83; David Snyder, "Institutional Setting and Industrial Conflict," *American Sociological Review* 40 (June 1975), pp. 259–78; David Britt and Omer R. Galle, "Industrial Conflict and Unionization," *American Sociological Review* 37 (February 1972), pp. 46–57; E. McNeil, ed., *The Nature of Human Conflict* (Englewood Cliffs, N.J.: Prentice-Hall, 1965); Jessie Bernard, *American Community Behavior* (New York: Dryden Press, 1949), "Where is the Modern Sociology of Conflict?" *American Journal of Sociology* 56 (1950), pp. 111–16, and "Parties and Issues in Conflict," *Journal of Conflict Resolution* 1 (June 1957), pp. 111–21; Kenneth Boulding, *Conflict and Defense: A General Theory* (New York: Harper & Row, 1962); Thomas Carver, "The Basis of Social Conflict," *American Journal of Sociology* 13 (1908), pp. 628–37; James Coleman, *Community Conflict* (Glencoe, Ill.: Free Press, 1957); James C. Davies, "Toward A Theory of Revolution," *American Journal of Sociology* 27 (1962), pp. 5–19; Charles P. Loomis, "In Praise of Conflict and Its Resolution," *American Sociological Review* 32 (December 1967), pp. 875–90; Raymond Mack and Richard C. Snyder, "The Analysis of Social Conflict," *Journal of Conflict Resolution* 1 (June 1957), pp. 388–97; John S. Patterson, *Conflict in Nature and Life* (New York: Appleton-Century-Crofts, 1883); Anatol Rapoport, *Fights, Games and Debates* (Ann Arbor, Mich.: University of Michigan Press, 1960); Thomas C. Schelling, *The Strategy of Conflict* (Cambridge, Mass.: Harvard Univ. Press, 1960); Pitirim Sorokin, "Solidary, Antagonistic, and Mixed Systems of Interaction," in *Society, Culture, and Personality* (New York: Harper & Row, 1947); Nicholas S. Timasheff, *War and Revolution* (New York: Sheed and Ward, 1965); Robin M. Williams, Jr., *The Reduction of Intergroup Tensions* (New York: Social Science Research Council, 1947); and Clinton F. Fink, "Some Conceptual Difficulties in the Theory of Social Conflict," *Journal of Conflict Resolution* 12 (December 1968), pp. 429–31.

Weber to analyze elements of inequality, power, domination, and conflict in human societies. I have grouped this diverse range of approaches under the rubric of *conflict theory,* but I do so only with the important qualification that this label embraces very different types of theoretical activity—ranging from dialectical and functional theories of conflict processes to more encompassing philosophical schemes about the state of human oppression and domination in the modern world. My purpose in this chapter, therefore, is to examine the origins of this eclectic mix of approaches by summarizing the diverse strains in the work of Marx, Simmel, and Weber that have been used to build these very different types of conflict theorizing.

## KARL MARX (1818–1883) AND THE ORIGINS OF CONFLICT AND CRITICAL THEORY

As with any scholar whose work evolves over time, there are contradictions and inconsistencies in Marx's ideas. I do not see this as a cause for great dismay, as many commentators have. Indeed, any creative scholar's thought will change and evolve over time. And thus, Marx and Friedrich Engels's first work, *The German Ideology,*[5] is vastly different from Marx's later works, such as *Capital.*[6] In between these early and late works is Marx's and Engels's *The Communist Manifesto.*[7] There are, of course, other important works to consider, but I feel that these have been the most influential in the development of critical theory, which stresses the emancipatory themes in Marx's thought, and dialectical conflict theory, which has followed the more positivistic hints in Marx's work.

### Critical Strains in Marx's Thought

In 1846, Marx and Engels completed *The German Ideology,* which was initially turned down by the publisher.[8] Much of this work is an attack on the "Young Hegelians," who were advocates of the German philosopher Georg Hegel, and is of little interest today. Yet, in this attack are certain basic ideas that, I feel, have served as the impetus behind "critical theory," or the view that social theory must be critical of oppressive arrangements and propose emancipatory alternatives. This theme exists, of course, in all of Marx's work, but it is in this first statement by Marx that the key elements of contemporary critical theory are most evident.

---

[5]Karl Marx and Friedrich Engels, *The German Ideology* (New York: International Publishers, 1947; originally written in 1846).

[6]Karl Marx, *Capital: A Critical Analysis of Capitalist Production,* vol. 1 (New York: International Publishers, 1967; originally published in 1867).

[7]Karl Marx and Friedrich Engels, *The Communist Manifesto* (New York: International Publishers, 1971; originally published in 1848).

[8]Marx and Engels, *The German Ideology.*

Marx criticized the Young Hegelians severely because he had once been one of them and was now making an irrevocable break with them. He saw the Hegelians as hopeless idealists, in the philosophical sense. That is, they saw the world as reflective of ideas, with the dynamics of social life revolving around consciousness and other cognitive processes by which "ideal essences" work their magic on humans. Marx saw this emphasis on the "reality of ideas" as nothing more than a conservative ideology that supports people's oppression by the material forces of their existence. His alternative was "to stand Hegel on his head," but in this early work, there is still an emphasis on the relation between consciousness and self-reflection, on the one hand, and social reality, on the other. This dualism becomes central to contemporary critical theory.

Marx saw humans as being unique by virtue of their conscious awareness of themselves and their situation. They are capable of self-reflection and, hence, assessment of their positions in society. Such consciousness arises out of people's daily existence and is not a realm of ideas that is somehow independent of the material world, as much German philosophy argued. For Marx, people produce their ideas and conceptions of the world in light of the social structures in which they are born, raised, and live.

The essence of people's lives is the process of production, since for Marx, human "life involves before anything else eating and drinking, a habitation, clothing, and many other material things."[9] To meet these contingencies of life, production is necessary, but as production satisfies one set of needs, new needs arise and encourage alterations in the ways that productive activity is organized. The elaboration of productive activity creates a division of labor, which, in the end, is alienating because it increasingly deprives humans of their capacity to determine their productive activities. Moreover, as people work, they are exploited in ways that generate private property and capital for those who enslave them. Thus, as people work as alienated cogs in the division of labor, they produce that which enslaves them: private property and profits for those who control the modes and means of production. Marx provided a more detailed discussion of the evolution of productive forces to this capitalist stage, but for my purposes, his analysis of consciousness is more important.[10]

Marx argued that the capacity to use language, to think, and to analyze allows humans to alter their environment. People do not merely have to react to their material conditions in some mechanical way; they can also use their capacities for thought and reflection to construct new material conditions and corresponding social relations. Indeed, the course of history

---

[9]Ibid., p. 15.

[10]Indeed, Marx was as much an evolutionist as any functionalist, and in fact, there is much functional reasoning in his arguments. For illustrations, see Arthur L. Stinchcombe, *Constructing Social Theories* (New York: Harcourt, Brace & World, 1968).

involved such processes as people actively restructured the material conditions of their existence. The goal of social theory, Marx implicitly argues, is to use humans' unique facility to expose those oppressive social
relations and to propose alternatives. Marx's entire career was devoted
to this goal; and it is this emancipatory aspect of Marx's thought that
forms the foundation for critical theory, which I will examine in Chapter
9.

## Positivistic Strains in Marx's Thought

In developing this emancipatory project, Marx produced a formal theory
of conflict and change, which he might disavow as a positivistic theory
but which has been used nonetheless in developing contemporary conflict
theory. In elaborating his model of revolutionary class conflict and social
change, Marx delineated an image of social organization that still influences a major portion of contemporary sociological theory. Marx began
with a simple—and I think simplistic—assumption: Economic organization, especially the ownership of property, determines the organization
of the rest of a society. The class structure and institutional arrangements,
as well as cultural values, beliefs, religious dogmas, and other idea systems
are ultimately a reflection of the economic base of a society. He then
added another assumption: Inherent in the economic organization of any
society—save the ultimate communistic society—are forces inevitably generating revolutionary class conflict. Such revolutionary class conflict is
seen as dialectical and conceptualized as occurring in epochs, with successive bases of economic organization sowing the seeds of their own
destruction through the polarization of classes and subsequent overthrow
of the dominant by the subjugated class. Hence, a third assumption: conflict is bipolar, with exploited classes under conditions created by the
economy becoming aware of their true interests and eventually forming
a revolutionary political organization that stands against the dominant,
property-holding class.

I see the criticisms that can be leveled against these assumptions as
self-evident: (1) societies are more than mere reflections of economic
organization and patterns of property ownership; (2) social conflict is
rarely bipolarized across an entire society; (3) interests in a society do
not always cohere around social class; (4) power relations in a society are
not always direct reflections of ownership of property; and (5) conflict
does not always cause social change, dialectical or otherwise. In addition
to a whole series of incorrect predictions—such as the formation of the
modern proletariat into a revolutionary class during the present "capitalistic" epoch, the subsequent overthrow of capitalist economic systems,
and the formation of a communist society—the wisdom of following Marx's
lead can, I believe, be seriously questioned.

With abstraction above the specifics of Marx's economic determinism and excessive polemics, however, I and other theorists see a set of assumptions that directly challenge those imputed to functionalism and that can serve as an intellectual springboard for a conflict alternative in sociological theorizing:

1. While social relationships display systemic features, these relationships are rife with conflicting interests.
2. This fact reveals that social systems systematically generate conflict.
3. Conflict is therefore an inevitable and pervasive feature of social systems.
4. Such conflict tends to be manifested in the opposition of interests.
5. Conflict most frequently occurs over the distribution of scarce resources, most notably power and material wealth.
6. Conflict is the major source of change in social systems.

In addition to these assumptions, I think that the form and substance of Marx's causal analysis has been equally influential in the development of modern conflict theory. This analysis takes the general form of assuming that conflict is an inevitable and inexorable force in social systems and is activated under certain specified conditions. Some of these conditions are viewed as allowing for the transformation of latent class interests (lying in a state of "false consciousness") into manifest class interests ("class consciousness"), which, under additional conditions, lead to the polarization of society into classes joined in conflict. Thus, for Marx, there is a series of conditions that are cast into the role of intervening variables that accelerate or retard the inevitable transformation of class interests into revolutionary class conflict.

In addition to the form of the argument (which I will discuss more thoroughly in the next chapter), the substance of the Marxian model is of great importance in understanding modern sociological theory. Contrary to most contemporary Marxist theorists, I believe that this substantive contribution can best be seen if the propositions of his theoretical scheme are stated in a highly abstract form and divorced from his polemics and rhetoric about social class and revolution. I admit that much of the flavor of Marx's analysis is lost in such an exercise, but the indebtedness of modern sociological theory to Marxian propositions becomes more evident.[11] I have summarized these abstract propositions in Table 6–1.

In Table 6–1, Marx's assumptions about the nature of the social world and the key causal connections in this world are stated propositionally. For it is in a propositional form that Marx's contribution to conflict theory has been most frequently used by contemporary theorists (see following

---

[11]For criticism of my efforts along these lines, see Richard P. Abbelbaum, "Marx's Theory of the Falling Rate of Profit: Towards a Dialectical Analysis of Structural Social Change," *American Sociological Review* 43 (February 1978), pp. 64–73.

**TABLE 6–1**    Marx's Key Propositions

I.   The more unequal is the distribution of scarce resources in a system, the greater is the conflict of interest between dominant and subordinate segments in a system.

II.  The more subordinate segments become aware of their true collective interests, the more likely are they to question the legitimacy of the existing pattern of distribution of scarce resources.

    A.  The more social changes wrought by dominant segments disrupt existing relations among subordinates, the more likely are the latter to become aware of their true interests.

    B.  The more practices of dominant segments create alienative dispositions among subordinates, the more likely are the latter to become aware of their true collective interests.

    C.  The more members of subordinate segments can communicate their grievances to each other, the more likely they are to become aware of their true collective interests.

        1.  The more ecological concentration of members of subordinate groups, the more likely communication of grievances.

        2.  The more the educational opportunities of subordinate group members, the more diverse the means of their communication, and the more likely they are to communicate their grievances.

    D.  The more subordinate segments can develop unifying ideologies, the more likely they are to become aware of their true collective interests.

        1.  The greater the capacity to recruit or generate ideological spokespeople, the more likely ideological unification.

        2.  The less the ability of dominant groups to regulate the socialization processes and communication networks in a system, the more likely ideological unification.

III. The more subordinate segments of a system are aware of their collective interests and the greater is their questioning of the legitimacy of the distribution of scarce resources, the more likely are they to join overt conflict against dominant segments of a system.

    A.  The less the ability of dominant groups to make manifest their collective interests, the more likely subordinate groups are to join in conflict.

    B.  The more the deprivations of subordinates move from an absolute to relative basis, the more likely they are to join in conflict.

    C.  The greater the ability of subordinate groups to develop a political leadership structure, the more likely they are to join in conflict.

IV.  The greater is the ideological unification of members of subordinate segments of a system and the more developed is their political leadership structure, the more likely are dominant and subjugated segments of a system to become polarized.

V.   The more polarized are the dominant and subjugated, the more violent is their conflict.

VI.  The more violent is the conflict, the greater is the structural change of the system and the greater is the redistribution of scarce resources.

chapters 7, 8, and 9). In Proposition I of Table 6–1, the degree of inequality in the distribution of resources is held by Marx to influence the extent to which segments of a social system will reveal conflicts of interest. Proposition II then documents some of the conditions that would make members of deprived or subordinate segments of a population aware of their conflict of interest with those holding the largest share of scarce resources. For once segments of a population become aware of their true interests, they will begin to question the legitimacy of a system in which they come out on the short end of the distribution of scarce resources. Propositions II-A, B, C, and D deal, respectively, with the disruption in the social situation of deprived populations, the amount of alienation people feel as a result of their situation, the capacity of members of deprived segments to communicate with each other, and their ability to develop a unifying ideology that codifies their true interests. Marx sees these conditions as factors that increase and heighten awareness of subordinates' collective interests and, hence, decrease their willingness to accept as legitimate the right of superordinates to command a disproportionate share of resources.

In turn, some of these forces heightening awareness are influenced by such structural conditions as ecological concentration (II-C-1), educational opportunities (II-C-2), the availability of ideological spokespeople (II-D-1), and the control of socialization processes and communication networks by superordinates (II-D-2). In Proposition III, Marx hypothesizes that the increasing awareness by deprived classes of their true interests and the resulting questioning of the legitimacy of the distribution of resources serve to increase the likelihood that the disadvantaged strata will begin to organize collectively their opposition against the dominant segments of a system. This organization is seen as especially likely under several conditions: the more disorganized the dominant segments with respect to understanding their true interests (III-A), the more the subordinates' deprivations escalate as they begin to compare their situation with that of the privileged (III-B), and the more the ease with which the deprived can develop political leadership to carry out the organizational tasks of mobilizing subordinates (III-C). In Proposition IV, Marx emphasizes that once deprived groups possess a unifying ideology and political leadership, their true interests begin to take on clear focus and their opposition to superordinates begins to increase. As polarization increases, the less possibility there is for reconciliation, compromise, or mild conflict, since now the deprived are sufficiently alienated, organized, and unified to press for a complete change in the pattern of resource distribution (V)—thus making violent confrontation the only way to overcome the inevitable resistance of superordinates. Finally (VI), Marx notes that the more violent the conflict, the greater is the change in patterns of organization in a system, especially its distribution of scarce resources.

Thus, for those who have tried to use these ideas to build positivistic theory, I see the Marxian legacy as consisting of a set of conflict-oriented assumptions, a particular form of causal analysis that stresses the importance of intervening conditions for accelerating or retarding inexorable conflict processes, and a series of abstract propositions. My sympathies reside with the more positivistic approach in Marx's work, but there are many who would disagree. Indeed, I would guess that most contemporary Marxists disavow positivism and the search for universal and timeless laws of human organization. And they certainly do not condone my and others' efforts to translate Marx's ideas into the language of positivism (as I did in Table 6-1). Such is clearly the case, as I will document in Chapter 9, for most critical theorists, but it is also true for the vast majority of Marxist sociologists. But in terms of actual theory development, I think that the more positivistic efforts to translate Marx's ideas have been more dominant than the work of Marxists and critical theorists. And even the most prominent critical theorist, Jurgen Habermas, who is the topic of Chapter 9, has increasingly sought to make such theory more objective. All this will become more evident, I think, as we proceed into the next chapters. But for the present, let me return to examining the origins of contemporary conflict theory.

## GEORG SIMMEL AND CONFLICT THEORIZING

### Functional Strains in Simmel's Thought

Georg Simmel was committed to developing a body of theoretical statements that captured the *form of basic social processes*, an approach he labeled *formal sociology.* Primarily on the basis of his own observations, he sought to abstract the essential properties from processes and events in a wide variety of empirical contexts. In doing so, Simmel hoped to develop abstract statements that depicted the most fundamental social processes of social organization. Nowhere is his genius in such activity more evident than in a short essay on conflict, which serves as a major source of insight for contemporary conflict theory in sociology.[12]

Much like Marx, Simmel viewed conflict as ubiquitous and inevitable in society. Unlike Marx, however, he did not view social structure as a domination and subjugation, but rather as an inseparable mingling associative and dissociative processes, which are separable only in analysis:

> The structure may be *sui generis*, its motivation and form being wholly self-consistent, and only in order to be able to describe and understand it, do we put it together, *post factum*, out of two tendencies, one monistic, the other antagonistic.[13]

---

[12]All subsequent references to this work are taken from Georg Simmel, *Conflict and the Web of Group Affiliation*, trans. K. H. Wolff (Glencoe, Ill.: Free Press, 1956).

[13]Ibid., p. 23. However, with his typical caution, Simmel warns: "This fact should not lead us to overlook the numerous cases in which contradictory tendencies really co-exist in separation and can thus be recognized at any moment in the over-all situation" (pp. 23–24).

Part of the reason for this emphasis, I think, lies in Simmel's "organismic" view of the social world. In displaying formal properties, social processes evidence a systemic character—a notion apparently derived from the organismic doctrines dominating the sociology of his time. This subtle organicism led Simmel to seek out the consequences of conflict for social continuity rather than change:

> Conflict is thus designed to resolve dualisms; it is a way of *achieving some kind of unity*, even if it be through the annihilation of one of the conflicting parties. This is roughly parallel to the fact that it is the most violent *symptom of a disease* which represents the effort of the *organism* to free itself of disturbances and damages caused by them. [Italics added.][14]

In apparent contradiction to the harmony implied by this organicism, Simmel postulated an innate "hostile impulse" or a "need for hating and fighting" among the units of organic wholes, although this instinct is mixed with others for love and affection and is circumscribed by the force of social relationships. Therefore, Simmel viewed conflict as a reflection not only of conflicts of interest but also of hostile instincts. Such instincts can be exacerbated by conflicts of interest or mitigated by harmonious relations as well as by instincts for love. But in the end, Simmel still viewed one of the ultimate sources of conflict to lie in the innate biological makeup of human actors.

In what I see as an effort to reconcile his assumptions about the nature of the social organism with notions of hating and fighting instincts, Simmel devoted considerable effort to analyzing the positive consequences of conflict for the maintenance of social wholes and their subunits. In this way, hostile impulses were seen not so much as a contradiction or cancer to the organic whole but as one of many processes maintaining the "body social." Thus, although Simmel recognized that an overly cooperative, consensual, and integrated society would show "no life process," his analysis of conflict is still loaded in the direction of how conflict promotes solidarity and unification.

It is this aspect of Simmel's work on conflict that reveals an image of social organization decidedly different from that emphasized by Marx:

1. Social relationships occur within systemic contexts that can only by typified as an organic intermingling of associative and dissociative processes.
2. Such processes are a reflection of both the instinctual impulses of actors and the imperatives dictated by various types of social relationships.
3. Conflict processes are therefore a ubiquitous feature of social systems, but they do not necessarily, in all cases, lead to breakdown of the system and/or to social change.

---

[14]Ibid, p. 13.

4. In fact, conflict is one of the principal processes operating to preserve the social whole and/or some of its subparts.

These assumptions are reflected in a large number of specific propositions, which Simmel apparently developed from direct observations of events occurring around him and from readings of historical accounts of conflict.[15] In these propositions, Simmel views conflict as a *variable* that manifests different states of intensity or violence. The polar ends of this variable continuum are "competition" and the "fight." Competition involves the more regulated and parallel strivings of parties toward a mutually exclusive end, and fight denotes the less regulated and more direct combative activities of parties against each other.[16] Although he does not elaborate extensively on the variable properties of conflict or consistently employ his labels, Simmel's distinctions have inspired a long debate among contemporary sociologists on what is and what is not conflict.[17] My sense is that this debate has often degenerated into terminological quibbling, but at its heart is the important issue of clarifying the concepts to be employed in propositions on conflict processes—a theoretical issue that Simmel clearly recognized as crucial.

Simmel's organicism probably was critical in forcing this conceptualization of conflict as a variable phenomenon. Unlike Marx, who saw conflict as ultimately becoming violent and revolutionary and leading to the structural change of the system, Simmel was quite often led to the analysis of the opposite phenomena—less intense and violent conflicts that promoted the solidarity, integration, and orderly change of the system.[18] Yet, within the apparent constraints of his subtle organicism, Simmel enumerated a number of suggestive propositions on the intensity of conflict, that is, the degree of direct action and violence of parties against each other. As with Marx, I think that the full impact of Simmel's analysis on modern theory can be seen more readily when his propositions are stated formally and abstractly. I have listed these propositions in Table 6-2.

---

[15] Simmel was not concerned with developing scientific theory, but rather, he was interested in inducting social forms from interaction processes. This emphasis on forms makes many of Simmel's analytical statements rather easily converted into propositions. I should emphasize, however, that transforming Simmel's analytical statements into propositions involves some risk of misinterpretation.

[16] Simmel, *Conflict*, p. 58.

[17] For an excellent summary of this debate, see C. F. Fink, "Some Conceptual Difficulties in the Theory of Social Conflict." See also my closing remarks in Chapter 8.

[18] Pierre van de Berghe has argued that a dialectical model of conflict is ultimately one where unification, albeit temporary, emerges out of conflict. But, as I will examine extensively in the next chapter, the differences between Marx and Simmel have inspired vastly different theoretical perspectives in contemporary sociology. See Pierre van de Berghe, "Dialectic and Functionalism: Toward a Theoretical Synthesis," *American Sociological Review* 28 (October 1963), pp. 695–705.

---

**TABLE 6–2**  Simmel's Propositions on Conflict Intensity

---

I. The greater is the degree of emotional involvement of parties to a conflict, the more likely is the conflict to be violent.

   A. The greater is the respective solidarity among members of conflict parties, the greater is the degree of their emotional involvement.

   B. The greater is the previous harmony between members of conflict parties, the greater is the degree of their emotional involvement.

II. The more that conflict is perceived by members of conflict groups to transcend individual aims and interests, the more likely is the conflict to be violent.

III. The more that conflict is a means to a clearly specified end, the less likely is the conflict to be violent.

---

Propositions I, I–A, and I–B overlap somewhat with those developed by Marx. In a vein similar to Marx, Simmel emphasized that violent conflict is the result of emotional arousal. Such arousal is particularly likely when conflict groups possess a great deal of internal solidarity and when these conflict groups emerge out of previously harmonious relations. Marx postulated a similar process in his contention that polarization of groups previously involved in social relations (albeit exploitive ones) leads to violent conflict. In Proposition II, Simmel indicated that, coupled with emotional arousal, the extent to which members see the conflict as transcending their individual aims increases the likelihood of violent conflict. Proposition III is Simmel's most important, I think, because it contradicts Marx's hypothesis that objective consciousness of interests will lead to organization for violent conflict. In this proposition, Simmel argued that the more clearly articulated their interests, the more focused are the goals of conflict groups. With clearly articulated goals, it becomes possible to view violent conflict as only one of many means for their achievement, since other less combative conflicts, such as bargaining and compromise, can often serve to meet the specific objectives of the group. Thus, for Simmel, consciousness of common interests (Proposition II) can, under unspecified conditions, lead to highly instrumental and nonviolent conflict. In the context of labor-management relations, for example, I think that Simmel's proposition is more accurate than Marx's, for violence has more often accompanied labor-management disputes in the initial formation of unions, when interests and goals are not well articulated. As interests become clarified, violent conflict has been increasingly replaced by less violent forms of social interaction.[19]

Simmel then turned his attention to the consequences of conflict for (1) the conflict parties and (2) for the systemic whole in which the conflict

---

[19]Admittedly, Marx's late awareness of the union movement in the United States forced him to begin pondering this possibility, but he did not incorporate this insight into his theoretical scheme.

**TABLE 6–3**   Simmel's Propositions on the Functions of Conflict for the
Respective Parties

I. The more violent are intergroup hostilities and the more frequent is conflict
   among groups, the less likely are group boundaries to disappear.
II. The more violent is the conflict and the less integrated is the group, the more
   likely is despotic centralization of conflict groups.
III. The more violent is the conflict, the greater will be the internal solidarity of
   conflict groups.
   A. The more violent is the conflict and the smaller are the conflict groups, the
      greater will be their internal solidarity.
      1. The more violent is the conflict and the smaller are the conflict groups,
         the less will be the tolerance of deviance and dissent in each group.
   B. The more violent is the conflict and the more a group represents a minority
      position in a system, the greater will be the internal solidarity of that group.
   C. The more violent is the conflict and the more a group is engaged in purely
      self-defense, the greater will be its internal solidarity.

occurs. Simmel first analyzed how violent conflicts *increase* solidarity and
internal organization of the conflict parties, but when he shifted to an
analysis of the functions of conflict for the social whole, he drew attention
primarily to the fact that conflict promotes system integration and adaptation. I think it reasonable to ask, however: how can violent conflicts
promoting increasing organization and solidarity of the conflict groups
suddenly have these positive functions for the systemic whole in which
the conflict occurs? For Marx, such a process is seen to lead to polarization
of conflict groups and then to the violent conflicts, which radically alter
the systemic whole. But for Simmel, the increased level of organization
within conflict groups enables them to realize many of their goals without
overt violence (but perhaps with a covert threat of violence), and such
partial realization of clearly defined goals cuts down internal system tension and hence promotes integration. Let me document Simmel's reasoning with his propositions.

In Table 6–3, I have listed Simmel's propositions on the functions of
violent conflict for the parties to the conflict. In these propositions, violent
conflict is seen, under certain conditions, to increase the degree of centralization and the level of internal solidarity of groups. Unlike Marx,
however, Simmel's does not assume that conflict begets increasingly violent conflicts between ever more organized and polarized segments that,
in the end, will cause radical change in the system. This difference between
their analyses is most clear when Simmel's propositions on the consequences of conflict for the systemic whole are reviewed. The most notable
feature of several key propositions, which I have listed in Table 6–4, is
that Simmel was initially concerned with less violent conflicts and with
their integrative functions for the social whole, and only then, did he turn

---

**TABLE 6–4** Simmel's Propositions on the Functions of Conflict for the Systemic Whole

---

I. The less violent is the conflict between groups of different degrees of power in a system, the more likely is the conflict to have integrative consequences for the social whole.

  A. The less violent and more frequent is the conflict, the more likely is the conflict to have integrative consequences for the social whole.

    1. The less violent and more frequent is the conflict, the more members of subordinate groups can release hostilities and have a sense of control over their destiny and thereby maintain the integration of the social whole.

    2. The less violent and more frequent is the conflict, the more likely are norms regularizing the conflict to be created by the conflicting parties.

  B. The less violent is the conflict and the more the social whole is based on functional interdependence, the more likely is the conflict to have integrative consequences for the social whole.

    1. The less violent is the conflict in systems with high degrees of functional interdependence, the more likely is it to encourage the creation of norms regularizing the conflict.

II. The more violent and the more prolonged are conflict relations between groups, the more likely is the formation of coalitions among previously unrelated groups in a system.

III. The more prolonged is the threat of violent conflict between groups, the more enduring are the coalitions of each of the conflict parties.

---

to more violent conflicts. And even here, he emphasized their integrative consequences for the social whole.

I think that Proposition I in Table 6-4 provides an important qualification to Marx's analysis. Marx visualized mild conflicts as intensifying as the combatants become increasingly polarized; and in the end, the resulting violent conflict would lead to radical social change in the system. In contrast, Simmel argued that conflicts of low intensity and high frequency in systems of high degrees of interdependence do not necessarily intensify or lead to radical social change. On the contrary, they release tensions and become normatively regulated, thereby promoting stability in social systems. Further, Simmel's previous propositions on violent conflicts present the possibility that with the increasing organization of the conflicting groups, the degree of violence of their conflict will decrease as their goals become better articulated. The consequence of such organization and articulation of interests will be a greater disposition to initiate milder forms of conflict, involving competition, bargaining, and compromise. What I see as critical for developing a sociology of conflict is that Simmel's analysis provides more options than Marx's propositions on conflict outcomes. First, conflicts do not necessarily intensify to the point of violence; and when they do not, they can have, under conditions that need to be further explored, integrative outcomes for the social whole. Marx's analysis precludes exploration of these processes. Second, Simmel's propositions allow for inquiry into the conditions under which initially violent conflicts can become less intense and thereby have integrative consequences for the social whole. This insight dictates a search for the conditions under which the level of conflict violence and its consequences for system parts and the social whole can shift and change over the course of the conflict process. I see this expansion of options as representing a much broader and firmer foundation for building a theory of conflict.

Finally, Propositions II and III in Table 6-4 note the functions of violent conflict for integrating systemic wholes. These propositions could represent a somewhat different way to state Marx's polarization hypothesis, since conflict was seen by Simmel as drawing together diverse elements in a system as their respective interests become more clearly recognized. But Simmel was not ideologically committed to dialectical assumptions. Thus, unlike Marx, he appeared to be arguing only that violent conflicts pose threats to many system units that, depending upon calculations of their diverse interests, will unite to form larger social wholes. Such unification will persist as long as the threat of violent conflict remains. Should violent conflict no longer be seen as necessary, with increasing articulation of interests and the initiation of bargaining relations, then Simmel's Propositions 1-A and 1-B on the consequences of conflict for the social whole would become operative.

Simmel's abstract propositions on conflict processes represent, I feel, an important qualification of Marx's reasoning. While various conflict theorists have focused on either Marx or Simmel as their principle resource, there has been sufficient cross-fertilization to knock off the extremes in their respective analyses—for Marx, the overemphasis on organization and polarization and for Simmel, the unmitigated functionalism and analysis of positive consequences.

## Simmel's Implicit Attack on Marx's Emancipatory Project

There is yet another sense in which Simmel's ideas represent an important qualification to Marx's reasoning. Marx's more emancipatory side saw modern capitalism, especially as it creates a division of labor and inequality, as oppressing individuals. His ideas about conflict are, of course, a reflection of his view that capitalism produces the conditions that will lead to a revolutionary conflict ushering in a new form of human organization where individuals are freed from the capitalists domination. Thus, capitalism expands the division of labor, makes workers' appendages to machines, concentrates them in urban areas, quantifies social relations through money and markets, and forces workers to be mere role players (as opposed to fully involved participants) in social relations. In so doing, it creates the personal alienation and resentments as well as the social structural conditions that will lead subordinates to become aware of their domination and to organize in an effort to change their plight (the propositions in Table 6-1 simply represent more abstract statements of these ideas).

Simmel called into question much of Marx's analysis in his *The Philosophy of Money*,[20] where, as I will document in Chapter 10, he also produced an important theory of social exchange. But for my present purposes, I only want to stress the critique of Marx in this work. One of the most important themes in Marx's writing, which critical theorists later elaborated, is that capitalism quantifies social life with money and, in so doing, it makes exchanges in markets paramount. The result is that human social relations are increasingly quantified, as is personified in the labor market where workers sell themselves as a commodity. Moreover, the growing division of labor makes workers mere cogs in an impersonal organizational machine. And as I mentioned above, such processes would, Marx believed, be so oppressive as to initiate revolutionary pressures for their elimination. In contrast to Marx, however, Simmel looked at these forces much differently. Although a certain level of alienation from work and commodification of relations through the use of money is inevitable with increasing differentiation and expansion of productive forces and markets, people are also freed from traditional constraints. They have more options as to how they spend their money and what they do; they can move about with more freedom and form new and varied social relations; they can live lifestyles that reflect their tastes and values; and in general, they are more liberated than their counterparts in less complex and traditional societies.

This critique of Marx was, however, to be rejected by the early critical theorists who did not want to visualize modern societies as liberating. And yet, they were confronted with the failure of Marx's predictions about the coming emancipation of society with the communist revolution. In an attempt to reconstruct Marx's vision of humans' capacity to make history, they were forced to accept Weber's highly pessimistic view of the constraints of modern society and to reject Simmel's more benign views. But in so doing, they became trapped in a dilemma: If capitalism is structurally not self-transforming in terms of Marx's revolutionary model, if modern life is not so liberating as Simmel felt, and if Weber's analysis of increasing constraint in societies must therefore be accepted as true, then how is liberation to occur? What force is to drive people's emancipation from domination? Early critical theorists would not accept Simmel's judgment—that is, that people are more *free* than in traditional societies—and so they conceptually retreated into a contemplative subjectivism. They viewed the liberating force as somehow springing from

---

[20]Georg Simmel, *The Philosophy of Money* (Boston: Routledge & Kegan Paul, 1978; originally published in 1907).

human nature and its capacity for conscious reflection; and as I will document in Chapter 9, they moved away from Marx who had "turned Hegel on his head" and put "Hegel back on his feet."

Thus, Weber becomes a critical link in the reinterpretation of Marx in this century by critical theorists. But Weber also presents, I feel, an important corrective to Marx's more formal theory of revolutionary conflict. Weber's analysis of stratification and social change presents some important propositions that consistently reappear in the more positivistic conflict theoretic literature. And so to understand the development of either critical theory or positivistically oriented conflict theory, we need to examine some of the works of Max Weber.

## MAX WEBER'S (1864–1920) THEORY OF CONFLICT

### Positivistic Strains in Weber's Thought

Max Weber did not believe that sociology could be a natural science, as positivists claim. Instead, he devoted his efforts to historical analyses, especially of the transition to industrial-bureaucratic social orders. Yet, despite his misgivings about timeless laws about invariant properties of the social universe, I see his work as filled with more abstract generalizations that imply more enduring and invariant social processes. Nowhere is this "implicit positivism" more evident than in Weber's analysis of stratification, conflict, and change. For in his seminal ideas on these topics, he developed a number of important conflict principles, which are similar to those espoused by Marx but which, at the same time, subtly shift points of emphasis. I believe that much contemporary conflict implicitly uses these principles, although this debt to Weber frequently goes unacknowledged.

Most of these principles can be found in his discussion of the transition from societies based on traditional authority to those organized around rational-legal authority.[21] In systems where the sanctity of traditions legitimates political and social activity, there are three conditions that encourage the emergence of charismatic leaders who organize conflict groups that challenge such traditional authority. One condition is a situation where there is a high degree of correlation among power, wealth, and prestige or, in his terms, incumbency in positions of political power (party), occupancy in advantaged economic positions (class), and membership in high-ranking social circles (status groups). That is, when economic elites, for example, are also social and political elites and vice versa,

---

[21]For a fuller discussion, see my and Leonard Beeghley's *The Emergence of Sociological Theory* (Homewood, Ill.: Dorsey Press, 1981), pp. 232–45 and 256–59. For original sources, see Max Weber, *Economy and Society* (New York: Bedminister Press, 1968).

then those who are excluded from power, wealth, and prestige become resentful and receptive to conflict alternatives.

Another condition is dramatic discontinuity in the distribution of rewards, or the existence of divisions in social hierarchies that give privilege to some and very little to others. When only a few hold power, wealth, and prestige and the rest are denied these rewards, then tensions and resentments exist. Such resentments become a further inducement for those without power, prestige, and wealth to engage in conflict with those who hoard these resources.

A final condition encouraging conflict is low rates of social mobility. When those of low rank have little chance to move up social hierarchies or to enter a new class, party, or status group, then resentment accumulates. Those denied opportunities to increase their access to resources become restive and willing to challenge the system of traditional authority.

The critical force that galvanizes the resentments inhering in these three conditions is charisma. Weber felt that whether or not charismatic leaders emerge is, to a great extent, a matter of historical chance. But if such leaders do emerge to challenge traditional authority and to mobilize resentments over the hoarding of resources by elites and the lack of opportunities to gain access to wealth, power, or prestige, then structural change would ensue.

When successful, such leaders confront organizational problems of consolidating their gains. One result is that charisma becomes routinized, as leaders create formal rules, procedures, and structures for organizing followers after their successful mobilization to pursue conflict. If routinization takes a traditional form, thus creating a new system of traditional authority, renewed conflict can be expected as membership in class, status, and party becomes highly correlated; as the new elites hoard resources; and as mobility is blocked. However, if rational-legal routinization occurs, then authority is based upon equally applied laws and rules; and performance and ability become the basis for recruitment and promotion in bureaucratic structures. Under these conditions, conflict potential will be mitigated.

I have, of course, ripped Weber's discussion out of its historical context, but this is just what contemporary conflict theorists do when using Weber's work to develop principles about social conflict. In Table 6-5, I have abstracted even further these ideas and presented them as a series of propositions. When stated in this way, I think their similarity and differences with those by Marx become more evident. For me, the unique feature of Weber's Proposition I is the recognition that inequality exists along several dimensions and that the level of correlation among incumbents along these dimensions is critical. Moreover, the degree of discontinuity in the distribution of resources and the rates of social mobility are also crucial.

---

**TABLE 6–5**  Weber's Propositions on Inequality and Conflict

---

I. The greater is the degree of withdrawal of legitimacy from political authority, the more likely is conflict between superordinates and subordinates.

   A. The greater is the correlation of membership in class, status group, and party (or alternatively, access to power, wealth, and prestige), the more intense is the level of resentment among those denied membership (or access), and hence, the more likely are they to withdraw legitimacy.

   B. The greater is the discontinuity in social hierarchies, the more intense is the level of resentment among those low in the hierarchies, and hence, the more likely are they to withdraw legitimacy.

   C. The lower are the rates of mobility up social hierarchies of power, prestige, and wealth, the more intense is the level of resentment among those denied opportunities, and hence, the more likely are they to withdraw legitimacy.

II. The more charismatic leaders can emerge to mobilize resentments of subordinates in a system, the greater will be the level of conflict between superordinates and subordinates.

   A. The more conditions I–A, I–B, and I–C are met, the more likely is the emergence of charismatic leadership.

III. The more effective are charismatic leaders in mobilizing subordinates in successful conflict, the greater are the pressures to routinize authority through the creation of a system of rules and administrative authority.

IV. The more a system of rules and administrative authority increases conditions I–A, I–B, and I–C, the greater will be the withdrawal of legitimacy from political authority, and the more likely is conflict between superordinates and subordinates.

---

    Unlike Marx, who tended to overemphasize the economic basis of inequality and to argue for a simple polarization of societies into propertied and nonpropertied (exploited) classes, Weber's Proposition I allows more theoretical options. He tells us to look at variations in the distribution of power, wealth, and prestige and the extent to which holders of one resource control the other resources. He tells us to examine the degree of discontinuity in the distribution of these resources—in other words, the extent to which there are clear lines demarking privilege and nonprivilege. Finally, he advises us to examine the degree of mobility— the chance to gain access to power, wealth, and prestige—in order to understand the resentments and tensions that make people prone to conflict. Marx's scheme denotes the same processes but with a much heavier and polemical hand. I think that Weber's proposition encourages theorists to explore more variations along more dimensions than does Marx's scheme.

    In Propositions II, III, and IV in Table 6–5, Weber emphasizes the importance of political leadership and organization. Political leaders emerge to galvanize resentments, and their effectiveness determines the course of conflict. But for Weber, leadership is not inevitable, nor is it necessarily liberating. Indeed, it can restore a new system of inequality and privilege that will initiate a new wave of escalating resentments and potential conflict. Marx, on the other hand, makes similar points but with much more optimism about leaders' capacity to further the evolutionary progress of societies toward his utopian end state, communism.

## Weber's Pessimism and the Dilemma for Critical Theorists

As I indicated earlier, Weber was concerned with the historical transition from traditional societies to modern capitalist societies. In his description and explanation of this transition, as it occurred in the Western European nations, is a devastating critique of Marx's optimism that the conditions for the revolutionary transition to a new utopian society were being created. Weber's analysis is complex, and the historical detail that he presents to document his case is impressive, but his argument is captured by the word *rationalization*. Weber argued that the rationality that defines modern societies is "means-ends rationality." The nature of such rationality involves selecting the best means to achieve a defined end. The process of rationalization involves, Weber felt, the increasing penetration of means-ends rationality into ever more spheres of life and the consequent destruction of traditions. For as bureaucracies expand in the economic and governmental sphere and as markets allow individuals to pursue their personal ends rationally, then the traditional moral fabric is broken. Weber agreed with Simmel that this rationalization of life brings individuals a new freedom from domination by religious dogmatism, community, class, and other traditional forces; but in their place, it creates a new kind of domination by impersonal economic forces, such as markets and corporate bureaucracies, and by the vast administrative apparatus of the ever-expanding state. Human options were, in Weber's view, becoming ever more constrained by the "iron cage" of rational-legal systems. And unlike Marx, he did not see such a situation as rife with revolutionary potential; on the contrary, he saw the social world as ever more administered by impersonal bureaucratic forces.

This pessimistic view seemed, by the early 1930s, to be a far more reasonable assessment of modern society than Marx's utopian dream. Indeed, the communist revolution in Russia had degenerated into Stalinism and bureaucratic totalitarianism by "the party"; in the West, particularly the United States, workers seemed ever more willing to sell themselves in markets and work in large-scale organizations; and political fascism in Germany and Italy seemed to be increasing as dictators created large authoritarian bureaucracies. How, then, was the first generation of critical theorists to reconcile Weber's more accurate assessment of empirical trends with Marx's optimistic emancipatory vision? Such is the central question of all critical theory. And so, just as Weber's ideas forced revision of Marx's more formal propositions among modern positivists, so his analysis of the process of rationalization required critical theorists to reformulate the emancipatory dream of Marx.

## THE PROLIFERATION OF CONFLICT SOCIOLOGY

From the reexamination of Marx, Weber, and Simmel came a powerful critique of positivist sociology in general and Parsons's conceptual scheme in particular. As the Parsonian scheme and functionalism receded, conflict sociology gained greater prominence. Although not as dominant as the Parsonian scheme once was, conflict sociology has been the most conspicuous successor to functionalism. Aside from self-conscious conflict theories, the basic tenets of conflict sociology—inequality, tension, conflict—are now incorporated into many other theoretical orientations in sociology.[22]

Within the narrower confines of conflict sociology itself, there is an enormous diversity of activity. All that I can possibly hope to do with such a proliferating perspective is examine the range of activity encompassed by the label *conflict theory.* Of course, I will examine in later sections other approaches that incorporated elements of the more self-conscious conflict theorists. But in the chapters to follow, I will explore three very different conflict theories: the dialectical approach of Ralf Dahrendorf, the conflict functionalism of Lewis Coser, and the critical theory of Jurgen Habermas. I will miss much theoretical activity in focusing on these three approaches, but my sense is that these three are the most central and, thus, worthy of detailed analysis.

----

[22]For example, there is the structuralist Marxism of Louis Althusser and Maurice Godelier (who will not be examined in this book), the exchange theory of Peter Blau (whose blending of conflict ideas into exchange theories is examined in Chapter 12), the conflict exchange approach of Randall Collins (the subject of Chapter 21), and the structuration theory of Anthony Giddens (who is examined in Chapter 22).

# CHAPTER 7

# The Dialectical Conflict Theory of Ralf Dahrendorf

In the late 1950s, Ralf Dahrendorf persistently argued that the Parsonian scheme and functionalism in general presents an overly consensual, integrated, and static vision of society. In Dahrendorf's view, society has two faces—one of consensus, the other of conflict. And it is time to begin analysis of society's ugly face and abandon the utopian image created by functionalism. To leave utopia, Dahrendorf offered the following advice:

> Concentrate in the future not only on concrete problems but on such problems as involve explanations in terms of constraint, conflict, and change. This second face of society may aesthetically be rather less pleasing than the social system—but, if all sociology had to offer were an easy escape to Utopian tranquility, it would hardly be worth our efforts.[1]

To escape utopia, therefore, requires that a one-sided conflict model be substituted for the one-sided functional model. Although this conflict perspective was not considered by Dahrendorf to be the only face of society, it is a necessary supplement that will make amends for the past inadequacies of functional theory.[2] The model that emerges from this

---

[1] Ralf Dahrendorf, "Out of Utopia: Toward a Reorientation of Sociological Analysis," *American Journal of Sociology* 64 (September 1958), p. 127.

[2] As Dahrendorf emphasizes: "I do not intend to fall victim to the mistake of many structural-functional theorists and advance for the conflict model a claim to comprehensive and exclusive applicability . . . it may well be that in a philosophical sense, society has two faces of equal reality: one of stability, harmony, and consensus and one of change, conflict, and constraint" (ibid.). Such disclaimers are, in reality, justifications for arguing for the primacy of conflict in society. By claiming that functionalists are one-sided, it becomes fair game to be equally one-sided in order to "balance" past one-sidedness.

theoretical calling is a dialectical-conflict perspective, which, I feel, still represents one of the best efforts to incorporate the insights of Marx and, to a lesser extent, Weber into a coherent set of theoretical propositions. I have my doubts that this dialectical conflict theory is more isomorphic than functional with what occurs in the actual world, but I do think that it represents an important corrective to Parsonian functionalism, which tended to overemphasize social integration.

In his analysis, Dahrendorf is careful to note that processes other than conflict are evident in social systems and that even the conflict phenomena he examines are not the only kinds of conflict in societies. Having said this, however, my sense is that Dahrendorf believes his conflict model represents a more comprehensive theory of society that provides a more adequate base for theorizing about human social organization than either functionalism or other alternatives.

## DAHRENDORF'S IMAGE OF THE SOCIAL ORDER

For Dahrendorf, the process of institutionalization involves the creation of "imperatively coordinated associations" (hereafter referred to as *ICAs*) that, in terms of criteria not specified, represent a distinguishable organization of roles. This organization is characterized by power relationships, with some clusters of roles having power to extract conformity from others. I see Dahrendorf as somewhat vague on the point, but it appears that any social unit—from a small group or formal organization to a community or an entire society—can be considered for analytical purposes an ICA if an organization of roles displaying power differentials exists. Furthermore, although power denotes the coercion of some by others, these power relations in ICAs tend to become legitimated and can therefore be viewed as authority relations in which some positions have the "accepted" or "normative right" to dominate others. Dahrendorf thus conceives the social order as maintained by processes creating authority relations in the various types of ICAs existing throughout all layers of social systems.[3]

At the same time, however, power and authority are the scarce resources over which subgroups within a designated ICA compete and fight. They are thus the major sources of conflict and change in these institutionalized patterns. This conflict is ultimately a reflection of where clusters of roles in an ICA stand in relation to authority, since the "objective interests" inherent in any role is a direct function of whether that role possesses authority and power over other roles. However, even though

---

[3]Ralf Dahrendorf, "Toward a Theory of Social Conflict," *Journal of Conflict Resolution* 2 (June 1958), pp. 170–83; Ralf Dahrendorf, *Class and Class Conflict in Industrial Society* (Stanford, Calif.: Stanford University Press, 1959), pp. 168–69; Ralf Dahrendorf, *Gesellschaft un Freiheit* (Munich: R. Piper, 1961); Ralf Dahrendorf, *Essays in the Theory of Society* (Stanford, Calif.: Stanford University Press, 1967).

roles in ICAs possess varying degrees of authority, any particular ICA can be typified in terms of just two basic types of roles, ruling and ruled. The ruling cluster of roles has an interest in preserving the status quo, and the ruled cluster has an interest in redistributing power, or authority. Under certain specified conditions, awareness of these contradictory interests increases, with the result that ICAs polarize into two conflict groups, each now aware of its objective interests, which then engage in a contest over authority. The resolution of this contest or conflict involves the redistribution of authority in the ICA, thus making conflict the source of change in social systems. In turn, the redistribution of authority represents the institutionalization of a new cluster of ruling and ruled roles that, under certain conditions, polarize into two interest groups that initiate another contest for authority. Social reality is thus typified in terms of this unending cycle of conflict over authority within the various types of ICAs comprising the social world. Sometimes the conflicts within diverse ICAs in a society overlap, leading to major conflicts cutting across large segments of the society, while, at other times and under different conditions, these conflicts are confined to a particular ICA.

As I think is clear, this image of social organization represents a revision of Marx's portrayal of social reality:

1. Social systems are seen by both Dahrendorf and Marx as in a continual state of conflict.
2. Such conflict is presumed by both authors to be generated by the opposed interests that inevitably inhere in the social structure of society.
3. Opposed interests are viewed by both Marx and Dahrendorf as reflections of differences in the distribution of power among dominant and subjugated groups.
4. Interests are seen by both as tending to polarize into two conflict groups.
5. For both, conflict is dialectical, with resolution of one conflict creating a new set of opposed interests that, under certain conditions, will generate further conflict.
6. Social change is thus seen by both as a ubiquitous feature of social systems and the result of inevitable conflict dialectics within various types of institutionalized patterns.

Much like Marx, this image of institutionalization as a cyclical or dialectic process has led Dahrendorf into the analysis of only certain key causal relations: (1) conflict is assumed to be an inexorable process arising out of opposing forces within social-structural arrangements; (2) such conflict is accelerated or retarded by a series of intervening structural conditions or variables; (3) conflict resolution at one point in time creates a structural situation that, under specifiable conditions, inevitably leads to further conflict among opposed forces.

For Marx, the source of conflict ultimately lies beneath cultural values and institutional arrangements, which represent edifices constructed by those with power. In reality, the dynamics of a society are found in its substructure, where the differential distribution of property and power inevitably initiates a sequence of events leading to revolutionary class conflict. While borrowing much of Marx's rhetoric about power and coercion in social systems, Dahrendorf actually ends up positing a much different source of conflict: the institutionalized authority relations of ICAs. Such a position is much different from that of Marx, who viewed such authority relations as simply a superstructure erected by the dominant classes, which, in the long run, would be destroyed by the conflict dynamics occurring below institutional arrangements. While Dahrendorf acknowledges that authority relations are imposed by the dominant groups in ICAs and frequently makes reference to "factual substrates," the source of conflict becomes, upon close examination, the legitimated authority role relations of ICAs. I think that this drift away from Marx's emphasis on the institutional substructure forces Dahrendorf to seek the source of conflict in those very relations that integrate, albeit temporarily, an ICA. By itself, I see this shift in emphasis as desirable, since Dahrendorf clearly recognizes that not all power is a reflection of property ownership—a fact Marx's polemics tended to underemphasize. But as I will later observe, viewing power only in terms of authority can lead to analytical problems as severe as those in Marx's model and, in fact, somewhat reminiscent of those in Parsons' "social systems."

Although emphasizing different sources of conflict, Dahrendorf's and Marx's models reveal similar causal chains of events leading to conflict and the reorganization of social structure. Relations of domination and subjugation create an "objective" opposition of interests; awareness or consciousness by the subjugated of this inherent opposition of interests occurs under certain specifiable conditions; under other conditions, this newfound awareness leads to the political organization and then polarization of subjugated groups, who then join in conflict with the dominant group; the outcome of the conflict will usher in a new pattern of social organization; this new pattern of social organization will have within it relations of domination and subjugation that set off another sequence of events leading to conflict and then change in patterns of social organization.

The intervening conditions affecting these processes are outlined by both Marx and Dahrendorf only with respect to the formation of awareness of opposed interests by the subjugated, the politicization and polarization of the subjugated into a conflict group, and the outcome of the conflict. The intervening conditions under which institutionalized patterns generate dominant and subjugated groups and the conditions under which these can be typified as having opposed interests remain unspecified—apparently because they are in the nature of institutionalization, or ICAs, and do not have to be explained.

In Figure 7-1, I have outlined the causal imagery of Marx and Dahrendorf. At the top of the figure are Marx's analytical categories, stated in their most abstract form. The other two rows specify the empirical categories of Marx and Dahrendorf, respectively. Separate analytical categories for the Dahrendorf model are not enumerated because they are the same as those in the Marxian model. As I think is clear, the empirical categories of the Dahrendorf scheme differ greatly from those of Marx. But the form of analysis is much the same, since each considers as nonproblematic and not in need of causal analysis the empirical conditions of social organization, the transformation of this organization into relations of domination and subjugation, and the creation of opposed interests. The causal analysis for both begins with an elaboration of the conditions leading to growing class consciousness (Marx) or awareness among quasi groups (Dahrendorf) of their objective interests; then analysis shifts to the creation of a politicized class "for itself" (Marx) or a true "conflict group" (Dahrendorf); and finally, emphasis focuses on the emergence of conflict between polarized and politicized classes (Marx) or conflict groups (Dahrendorf).

## CRITICISMS OF THE DIALECTICAL CONFLICT MODEL

### Problems in the Causal Analysis

The most conspicuous criticism of Dahrendorf's causal imagery comes from Peter Weingart. He has argued that in deviating from Marx's conception of the "substructure of opposed interests" existing below the cultural and institutional edifices of the ruling classes, Dahrendorf forfeits a genuine causal analysis of conflict and, therefore, an explanation of how patterns of social organization are changed.[4] This criticism asks questions reminiscent of Dahrendorf's portrayal of Parsonian functionalism: How is it that conflict emerges from legitimated authority relations among roles in an ICA? How is it that the same structure that generates integration also generates conflict? Although for the Marxian scheme there are, I think, rather severe analytical and empirical problems, the causal analysis is clear, since the source of conflict—the opposition of economic interests—is clearly distinguished from the institutional and cultural arrangements maintaining a temporary order—the societal superstructure. Dahrendorf, however, has failed to make explicit this distinction and thus falls into the very analytical trap he has imputed to functional theory:

---

[4]Peter Weingart, "Beyond Parsons? A Critique of Ralf Dahrendorf's Conflict Theory," *Social Forces* 48 (December 1969), pp. 151-65. See also Jonathan H. Turner, "From Utopia to Where: A Strategy for Reformulating the Dahrendorf Conflict Model," *Social Forces* 52 (December 1973), pp. 236-44.

**FIGURE 7-1** The Dialectical Causal Imagery

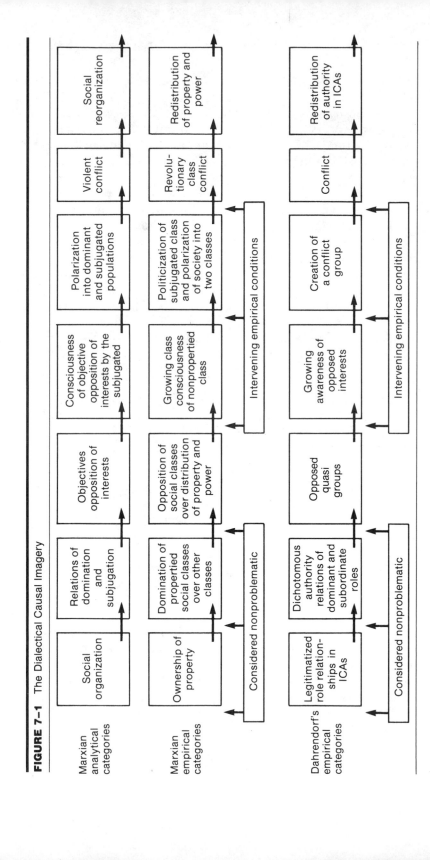

change inducing conflict must mysteriously arise from the legitimated relations of the social system.

In an attempt to escape this analytical trap, I think that Dahrendorf's causal analysis often becomes confusing. One tack Dahrendorf employs is to assert that many roles also have a nonintegrative aspect because they represent fundamentally opposed interests of the incumbents. These opposed interests are reflected in role conflict, which seemingly reduces the issues of role strain and conflict to dilemmas created by objectively opposed interests—surely a dubious assertion that is correct only some of the time. In equating interests and role expectations, Dahrendorf would seemingly have to hypothesize that all institutionalized patterns, or ICAs, display two mutually contradictory sets of role expectations—one to obey, the other to revolt—and that actors must decide which set they will follow. Presumably, actors wish to realize their objective interests and hence revolt against the role expectations imposed upon them by the dominant group. This approach forces the Dahrendorf model to reduce the origins of conflict to the wishes, wills, and sentiments of a person or group—a reductionist imperative that I am sure Dahrendorf would reject but one that his causal imagery would seemingly dictate.[5]

Many of these problems might be overcome, I feel, if Dahrendorf had provided a series of theoretical statements that would indicate the conditions under which legitimatized role relationships in ICAs create dichotomous authority relations of domination and subjugation. To simply assume that this is the case is to avoid what I see as the critical causal link in his analytical scheme. I believe that these propositions—or, as Dahrendorf describes them, "intervening empirical conditions"—are a necessary part of the model. Without them it is unclear how the types of authority, coercion, and domination that lead to conflict ever emerge in the first place. Assuming that they just emerge or are an endemic part of social structure is to define away the theoretically important question about what types of authority in what types of ICAs lead to what types of domination and subjugation that, in turn, lead to what types of opposed interests and what types of conflict. These are all phenomena that must be conceptualized as variables and incorporated into the causal chains of the dialectical-conflict model. Referring to Figure 7-1, this task would involve stating the "intervening empirical conditions" at each juncture of all of Dahrendorf's empirical categories. What is now considered nonproblematic would become as problematic as subsequent empirical conditions.

Initiating this task is difficult,[6] but to do so would enable Dahrendorf to avoid some of the more standard criticisms of this causal imagery:

---

[5]Weingart, "Beyond Parsons?"

[6]For my best effort on this score, see Jonathan H. Turner, "A Strategy for Reformulating the Dialectical and Functional Theories of Conflict," *Social Forces* 53 (March 1975), pp. 433–44.

(1) conflict not only causes change of social structure but changes of structure also cause conflict (under conditions that need to be specified in greater detail than Simmel's initial analysis); and (2) conflict can inhibit change (again, under conditions that need to be specified).[7] Unless these conditions are part of the causal imagery, conflict theory merely states the rather obvious fact that change occurs, without answering the theoretical questions of why, when, and where such change occurs.

Despite the vagueness of Dahrendorf's causal analysis, I see the great strength of his approach residing in the formulation of explicit propositions. These state the intervening empirical conditions that cause quasi groups to become conflict groups, as well as the conditions affecting the intensity (involvement of group members) and violence (degree of regulation) of the conflict and the degree and the rate of structural change caused by it. More formally, Dahrendorf outlines three types of intervening empirical conditions: (1) conditions of organization that affect the transformation of latent quasi groups into manifest conflict groups; (2) conditions of conflict that determine the form and intensity of conflict; and (3) conditions of structural change that influence the kind, speed, and the depth of the changes in social structure.[8]

Thus, the variables in the theoretical scheme are the (1) degree of conflict-group formation; (2) the degree of intensity of the conflict; (3) the degree of violence of the conflict; (4) the degree of change of social structure; and (5) the rate of such change. I think it significant, for criticisms to be delineated later, that concepts such as ICAs, legitimacy, authority, coercion, domination, and subjugation are not explicitly characterized as variables requiring statements on the conditions affecting their variability. Rather, these concepts are simply defined and interrelated to each other in terms of definitional overlap or stated as assumptions about the nature of social reality.

For those phenomena that are conceptualized as variables, Dahrendorf's propositions appear to be an elaboration of those developed by Marx. I have reworked them a bit and placed them in Table 7-1.[9]

Like Marx, Dahrendorf sees conflict as related to subordinates' growing awareness of their interests and formation into conflict groups (Proposition I). Such awareness and group formation is a positive function of the degree to which (*a*) the technical conditions (leadership and unifying ideology), (*b*) the political conditions (capacity to organize), and (*c*) the

---

[7]For a convenient summary of these, see Percy Cohen, *Modern Sociological Theory* (New York: Basic Books, 1968), pp. 183–91.

[8]Dahrendorf, "Toward a Theory of Social Conflict."

[9]The propositions listed in the table differ from a list provided by Dahrendorf, *Class and Class Conflict*, pp. 239–40 in two respects: (1) they are phrased consistently as statements of covariance, and (2) they are phrased somewhat more abstractly without reference to "class," which in this particular work was Dahrendorf's primary concern.

---

**TABLE 7–1**  Dahrendorf's Abstract Propositions

  I. The more members of quasi groups in ICAs can become aware of their objective interests and form a conflict group, the more likely is conflict to occur.

    A. The more the "technical" conditions of organization can be met, the more likely is the formation of a conflict group.

      1. The more a leadership cadre among quasi groups can be developed, the more likely are the technical conditions of organization to be met.

      2. The more a codified idea system, or charter, can be developed, the more likely are the technical conditions of organization to be met.

    B. The more the "political" conditions of organization can be met, the more likely is the formation of a conflict group.

      1. The more the dominant groups permit organization of opposed interests, the more likely are the political conditions of organization to be met.

    C. The more the "social" conditions of organization can be met, the more likely is the formation of a conflict group.

      1. The more opportunity for members of quasi groups to communicate, the more likely are the social conditions of organization to be met.

      2. The more recruiting is permitted by structural arrangements (such as propinquity), the more likely are the social conditions to be met.

  II. The less the technical, political, and social conditions of organization are met, the more intense is the conflict.

  III. The more the distribution of authority and other rewards are associated with each other (superimposed), the more intense is the conflict.

  IV. The less the mobility between super- and subordinate groups, the more intense is the conflict.

  V. The less the technical, political, and social conditions of organization are met, the more violent is the conflict.

  VI. The more the deprivations of the subjugated in the distribution of rewards shifts from an absolute to relative basis, the more violent is the conflict.

  VII. The less the ability of conflict groups to develop regulatory agreements, the more violent is the conflict.

  VIII. The more intense the conflict, the more structural change and reorganization it will generate.

  IX. The more violent the conflict, the greater is the rate of structural change and reorganization.

---

social conditions (ability to communicate) are met. These ideas clearly come from Marx's discussion (see Table 6-1). However, Proposition II borrows from Simmel and contradicts Marx. It emphasizes that if groups are *not* well organized—that is, if the technical, political, and social conditions are not met—then conflict is likely to be emotionally involving (see Table 6-2). Then Dahrendorf borrows from Weber in Proposition III by stressing that the superimposition of rewards—that is, the degree of correlation among those who enjoy privilege with respect to power, wealth, prestige—also increases the emotional involvement of subordinates who pursue conflict (see Table 6-5). Proposition IV also takes as much from Weber as from Marx because it sees the lack of mobility into positions of authority as escalating the emotional involvement of subordinates. Proposition V is clearly from Simmel and contradicts Marx, in that the violence of conflict is related to the lack of organization and clear articulation of interests. But Proposition VI returns to Marx's emphasis that sudden escalation in people's perception of deprivation—that is, relative deprivation—increases the likelihood of violent conflict. In Proposition VII, however, Dahrendorf returns to Simmel and argues that violence is very much related to the capacity of a system to develop regulatory procedures for dealing with grievances and releasing tensions. And in Propositions VIII and IX, Dahrendorf moves again to Marx's emphasis on how conflict produces varying rates and degrees of structural change in a social system.

I feel that Dahrendorf must be commended for placing the propositions in a reasonably systematic format—a difficult task too infrequently performed by theorists in sociology. However, even though this propositional inventory is highly suggestive, I see a number of criticisms that need to be addressed.

One of the most obvious criticisms of the Dahrendorf perspective is the failure to visualize crucial concepts as variables. Indeed, my rephrasing has converted some of Dahrendorf's concepts into variables. But still, most conspicuous for their nominal character are such central concepts of authority, domination-subjugation, and interest. Since it is from legitimated authority relations that conflict ultimately springs, I find it somewhat surprising that this concept is not viewed as a variable, varying at a minimum in terms of such properties as intensity, scope, and legitimacy. Rather, Dahrendorf has chosen to define away the problem:

> No attempt will be made in this study to develop a typology of authority. But it is assumed throughout that the existence of domination and subjugation is a common feature of all possible types of authority and, indeed, of all possible types of association and organization.[10]

A typology of authority might offer some indication of the variable states of authority and related concepts—a fact Dahrendorf ignores by simply arguing that authority implies domination and subjugation, which in turn gives him the structural dichotomy necessary for this dialectical theory of conflicting interests. He refuses to speculate on what types of authority displaying what variable states lead to what types of variations in domination and subjugation that, in turn, cause what variable types of opposed interests leading to what variable types of conflict groups. Thus, I see Dahrendorf as linking only by assumption and definition crucial variables that causally influence each other as well as the more explicit variables of his scheme: the degree of conflict, the degree of intensity of conflict, the degree of violence in conflict, the degree of change,

---

[10]Ibid., p. 169.

and the rate of social change. In fact, it is likely that these unstated variable properties of authority, domination, and interests have as much influence on the scheme's explicit variables as the "intervening empirical conditions" that Dahrendorf chooses to emphasize. Furthermore, as I noted earlier, when viewed as variables, the concepts of authority, domination-subjugation, and interests require their own intervening empirical conditions. These conditions may in turn influence other subsequently intervening conditions in much the same way as the "conditions of organization" also influence the subsequent intensity and violence of conflict in the scheme.

My criticisms suggest an obvious solution: to conceptualize ICAs, legitimacy, authority, domination-subjugation, and interests as variable phenomena and to attempt a statement of the intervening empirical conditions influencing their variability. Expanding the propositional inventory in this way would, I feel, reduce the vagueness of the causal imagery in the present scheme. Such an alteration would also cut down on the rather protracted set of dialectical assumptions—which are of dubious isomorphism in reality—and address a theoretical (rather than philosophical) question: under what conditions do ICAs create legitimated authority relations that generate clear relations of domination and subjugation leading to strongly opposed interests?

## Methodological Problems

To his credit, Dahrendorf provides formal definitions of major concepts and suggests operational clues about their application in concrete empirical settings, as is evident in his analysis of class conflict in industrial societies.[11] Furthermore, the incorporation of at least *some* concepts into an explicit propositional inventory—albeit an incomplete one—makes the scheme appear more testable and amendable to refutation.

A number of methodological problems remain, however. One of these concerns the extremely general definitions given to concepts. Although these definitions are stated formally, they are often so general that they can be used in an ad hoc and ex post facto fashion to apply to such a wide variety of phenomena that their current utility for the development and testing of theory can be questioned. For example, I think that the concepts of power, legitimacy, authority, interests, domination, and even conflict are defined so broadly that instances of these concepts can be found in almost any empirical situation. Thus, Dahrendorf can rather easily confirm his assumption that social life is rife with conflict. But how is one to measure these vaguely and globally defined concepts? I noted this problem earlier when discussing Dahrendorf's reluctance to

---

[11]Ibid., pp. 241–318.

view crucial concepts, such as authority and domination, as variables. If these concepts were so conceptualized, I feel that it would be easier for investigators to put empirical handles on them, since definitional statements about their variable states would specify more precisely the phenomena denoted by the concept. Dahrendorf rarely does this service, preferring to avoid typologies; and even when concepts are defined as variables, Dahrendorf avoids the issue with such statements as the following: "The intensity of class conflict varies on a scale (from 0 to 1)." Coupled with the formal definition of conflict intensity as the "energy expenditure and degree of involvement of conflicting parties," empirical investigators are given few operational guidelines about how such a concept might be measured. Were these definitions supplemented with, at a minimum, a few examples of prominent points along the 0 to 1 scale, then the concepts and propositions of the scheme would be more amenable to empirical investigation. As the definitions stand now, Dahrendorf does the very thing for which he has so resoundingly criticized Parsons: he uses vague concepts in a way that will inevitably confirm his overall scheme. More attention to precise definitions would give the concepts more power as theoretical constructs and as guidelines for investigators.

In sum, then, the Dahrendorf scheme presents a number of problems for empirical investigators. Such a statement can be made for almost all theoretical perspectives in sociology and by itself is not a unique indictment. For the Dahrendorf scheme, however, it appears that methodological problems could be minimized with just a little additional work. To the extent that my suggested corrections are made, it is likely that the dialectical-conflict perspective will offer a fruitful strategy for developing sociological theory.

## FROM UTOPIA TO WHERE?
## A CONCLUDING COMMENT

As I emphasized at the beginning of this chapter, Dahrendorf has been one of the harshest critics of functional forms of theorizing, likening them to an ideological utopia. In order to set sociological theorizing on the road out of utopia, Dahrendorf felt compelled to delineate a dialectical-conflict scheme that presumably mirrors more accurately than Parsonian functionalism the real character of the social world. In so doing, I presume that Dahrendorf views his theoretical perspective and strategy as providing a more adequate set of theoretical guidelines for understanding the nature and dynamics of human social organization.

What I find curious about Dahrendorf's approach is that, upon close examination, it appears quite similar to the one he imputed to Parsonian functionalism. For example, a number of commentators[12] have noted that

---

[12]For the best of these critiques, see Weingart, "Beyond Parsons."

both Parsons and Dahrendorf view the social world in terms of institutionalized patterns—for Parsons, the "social systems," for Dahrendorf,
"imperatively coordinated associations."[13] Both view societies as composed of subsystems involving the organization of roles in terms of legitimate normative prescriptions. For Dahrendorf, these legitimated normative patterns reflect power differentials in a system; and, despite his
rhetoric about the coercive nature of these relations, I see this vision of
power as remarkably similar to Parsons's conception of power as the
legitimate right of some status-roles to regulate the expectations attendant
upon other statuses.[14] Furthermore, in Dahrendorf's model, deviation from
the norms established by status-roles will lead dominant groups to attempt
to employ negative sanctions—a position that is very close to Parsons's
view that power exists to correct for deviations within a system.[15]

The apparent difference between Dahrendorf's and Parsons's emphasis with respect to the functions of power in social systems (or ICAs)
is that Dahrendorf argues explicitly that power differentials cause both
integration (through legitimated authority relations) and disintegration
(through the persistence of opposed interests). However, to state that
conflict emerges out of legitimated authority is nothing more than to state,
a priori, that opposed interests exist and cause conflict. The emergence
of conflict follows from vague assumptions about such processes as the
"inner dialectic of power and authority" and the "historical function of
authority,"[16] rather than from carefully documented causal sequences.
Thus, I think that the genesis of conflict in Dahrendorf's model remains
as unexplained as it does in his portrayal of the inadequacies of the functional utopia, primarily because its emergence is set against a background
of unexplained conceptions of system norms and legitimated authority.

Dahrendorf's problem in explaining why and how conflict groups can
emerge from a legitimated authority structure is partly a reflection of
hidden assumptions about functional requisites. In a subtle and yet consistent fashion, he assumes that authority is a functional requisite for
system integration and that the conflict that somehow emerges from authority relations is a functional requisite for social change. As Dahrendorf
argues, "the historical function of authority" is to generate conflict and
thereby maintain the vitality of social systems. From this notion of the
requisite for change, it is all too easy to assert that conflict exists to meet
the system's needs for change—an illegitimate teleology that echoes Marx's

---

[13]Ibid.; Pierre L. van den Berghe, "Dialectic and Functionalism: Toward a Theoretical
Synthesis," *American Sociological Review* 28 (October 1963), pp. 695–705.

[14]For example, see Talcott Parsons and Edward Shils, eds., *Toward a General Theory
of Action* (New York: Harper & Row, 1962), pp. 197–205.

[15]Ibid., p. 230.

[16]Weingart, "Beyond Parsons," p. 161.

teleological assumption that cycles of dialectical change are necessary to create the communist utopia.

More fundamentally, however, is Dahrendorf's inability to explain the organization of ICAs. To assert that they are organized in terms of power and authority defines away a theoretically interesting problem of how, why, and through what processes the institutionalized patterns generating both integration and conflict come to exist. On the other hand, Parsons's analysis does attempt—however inadequately—to account for how institutionalized patterns, or social systems, become organized: by actors adjusting their various orientations, normative prescriptions emerge, which affect the subsequent organization of action; such organization is maintained by various mechanisms of social control—interpersonal sanctions, ritual activity, safety-valve structures, role segregation, and, on some occasions, power—and by mechanisms of socialization—the internalization of relevant values and the acquisition of critical interpersonal skills. Quite naturally, because of his commitment to developing systems of concepts instead of formats of propositions, Parsons gives only a vague clue about the variables involved in the process of institutionalization by which the types of opposed interests that lead to the organization of conflict groups and social change are created. However, Parsons at least attempts to conceptualize the variables involved in creating and maintaining the very social order that Dahrendorf glosses over in his formulation of the ICA concept. Yet it is from the institutionalized relations in ICAs that conflict-ridden cycles of change are supposed to emerge. Asserting one's way out of utopia, as I think Dahrendorf does, will not obviate the fundamental theoretical question facing sociological theory: how is social organization, in all its varied and changing forms, possible?

In sum, then, I think that Dahrendorf has used the rhetoric of coercion, dialectics, domination, subjugation, and conflict to mask a vision of social reality that is very close to the utopian image he has imputed to Parsons's work. In Dahrendorf's ICA is Parsons's social system; in his concepts of roles and authority is Parsons's concern with social control; in his portrayal of conflict, the origin of conflict is just as unclear as he assumes it to be in Parsons's work; and even in the analysis of social change, conflict is considered, in a way reminiscent of Parsons, to meet the functional need for change. Thus, we can at least be suspicious about Dahrendorf's claim that we are on the road out of utopia. Yet, in making this harsh judgment, I still think that the propositions in Table 7–1 will be very useful in understanding some conflict processes. They will not, I feel, be as fundamental to understanding the nature of social reality as Dahrendorf seems to imply. But I find them very useful for helping to increase our knowledge of conflict processes in social systems. But I think that there is more to social reality than dialectical conflict, and this is where Dahrendorf and most conflict theorists go wrong: they assume, or should I say, presume, too much of their more limited and delimited schemes about conflict.

# CHAPTER 8

# The Conflict Functionalism of Lewis A. Coser

In the 1960s and 1970s, I see the criticisms of functionalism as looking much the same. They all berated Parsons and other functionalists for viewing society as overly institutionalized and equilibrating. At the same time, the conflict schemes offered as alternatives revealed considerable diversity. The divergence in conflict theory is particularly evident when the conflict functionalism of Lewis Coser is compared with Ralf Dahrendorf's dialectical-conflict perspective. Although Coser consistently criticized Parsonian functionalism for its failure to address the issue of conflict, he has also been sharply critical of Dahrendorf and other dialectical theorists for underemphasizing the positive functions of conflict for maintaining social systems.

In his first major work on conflict, Coser launched what became the standard polemic against functionalism: conflict is not given sufficient attention, with related phenomena such as deviance and dissent too easily viewed as "pathological" for the equilibrium of the social system.[1] Parsons, in his concern for developing a system of concepts denoting the process of institutionalization, underemphasized conflict in his formal analytical works, seemingly viewing conflict as a disease that needs to be treated by the mechanisms of the body social.[2] I think that this rather one-sided portrayal of Parsons's work allows Coser to posit the need for redressing the sins of Parsonian functionalism with a one-sided conflict scheme. Apparently such analytical compensation was to be carried out for well

---

[1]Lewis A. Coser, *The Functions of Social Conflict* (London: Free Press of Glencoe, 1956).
[2]Ibid., pp. 22–23.

over a decade, since after the 10th anniversary of his first polemic Coser was moved to reassert his earlier claim that it was "high time to tilt the scale in the direction of greater attention to social conflict."[3] Yet, while Coser has consistently maintained that functional theorizing "has too often neglected the dimensions of power and interest," he does not follow either Marx's or Dahrendorf's emphasis on the disruptive consequences of violent conflict.[4] On the contrary, Coser seeks to correct Dahrendorf's analytical excesses by emphasizing the integrative and "adaptability" functions of conflict for social systems. Thus, Coser justifies his efforts by criticizing functionalism for ignoring conflict and conflict theory for underemphasizing the functions of conflict.[5]

## IMAGES OF SOCIAL ORGANIZATION

As I emphasized in Chapter 2, Émile Durkheim can be considered one of the fathers of functionalism. And thus, I think it is interesting to note that a "conflict functionalist" is critical of Durkheim's approach.[6] In particular, Coser views Durkheim as taking a conservative orientation to the study of society, an orientation that "prevented him from taking due cognizance of a variety of societal processes, among which social conflict is the most conspicuous." Furthermore, this abiding conservatism forced Durkheim to view violence and dissent as deviant and pathological to the social equilibrium, rather than as opportunities for constructive social changes. Although Coser appears intent on rejecting the organicism of Durkheim's sociology, I find his own work filled with organismic analogies. For example, in describing the "functions of violence," Coser likens violence to pain in the human body, since both can serve as a danger signal that allows the body social to readjust itself.[7] To take another example,

---

[3]Lewis A. Coser, "Some Social Functions of Violence," *Annuals of the American Academy of Political and Social Science* 364 (March 1966), p. 10.

[4]Lewis A. Coser, *Continuities in the Study of Social Conflict* (New York: Free Press, 1967), p. 141.

[5]A listing of some of Coser's prominent works, to be utilized in subsequent analysis, reveals the functional flavor of his conflict perspective: *Functions of Social Conflict*; "Some Social Functions of Violence"; "Some Functions of Deviant Behavior and Normative Flexibility," *American Journal of Sociology* 68 (September 1962), pp. 172-81; and "The Functions of Dissent," in *The Dynamics of Dissent* (New York: Grune & Stratton, 1968), pp. 158-70. Other prominent works with less revealing titles but critical substance include: "Social Conflict and the Theory of Social Change," *British Journal of Sociology* 8 (September 1957), pp. 197-207; "Violence and the Social Structure," in *Science and Psychoanalysis*, ed. J. Masserman, vol. 7 (New York: Grune & Stratton, 1963), pp. 30-42. These and other essays are collected in Coser's *Continuities in the Study of Social Conflict*. One should also consult his *Masters of Sociological Thought* (New York: Harcourt Brace Jovanovich, 1977).

[6]Lewis Coser, "Durkheim's Conservatism and Its Implications for His Sociological Theory," in *Émile Durkheim, 1858-1917: A Collection of Essays*, ed. K. H. Wolff (Columbus: Ohio State University Press, 1960); also reprinted in Coser's *Continuities*, pp. 153-80.

[7]Coser, "Some Functions of Violence," pp. 12-13.

in his analysis of the "functions of dissent," Coser rejects the notion that dissent is explainable in terms of individual sickness and embraces the assumption that "dissent may more readily be explained as a reaction to what is perceived as a sickness in the body social."[8] I do not think that this form of analogizing fatally wounds Coser's analysis, but it does reveal that he has not rejected organicism. Apparently, Coser has felt compelled to criticize Durkheim's organicism because it did not allow the analysis of conflict as a process that could promote the further adaptation and integration of the body social.[9]

In rejecting the analytical constraints of Durkheim's analogizing, Coser embraces Georg Simmel's organicism (see Chapter 6). Conflict is viewed as a process that, under certain conditions, functions to maintain the body social or some of its vital parts. From this vantage point, Coser develops an image of society that stresses:

1. The social world can be viewed as a system of variously interrelated parts.
2. All social systems reveal imbalances, tensions, and conflicts of interests among variously interrelated parts.
3. Processes within and between the system's constituent parts operate under different conditions to maintain, change, and increase or decrease a system's integration and adaptability.
4. Many processes, such as violence, dissent, deviance, and conflict, which are typically viewed as disruptive to the system, can also be viewed, under specifiable conditions, as strengthening the system's basis of integration as well as its adaptability to the environment.

From these assumptions, Coser articulates a rather extensive set of propositions about the functions (and to a limited extent, the dysfunctions) of conflict for social systems. Coser offers some propositions about the conditions under which conflict leads to disruption and malintegration of social systems, but I see the main thrust of his analysis as revolving around statements on how conflict maintains or reestablishes system integration and adaptability to changing conditions. In so doing, I see Coser's analysis as emphasizing: (1) imbalances in the integration of system parts lead to (2) the outbreak of varying types of conflict among these parts, which, in turn, causes (3) temporary reintegration of the system, which causes (4) increased flexibility in the system's structure, increased capability to resolve future imbalances through conflict, and increased capacity to adapt to changing conditions.

---

[8]Coser, "The Functions of Dissent," pp. 159-60.

[9]I should note that such an emphasis on the "positive functions" of conflict could be construed as the pinnacle of conservative ideology—surpassing that attributed to Parsons. Even conflict promotes integration rather than disruption, malintegration, and change. Such a society, as Dahrendorf would argue, no longer has an ugly face and is as utopian as that of Parsons's. For Coser's reply to this kind of charge, see *Continuities*, pp. 1 and 5.

The causal imagery presents, I feel, a number of obvious problems. The most important of these is that processes are too frequently viewed as contributing to system integration and adaptation. Such an emphasis on the positive functions of conflict may reveal hidden assumptions of system needs that can be met only through the functions of conflict. Although Coser is careful to point out that he is simply correcting for analytical inattention to the positive consequences of conflict, the strategy is nonetheless one-sided.[10] Despite these shortcomings, I think that Coser mitigates his functionalism by translating his image of social organization into a series of abstract propositions about conflict in social systems. As a result, the scheme takes on considerably more clarity than when stated as a cluster of assumptions. Equally significant, the scheme becomes more testable and amenable to reformulation on the basis of empirical findings. Let me now turn to these propositions, since they are the great strength of Coser's conflict functionalism.

## PROPOSITIONS ON CONFLICT PROCESSES

Using both the substance and style of Georg Simmel's provocative analysis, Coser has expanded the scope of Simmel's initial insights, incorporating propositions not only from Marx but also from Weber and the contemporary literature on conflict. Although the scheme reveals a large number of problems, stemming from his primary concern with the functions of conflict, I feel that Coser's conflict perspective still remains one of the most comprehensive in the current literature. This comprehensiveness can, I think, be made evident by a partial list of the phenomena covered by his propositions: (1) the causes of conflict; (2) the violence of conflict; (3) the duration of conflict; and (4) the functions of conflict. Under each of these headings a variety of specific variables are incorporated into propositions.

One drawback to Coser's propositional inventory is that it has not been presented in a systematic or ordered format. Rather, the propositions appear in a number of discursive essays on substantive topics and in his analysis of Simmel's essay on conflict. Although each discrete proposition is usually stated quite clearly, I have had to extract and order the propositions. There is, of course, some danger of misinterpretation in this kind of exercise. Yet, I feel Coser's approach is much stronger when stated as a series of formal propositions.

---

[10]It is somewhat tragic for theory building in sociology that the early promising lead of Robin M. Williams, Jr., in his *The Reduction of Intergroup Tensions: A Survey of Research on Problems of Ethnic, Social, and Religious Group Relations* (New York: Social Science Research Council, 1947) was not consistently followed. Most of the propositions developed by Dahrendorf and Coser were summarized in this volume 10 years prior to their major works. More important, they are phrased more neutrally, without an attempt to reveal society's "ugly face" or correct for inattention to the "functions of conflict."

---

**TABLE 8-1**   Coser's Propositions on the Causes of Conflict

---

I. The more subordinate members in a system of inequality question the legitimacy of the existing distribution of scarce resources, the more likely are they to initiate conflict.

   A. The fewer are the channels for redressing grievances over the distribution of scarce resources by subordinates, the more likely are they to question legitimacy.

      1. The fewer are the internal organizations segmenting emotional energies of subordinates, the more likely are they to be without grievance alternatives and, as a result, to question legitimacy.

      2. The greater are the ego deprivations of those without grievance channels, the more likely are they to question legitimacy.

   B. The more membership in privileged groups is sought by subordinates and the less mobility allowed, the more likely are they to withdraw legitimacy.

II. The more deprivations of subordinates are transformed from absolute to relative, the greater will be their sense of injustice, and hence, the more likely are they to initiate conflict.

   A. The less is the degree to which socialization experiences of subordinates generate internal ego constraints, the more likely are they to experience relative deprivation.

   B. The less are the external constraints applied to subordinates, the more likely are they to experience relative deprivation.

---

## The Causes of Conflict

In Table 8-1, I have formalized Coser's discursive analysis on the causes of conflict.[11] Much like Weber (see Table 6-5), Coser emphasizes in Proposition I that the withdrawal of legitimacy from an existing system of inequality is a critical precondition for conflict. In contrast, dialectical theorists such as Dahrendorf tend to view the causes of conflict as residing in "contradictions" or "conflicts of interests." As subordinates become aware of their interests, they pursue conflict; and hence, the major theoretical task is to specify the conditions raising levels of awareness. But Coser is arguing that conflicts of interest are likely to be exposed only after the deprived withdraw legitimacy from the system. Coser emphasizes that the social order is maintained by some degree of consensus over existing arrangements and that "disorder" through conflict occurs when conditions decreasing this consensus or legitimacy over existing arrangements are present. Two such conditions are specified in Propositions I-A and I-B, both of which owe their inspiration more to Weber than Marx.

---

[11]Again, it should be emphasized that it is dangerous and difficult to pull from diverse sources discrete propositions and attempt to relate them systematically without doing some injustice to the theorist's intent. However, unless this kind of exercise is performed, the propositions will contribute little to the development of sociological theory. The propositions in Table 8-1 were extracted from: *Functions of Social Conflict*, pp. 8–385, "Social Conflict and the Theory of Social Change," pp. 197–207; "Internal Violence as a Mechanism for Conflict Resolution"; and "Violence and Social Structure."

Proposition I-A argues that when channels for expressing grievances do not exist, the withdrawal of legitimacy is likely, especially if there are few organizations to deflect and occupy people's energy (I-A-1) and if there are felt ego deprivations (I-A-2). Proposition I-B specifies that if the deprived desire membership in higher ranks or if they have been led to believe that some mobility is possible, a withdrawal of legitimacy will be likely when little mobility is allowed.

Proposition II indicates, however, that the withdrawal of legitimacy, in itself, is not likely to result in conflict. People must first become emotionally aroused. The theoretical task then becomes one of specifying the conditions that translate the withdrawal of legitimacy into emotional arousal, as opposed to some other emotional state, such as apathy and resignation. Here, Coser draws inspiration from Marx's notion of relative deprivation. For as Marx observed and as a number of empirical studies have documented, absolute deprivation does not always foster revolt.[12] When people's expectations for a better future suddenly begin to exceed perceived avenues for realizing these expectations, only then do they become sufficiently aroused to pursue conflict. The level of arousal will, in turn, be influenced by their commitments to the existing system, by the degree to which they have developed strong internal constraints, and on the nature and amount of social control in a system. Such propositions, for example, lead to predictions that in systems with absolute dictators, who ruthlessly repress the masses, revolt by the masses is less likely than in systems where some freedoms have been granted and where the deprived have been led to believe that things will be getting better. Under these conditions, the withdrawal of legitimacy can be accompanied by released passions and emotions.

## The Violence of Conflict

In Table 8-2, I have extracted and listed Coser's most important propositions on the level of violence in a conflict.[13] I find Coser somewhat vague in his definition of conflict violence, but he appears to be denoting the degree to which conflict parties seek to injure or eliminate each other. As most functional theorists are likely to emphasize, Coser's Proposition I is directed at specifying the conditions under which conflict will be less violent. In contrast, dialectical theorists, such as Marx, often pursue just

---

[12]James Davies, "Toward a Theory of Revolution," *American Journal of Sociology* 27 (1962), pp. 5-19; Ted Robert Gurr, *Why Men Rebel* (Princeton, N.J.: Princeton University Press, 1970) and "Sources of Rebellion in Western Societies: Some Quantitative Evidence," *The Annals* 38 (1973), pp. 495-501.

[13]These propositions are taken from Coser's *Functions of Social Conflict*, pp. 45-50. Again, I have made them more formal than Coser's more discursive text.

---

**TABLE 8–2**  Coser's Propositions on the Violence of Conflict

   I. The more groups engage in conflict over realistic issues (obtainable goals), the more likely are they to seek compromises over the means to realize their interests, and hence, the less violent is the conflict.

  II. The more groups engage in conflict over nonrealistic issues, the greater is the level of emotional arousal and involvement in the conflict, and hence, the more violent is the conflict.

   A. The more conflict occurs over core values, the more likely is it to be over nonrealistic issues.

   B. The more a realistic conflict endures, the more likely is it to become increasingly nonrealistic.

 III. The less functionally interdependent are relations among social units in a system, the less is the availability of institutional means for absorbing conflicts and tensions, and hence, the more violent is the conflict.

   A. The greater are the power differentials between super- and subordinates in a system, the less functionally interdependent are relations.

   B. The greater is the level of isolation of subpopulations in a system, the less functionally interdependent are relations.

---

the opposite fact: to specify the conditions under which conflict will be more violent. Yet, the inverse of Coser's first proposition can indicate a condition under which conflict will be violent. The key concept in this proposition is "realistic issues." For Coser, realistic conflict involves the pursuit of specific aims against real sources of hostility, with some estimation of the costs to be incurred in such pursuit. As I noted in Chapter 6, Simmel recognized that when clear goals are sought, compromise and conciliation are likely alternatives to violence. Coser restates this proposition but adds Proposition II on conflict over "nonrealistic issues," such as ultimate values, beliefs, ideology, and vaguely defined class interests. When nonrealistic, then the conflict will be violent. Such nonrealism is particularly likely when conflict is over core values, which emotionally mobilize participants and make them unwilling to compromise (Proposition II-A). Moreover, if conflicts endure for a long period of time, then it becomes increasingly nonrealistic as parties become emotionally involved, as ideologies become codified, and as "the enemy" is portrayed in increasingly negative terms (Proposition II-B).

Proposition III adds a more structural variable to the analysis of conflict violence. In systems where there are high degrees of functional interdependence among actors—that is, where there are mutual exchanges and cooperation—then conflict is less likely to be violent. However, if there is great inequality in power among units (Proposition III-A) or isolation of subpopulations (Proposition III-B), functional interdependence decreases, and hence when conflict occurs, it will tend to be nonrealistic and violent.

---

**TABLE 8–3**   Coser's Propositions on the Duration of Conflict

---

  I. The less limited are the goals of the opposing parties to a conflict, the more prolonged is the conflict.

  II. The less is the degree of consensus over the goals of conflict, the more prolonged is the conflict.

  III. The less the parties in a conflict can interpret their adversary's symbolic points of victory and defeat, the more prolonged is the conflict.

  IV. The more leaders of conflicting parties can perceive that complete attainment of goals is possible at only very high costs, the less prolonged is the conflict.

    A. The more equal is the power between conflicting groups, the more likely are leaders to perceive the high costs of complete attainment of goals.

    B. The more clear-cut are the indexes of defeat or victory in a conflict, the more likely are leaders to perceive the high costs of complete attainment of goals.

  V. The greater is the capacity of leaders of each conflict party to persuade followers to terminate conflict, the less prolonged is the conflict.

    A. The more centralized are the conflict parties, the greater is a leader's capacity to persuade followers.

    B. The fewer are the internal cleavages within conflict parties, the greater is a leader's capacity to persuade followers.

---

## The Duration of Conflict

Despite the recognition that conflict is a process, unfolding over time, I find it surprising that few theorists have incorporated the variable of time in their work. I emphasize, however, that this oversight is not just true of conflict theory but also of all theory in sociology, although some recent theoretical efforts have made time an explicit property of social structure (see chapters 21 and 22). Coser's incorporation of the time variable is extremely limited. He views time in terms of the duration of conflict and as a dependent variable, when it can also be an independent variable (see Proposition II-B in Table 8-2, for example). Just how the duration of conflict operates as an independent variable, influencing such variables as conflict intensity, violence, or functions, is never specified. Thus, Coser's analysis is confined to the more limited, yet I think important, question: what variables influence the length of conflict relations? In Table 8-3, I have extracted some of these propositions on conflict duration.[14]

In Propositions I and II, Coser underscores the fact that conflicts with a broad range of goals or with vague ones will be prolonged. When goals are limited and articulated, it is possible to know when they have been attained. With perception of attainment, the conflict can be terminated. Conversely, with a wide variety or long list of goals, a sense of attainment is less likely to occur—thus prolonging the conflict. In Prop-

---

[14]These propositions come from Coser, "The Termination of Conflict," in *Continuities*, pp. 37-52; Coser, *Functions of Social Conflict*, pp. 20, 48-55, 59, 128-33; *Continuities in the Study of Social Conflict*, pp. 37-52.

osition III, Coser emphasizes that knowledge of what would symbolically constitute victory and defeat will influence the length of conflict. Without the ability to recognize defeat or victory, then conflict is likely to be prolonged to a point where one party destroys the other. Propositions IV and V deal with the role of leadership in conflict processes. The more leaders can perceive that complete attainment of goals is not possible and the greater is their ability to convince followers to terminate conflict, the less prolonged is the conflict.

Thus, I see Coser's overall image of conflict duration as follows. Where the goals of conflict parties are extensive, where there is dissent over goals, where conflict parties cannot interpret symbolic points of victory and defeat, where leaders cannot assess the costs of victory, and where leaders cannot effectively persuade followers, then the conflict will be of longer duration than when the converse conditions hold true. In turn, as I think is evident, these variables are interrelated. For example, clear and limited goals help members to determine symbolic points of victory or defeat and leaders to assess the costs of victory. Although these inter-relations are not fully or systematically developed, Coser has provided an important lead in the study of the time dimension in the conflict process.

## The Functions of Social Conflict

As I emphasized in the chapters on functionalism, the concept of "func-tion" presents a number of problems. If some process or structure has functions for some other feature of a system, there is often an implicit assumption about what is good and bad for a system. If this implicit evaluation is not operative, how does one assess when an item is functional or dysfunctional? Even seemingly neutral concepts, such as survival or adaptability, merely mask the implicit evaluation that is taking place. Sociologists are usually not in a position to determine what is survival and adaptation. To say that an item has more survival value or increases adaptation is frequently a way to mask an evaluation of what is "good."

In Coser's propositions on the functions of conflict, I think that this problem exists. Conflict is good when it promotes integration based on solidarity, clear authority, functional interdependence, and normative control. In Coser's terms, it is more *adaptive*. Other conflict theorists might argue that conflict in such a system is bad because integration and adaptability in this specific context could be exploitive. And so, with these qualifications, let me now turn to Coser's propositions.

Coser divides his analysis of the functions of conflict along lines sim-ilar to those by Simmel: the functions of conflict for (1) the respective parties to the conflict and (2) the systemic whole in which the conflict occurs. In Table 8–4, I have delineated the propositions on the functions of conflict for the parties.[15]

---

[15]These propositions are taken from Coser, *Functions of Social Conflict*, pp. 37–38, 45, 69–72, 92–95.

---

**TABLE 8–4**    Coser's Propositions on the Functions of Conflict for the Respective Parties

---

I. The more violent or intense is the conflict, the more clear-cut are the boundaries of each respective conflict party.

II. The more violent or intense is the conflict and the more internally differentiated are the conflict parties, the more likely is each conflict party to centralize its decision-making structure.

III. The more violent or intense is the conflict and the more it is perceived to affect the welfare of all segments of the conflict parties, the more conflict promotes structural and ideological solidarity among members of each conflict party.

IV. The more violent or intense is the conflict, the more conflict leads to the suppression of dissent and deviance within each conflict party as well as forced conformity to norms and values.

V. The more conflict between parties leads to forced conformity, the greater is the accumulation of hostilities, and the more likely is internal group conflict to surface in the long run.

---

In the propositions listed in Table 8-4, the intensity of conflict—that is, people's involvement in and commitment to pursue the conflict—and its level of violence increase the demarcation of boundaries (Proposition I), centralization of authority (Proposition II), ideological solidarity (Proposition III), and suppression of dissent and deviance (Proposition IV) within each of the conflict parties. Conflict intensity is presumably functional because it increases integration, although Proposition V indicates that centralization of power as well as the suppression of deviance and dissent create malintegrative pressures in the long run. Thus, there appears to be an inherent dialectic in conflict group unification—one which creates pressures toward disunification. Unfortunately, Coser does not specify the conditions under which these malintegrative pressures are likely to surface. In focusing on positive functions—that is, forces promoting integration—I think that the analysis ignores a promising area of inquiry. This bias becomes even more evident when Coser shifts attention to the functions of conflict for the systemic whole within which the conflict occurs. I have listed these propositions in Table 8-5.[16]

I have not presented Coser's propositions in their full complexity in Table 8-5, but the essentials of his analysis are clear.[17] In Proposition I, complex systems that have a large number of interdependencies and ex-

---

[16]Ibid., pp. 45–48; Lewis A. Coser, "Internal Violence as Mechanisms for Conflict Resolution"; "Social Conflict and the Theory of Social Change," *British Journal of Sociology* 8 (September 1957), pp. 197-207; "Some Social Functions of Violence," *Annals of the American Academy of Political and Social Science* 364 (March 1966), p. 10; "The Functions of Dissent," in *The Dynamics of Dissent*, ed. L. A. Coser (New York: Grune & Stratton, 1968); and "Social Conflict and the Theory of Social Change."

[17]See third edition of *The Structure of Social Theory* (Homewood, Ill.: The Dorsey Press, 1982).

---

**TABLE 8–5**  Coser's Propositions on the Functions of Conflict for the Social Whole

---

  I. The more differentiated and functionally interdependent are the units in a system, the more likely is conflict to be frequent but of low degrees of intensity and violence.

 II. The more frequent are conflicts, the less is their intensity, and the lower is their level of violence, then the more likely are conflicts in a system to (*a*) increase the level of innovation and creativity of system units, (*b*) release hostilities before they polarize system units, (*c*) promote normative regulation of conflict relations, (*d*) increase awareness of realistic issues, and (*e*) increase the number of associative coalitions among social units.

III. The more conflict promotes (*a*), (*b*), (*c*), (*d*), and (*e*) above, then the greater will be the level of internal social integration of the system and the greater will be its capacity to adapt to its external environment.

---

changes are more likely to have frequent conflicts that are less emotionally involving and violent than those systems that are less complex and where tensions accumulate. It is in the nature of interdependence, Coser argues, for conflicts to erupt frequently, but since they emerge periodically, emotions do not build to the point where violence is inevitable. Conversely, systems where there are low degrees of functional interdependence will often polarize into hostile camps; and when conflict does erupt, it will be intense and violent. In Proposition II, frequent conflicts of low intensity and violence are seen to have certain positive functions. First, they will force those in conflict to reassess and reorganize their actions (Proposition II*a*). Second, such conflicts will release tensions and hostilities before they build to a point where adversaries become polarized around non-realistic issues (Proposition II*b*). Third, frequent conflicts of low intensity and violence encourage the development of normative procedures—laws, courts, mediating agencies, and the like—to be developed in order to regulate tensions (Proposition II*c*). Fourth, these kinds of conflicts also increase a sense of realism over what the conflict is about. That is, frequent conflicts where intensity and violence are kept under control allow conflict parties to articulate their interests and goals, thereby allowing them to bargain and compromise (Proposition II*d*). Fifth, conflicts promote coalitions among units who are threatened by the action of one party or another. If conflicts are frequent and of low intensity and violence, such coalitions come and go, thereby promoting flexible alliances (Proposition II*e*). However, if conflicts are infrequent and emotions accumulate, coalitions often polarize threatened parties into ever more hostile camps, with the result that when conflict does occur it is violent. And Proposition III simply asserts Coser's functional conclusion that when conflicts are frequent and when violence and intensity are reduced, conflict will promote flexible coordination within the system and increased capacity to adjust and adapt to environmental circumstances. This increased flexibility and adaptation is possible because of the processes listed in Proposition II.

## COSER'S FUNCTIONAL APPROACH: AN ASSESSMENT

I think that Coser's approach has done much to correct for the one-sidedness of Dahrendorf's analysis, while it has reintroduced Simmel's ideas into conflict theory. Yet, Coser's scheme represents an analytical one-sidedness that, if followed exclusively, would produce a skewed vision of the social world. Coser begins with statements about the inevitability of force, coercion, constraint, and conflict, but his analysis quickly turns to the integrative and adaptive consequences of such processes. This emphasis could rather easily transform the integrative and adaptive functions of conflict into functional needs and requisites that necessitate, or even cause, conflict to occur. Such teleology was inherent in Marx's work, where revolutionary conflict was viewed as necessary to meet the need for a communist society. But Coser's teleological inspiration appears to have come more from Simmel's organic model than Marx's dialectical scheme. Once he documents how conflict contributes to the systemic whole, or body social, Coser inadvertently implies that the body social causes conflict in order to meet its integrative needs. Although conflict is acknowledged by Coser to cause change in social systems, it is still viewed primarily as a crucial process in promoting integration and adaptation.

I think that Coser, like so many conflict theorists, creates a problem when he tries to correct for past weaknesses in other approaches. For in trying to compensate for the one-sidedness of dialectical theory *and* functionalism, Coser presents yet one more skewed approach. In my presentation of propositions in Tables 8–1 through 8–5, I have sought to mitigate against this overemphasis on the positive functions of conflict, but the actual scheme itself is heavily functional. I have not listed the many other functional statements here,[18] primarily because I have emphasized the strong points in Coser's scheme—that is, the propositions on the causes, violence, and duration of conflict (see Tables 8–1, 8–2, 8–3). Tables 8–4 and 8–5 on the functions of conflict could, in fact, be longer than the others combined, but I decided to limit my summary to only the strong points. As a consequence, I have distorted Coser's ideas somewhat.

Thus, the major substantive problem in Coser's scheme is its functionalism. To correct this problem, I see little need to redirect his propositions on the causes, violence, and duration of conflict. These propositions address, I feel, important questions neutrally and do not attempt to balance or correct for past theoretical one-sidedness with another kind

---

[18]Ibid.

of one-sidedness. Indeed, they display an awareness of key aspects of conflict in social systems; and with supplementation and reformulation, they offer an important theoretical lead. The substantive one-sidedness in the scheme comes with Coser's borrowing and then supplementing Simmel's functional propositions; and it is here that drastic changes in the scheme must come. One corrective strategy, which does not smack of another form of one-sidedness, is to ask the more neutral theoretical question: under what conditions can what kinds of outcomes of conflict for what types of systems and subsystems be expected? Although this is not a startling theoretical revelation, I think that it keeps assessments of conflict processes away from what ultimately must be evaluative questions of functions and dysfunctions. If the question of outcomes of conflicts is more rigorously pursued, the resulting propositions will present a more balanced and substantively accurate view of social reality.

Because of the long and unfortunate organic connotations of words such as "function," I believe that it is wise to drop their use in sociology. They all too frequently create logical and substantive problems of interpretation. Coser appears well aware of these dangers, but he has invited misinterpretation by continually juxtaposing notions of "the body social" and the "functions" of various conflict processes and related phenomena, such as dissent and violence. Had he not done this, he would have better achieved his goal of correcting for the inadequacies of functional and conflict theorizing in sociology. Instead, he has created a heavily functional scheme.

In sum, then, I think that it makes little sense to have new perspectives that correct for the deficiencies of either dialectical or functional conflict theory. Sociological theory has far too long engaged in this kind of activity; and it is far more appropriate, I feel, to visualize conflict as one of many important processes in the social universe and to develop some abstract principles about this process that avoid problems inherent in all forms of functional analysis.

Let me close this chapter by addressing problems in both Coser's and Dahrendorf's approaches. For in redirecting both the functional and dialectical schemes, I think that more interesting propositions on conflict processes will emerge.

## REDIRECTING CONFLICT THEORY: OVERCOMING UNRESOLVED ISSUES

### What is Conflict?

To my constant surprise, one of the most controversial issues in conflict theory is the definition of conflict. What is and what is not conflict? A quick review of the conflict theory literature will produce a surprisingly diverse array of terms denoting different aspects of conflict: hostilities, war, competition, antagonism, tension, contradiction, quarrels, disagreements, inconsistencies, controversy, violence, opposition, revolution, dispute, and many other terms. This issue boils down to the question of what kind of behavior among either individuals or collective units is to be defined as conflict? For example, does conflict involve only overt action of one party against another? Or can it include covert tensions among these parties? Or does conflict embrace competition where parties strive for mutually exclusive goals without directly confronting each other? Or is conflict only antagonisms involving overt violence and efforts to injure another party?

There is no consensus on these issues. Dahrendorf and Coser both employed broad definitions. For example, Dahrendorf uses the concept of conflict for "contests, competitions, disputes, and tensions as well as for manifest clashes between social forces."[19] His definition is consistent with his dialectical assumptions: ICAs reveal "conflicts of interest" among quasi groups, which under technical, social, and political conditions become true conflict groups willing to engage in overt action against each other. I assume that as long as one wants to prove that the social world is rife with contradictions, a broad definition of conflict is desirable. For when conflict can be *any* overt or covert state that hints of antagonism, I imagine that it is rather easy to document the ubiquity of conflict. And demonstrating the pervasiveness of conflict has indeed been one of Dahrendorf's and other conflict theorists' primary intellectual goals.

Similarly, Coser's broad definition serves his intellectual purposes: to demonstrate the ubiquity of conflict and to document its functions for system integration. If Coser viewed conflict as only violent confrontations, then its integrative functions might be less visible, since conflict parties might indeed destroy each other. But if conflict can be any antagonistic disposition of subgroups in a system, we are more likely to find instances where these antagonisms have promoted integration and adaptability among the parties or the systemic whole.

Presently, I see most conflict theorists as favoring a broad definition. After exhaustively reviewing numerous definitions, for example, Clinton Fink argues for a broad definition: conflict is "any social situation or process in which two or more entities are linked by at least one form of antagonistic psychological relation or at least one form of antagonistic interaction."[20] In turn, the concept of antagonism embraces such states as incompatible goals, mutually exclusive interests, emotional hostility, dissent, violent struggle, and regulated mutual interference.

---

[19] Ralf Dahrendorf, *Class and Class Conflict in Industrial Society* (Stanford: Stanford University Press, 1957), p. 135.

[20] Clinton F. Fink, "Some Conceptual Difficulties in the Theory of Social Conflict," *Journal of Conflict Resolution* 12 (December 1968), p. 456.

Few would, for example, want to consider the kind of definition that I prefer: "A conflict is direct and overt interaction between parties in which the actions of each party are directed at inhibiting their adversary's attainment of its goals." Such a definition makes conflict an overt and direct interaction between parties, but it allows for considerable variability in how one party inhibits the actions of the other. Such actions can be normatively regulated or unregulated and violent. Other forms of interaction could be labeled with different terms; and as a result, I think that we could avoid the lumping together of apples and oranges under the generic rubric of conflict. At present, I see the term as so global and encompassing that it embraces diverse forms of relationships, which, in all probability, are highly distinctive and reveal somewhat different laws of operation.

One of the few conflict theorists who has sought to develop a more limited definition that also embraces diverse forms of conflict is Robin Williams, Jr. Although he is not always this explicit, he defines conflict in one essay as:

> Interaction in which one party intends to deprive, control, injure, or eliminate another, against the will of that other. Pure conflict is a *fight*; its goal is to immobilize, neutralize, destroy, or otherwise harm an opponent. In the impure world of actuality, some overt struggles are conducted accordingly to rules and for limited goals; oppositional behavior may then have the primary goal of winning rather than of injuring the opponent; we then usually call the encounter a *game*. Some games merge into *debates* in which the primary aim is to convince or persuade opponents or others of the rightness or correctness or attractiveness of one's views or claims.[21]

This definition views conflict as direct interaction that takes a variety of specific forms but also involves efforts to "deprive, control, injure, or eliminate" the other. I feel that this kind of explicit definition of conflict is what we need in conflict theory. As long as the background conditions, such as contradictions, oppositions of interests, or hostilities, are viewed as conflict, then we will have difficulty separating the causes of conflict— that is, these and other background conditions—from the conflict itself. When the preconditions of conflict are lumped together with the actual emission of conflict acts, then theories are likely to be vague. The future of conflict theory thus depends on making explicit what is and what is not conflict and in distinguishing different types or forms of conflict from each other.

---

[21]Robin M. Williams, Jr., "Social Order and Social Conflict," *Proceedings of the American Philosophical Society* 114 (June 1970), pp. 217–25. Yet, in a more thorough analysis of the "law of social conflict," Williams does not present this kind of explicit definition. See "Conflict and Social Order: A Research Strategy for Complex Propositions," *Journal of Social Issues* 28 (1972), pp. 11–26.

## Conflict among or between What?

In addition to definitional problems over just what conflict is, I think that there is also a unit of analysis problem in conflict theory. Typically, just what the units are in conflict is left vague—whether they be individuals, groups, organizations, classes, nations, communities, and the like. For example, in Dahrendorf's scheme, conflict occurs between such units as quasi groups and conflict groups in equally vague ICAs. In Coser's portrayal, parties and groups are the units in conflict, although his essays often deal with explicit empirical referents.

Leaving the units vague has the virtue of making theory abstract and hence applicable to all social units, from individuals to nation-states. Thus, theoretical statements can potentially be more powerful, explaining conflict among all social forms. On the other hand, I see it as likely that the type of the unit does influence the nature of the conflict. Conflict between individuals and nations may have certain common properties and thus be subsumable under some general laws, but there are also likely to be clear differences in conflict between such disparate units.

The failure to address this issue has, I believe, given conflict sociology a bipolarity: On the one hand, there are numerous abstract schemes, such as Dahrendorf's and Coser's, that seek to uncover basic laws of conflict among a wide variety of social units. On the other hand, there are numerous middle-range theories of international, interpersonal, racial, class, sexual, religious, ethnic, organizational, community, and occupational conflict, to name just a few empirical areas where research and theory on conflict are prominent.

Recognizing this polarity, a number of theorists have sought to isolate those basic units that might reveal their own laws of conflict. For example, Dahrendorf's work posits conflict between and within five different levels of organization: roles, groups, sectors, societies, and suprasocietal units.[22] Other classifications, such as one by Johan Galtung, distinguish conflicts between and within just two levels: the individual and the collective.[23] In this scheme, intrapersonal and interpersonal conflicts are presumed to be of a different nature than intranational and international ones. In turn, intrapersonal (within a person) differ from interpersonal (between person) conflicts, and intranational (within society) and international (between societies) reveal fundamental differences.

At present, then, conflict theory has yet to agree on how conflict varies among different types of units. Yet I note that conflict theory has at least addressed the issue of units. Sociological theory has rarely con-

---

[22]These distinctions are made in Dahrendorf's untranslated work. Cited in Robert C. Angel's "The Sociology of Human Conflict," *The Nature of Human Conflict,* ed. E. McNeil (Englewood Cliffs, N.J.: Prentice-Hall, 1965), p. 14.

[23]Johan Galtung, "Institutionalized Conflict Resolution: A Theoretical Paradigm," *Journal of Peace Research* 2 (1965), pp. 348-96.

cerned itself with how social relations vary with different types of units. For example, Parsonian functionalism developed an elaborate conceptual scheme around processes occurring in one type of unit—the social system—which could be anything from a small group to a system of societies. Little attention was devoted to indicate how social processes varied with different types of social units.

As conflict theorists begin to define conflict more explicitly and to develop theories that distinguish among phenomena denoted by such labels as fights, games, war, revolution, competitions, and disputes, I think that the units of analysis will become more relevant. For I believe that the type of conflict will vary with the type of unit. Or at least, certain types of units will be found to be more likely to engage in one type of conflict than in another. For example, a fight may be an interpersonal conflict, whereas a revolution is a type of conflict among other types of social units, such as social classes. Until these kinds of problems in distinguishing types of units and types of conflicts are resolved, conflict theory will tend to remain somewhat vague. Coser's and Dahrendorf's schemes illustrate this fact, for although I see them both as highly insightful, they are nonetheless vague.[24]

## Escape from Functionalism?

In addition to my comments earlier, a number of recent commentaries have sought to document the implicit functionalism in conflict theory.[25] Such functional imagery is, of course, explicit in the conflict functionalism of Lewis Coser. In asserting an implicit functionalism in conflict theory, the charge is made that end states or the consequences of conflict often take analytical precedence over the causes of conflict. This charge is, I can imagine, particularly bothersome to dialectical theorists who have sought to take sociology out of its functional utopia. And yet, I think that it has the ring of truth.

There can be little doubt that the consequences of conflict are given prominent attention by theorists. The issue of whether or not this emphasis on consequences distorts analysis is, however, less clear. In Figure 8-1, I have presented the over-all causal imagery in Dahrendorf's and Coser's analysis, as well as in the analyses of most conflict theorists.

---

[24]Lest there be a misunderstanding, I should emphasize that this point is not intended as a critique of highly abstract conflict schemes. Indeed, these tend to be far superior to the lower-level empirical analyses, which abound in the literature. But the schemes of Coser, Dahrendorf, Williams, Gamson, Gurr, and others are now sufficiently developed that unit of analysis questions can be profitably addressed.

[25]Arthur L. Stinchcombe, *Constructing Social Theories* (New York: Harcourt Brace Jovanovich, 1968), p. 94; Piotr Sztompka, *System and Function: Toward a Theory of Society* (New York: Academic Press, 1974).

**FIGURE 8-1**    Overall Causal Imagery of Conflict Theory

I think it evident from Figure 8-1 and my discussion in these last two chapters that conflict theory emphasizes inequality as the ultimate source of conflict. Under varying conditions, which differ in each theory, inequality causes conflict, which then, under differing conditions, changes the organization of the social system. The feedback arrow at the top of the figure underscores the dialectical assumption that reorganization of the system sets off the conflict-producing process again. This sequence is unending, because social systems are always assumed to reveal inherent conflict-producing tendencies. As is obvious, of course, dialectical and functional conflict theories focus on different types of conflict and on varying forms of system reorganization. Dialectical theories concentrate on more severe and violent conflicts causing redistribution of resources into a new pattern of inequality that, in turn, will cause a new wave of conflict and resource distribution. In contrast, functional theories focus on less severe and violent conflicts and on their consequences for promoting integration within and between conflict parties and for increasing overall system adaptability and flexibility.

Both dialectical and functional conflict theories, then, are not merely interested in what causes conflict. They are also interested in what conflict *does for the systemic whole* in which it occurs. Conflict is both a dependent variable—that is, a process caused by other forces—and an independent variable—that is, a process that causes alterations in still other processes. This distinction between conflict as a dependent and independent variable is not always clear, however. It appears to me that theorists' desire to present social organization as either constantly in change or in adaptive upgrading obscures the causes of conflict. Conflict is seen to emerge and cause changes, but theories sometimes fail to specify what kind of conflict revealing what properties causes what alterations in what subsystems or systemic wholes.

This problem is compounded by the failure to define conflict and to specify what conflict units are involved in what kinds of conflict. The result is a vagueness about what conflict theorists are trying to explain: the causes of different forms of conflict or the social functions of ill-defined conflict processes? The simple answer to these questions about the causes or consequences of conflict is that both are being explained. Yet, as with all other forms of functionalism, the desire to explain the functions of a social phenomenon—whether it be conflict, religion, or a mechanism of social control—sometimes leads theorists to short-circuit the explanation of what caused the phenomena in the first place. Coser and Dahrendorf do provide suggestive causal statements, but their analysis of functions also appears to be obscured by their desires to demonstrate the system change and system integration consequences of conflict, respectively.

Thus, conflict theorists must, I feel, be more explicit in deciding if conflict is to be an independent, intervening, or dependent variable in their theoretical schemes. And as a variable, I think that they will then ask the interesting theoretical questions: What are its varying states and what causes these varying states? And what variations in other social processes and structures do these varying states of conflict cause?

For behind these questions is, I sense, the more fundamental issue of sorting out causes and consequences—the problem that has always plagued functionalism (see Chapters 2–5). To delineate the causes of varying types of conflicts is a much easier task than specifying what they do for system parts and systemic wholes. For example, it might be possible to document the causes of violent revolution between social classes, but to assess what this revolution did for the social whole can prove illusive. What the violence brought in the first week is different from the first year, and the first year's results will differ, in all probability, from the first decade. Or what were the consequences of the revolution for what units—individuals, classes, political parties, the integration of the nation, international affairs, and so on for any conceivable system referent? Thus, the scope, the time, and the structures influenced by a particular conflict present problems of analysis—problems that inhere in a functional orientation.

In sum, then, I see these three problems—the definition of conflict, the units of conflict, and the confusion over causes and functions—as presenting a challenge to conflict theory. Theorists must first decide what is and what is not conflict. If the definition remains too broad, then almost any social process can be labeled conflict, since all that must be revealed is a hint of antagonism, psychological hostility, frustration, dissent, or any of the hundreds of terms currently subsumed under this concept. Theorists will also have to decide on the scope and level of abstraction of their theories. Are they seeking to develop general laws that can subsume all the more specific conflict processes in the world? Or are they attempting to develop a more middle-range theory about a specific type of conflict—if so, what type of conflict among what types of units? And finally, theorists must make clear what they are seeking to do: explain the causes or functions of conflict? As Durkheim emphasized, causal and functional analysis are separate tasks. It is unlikely, as the deficiencies in Durkheim's, Malinowski's, Parsons's, and Merton's theories underscore, that one theory can do both a causal and functional analysis. Hence, it is in the context of these unresolved problems, I feel, that the future of conflict theory resides.

# CHAPTER 9

# The Critical Theorizing of Jurgen Habermas

As I emphasized in Chapter 6 on the origins of conflict theorizing, the emancipatory theme in Karl Marx's thought has been carried over into this century in a number of guises, one of which is critical theory.[1] Such theorizing is explicitly evaluational in that it sees as its purpose the emancipation of individuals from domination. However, as I also mentioned in Chapter 6, the first generation of critical theorists confronted a modern world that did not appear rife with emancipatory potential. Indeed, Max Weber's analysis of rationalization and the extension of bureaucratic systems of control into ever more spheres of life seemed to be a more apt prognosis of the future than Marx's utopian dream.

Thus, the first generation of critical theorists, who are frequently referred to as the Frankfurt School because of their location in Germany and their explicit interdisciplinary effort to interpret the oppressive events of the 20th century, confronted a real dilemma: how to reconcile Marx's

---

[1]Some basic reviews and analyses of critical theory and sociology include: Paul Connerton, ed., *Critical Sociology* (New York: Penguin Books, 1970); Raymond Geuss, *The Idea of a Critical Theory* (New York: Cambridge University Press, 1981); David Held, *Introduction to Critical Theory* (Berkeley, Calif.: University of California Press, 1980); Trent Schroyer, *The Critique of Domination: The Origins and Development of Critical Theory* (New York: George Braziller, Inc., 1973); Albrecht Wellmer, *Critical Theory of Society* (New York: Seabury Press, 1974); Ellsworth R. Fuhrman and William E. Snizek, "Some Observations on the Nature and Content of Critical Theory," *Humboldt Journal of Social Relations* 7 (Fall-Winter 1979- 80), pp. 33–51; Zygmunt Bauman, *Towards a Critical Sociology* (Boston: Routledge & Kegan Paul, 1976); Robert J. Antonio, "The Origin, Development, and Contemporary Status of Critical Theory," *The Sociological Quarterly* 24 (Summer 1983), pp. 325–51; Jim Faught, "Objective Reason and the Justification of Norms," *California Sociologist* 4 (Winter 1981), pp. 33-53.

emancipatory dream with the stark reality of modern society as conceptualized by Weber.[2] Indeed, when the Frankfurt Institute for Social Research was founded in 1923, there seemed little reason to be optimistic about developing a theoretically informed program for freeing people from unnecessary domination. The defeat of the left-wing working-class movements, the rise of fascism in the aftermath of World War I, and the degeneration of the Russian Revolution into Stalinism had, by the 1930s, made it clear that Marx's analysis needed drastic revision. Moreover, the expansion of the state, the spread of bureaucracy, and the emphasis on means-ends rationality through the application of science and technology all signaled that Weber's analysis had to be confronted.

The members of the Frankfurt School wanted to maintain Marx's notion of praxis—that is, a blending of theory and action or the use of theory to stimulate action, and vice versa. And they wanted theory to expose oppression and to propose less constrictive options. Yet, they were confronted with the spread of political and economic domination. Thus, the development of modern critical theory in sociology was born in a time when there was little reason to be optimistic about realizing emancipatory goals.

Three members of the Frankfurt School are most central: George Lukács, Max Horkheimer, and Theodor Adorno.[3] Lukács's major work appeared in the 1920s,[4] whereas Horkheimer[5] and Adorno[6] were active well into the 1960s. In many ways, I view Lukács as the key link in the transition from Marx and Weber to modern critical theory, for Horkheimer and Adorno were reacting to much of Lukács's analysis and approach.

---

[2]For descriptions of this activity, see Martin Jay, *The Dialectical Imagination* (Boston: Little, Brown, 1973) and "The Frankfurt School's Critique of Marxist Humanism," *Social Research* 39 (1972), pp. 285–305; David Held, *Introduction to Critical Theory*, pp. 29–110; Robert J. Antonio, "The Origin, Development, and Contemporary Status of Critical Theory," *The Sociological Quarterly* 24 (Summer 1983), pp. 325–51; Phil Slater, *Origin and Significance of The Frankfurt School* (London: Routledge & Kegan Paul, 1977).

[3]Other prominent members included: Friedrich Pollock (economist), Erich Fromm (psychoanalyst, social psychologist), Franz Neumann (political scientist), Herbert Marcuse (philosopher), and Leo Loenthal (sociologist). During the Nazi years, the school relocated in America, and many of its members never returned to Germany.

[4]George Lukács, *History and Class Consciousness* (Cambridge, Mass.: MIT Press, 1968; originally published in 1922).

[5]Max Horkheimer, *Critical Theory: Selected Essays* (New York: Herder and Herder, 1972) is a translation of essays written in German in the 1930s and 1940s; *Eclipse of Reason* (New York: Oxford University Press in 1947; reprinted by Seabury Press in 1974) was the only book by Horkheimer originally published in English. It takes a slightly different turn than earlier works, but it does present ideas that emerged from his association with Theodor Adorno; and *Critique of Instrumental Reason* (New York: Seabury Press, 1974). See David Held, *Introduction to Critical Theory*, pp. 489–91 for a more complete listing of Horkheimer's works in German.

[6]Theodor W. Adorno, *Negative Dialectics* (New York: Seabury Press, 1973; originally published 1966); and with Max Horkheimer, *Dialectic of Enlightenment* (New York: Herder and Herder, 1972; originally published in 1947). See Held, *Introduction to Critical Theory*, pp. 485–87 for a more complete listing of his works.

All of these scholars are important for the purposes of this chapter because they directly influenced the intellectual development and subsequent work of Jurgen Habermas, the most prolific contemporary critical theorist. Thus, to appreciate fully the nature of critical theory in general and Habermas' work in particular, I will briefly examine Lukács's, Horkheimer's, and Adorno's ideas and how Habermas interpreted and reacted to them.[7] Then, I will move directly into a more detailed review and analysis of Habermas's work as it has developed over the last decades.

## EARLY CRITICAL THEORY: LUKÁCS, HORKHEIMER, ADORNO

In Habermas's eyes, George Lukács blended Marx and Weber together by seeing a convergence of Marx's ideas about commodification of social relations through money and markets with Weber's thesis about the penetration of rationality into ever more spheres of modern life. Borrowing from Marx's analysis of the "fetishism of commodities," Lukács employed the concept of "reification" to denote the process by which social relationships become "objects" that can be manipulated, bought, and sold. Then, reinterpreting Weber's notion of "rationalization" to mean a growing emphasis on the process of "calculation" of exchange values, Lukács combined Weber's and Marx's analysis. As traditional societies change, he argued, there is less reliance on moral standards and processes of communication to achieve societal integration; instead, there is more utilization of money, markets, and rational calculations. As a result, relations are coordinated by exchange values and by people seeing each other as "things."[8]

As Habermas contends, Lukács painted himself into a conceptual corner: if indeed such is the historical process, how is it to be stopped? Lukács's answer is to resurrect Hegel and "stand him back on his feet" in opposition to Marx's effort to "stand Hegel on his head." That is, rather than look to contradictions in material conditions—economic and political forces—one must examine the dialectical forces inherent in human consciousness. For there are limits, Lukács argued, to how much reification and rationalization people will endure. There is an inner quality in human subjects that keeps rationalization from completely taking over.[9]

---

[7]Chapter 4, "From Lukács to Adorno: Rationalization as Reification," pp. 339-99 in Jurgen Habermas, *The Theory of Communicative Action*, vol. 1 (Boston: Beacon Press, 1984) contains Habermas's critique of Lukács, Horkheimer, and Adorno.

[8]Lukács, *History and Class Consciousness*.

[9]Ibid., pp. 89-102. In a sense, Lukács becomes another "Young Hegelian" whom Marx would have criticized. Yet, in Marx's own analysis, he sees alienation, per se, as producing resistance by workers to further alienation by the forces of production. This is the image that Lukács seems to take from Marx.

This emphasis on the process of consciousness is very much a part of critical theory that borrows much from the early Marx[10] and that, at the Frankfurt School, had a heavy dose of Freud and psychoanalytic theory. But as Habermas was to emphasize, early critical theory was too subjectivist and failed to analyze intersubjectivity, or the ways people interact through mutually shared conscious activity. Emphasizing the inherent resistance of subjects to their total reification, Lukács could only propose that the critical theorist's role is to expose reification at work by analyzing the historical processes that have dehumanized people. As a consequence, Lukács made critical theory highly contemplative, emphasizing that the solution to the problem of domination resides in making people more aware and conscious of their situation through a detailed, historical analysis of reification.

Both Horkheimer and Adorno were highly suspicious of Lukács's Hegelian solution to the dilemma of reification and rationalization. These processes do not imply their own critique, as Hegel would have suggested. Subjective consciousness and material reality cannot be separated. Consciousness does not automatically offer resistance to those material forces that commodify, reify, and rationalize it. Critical theory must, therefore, actively seek to (1) describe historical forces that dominate human freedom and (2) expose ideological justifications of these forces. Such is to be achieved through interdisciplinary research among variously trained researchers and theorists who confront each others' ideas and use this dialogue to analyze concrete social conditions and to propose courses of ameliorative action. This emphasis on praxis—the confrontation between theory and action in the world—involves the development of ideas about what oppresses and what to do about it in the course of human struggles. As Horkheimer argued: "[The] value of theory is not decided alone by the formal criteria of truth ... but by its connection with tasks, which in the particular historical moment are taken up by progressive social forces.[11] Such critical theory is, Horkheimer claimed, guided by a "particular practical interest" in the emancipation of people from class domination.[12] Thus, critical theory is tied, in a sense that Marx might have appreciated, to people's practical interests.

As Adorno and Horkheimer interacted and collaborated, their positions converged (although by the late 1950s and early 1960s, Horkheimer had seemingly rejected much of his earlier work). Adorno was, in my eyes,

---

[10]Karl Marx and Friedrich Engels, *The German Ideology* (New York: International Publishers, 1947; originally written in 1846).

[11]Max Horkheimer, "Zum Rationalismusstreit in der gegenwartigen Philosophe," originally published in 1935, reprinted in *Kritische Theorie*, vol. 1, ed. A. Schmidt (Frankfurt: Fischer Verlag, 1968), pp. 146-7. This and volume 2, by the way, represent a compilation of many of Horkheimer's essays while at the Institute in Frankfurt.

[12]Habermas is to take up this idea, but he will extend it in several ways.

more philosophical and research oriented than Horkheimer; his empirical work on "the authoritarian personality" had a major impact on research in sociology and psychology, but I think that his theoretical impact came from his collaboration with Horkheimer and, in many ways, through Horkheimer's singled authored work.[13] Adorno was very pessimistic about the chances of critical theory making great changes, although his essays were designed to expose patterns of recognized and unrecognized domination of individuals by social and psychological forces. At best, his "negative dialectics" could allow humans to "tread water" until historical circumstances were more favorable to emancipatory movements. The goal of negative dialectics is to sustain a constant critique of ideas, conceptions, and conditions. This critique cannot by itself change anything, for it occurs only on the plane of ideas and concepts. But it can keep ideological dogmatisms from obscuring conditions that might eventually allow for emancipatory action.

I have not done justice to either Horkheimer or Adorno, but my goal is not to summarize their ideas in total, but only those portions to which Jurgen Habermas reacted. Both Horkheimer and Adorno emphasized that humans' "subjective side" is restricted by the spread of rationalization. In conceptualizing this process, they created a kind of dualism between the subjective world and the realm of material objects, seeing the latter as working to oppress the former. And so, from their viewpoint, critical theory must expose this dualism; and it must see how this invasion of "instrumental reason" (means-ends rationality)[14] has invaded the human spirit. In this way, some resistance can be offered to these oppressive forces.

Habermas sees this kind of philosophical analysis—even with the caveats to praxis—as terribly vague, excessively contemplative, and amazingly detached from what people actually do when they interact and use their conscious faculties.[15] Such critical theory is also fatalistic, seeing the forces of production as immobilizing the forces of subjective consciousness and ameliorative action. What Habermas proposes, then, is a shift in orientation away from the subjective consciousness of the individual to the processes by which humans create *inter*subjective understandings and to the processes by which they actually coordinate their actions. For if there is oppression and domination, it can only be relieved by understanding the specific mechanisms that integrate societies. For to change a society requires detailed insight into what binds it together. And

---

[13]Theodor W. Adorno, et al., *The Authoritarian Personality* (New York: Harper & Row, 1950).

[14]Means-ends rationality is action designed to use the most efficient means to achieve stated ends or goals. For Max Weber's use of this concept, see Chapter 6.

[15]Habermas, *The Theory of Communicative Action*, vol. 1, Chapter 4.

so, it is in the analysis of these integrating processes that critical theory can propose realistic emancipatory solutions.

# THE CRITICAL APPROACH OF JURGEN HABERMAS

Jurgen Habermas has been an enormously productive scholar in the past two decades. This fact makes it difficult to summarize his work in a simple way. Moreover, to be kind about the matter, Habermas's style of exposition is somewhat dense. Part of this denseness is his style of prose,[16] but much of it is Habermas's Germanic approach, which involves an effort to analyze all the relevant viewpoints on a topic before he presents his case. As a result, Habermas's main line of argument is often buried in tangential analyses of scholars and issues that he perceives to be relevant and essential to his point.[17] Consequently, there are varying interpretations of Habermas's views; and I suspect that in working through his work, I may misinterpret him. This danger of misinterpretation is particularly acute because I will try to extract the central themes from a conceptual scheme that has evolved and changed over the years. Yet, I see a certain continuity in the argument; and it is this aspect of his work that I will emphasize.

## The Central Problem of Critical Theory

Underlying Habermas's work, I believe, are a series of unarticulated questions. These include: (1) How is social theory to develop ideas that keep Karl Marx's emancipatory project alive and, yet at the same time, recognize the empirical inadequacy of his prognosis for advanced capitalist societies? (2) How is social theory to confront Max Weber's historical analysis of rationalization[18] in a way that avoids his pessimism and thereby keeps Marx's emancipatory goals at the center of theory? (3) How is social theory to avoid the retreat into subjectivism of earlier critical theorists, such as Lukács, Horkheimer, and Adorno, who increasingly focused on states of subjective consciousness *within individuals* and, as a consequence, lost Marx's insight that society is constructed from, and must therefore be emancipated in terms of, the processes that sustain *social relations among* individuals? (4) How is social theory to conceptualize and develop a theory that reconciles the forces of material production and political organization with the forces of intersubjectivity among reflective and conscious individuals in such a way that it avoids (*a*) Weber's

---

[16]Indeed, the English translations of his work are difficult, but the German versions are even worse. Translators consistently improve Habermas's prose, but it still remains highly obscure.

[17]In some ways, I find these tangents more interesting than the main argument.

[18]That is, the spread of means-end rationality into ever more spheres of life.

pessimism about the domination of consciousness by rational economic and political forces? (*b*) Marx's naive optimism about inevitability of class consciousness and revolt? and (*c*) Early critical theorists' retreat into the subjectivism of Hegel's dialectic, where oppression mysteriously mobilizes its negation through increases in subjective consciousnesses and resistance?

At different points in his career, Habermas focused on one or the other of these questions, but my sense is that all four have always guided his approach, at least implicitly. Habermas has been accused of abandoning the critical thrust of his earlier works, but I think that this conclusion is incorrect. For in trying to answer these questions, he has increasingly recognized that mere critique of oppression is not enough. Such critique becomes a "reified object itself"; and although early critical theorists knew this, they never developed conceptual schemes that accounted for the underlying dynamics of societies. For critique to be useful in liberating people from domination, it is necessary, Habermas seems to say, for the critique to be couched in terms of the fundamental processes that integrate social systems. In this way, the critique has some possibility for suggesting ways to create new types of social relations. Without theoretical understanding of how society works, critique is only superficial debunking and becomes an exercise in futility. It is this willingness to theorize about the underlying dynamics of society, to avoid the retreat into subjectivism, to reject superficial criticism and, instead, to base critique on reasoned theoretical analysis and to incorporate ideas from many diverse theoretical approaches that makes Habermas's work theoretically significant.

In presenting his ideas, I will briefly summarize his earlier works, showing how they have culminated in the synthesis of his ideas in the two-volume work *The Theory of Communicative Action.*[19]

## Habermas's Analysis of "The Public Sphere"[20]

In his first major publication, *Structural Transformation of the Public Sphere,* Habermas traces the evolution and dissolution of what he termed *the public sphere.*[21] This sphere is a realm of social life where people can bring up matters of general interest; where they can discuss and debate these issues without recourse to custom, dogma, and force; and where they can resolve differences of opinion by rational argument. To say the least, I find this conception of a public sphere as rather romanticized, but the imagery of free and open discussion that is resolved by rational argumentation becomes a central theme in Habermas's subsequent approach.

---

[19]Habermas, *The Theory of Communicative Action.*

[20]Some useful reviews and critiques of Habermas's work include: John B. Thompson and David Held, eds., *Habermas: Critical Debates* (London: Macmillan Press LTD, 1982); David Held, *An Introduction to Critical Theory,* chapters 9–12.

[21]Jurgen Habermas, *Struckturwandel der Offentlichkeit* (Neuwied: Luchterhand, 1962).

Increasingly throughout his career, Habermas sees emancipation from domination as possible through "communicative action," which is a reincarnation of the public sphere in more conceptual clothing.

In this early work, however, Habermas appears more interested in history and views the emergence of the public sphere as occurring in the 18th century, when various forums for public debate—clubs, cafés, journals, newspapers—proliferated. He concludes that these forums helped erode the basic structure of feudalism, which is legitimated by religion and custom rather than by agreements that have been reached through public debate and discourse. The public sphere was greatly expanded, Habermas argues, by the extension of market economies and the resulting liberation of the individual from the constraints of feudalism. Free citizens, property holders, traders, merchants, and members of other new sectors in society could now be actively concerned about the governance of society and could openly discuss and debate issues. But, in a vein similar to Weber's analysis of rationalization, Habermas argues that the public sphere was eroded by some of the very forces that stimulated its expansion. As market economies experience instability, the powers of the state are extended in an effort to stabilize the economy; and with the expansion of bureaucracy to ever more contexts of social life, the public sphere is constricted. And increasingly, the state seeks to redefine problems as technical and soluble by technologies and administrative procedures rather than by public debate and argumentation.

The details of this argument are less important, I think, than the fact that this work established Habermas's credentials as a critical theorist. All the key elements of critical theory are there—the decline of freedom with the expansion of capitalism and the bureaucratized state; and the seeming power of the state to construct and control social life. The solution to these problems is to resurrect the public sphere, but how is this to be done in light of the growing power of the state? Thus, in this early work, I see Habermas as having painted himself into the same conceptual corner as his teachers in the Frankfurt School. The next phase of his work extends this critique of capitalist society, but it also tries to redirect critical theory so that it does not have to retreat into the contemplative subjectivism of Lukács, Horkheimer, and Adorno. He begins this project in the late 1960s with an analysis of knowledge systems and critique of science.

## The Critique of Science

In his *The Logic of the Social Sciences*[22] and *Knowledge and Human Interest*,[23] Habermas analyzes systems of knowledge in an effort to elaborate

---

[22]Jurgen Habermas, *Zur Logik der Sozialwissenschaften* (Frankfurt: Suhrkamp, 1970).
[23]Jurgen Habermas, *Knowledge and Human Interest*, trans. J. Shapiro (London: Hei-

a framework for critical theory. The ultimate goal of this analysis is to establish the fact that science is but one type of knowledge that exists in order to meet only one set of human interests. To realize this goal, Habermas posits three basic types of knowledge that encompass the full range of human reason: (1) There is *empirical-analytic* knowledge, which are those types of knowledge concerned with understanding the lawful properties of the material world. (2) There is *hermeneutic-historical* knowledge, which is devoted to understanding of meanings, especially through the interpretations of historical texts. And (3) there is *critical* knowledge, which is devoted to uncovering conditions of constraint and domination. These three types of knowledge reflect three basic types of human interests: (1) a *technical* interest in the reproduction of existence through control of the environment, (2) a *practical* interest in understanding the meaning of situations, and (3) an *emancipatory* interest in freedom for growth and improvement. Such interests do not reside in individuals, but in more general imperatives for reproduction, meaning, and freedom that presumably are built into the species as it has become organized into societies. These three interests create, therefore, three types of knowledge. The interest in material reproduction has produced science or empirical/analytic knowledge; the interest in understanding of meaning has led to the development of hermeneutic/historical knowledge; and the interest in freedom has required the development of critical theory.

These interests in technical control, practical understanding, and emancipation generate different types of knowledge through three types of media: (1) "work" for realizing interests in technical control through the development of empirical/analytic knowledge; (2) "language" for realizing practical interests in understanding through hermeneutic knowledge; and (3) "authority" for realizing interests in emancipation through the development of critical theory. There is a kind of functionalism in this analysis: needs for "material survival and social reproduction," for "continuity of society through interpretive understanding," and for "utopian fulfillment" create interests. Then, through the media of work, language, and authority, these needs produce three types of knowledge: the scientific, hermeneutical, and critical.

This kind of typologizing is, of course, reminiscent of Weber and Parsons; and in many ways it is even more vague than Parsons's typologizing. Nonetheless, it is the vehicle through which Habermas makes the central point: positivism and the search for natural laws is only one type of knowledge, although the historical trend has been for the empir-

---

nemann, 1970; originally published in German in 1968). The basic ideas in *Zur Logik der Sozialwissenschaften* and *Knowledge and Human Interest* were stated in Habermas's inaugural lecture at the University of Frankfurt in 1965 and were first published in "Knowledge and Interest," *Inquiry* 9 (1966), pp. 285–300.

---

**FIGURE 9-1**  Types of Knowledge, Interests, Media (and Functional Needs)

| Functional Needs | Interests | Knowledge | Media |
|---|---|---|---|
| Material survival and social reproduction generates pressures for: | technical control of environment, which leads to the development of: | empirical/analytic knowledge, which is achieved through: | work. |
| Continuity of social relations generates pressures for: | practical understanding through interpretations of others' subjective states, which leads to development of: | hermeneutic and historical knowledge, which is achieved through: | language. |
| Desires for utopian fulfillment generates pressures for: | emancipation from unnecessary domination, which leads to development of: | critical theory, which is achieved through: | authority. |

---

ical/analytic to dominate the other two types of knowledge. Thus, interests in technical control through work and the development of science have dominated the interests in understanding and emancipation. And so, if social life seems meaningless and cold, it is because technical interests in producing science have come to dictate what kind of knowledge is permissible and legitimate. Thus, Weber's "rationalization thesis" is restated with the typological distinction among interest, knowledge, and media. There is, I should emphasize again, an implicit functionalism here: two sets of universal functional needs—for "continuity through interpretive understanding" and for "utopian fulfillment"—are not being met by virtue of the ascendancy of concern with practical interests. And by implication, then, one of the underlying causes of the problems in advanced capitalism is the failure to meet the functional needs of Habermas' implicit functionalism. I will not pursue this point further, but it is worth considering. I have summarized Habermas' excessive typological argument in Figure 9-1. I have, however, revised it somewhat in order to make the argument clear.

This typology allows Habermas to achieve several goals. First, he can attack the assumption that science is value free because, like all knowledge, it is attached to a set of interests. Second, he can revise the Weberian thesis of rationalization in such a way that it dictates a renewed emphasis on hermeneutics and criticism. For it is these other two types of knowledge that are being driven out by empirical/analytic knowledge, or science. Therefore, it is necessary to re-emphasize these neglected types of knowledge. Third, he can justify certain topic areas that come to consume his work. Let me elaborate on this last point.

By viewing positivism in the social sciences as type of empirical/
analytic knowledge, Habermas can associate it with human interests in
technical control. He can, therefore, visualize social science as a tool of
economic and political interests. Science thus becomes an ideology, and
in fact, Habermas sees it as the underlying cause of the legitimation crises
of advanced capitalist societies (more on this shortly). In dismissing positivism in this way, he can orient his own project to hermeneutics with
a critical twist. That is, he can visualize the major task of critical theory
as the analysis of those processes by which people achieve interpretative
understanding of each other in ways that give social life a sense of continuity. Increasingly, Habermas has come to focus on the communicative
processes among actors as the theoretical core for critical theorizing. Goals
of emancipation cannot be realized without knowledge about how people
interact and communicate. Such an emphasis represents a restatement
in a new guise of Habermas's early analysis of the public sphere, but now
the process of public discourse and debate is viewed as the essence of
human interaction in general. Moreover, to understand interaction, it is
necessary to analyze language and linguistic processes among individuals.
Knowledge of these processes can, in turn, give critical theory a firm
conceptual basis from which to launch a critique of society and to suggest
paths for the emancipation of individuals. Yet, to justify this emphasis
on hermeneutics and criticism, Habermas must first analyze the crises of
capitalist societies in terms of the overextension of empirical/analytic
systems of knowledge.

## Legitimation Crises in Society

As Habermas's earlier work had argued, there are several historical trends
in modern societies: (1) the decline of the public sphere, (2) the increasing
intervention of the state into the economy, and (3) the growing dominance
of science in the service of the state's interests in technical control. These
ideas are woven together in *Legitimation Crisis,* which I see as a further
critique of capitalist society and positivistic science.[24] But in locating the
crises of capitalist society in the ascendance of interests in technical
control, Habermas can justify his own critical project, especially as it
takes a hermeneutic turn—that is, as it moves toward an analysis of the
processes by which actors interpret each others' subjective states.

The basic argument in *Legitimation Crisis* is that as the state increasingly intervenes in the economy, it also seeks to translate political
issues into "technical problems." Issues are not topics for public debate,
but rather, they represent technical problems that require the use of technologies by experts in bureaucratic organizations. As a result, there is a

---

[24]Jurgen Habermas, *Legitimation Crisis*, trans. T. McCarthy (London: Heinemann, 1976;
originally published in German in 1973).

"depoliticization" of practical issues by redefining them as technical problems. To do this, the state propagates a "technocratic consciousness" that, to Habermas, represents a new kind of ideology. Unlike previous ideologies, however, it does not promise a future utopia, but like other ideologies it is seductive in its ability to veil problems, to simplify perceived options, and to justify a particular way of organizing social life. At the core of this technocratic consciousness is an emphasis on "instrumental reason," or what Weber termed *means-ends rationality*. That is, criteria of the efficiency of means in realizing explicit goals increasingly come to guide evaluations of social action and people's approach to problems. This emphasis on instrumental reason operates to displace other types of action, such as behaviors oriented to mutual understanding. This displacement occurs in a series of stages: science is first used by the state to realize specific goals; then, the criterion of efficiency is used by the state to reconcile competing goals of groupings; next, basic cultural values are themselves assessed and evaluated in terms of their efficiency and rationality; and finally, in Habermas's version of *Brave New World,* decisions are completely delegated to computers, which seek the most rational and efficient course of action.

This reliance on the ideology of technocratic consciousnesses creates, Habermas argues, new dilemmas of political legitimation. For Habermas, capitalist societies can be divided into three basic subsystems: (1) the economic, (2) the politico-administrative, and (3) the cultural (what he later calls *lifeworld*). From this division of societies into these subsystems, Habermas then posits four points of crises: (1) an "economic crisis" occurs if the economic subsystem cannot generate sufficient productivity to meet people's needs; (2) a "rationality crisis" exists when the politico-administrative subsystem cannot generate a sufficient number of instrumental decisions; (3) a "motivation crisis" exists when actors cannot use cultural symbols to generate sufficient meaning for them to feel committed to participate fully in the society; and (4) a "legitimation crisis" arises when actors do not possess the "requisite number of generalized motivations" or diffuse commitments to the political subsystem's right to make decisions. Much of this analysis of crises is couched in Marxian terms but emphasizes that economic and rationality crises are perhaps less important than either motivational or legitimation crisis. For as technocratic consciousness penetrates all spheres of social life and creates productive economies as well as an intrusive state, the crisis tendencies of late capitalism shift from the inability to produce sufficient economic goods or political decisions to the failure to generate (*a*) diffuse commitments to political processes and (*b*) adequate levels of meaning among individual actors.

I have, of course, simplified Habermas's argument, but my main intent is only to highlight those aspects of his work that become prominent in his most recent theoretical synthesis. In *Legitimation Crisis* is an early form of what becomes an important distinction: "systemic" processes revolving around the economy and politico-administrative apparatus of the state must be distinguished from "cultural" processes. This distinction will later be conceptualized as *system* and *lifeworld,* respectively, but the central point is this: in tune with his Frankfurt School roots, Habermas is shifting emphasis from Marx's analysis of the economic crisis of production to crises of meaning and commitment; and if the problems or crises of capitalist societies are in these areas, then critical theory must focus on the communicative and interactive processes by which humans generate understandings and meanings among themselves. For if instrumental reason, or means-ends rationality, is driving out action based on mutual understanding and commitment, then the goal of critical theory is to expose this trend and to suggest ways of overcoming it, especially since legitimation and motivational crises make people aware that something is missing from their lives and, therefore, receptive to more emancipatory alternatives. And so, the task of critical theory is to develop a theoretical perspective that allows for the restructuring of meaning and commitment in social life. This goal will be realized, Habermas argues, by further understanding of how people communicate, interact, and develop symbolic meanings.

## Early Analyses of Speech and Interaction

In 1970, Habermas wrote two articles that marked a return to the idea of the public sphere, but with a new, more theoretical thrust. They also signaled an increasing emphasis on the process of speech, communication, and interaction. In his "On Systematically Distorted Communication," Habermas outlines the nature of undistorted communication.[25] True to Habermas's Weberian origins, this outline is an ideal type. The goal is to determine the essentials and essence of undistorted communication so that those processes that distort communication, such as domination, can be better exposed. What, then, are the features of undistorted communication? Habermas lists five: (1) expressions, actions, and gestures are noncontradictory; (2) communication is public and conforms to cultural standards of what is appropriate; (3) actors can distinguish between the properties of language, per se, and the events and processes that are described by language; (4) communication leads to, and is the product of, intersubjectivity, or the capacity of actors to understand each others' subjective states and to develop a sense of shared collective meanings; and (5) conceptualizations of time and space are understood by actors to mean different things when externally observed and when subjectively

---

[25]Jurgen Habermas, "On Systematically Distorted Communication," *Inquiry* 13 (1970), pp. 205–18.

experienced in the process of interaction.[26] The details of his analysis on the distortion of communication are less essential than the assertions about what critical theory must conceptualize. For Habermas, the conceptualization of undistorted communication is used as a foil for mounting a critique against those social forces that make such idealized communication difficult to realize. Moreover, as his subsequent work testifies, Habermas emphasizes condition (4), or communication and intersubjectivity among actors.

This emphasis becomes evident in his other article published in 1970, entitled "Toward a Theory of Communicative Competence."[27] Again, I do not think the details of this argument are as critical as the overall intent, especially since his ideas undergo subsequent modification. Habermas argues that for actors to be competent, they must know more than the linguistic rules of how to construct sentences and to talk; they must also master "dialogue-constitutive universals," which are part of the "social linguistic structure of society." Behind this jargon is the idea that the meaning of language and speech is contextual and that actors use implicit stores or stocks of knowledge to interpret the meaning of utterances. Habermas then proposes yet another ideal type, "the ideal speech situation," in which actors possess all of the relevant background knowledge and linguistic skills to communicate without distortion.

Thus, in the early 1970s, Habermas began to view the mission of critical theory as emphasizing the process of interaction as mediated by speech. But such speech acts draw upon stores of knowledge—rules, norms, values, tacit understandings, memory traces, and the like—for their interpretation. I see these ideals of the speech process as a restatement of the romanticized public sphere, where issues were openly debated, discussed, and rationally resolved. What Habermas has done, of course, is to restate this view of "what is good and desirable" in more theoretical and conceptual terms, although it could be argued that there is not much difference between the romanticized portrayal of the public sphere and the ideal-typical conceptualization of speech. But with this conceptualization, the goal of critical theory must be to expose those conditions that distort communication and that inhibit realization of the ideal speech situation. Habermas's utopia is thus a society where actors are able to communicate without distortion, to achieve a sense of each others' subjective states, and to openly reconcile their differences through argumentation that is free of external constraint and coercion. In other words, he wants to restore the public sphere but in a more encompassing way—that is, in people's day-to-day interactions.

---

[26]I am simplifying here. See also Jim Faught's discussion in his "Objective Reason and the Justification of Norms."

[27]Jurgen Habermas, "Toward a Theory of Communicative Competence," *Inquiry* 13 (1970), pp. 360–75.

Habermas moves in several different directions in trying to construct a rational approach for realizing this utopia. He borrows metaphorically from psychoanalytic theory as a way to uncover the distortions that inhibit open discourse,[28] but I think that this psychoanalytic journey is far less important than his growing concentration on the process of communicative action and interaction as the basis for creating a society that reduces domination and constraint. Thus, by the mid-1970s, he labeled his analysis *universal pragmatics* whose centerpiece is the "theory of communicative action."[29] I will discuss this theory in more detail shortly, but let me briefly indicate its key elements. Communication involves more than words, grammar, and syntax; it also involves what Habermas terms *validity claims.* There are three types of claims: (1) those asserting that a course of action as indicated through speech is the most effective and efficient means for attaining ends; (2) those claiming that an action is correct and proper in accordance with relevant norms; and (3) those maintaining that the subjective experiences as expressed in a speech act are sincere and authentic. All speech acts implicitly make these three claims, although a speech act may emphasize one more than the other two. Those responding to communication can accept or challenge these validity claims, and if challenged, then the actors contest, debate, criticize, and revise their communication. They use, of course, shared "stocks of knowledge" about norms, means-ends effectiveness, and sincerity to make their claims as well as to contest and revise them. This process that, I should add, restates the public sphere in yet one more guise is often usurped when claims are settled by recourse to power and authority. But if claims are settled by the "giving of reasons for" and "reasons against" the claim in a mutual give-and-take among individuals, then Habermas sees it as "rational discourse." Thus, built into the very process of interaction is the potential for rational discourse that can be used to create a more just, open, and free society. Such discourse is not merely means-ends rationality, for it involves adjudication of two other validity claims: those concerned with normative appropriateness and those with subjective sincerity. Actors thus implicitly assess and critique each other in terms of effectiveness, normative appropriateness, and sincerity of their respective speech acts; and so, the goal of critical theory is to expose those societal conditions that keep such processes from occurring for *all three types* of validity claims.

---

[28]Habermas sometimes calls this aspect of his program "depth hermeneutics." And the idea is to create a methodology of inquiry for social systems that parallels the approach of psychoanalysis—that is, dialogue, removal of barriers to understanding, analysis of underlying causal processes, and efforts to use this understanding to dissolve distortions in interaction.

[29]For an early statement, see "Some Distinctions in Universal Pragmatics: A Working Paper," *Theory and Society* 3 (1976), pp. 155-67.

In this way, Habermas has moved critical theory from Lukács's, Horkheimer's, and Adorno's emphasis on subjective consciousness to a concern with *inter*subjective consciousness and the interactive processes by which intersubjectivity is created, maintained, and changed through the validity claims in each speech act. Moreover, rather than viewing the potential for liberating alternatives as residing in subjective consciousness, Habermas can assert that emancipatory potential inheres in each and every communicative interaction. And since speech and communication are the basis of interaction and since society is ultimately sustained by interaction, the creation of less restrictive societies will come about by realizing the inherent dynamics of the communication process.

## Habermas's Reconceptualization of Social Evolution

All critical theory is historical in the sense that it tries to analyze the long-term development of oppressive arrangements in society. Indeed, as I have emphasized, the central problem of critical theory is to reconcile Marx's and Weber's respective analysis of the development of advanced capitalism. It is not surprising, therefore, that Habermas produces a historical-evolutionary analysis, but in contrast to Weber, he needs to see emancipatory potential in evolutionary trends. Yet at the same time, he needs to avoid the incorrect prognosis in Marx's analysis and to retain the emancipatory thrust of Marx's approach. Habermas's first major effort to effect this reconciliation appears in his *The Reconstruction of Historical Materialism*,[30] parts of which have been translated and appear in *Communication and the Evolution of Society*.[31]

Habermas's approach to evolution pulls together many of the themes that I have discussed above, and so, a brief review of his general argument can set the stage for an analysis of his most recent theoretical synthesis, *The Theory of Communicative Action*.[32] In many ways, Habermas reintroduces traditional functionalism into Marx's and Weber's evolutionary descriptions, but with both a phenomenological and structuralist emphasis (see chapters 14, 18, and 19). As with all functional theory, he views evolution as the process of structural differentiation and the emergence of integrative problems. He also borrows a page from Herbert Spencer, Talcott Parsons, and Niklas Luhmann when he argues that the integration of complex systems leads to an adaptive upgrading, increasing the

[30]Jurgen Habermas, *Zur Rekonstruktion des Historischen Materialismus* (Frankfurt: Suhrkamp, 1976).

[31]Jurgen Habermas, *Communication and the Evolution of Society*, trans. T. McCarthy (London: Heinemann, 1979).

[32]For an earlier statement, see Jurgen Habermas, "Towards a Reconstruction of Historical Materialism," *Theory and Society* 2 (3, 1975), pp. 84-98.

capacity of the society to cope with the environment.[33] That is, complex systems that are integrated are better adapted to their environments than less complex systems. The key issue, then, is what conditions increase or decrease integration? For without integration, differentiation produces severe problems.

Habermas's analysis of system integration is both protracted and vague; and so, I will offer only a cursory review. He argues that contained in the world views or stocks of knowledge of individual actors are learning capacities and stores of information that determine the overall learning level of a society. In turn, this learning level determines the society's steering capacity to respond to environmental problems. At times, Habermas refers to these learning levels as *organization principles.* Thus, as systems confront problems of internal integration and external contingencies, the stocks of knowledge and world views of individual actors are translated into organization principles and steering capacities, which, in turn, set limits on just how a system can respond. For example, a society with only religious mythology will be less complex and less able to respond to environmental challenges than a more complex one with large stores of technology and stocks of normative procedures determining its organization principles. But societies can "learn"[34] that when confronted with problems beyond the capacity of their current organization principles and steering mechanisms, they can draw upon the "cognitive potential" in the world views and stocks of knowledge of individuals who reorganize their actions. The result of this learning creates new levels of information that allow for the development of new organization principles for securing integration in the face of increased societal differentiation and complexity.

I have only skimmed the surface of Habermas's views, but the details are perhaps best left out since they are ambiguous. Yet, there is an implicit line of argument that I should emphasize: the basis for societal integration lies in the processes by which actors communicate and develop mutual understandings and stores of knowledge. To the extent that these interactive processes are arrested by the patterns of economic and political organization, then the society's learning capacity is correspondingly diminished. One of the main integrative problems of capitalist societies is the integration of the material forces of production (economy as administered by the state), on the one side, and the cultural stores of knowledge that are produced by communicative interaction, on the other side. Societies that differentiate materially in the economic and political realms

---

[33]He borrows from Niklas Luhmann here (see Chapter 5), although much of Habermas's approach is a reaction to Luhmann.

[34]Habermas analogizes here to Piaget's and Kohlberg's analysis of the cognitive development of children, seeing societies as able to "learn" as they become more structurally complex.

without achieving integration on a normative and cultural level (i.e., shared understandings) will remain unintegrated and experience crises.

Built into these dynamics, however, is their resolution. The processes of "communicative interaction" that produce and reproduce unifying cultural symbols must be given equal weight to the "labor" processes that generate material production and reproduction. It is at this point that Habermas develops his more synthetic approach in *The Theory of Communicative Action.*

## The Theory of Communicative Action

The two-volume *The Theory of Communicative Action* pulls together into a reasonably coherent framework various strands of Habermas's thought.[35] Yet, true to his general style of scholarship, Habermas wanders over a rather large intellectual landscape. In Thomas McCarthy's words, Habermas develops his ideas through "a somewhat unusual combination of theoretical constructions with historical reconstructions of the ideas of 'classical' social theorists."[36] Such thinkers as Marx, Weber, Durkheim, Mead, Lukács, Horkheimer, Adorno, and Parsons are, for Habermas, "still very much alive" and are treated as "virtual dialogue partners."[37] As a consequence, the two volumes meander through selected portions of various thinkers' work with an eye toward critiquing and yet utilizing key ideas. After the dust settles, however, the end result is a very creative synthesis of ideas into a critical theory.

Habermas's basic premise is summarized near the end of volume 1:

> If we assume that the human species maintains itself through the socially coordinated activities of its members and that this coordination is established through communication and in certain spheres of life, through communication aimed at reaching agreement—then the reproduction of the species also requires satisfying the conditions of a rationality inherent in communicative action.[38]

In other words, intrinsic to the process of communicative action, where actors implicitly make, challenge, and accept each others' validity

---

[35]Jurgen Habermas, *The Theory of Communicative Action,* 2 vols. Only volume 1 is, at this writing, translated. Its subtitle, *Reason and the Rationalization of Society,* gives some indication of its thrust. The translator, Thomas McCarthy, has done an excellent service in translating what is very difficult prose. Also, his "Translators Introduction" to volume 1, pp. v–xxxvii is the best summary of Habermas's recent theory that I have come across. Perhaps by the time this book is published, McCarthy will have finished the translation of volume 2. My understanding of volume 2 is limited by my lack of fluency in German, but I have waded through the text and consulted German colleagues. I would, in particular, like to thank Angscar Weyman, Universitat Bremen.

[36]Thomas McCarthy, "Translators Introduction," p. vii.

[37]Ibid.

[38]Jurgen Habermas, *The Theory of Communicative Action,* vol. 1, p. 397.

claims, resides a rationality that can potentially serve as the basis for reconstructing the social order in less oppressive ways. The first volume of *The Theory of Communicative Action* thus focuses on action and rationality in an effort to reconceptualize both processes in a manner that shifts emphasis from the subjectivity and consciousness of the individual to the process of symbolic interaction. In a sense, volume 1 is Habermas's microsociology, whereas volume 2 is his macrosociology. In this second volume, Habermas introduces the concept of system and tries to connect it to microprocesses of action and interaction through a reconceptualization of the phenomenological concept of lifeworld (see Chapters 14 and 18).

**The overall project.**     Let me begin by briefly summarizing the overall argument, and then, I will return to volumes 1 and 2 with a more detailed analysis. There are four types of action—(1) teleological, (2) normative, (3) dramaturgical, and (4) communicative. Only communicative action contains the elements whereby actors reach intersubjective understanding. Such communicative action—which is, in fact, interaction—presupposes a set of background assumptions and stocks of knowledge, or in Habermas's terms, a *lifeworld.* Also operating in any society are "system" processes, which revolve around the material maintenance of the species and its survival. The evolutionary trend is for system processes and lifeworld processes to become internally differentiated *and* differentiated from each other. The integration of a society depends upon a balance between system and lifeworld processes. As modern societies have evolved, however, this balance has been upset as system processes revolving around the economy and the state (also law, family, and other reproductive structures) have "colonized" and dominated lifeworld processes concerned with mutually shared meanings, understandings, and intersubjectivity. As a result, modern society is poorly integrated.

These integrative problems in capitalist societies are manifested in crises concerning the "reproduction of the lifeworld"; that is, the acts of communicative interaction that reproduce this lifeworld are displaced by "delinguistified media," such as money and power, that are used in the reproduction of system processes (economy and government). The solution to these crises is a rebalancing of relations between lifeworld and system. This rebalancing is to come through the resurrection of the public sphere in the economic and political arenas and in the creation of more situations where communicative action (interaction) can proceed uninhibited by the intrusion of system's media, such as power and money. The goal of critical theory is, therefore, to document those facets of society where the lifeworld has been colonized and to suggest approaches whereby situations of communicative action (interaction) can be reestablished. Such is Habermas's general argument; and now, I will fill in some of the details.

**The reconceptualization of action and rationality.** In volume 1 of *The Theory of Communicative Action*, Habermas undertakes a long and detailed analysis of Weber's conceptualization of action and rationalization. He does so because he wants to reconceptualize rationality and action in ways that allow him to view rational action as a potentially liberating rather than as an imprisoning force.[39] In this way, he feels, he can avoid the pessimism of Weber and the retreat into subjectivity by Lukács, Adorno, and Horkheimer.

Habermas argues by adding typological distinctions on top of each other, which, to say the least, makes the exposition somewhat ponderous. I will simplify a bit and discuss only the critical distinctions. There are, he concludes, several different types of action:[40]

1. *Teleological action* is behavior oriented to calculating various means and selecting the most appropriate means to realize explicit goals. Such action becomes strategic when other acting agents are involved in one's calculations. Habermas also calls this action "instrumental" because it is concerned with means to achieve ends. Most importantly, he emphasizes that this kind of action is too often considered to be "rational action" in previous conceptualizations of rationality. For as he is to argue, this view of rationality is too narrow and forces critical theory into a conceptual trap: if teleological or means-ends rationality is what has taken over the modern world and what has, as a consequence, oppressed people, then how can critical theory propose rational alternatives? Would not such a rational theory be yet one more oppressive application of means-ends rationality? The answers to these questions lie in recognizing that there are several types of action and that true rationality does not reside in teleological action, but in communicative action.

2. *Normatively regulated action* is behavior that is oriented to common values of a group. Thus, normative action is directed toward complying with normative expectations of collectively organized groupings of individuals.

3. *Dramaturgical action* is action that involves conscious manipulation of oneself before an audience or public. It is ego-centered in that it involves actors mutually manipulating their behaviors to present their own intentions, but it is also social in that such manipulation is done in the context of organized activity.

4. *Communicative action* is interaction among agents who use speech and nonverbal symbols as a way of understanding their mutual situation and their respective plans of action in order that they can agree on how to coordinate their behaviors.

---

[39]Recall that its subtitle is *Reason and The Rationalization of Society*.
[40]Jurgen Habermas, *The Theory of Communicative Action*, pp. 85–102.

These four types of action presuppose different kinds of "worlds." That is, each action is oriented to a somewhat different aspect of the universe that can be divided into the (1) "objective or external world" of manipulable objects, (2) "social world" of norms, values, and other socially recognized expectations, and (3) "subjective world" of experiences. Teleological action is concerned primarily with the objective world; normatively regulated action with the social; and dramaturgical with the subjective and external. But it is only with communicative action that actors "refer simultaneously to things in the objective, social, and subjective worlds in order to negotiate common definitions of the situation."[41]

Such communicative action is, therefore, potentially more rational than all of the others because it deals with all three worlds and because it proceeds in terms of speech acts that assert three types of validity claims. Such speech acts assert that (1) statements are true in "propositional content," or in reference to the external and objective world; (2) statements are correct with respect to the existing normative context, or social world; and (3) statements are sincere and manifest the subjective world of intention and experiences of the actor.[42] The process of communicative action in which these three types of validity claims are made, accepted, or challenged by others is inherently more rational than other types of action. For if a validity claim is not accepted, then it is debated and discussed in an effort to reach understanding without recourse to force and authority.[43] The process of reaching understanding through validity claims, their acceptance, or their discussion takes place against

> the background of a culturally ingrained preunderstanding. This background remains unproblematic as a whole; only that part of the stock of knowledge that participants make use of and thematize at a given time is put to the test. To the extent that definitions of situations are negotiated by participants *themselves*, this thematic segment of the lifeworld is at their disposal with the negotiation of each new definition of the situation.[44]

Thus, in the process of making validity claims through speech acts, actors use existing definitions of situations or create new ones that establish order to their social relations. Such definitions become part of the stocks of knowledge in their lifeworlds, and they become the standards by which validity claims are made, accepted, and challenged. Thus, in reaching an understanding through communicative action, the lifeworld serves as a point of reference for the adjudication of validity claims, which encompass the full range of worlds—the objective, social, and subjective.

---

[41]Ibid., p. 95.

[42]Ibid., p. 99.

[43]Recall Habermas's earlier discussion of nondistorted communication and the ideal speech act. This is his most recent reconceptualization of these ideas.

[44]Ibid., p. 100. Emphasis in original.

And so in Habermas's eyes, there is more rationality inherent in the very process of communicative interaction than in means-ends or teleological action.[45] As Habermas summarizes in a rare moment of succinctness:

> We have . . . characterized the rational structure of the processes of reaching understanding in terms of (a) the three world-relations of actors and the corresponding concepts of the objective, social, and subjective worlds; (b) the validity claims of propositional truth, normative rightness, and sincerity or authenticity; (c) the concept of a rationally motivated agreement, that is, one based on the intersubjective recognition of criticizable validity claims; and (d) the concept of reaching understanding as the cooperative negotiation of common definitions of the situation.[46]

Thus, as people communicatively act (interact), they use and at the same time produce common definitions of the situation. Such definitions are part of the lifeworld of a society; and if they have been produced and reproduced through the communicative action, then they are the basis for the rational and non-oppressive integration of a society. Let me now turn to Habermas's discussion of this lifeworld that serves as the "court of appeals" in communicative action.

**The lifeworld and system processes of society.** For Habermas, the lifeworld is a "culturally transmitted and linguistically organized stock of interpretative patterns." But what are these "interpretative patterns" about? What do they pertain to? His answer, as one comes to expect from Habermas, is yet another typology. There are three different types of interpretative patterns in the lifeworld: there are interpretative patterns with respect to culture, or systems of symbols; there are those pertaining to society, or social institutions; and there are those oriented to personality, or aspects of self and being. That is, (1) actors possess implicit and shared stocks of knowledge about cultural traditions, values, beliefs, linguistic structures and their use in interaction; (2) they also know how to organize social relations and what kinds and patterns of coordinated interaction are proper and appropriate; and (3) they understand what people are like, how they should act, and what is normal or aberrant.

These three types of interpretative patterns correspond, Habermas asserts, to the following functional needs for reproducing the lifeworld (and by implication, for integrating society): (1) Reaching understanding through communicative action serves the function of transmitting, preserving, and renewing cultural knowledge; (2) communicative action that coordinates interaction meets the need for social integration and group

---

[45]Ibid., p. 302.
[46]Ibid., p. 137.

solidarity; and (3) communicative action that socializes agents meets the need for the formation of personal identities.[47]

Thus, the three components of the lifeworld—culture, society, personality—meet corresponding needs of society—cultural reproduction, social integration, and personality formation—through three dimensions along which communicative action is conducted—reaching understanding, coordinating interaction, and socialization. As Habermas summarizes in volume 2:

> In coming to an understanding with one another about their situation, participants in communication stand in a cultural tradition which they use and at the same time renew; in coordinating their actions via intersubjective recognition of criticizable validity claims, they rely upon their membership in groupings and at the same time reenforce their integration; through participating in interaction with competent persons, growing children internalize value orientations and acquire generalized capacities for action.[48]

These lifeworld processes are interrelated with system processes in a society. Action in economic, political, familial, and other institutional contexts draws upon, and reproduces, the cultural, societal, and personality dimensions of the lifeworld. Yet, evolutionary trends are for differentiation of the lifeworld into separate stocks of knowledge with respect to culture, society, and personality and for differentiation of system processes into distinctive and separate institutional clusters, such as economy, state, family, and law. Such differentiation creates problems of integration and balance between the lifeworld and system.[49] And therein reside the dilemmas and crises of modern societies.

**Evolutionary dynamics and societal crises.**   In a sense, Habermas blends traditional analysis by functionalists on societal and cultural differentiation with a Marxian dialectic whereby the seeds for emancipation are sown in the creation of an ever more rationalized and differentiated society. Borrowing from Durkheim's analysis of mechanical solidarity, Habermas argues that "the more cultural traditions predecide which validity claims, when, where, for what, from whom, and to whom must be accepted, the less the participants themselves have the possibility of making explicit and examining the potential groups in which their yes/

---

[47]We are now into volume 2, ibid., pp. 205–40, which is entitled *System and Lifeworld: A Critique of Functionalist Reason,* which is, I think, a somewhat ironic title because of the heavily functional arguments in volume 2. But as I pointed out earlier, even Habermas's earlier work has always had an implicit functionalism.

[48]Ibid., p. 208.

[49]This is the old functionalist argument of "differentiation" produces "integrative problems," which is as old as Spencer and which is Parsons reincarnated with a phenomenological twist.

no positions are based."[50] But "as mechanical solidarity gives way to organic solidarity based upon functional interdependence," then "the more the worldview that furnishes the cultural stock of knowledge is decentered" and "the less the need for understanding is covered *in advance* by an interpreted lifeworld immune from critique," and therefore, "the more this need has to be met by the interpretative accomplishments of the participants themselves." That is, if the lifeworld is to be sustained and reproduced, it becomes ever more necessary with growing societal complexity for social actions to be based upon communicative processes. The result is that there is greater potential for rational communicative action because less and less of the social order is preordained by a simple and undifferentiated lifeworld. But system processes have operated to reduce this potential; and the task of critical theory is to document how system processes have worked to colonize the lifeworld and thereby arrest this potentially superior rationality inherent in the speech acts of communicative action.

How have system processes restricted this potential contained in communicative action? As the sacred/traditional basis of the lifeworld organization has dissolved and been replaced by linguistic interaction around a lifeworld differentiated along cultural, social, and personality axes, there is a countertrend in the differentiation of system processes. System evolution involves the expansion of material production through the greater use of technologies, science, and "delinguistified steering mechanisms" such as money and power to carry out system processes.[51] These media do not rely upon the validity claims of communicative action; and when they become the media of interaction in ever more spheres of life—markets, bureaucracies, welfare state policies, legal systems, and even family relations—the processes of communicative action so essential for lifeworld reproduction are invaded and colonized. Thus, system processes use power and money as their media of integration, and in the process, they "decouple the lifeworld" from its functions for societal integration.[52] There is an irony here because differentiation of the lifeworld facilitated the differentiation of system processes and the use of money and power[53]; and so, "the rationalized lifeworld makes possible the rise of growth of subsystems which strike back at it in a destructive fashion."[54]

Through this ironical process, capitalism creates market dynamics using money, which, in turn, spawn a welfare state employing power in

---

[50]I have shifted now, back to portions of volume 1. All quotes here are from p. 70 of volume 1.

[51]Here Habermas is borrowing from Simmel's analysis in *The Philosophy of Money* (see Chapter 6) and Parsons's conceptualization of generalized media (see Chapter 3).

[52]I am now back in volume 2 of *The Theory of Communicative Action*, pp. 256–76.

[53]Habermas appears in these arguments to borrow heavily from Parsons's analysis of evolution (see Chapter 3).

[54]Volume 2, p. 227.

ways that reduce political and economic crises but which increase those crises revolving around lifeworld reproduction. For the new crises and conflicts "arise in areas of cultural reproduction, of social integration and of socialization."[55]

**The goal of critical theory.**   Habermas has now circled back to his initial concerns and those of early critical theorists. He has recast the Weberian thesis by asserting that true rationality inheres in communicative action, not teleological (and strategic or instrumental) action, as Weber claimed. And he has redefined the critical theorist's view on modern crises; they are not ones of rationalization, but ones of colonization of those truly rational processes that inhere in the speech acts of communicative action, which reproduce the lifeworld so essential to societal integration. Thus, built into the integrating processes of differentiated societies (note, not the subjective processes of individuals, as early critical theorists claimed) is the potential for a critical theory that seeks to restore communicative rationality in the face of impersonal steering mechanisms. If system differentiation occurs in terms of delinguistified media, like money and power, and if these reduce the reliance upon communicative action, then crises are inevitable. The resulting collective frustration over the lack of meaning in social life can be used by critical theorists to mobilize people to restore the proper balance between system and lifeworld processes. Thus, it is not crises of material production that will be the impetus for change, as Marx contended. It is the crises of lifeworld reproduction that will serve as the stimulus to societal reorganization. And returning to his first work, Habermas sees such reorganization as involving (1) the restoration of the public sphere in politics, where relinguistified debate and argumentation rather than delinguistified power and authority, are used to make political decisions (thus reducing "legitimation crises") and (2) the extension of communicative action back into those spheres—family, work, and social relations—that have become increasingly dominated by delinguistified steering media (thereby eliminating "motivational crises").

The potential for this reorganization inheres in the nature of societal integration through the rationality inherent in the communicative actions that reproduce the lifeworld. It is the purpose of critical theory to release this rational potential.

## AN ASSESSMENT OF HABERMAS'S CRITICAL THEORY AND PROJECT

Because it does not claim to be science or theory in the sense outlined in Chapter 1, critical theory is difficult to assess in other than its own

---

[55]Ibid., p. 576.

terms.[56] Yet, I have examined Habermas's project in detail because, unlike many in this area, it does try to develop a theoretical perspective for understanding the dynamics of human organization. In assessing Habermas's approach, therefore, I will focus only on those portions of his project that analyze human organization. I will leave to others the assessment of his ideological argument, which, I must confess, I find hopelessly naive. Naturally, Habermas's critical approach owes its guiding inspiration to the tradition of the Frankfurt School, and his formulation of concepts has thereby been biased by these ideological commitments. But nonetheless, I will concentrate primarily on one central question: does Habermas's approach give us new insight and understanding into the processes of human action, interaction, and organization?

I admit that this question is somewhat unfair, because much of the creativity in Habermas's approach is the blending of theory and ideology. But since my commitments are to the separation of science from ideology (of course, I recognize the problems involved), I would have few positive remarks for theory that is so explicitly ideological (of course, Habermas would counter that science is ideological because it serves certain interests). Thus, just as I did for Marx in Chapter 6, I will try to stress the merits of Habermas's approach *as theory*, divorced from his critical project.

## Evaluating Habermas's Conception of Action

Habermas's distinction among teleological (plus its strategic and instrumental variants), normative, dramaturgical, and communicative action does direct our attention to different phases of behavior. The distinction between teleological and normative adds little beyond Parsons's formulation in 1937.[57] The dramaturgical does incorporate Goffman's ideas into action theory, but Habermas does not extend Goffman's conceptualization in any way.[58] The only unique portion of the approach, then, is the conceptualization of communicative action, which is, in reality, a perspective for the analysis of interaction.

## Habermas's Conception of Interaction

In the analysis of communicative action, Habermas does blend elements of George Herbert Mead's behaviorist/interactionist approach and Alfred Schutz's phenomenological/interactionist ideas (see Chapter 14) with

---

[56]Indeed, it is both "ideological" and "scientific" in terms of the scheme drawn in Figure 1-1.

[57]Talcott Parsons, *The Structure of Social Action* (New York: McGraw-Hill, 1937) does not go much beyond Weber's analysis.

[58]Erving Goffman, *The Presentation of Self in Everyday Life* (Garden City, N.Y.: Doubleday Publishing, 1959).

portions of ethnomethodology (see Chapter 18) and linguistic analysis. I have not discussed Habermas's detailed presentation of speech processes, but they figure prominently in his classification of types of action and the nature of validity claims in speech acts.[59] Moreover, the emphasis on the processes of reaching understanding and intersubjectivity through speech acts and implicit background assumptions contained in the lifeworld does, I think, represent a creative synthesis of linguistics, ethnomethodology, phenomenology, and symbolic interactionism. Speech acts are seen as contextual or indexical in that their meaning is shaped by implicit stocks of knowledge; and actors use these stocks to interpret each others' gestures and achieve a sense of intersubjectivity. There is nothing new in the formulation as I have just stated it, but the notion that speech acts make three types of validity claims—propositional truth, normative appropriateness, and subjective sincerity—is a very interesting idea. That is, Habermas is asserting that in achieving understanding and intersubjectivity through the contextual interpretations of speech acts, humans make implicit validity claims along these dimensions. Furthermore, Habermas's contention that this sense of understanding and intersubjectivity depends upon such validity claims being made, accepted, or challenged without recourse to authority is, likewise, an interesting proposition. Thus, although I am not sure that Habermas's ideas denote how interaction actually occurs, he has given interactionist theory some new ideas that, I feel, need to be considered carefully.

## Habermas's Macrosociology: System and Lifeworld

By viewing lifeworld as consisting of interpretative patterns with respect to culture, society, and personality, Habermas has done three things. First, he has tied Talcott Parsons's analytical distinctions among personality, social, and cultural systems to the process of interaction.[60] That is, people use linguistically articulated patterns as well as more implicit and tacit stocks of knowledge about culture, society, and personality in their day-to-day interactions. These distinctions are not just those of analytical theory; they are also implicit "folk categories" of actual people and are part of the active lifeworld among interacting and communicating actors.

Secondly, Habermas has made less mysterious and vague the lifeworld as it has been conceptualized by phenomenologists and ethnomethodologists. It is not just an amorphous mass of implicit and tacit understandings; rather, it is a series of folk ideas about several classes of phenomena—culture (symbols), society (social organization), and personality (self and ego).

---

[59]Habermas, *The Theory of Communicative Action*, vol. 1, pp. 273–344.

[60]See Chapter 3. See also Talcott Parsons, *The Social System* (New York: Free Press, 1951).

Third, Habermas has extended and refined functionalists' arguments about social integration as being dependent upon value consensus and other cultural forces, while he has synthesized them with the more processual arguments of interactionists. By viewing the lifeworld as interpretative patterns with respect to culture, society, and personality and as the background context for speech acts and validity claims, societal integration is reconceptualized as being sustained through the active processes of interaction that utilize and reproduce the interpretative patterns of the lifeworld. Culture is not some ex cathedra force external to actors, pushing and shoving them around. Instead, it is part of a more encompassing stock of knowledge and a crucial resource that is used in interaction. And in being actively used, it is reproduced in ways that allow actors to understand each others' subjective points of view and to coordinate their actions.[61] As such, it has functions for sustaining the macrostructures of societies.

System processes are given a rather standard interpretation of institutional structures involved in material reproduction of the species through the institutionalization of economic, political, legal, and family activities. But there are creative points of synthesis in Habermas's argument when he views lifeworld and system processes as interdependent. That is, institutionalized structures like economy and polity function better when the behaviors that reproduce them are conducted in terms of communicative interactions utilizing and reproducing the interpretative patterns of the lifeworld. And Habermas's view of the integrative problems of modern societies as a decoupling of lifeworld and system is, I feel, an interesting way to reconceptualize the basic integrative problems of differentiated systems. For when Habermas talks about a decoupling, he is doing more than merely restating Durkheim's anomie thesis, Marx's alienation argument, or Parsons's discussion of imbalances of information or energy in his cybernetic hierarchy of control.[62] He is also specifying the particular *processes of interaction* that are being decoupled from institutionalized patterns. In so doing, Habermas is far less vague than notions of malintegration so typical of functional theory. He is indicating more precisely what is being lost—certain types of speech acts involving validity claims and discourse that utilize lifeworld processes to create the mutual understandings that integrate the social order.

## Habermas's View of Evolution

Habermas interprets evolution in highly functional terms as a dual process of (1) differentiation and (2) creation of integrative problems, especially

---

[61]Habermas has also refined Mead's view of "role-taking" with the "generalized other" in this conceptualization. See Chapter 14.

[62]See Chapter 3, Figure 3–7.

those of sustaining common meanings among actors in differentiated niches in a complex society. He borrows from Durkheim's and Parsons' view of evolution as a process of differentiation between and within symbolic and structural realms, with the essential dilemma of modern societies revolving around how to put these two realms back together again so that actions in social structures are meaningful to individuals. But unlike most functional theory, he turns to interactionism (see Chapters 14–18) for his answer: restore the processes of communicative action, or symbolic interaction.

My sense is that he merely restated the problem in interactionist terms, without telling us *how* and *through what procedures* communicative action is to be restored. Moreover, I agree with Niklas Luhmann's critique that humans do in fact reach understanding in their interactions in complex systems dominated by the steering media of power and money.[63] Habermas has, I think, a rather romanticized view of what human interaction is really like and of what humans actually need in their social relations in order to be content. He assumes incorrectly, I believe, that the symbolic interactions that generate intersubjectivity do not occur in structures dominated by power and money; my sense is that they do, as is amply evidenced by studies of "the informal system" in bureaucratic structures.

And this line of argument brings me to my last observation of Habermas's approach. There is a kind of naive romanticism in all of his work, from his first discussion of the public sphere to the present. He employs a totally artificial yardstick—first the yardstick of undistorted communication, then one on the ideal speech situation, and finally the criterion of communicative action—for assessing what's wrong with modern societies. When one begins the analysis of human social organization with a set of standards that, I suspect, have never been met in human affairs, then one's interpretation of events will be rather dramatically obscured. Although Habermas has blended many diverse traditions in creative ways and offered, as I have indicated, a number of interesting conceptual leads, I do not think that these denote the operative dynamics of human social systems. And this is where all critical theory goes wrong— from Marx's dream of the communist society to Habermas's desire for a society integrated by communicative action. When ideology and hope for a future society are the beginning points of analysis, I doubt if the end points will be as accurate as would be the case if these ideological hopes were never a part of the theoretical project. Yet, it is a credit to both Marx's and Habermas's genius that, despite this great flaw, they have both produced a body of concepts that, when stripped of the ideological trappings, can be useful in building scientific theory.

---

[63]Niklas Luhmann, *The Differentiation of Society* (New York: Columbia University Press, 1982). Indeed, Luhmann and Habermas have had a number of stimulating debates on the issue, with Luhmann emerging the victor in my opinion.

## PART THREE

## Exchange Theory

# CHAPTER 10

# Early Forms of Exchange Theorizing

The intellectual lineage culminating in modern exchange theory is very diverse. What typifies this heritage as much as its diversity are the frequently vague connections between contemporary exchange theorists and their predecessors. Indeed, I find current exchange theories to be a curious and unspecified mixture of utilitarian economics, functional anthropology, conflict sociology, and behavioral psychology. As a result, tracing the roots of exchange theory is an eclectic and uncertain enterprise. At best, I can only summarize various types of early exchange theory, leaving unanswered the question of how each modern theorist has drawn from this diverse legacy.

## UTILITARIANISM: THE LEGACY OF CLASSICAL ECONOMICS

The names of Adam Smith, David Ricardo, John Stuart Mill, and Jeremy Bentham loom large in the history of economic theorizing between 1770–1850. Each made a unique contribution to both economic and social thought, but I see several common assumptions in all of their works that enable their thought to be labeled *utilitarianism*. For these classical economists, humans are viewed as rationally seeking to maximize their material benefits, or utility, from transactions or exchanges with others in a free and competitive marketplace. As rational units in a free marketplace, people have access to all necessary information, can consider all available alternatives, and, on the basis of this consideration, rationally select the course of activity that will maximize material benefits. Entering into these rational considerations are calculations of the costs involved in pursuing various alternatives. Such costs must be weighed against material benefits in an effort to determine which alternative will yield the maximum payoff or profit (benefits less costs).[1]

With the emergence of sociology as a self-conscious discipline, there was considerable borrowing, revision, and reaction to this conception of humans. In fact, the debate between the intellectual descendants of utilitarianism and those reacting to this perspective has raged since sociology's inception. For example, as I outlined in Chapter 3, Talcott Parsons attempted to reformulate utilitarian principles and weld them to other theoretical traditions in an effort to develop a general perspective on social action.[2] Similarly, modern exchange theorists have attempted to reformulate utilitarian principles into various theories of social exchange.[3] This reformulation asserts the following alternative assumptions:

1. Humans do not seek to maximize profits, but they always attempt to make some profit in their social transactions with others.
2. Humans are not perfectly rational, but they do engage in calculations of costs and benefits in social transactions.
3. Humans do not have perfect information on all available alternatives, but they are usually aware of at least some alternatives, which form the basis for assessments of costs and benefits.
4. Humans always act under constraints, but they still compete with each other in seeking to make a profit in their transactions.
5. Humans always seek to make a profit in their transactions, but they are limited by the resources that they have when entering an exchange relation.

In addition to these alterations of utilitarian assumptions, exchange theory removes human interaction from the limitations of material transactions in an economic marketplace. Rather, these alternative assumptions are seen to apply to all social contexts, requiring that I add two more:

6. Humans do engage in economic transactions in clearly defined marketplaces in all societies, but these transactions are only a special case of more general exchange relations occurring among individuals in virtually all social contexts.

---

[1]For interesting discussions of utilitarian thought as it bears on the present discussion, see Elie Halévy, *The Growth of Philosophical Radicalism* (London: Farber & Farber, 1928); John Plamenatz, *Man and Society* (New York: McGraw-Hill, 1963).

[2]This effort continues, as we saw with Jurgen Habermas's work in the last chapter. And in both sociology and economics today, there is concern—excessive concern, in my view—with the notion of "rationality."

[3]The most blatant of these efforts, which I will not examine in the following chapters, is James Coleman's "Foundations for a Theory of Collective Decisions," *American Journal of Sociology* 71 (1966), pp. 615–27.

7. Humans do pursue material goals in exchanges, but they also mobilize and exchange nonmaterial resources, such as sentiments, services, and symbols.

Aside from this revised substantive legacy, I believe that some forms of modern exchange theory have also adopted the strategy of the utilitarians for constructing social theory. In assuming humans to be rational, utilitarians argued that exchanges among people could also be studied by a rational science, one in which the "laws of human nature" would stand at the top of a deductive system of explanation.[4] Thus, utilitarians borrowed the early physical-science conception of theory as a logico-deductive system of axioms or laws and various layers of lower-order propositions that could be rationally deduced from the laws of "economic man." Thus, most exchange theories are presented in a propositional format, typically in what I called a formal propositional scheme in Chapter 1.

In reviewing the tenets of utilitarianism, however, I think that only part of the historical legacy of exchange theory is revealed. For utilitarianism excited considerable debate and controversy in early anthropology. In fact, I sense that much of the influence of utilitarianism on current exchange theory has been indirect, passing through social anthropology around the turn of this century.

# EXCHANGE THEORY IN ANTHROPOLOGY[5]

## Sir James Frazer (1854–1941)

In 1919, Sir James George Frazer's second volume of *Folklore in the Old Testament* conducted what was probably the first explicit exchange-theoretic analysis of social institutions.[6] In examining a wide variety of kinship and marriage practices among primitive societies, Frazer was struck by the clear preference of Australian aborigines for cross-cousin over parallel-cousin marriages: "Why is the marriage of cross-cousins so often favored? Why is the marriage of ortho-cousins [that is, parallel cousins] so uniformly prohibited?"[7]

---

[4] Jurgen Habermas would, of course, make this a much more complicated issue. See his *The Theory of Communicative Action*, vol. 1 (Boston: Beacon Press, 1981).

[5] For a similar treatment of these materials, see Peter Ekeh, *Social Exchange Theory and the Two Sociological Traditions* (Cambridge, Mass.: Harvard Univ. Press, 1975).

[6] Sir James George Frazer, *Folklore in the Old Testament*, vol. 2 (New York: Macmillan, 1919); see also his *Totemism and Exogamy: A Treatise on Certain Early Forms of Superstition and Society* (London: Dawsons of Pall Mall, 1968; original publication 1910); and his Preface to Bronislaw Malinowski's *Argonauts of the Western Pacific* (London: Routledge & Kegan Paul, 1922), pp. vii–xiv.

[7] Quote taken from Ekeh's *Social Exchange Theory*, pp. 41–42, discussion of Frazer (original quote in Frazer, *Folklore*, p. 199).

While the substantive details of Frazer's descriptions of the aborigines' practices are fascinating in themselves (if only for their inaccuracy), I think that it is the form of his explanation that marks his theoretical contribution. In a manner clearly indebted to utilitarian economics, Frazer launched an economic interpretation of the predominance of cross-cousin marriage patterns. In this explanation, Frazer invoked the "law" of "economic motives," since in having "no equivalent in property to give for a wife, an Australian aborigine is generally obliged to get her in exchange for a female relative, usually a sister or daughter."[8] Thus, the material or economic motives of individuals in society (lack of property and desire for a wife) explain various social patterns (cross-cousin marriages). What is more, Frazer went on to postulate that once a particular pattern emanating from economic motives becomes established in a culture, it constrains other social patterns that can potentially emerge.

For Frazer, the social-structural patterns that come to typify a particular culture are a reflection of economic motives in humans, who, in exchanging commodities, attempt to satisfy their basic economic needs. Although Frazer's specific explanation was to be found sadly wanting by subsequent generations of anthropologists, especially Malinowski and Lévi-Strauss, modern exchange theory in sociology invokes a similar conception of social organization:

1. Exchange processes are the result of efforts by people to realize basic needs.
2. When yielding payoffs for those involved, exchange processes lead to the patterning of interaction.
3. Such patterns of interaction not only serve the needs of individuals, but they also constrain the kinds of social structures that can subsequently emerge.

In addition to anticipating the general profile of modern explanations on how elementary exchange processes create more complex patterns in a society, Frazer's analysis also foreshadowed another concern of contemporary exchange theory: the differentiation of social systems in terms of privilege and power. Much as Marx had done a generation earlier, Frazer noted that those who possess resources of high economic value can exploit those who have few such resources, thereby enabling them to possess high privilege and presumably power. Hence, the exchange of women among the aborigines was observed by Frazer to lead to the differentiation of power and privilege in at least two separate ways: First, "Since among the Australian aboriginals women had a high economic and commercial value, a man who had many sisters or daughters was rich and a man who had none was poor and might be unable to procure a wife at all."[9] Second,

---

[8]Ibid., p. 195.

[9]Frazer, *Folklore*, p. 198.

"the old men availed themselves of the system of exchange in order to procure a number of wives for themselves from among the young women, while the young men having no women to give in exchange, were often obliged to remain single or to put up with the cast-off wives of their elders."[10] Thus, at least implicitly, Frazer supplemented the conflict theory contribution with a fourth exchange principle:

4. Exchange processes operate to differentiate groups in terms of their relative access to valued commodities, resulting in differences in power, prestige, and privilege.

As provocative and seemingly seminal as Frazer's analysis appears, I doubt if it had a direct impact on modern exchange theory. Rather, it is to those in anthropology who reacted against Frazer's utilitarianism that contemporary theory remains indebted.

## Bronislaw Malinowski and Nonmaterial Exchange

Despite Malinowski's close ties with Frazer, he developed an exchange perspective that radically altered the utilitarian slant of Frazer's analysis of cross-cousin marriage. Indeed, Frazer himself in his preface to Malinowski's *Argonauts of the Western Pacific* recognized the importance of Malinowski's contribution to the analysis of exchange relations.[11] In his now-famous ethnography of the Trobriand Islanders—a group of South Seas Island cultures—Malinowski observed an exchange system termed the *Kula Ring,* a closed circle of exchange relations among individuals in communities inhabiting a wide ring of islands.[12] What was distinctive in this closed circle, Malinowski observed, was the predominance of exchange of two articles—armlets and necklaces—which the inhabitants constantly exchanged in opposite directions. Traveling one direction around the Kula Ring, armlets were exchanged for necklaces moving in the opposite direction around the ring. In any particular exchange between individuals, then, an armlet would always be exchanged for a necklace.

In interpreting this unique exchange network, Malinowski was led to distinguish material or economic from nonmaterial or symbolic exchanges. In contrast with the utilitarians and Frazer, who did not conceptualize nonmaterial exchange relations, Malinowski recognized that the Kula was not only an economic or material exchange network but also a symbolic exchange, cementing a web of social relationships: "One transaction does not finish the Kula relationship, the rule being 'once in the Kula, always in the Kula,' and a partnership between two men is a permanent and

---

[10]Ibid., pp. 200–201.

[11]Frazer, Preface to *Argonauts* (see note 12).

[12]Bronislaw Malinowski, *Argonauts of the Western Pacific* (London: Routledge & Kegan Paul, 1922), p. 81.

lifelong affair."[13] Although purely economic transactions did occur within the rules of the Kula, the ceremonial exchange of armlets and necklaces was observed by Malinowski to be the Kula's principle function.

The natives themselves, Malinowski emphasized, recognized the distinction between purely economic commodities and the symbolic significance of armlets and necklaces. However, to distinguish economic from symbolic commodities does not mean that the Trobriand Islanders failed to assign graded values to the symbolic commodities; indeed, they made gradations and used them to express and confirm the nature of the relationships among exchange partners as equals, superordinates, or subordinates. But as Malinowski noted, "in all forms of [Kula] exchange in the Trobriands, there is not even a trace of gain, nor is there any reason for looking at it from the purely utilitarian and economic standpoint, since there is no enhancement of mutual utility through the exchange."[14] Rather, the motives behind the Kula were social psychological, for the exchanges in the ring were viewed by Malinowski to have implications for the needs of both individuals and society (recall from Chapter 2 that Malinowski was also a founder of functional theory). From Malinowski's functionalist framework, he interpreted the Kula to mean "the fundamental impulse to display, to share, to bestow [and] the deep tendency to create social ties."[15] For Malinowski, then, an enduring social pattern such as the Kula Ring is considered to have positively functional consequences for satisfying individual psychological needs and societal needs for social integration and solidarity.

As Robert Merton and others were to emphasize (see Chapter 4), this form of functional analysis presents many logical difficulties. Despite these, I believe that Malinowski's analysis made several enduring contributions to modern exchange theory:

1. In Malinowski's words, "the meaning of the Kula will consist in being instrumental to dispel [the] conception of a rational being who wants nothing but to satisfy his simplest needs and does it according to the economic principle of least effort."[16]
2. Psychological rather than economic needs are the forces that initiate and sustain exchange relations and are therefore critical in the explanation of social behavior.
3. Exchange relations can also have implications beyond two parties, for as the Kula demonstrates, complex patterns of indirect exchange can operate to maintain extended and protracted social networks.

---

[13]Ibid., pp. 82–83.
[14]Ibid., p. 175.
[15]Ibid., p. 175.
[16]Ibid., p. 516.

4. Symbolic exchange relations are the basic social process underlying both differentiation of ranks in a society and the integration of society into a cohesive and solidary whole.

With these points of emphasis, Malinowski helped free exchange theory from the limiting confines of utilitarianism. By stressing the importance of symbolic exchanges for both individual psychological processes and patterns of social integration, he anticipated the conceptual base for two basic types of exchange perspectives, one emphasizing the importance of psychological processes and the other stressing the significance of emergent cultural and structural forces on exchange relations.

## Marcel Mauss and the Emergence of Exchange Structuralism

Reacting to what he perceived as Malinowski's tendency to overemphasize psychological instead of social needs, Marcel Mauss reinterpreted Malinowski's analysis of the Kula.[17] In this effort, he formulated the broad outlines of a "collectivistic," or structural exchange, perspective.[18] For Mauss, the critical question in examining an exchange network as complex as that of the Kula was:

> In primitive or archaic types of societies what is the principle whereby the gift received has to be repaid? What force is there in the thing which compels the recipient to make a return?[19]

The "force" compelling reciprocity was, for Mauss, society or the group. As he noted: "It is groups, and not individuals, which carry on exchange, make contracts, and are bound by obligations."[20] The individuals actually engaged in an exchange represent the moral codes of the group. Exchange transactions among individuals are conducted in accordance with the rules of the group, while reinforcing these rules and

---

[17]Marcel Mauss, *The Gift*, trans. I. Cunnison (New York: Free Press, 1954; originally published as *Essai sur le don en sociologie et anthropologie* [Paris: Presses universitaires de France, 1925]). It should be noted that Mauss rather consistently misinterpreted Malinowski's ethnography, but it is through such misinterpretation that he came to visualize a "structural" alternative to "psychological" exchange theories.

[18]In Peter Ekeh's excellent discussion of Mauss and Lévi-Strauss (*Social Exchange Theory*, pp. 55–122), the term *collectivist* is used in preference to *structural* and is posited as the alternative to *individualistic* or psychological exchange perspectives. I prefer the terms *structural* and *psychological;* thus, although I am indebted to Ekeh's discussion, these terms will be used to make essentially the same distinction. My preference for these terms will become more evident in subsequent chapters, since in contrast with Ekeh's analysis, I consider Peter M. Blau and George C. Homans to have developed, respectively, structural and psychological theories. Ekeh considers the theories of both Blau and Homans to be individualistic, or psychological.

[19]Mauss, *The Gift*, p. 1.

[20]Ibid., p. 3.

codes. Thus, for Mauss, the over-concern with individuals' self-interests by utilitarians and the overemphasis on psychological needs by Malinowski are replaced by a conception of individuals as representatives of social groups. In the end, exchange relations create, reinforce, and serve a group morality that is an entity *sui generis*, to borrow a famous phrase from Mauss's mentor, Émile Durkheim. Furthermore, in a vein similar to that of Frazer, once such a morality emerges and is reinforced by exchange activities, it comes to regulate other activities in the social life of a group, above and beyond particular exchange transactions.

Mauss's work has received scant attention from sociologists, but I see him as the first to forge a reconciliation between the exchange principles of utilitarianism and the structural, or collectivistic, thought of Durkheim. In recognizing that exchange transactions give rise to and, at the same time, reinforce the normative structure of society, Mauss anticipated the structural position of some contemporary exchange theories. Mauss's influence on modern theory has been indirect, however, for I think that it is through the structuralism of Claude Lévi-Strauss that the French collectivist tradition of Durkheim and Mauss influenced the exchange perspectives of contemporary sociological theory.

## Claude Lévi-Strauss and Structuralism

In 1949, Claude Lévi-Strauss launched an analysis of cross-cousin marriage in his classic work, *The Elementary Structures of Kinship*.[21] In restating Durkheim's objections to utilitarians, Lévi-Strauss took exception to Frazer's utilitarian interpretation of cross-cousin marriage patterns. And in a manner similar to Mauss's opposition to Malinowski's emphasis on psychological needs, Lévi-Strauss developed a sophisticated structural-exchange perspective.[22]

In rejecting Frazer's interpretation of cross-cousin marriage, Lévi-Strauss first questions the substance of Frazer's utilitarian conceptualization. Frazer, he notes, "depicts the poor Australian aborigine wondering how he is going to obtain a wife since he has no material goods with which to purchase her, and discovering exchange as the solution to this apparently insoluble problem: 'men exchange their sisters in marriage because that was the cheapest way of getting a wife.' " In contrast, Lévi-Strauss emphasizes that "it is the exchange which counts and not the

---

[21]Claude Lévi-Strauss, *The Elementary Structures of Kinship* (Boston: Beacon Press, 1969). This is a translation of Lévi-Strauss's 1967 revision of the original *Les structures élémentaires de la parenté* (Paris: Presses universitaires de France, 1949). The full impact of this work was probably never felt in sociology, since until 1969 it was not available in English. Yet, as will be noted in Chapter 11 on Homans, this work did have a profound impact on Homans's thinking, primarily because Homans felt compelled to reject Lévi-Strauss's analysis. I will examine Lévi-Strauss's work again in Chapter 19.

[22]See Ekeh's discussions for a more detailed analysis of Lévi-Strauss.

things exchanged." For Lévi-Strauss, exchange must be viewed in terms of its functions for integrating the larger social structure. Lévi-Strauss then attacks Frazer's and the utilitarian's assumption that the first principles of social behavior are economic. Such an assumption flies in the face of the fact that social structure is an emergent phenomenon that operates in terms of its own irreducible laws and principles.

Lévi-Strauss also rejects psychological interpretations of exchange processes, especially the position advocated by behaviorists (see later section). In contrast with psychological behaviorists, who see little real difference between the laws of behavior among animals and humans, Lévi-Strauss emphasizes that humans possess a cultural heritage of norms and values that separates their behavior and societal organization from that of animal species. Human action is thus qualitatively different from animal behavior, especially with respect to social exchange. Animals are not guided by values and rules that specify when, where, and how they are to carry out social transactions. Humans, however, carry with them into any exchange situation learned definitions of how they are to behave—thus assuring that the principles of human exchange will be distinctive.

Furthermore, exchange is more than the result of psychological needs, even those that have been acquired through socialization. Exchange cannot be understood solely in terms of individual motives, because exchange relations are a reflection of patterns of social organization that exist as an entity, *sui generis*. Exchange behavior is thus regulated from without by norms and values, resulting in processes that can only be analyzed in terms of their consequences, or functions, for these norms and values.

In arguing this point of view, Lévi-Strauss posits several fundamental exchange principles. First, all exchange relations involve costs for individuals, but in contrast with economic or psychological explanations of exchange, such costs are attributed to society—to those customs, rules, laws, and values that require behaviors incurring costs. Yet, individuals do not assign the costs to themselves, but to the "social order." Second, for all those scarce and valued resources in society—whether material objects, such as wives, or symbolic resources, like esteem and prestige—their distribution is regulated by norms and values. As long as resources are in abundant supply or not highly valued in a society, their distribution goes unregulated, but once they become scarce and highly valued, their distribution is soon regulated. Third, all exchange relations are governed by a norm of reciprocity, requiring those receiving valued sources to bestow on their benefactors other valued resources. In Lévi-Strauss's conception of reciprocity there are various patterns of reciprocation specified by norms and values. In some situations, norms dictate "mutual" and direct rewarding of one's benefactor, whereas in other situations the reciprocity can be "univocal" involving diverse patterns of indirect exchange in which actors do not reciprocate directly but only through various third (fourth, fifth, and so forth) parties. Within these two general types of exchange reciprocity—mutual and univocal—numerous subtypes of exchange networks can be normatively regulated.

For Lévi-Strauss, these three exchange principles offer a more useful set of concepts to describe cross-cousin marriage patterns, because they can now be viewed in terms of their functions for the larger social structure. Particular marriage patterns and other features of kinship organization no longer need be interpreted merely as direct exchanges among individuals, but can be conceptualized as univocal exchanges between individuals and society. In freeing exchange from the analysis of only direct and mutual exchanges, Lévi-Strauss offers a tentative theory of societal integration and solidarity. His explanation extends Durkheim's provocative analysis and indicates how various subtypes of direct and univocal exchange both reflect and reinforce different patterns of societal integration and organization.

This theory of integration is, in itself, of theoretical importance. But I think it more significant for present purposes to stress Lévi-Strauss's impact on current sociological exchange perspectives. My sense is that two points of emphasis exerted strong influence on modern sociological theory.

1. Various forms of social structure rather than individual motives are the critical variables in the analysis of exchange relations.
2. Exchange relations in social systems are frequently not restricted to direct interaction among individuals, but protracted into complex networks of indirect exchange. On the one hand, these exchange processes are caused by patterns of social integration and organization; on the other hand, they promote diverse forms of such organization.

In looking back on this anthropological heritage, I believe that Lévi-Strauss's work represents the culmination of a reaction to economic utilitarianism as it was originally incorporated into anthropology by Frazer. Malinowski recognized the limitations of Frazer's analysis of only material or economic motives in direct exchange transactions. As the Kula Ring demonstrates, exchange can be generalized into protracted networks involving noneconomic motives that have implications for societal integration. Mauss drew explicit attention to the significance of social structure in regulating exchange processes and to the consequences of such processes for maintaining social structure. Finally, in this intellectual chain of events in anthropology, Lévi-Strauss began to indicate how different types of direct and indirect exchange are linked to different patterns of social organization. This intellectual heritage has influenced both the substance and strategy of exchange theory in sociology, but it has done so only after considerable modification of assumptions and concepts by a particular strain of psychology: behaviorism.

# PSYCHOLOGICAL BEHAVIORISM AND EXCHANGE THEORY

As a psychological perspective, behaviorism began from insights derived from observations of an accident. The Russian physiologist Ivan Petrovich Pavlov (1849–1936) discovered that experimental dogs associated food with the person bringing it.[23] He observed, for instance, that dogs on whom he was performing secretory experiments would salivate not only when presented food but also when they heard their feeder's footsteps approaching. After considerable delay and personal agonizing, Pavlov undertook a series of experiments on animals to understand such "conditioned responses."[24] From these experiments, he developed several principles that later were to be incorporated into behaviorism. These include: (1) A stimulus consistently associated with another stimulus producing a given physiological response will, by itself, elicit that response. (2) Such conditioned responses can be extinguished when gratifications associated with stimuli are no longer forthcoming. (3) Stimuli that are similar to those producing a conditioned response can also elicit the same response as the original stimulus. (4) Stimuli that increasingly differ from those used to condition a particular response will decreasingly be able to elicit this response. Thus, Pavlov's experiments exposed the principles of conditioned responses, extinction, response generalization, and response discrimination. Although Pavlov clearly recognized the significance of these findings of human behavior, his insights came to fruition in America under the tutelage of Edward Thorndike and John B. Watson—the founders of behaviorism.[25]

Edward Lee Thorndike conducted the first laboratory experiments on animals in America. In the course of these experiments, he observed that animals would retain response patterns for which they are rewarded.[26] For example, in experiments on kittens placed in a puzzle box, Thorndike found that they would engage in trial-and-error behavior until emitting the response that allowed them to escape. And with each placement in the box, the kittens would engage in less trial-and-error behavior, thereby indicating that the gratifications associated with a response allowing the kittens to escape caused them to learn and retain this response. From these and other studies, which were conducted at the same time as Pavlov's,

---

[23]See, for relevant articles, lectures, and references, I. P. Pavlov, *Selected Works*, ed. K. S. Kostoyants, trans. S. Belsky (Moscow: Foreign Languages Publishing House, 1955); and *Lectures on Conditioned Reflexes*, 3d ed., trans. W. H. Grant (New York: International Publishers, 1928).

[24]I. P. Pavlov, "Autobiography" in *Selected Works*, pp. 41–44.

[25]For an excellent summary of their ideas, see Robert I. Watson, *The Great Psychologists*, 3d ed. (Philadelphia: J. B. Lippincott, 1971), pp. 417–46.

[26]Edward L. Thorndike, "Animal Intelligence: An Experimental Study of the Associative Processes in Animals," *Psychological Review Monograph*, Supplement 2 (1898).

Thorndike formulated three principles or laws: (1) the "law of effect," which holds that acts in a situation producing gratification will be more likely to occur in the future when that situation recurs; (2) the "law of use," which states that situation-response connection is strengthened with repetitions and practice; and (3) the "law of disuse," which argues that the connection will weaken when practice is discontinued.[27]

These laws converge with those presented by Pavlov, but there is one important difference. Thorndike's experiments involved animals engaged in free trial-and-error behavior, whereas Pavlov's work was on the conditioning of physiological—typically glandular—responses in a tightly controlled laboratory situation. Thorndike's work could thus be seen as more directly relevant to human behavior in natural settings.

John B. Watson was one of only several thinkers to recognize the significance of Pavlov's and Thorndike's work, but he soon became the dominant advocate of what was becoming explicitly known as behaviorism.[28] Watson's opening shot for the new science of behavior was fired in an article entitled "Psychology as the Behaviorist Views It":

> Psychology as the behaviorist views it is a purely objective experimental branch of natural science. Its theoretical goal is the prediction and control of behavior. Introspection forms no essential part of its methods, nor is the scientific value of its data dependent upon the readiness with which they lend themselves to interpretation in terms of consciousness. The behaviorist, in efforts to get a unitary scheme of animal response, recognizes no dividing line between man and brute.[29]

Watson thus became the advocate of the extreme behaviorism against which many vehemently reacted.[30] For Watson, psychology is the study of stimulus-response relations, and the only admissible evidence is overt behavior. Psychologists are to stay out of the "mystery box" of human consciousness and to study only observable behaviors as they are connected to observable stimuli.[31]

---

[27]See Edward L. Thorndike, *The Elements of Psychology* (New York: Seiler, 1905), *The Fundamentals of Learning* (New York: Teachers College Press, 1932), and *The Psychology of Wants, Interests, and Attitudes* (New York: D. Appleton, 1935).

[28]Others who recognized their importance included: Max F. Meyer, *Psychology of the Other-One* (Columbus: Missouri Book, 1921); and Albert P. Weiss, *A Theoretical Basis of Human Behavior* (Columbus: Adams Press, 1925).

[29]J. B. Watson, "Psychology as the Behaviorist Views It," *Psychological Review* 20 (1913), pp. 158-77. For other basic works by Watson, see *Psychology from the Standpoint of a Behaviorist*, 3d ed. (Philadelphia: J. B. Lippincott, 1929); *Behavior: An Introduction to Comparative Psychology* (New York: Henry Holt, 1914).

[30]For example, in his *Mind, Self, and Society* (Chicago: University of Chicago Press, 1934), Mead has 18 references to Watson's work.

[31]For a more detailed discussion of the emergence of behaviorism, see Jonathan H. Turner and Leonard Beeghley, *The Emergence of Sociological Theory* (Homewood, Ill.: Dorsey Press, 1981).

In many ways, I see behaviorism as similar to utilitarianism, since it operates on the principle that humans are reward-seeking organisms that pursue alternatives that will yield the most reward and the least punishment. Rewards are simply another way of phrasing the economist's concept of "utility," and "punishment" is somewhat equivalent to the notion of "cost." For the behaviorist, reward is any behavior that reinforces or meets the needs of the organism, whereas punishment denies rewards or forces the expenditure of energy to avoid pain (thereby incurring costs).

Modern exchange theories have borrowed from behaviorists the notion of reward and used it to reinterpret the utilitarian exchange heritage. In place of utility, the concept of reward has been inserted, primarily because it allows exchange theorists to view behavior as motivated by psychological needs. However, the utilitarian concept of cost appears to have been retained in preference to the behaviorist's formulation of punishment, since the notion of cost allows exchange theorists to visualize more completely the alternative rewards that organisms forego in seeking to achieve a particular reward.

Despite these modifications of the basic concepts of behaviorism, its key theoretical generalizations have been incorporated with relatively little change into some forms of sociological exchange theory. Let me list these:

1. In any given situation, organisms will emit those behaviors that will yield the most reward and least punishment.
2. Organisms will repeat those behaviors that have proved rewarding in the past.
3. Organisms will repeat behaviors in situations that are similar to those in the past in which behaviors were rewarded.
4. Present stimuli that on past occasions have been associated with rewards will evoke behaviors similar to those emitted in the past.
5. Repetition of behaviors will occur only as long as they continue to yield rewards.
6. An organism will display emotion if a behavior that has previously been rewarded in the same or similar situation suddenly goes unrewarded.
7. The more an organism receives rewards from a particular behavior, the less rewarding that behavior becomes (due to satiation) and the more likely is the organism to emit alternative behaviors in search of other rewards.

Since these principles were discovered in laboratory situations where experimenters typically manipulated the environment of the organism, it is difficult to visualize the experimental situation as interaction. The experimenter's tight control of the situation precludes the possibility that the animal will affect significantly the responses of the experimenter. This fact has forced modern exchange theories using behaviorist principles to incorporate the utilitarian's concern with transactions, or exchanges. In this way, humans can be seen as mutually affecting each other's opportunities for rewards. In contrast to animals in a Skinner box or some similar laboratory situation, humans exchange rewards. Each person represents a potentially rewarding stimulus situation for the other.

As sociological exchange theorists have attempted to apply behaviorist principles to the study of human behavior, they have inevitably confronted the problem of the black box: humans differ from laboratory animals in their greater ability to engage in a wide variety of complex cognitive processes. Indeed, as the utilitarians were the first to emphasize, what is distinctly human is the capacity to abstract, to calculate, to project outcomes, to weigh alternatives, and to perform a wide number of other cognitive manipulations. Furthermore, in borrowing behaviorist's concepts, contemporary exchange theorists have also had to introduce the concepts of an introspective psychology and structural sociology. Humans not only think in complex ways; their thinking is emotional and circumscribed by many social and cultural forces (first incorporated into the exchange theories of Mauss and Lévi-Strauss). Once it is recognized that behaviorist principles must incorporate concepts denoting both internal psychological processes and constraints of social structure and culture, it is also necessary to visualize exchange as frequently transcending the mutually rewarding activities of individuals in direct interaction. The organization of behavior by social structure and culture, coupled with humans' complex cognitive abilities, allows protracted and indirect exchange networks to exist.

In looking back upon the impact of behaviorism on some forms of contemporary exchange theory, then, I see a convergence of concepts and principles. Although the vocabulary and general principles of behaviorism are clearly evident, the concepts have been redefined and the principles altered to incorporate the insights of the early utilitarians as well as the anthropological reaction to utilitarianism. The end result has been for proponents of an exchange perspective employing behaviorist concepts and principles to abandon much of what made behaviorism a unique perspective as they have dealt with the complexities introduced by human cognitive capacities and their organization into sociocultural groupings.

## THE SOCIOLOGICAL TRADITION AND EXCHANGE THEORY

Thus far, I have concentrated on the influence of conceptual work in economics, anthropology, and psychology on exchange theory. The vocabulary of exchange theory clearly comes from utilitarianism and behaviorism. Anthropological work forced the recognition that cultural and social dynamics need to be incorporated into exchange theory. When looking at early sociological work, however, the impact of early sociological theorists on modern exchange theory is difficult to assess. I think that this difficulty is the result of several factors. First, much sociological theory represented a reaction against utilitarianism and extreme behaviorism and, therefore, has been reluctant to incorporate concepts from these fields. Second, the most developed of the early exchange theories—that provided by Georg Simmel in his *The Philosophy of Money*—remained untranslated into English until recent years.[32] Yet, I suspect that German-reading theorists, such as Peter Blau and Talcott Parsons, were to some degree influenced by Simmel's ideas. Third, the topics of most interests to many sociological exchange theorists—differentiations of power and conflict in exchanges—have more typically been conceptualized as conflict theory than exchange theory. But as I will document, sociological theories of exchange converge with those on conflict processes; and I have little doubt that Marx's ideas exerted considerable influence on modern exchange theories.

Thus, while I am not sure of the exact lines of influence, I think that Marx's and Simmel's work has been involved—perhaps only subliminally—in the development of sociological exchange theory. Let me draw out this line of argument for Marx and then for Simmel.

## Marx's Theory of Exchange and Conflict

Most contemporary theories of exchange examine the dynamics of exchange that follow from the fact that actors typically have unequal levels of resources with which to bargain. Those with resources valued by others are in a position to strike a better bargain, especially if those others who value their resource do not possess equally valued resources to offer in exchange. This fact of social life is, I feel, the situation described in Marx's conflict theory.[33] Capitalists have the power to control the distribution of material rewards, whereas all that workers have is their labor to offer in exchange. Although labor is valued by the capitalist, it is in plentiful supply, and thus, no one worker is in a position to bargain effectively with an employer. As a consequence, capitalists can get labor at a low cost and can force workers to do what they want. As capitalists press their advantage, they create the very conditions that allow workers to develop resources—political, organizational, ideological—which they can then use to strike a better bargain with capitalists and, in the end, to overthrow them.

Granted, I am simplifying Marx's implicit exchange theory, but my point is clear: dialectical conflict theory is, I think, a variety of exchange theory. Let me list some of these exchange dynamics more explicitly:

---

[32]Georg Simmel, *The Philosophy of Money*, trans. T. Bottomore and D. Frisby (Boston: Routledge & Kegan Paul, 1978; originally published in 1907).

[33]See Chapter 6.

1. Those who need scarce and valued resources that others possess but who do not have equally valued and scarce resources to offer in return will be dependent upon those who control these resources.
2. Those who control valued resources have power over those who do not. That is, the power of one actor over another is directly related to (*a*) the capacity of one actor to monopolize the valued resources needed by other actors and (*b*) the inability of those actors who need these resources to offer equally valued and scarce resources in return.
3. Those with power will press their advantage and will try to extract more resources from those dependent upon them in exchange for fewer (or the same level) of the resources that they control.
4. Those who press their advantage in this way will create conditions that encourage those who are dependent on them to (*a*) organize in ways that increase the value of their resources and, failing this, to (*b*) organize in ways that enable them to coerce those on whom they are dependent.

If the words *capitalist* and *proletarian* are inserted at the appropriate places in the above list, I think that Marx's exchange model becomes readily apparent. Dialectical conflict theory is thus a series of propositions about exchange dynamics in systems where the distribution of resources is unequal. And, as I think will become evident in the next chapters, sociological exchange theories have emphasized these dynamics that inhere in the unequal distribution of resources. Such is, I feel, Marx's major contribution to exchange theory.

## Georg Simmel's Exchange Theory

In Georg Simmel's *The Philosophy of Money*[34] is a critique of Marx's "value theory of labor"[35] and, in its place, a clear exposition of exchange theory. Since this important work remained untranslated until recently, I am not sure just how much influence it had on sociological exchange theory. Yet, since a number of exchange theorists are fluent in German, I suspect that Simmel's work has shaped modern exchange theory more than is commonly realized or acknowledged.

*The Philosophy of Money* is, as its title indicates, about the impact of money on social relations and social structure. I need not go into the details of Simmel's insightful analysis and critique of Marx for our present purposes. I only want to extract the purely exchange-theoretic principles

---

[34]Simmel, *The Philosophy.*

[35]Ibid. Simmel did not see value as inhering in "labor power," but it is what people desired and the level of scarcity in what they desired.

from Simmel's discussion. For Simmel, social exchange involves the following elements:

1. The desire for a valued object that one does not have.
2. The possession of the valued object by an identifiable other.
3. The offer of an object of value to secure from another the desired object.
4. The acceptance of this offer by the possessor of the valued object.[36]

Contained in this portrayal of social exchange are several additional points that Simmel emphasized. First, value is idiosyncratic and is, ultimately, tied to an individual's impulses and needs. Of course, what is defined as valuable is typically circumscribed by cultural and social patterns, but how valuable an object is will be a positive function of (a) the intensity of a person's needs and (b) the scarcity of the object. Second, much exchange involves efforts to manipulate situations so that the intensity of needs for an object are concealed and the availability of an object is made to seem less than what it actually is. Inherent in exchange, therefore, is a basic tension that can often erupt into other social forms, such as conflict. Third, to possess an object is to lessen its value and to increase the value of objects that one does not possess. Fourth, exchanges will only occur if both parties perceive that the object given is less valuable than the one received.[37] Fifth, collective units as well as individuals participate in exchange relations and, hence, are subject to the four processes listed above. Sixth, the more liquid the resources of an actor in an exchange—that is, the more that resources can be used in many types of exchanges—the greater will be that actor's options and power. For if an actor is not bound to exchange with any other and can readily withdraw resources and exchange them with another, then that actor has considerable power to manipulate any exchange.

Economic exchange involving money is only one case of this more general social form. But it is a very special case. For when money becomes the predominate means for establishing value in social relationships, the properties and dynamics of social relations are transformed. This process of displacing other criteria of value, such as logic, ethics, and aesthetics, with a monetary criterion is precisely the long-term evolutionary trend in societies. This trend is, as I mentioned earlier, both a cause and effect of money as the medium of exchange. Money emerged to facilitate exchanges and to realize even more completely humans' basic needs. But

---

[36]Simmel, *The Philosophy*, pp. 85–88.

[37]Surprisingly, Simmel did not explore in any great detail the consequences of unbalanced exchanges, where people are forced to give up a more valuable object for a less valuable one. Simmel simply assumed that at the time of exchange, one party felt that an increase in value had occurred. Retrospectively, a redefinition may occur, but the exchange would not occur if at the moment people did not perceive that they had received more value than they had given up.

---

**TABLE 10–1**   Georg Simmel's Exchange Principles

---

*The Attraction Principle*

I. The more actors perceive as valuable each other's respective resources, the more likely is an exchange relationship to develop among these actors.

*The Value Principle*

II. The greater is the intensity of an actor's needs for a resource of a given type, and the less available is that resource, the greater is the value of that resource to the actor.

*The Power Principle*

III. The more an actor perceives as valuable the resources of another actor, the greater is the power of the latter over the former.

IV. The more liquid are an actor's resources, the greater will be the exchange options and alternatives, and hence, the greater will be the power of that actor in social exchanges.

*The Tension Principle*

V. The more actors in a social exchange manipulate the situation in an effort to misrepresent their needs for a resource and/or conceal the availability of resources, the greater is the level of tension in that exchange and the greater is the potential for conflict.

---

once established, the use of money has the power to transform the structure of social relations in society.

Thus, the key insight in *The Philosophy of Money* is that the use of different criteria for assessing value has an enormous impact on the form of social relations. Thus, as money replaces barter and other criteria for determining values, social relations are fundamentally changed. But they are transformed in accordance with some basic principles of social exchange, which are never codified by Simmel but which, as I have indicated above, are very clear. In Table 10-1, I have codified these ideas into abstract exchange principles, because I see them as *the* basic processes depicted in sociological analysis of exchange. At the risk of repeating myself, let me summarize again the ideas behind the propositions. Principle I states that interaction occurs because actors value each other's resources, and in accordance with Principle II, value is a dual function of (*a*) actors' needs for resources and (*b*) the scarcity of resources. Principles III and IV underscore the fact that power is a part of the exchange process. Actors who have resources that others value are in a position to extract compliance from those seeking these resources (Principle III), and actors who have liquid or generalized resources, such as money, will be more likely to have power, since liquid resources can be more readily exchanged with alternative actors. Principle V states that as actors seek to manipulate situations in order to conceal the availability of resources and their needs for resources, tensions are created, and these tensions can result in conflict.

# MODERN EXCHANGE THEORY: A PREVIEW

Exchange theory is now one of the most prominent theoretical perspectives in sociology. A number of exchange perspectives have emerged in recent decades. Typically, they begin with inspiration from either the behaviorist tradition in psychology or the utilitarian heritage in economic theory. But as we will observe, these two traditions merge in modern exchange theory, especially as they deal with the related issues of inequality, power, and conflict.

In the chapters to follow, I will begin with the behavioristic approach of George C. Homans, and then, I will examine the more economic strategy of Peter M. Blau. As I believe will become clear, these two theorists begin at somewhat different places, and they advocate varying theoretical strategies, but I see their ideas as converging around the questions of tension and conflict in exchange systems. I will close with the network exchange approach of the late Richard Emerson and his frequent coauthor Karen Cook. Borrowing from behaviorism but extending Simmel's analysis of social forms, they have given theoretical underpinnings to network sociology. These three approaches offer, I feel, the best of the contemporary exchange theories.

# CHAPTER 11

# The Exchange Behaviorism of George C. Homans

One of the most prominent theorists of this century is George C. Homans, who, in recent decades, has advocated an exchange theoretic approach that borrows key concepts and propositions from behavioristic psychology.[1] Homans's early work emphasized "what people do" and "how they behave" in concrete settings, but it was highly inductive. It stressed pulling from empirical contexts generalizations in an effort to tie theory to ongoing social processes. But as I emphasized in Chapter 1, empirical generalizations are not theory; rather, they are what a theory is supposed to explain. And so, as Homans sought to explain a variety of empirical findings and generalizations, he shifted to a more deductive theoretical strategy. He labels this strategy *axiomatic,* but as I indicated in Chapter 1, axiomatic theorizing in sociology is not really possible. A better name is *formal theorizing* where the strict requirements of axiomatic theory are relaxed. But the basic idea is the same: to make deductions from abstract principles to empirical generalizations; and to the extent that the abstract statement subsumes or "covers" the empirical generalization, then the abstract statement explains the generalization (consult Figure 1-4).

I think that Homans's transition from empirical generalizations to deductive explanations is instructive. For as I argued in Chapter 1, one does not mechanically generalize from empirical findings to abstract laws. Empirical generalizations always have contextual content; and it is not

---

[1] I would like to thank George C. Homans for his constructive criticisms of this chapter as it appeared in an earlier edition of this book.

easy to simply raise the level of abstract and create abstract theory. Rather, a creative leap in abstraction is necessary, and then, armed with more abstract principles, one makes deductions back down to empirical generalizations. Homans's "creative leap" involved borrowing from behavioristic psychology, and so, perhaps I should view his exchange work as creative borrowing. Nonetheless, Homans recognized that induction from empirical contexts can only go so far; at some point, one must construct deductive propositional schemes to explain what one has induced from these contexts.

## THE EARLY INDUCTIVE STRATEGY

By 1950, with the publication of *The Human Group*, Homans's work revealed a clear commitment to an inductive strategy for building sociological theory.[2] In studies ranging from the analysis of a work group in a factory and a street gang to the kinship system of a primitive society and the structure of an entire New England community, he stressed the importance of observing people's actual behaviors and activities in various types of groups. By observing what people actually do, it is possible to develop concepts that are attached to the ongoing processes of social systems. Such concepts are termed by Homans *first-order abstractions*, since they merely represent names that observers use to signify a single class of observations in a group. Homans chose these words carefully. He wanted to emphasize their difference from the "second-order abstractions" commonly employed by sociologists. As distinct from the abstractions he prefers, *second-order abstractions* refer to several classes of observations and are thereby somewhat detached from ongoing events in actual groups. For example, "status" and "role" are favorite concepts used by sociologists to denote processes in groups, but upon careful reflection, it is evident that one does not observe directly a status or role; rather, they are highly abstract names that subsume numerous types and classes of events occurring in groups.

The typical practice of jumping to second-order abstractions in building theory was viewed by Homans as premature:

> [Sociologists should initially] attempt to climb down from the big words of social science, at least as far as common sense observation. Then, if we wish, we can start climbing up again, but this time with a ladder we can depend on.[3]

In constructing a firm bottom rung to the abstraction ladder, Homans introduced three first-order abstractions that provided labels or names to the actual events occurring in groups: *activities*, *interaction*, and

---

[2]George C. Homans, *The Human Group* (New York: Harcourt Brace Jovanovich, 1950).
[3]Ibid., p. 13.

*sentiments.* Activities pertain to what people do in a given situation; interaction denotes the process in which one unit of activity stimulates a unit of activity in another person; and sentiments refer to actions that signal the internal psychological states of people engaged in activities and interaction.

The three first-order abstractions, or *elements,* as Homans was fond of calling them, exist within an "external system." For Homans, this external system represents the environmental parameters of a particular group under study. As he was to later label this analytical approach, the external system summarizes the "givens" of a particular situation, which, for the purposes at hand, are not examined extensively. Of more interest, however, is the "internal system," which operates within the constraints imposed by the external system and which is composed of the interrelated activities, interactions, and sentiments of group members. The fact that activities, interactions, and sentiments are interrelated is of great analytical significance: changes in one element lead to changes in the other elements.

Of critical importance in the analysis of internal systems is the process of "elaboration" in which new patterns of organization among activities, interaction, and sentiments are constantly emerging by virtue of their interrelatedness with each other and with the external system. A group thus "elaborates itself, complicates itself, beyond the demands of the original situation"; in so doing, it brings about new types of activities, forms of interaction, and types of sentiments.

In *The Human Group,* Homans's strategy was to present a descriptive summary of five case studies on diverse groups. From each summary, Homans incorporates the elements of the internal system into propositions that describe the empirical regularities he had observed in the case study.[4] As he proceeds in his summaries, Homans attempts to substantiate the generalizations in one study from the next, while using each successive study as a source for additional generalizations. With this strategy, he hoped to generate a body of interrelated generalizations describing the various ways different types of groups elaborate their internal systems of activities, interactions, and sentiments. In this way, the first rungs of the abstraction ladder used in sociological theorizing would be dependable, providing a firm base for subsequent theorizing at a more abstract level.

Let me offer an example from Homans's summary of the famous Bank Wiring Room in the Hawthorne Western Electric Plant. In this setting, Homans "observed" these regularities:[5] (1) If the frequency of interaction

---

[4]In his work, Homans rarely makes direct observations himself. Rather, he has tended to rely on the observations of others, making from their reports inferences about events. As would be expected, Homans has often been criticized for accepting too readily the imprecise and perhaps inaccurate observations of others as an inductive base for theorizing.

[5]This extended example is adapted from the discussion of Homans' propositions in M.

between two or more persons increases, the degree of their liking for one another will increase, and vice versa.[6] (2) Persons whose sentiments of liking for one another increase will express these sentiments in increased activity, and vice versa.[7] (3) The more frequently persons interact with one another, the more alike their activities and their sentiments tend to become, and vice versa.[8] (4) The higher the rank of a person within a group, the more nearly his activities conform to the norms of the group, and vice versa.[9] (5) The higher the person's social rank, the wider will be the range of this person's interactions.[10]

These propositions describe some of the group-elaboration processes that Homans "observed" in the Bank Wiring Room. Propositions 1 and 2 summarize Homans's observations that the more the workers interacted, the more they appeared to like one another, which, in turn, seemed to cause further interactions above and beyond the work requirements of the external system. Such elaboration of interactions, sentiments, and activities also results in the differentiation of subgroups that reveal their own levels of output, topics of conversation, and patterns of work assistance. This tendency is denoted by Proposition 3. Another pattern of differentiation in the Bank Wiring Room is described by Proposition 4, whereby the ranking of individuals and subgroups occurs when group members compare their activities with those of other members and the output norms of the group. Proposition 5 describes the tendency of high-ranking members to interact more frequently with all members of the group, offering more on-the-job assistance.

Having tentatively established these and other empirical regularities in the Bank Wiring Room, Homans then analyzes the equally famous Norton Street Gang, described in William Whyte's *Street Corner Society*. In this second case study, Homans follows his strategy of confirming his earlier propositions, while inducing further generalizations: (6) The higher a person's social rank, the larger will be the number of persons that originate interaction for him or her, either directly or through intermediaries.[11] (7) The higher a person's social rank, the larger will be the number of persons toward whom interaction is initiated, either directly or through intermediaries.[12] (8) The more nearly equal in social rank a

J. Mulkay, *Functionalism and Exchange and Theoretical Strategy* (New York: Schocken Books, 1971), pp. 135–41. As was done by Mulkay, some of Homans' propositions are reworded for simplification.

[6] Homans, *Human Group,* p. 112.

[7] Ibid., p. 118.

[8] Ibid., p. 120.

[9] Ibid., p. 141.

[10] Ibid., p. 145.

[11] Ibid., p. 182.

[12] Ibid.

number of people are, the more frequently they will interact with one another.[13]

I see Propositions 6 and 7 as simply corollaries of Proposition 5. It follows, almost by definition, that those with a wide range of interactions will receive and initiate more interaction. However, Propositions 6 and 7 are induced separately from his observations of the Bank Wiring Room. For the Norton Street Gang, Homans observes that Doc, the leader of the gang, was the center of a complex network of communication. Such a pattern of communication was not observable in the Bank Wiring Room because stable leadership ranks had not emerged. Proposition 8 describes another process Homans sees in groups with clear leadership: the internal system tends to differentiate into super- and subordinate subgroups, whose members appear to interact more with each other than those of higher or lower rank.

After using the group-elaboration processes in the Norton Street Gang to confirm and supplement the propositions induced from the Bank Wiring Room, Homans then examines the Tikopia family, as described in Raymond Firth's famous ethnography. As with the Norton Street Gang, the Tikopia family. system was used to confirm earlier propositions and as a field from which to induce further propositions: (9) The more frequently persons interact with one another, when no one of them originates interaction with much greater frequency than the others, the greater is their liking for one another and their feeling of ease in one another's presence.[14] (10) When two persons interact with one another, the more frequently one of the two originates interaction for the other, the stronger will be the latter's sentiment of respect (or hostility), and the more nearly will the frequency of interaction be kept to a minimum.[15]

These propositions reveal, I should emphasize, another facet of Homans's inductive strategy. They establish some conditions under which Proposition 1 will hold true. In Proposition 1, Homans notes that increased interaction between two persons increases their liking, but in the Tikopia family system Homans discovered that this generalization holds true only under conditions where authority of one person over another is low. In the Tikopia family system, brothers revealed sentiments of liking as a result of their frequent interactions, primarily because they do not have authority over one another. However, frequent interaction with their father, who does have authority, was tense because the father initiated the interaction and because it usually involved the exercise of his authority.

Perhaps less critical than the substance of Propositions 9 and 10, I think, is the strategy they reveal. Homans has used an inductive technique

---

[13]Ibid., p. 184.
[14]Ibid., p. 243.
[15]Ibid., p. 247.

to develop a large number of propositions that describe empirical regularities. By continually testing them in different types of groups, he can confirm them or, as is the case with Propositions 9 and 10, qualify these earlier propositions. By following this strategy, Homans argued in this early work that it is possible to develop a large body of empirical statements that reveal the form: $y$ varies with $x$, under specifiable conditions. Stated in this form and with a clear connection to actual events in human groupings, such propositions encourage the development of more abstract concepts and theoretical statements. In addition, these statements are induced from a firm empirical footing that allows the abstract statements of sociology to be tested against the facts of ongoing group life. The next step in developing theory is to subsume these kinds of generalizations under more abstract laws. For as I emphasized in Chapter 1, empirical generalizations by themselves are not explanations. They are regularities that require a theoretical explanation. And so, it is not surprising that Homans eventually began to add another theoretical strategy to his general approach: formal theorizing, dressed up in the vocabulary of axiomatic theory (see Chapter 1 and Figure 1–4).

## THE ADDITION OF A DEDUCTIVE STRATEGY

Homans visualizes the process of deduction and induction in the following way:

> The process of borrowing or inventing the more general propositions I call *induction*, whether or not it is the induction of the philosophers; the process of deriving the empirical propositions from the more general ones I call explanation, and this is the *explanation* of the philosophers.[16]

*The Human Group* was, therefore, an exercise in induction, and now, the task of the theorist is explanation through deduction. And it is to this deductive approach—what I called formal theory in Chapter 1—that Homans turned in the 1960s with the publication of *Social Behavior: Its Elementary Forms*.[17] Such an approach emerged from Homans's long-standing criticism of most sociological theory, especially the functional strategy of Talcott Parsons (see Chapter 3). For over the years, Homans has mounted an increasingly pointed criticism of sociological theorizing, with the hope that "we bring what we say about theory into line with what we actually do, and so put an end to our intellectual hypocrisy."[18] On the road out of "intellectual hypocrisy" is a rejection of Talcott

---

[16]George C. Homans, *Social Behavior: Its Elementary Forms* (New York: Harcourt Brace Jovanovich, 1961), p. 10.

[17]Ibid.

[18]Ibid.

Parsons's classificatory strategy of developing systems of concept and categorical schemes (what I termed conceptual schemes in Chapter 1).

> Some students get so much intellectual security out of such a scheme, because it allows them to give names to, and to pigeonhole, almost any social phenomenon, that they are hesitant to embark on the dangerous waters of actually saying something about the relations between the phenomena—because they must actually take the risk of being found wrong.[19]

For Homans, a more proper strategy is the construction of deductive systems of propositions. At the top of the deductive system are the general axioms, from which lower-order propositions are logically deduced. The lowest-order propositions in the scheme are those composed of first-order abstractions that describe actual events in the empirical world. Because these empirical generalizations are logically related to a hierarchy of increasingly abstract propositions, culminating in logical articulation with the axioms, the empirical generalizations are assumed to be explained by the axioms (consult Figures 1-4 and 1-7 in Chapter 1). Thus, for Homans, to have deduced logically an empirical regularity from a set of more general propositions and axioms is to have explained the regularity.[20] Armed with this commitment to axiomatic theory, Homans articulates his exchange approach.

## THE EXCHANGE MODEL

### Sources of Homans's Psychological Exchange Perspective

I see Homans's exchange scheme first surfacing in a polemical reaction to Lévi-Strauss's structural analysis of cross-cousin marriage patterns. In collaboration with David Schneider, Homans previews what become

---

[19]George C. Homans, *The Nature of Social Science* (New York: Harcourt, Brace, & World, 1967), p. 13. Parsons has replied that such systems of concepts can be theory: "I emphatically dispute this [deductive theory] is all that can legitimately be called theory. In biology, for example, I should certainly regard the basic classificatory schemes of taxonomy, for example in particular the comparative anatomy of vertebrates, to be theoretical. Moreover very important things are, with a few additional facts, explained on such levels such as the inability of organisms with lungs and no gills to live for long periods under water" (Talcott Parsons, "Levels of Organization and the Mediation of Social Interaction," *Sociological Inquiry* 34 [Spring 1964], pp. 219-20).

[20]Homans has championed this conception of theory in a large number of works; see, for example, Homans, *Social Behavior*; Homans, *Nature of Social Science*; George C. Homans, "Fundamental Social Processes," in *Sociology,* ed. N. J. Smelser (New York: John Wiley & Sons, 1967), pp. 27-78; George C. Homans, "Contemporary Theory in Sociology," in *Handbook of Modern Sociology,* ed. R. E. L. Faris (Skokie, Ill.: Rand-McNally, 1964), pp. 251-77; and George C. Homans, "Bringing Men Back In," *American Sociological Review* 29 (December 1964), pp. 809-18. For an early statement of his position, see George C. Homans, "Social Behavior as Exchange," *American Journal of Sociology* 63 (August 1958), pp. 597-606. For a recent statement, see "Discovery and the Discovered in Social Theory," *Humboldt Journal of Social Relations* 7 (Fall-Winter 1979-80), pp. 89-102.

prominent themes in his writings: (1) a skeptical view of any form of functional theorizing, (2) an emphasis on psychological principles as the axioms of social theory, and (3) a preoccupation with exchange-theoretic concepts.[21]

In their assessment of Lévi-Strauss's exchange functionalism, Homans and Schneider take exception to virtually all that made Lévi-Strauss's theory. First, the conceptualization of different forms of indirect, generalized exchange is rejected. In so conceptualizing exchange, Lévi-Strauss "thinned the meaning out of it." Second, Lévi-Strauss's position that different forms of exchange symbolically reaffirm and integrate different patterns of social organization is questioned, for an "institution is what it is because it results from the drives, or meets the immediate needs, of individuals or subgroups within a society."[22] The result of this rejection of Lévi-Strauss's thought is for Homans and Schneider to argue that exchange theory must initially emphasize face-to-face interaction, focus primarily on limited and direct exchanges among individuals, and recognize that social structures are created and sustained by the behaviors of individuals.[23]

With this critique of the anthropological tradition, which, I should emphasize, emerged as a reaction to utilitarianism, Homans resurrects the utilitarian's concern with individual self-interest in the conceptual trappings of psychological behaviorism. For indeed, as Homans and Schneider emphasize: "We may call this an individual self-interest theory, if we remember that interests may be other than economic."[24] As becomes evident by the early 1960s, this self-interest theory is to be cast in the behaviorist language of B. F. Skinner. Given Homans's commitment to axiomatic theorizing and his concern with face-to-face interaction among individuals, it was perhaps inevitable that he would look toward Skinner and, indirectly, to the early founders of behaviorism—Pavlov, Thorndike, and Watson (see Chapter 10). But Homans borrows directly from Skinner's reformulations of early behaviorist principles.[25] Stripped of its

---

[21]George C. Homans and David M. Schneider, *Marriage, Authority, and Final Causes: A Study of Unilateral Cross-Cousin Marriage* (New York: Free Press, 1955). There are, however, hints of this interest in exchange theory in Homans's first major work, *English Villagers of the 13th Century* (New York: Russell & Russell, 1941).

[22]Homans and Schneider, *Marriage*, p. 15.

[23]In so doing, Homans advocates the principle of "methodological individualism," which sees social reality as the result of aggregated individual actions and behaviors. If social structure is aggregations of individual behavior, then the highest order principles in the deductive schemes of sociology must be about individual behavior. For another version of this, see Chapter 21 on Randall Collins's exchange perspective.

[24]Homans and Schneider, *Marriage*, p. 15.

[25]Homans, *Social Behavior*, pp. 1–83. For an excellent summary of the Skinnerian principles incorporated into Homans's scheme, see Richard L. Simpson, "Theories of Social Exchange" (Morristown, N.Y.: General Learning Press, 1972), pp. 3–4. As an interesting aside, Peter P. Ekeh, *Social Exchange Theory and the Two Sociological Traditions* (Cam-

subtlety, as Homans prefers, Skinnerian behaviorism states as its basic principle that if an animal has a need it will perform activities that in the past have satisfied this need. A first corollary to this principle is that organisms will attempt to avoid unpleasant experiences but will endure limited amounts of such experiences as a cost in emitting the behaviors that satisfy an overriding need. A second corollary is that organisms will continue emitting certain behaviors only as long as they continue to produce desired and expected effects. A third corollary of Skinnerian psychology emphasizes that as needs are satisfied by a particular behavior, animals are less likely to emit the behavior. A fourth corollary states that if in the recent past a behavior has brought rewards and if these rewards suddenly stop, the organism will appear angry and gradually cease emitting the behavior that formerly satisfied its needs. A final corollary holds that if an event has consistently occurred at the same time as a behavior that was rewarded or punished, the event becomes a stimulus and is likely to produce the behavior or its avoidance.

These principles were derived from behavioral psychologists' highly controlled observations of animals, whose needs could be inferred from deprivations imposed by the investigators. Although human needs are much more difficult to ascertain than those of laboratory pigeons and mice and despite the fact that humans interact in groupings that defy experimental controls, Homans believes that the principles of operant psychology can be applied to the explanation of human behavior in both simple and complex groupings. One of the most important adjustments of Skinnerian principles to fit the facts of human social organization involves the recognition that needs are satisfied by other people and that people reward and punish each other. In contrast with Skinner's animals, which only indirectly interact with Skinner through the apparatus of the laboratory and which have little ability to reward Skinner (except perhaps to confirm his principles), humans constantly give and take, or exchange, rewards and punishments.[26]

The conceptualization of human behavior as exchange of rewards (and punishments) among interacting individuals leads Homans to incorporate, in altered form, the first principle of elementary economics: humans rationally calculate the long-range consequences of their actions in a marketplace and attempt to maximize their material profits in their transactions. I emphasize, however, that Homans qualifies this simplistic notion:

bridge, Mass.: Harvard Univ. Press, 1975) has argued that had Homans not felt so compelled to reject Lévi-Strauss, he would not have embraced Skinnerian principles. Ekeh goes so far as to offer a hypothetical list of axioms that Homans would have postulated, had he not cast his scheme into the terminology of behaviorism.

[26]For a more detailed analysis of this point and the problems it presents, see Richard M. Emerson, "Social Exchange Theory," in *Annual Review of Sociology* 2 (Palo Alto, Calif.: Annual Reviews, 1976).

Indeed we are out to rehabilitate the economic man. The trouble with him was not that he was economic, that he used resources to some advantage, but that he was antisocial and materialistic, interested only in money and material goods and ready to sacrifice even his old mother to get them.[27]

Thus, to be an appropriate explanation of human behavior, this basic economic assumption must be altered in four ways: (1) People do not always attempt to maximize profits; they seek only to make some profit in exchange relations. (2) Humans do not usually make either long-run or rational calculations in exchanges; for, in everyday life, "the Theory of Games is good advice for human behavior but a poor description of it." (3) The things exchanged involve not only money but also other commodities, including approval, esteem, compliance, love, affection, and other less materialistic goods. (4) The marketplace is not a separate domain in human exchanges, for all interaction involves individuals exchanging rewards (and punishments) and seeking profits.

## The Basic Concepts

In an effort to meet the objections of his critics, Homans has altered somewhat his concepts since the original publication of his theory. Below, I have summarized the concepts of the theory in their most recent form:[28]

1. *Stimulus*—cues in the environment to which an organism responds with action.
2. *Action*—behaviors emitted by organisms directed at getting rewards and avoiding punishments.
3. *Reward*—the capacity to bestow gratification or to meet the needs of an organism that a stimulus possesses.
4. *Punishment*—the capacity to harm, injure, or to block the satisfaction of needs that a stimulus possesses.
5. *Value*—the degree of reward that a stimulus possesses.
6. *Cost*—rewards foregone or punishment incurred in engaging in one line of action.
7. *Perception*—the capacity to perceive, weigh, and assess rewards and costs.

---

[27]Homans, *Social Behavior*, p. 79. Kenneth Boulding ("An Economist's View of 'Social Behavior: Its Elementary Forms,'" *American Journal of Sociology* 67 [January 1962], p. 458) has noted that in Homans's work "economic man is crossed with the psychological pigeon to produce what the unkind might call the Economic Pigeon theory of human interaction." For a more detailed and serious analysis of Homans's meshing of elementary economics and psychology, see Ekeh, *Social Exchange Theory*, pp. 162–71.

[28]George Caspar Homans, *Social Behavior: Its Elementary Forms* (New York: Harcourt Brace Jovanovich, 1974), pp. 15–47. In contrast to the first edition of *The Structure of Sociological Theory*, which concentrated on the earlier edition of Homans's book, I have relied almost exclusively on the revised edition of *Social Behavior*. For a discussion of Homans's original formulation of his exchange theory, the reader is referred to pp. 235–47 of my *The Structure of Sociological Theory* (Homewood, Ill.: Dorsey Press, 1974).

8. *Expectation*—the level of rewards, punishments, or costs that an organism has come to associate with a particular stimulus.

These are the key concepts used in Homans's statement of his "elementary exchange principles."[29] He adds other concepts when applying these principles to human behavior. These new concepts, however, merely extend those listed here.

## Elementary Principles of Social Behavior

Homans labels propositions in terms of the variables that each highlights.[30] These labels are listed alongside the appropriate propositions as I have listed them in Table 11-1.

In Propositions I through III in Table 11-1, the principles of Skinnerian psychology are restated. The more valuable an activity (III), the more often such activity is rewarded (I), and the more a situation approximates one in which activity has been rewarded in the past (II), then the more likely a particular activity will be emitted. Proposition IV indicates the condition under which the first three fall into temporary abeyance. In accordance with the reinforcement principle of satiation or the economic law of marginal utility, humans eventually define rewarded activities as less valuable and begin to emit other activities in search of different rewards (again, however, in accordance with the principles enumerated in Propositions I-III). Proposition V introduces a more complicated set of conditions that qualify Propositions I through IV. From Skinner's observation that pigeons reveal anger and frustration when they do not receive an expected reward, Homans reasons that humans will probably reveal the same behavior.

In addition to these principles, Homans introduces a "rationality proposition," which summarizes the stimulus, success, and value propositions. I have also placed this proposition in Table 11-1 because it is so prominent in Homans's actual construction of deductive explanations. Let me translate the somewhat awkward vocabulary of Principle VI as Homans wrote it. People make calculations about various alternative lines of action. They perceive or calculate the value of the rewards that might be yielded by various actions. But they also temper this calculation in terms of the perceptions of how probable the receipt of rewards will be. Low probability of receiving highly valued rewards would lower their reward potential. Conversely, high probability of receiving a lower valued reward increases their overall reward potential. This relationship can be stated by the following formula:

---

[29]The concept of *cost* does not appear in Homans's actual axioms, but it is so prominent in his scheme that it is listed here with his other important concepts.

[30]See Homans, *Social Behavior*, pp. 11–68. Masculine pronouns are maintained, since this is how Homans wrote the propositions.

$$\text{Action} = \text{Value} \times \text{Probability}$$

People are, Homans asserts, rational in the sense that they are likely to emit that behavior, or action, among alternatives in which value on the right side of the equation is largest. For example, if $Action_1$ is highly valued (say, 10) but the probability of getting it by emitting $Action_1$ is low (.20) and if $Action_2$ is less valued (say, 5) but the probability of receiving it is greater (.50) than $Action_1$, then the actor will emit $Action_2$ (because $10 \times .20 = 2$ yields less reward than $5 \times .50 = 2.5$).

This proposition was implicit in Homans's earlier version of his exchange theory, but he has now made it explicit. This proposition, as noted above, summarizes the implications of the stimulus, value, and success propositions, because it indicates why actors would choose one stimulus situation that has been rewarding over another. And in fact, Homans had tended to use the rationality proposition in his explanations long before he made it explicit.[31] I see such a proposition as reevoking utilitarian notions of rational calculation but in the vocabulary of psychological behaviorism.

As summarized in Table 11-1, these basic principles or laws are seen by Homans to explain, in the sense of deductive explanation, patterns of human organization. As is obvious, they are psychological in nature. What is more, these psychological axioms constitute from Homans's viewpoint the only general sociological propositions, since "there are no general sociological propositions that hold good of all societies or social groups as such."[32]

However, the fact that psychological propositions are the most general does not make any less relevant or important sociological propositions stating the relationships among group properties or between group properties and those of individuals. On the contrary, these are the very propositions that are to be deduced from the psychological axioms. Thus, sociological propositions will be conspicuous in the deductive system emanating from the psychological principles. Homans stresses that sociology will finally bring what it says about theory into what it actually does when it arranges both abstract sociological statements and specific empirical generalizations in a deductive system with the psychological axioms at its top. For, as he continually emphasizes, to deduce propositions from one another is to explain them.

## Homans's Construction of Deductive Systems

The fact that the basic axioms to be used in sociological explanation seem to be obvious truisms should not be a cause for dismay. Too often, Homans

---

[31]See the first edition of *The Structure of Sociological Theory* and my "Building Social Theory: Some Questions about Homans' Strategy," *Pacific Sociological Review* 20 (April 1977), pp. 203–20.

[32]Homans, "Bringing Men Back In."

**TABLE 11–1**  Homans's Exchange Principles

I. *Success Proposition:* For all actions taken by persons, the more often a particular action of a person is rewarded, the more likely the person is to perform that action.

II. *Stimulus Proposition:* If in the past the occurrence of a particular stimulus or set of stimuli has been the occasion on which a person's action has been rewarded, then the more similar the present stimuli are to the past ones, the more likely the person is to perform the action or some similar action now.

III. *Value Proposition:* The more valuable to a person is the result of his action, the more likely he is to perform the action.

IV. *Deprivation-Satiation Proposition:* The more often in the recent past a person has received a particular reward, the less valuable any further unit of that reward becomes for him.

V. *Aggression-Approval Propositions:* (*a*) When a person's action does not receive the reward he expected or receives punishment he did not expect, he will be angry and become more likely to perform aggressive behavior, and the results of such behavior become more valuable to him. (*b*) When a person's action receives the reward expected, especially greater reward than expected, or does not receive punishment he expected, he will be pleased and become more likely to perform approving behavior, and the results of such behavior become more valuable to him.

VI. *Rationality Proposition:* In choosing between alternative actions, a person will choose that one for which, as perceived by him or her at the time, the value of the result, multiplied by the probability of getting that result, is greater.

insists, social scientists assume that the basic laws of social organization will be more esoteric—and certainly less familiar—since for them the game of science involves the startling discovery of new, unfamiliar, and presumably profound principles. In reference to these social scientists, Homans writes:

> All this familiarity has bred contempt, a contempt that has got in the way of the development of social science. Its fundamental propositions seem so obvious as to be boring, and an intellectual, by definition a wit and a man of the world, will go to great lengths to avoid the obvious.[33]

However, if the first principles of sociology are obvious, despite the best efforts of scientists to the contrary, Homans suggests that sociology cease its vain search for the esoteric and begin constructing deductive systems that recognize the fact that the most general propositions are not only psychological but familiar. In fact, if sociologists crave complexity, this task should certainly be satisfying, since the deductive systems connecting these simple principles to observed empirical regularities will be incredibly complex.

Unfortunately, Homans himself never offers a well-developed explanation. He has tended to simply invoke, in a rather ad hoc fashion, his

---

[33]Homans, *Nature of Social Science,* p. 73.

axioms and to reconcile them in a very loose and imprecise manner with empirical regularities. Or he has constructed brief deductive schemes to illustrate his strategy. These limitations in themselves constitute an important criticism of Homans's work, because he has not fully implemented his own theoretical strategy. Yet I do not see Homans's failure to actually do what he says should be done as negating the utility of the strategy. Let me examine one of Homans's deductive schemes to assess its potential as well as its problems.

One of Homans's explanations is reproduced below. Homans recognizes that this is not a complete explanation, but he argues that it is as good as any other that exists. Moreover, although certain steps in the deductive scheme are omitted, it is the proper way to develop scientific explanations from Homans's point of view. In this scheme, Homans seeks to explain Golden's Law that industrialization and the level of literacy in the population are highly correlated. As I emphasized in Chapter 1, such empirical generalizations are often considered to be theory, but Homans has correctly perceived that this "law" is only an empirical generalization that belongs at the bottom of the deductive scheme (see Figure 1-4). Propositions move from the most abstract statement, or the axiom(s),[34] to the specific empirical regularity to be explained. Golden's Law is thus explained in the following manner.

1. Men are more likely to perform an activity the more valuable they perceive the reward of that activity to be.
2. Men are more likely to perform an activity the more successful they perceive the activity to be in getting that reward.[35]
3. Compared with agricultural societies, a higher proportion of men in industrial societies are prepared to reward activities that involve literacy. (Industrialists want to hire bookkeepers, clerks, and persons who can make and read blueprints, manuals, and so forth.)
4. Therefore a higher proportion of men in industrial societies will perceive the acquisition of literacy as rewarding.
5. And [by (1)] a higher proportion will attempt to acquire literacy.
6. The provision of schooling costs money, directly or indirectly.
7. Compared with agricultural societies, a higher proportion of men in industrial societies is, by some standard, wealthy.
8. Therefore a higher proportion is able to provide schooling (through government or private charity), and a higher proportion is able to pay for their own schooling without charity.

---

[34]Note that I am using Homans's vocabulary, but as I emphasized in Chapter 1, "axiomatic" theory for sociology is unrealistic.

[35]Note that "axioms" 1 and 2 here are simply an earlier version of Homans's rationality principle (VI) listed in Table 11-1.

9. And a higher proportion will perceive the effort to acquire literacy as apt to be successful.

10. And [by (2) as by (1)] a higher proportion will attempt to acquire literacy.

11. Since their perceptions are generally accurate, a higher proportion of men in industrial societies will in fact acquire literacy. That is, the literacy rate is apt to be higher in an industrial than in an agricultural society.[36]

Propositions 1 and 2 are an earlier statement of the rationality proposition that summarizes the success, stimulus, and value propositions. It is from these first two propositions, or axioms, that others are derived in an effort to explain Golden's Law (Proposition 11 in the scheme above). Examining some of the features of this explanation can provide insight into Homans's deductive strategy.

In this example, the transition between Propositions 2 and 3 ignores so many necessary variables as to simply describe in the words of behavioral psychology what Homans perceives to have occurred. Why are people in industrial societies prepared to reward literacy? This statement does not explain; it describes and thus opens a large gap in the logic of the deductive system. For Homans, this statement is a given. It states a boundary condition, for the theory is not trying to explain why people are prepared to reward literacy. Another story is required to explain this event. Thus, Homans argues that "no theory can explain everything" and that it is necessary to ignore some things and assume them to be givens for the purposes of explanation at hand. The issue remains, however. Has not Homans defined away the most interesting sociological issue—what makes people ready to reward literacy in a society's historical development? For Homans, people are just ready to do so.

Another problem in this scheme comes with the placement of the word *therefore.* This transitive is typically used immediately following a statement of the givens that define away important classes of sociological variables. For example, the "therefore" preceding key propositions (4 and 8) begs questions such as: Why do people perceive literacy as rewarding? What level of industrialization would make this so? What level of educational development? What feedback consequences does desire for literacy have for educational development? By ignoring the why and what of these questions, Homans can then in Propositions 5 and 10 reinsert the higher order axioms (1 and 2) of the explanation, thereby giving the scheme an appearance of deductive continuity. In fact, however, answers

---

[36]George C. Homans, "Reply to Blain," *Sociological Inquiry* 41 (Winter 1971), pp. 19–24. This article was written in response to a challenge by Robert Blain for Homans to explain a sociological law: "On Homans' Psychological Reductionism," *Sociological Inquiry* 41 (Winter 1971), pp. 3–25.

to the critical sociological questions have been avoided, such as why people perceive as valuable and rewarding certain crucial activities.

Homans's reply to such criticisms is, I think, important to note.[37] First, he emphasizes that this deductive scheme was just an example or illustrative sketch, leaving out many details. Second, and more importantly, Homans contends that it is unreasonable for the critic to expect that a theory can and must explain every given condition (Propositions 3 and 7, for example). He offers the example of Newton's laws, which can help explain the movement of the tides (by virtue of gravitational forces of the moon relative to the axis of the earth), but these laws cannot explain why oceans are present and why the earth exists. I think that this latter argument is reasonable, in principle, since deductive theories explain only a delimited range of phenomena, as can be recalled by reference to Figure 1–6 in Chapter 1. But let me anticipate a point that I will emphasize shortly: while Homans does not need to explain the givens of a deductive scheme, all of the interesting sociological questions are contained in those givens. Moreover, these questions beg for the development of abstract *sociological* laws to explain them (Golden's Law is not an abstract principle, only an empirical generalization). And so, I wonder why Homans devotes his time to the construction of quasi-axiomatic (formal) systems that contain no sociological laws. Why concentrate on the psychological laws from which sociological laws are to be ultimately deduced when the real task of sociology is to develop these sociological laws? But this is one of many criticisms leveled at Homans' scheme in particular and, to some extent, at all exchange theory. Let me now turn to these criticisms and discuss them in more detail.

## CRITICISMS OF HOMANS'S STRATEGY AND EXCHANGE THEORY

### The Issues of Rationality

Homans's proposition on rationality could potentially open his exchange scheme to criticisms leveled against utilitarianism: do actors rationally calculate the costs and rewards? Homans partially meets this criticism by recognizing that people make calculations by weighing costs, rewards, and the probabilities of receiving rewards or avoiding punishments. But people do so in terms of value—that is, in terms of what bestows gratifications on them. Just what is rewarding is thus a personal matter and unique to all individuals. Depending on their past experiences, people

---

[37]Personal communication to the author.

establish their own values. Rationality, then, occurs in terms of calculations of personal value.[38]

There is, however, another implicit assumption that leaves Homans, and most exchange schemes, open to criticism. Do all human actions involve calculations? Do people always weigh and assess costs and rewards in all situations?[39] Often, critics argue, people just receive rewards without prior calculations. For example, when a person receives a gift or becomes the beneficiary of another's desires to bestow rewards, prior calculations are not involved. Rewards or reinforcement are, of course, still involved, but the principle of rationality excludes much interaction. Thus, Homans may have unduly limited his theory.

## The Issue of Tautology

More fundamental to the exchange perspective is the problem of tautology. If one examines the definition of key concepts—value, reward, and action—they appear to be defined in terms of each other. Rewards are gratifications that have value. Value is the degree of reward, or reinforcement. Action is reward-seeking activity. The question arises, then, as to whether it is possible to build a theory from axioms that are tautological. For example, Homans's proposition that "The more valuable to a person is the result of his action, the more likely he is to perform the action" could be considered a tautology. Value is defined as the degree of reward, and action is defined as reward-seeking behavior.[40]

Homans acknowledges the circularity, but views the problem as resolved by the use of deductive theory. Indeed, he argues that many axioms in deductive systems will be statements of equivalence, with concepts defined in terms of each other (for example, $f = ma$ and $E = mc^2$ in physics). For if the axioms are viewed as part of a deductive system, the

[38]Parsons, who similarly has dealt with the rationality issue ("Levels of Organization," in *Institutions and Social Exchange*, ed. H. Turk and R. L. Simpson [Indianapolis, Ind.: Bobbs-Merrill, 1971], p. 219), notes: "History thus seems to become for Homans the ultimate residual category, recourse to which can solve any embarrassment which arises from inadequacy of the more specific parts of the conceptual scheme. The very extent to which he has narrowed his conceptualization of the variables, in particular adopting the atomistic conception of values, . . . increases the burden thrown upon history and with it the confession of ignorance embodied in the statement, 'things are as they are because of ways in which they have come to be that way.'"

[39]Robert Bierstedt, "Review of Blain's Exchange and Power," *American Sociological Review* 30 (1965), pp. 789–90.

[40]For enlightening discussions of this problem, see Morton Deutsch, "Homans in the Skinner Box," in *Institutions and Social Exchange*, ed. H. Turk and R. L. Simpson (Indianapolis, Ind.: Bobbs-Merrill, 1971), pp. 81-92; Bengt Abrahamsson, "Homans on Exchange: Hedonism Revived," *American Journal of Sociology* 76 (September 1970), pp. 273–85; Pitirim Sorokin, *Sociological Theories of Today* (New York: Harper & Row, 1966), especially Chapter 15, "Pseudo-Behavioral and Empirical Sociologies," and Mulkay, *Functionalism and Exchange*, pp. 166–69.

problem of tautology is soon obviated. Although value and action cannot be measured independently when stated so abstractly, the deductive system allows for their independent measurement at the empirical level. Thus, "a tautology can take part in the deductive system whose conclusion is not a tautology."[41] Thus, Homans argues that the tautological nature of highly abstract axioms in a deductive system can be obviated when precise and clear derivations from the axioms are performed. In this process, independent definitions and indicators of key concepts can be provided. If these deductive steps are left out, however, and vague axioms are simply reconciled in an ad hoc fashion to empirical events, the problem of tautology will persist. And it is here that critics note: in virtually every explanation of social behavior in Homans's recent work, rigorous deductive systems are absent.[42] But in fairness, I think that Homans has been only attempting to suggest the utility of his concepts for future construction of deductive systems and to point out to sociologists that the ultimate explanatory principles of sociology are those about individual behavior.

## The Issue of Reductionism

Periodically, old philosophical issues are resurrected and debated fervently. Homans's exchange perspective has rekindled one such debate: the issue of reductionism. Homans's statements on the issue are sometimes tempered and at other times polemic, but the thrust of his argument has been made amply clear. He writes:

> The institutions, organizations, and societies that sociologists study can always be analyzed, without residue, into the behavior of individual men. They must therefore be explained by propositions about the behavior of individual men.[43]

This position has been particularly disturbing to some sociologists, since it appears to pose a problem: if we accept the contention that

---

[41]Homans, *Social Behavior*, p. 35.

[42]Ronald Maris ("The Logical Adequacy of Homans' Social Theory," *American Sociological Review* 35 [December 1970], pp. 1069–81) came to a somewhat different conclusion about the logical adequacy of Homans's theoretical manipulations. With the aid of symbolic logic and the addition of some assumptions, "Homans' theory of elementary social behavior has not been proven inadequate." But the criticisms of Maris's logical manipulation are sufficient to suggest that his analysis is not the definitive answer to the logical adequacy of Homans's deductions. For examples of these criticisms, see Don Gray, "Some Comments concerning Maris on 'Logical Adequacy' "; Stephen Turner, "The Logical Adequacy of 'The Logical Adequacy of Homans' Social Theory' "; and Robert Price, "On Maris and the Logic of Time"; all in *American Sociological Review* 36 (August 1971), pp. 706–13. Maris's "Second Thoughts: Uses of Logic in Theory Construction" can also be found in this issue. For a more adequate construction of a logically sophisticated exchange perspective, see B. F. Meeker, "Decisions and Exchange," *American Sociological Review* 36 (June 1971), pp. 485–95.

[43]George C. Homans, "Commentary," *Sociological Inquiry* 34 (Spring 1964), p. 231.

sociological propositions are reducible to those about individuals, then those about individuals are reducible to physiological propositions, which, in turn, are reducible to biochemical propositions, and so on in a reductionist sequence ending in the basic laws of physical matter. Homans has not been very helpful in alleviating sociologists' concern with whether he is advocating this kind of reductionism. In fact, he advocates the position that although the psychological axioms "cannot be derived from physiological propositions, . . . this condition is unlikely to last forever."[44] His tempered statements, however, are more revealing. Even if the laws of sociology are reducible to those of psychology and, at some future date, those of psychology to physiology, we will still need sociological laws. For example, to know that portions of Newtonian mechanics can be deduced from Einsteinian relativity theory does not stop us from using Newton's laws. Similarly, I think that Homans would argue: we need not reduce every sociological law to psychology each time we construct an explanation of an event.

This position argues against critics who have charged that Homans is a "nominalist" who asserts that society and its various collective forms (groups, institutions, organizations, and so forth) are mere names sociologists arbitrarily assign to the only "really real" phenomenon, the individual. For Homans is very clear on the matter:

> I, for one, am not going to back into the position of denying the reality of social institutions. . . . The question is not whether the individual is the ultimate reality or whether social behavior involves something more than the behavior of individuals. The question is, always, how social phenomena are to be explained.[45]

I think that the thrust of the last phase has been underemphasized in the criticisms of Homans's reductionism. Critics have too often implied that his reductionism forces him to embrace a particular variety of nominalism. Yet, for Homans, the issue has always been one of how to explain with deductive—or axiomatic—systems the groups and institutions studied by sociologists.

**Homans and the fallacy of "misplaced concreteness."**    I see the most persistent criticism of Homans's reductionist strategy as revolving around charges that he has fallen into the fallacy of misplaced concreteness.[46] As originally conceived by the philosopher Alfred North Whitehead, scientists had at one time fallen into the trap of thinking that

---

[44]Homans, "Commentary," p. 225.

[45]Homans, *Nature of Social Science*, pp. 61–62.

[46]For examples of this line of criticism, see Parsons, "Levels of Organization"; and Blain, "On Homans' Psychological Reductionism," *Sociological Inquiry* 41 (Winter 1971), pp. 10–19.

they could analyze the universe into its constituent parts and thereby eventually discover the basic elements or building blocks of all matter.[47] Once *the* basic building block had been found, it would only then be necessary to comprehend the laws of its operation for an understanding of everything else in the universe. In the eyes of Whitehead and others, these scientists had erroneously assumed that the basic parts of the universe were the only reality. In so doing, they had "misplaced" the concreteness of phenomena. In reality, the *relationships* among parts forming a whole are just as real as the constituent parts. The organization of parts is not the sum of the parts, but rather, the constitution of a new kind of reality.

Has Homans fallen into this fallacy? Numerous critics think that he has when he implies that the behavior of persons or "men" are the basic units, whose laws need only be understood to explain more complex sociocultural arrangements. I think that these critics are overreacting to Homans's reductionism, perhaps confusing his reductionist strategy with the mistaken assumption that Homans is a nominalist in disguise. Actually, Homans has never denied the importance of sociological laws describing complex sociocultural processes; on the contrary, they are critical propositions in any deductive system that attempts to explain these processes. In my view, all that Homans asserts is: these sociological laws are not the most general; they are subsumable under more general psychological laws (his axioms), which, with more knowledge and sophisticated intellectual techniques, will be subsumable under a still more general set of laws. At no point in this reductionist philosophy is Homans asserting that the propositions subsumed by a more general set of laws are irrelevant or unimportant. Thus, Homans has not misplaced the concreteness of reality. He has not denied the existence of emergent properties such as groups, organizations, and institutions, nor the theoretical significance of the laws describing these emergent phenomena. Homans is not a nominalist in disguise, but a sociological realist, who is advocating a particular strategy for understanding sociocultural phenomena.

**The utility of Homans's reductionist strategy.**    Once it becomes evident that Homans's reductionism is a theoretical strategy that does not deny the metaphysical or ontological existence of emergent phenomena, the next question becomes: is this strategy useful in explaining phenomena? Some critics have emphasized that a reductionist strategy will affect the kinds of theoretical and research questions sociologists will ask.[48] If one is concerned primarily with psychological laws as explanatory

---

[47]Alfred North Whitehead, *Science and the Modern World* (New York: Macmillan, 1925).

[48]For example, see Blain, "On Homans' Psychological Reductionism"; and Walter Buckley, *Sociology and Modern Systems Theory* (Englewood Cliffs, N.J.: Prentice-Hall, 1967), pp. 109-11.

principles, it is likely that research questions and theoretical generalizations will begin to revolve around psychological and social-psychological phenomena, because these phenomena are the most readily derived from psychological axioms. Thus, despite a recognition that complex sociological phenomena are real, the adoption of a reductionist strategy for building theory will inadvertently result in the avoidance of the macro patterns of social organization studied by many sociologists. To the extent that such one-sided research and theory building are the result of a reductionist strategy, then this strategy is undesirable and can be questioned on these grounds alone. However, critics charge that there are more fundamental grounds on which to reject Homans's strategy: adherence to his strategy at the present time will lead to logically imprecise and empirically empty theoretical formulations.

This indictment is, of course, severe and needs to be documented. I sense that Homans may be correct in holding that a deductive axiomatic strategy necessitates reductionism, for the goal of such a strategy is to subsume under ever more general axioms what we previously considered the most general ones. Such a process of subsumption may indeed lead first to the subsumption of sociological axioms under psychological axioms and then to the subsequent subsumption of these latter axioms under physiological, biochemical, and physical laws. Just as many of the laws of chemistry can be subsumed under the laws of physics, so sociological laws may be subsumed by the laws of psychology. However, I believe that deduction of sociological laws from psychological axioms should occur in a two-step process: (1) A series of well-established sociological laws from which it is possible to deduce a wide variety of sociological propositions that have received consistent empirical support must be developed. (2) Then, and only then, a clear body of psychological axioms, which are amendable to similar reductions and which have received consistent empirical support, can be used to explain the sociological laws.[49] I think that Step 1 must occur prior to Step 2, as it typically has in the physical sciences. Homans has recognized the fact that the social sciences have not achieved Step 1 when he notes that the "issue for the social sciences is not whether we should be reductionists, but rather, if we were reductionists, whether we could find any propositions to reduce."[50]

Yet, I believe that Homans fails to realize the full implications of his statement. Without well-established sociological laws to subsume, the critics can correctly ask: What is the utility of attempting to subsume what does not exist? Would it not be far wiser to expend our efforts in developing sociological laws and let the issue of reductionism take care of itself when these laws are established? To attempt prematurely to develop psy-

---

[49]Turner, "Building Social Theory."

[50]Homans, *Nature of Social Science*, p. 86.

chological axioms and then deduce sociological propositions from them in the absence of well-established sociological laws is likely to generate logically imprecise deductions, as I illustrated with Homans's explanation of Golden's Law. What Homans typically does in his deductions is to take as givens all the interesting sociological questions, answers to which would lead to the development of the sociological laws needed to fill out properly his deductive system. The end result is that an empirical generalization—say, Golden's Law—may be explained without any of the desirable components of a deductive system—clear sociological laws.

Such deductive systems will ultimately boil down to statements such as: things are as they are because they are rewarding. What this does is to repeat the empirical generalization to be explained in the words of behavioral psychology, without logically deducing the generalization from sociological laws, which, in turn, are deduced (if one is so inclined) from psychological laws.[51]

## HOMANS'S IMAGE OF SOCIETY

What has always intrigued me about Homans's approach is the substantive image of society that he presents. I share his commitment to deductive theory, although I think that he is premature in his overconcern with psychological laws. But these kinds of criticisms aside, Homans has approached the substantive issues that divide sociologists in a very creative way. The most prominent of these substantive issues is the micro versus macro controversy that I outlined in Chapter 1. That is, how do we reconcile the microprocesses of behavior, action, and interaction of individuals with the macrostructures and institutions of society? How do we explain their relationship? One answer is through deductive reduction; that is, if sociological laws about social structures can be deduced from those about individual behavior, then the micro-macro schism is resolved by the logic of deductive reasoning. I find this answer less compelling than the substantive image that Homans discursively develops in both

---

[51]The concepts of behavioral psychology do not have to muddle empirical generalizations, so long as one does not prematurely try to deduce sociological propositions to crude psychological propositions. In fact, operant principles can be used quite fruitfully to build (note: not reduce) more complex exchange principles that pertain to sociological processes (note: not psychological). For an impressive attempt at employing operant principles as a starting point and then changing them to fit the facts of emergent properties, see Richard M. Emerson's various works, especially "Power-Dependence Relations," *American Sociological Review* 27 (February 1962), pp. 31–41; "Power-Dependent Relations: Two Experiments," *Sociometry* 27 (September 1964), pp. 282–98; "Operant Psychology and Exchange Theory," in *Behavior Sociology: The Experimental Analysis of Social Process,* ed. R. L. Burgess and D. Bushell, Jr. (New York: Columbia University Press, 1969), pp. 379–405; and "Exchange Theory, Part I: A Psychological Basis for Social Exchange" and "Exchange Theory, Part II: Exchange Relations and Network Structures," in *Sociological Theories in Progress,* ed. J. Berger, M. Zelditch, Jr., and B. Anderson (New York: Houghton Mifflin, 1972), pp. 38–87.

**FIGURE 11-1**   Homans's Image of Social Organization

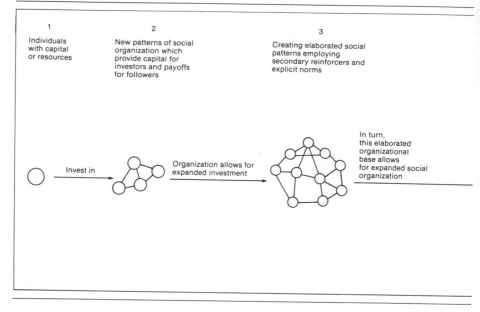

*The Human Group* and *Social Behavior*. For I think that the *substantive* vision of the social world first communicated in *The Human Group* and expanded upon in the later exchange works is provocative and likely to be the most enduring feature of Homans's theoretical perspective. And thus, let me close this chapter on Homans's approach with a review of this more substantive image of society.

In *The Human Group*, Homans's numerous empirical generalizations describe the processes of group elaboration and disintegration. Groups are observed to differentiate into subgroups, to form leadership ranks, to codify norms, to establish temporary equilibriums, and then, in his last case study of a dying New England town, to reveal the converse of these processes. In the later exchange works, the concepts of *activities, inter-actions,* and *sentiments,* which are incorporated into the propositions describing such group elaboration, are redefined in order to give Homans the opportunity to explain why these processes should occur. Human activity becomes action directed toward the attainment of rewards and avoidance of punishments. Interaction becomes social behavior where the mutual actions of individuals have cost and reward implications for the parties to the interaction. People are now seen as emitting those activities that increase the likelihood of profits—rewards less costs—measured against a set of expectations. Such rewarding and costly exchanges of activities are not viewed as necessarily involving the exchange of material rewards and punishments, but more frequently "psychic profits."

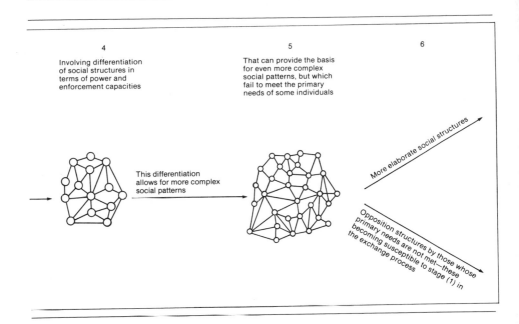

4

Involving differentiation
of social structures in
terms of power and
enforcement capacities

5

That can provide the basis
for even more complex
social patterns, but which
fail to meet the primary
needs of some individuals

6

This differentiation
allows for more complex
social patterns

More elaborate social structures

Opposition structures by those whose
primary needs are not met—these
becoming susceptible to stage (1) in
the exchange process

Just as he did in *The Human Group*, Homans enumerates concepts that enable him to denote processes of group elaboration in his more recent work. In *Social Behavior*, the particular explanations are of less interest, I feel, than Homans's descriptions of how vital group processes—interaction, influence, conformity, competition, bestowal of esteem, justice, ranking, and innovation—ebb and flow as actors seek psychic profits in their exchanges of rewards and punishments. In these descriptions, considerable intuitive insight into the basic processes of human interaction is evident. It was these insights that made *The Human Group* appealing, and I think that it is this same feature of *Social Behavior* that makes it an important work.

Despite the suggestiveness of his descriptions of basic processes in earlier chapters, the most theoretically interesting section of *Social Behavior* is the closing chapter, "The Institutional and the Subinstitutional." Introduced apologetically as a last-gasp "orgy," Homans nevertheless returns to an issue first raised in *The Human Group*: the relationship of processes in groups to the structures of larger societies, or "civilizations," as he phrased the issue then. As he emphasized in the last paragraph of *The Human Group*, the development of civilizations is ultimately carried out by persons in groups:

At the level of the small group, society has always been able to cohere. We infer, therefore, that if civilization is to stand, it must maintain, in the relation between the groups that make up society and the central direction of society, some of the features of the small group itself.[52]

In *Social Behavior,* Homans has a more sophisticated answer to why it appears that society coheres around the small group: society is elaborated and structured from fundamentally the same exchange processes that cause the elaboration of the small group. All social structures are thus built up from basically the same exchange processes. In the explication of why this should be so, Homans provides an interesting image of how patterns of social organization are created, maintained, changed, and broken down. This image is not developed into what can be considered adequate theory, as has already been shown. But it does provide a vision of the social world that can perhaps initiate a more useful exchange-theoretic perspective on the processes underlying various patterns of social organization.

To explicate the relationship between elementary exchange processes and more complex patterns of social organization, Homans—much like Parsons a decade earlier—provides a sketch of the process of institutionalization, which I have illustrated in Figure 11-1.[53] At points in history, some people have the "capital" to reinforce or provide rewards for others, whether it comes from their possessing a surplus of food, money, a moral code, or valued leadership qualities. With such capital, "institutional elaboration" can occur, since some can invest their capital by trying to induce others (through rewards or threats of punishments) to engage in novel activities. These new activities can involve an "intermeshing of the behavior of a large number of persons in a more complicated or roundabout way than has hitherto been the custom." Whether this investment involves conquering territory and organizing a kingdom or creating a new form of business organization, those making the investment must have the resources—whether it be an army to threaten punishment, a charismatic personality to morally persuade followers, or the ability to provide for people's subsistence needs—to keep those so organized in a situation where they derive some profit. At some point in this process, such organization can become more efficient and hence rewarding to all when the rewards are clearly specified in terms of generalized reinforcers, such as money, and when the activities expended to get their rewards are more clearly specified, such as when explicit norms and rules emerge. In turn, this increased efficiency allows for greater organization of activities. This

[52]Homans, *Human Group,* p. 468.

[53]Homans, *Social Behavior,* Chapter 16. The reader should find interesting a comparison of this model of institutionalization and that provided by Parsons, since Homans implicitly sees this model as an alternative to that presented by functionalists such as Parsons. But a careful reading of Talcott Parsons, *The Social System* (New York: Free Press, 1951), pp. 1–91 and his more recent work on evolution would reveal a remarkable similarity between his conceptualization of this basic process and that of Homans.

new efficiency increases the likelihood that generalized reinforcers and explicit norms will be used to regulate exchange relations and hence increase the profits to those involved. Eventually, the exchange networks involving generalized reinforcers and an increasingly complex body of rules require differentiation or subunits—such as a legal and banking system—that can maintain the stability of the generalized reinforcers and the integrity of the norms.

Out of this kind of exchange process, then, social organization—whether at a societal, group, organizational, or institutional level—is constructed. The emergence of most patterns of organization is frequently buried in the recesses of history, but such emergence is typified by these accelerating processes: (1) People with capital (reward capacity) invest in creating more complex social relations that increase their rewards and allow those whose activities are organized to realize a profit. (2) With increased rewards, these people can invest in more complex patterns of organization. (3) Increasingly complex patterns of organization require, first of all, the use of generalized reinforcers and then the codification of norms to regulate activity. (4) With this organizational base, it then becomes possible to elaborate further the pattern of organization, creating the necessity for differentiation of subunits that assure the stability of the generalized reinforcers and the integrity of norms. (5) With this differentiation, it is possible to expand even further the networks of interaction, since there are standardized means for rewarding activities and codifying new norms as well as enforcing old rules.

However, these complex patterns of social organization employing formal rules and secondary or generalized reinforcers can never cease to meet the more primary needs of individuals.[54] Institutions first emerged to meet these needs; and no matter how complex institutional arrangements become and how many norms and formal rules are elaborated, these extended interaction networks must ultimately reinforce humans' more primary needs. When these arrangements cease meeting the primary needs from which they ultimately sprang, an institution is vulnerable and apt to collapse if alternative actions, which can provide primary rewards, present themselves as a possibility. In this situation, low- or high-status persons—someone who has little to lose by nonconformity to existing prescriptions—will break from established ways to expose to others a more rewarding alternative. Institutions may continue to extract conformity for a period, but they will cease to do so when they lose the capacity to provide primary rewards. Thus, complex institutional arrangements must ultimately be satisfying to individuals, not simply because of the weight of culture or norms, but because they are constructed to serve people:

> Institutions do not keep going just because they are enshrined in norms, and it seems extraordinary that anyone should ever talk as if they did. They

---

[54]Unfortunately, Homans never defines "primary need."

keep going because they have pay-offs, ultimately pay-offs for individuals. Nor is society a perpetual-motion machine, supplying its own fuel. It cannot keep itself going by planting in the young a desire for these goods and only those goods that it happens to be in shape to provide. It must provide goods that men find rewarding not simply because they are sharers in a particular culture but because they are men.[55]

The fact that institutions of society must also meet primary needs sets the stage for a continual conflict between institutional elaboration and the primary needs of humans. As one form of institutional elaboration meets one set of needs, it may deprive people of other important rewards—opening the way for deviation and innovation by those presenting the alternative rewards that have been suppressed by dominant institutional arrangements. In turn, the new institutional elaborations that may ensue from innovators who have the capital to reward others will suppress other needs, which, through processes similar to its inception, will set off another process of institutional elaboration.

In sum, this sketch of how social organization is linked to elementary processes of exchange represents an interesting perspective for analyzing how patterns of social organization are built up, maintained, altered, and broken down. Although there are obvious conceptual problems—for example, the difficulty of distinguishing primary rewards from other types—the image of society presented by Homans is provocative. It can perhaps lead Homans to a fruitful strategy for developing a theory of exchange relations.

---

[55]Homans, *Social Behavior*, p. 366.

# CHAPTER 12

# The Structural Exchange
# Theory of Peter M. Blau

Peter M. Blau has been one of the most productive social theorists over the last three decades. In his early work on informal processes within bureaucracies, he noted how frequently employees exchanged assistance with their work for respect, information for social approval, and other processes of giving and receiving nonmaterial rewards. Yet, in looking back on this early empirical work, he recently remarked, "I was not aware, or did not remember, that conceptions of social exchange had been used by many others before, from Aristotle to Mauss."[1] In some ways, I think that this ignorance may have been an advantage because in rediscovering exchange processes, Blau created a constructive blend of exchange, functional, and dialectical conflict theories. And although Blau has in recent years abandoned his exchange approach for another theoretical strategy (see Chapter 20),[2] I think that his exchange orientation is still very important and worthy of a more detailed analysis.[3]

---

[1]Peter M. Blau, "Contrasting Theoretical Perspectives," paper delivered at the German-American Theory Conference, 1984, p. 2.

[2]Peter M. Blau, *Inequality and Heterogeneity* (New York: Free Press, 1977).

[3]Peter M. Blau's major exchange work is *Exchange and Power in Social Life* (New York: John Wiley & Sons, 1964). This formal and expanded statement on his exchange perspective was anticipated in earlier works. For example, see Peter M. Blau, "A Theory of Social Integration," *American Journal of Sociology* 65 (May 1960), pp. 545–56; and Peter M. Blau, *The Dynamics of Bureaucracy,* 1st and 2d eds. (Chicago: University of Chicago Press, 1955, 1963). It is of interest to note that George C. Homans in *Social Behavior: Its Elementary Forms* (New York: Harcourt, Brace & World, 1961) makes frequent reference to the data summarized in this latter work. For a more recent statement of Blau's position, see Peter M. Blau, "Interaction: Social Exchange," in *International Encyclopaedia of the Social Sciences,* vol. 7 (New York: Macmillan, 1968), pp. 452–58.

# BLAU'S THEORETICAL STRATEGY

In contrast with Homans's concern with developing deductive explanations, Blau offers what he terms a *theoretical prolegomenon*—or a conceptual sketch that can serve as a preliminary to more mature forms of theorizing. In many ways, Blau's strategy resembles Talcott Parsons's, for he appears less concerned with developing a rigorous system of propositions than with enumerating concepts that can capture in loosely phrased and related propositions the fundamental processes occurring at diverse levels of social organization. While there is less categorization than in Parsons's conceptual efforts, Blau is concerned with developing an initial bundle of concepts and propositions that can provide insight into the operation of a wide range of sociological processes, from the behavior of individuals in small-group contexts to the operation of whole societies.

Yet, as his more recent theorizing reveals and as he was led to remark in a retrospective look at his exchange approach, sociologists should be concerned with exchange analysis because "it is one of the few subject matters, outside of mathematical sociology, that lends itself to the development of systematic axiomatic theory."[4] Thus, although he does not develop his exchange ideas into an axiomatic format as does George Homans (see Chapter 11), he clearly had this goal in mind. And as we will see in Chapter 20, he has tried in recent years to implement a more formal deductive approach. And so, as I proceed with Blau's approach, I will convert his ideas into formal principles. Such conversion is, I feel, in the spirit of his underlying theoretical strategy.

But at this stage in his theoretical work on exchange, Blau tries to use a bundle of exchange concepts and implicit principles to bridge the micro-macro gap. For he thought that exchange theory could provide a means for analyzing individual interactions as well as more structural relations in terms of the same basic framework. Although he is no longer so convinced that this can be the case, he sought in *Exchange and Power in Social Life* to (1) conceptualize some of the simple and direct exchange processes occurring in relatively small interaction networks and (2) then expand the conceptual edifice to include some of the complexities inherent in less direct exchange processes in larger social systems. In a vein similar to Homans's analysis, Blau first examines "elementary" forms of social exchange with an eye to how they help in the analysis of "subinstitutional" behavior. However, unlike Homans, who terminates his analysis by simply presenting a conceptual "orgy" in *Social Behavior,*[5] Blau begins to supplement the exchange concepts describing elementary processes in an effort to understand more complex processes of institutionalization.

---

[4] Blau, "Contrasting Theoretical Perspectives."

[5] Homans, "The Institutional and the Subinstitutional," *Social Behavior,* rev. ed., Chapter 16.

Thus, in a manner reminiscent of Parsons's analysis of the process of institutionalization in *The Social System*[6] (see Chapter 3), Blau begins with a conceptualization of basic interactive processes; then, utilizing and supplementing the concepts developed in this analysis, he shifts to the analysis of more elaborate institutional complexes.

## BASIC EXCHANGE PRINCIPLES

I find that Blau does not define the variables in his exchange scheme as explicitly as Homans does. Rather, considerably more attention is devoted to defining exchange as a particular type of association, involving "actions that are contingent on rewarding reactions from others and that cease when these expected reactions are not forthcoming."[7] For Blau, exchange occurs only among those relationships in which rewards are expected and received from designated others. Much like Parsons's conception of voluntarism and Homans's rationality proposition, Blau conceptualizes as exchange activities only those behaviors that are oriented to specified goals, or rewards, and that involve actors selecting from various potential alternatives, or costs, a particular line of action that will yield an expected reward. In pursuing rewards and selecting alternative lines of behavior, actors are conceptualized as seeking a profit (rewards less costs) from their relations with others. Thus, Blau employs the basic concepts of all exchange theories—reward, cost, and profit—but he limits their application to relations with others from whom rewards are expected and received. This definition of exchange is considerably more limited than Homans's definition, which encompasses all activity as exchange, regardless of whether rewards are expected or received.

In common with Homans, however, Blau recognizes that in focusing on associations involving "an exchange of activity, tangible or intangible, and more or less rewarding and costly, between two persons," an elementary economic model is being employed.[8] Indeed, social life is conceived to be a marketplace in which actors negotiate with each other in an effort to make a profit. But Blau shares the skepticism that led Homans to reject the theory of games as good advice but a poor description of human behavior and that induced Parsons's earlier in *The Structure of Social Action* to discard the extremes of utilitarianism.[9] Blau recognizes that, unlike the simple "economic man" of classical economics (and of more recent rationalistic models of human behavior), humans (1) rarely pursue one specific goal to the exclusion of all others, (2) are frequently

---

[6]Talcott Parsons, *The Social System* (New York: Free Press, 1951), especially pp. 1–200.

[7]Blau, *Exchange and Power*, p. 6.

[8]Ibid., p. 88.

[9]Talcott Parsons, *The Structure of Social Action* (New York: McGraw-Hill, 1937).

---

**TABLE 12–1**   Blau's Implicit Exchange Principles

I. *The Rationality Principle*
The more profit people expect from one another in emitting a particular activity, the more likely they are to emit that activity.

II. *The Reciprocity Principles*

A. The more people have exchanged rewards with one another, the more likely are reciprocal obligations to emerge and guide subsequent exchanges among these persons.

B. The more the reciprocal obligations of an exchange relationship are violated, the more are deprived parties disposed to sanction negatively those violating the norm of reciprocity.

III. *The Justice Principles*

A. The more exchange relations have been established, the more likely they are to be governed by norms of ''fair exchange.''

B. The less norms of fairness are realized in an exchange, the more are deprived parties disposed to sanction negatively those violating the norms.

IV. *The Marginal Utility Principle*
The more expected rewards have been forthcoming from the emission of a particular activity, the less valuable is the activity, and the less likely is its emission.

V. *The Imbalance Principle*
The more stabilized and balanced are some exchange relations among social units, the more likely are other exchange relations to become imbalanced and unstable.

---

inconsistent in their preferences, (3) virtually never have complete information of alternatives, and (4) are never free from social commitments limiting the available alternatives. Furthermore, in contrast with a purely economic model of human transactions, social associations involve the exchange of rewards whose value varies from one transaction to another without a fixed market value and whose value cannot be expressed precisely in terms of a single, accepted medium of exchange (such as money). In fact, the vagueness of the values exchanged in social life is a "substantive fact, not simply a methodological problem."[10] As Blau emphasizes, the values people hold are inherently diffuse and ill defined.[11]

As I just indicated, Blau does not develop explicit exchange axioms or principles. But in Table 12–1, I have listed his basic ideas in propositional form. Proposition I, which I have termed the *rationality principle,* combines Homans's Axioms 1, 2, and 3, where rewarding stimulus situations, the frequency of rewards, and the value of rewards increase the

---

[10]Blau, *Exchange and Power,* p. 95.

[11]As I noted for Homans's scheme, this "fact" creates both methodological and logical problems. If value cannot be precisely measured, how is it possible to discern just how value influences behavior? If value cannot be measured independently of the behavior it is supposed to regulate, then propositions will be tautologous and of little use in building sociological theory.

likelihood that actions would be emitted. Actually, as we saw in the last chapter, Homans's own deductive systems—for example, the one he constructed to explain Golden's Law—collapses his first three axioms into a similar rationality principle: "In choosing between alternative actions, a person will choose that one for which as perceived by him at the time, the value of the result, multiplied by the probability of getting the result, is greater."[12] In practice, then, Homans and Blau utilize the same basic principle. Blau's use of the concept "reward expectation" would encompass the same phenomena denoted by Homans's "perception of reward" and "probability" of getting a reward.

Propositions II-A and II-B on reciprocity borrow from Malinowski's and Lévi-Strauss's initial discussion as reinterpreted by Alvin Gouldner.[13] Blau postulates that "the need to reciprocate for benefits received in order to continue receiving them serves as a 'starting mechanism' of social interaction."[14] Equally important, once exchanges have occurred, a "fundamental and ubiquitous norm of reciprocity" emerges to regulate subsequent exchanges. Thus, inherent in the exchange process, per se, is a principle of reciprocity. Over time, and as the conditions of Principle I are met, a social "norm of reciprocity," whose violation brings about social disapproval and other negative sanctions, emerges in exchange relations. And I should emphasize here in anticipation of later discussion that violations of the norm of reciprocity become significant in Blau's subsequent analysis of opposition and conflict.

Much like Homans, Blau recognizes that people establish expectations about what level of reward particular exchange relations should yield. Unlike Homans, however, Blau recognizes that these expectations are normatively regulated. These norms are termed *norms of fair exchange* since they determine what the proportion of rewards to costs should be in a given exchange relation. And like Homans, Blau asserts that aggression is forthcoming when these norms of fair exchange are violated. I have incorporated these ideas into Propositions III-A and III-B, terming them *the justice principles*.[15]

Following economists' analyses of transactions in the marketplace, Blau introduces a principle on "marginal utility" (Proposition IV). The more a person has received a reward, the more satiated he or she is with that reward, and the less valuable are further increments of the reward.[16]

---

[12]Homans, *Social Behavior*, p. 43.

[13]Alvin W. Gouldner, "The Norm of Reciprocity," *American Sociological Review* 25 (April 1960), pp. 161–78.

[14]Blau, *Exchange and Power*, p. 92.

[15]See Peter M. Blau, "Justice in Social Exchange," in *Institutions and Social Exchange: The Sociologies of Talcott Parsons and George C. Homans*, ed. H. Turk and R. L. Simpson (Indianapolis, Ind.: Bobbs-Merrill, 1971), pp. 56–68; see also: Blau, *Exchange and Power*, pp. 156–57.

[16]Blau, *Exchange and Power*, p. 90.

I should note that this marginal utility principle is the same as Homans's axiom on "deprivation-satiation." For both Blau and Homans, then, actors will seek alternative rewards until their level of satiation declines.

Blau's exchange model is vitally concerned with the conditions under which conflict and change occur in social systems, and so, these justice principles become crucial generalizations. As I will document shortly, the deprivations arising from violating the norms of fair exchange can lead to retaliation against violators.

Proposition V on imbalance completes my listing of Blau's abstract laws. For Blau, as for all exchange theorists, established exchange relations are seen to involve costs or alternative rewards foregone. Since most actors must engage in more than one exchange relation, the balance and stabilization of one exchange relation is likely to create imbalance and strain in other necessary exchange relations. For Blau, social life is thus filled with dilemmas in which people must successively trade off stability and balance in one exchange relation for strain in others as they attempt to cope with the variety of relations they must maintain. In his last chapter on institutionalization, Homans hinted at this principle when he emphasized that, in satisfying some needs, institutional arrangements deny others and thereby set into motion a perpetual dialectic between dominant institutions and change-oriented acts of innovation and deviance.[17] It is from this concluding insight of Homans into the dialectical nature of relationships between established social patterns and forces of opposition that Blau is to begin his analysis of exchange in social life. Indeed, we might even term Blau's approach a *dialectical exchange theory* because inherent in exchange relations are potentials for conflict. Indeed, as I have indicated in the last chapter, Marxian conflict theory and exchange theory have much in common, for both are concerned with the conditions under which actors feel deprived of expected rewards and are mobilized to redress their grievances.

## BASIC EXCHANGE PROCESSES IN SOCIAL LIFE

### Elementary Systems of Exchange

Blau initiates his discussion of elementary exchange processes with the assumption that people enter into social exchange because they perceive the possibility of deriving rewards (Principle I). Blau labels this perception *social attraction* and postulates that unless relationships involve such attraction, they are not relationships of exchange. In entering an exchange relationship, each actor assumes the perspective of another and thereby derives some perception of the other's needs. Actors then manipulate their

---

[17]Homans, *Social Behavior,* pp. 390–98 (1961 ed.); pp. 366–73 (1974 ed.).

presentation of self so as to convince each other that they have the valued qualities others appear to desire. In adjusting role behaviors in an effort to impress others with the resources that they have to offer, people operate under the principle of reciprocity, for by indicating that one possesses valued qualities, each person is attempting to establish a claim on others for the receipt of rewards from them. All exchange operates under the presumption that people who bestow rewards will receive rewards in turn as payment for value received.

Actors attempt to impress each other through competition in which they reveal the rewards they have to offer in an effort to force others, in accordance with the norm of reciprocity, to reciprocate with an even more valuable reward. Social life is thus rife with people's competitive efforts to impress each other and thereby extract valuable rewards. But as interaction proceeds, it inevitably becomes evident to the parties to an exchange that some people have more valued resources to offer than others, putting them in a unique position to extract rewards from all others who value the resources that they have to offer.

It is at this point in exchange relations that groups of individuals become differentiated in terms of the resources that they possess and the kinds of reciprocal demands they can make on others. Blau then asks an analytical question: What generic types or classes of rewards can those with resources extract in return for bestowing their valued resources upon others? Blau conceptualizes four general classes of such rewards: money, social approval, esteem or respect, and compliance. Although Blau does not make full use of his categorization of rewards, he offers some suggestive clues about how these categories can be incorporated into abstract theoretical statements. Let me elaborate upon his argument.

Blau first ranks these generalized reinforcers in terms of their value in exchange relations. In most social relations, money is an inappropriate reward and hence is the least valuable reward. Social approval is an appropriate reward, but for most humans it is not very valuable, thus forcing those who derive valued services to offer with great frequency the more valuable reward of esteem or respect to those providing valued services. In many situations, the services offered can command no more than respect and esteem from those receiving the benefit of these services. At times, however, the services offered are sufficiently valuable to require those receiving them to offer, in accordance with the principles of reciprocity and justice, the most valuable class of rewards—compliance with one's requests.

When people can extract compliance in an exchange relationship, they have power. They have the capacity to withhold rewarding services and thereby punish or inflict heavy costs on those who might not comply. To conceptualize the degree of power possessed by individuals, Blau formulates four general propositions that determine the capacity of powerful

---

**TABLE 12–2**   Blau's Conditions for the Differentiation of Power in Social Exchange

---

I. The fewer services people can supply in return for the receipt of particularly valued services, the more those providing these particularly valued services can extract compliance.

II. The fewer alternative sources of rewards people have, the more those providing valuable services can extract compliance.

III. The less those receiving valuable services from particular individuals can employ physical force and coercion, the more those providing the services can extract compliance.

IV. The less those receiving the valuable services can do without them, the more those providing the services can extract compliance.

---

individuals to extract compliance. I have listed, and reformulated them somewhat, in Table 12-2.[18]

These four propositions list the conditions leading to differentiation of members in social groups in terms of power. To the extent that group members can supply some services in return, seek alternative rewards, potentially use physical force, or do without certain valuable services, individuals who can provide valuable services will be able to extract only esteem and approval from group members. Such groups will be differentiated in terms of prestige rankings but not power. Naturally, as Blau emphasizes, most social groups reveal complex patterns of differentiation of power, prestige, and patterns of approval, but of particular interest to him are the dynamics involved in generating power, authority, and opposition.

In focusing almost exclusively on the questions of power, authority, and opposition, I think that Blau fails to complete his analysis of how different types of social structures are influenced by the exchange of different classes of rewards. The logic of Blau's argument would, I believe, require additional propositions that would indicate how various types of rewards lead to the differentiation of groups, not only in terms of power and authority but also with respect to prestige rankings and networks of social approval. Interesting theoretical questions left unanswered include: What are the conditions for the emergence of different types of prestige rankings? What are the conditions for the creation of various types of approval networks? Presumably, answers to these questions are left for others to provide. Blau chooses to focus primarily on the problem of how power is converted into authority and how, in accordance with his basic exchange principles listed in Table 12-1, various patterns of integration and opposition become evident in human groupings.

---

[18]Blau, *Exchange and Power,* pp. 118–19.

For Blau, power differentials in groups create two contradictory forces: (1) strains toward integration and (2) strains toward opposition and conflict.

**Strains toward integration.**    Differences in power inevitably create the potential for conflict. However, such potential is frequently suspended by a series of forces promoting the conversion of power into authority, in which subordinates accept as legitimate the leaders' demands for compliance. Principles II and III in Table 12-1 denote two processes fostering such group integration: exchange relations always operate under the presumption of reciprocity and justice, forcing those deriving valued services to provide other rewards in payment. In providing these rewards, subordinates are guided by norms of fair exchange, in which the costs that they incur in offering compliance are to be proportional to the value of the services that they receive from leaders. Thus, to the extent that actors engage in exchanges with leaders and to the degree that the services provided by leaders are highly valued, subordination must be accepted as legitimate in accordance with the norms of reciprocity and fairness that emerge in all exchanges. Under these conditions, groups elaborate additional norms specifying just how exchanges with leaders are to be conducted in order to regularize the requirements for reciprocity and to maintain fair rates of exchange. Leaders who conform to these emergent norms can usually assure themselves that their leadership will be considered legitimate. In fact, Blau emphasizes that if leaders abide by the norms regulating exchange of their services for compliance, norms carrying negative sanctions typically emerge among subordinates stressing the need for compliance to leaders' requests. Through this process, subordinates exercise considerable social control over each other's actions and thereby promote the integration of super- and subordinate segments of groupings.

Authority, therefore, "rests on the common norms in a collectivity of subordinates that constrain its individual members to conform to the orders of a superior."[19] In many patterns of social organization, these norms simply emerge out of the competitive exchanges among collective groups of actors. Frequently, however, in order for such "normative agreements" to be struck, participants in an exchange must be socialized into a common set of values that define not only what constitutes fair exchange in a given situation but also the way such exchange should be institutionalized into norms for both leaders and subordinates. Although it is quite possible for actors to arrive at normative consensus in the course of the exchange process itself, an initial set of common values facilitates the legitimation of power. Actors can now enter into exchanges with a common definition of the situation, which can provide a general framework

---

[19]Ibid., p. 208.

for the normative regulation of emerging power differentials. Without common values, the competition for power is likely to be severe. In the absence of guidelines about reciprocity and fair exchange, considerable strain and tension will persist as definitions of these are worked out. For Blau, then, legitimation "entails not merely tolerant approval but active confirmation and promotion of social patterns by common values, either preexisting ones or those that emerge in a collectivity in the course of social interaction."[20]

With the legitimation of power through the normative regulation of interaction, as confirmed by common values, the structure of collective organization is altered. One of the most evident changes is the decline in interpersonal competition, for now actors' presentations of self shift from a concern of impressing others with their valuable qualities to an emphasis on confirming their statuses as loyal group members. Subordinates come to accept their statuses and manipulate their role behaviors to assure that they receive social approval from their peers as a reward for conformity to group norms. Leaders can typically assume a lower profile, since they must no longer demonstrate their superior qualities in each and every encounter with subordinates—especially since norms now define when and how they should extract conformity and esteem for providing their valued services. Thus, with the legitimation of power as authority, the interactive processes (involving the way group members define the situation and present themselves to others) undergo a dramatic change, reducing the degree of competition and thereby fostering group integration.

With these events, the amount of direct interaction between leaders and subordinates usually declines, since power and ranking no longer must be constantly negotiated. This decline in direct interaction marks the formation of distinct subgroupings as members seek to interact with those of their own social rank, avoiding the costs of interacting with either their inferiors or superiors.[21] In interacting primarily among themselves, subordinates avoid the high costs of interacting with leaders; and although social approval from their peers is not a particularly valuable reward, it can be extracted with comparatively few costs—thus allowing for a sufficient profit. Conversely, leaders can avoid the high costs (in terms of time and energy) of constantly competing and negotiating with inferiors over when and how compliance and esteem are to be bestowed upon them. Instead, by having relatively limited and well-defined contact with subordinates, they can derive the high rewards that come from compliance and esteem without incurring excessive costs in interacting with subordinates—thereby allowing for a profit.

---

[20]Ibid., p. 221.

[21]As will be recalled from Chapter 11, these processes were insightfully described by George C. Homans in *The Human Group* (New York: Harcourt, Brace & World, 1950).

**Strains toward opposition.**   Thus far, I see Blau's exchange perspective as decidedly functional. Social exchange processes—attraction, competition, differentiation, and integration—are analyzed in terms of how they contribute to creating a legitimated set of normatively regulated relations. In a manner similar to Parsons's discussion of institutionalization, Blau emphasizes the importance of common values as a significant force in creating patterns of social organization. However, Blau is keenly aware that social organization is always rife with conflict and opposition, creating an inevitable dialectic between integration and opposition in social structures. Recognition of this fact leads Blau to assert:

> The functional approach reinforces the overemphasis on integrative social forces . . . whereas the dialectical perspective counteracts it by requiring explicit concern with disruptive tendencies in social structures. The pursuit of systematic analysis and the adoption of a dialectical perspective create a dilemma for the sociologist, who must rivet his attention on consistent social patterns for the sake of the former and on inconsistencies in accordance with the latter. This dilemma, like others, is likely to give rise to alternating developments, making him veer in one direction at one time and in the opposite at another.[22]

What I think is especially important about Blau's perspective is that, in adopting dialectical assumptions, he does not reject the useful tenets of functionalism. Blau recognizes that patterns of social organization are created and maintained *as well as* changed and broken down, leading him to seek the principles that can explain this spectrum of events. Thus, unlike Dahrendorf's conflict model, in which the organization of authority relations in imperatively coordinated associations (ICAs) and the opposition of quasi groups were merely taken as givens, Blau seeks to address the question of how, and through what processes, authority structures such as ICAs are created. In so doing, Blau is in a much better analytical position than Dahrendorf and other dialectical theorists to document how the creation of social structure can also set in motion forces for conflict and change. As I emphasized in my earlier discussion of conflict theory, to assert that conflict is endemic to authority relations in social structure and then to analyze how conflict changes structures is to define away the interesting theoretical question: under what conditions, in what types of structures, revealing what types of authority that have arisen through what processes, is what type of conflict likely to emerge? I feel that Blau's discussion of strains for integration represents an attempt to answer this question and provide a more balanced theoretical framework for discussing opposition and conflict in social systems.

---

[22]Peter M. Blau, "Dialectical Sociology: Comments," *Sociological Inquiry* 42 (Spring 1972), p. 185. This article was written in reply to an attempt to document Blau's shift from a functional to dialectical perspective; see Michael A. Weinstein and Deena Weinstein, "Blau's Dialectical Sociology," ibid., pp. 173–82.

Blau's exchange principles, which I summarized in Table 12-1, allow for the conceptualization of these strains for opposition and conflict. As Principle II-B on reciprocity documents, the failure to receive expected rewards in return for various activities leads actors to attempt to apply negative sanctions that, when ineffective, can drive people to violent retaliation against those who have denied them an expected reward. Such retaliation is intensified by the dynamics summarized in Principle III-B on justice and fair exchange, since when those in power violate such norms, they inflict excessive costs on subordinates, creating a situation that, at a minimum, leads to attempts to sanction negatively and, at most, to retaliation. Finally, Principle V on the inevitable imbalances emerging from multiple exchange relations emphasizes that to balance relations in one exchange context by meeting reciprocal obligations and conforming to norms of fairness is to put into imbalance other relations. Thus, the imbalances potentially encourage a cyclical process in which actors seek to balance previously unbalanced relations and thereby throw into imbalance currently balanced exchanges. In turn, exchange relations that are thrown into imbalance violate the norms of reciprocity and fair exchange, thus causing attempts at negative sanctioning and, under some conditions, retaliation. For Blau, then, built into all exchange relationships are sources of imbalance. When severely violating norms of reciprocity and fair exchange, these imbalances can lead to open conflict among individuals in group contexts.

I see these suggestive ideas as simply stating what can occur, without specifying the conditions under which the forces that they denote will actually be set into motion. Unfortunately, Blau provides few specific propositions that indicate when opposition will be activated. And when Blau does undertake a limited discussion of the conditions leading to increasingly intense forms of opposition, I see his propositions as resembling Dahrendorf's discussion of the technical, political, and social conditions of conflict group organization.

In Table 12-3, I summarize Blau's ideas in propositional form.[23] To appreciate the degree to which these propositions resemble those in conflict theory, I suggest that Table 12-3 be compared with Tables 6-1 and 7-1. For in the end, I believe that dialectical conflict theory and exchange theory are converging perspectives. In fact, I would go so far as to argue that conflict theory is a derivative of exchange theory, although I am sure that many would argue just the reverse. In either case, the perspectives converge.

From the discursive context in which the propositions in Table 12-3 are imbedded comes a conceptualization of opposition. Blau hypothesizes that the more imbalanced exchange relations are experienced col-

---

[23]Blau, *Exchange and Power,* pp. 224–52.

**TABLE 12–3**  Blau's Principles of Exchange Conflict

I. The more exchange relations between super- and subordinates become imbalanced, the greater is the probability of opposition to those with power.
   A. The more norms of reciprocity are violated by the superordinates, the greater is the imbalance.
   B. The more norms of fair exchange are violated by superordinates, the greater is the imbalance.

II. The more individuals experience collectively relations of imbalance with superordinates, the greater is their sense of deprivation, and the greater is the probability of opposition to those with power.
   A. The less is the spatial dispersion of subordinates, the more likely are they to experience collectively relations of imbalance with superordinates.
   B. The more subordinates can communicate with each other, the more likely are they to experience collectively relations of imbalance with superordinates.

III. The more subordinates can experience collectively deprivations in exchange relations with superordinates, the more likely are they to codify ideologically their deprivations and the greater their opposition to those with power.

IV. The more deprivations of subordinates are ideologically codified, the greater is their sense of solidarity, and the greater is the probability of opposition.

V. The greater is the sense of solidarity among subordinates, the more they can define their opposition as a noble and worthy cause, and the greater is the probability of their opposition to those with power.

VI. The greater is the sense of ideological solidarity, the more likely are subordinates to view opposition as an end in itself, and the greater is the probability of opposition to those with power.

lectively, the greater is the sense of deprivation and the greater is the potential for opposition. While he does not explicitly state the case, he appears to hold that increasing ideological codification of deprivations, the formation of group solidarity, and the emergence of conflict as a way of life will increase the intensity of the opposition—that is, members' emotional involvement in and commitment to opposition to those with power. I think that these propositions offer a suggestive lead for conceptualizing inherent processes of opposition in exchange relations. Moreover, unlike Dahrendorf's dialectical model, Blau's scheme presents theoretical insight into how the creation of relations of authority can also cause opposition. Indeed, I see Blau's conceptualization of the processes of institutionalization *and* conflict in terms of the same abstract exchange principles as representing a significant improvement over Dahrendorf's model, which failed to specify either how institutionalized patterns of latent conflicts first emerge in authority systems. I also believe that Blau's presentation represents an improvement over Homans's analysis of institutionalization and of the inherent conflict between the institutional and subinstitutional. In Blau's scheme there is a more adequate conceptualization of the process of institutionalization of those power relations from which opposition, innovation, and deviance ultimately spring.

Despite these strengths, however, I think that Blau's model can be improved by: (*a*) more precise formulation of the conditions under which exchange imbalances are likely for various types of social units; and then (*b*) specification of the conditions leading to various levels of intensity, violence, and duration in relations of opposition among various types of social units.

In looking back on Blau's discussion of microexchange processes, it is clear that he visualizes a series of basic exchange processes in human groupings: attraction, competition, differentiation, integration, and opposition. Of particular interest are the processes of differentiation in terms of power and how this pattern of differentiation creates strains for both integration and opposition—thus giving social reality a dialectical character.

Also noteworthy in the perspective is the attempt to utilize concepts developed in the analysis of elementary exchange processes in order to examine more complex exchange processes among the macrosocial units of social systems. Of great significance is Blau's recognition of the necessity for reformulating and supplementing elementary exchange concepts when analyzing more complex social processes. But, as I indicated earlier, Blau is now convinced that this strategy was unsuccessful. For he had hoped that exchange theory:

> could serve as a microsociological foundation for building a macrosociological theory of social structure. This is what I attempted . . . but I was more successful in the microsociological analysis of exchange processes than in employing the micro principles as the groundwork for building a vigorous macrostructural theory.[24]

And so, as a result, he shifted his theoretical approach to macrostructure, as I will discuss in Chapter 20. But I am not so convinced that Blau was correct in abandoning this exchange approach for macroprocesses, and therefore, I still think it useful to summarize the key elements of his macroexchange perspective.

## Exchange Systems and Macrostructure

While the general processes of attraction, competition, differentiation, integration, and opposition are evident in the exchanges among macrostructures, Blau sees several fundamental differences between these exchanges and those among microstructures.

1. In complex exchanges among macrostructures, the significance of "shared values" increases, for it is through such values that indirect exchanges among macrostructures are mediated.

---

[24]Blau, "Contrasting Theoretical Perspectives."

2. Exchange networks among macrostructures are typically institutionalized. Although spontaneous exchange is a ubiquitous feature
of social life, there are usually well-established historical arrangements that circumscribe the operation of the basic exchange processes of attraction, competition, differentiation, integration, and
even opposition among collective units.
3. Since macrostructures are themselves the product of more elementary exchange processes, the analysis of macrostructures requires the analysis of more than one level of social organization.[25]

**Mediating values.**     For Blau, the "interpersonal attraction" of elementary exchange among individuals is replaced by shared values at the
macro level. These values can be conceptualized as "media of social transactions" in that they provide a common set of standards for conducting
the complex chains of indirect exchanges among social structures and
their individual members. Such values are viewed by Blau as providing
effective mediation of complex exchanges by virtue of the fact that the
individual members of social structures have usually been socialized into
a set of common values, leading them to accept them as appropriate.
Furthermore, when coupled with codification into laws and enforcement
procedures by those groups and organizations with power, shared values
provide a means for mediating the complex and indirect exchanges among
the macrostructures of large-scale systems. In mediating indirect exchanges among groups and organizations, shared values provide standards
for the calculation of: (a) expected rewards, (b) reciprocity, and (c) fair
exchange.

Thus, since individuals are not the units of complex exchanges, Blau
emphasizes that in order for complex patterns of social organization to
emerge and persist, it is necessary for a "functional equivalent" of direct
interpersonal attraction to exist. Values assume this function and assure
that exchange can proceed in accordance with the principles presented
in Table 12-1. And even when complex exchanges do involve people, their
interactions are frequently so protracted and indirect that one individual's
rewards are contingent on others who are far removed, requiring that
common values guide and regulate the exchanges.

I think that there is considerable similarity between Blau's concern
with "mediating values" and Parsons's analysis of "generalized media of
exchange" (see Chapter 3).[26] Although the respective conceptualizations

[25]Ibid., pp. 253–311.

[26]See discussion in Chapter 3, as well as Talcott Parsons, "On the Concept of Political
Power," *Proceedings of the American Philosophical Society* 107 (June 1963), pp. 232–62;
Talcott Parsons, "On the Concept of Influence," *Public Opinion Quarterly* 7 (Spring 1963),
pp. 37–67; and Talcott Parsons, "Some Problems of General Theory," in *Theoretical So-
ciology: Perspectives and Developments*, ed. J. C. McKinney and E. A. Tiryakian (New
York: Appleton-Century-Crofts, 1970), pp. 28–68. See also T. S. Turner, "Parsons' Concept
of Generalized Media of Social Interaction and Its Relevance for Social Anthropology,"
*Sociological Inquiry* 38 (Spring 1968), pp. 121–34.

of the general classes and types of media differ, each is concerned with how social relationships utilize in varying contexts distinctive symbols, not only to establish the respective values of actions among exchange units but also to specify just how the exchange should be conducted. For without shared values, exchange is tied to the direct interpersonal inter-actions of individuals. Since virtually all known social systems involve indirect exchange relations among various types of social units—from individuals and groups to organizations and communities—it is necessary to conceptualize just how this can occur. For Blau, mediating values are a critical condition for the development of complex exchange systems. Without them, social organization beyond face-to-face interaction would not be possible.

**Institutionalization.**    While values facilitate processes of indirect exchange among diverse types of social units, institutionalization denotes those processes that regularize and stabilize complex exchange processes.[27] As people and various forms of collective organization become dependent upon particular networks of indirect exchange for expected rewards, pres-sures for formalizing exchange networks through explicit norms increase. This formalization and regularization of complex exchange systems can be effective under three minimal conditions: (1) The formalized exchange networks must have profitable payoffs for most parties to the exchange. (2) Most individuals organized into collective units must have internalized through prior socialization the mediating values used to build exchange networks. And (3) those units with power in the exchange system must receive a level of rewards that moves them to seek actively the formali-zation of rules governing exchange relations.

Institutions are historical products whose norms and underlying me-diating values are handed down from one generation to another, thereby limiting and circumscribing the kinds of indirect exchange networks that can emerge. Institutions exert a kind of external constraint on individuals and various types of collective units, bending exchange processes to fit their prescriptions and proscriptions. Institutions thus represent sets of relatively stable and general norms regularizing different patterns of in-direct and complex exchange relations among diverse social units.

I see this conception of institutionalization as similar to the somewhat divergent formulations of both Parsons and Homans. Although institu-tions represent for both of them the regularization through norms of interaction patterns, Parsons visualizes institutions as normative struc-tures, infused with values that allow for the patterning of interaction among diversely oriented and goal-seeking actors, whereas Homans con-siders institutions as the formalization through norms and generalized

---

[27]Blau, *Exchange and Power*, pp. 273–80.

reinforcers of exchange relations that ultimately have payoffs for each individual involved. Despite their respective points of emphasis, however, both are concerned with the basic process through which norms emerge to facilitate the attainment of goals and rewards by social units. Both view the formalization of such institutional norms as allowing for expanded networks of interaction or exchange among various social units. Blau draws from both these perspectives by emphasizing, in a vein similar to Homans, that institutionalized patterns of interaction must have payoffs for the reward-seeking individuals involved and, in a way reminiscent of Parsons, that shared values must exist prior to effective institutionalization of indirect exchange relations. In this way, Blau apparently has sought to weld exchange-theoretical principles to the functionalist's concern with how values and norms account for the emergence and persistence of complex social systems.

In doing so, Blau, I sense, recognizes Homans's failure to develop concepts that describe the various types and classes of institutionalized exchange systems. In an effort to correct for this oversight, Blau develops a typology of institutions embracing both the substance and style of the Parsonian formulation. Just as Parsons employed the pattern variables (see Chapter 3) to describe the values guiding institutionalized patterns, Blau attempts to classify institutions in terms of the values they appear to embody in their normative structure. He posits three generic types of institutions: (1) Integrative institutions "perpetuate particularistic values, maintain social solidarity, and preserve the distinctive character and identity of the social structure."[28] (2) Distributive institutions embody universalistic values and operate to "preserve the social arrangements that have been developed for the production and distribution of needed social facilities, contributions, and rewards of various kinds."[29] And (3) organizational institutions utilize values legitimating authority and serve "to perpetuate the authority and organization necessary to mobilize resources and coordinate collective effort in the pursuit of social objectives."[30]

However, Blau also recognizes that in this form of typologizing, the potential is great for connoting an image of society as static and equilibrium maintaining. Thus, drawing from Homans's recognition that institutions are accepted only as long as they have payoffs for humans' primary needs and from Dahrendorf's concern with the inherent sources of conflict and change in all relations of authority, Blau stresses that all

---

[28]Ibid., p. 278.

[29]Ibid.

[30]Ibid., p. 279. It is of interest to note that Blau implicitly defines institutions in terms of their functions for the social whole. Although these functions are not made explicit, they are similar to Parsons's requisites. For example, integrative institutions appear to meet needs for latency; distributive institutions, for adaptation; and organizational institutions, for integration and goal attainment.

institutionalized exchange systems reveal a counterinstitutional component "consisting of those basic values and ideals that have not been realized and have not found expression in explicit institutional forms, and which are the ultimate source of social change."[31] To the extent that these values remain unrealized in institutionalized exchange relations, individuals who have internalized them will derive little payoff from existing institutional arrangements and will therefore feel deprived, seeking alternatives to dominant institutions. These unrealized values, even when codified into an opposition ideology advocating open revolution, usually contain at least some of the ideals and ultimate objectives legitimated by the prevailing culture. This indicates that institutional arrangements "contain the seeds of their potential destruction" by failing to meet all of the expectations of reward raised by institutionalized values.

Blau does not enumerate extensively the conditions for mobilization of individuals into conflict groups, but his scheme explicitly denotes the source of conflict and change: counterinstitutional values whose failure of realization by dominant institutional arrangements create deprivations that, under unspecified conditions, can lead to conflict and change in social systems. In this way, Blau attempts to avoid the predictable charges leveled against almost any form of functional analysis for failing to account for the sources of conflict, deviance, and change in social systems. Unlike the Dahrendorf model of dialectical conflict, however, Blau's scheme does not just assert the pervasiveness of conflict and change in social systems but also attempts to document how opposition forces, culminating in conflict and change, are created by the very processes that lead to the institutionalization of power in complex exchange systems.

Such tendencies for complex exchange systems to generate opposition are explicable in terms of the basic principles of exchange. When certain mediating values are not institutionalized in a social system, exchange relations will not be viewed as reciprocated by those who have internalized these values. Thus, in accordance with Blau's principles on reciprocity (see Table 12-1), these segments of a collectivity are more likely to feel deprived and to seek ways of retaliating against the dominant institutional arrangements, which, from the perspective dictated by their values, have failed to reciprocate. For those who have internalized values that are not institutionalized, it is also likely that perceptions of fair exchange have been violated, leading them, in accordance with the principles on justice, to attempt to sanction negatively those arrangements that violate alternative norms of fair exchange. Finally, in institutionalized exchange networks, the balancing of exchange relations with some segments of a collectivity inevitably creates imbalances in relations with other segments (the imbalance principle in Table 12-1), thereby violating norms of reciprocity and fairness and setting into motion forces of opposition.

---

[31]Blau, *Exchange and Power,* p. 279.

Unlike direct interpersonal exchanges, however, opposition in complex exchange systems is between large collective units of organization, which, in their internal dynamics, reveal their own propensities for integration and opposition. This fact requires that the analysis of integration and opposition in complex exchange networks be attuned to various levels of social organization. Such analysis needs to show, in particular, how exchange processes among macrostructures, whether for integration or opposition, are partly influenced by the exchange processes occurring among their constituent substructures.

**Levels of social organization.**    To a great extent, Blau believes, the "dynamics of macro structures rests on the manifold interdependence between the social forces within and among their substructures."[32] The patterns of interdependence among the substructures of distinguishable macrostructures are various, including: (a) joint membership by some members of macrostructures in constituent substructures; (b) mobility of members between various substructures of macrostructures; and (c) direct exchange relations among the substructures of different macrostructure.

To discern these dynamics of substructures and how they influence exchanges among macrostructures, Blau first questions what generic types of substructures exist, resulting in the isolation of four classes of substructures: "categories," "communities," "organized collectivities," and "social systems." Categories refer to an attribute, such as race, sex, and age, that "actually governs the relations among people and their orientations to each other."[33] Communities are "collectivities organized in given territories, which typically have their own government and geographical boundaries that preclude their being overlapping, though every community includes smaller and is part of larger territorial organizations."[34] Organized collectivities are "associations of people with a distinctive social organization, which may range from a small informal friendship clique to a large bureaucratized formal organization."[35] Social systems "consist not of the social relations in specific collectivities but of analytical principles or organization, such as the economy of a society or its political institutions."[36]

Values mediate the processes within these various types of substructures. However, discerning the complex relationships between the mediating values of substructures and those of macrostructures poses one of the most difficult problems of analysis. On the one hand, some values must cut across the substructures of a macrostructure if the latter is to

---

[32]Ibid., p. 284.
[33]Ibid., p. 285.
[34]Ibid.
[35]Ibid.
[36]Ibid.

remain minimally integrated; on the other hand, values of various sub-structures not only can segregate substructures from each other, but also generate conflict among them. Further, the relations among substructures involve the same basic exchange processes of attraction, competition, and differentiation in terms of the services they can provide for each other. It thus becomes evident that the analysis of exchange networks among macrostructures forces examination of the exchange processes of their substructures. Additionally, the relations among these substructures are complicated by the fact that they often have overlapping memberships or mobility of members between them, making the analysis of attraction, competition, differentiation, integration, and opposition increasingly difficult.

Blau simplifies the complex analytical task of examining the dynamics of substructures by positing that organized collectivities, especially formal organizations, are the most important substructures in the analysis of macrostructures. As explicit goal (reward) seeking structures that frequently cut across social categories and communities and that form the substructures of analytical social systems, collectivities are mainly responsible for the dynamics of macrostructures. Thus, the theoretical analysis of complex exchange systems among macrostructures requires that primary attention be drawn to the relations of attraction, competition, differentiation, integration, and opposition among various types of complex organizations. In emphasizing the pivotal significance of complex organizations, Blau posits a particular image of society that should guide the ultimate construction of sociological theory.

# THE ORGANIZATIONAL BASIS OF SOCIETY

Organizations in a society must typically derive rewards from each other, thus creating a situation in which they are both attracted to, and in competition with, each other. Out of this competition, hierarchical differentiation between successful and less successful organizations operating in the same sphere emerges. Such differentiation usually creates strains toward specialization in different fields among less successful organizations as they seek to provide particular goods and services for dominant organizations and each other. If such differentiation and specialization among organizations is to provide effective means for integration, separate political organizations must also emerge to regulate their exchanges. Such political organizations possess power and are viewed as legitimate only as long as they are considered by individuals and organizations to follow the dictates of shared cultural values. Typically, political organizations are charged with several objectives: (1) regulating complex networks of indirect exchange by the enactment of laws; (2) controlling through law competition among dominant organizations, thereby assuring the latter of scarce resources; (3) protecting existing exchange networks among organizations, especially those with power, from encroachment on these rewards by organizations opposing the current distribution of resources.

For Blau, then, it is out of the competition among organizations in a society that differentiation and specialization occur among macrostructures. While mediating values allow differentiation and specialization among organizations to occur, it is also necessary for separate political organizations to exist and regularize, through laws and the use of force, existent patterns of exchange among other organizations. Such political organizations will be viewed as legitimate as long as they normatively regulate exchanges that reflect the tenets of mediating values and protect the payoffs for most organizations, especially the most powerful. However, the existence of political authority inevitably encourages opposition movements, for now opposition groups have a clear target—the political organizations—against which to address their grievances. As long as political authority remains diffuse, opposition organizations can only compete unsuccessfully against various dominant organizations. With the legitimation of clear-cut political organizations charged with preserving current patterns of organization, opposition movements can concentrate their energies against one organization, the political system.

In addition to providing deprived groups with a target for their aggressions, political organizations inevitably must aggravate the deprivations of various segments of a population, because political control involves exerting constraints and distributing resources unequally. Those segments of the population that must bear the brunt of such constraint and unequal distribution usually experience great deprivation in terms of the principles of reciprocity and fair exchange, which, under various conditions, creates a movement against the existing political authorities. To the extent that this organized opposition forces redistribution of rewards, other segments of the population are likely to feel constrained and deprived, leading them to organize into an opposition movement. These facts indicate that the organization of political authority assures that, in accordance with the principle of imbalance, attempts to balance one set of exchange relations among organizations throw into imbalance other exchange relations, causing the formation of opposition organizations. Thus, built into the structure of political authority in a society are inherent forces of opposition that give society a dialectical and dynamic character.

Echoing the assumptions of Dahrendorf and Coser, Blau conceptualizes opposition as representing "a regenerative force that interjects new vitality into a social structure and becomes the basis of social reorganization."[37] However, the extent to which opposition can result in dramatic social change is limited by several counterforces:[38] (1) The

---

[37]Ibid., p. 301. Such a position is inevitable in light of Blau's explicitly stated belief that "our society is in need of fundamental reforms" (Blau, "Dialectical Sociology," p. 184).

[38]Blau, "Dialectical Sociology," p. 187; Blau, *Exchange and Power*, pp. 301-9.

**FIGURE 12–1** Blau's Image of Social Organization

interdependence of the majority of organizations upon each other for rewards gives each a vested interest in the status quo, thus providing strong resistance to opposition organizations. (2) Dominant organizations that have considerable power to bestow rewards on other organizations independently of political organizations have a particularly strong vested interest in existing arrangements, thereby assuring their resistance to change-oriented organizations. (3) By virtue of controlling the distribution of valued resources, both dominant and political organizations are in a strategic position to make necessary concessions to opposition groups, thereby diffusing their effective organization. (4) Opposition movements must overcome the internalization of values by the majority; and without control of the means of socialization, their ideological call for organization is likely to fall on unsympathetic ears. (5) Societies composed of exchange networks among complex organizations typically reveal high levels of social mobility up the organizational hierarchy, thus increasing the difficulties involved in organizing a stable constituency.[39]

In reviewing Blau's analysis of exchanges among organizations in a society, it is evident that he has attempted to cast many of the assumptions and propositions of Parsons, Dahrendorf, and Coser into an exchange perspective that extends Homans's insights beyond the analysis of individuals. In discussing the developments of exchange systems among organizations and of political authority, Blau focuses on the institutionalization of relations among what Parsons termed *social systems*. The fact

---

[39]However, Blau recognizes that high rates of mobility in a society can also increase the sense of relative deprivation of those who are denied opportunities for advancement, thereby making them likely constituents of an opposition organization.

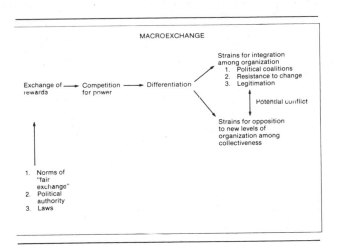

MACROEXCHANGE

that such institutionalization rests upon the internalization of shared values and that institutional patterns can be typologized in terms of the dominance of various clusters of values further underscores Blau's analytical debt to Parsons. In contrast with Parsons's less explicit analysis, Blau's discussion is concerned with mechanisms of social change. Embracing Marx's, Dahrendorf's, and Simmel's assumptions of the dialectical forces of opposition inherent in all micro and macro relations of power and authority, Blau visualizes the source of conflict in the unbalanced exchange relations, violating norms of reciprocity and fairness, which are inevitable concomitants of some organizations having a disproportionate hold upon valued resources.

Blau does not enumerate the conditions leading to the organization of opposition as explicitly as did either Marx or Dahrendorf ("conflict groups" for Dahrendorf and "class" for Marx). But his debt to Marx's work (see Chapter 6) is evident in his analysis on how levels of deprivation are influenced by (1) the degree of ecological concentration and the capacity to communicate among the deprived, (2) the capacity to codify an opposition ideology, (3) the degree of social solidarity among the deprived, and (4) the degree to which opposition organization is politicized and directed against the political organizations (see Table 12-3). Furthermore, Blau's incorporation of Dahrendorf's key propositions is shown in his recognition that the capacity of the population's deprived segments to organize opposition is affected by such variables as the rate of social mobility, the capacity of dominant groups to make strategic concessions, and the number of cross-cutting conflicts resulting from multigroup affiliations. Finally, although Blau does not develop his argument extensively, he clearly has followed Simmel's and Coser's lead in emphasizing that conflict and opposition are regenerative forces in societies that "constitute countervailing forces against . . . institutional rigidities, rooted in vested powers as well as traditional values, and . . . [that] are essential for speeding social change."[40]

In sum, then, Blau has offered a most varied image of society. By incorporating—albeit in an unsystematic manner—the fruitful leads of sociology's other dominant conceptual perspectives, Blau has indeed offered a suggestive theoretical prolegomenon that can serve as a guide to more explicit theoretical formulations. I have summarized both the micro- and macroprocesses of this prolegomenon in Figure 12-1. As is evident, Blau has synthesized several theoretical traditions, and in so doing, he offers something for everyone. For the functionalist, Blau offers the concept of mediating values, types of institutions, and the counterpart of mechanisms of socialization and control that operate to maintain macrosocial wholes. For the conflict theorist, Blau presents a dialectical-conflict perspective emphasizing the inevitable forces of opposition in relations of power and authority. For those concerned with interactions among individuals, Blau's analysis of elementary exchange processes places considerable emphasis on the actions of people in interaction. And for the critic of Homans's reductionism, Blau provides an insightful portrayal of exchanges among emergent social structures, which leaves the integrity of sociological theorizing intact.

In offering a theoretical resting place for the major perspectives in sociology, I think that Blau provides a useful example of how sociological theorizing should proceed: rather than becoming bogged down in controversies and debates among proponents of various theoretical positions, it is much wiser to borrow and integrate the useful concepts and assumptions of diverse perspectives. In offering this alternative to continued debate, Blau left a number of theoretical issues unresolved, but I think that the most important one is the question of how micro- and macroprocesses can be incorporated into one theoretical approach.[41] This issue is obscured by the insightfulness of his synthesis, and yet its resolution constitutes a critical next step in his theoretical strategy. And I suspect that the failure to resolve it is what caused Blau to abandon this exchange approach.

## THE UNRESOLVED ISSUE: MICRO VERSUS MACRO ANALYSIS

As I emphasized in Chapter 1, one of the issues that haunts sociological theory is: To what extent are structures and processes at micro and macro

---

[40]Blau, *Exchange and Power*, p. 302.

[41]For examples of criticisms on Blau's work, see M. J. Mulkay, "A Conceptual Elaboration of Exchange Theory: Blau," in his *Functionalism, Exchange, Theoretical Strategy* (New York: Schocken Books, 1971), especially pp. 206–12; Percy S. Cohen, *Modern Sociological Theory* (New York: Basic Books, 1968), pp. 123–27; and Anthony Heath, "Economic Theory and Sociology: A Critique of P. M. Blau's 'Exchange and Power in Social Life,' " *Sociology* 2 (September 1968), pp. 273–92.

levels of social organization subject to analysis by the same concepts and laws? At what levels of sociological organization do emergent properties require use of additional concepts and description in terms of their unique modes of analysis? In what ways are groups, organizations, communities, or social systems similar and different? These questions are extremely troublesome for sociological theorizing and constitute one of its most enduring problems. In his early exchange approach, Blau tried to resolve this problem in several ways: (1) by assuming that the basic exchange processes of attraction, competition, differentiation, integration, and opposition occur at all levels of social organization; (2) by explicating general exchange principles and incorporating abstract exchange concepts that can account for the unfolding of these processes at all levels of organization; (3) by enumerating additional concepts, such as mediating values and institutionalization, to account for emergent phenomena at increasingly macro levels of social organization; and (4) by classifying the generic types of organization—categories, communities, organized collectivities, and social systems—that denote different levels of organization, requiring somewhat different concepts for explication of their operation.

I see this as an interesting effort to bridge the micro-macro analytical gap in sociological theorizing. A number of problems remain, however. And it is to their resolution that efforts to improve upon Blau's scheme that I offer a few critical closing remarks.

First, Blau defines organized collectivities so broadly that they include phenomena ranging from small groups to complex organizations. It is likely that the concepts and theoretical generalizations appropriate to the small primary group, the secondary group, a crowd, a social movement, a small organization, and a large corporate bureaucracy will be somewhat different. Surely, there are emergent properties of social organization in a spectrum ranging from a small group to a complex organization. In fact, aside from the study of community, most subfields in sociology fall within Blau's category of organized collectivity. Thus, Blau has not resolved the problem of emergent properties; rather, I think that it has been defined away with an excessively broad category that subsumes most of the emergent properties of interest to sociologists.

Second, the addition of concepts to account for differences in levels of organization only highlights the micro-macro gap without providing a sense of what concepts are needed to understand increasingly macro phenomena. What Blau does is to assert that there are elementary exchange processes that occur at macro levels of organization and that require the addition of the concept, mediating values, if these emergent levels of organization are to be understood. But such an analysis begs the key question: When and at what levels of organization do such concepts become critical? Among dyads? Triads? Primary groups? Secondary groups? Small organizations? Large organizations? To phrase the issue differently, at what point do what kinds of values, operating in accordance with what laws, become analytically significant? Blau simply says that at some point mediating values become critical, and he thereby avoids answering the theoretically interesting question.

Third, Blau's presentation of exchange concepts and their incorporation into exchange principles is vague. My analysis and reformulation of Blau's ideas into tables and figures represent an attempt to make more explicit the implicit exchange principles employed in his analysis. Without explicit statements of the exchange laws that cut across levels of organization, Blau fails to address an issue that he claims to be of great significance in the opening pages of his major work:

> The problem is to derive the social processes that govern the complex structures of communities and societies from the simpler processes that pervade the daily intercourse among individuals and their interpersonal relations.[42]

To make such derivations, it is necessary to formulate explicitly the laws from which derivations from simpler to more complex structures are to be made. Too often, Blau hides behind the fact that, to use his words, his "intent is not to present a systematic theory of social structure; it is more modest than that."

Yet, even in his modesty, I believe that Blau synthesized diverse theoretical traditions into a suggestive exchange perspective. But he abandoned it, nonetheless. He simply stopped trying to view macroprocesses as fundamentally connected to microexchanges. I think that this shift in strategy was mistaken, but it does signal a dissatisfaction with his own exchange solution to the micro-macro issue.[43] My sense is that exchange theory is one of the few approaches that can bridge this gap with common principles. And thus, my belief is that it should be utilized, not abandoned, in an effort to integrate interpersonal and structural theories.

---

[42]Blau, *Exchange and Power,* p. 2.

[43]Patrick Spread, "Blau's Exchange Theory, Support, and the Macro Structure," *The British Journal of Sociology* 35 (June 1984), pp. 157–73.

# CHAPTER 13

# The Exchange Network Theory of Richard Emerson

As my review of George Homans's and Peter Blau's approaches has emphasized, power is one of the central concepts of exchange theory. Inequalities in resources generate differences in power among actors; and many of the dynamics of social systems revolve around transactions among actors who possess varying degrees of power. In particular, I find that Blau's approach converges with the dialectical conflict theory of Marx and Dahrendorf, who viewed inequality as causing opposition and conflict. Yet, as exchange theory has been used to analyze social structures and their inherent conflict potential, the conceptualization of "structure" has been very weak and, at best, metaphorical. Blau discusses levels of social organization and opposition groups, but as I noted in Chapter 12, he is not very precise in his analysis; and in fact, he has now abandoned exchange theory as a useful tool for theorizing about social structure (see Chapter 20). With his overconcern with deducing principles of structure from the axioms of behaviorist psychology, Homans never gets around to developing principles about the structural properties of systems. Thus, I think it fair to conclude that exchange theory has not adequately conceptualized inequality and power in social structures.

In recent decades, *social network analysis* has been offered as a new way to conceptualize social structures.[1] By viewing actors as points in a

---

[1] For some basic references on network analysis, see Jeremy F. Boissevain and J. Clyde Mitchell, eds., *Network Analysis* (The Hague, Holland: Mouton Publishers, 1973); Paul Holland and Samuel Leinhardt, eds., *Perspectives on Social Network Research* (New York:

system of interconnections, network analysis has been able to describe the flows of events among actors. Yet, network analysis has developed very little theory that explains the dynamics of network structures.[2] Instead, emphasis has been on the development of techniques for describing data sets from a network perspective. There are, of course, a few exceptions,[3] but they are so few in number that they confirm my general point: network sociology, for all its methodological sophistication, is decidedly atheoretical.

We have, then, a curious situation: On the one side, there is exchange theory, which denotes some of the crucial dynamics of human relationships but which, at the same time, does not develop an adequate conception of social structure. On the other side, we have network analyses, which possess a powerful set of techniques for describing social structures but which, despite its promise, does not evidence many theoretical ideas. Until his recent death, Richard Emerson was one of the few social theorists to realize the potential for blending exchange theory and network analysis.[4] Using a sophisticated version of exchange theory, Emerson had begun to analyze inequality and power in social networks, and as a result, his perspective promised to give exchange theory what it needed—a more precise conceptualization of structure—and to provide network analysis what it needed—a theory of social structure.[5]

---

Academic Press, 1979); Linton C. Freeman, *A Bibliography of Social Networks* (Monticello, Ill.: Council of Planning Librarians, 1976); J. Clyde Mitchell, ed., *Social Networks in Urban Situations* (Manchester, Conn.: Manchester University Press, 1969) and "Social Networks," *Annual Review of Anthropology* 3 (1974), pp. 279–99; Peter Marsden and Nan Lin, eds., *Social Structure and Network Analysis* (Beverly Hills, Calif.: Sage Publications, 1982). Also consult the journal *Social Networks*.

[2]Mark Granovetter, "The Theory-Gap in Social Network Analysis," in *Perspectives on Social Network Research*, ed. P. Holland and S. Leinhardt. Granovetter, I should add, is an exception to this statement. See, in particular, his "The Strength of Weak Ties," *American Journal of Sociology* 78 (1973), pp. 1360–80 and "The Strength of Weak Ties: A Network Theory Revisited," *Sociological Theory* 1 (1983), pp. 201–33. See also, for an example of an effort to theorize, Barry Wellman, "Network Analysis: Some Basic Principles," ibid., pp. 155–200. See also Ronald Burt, *Toward a Structural Theory of Action: Network Models of Social Structure, Perception, and Action* (New York: Academic Press, 1982).

[3]Ibid.

[4]There are others, of course. For example, see David Willer, "The Basic Concepts of the Elementary Theory," in *Networks, Exchange and Coercion*, ed. D. Willer and B. Anderson (New York: Elsevier/Greenwood, 1981). All of the essays in this volume are theoretical in nature.

[5]Emerson's perspective is best stated in his "Exchange Theory, Part I: A Psychological Basis for Social Exchange" and "Exchange Theory, Part II: Exchange Relations and Network Structures," in *Sociological Theories*, ed. J. Berger, M. Zelditch, and B. Anderson, pp. 38–87. Earlier empirical work that provided the initial impetus to, or the empirical support of, this theoretical perspective include: "Power-Dependence Relations," *American Sociological Review* 17 (February 1962), pp. 31–41; "Power-Dependence Relations: Two Experiments," *Sociometry* 27 (September 1964), pp. 282–98; John F. Stolte and Richard M. Emerson, "Structural Inequality: Position and Power in Network Structures," in *Behavioral*

Emerson's death at the peak of his career was thus a great tragedy, but fortunately, his colleague and collaborator, Karen S. Cook, has continued to explore this blending of exchange theory and network analysis.[6] In my review of this promising approach, I will emphasize the basic ideas in Emerson's work, but I will also indicate some of the ways that Cook has extended the theoretical foundation provided by Emerson.

## EMERSON'S EXCHANGE NETWORK APPROACH

Much like Homans's, Emerson's approach begins with a discussion of psychological behaviorism. His purpose is to extract basic concepts and principles of operant psychology that are useful in analyzing more complex social patterns. Unlike Homans, however, Emerson did not stop theoretical efforts once basic reinforcement principles are isolated. As I noted in Chapter 11, Homans tends to define away the complexities of social structure by viewing them as givens. Then in an ad hoc and ex post facto manner, he reconciles psychological axioms and empirical generalizations. And when Homans does address questions of social organization, he becomes metaphorical and abandons even the illusion of logical rigor in favor of what he termed an "intellectual orgy."

In contrast, Emerson's strategy involves a careful analysis of the logic of operant psychology, a selective borrowing of concepts and principles, and, most important, an extension of these principles that allows for a less metaphorical analysis of the complexity of social organization. His efforts represented, of course, only a tentative beginning. And perhaps more important than the state of the theory at his death is the strategy that it personified.

### The Overall Strategy

Emerson began by enumerating the basic propositions of operant psychology. Then, through the development of corollaries, he extended these

---

*Theory in Sociology,* ed. R. Hamblin (New Brunswick, N.J.: Transaction Books, 1977). Other more conceptual works include "Operant Psychology and Exchange Theory," in *Behavioral Sociology,* ed. R. Burgess and D. Bushell (New York: Columbia University Press, 1969) and "Social Exchange Theory," in *Annual Review of Sociology,* ed. A. Inkeles and N. Smelser, 2 (1976), pp. 335–62.

[6]For example, see Karen S. Cook and Richard Emerson, "Power, Equity and Commitment in Exchange Networks," *American Sociological Review* 43 (1978), pp. 712–39; Karen S. Cook, Richard M. Emerson, Mary R. Gillmore, and Toshio Yamagish, "The Distribution of Power in Exchange Networks," *American Journal of Sociology* 89 (1983), pp. 275–305; Karen S. Cook and Richard M. Emerson, "Exchange Networks and the Analysis of Complex Organizations," *Research in the Sociology of Organizations* 3 (1984), pp. 1–30. See also Karen S. Cook, "Exchange and Power in Networks of Interorganizational Relations," *Sociological Quarterly* 18 (Winter 1977), pp. 66–82; "Network Structures from an Exchange Perspective," in *Social Structure and Network Analysis,* ed. P. Marsden and N. Lin; and Karen S. Cook and Karen A. Hegtvedt, "Distributive Justice, Equity, and Equality," *American Sociological Review* 9 (1983), pp. 217–41.

propositions and made them more relevant to human social organization. Finally, he derived from these propositions and their corollaries a series of theorems to account for the operation of different social patterns. At various points in the development of his system of propositions, corollaries, and theorems, new concepts that will be incorporated into the corollaries and theorems are added.

Emerson never did perform the logical operations in deriving corollaries from basic operant propositions and in developing theorems from these propositions and corollaries. Yet in contrast to Homans's strategy, Emerson's work is extremely rigorous. Concepts are precisely defined and represented by symbolic notation. Propositions, corollaries, and theorems are stated in terms of covariance among these clearly defined concepts. Thus, considerable attention is devoted to concept formation and then to the use of these concepts in a system of propositions, corollaries, and theorems. Rarely do sociological theories reveal this degree of rigor.[7]

Emerson followed the substantive strategy of other exchange theorists by moving from microprocesses in simple structures to processes in more complex structures. As the structures under investigation become more complex, additional corollaries and theorems are developed. But the most important difference between Emerson's substantive approach and that of other perspectives is his concern with the _forms_ of exchange relations. The theorems delineate the processes inherent in a given form of exchange relationship. The nature of the units in this relationship can be either micro or macro—individual persons or corporate units such as groups, organizations, or nations. Much as the German sociologist Georg Simmel (see chapters 6, 10, and 19) focused on the "forms of sociation" and their underlying exchange basis, so Emerson sought to develop a set of theoretical principles that explain generic social forms. In this way, the distinction between micro- and macroanalysis is rendered less obstructive, because it is the _form of the relationship_ rather than the properties of the units that is being explained. And as a consequence, he did not have to abandon exchange theory, as did Blau, when he moved from micro- to macrostructural analysis, nor did he define away, as does Homans, social structure as mere givens in a deductive scheme.

Emerson's strategy involves many problems of exposition, however. His concern with rigorous concept formation involves the creation of a new language. Acquiring a familiarity with this language requires considerable time and effort. Moreover, the system of definitions, concepts, propositions, corollaries, and theorems soon becomes exceedingly complex, even though Emerson explores only a few basic types, or forms, of

---

[7]There are, of course, notable exceptions to this statement. See, for examples, Alfred Kuhn, _Unified Social Science_ (Homewood, Ill.: Dorsey Press, 1975) and the articles in Berger, Zelditch, and Anderson, _Sociological Theory in Progress_.

social relations. My analysis of Emerson's work therefore translates terms into more discursive language and omits discussion of certain corollaries and theorems. Also, in an effort to communicate succinctly the essence of Emerson's approach, I will not follow the exact sequence of his argument. In this way, I think that I can communicate more clearly the logic of Emerson's approach and its substantive implications.

## The Basic Exchange Concepts

Below I present an incomplete list of key concepts in Emerson's exchange perspective. While the definitions for each concept appear, on the surface, to be similar to those developed by Homans, important differences exist. These differences will become increasingly evident as I proceed, but for the moment, let me offer the definitions:

*Actor:* An individual or collective unit that is capable of receiving reinforcement from its environment.

*Reinforcement:* Features of the environment that are capable of bestowing gratification upon an actor.

*Behaviors:* Actions or movements of actors on their environment.

*Exchange:* Behaviors by actors that yield reinforcement from the environment.

*Value:* The strength of reinforcers to evoke and reinforce behavioral initiations by an actor, relative to other reinforcers and holding deprivation constant and greater than zero.

*Reward:* The degree of value attached to a given type of reinforcement.

*Alternatives:* The number of sources in the environment of an actor that can bestow a given type of reinforcer.

*Cost:* The magnitude and number of rewards of one type foregone to receive rewards of another type.

*Exchange relation:* Opportunities across time for an actor to initiate behaviors that lead to relatively enduring exchange transactions with other actors in the environment.

*Dependence:* A situation where an actor's reinforcement is contingent upon behaviors on the part of another actor, with the degree of dependence being a dual function of the strength of reinforcement associated with behavior and the number of alternatives for rewards.

*Balance:* The degree to which the dependency of one actor, A, for rewards from actor B is equal to the dependency of actor B for rewards from actor A.

> *Power:* The degree to which one actor can force another actor to incur costs in an exchange relation.

> *Resources:* Any reward that an actor can use in an exchange relation with other actors.

This list of concepts does not exhaust those employed by Emerson. With these concepts, however, I think it possible to gain considerable insight into the approach. Let me enhance several points about this list of concepts. First, Emerson analyzes only the exchange *relation* between actors. This approach bypasses the problem of tautology so evident in Homans's analysis by viewing an established relation—not the actors in the relation—as the smallest unit of analysis. In this way, questions about each actor's values become less central because attention is focused on the relationship between actors who exchange resources. This line of argument, of course, abandons explanation in terms of an individual actor's values. The emphasis is on the ratio of rewards exchanged among actors and on how this ratio shifts or stabilizes over the course of the exchange relationship. Propositions thus focus on explaining the variables outside the actors in the broader context of the social relationship that might influence the ratio of rewards in a given social relationship. Thus, behavior is no longer the dependent variable in propositions; rather, the exchange relationship becomes the variable to be explained. The goal is to discover laws that help account for particular patterns of exchange relations. This approach is contrary to traditional exchange theory, which seeks to explain why a person enters into an exchange relationship in terms of that person's values. But if the relationship is the unit of analysis, then the question of why the individual enters the relationship is no longer of prime concern. The fact is that the individual has entered a relationship and is willing to exchange rewards with another. When this exchange relationship among actors becomes the unit of analysis, Emerson argued, theory seeks to discover what events could effect variations in the entire relational unit, not in the individual behaviors of actors. For example, in a hypothetical exchange, person A gives esteem and respect to person B in return for advice. With the A,B relationship as the unit of analysis, the question is not what made either A or B enter the relationship, answers to which would take theory into A's and B's cognitive structure and thereby increase the probability of tautologous propositions. Rather, since the A,B unit already exists as an entity, theoretical questions should focus on what events would influence the ratio of esteem and advice exchanged in the A,B unit.

Second, as can be seen from the list of definitions above, the concepts of actor, reinforcement, exchange, value, reward, cost, and resource are all defined in terms of each other, but since they are not analyzed independently of the exchange relation, the problem of tautology is bypassed.

These concepts are the givens of any existing exchange relation. Thus, in contrast to Homans's approach, social structure is not a theoretical given. Instead, behavioral dispositions are the givens, and it is social structure that is to be explained.

Third, in accordance with the emphasis on the structure of the exchange relation, as opposed to the characteristics of the actors, the concepts of (a) dependence, (b) power, and (c) balance in exchange relations become central. The key questions in Emerson's scheme thus revolve around how dependence, power, and balance in exchange relations help explain the operation of more complex social patterns.

Fourth, actors are viewed as either individuals or collective units. The same processes in exchange relations are presumed to apply to both individuals and collectivities of individuals, thus obviating many problems in the micro versus macro schism in sociological theorizing. This emphasis is possible when attention is shifted away from the attributes of actors to the *form* of their exchange relationship.

Thus, while this partial list of Emerson's concepts appears to be similar to that developed by Homans and other behavioristically oriented exchange theorists, I see an important shift in emphasis from concern with the values and other cognitive properties of actors to a concern with the structure of an exchange relation. This concern with structure takes as a given the flow of valued resources among those involved in the exchange. Theoretical attention then focuses on the structural attributes of the exchange relation and on the processes that maintain or change the structural form of an ongoing exchange relationship.

## The Basic Exchange Processes

In Emerson's scheme, analysis begins with an existing exchange relation between at least two actors. This relationship has been formed from (1) perceived opportunities by at least one actor, (2) the initiation of behaviors, and (3) the consummation of a transaction between actors mutually reinforcing each other. If initiations go unreinforced, then an exchange relation will not develop. And unless the exchange transaction between actors endures for at least some period of time, it is theoretically uninteresting.

Emerson's approach thus starts with an established exchange relation and then asks: to what basic processes is this relationship subject? His answer: (1) the use of power and (2) balancing. If exchange relations reveal high dependency of one actor, B, on another actor, A, for reinforcement, then A has what Emerson termed a *power advantage* over B. This conceptualization of power is similar to Blau's formulation, although Emerson developed a different set of propositions for explaining its dynamics. To have a power advantage is to use it, with the result that actor A forces increasing costs on actor B within the exchange relationship.

In Emerson's view, a power advantage represents an imbalanced exchange relation. A basic proposition in Emerson's scheme is that, over time, imbalanced exchange relations tend toward balance. He visualized this process as occurring through a number of "balancing operations":

1. A decrease in the value for actor B of reinforcers, or rewards, from actor A.
2. An increase in the number of alternative sources for the reinforcers, or rewards, provided to B by A.
3. An increase in the value of reinforcers provided by B for A.
4. A reduction in the alternative sources for the rewards provided by B for A.

These balancing operations are, I think, somewhat similar to the propositions enumerated by Blau on the conditions for differentiation of power (see Table 12–2). But in contrast to Blau's emphasis on the inherent and incessant dialectic for change resulting from power imbalances, Emerson stressed that through at least one of these four balancing operations the dependency of B and A on each other for rewards will reach an equilibrium. Thus, exchange transactions reveal differences in power that, over time, tend toward balance. Naturally, in complex exchange relations involving many actors, A, B, C, D, . . ., $n$, the basic processes of dependence, power, and balance will ebb and flow as new actors and new reinforcers or resources enter the exchange relations.

## The Basic Exchange Propositions

In Table 13–1, I have selectively summarized the initial propositions that Emerson developed to explain exchange relations. The general strategy was to begin with behaviorist principles and then to derive theorems from these that explain the basic exchange processes, use of power, and balancing. In turn, corollaries to these theorems can be developed to account for the structural forms of exchange relations. Thus, the propositions in Table 13–1 represent only a starting point, whereas they were the end point in Homans's list of behaviorist axioms.

The crucial next step is to derive theorems from these behaviorist principles that pertain to the dynamics of power and balancing. In Table 13–2, I have summarized Emerson's initial set of theorems. These theorems describe the dynamics of power as a function of one actor's dependency on another for valued resources (Theorem 4), whereas balance is conceptualized as a process whereby dependency is reduced over time (see definition of balance and Theorem 5). Thus, power (P) is a positive function of the dependency (D) of actor B on the resources of actor A, or $P_{AB}$

**TABLE 13–1**   The Operant Propositions and Initial Corollaries

*Proposition 1:*   The greater is the behavioral repertoire of actor A in a situation and the greater are the variations in rewards for behaviors, the more likely is A to emit those behaviors yielding the greatest rewards.

  *Corollary 1.1:*   The more rewards decrease for A in an established exchange relation, the more variation in A's behavior.

  *Corollary 1.2:*   The more rewards in an established exchange relation approach a zero level of reinforcement, the fewer initiations by A.

  *Corollary 1.3:*   The greater the power advantage of A over B in an exchange relation, the more A will use its power advantage across continuing transactions.

  *Corollary 1.4:*   The more power is balanced in an exchange relation between A and B and the more A increases its use of power, the more B will increase its use of power.

*Proposition 2:*   The more frequent and valuable are the rewards received by actor A for a given behavior in a situation, the less likely is actor A to emit similar behaviors immediately.

  *Corollary 2.1:*   The more rewards of a given type received by A, the less frequent A's initiations for rewards of this type.

*Proposition 3:*   The more actor A must emit a given behavior for a given type of reward, and the greater strength and number of rewards of this type in a situation, the more likely is actor A to emit behaviors of a given type in that situation.

  *Corollary 3.1:*   The greater is the number of alternatives available to A for a given reward, the less dependent is A upon that situation.

  *Corollary 3.2:*   The more a situation provides multiple sources of reward for A, the more dependent is A on that situation.

  *Corollary 3.3:*   The greater is the value of rewards received by A in a given situation, the greater is the dependency of A on that situation.

  *Corollary 3.4:*   The greater is the uncertainty of A ever receiving a given reward in a given situation and the fewer alternative situations for receiving this reward, the greater is the dependency of A on that situation.

  *Corollary 3.5:*   The less is the value of a reward for A in an A,B exchange relation and the greater the alternative sources of that reward for A, the less cohesive is the exchange relation between A and B; or conversely, the more is the value of a reward for A, and the fewer alternative sources of that reward for A, the more cohesive is the relationship between A and B.

  *Corollary 3.6:*   The more an A,B exchange relationship at one point in time is transformed to A—B—C relationship, the greater the dependency of B upon A, and the fewer the alternatives for B in the A,B relationship, then B's dependency upon A will be greater than B's dependency upon C.

*Proposition 4:*   The more uncertain is an actor A of receiving a given type of reward in recent transactions, the more valuable is that reward for actor A.

  *Corollary 4.1:*   In a set of potential exchange relations, the more maintenance of one transaction precludes other transactions in this set, the greater the initial costs of this one transaction, but the less the costs across continuing transactions.

**TABLE 13–2**   The Initial Theorems

| | |
|---|---|
| *Theorem 1:* | The greater is the value of rewards to A in a situation, the more initiations by A reveal a curvilinear pattern, with initiations increasing over early transactions and then decreasing over time (From Corollaries 1.2 and 2.1). |
| *Theorem 2:* | The greater is the dependency of A on a set of exchange relations, the more likely A is to initiate behaviors in this set of relations (From Propositions 1 and 3). |
| *Theorem 3:* | The more the uncertainty of A increases in an exchange relation, the more the dependency of A on that situation increases, and vice versa. (From Corollary 3.3 and Proposition 4). |
| *Theorem 4:* | The greater is the dependency of B on A for rewards in an A,B exchange relationship, the greater is the power of A over B and the more imbalanced is the relationship between A and B (From Propositions 1 and 3 and definitions of cost, dependence, and power). |
| *Theorem 5:* | The greater is the imbalance of an A,B exchange relation at one point in time, the more likely it is to be balanced at a subsequent point in time (From Corollaries 1.1, 1.3, 3.1, 3.3, and Proposition 4). |

$= D_{BA}$. Balance is a situation where B's dependency for resources from A is equal to A's dependency for resources from B, or $D_{BA} = D_{AB}$.

Thus far, Emerson has derived some basic theorems on power and balance from a long list of behaviorist principles (Table 13–1). This list of behaviorist assumptions now recedes, and the main task is to introduce corollaries and new theorems to account for the structural form of an ongoing exchange relation. It is at this point that Emerson introduced ideas from network analysis.

## Structure, Networks, and Exchange

I will simplify Emerson's portrayal of social networks, but I should emphasize that network analysis is highly sophisticated and can be heavily mathematical. But for our purposes here, I need only offer a simplified view in order to communicate Emerson's basic approach. In addressing the forms of exchange relations, Emerson represented networks of relations among actors in graphic form. Although he followed the conventions of digraph theory and developed a number of definitions, I think that only two definitions are critical:

> ***Actors:*** Points A, B, C, . . ., $n$ in a network of relations. Different letters represent actors with different resources to exchange. The same letters—that is, $A_1$, $A_2$, $A_3$, and so forth—represent different actors exchanging similar resources.

> ***Exchange relations:*** A——— B, A———·B ——— C, $A_1$———$A_2$, and other patterns that can connect different actors to each other forming a network of relations.

With these two definitions, I think it possible to summarize the basic thrust of Emerson's network approach. But I should caution again that his analysis is more complex, especially in summarizing the nature of relations in an exchange network. The next conceptual task is to visualize the forms of networks that can be represented with these two definitions. For each basic form, new corollaries and theorems are added as Emerson documented the way in which the basic processes of dependence, power, and balance operate. His discussion is only preliminary, but it does illustrate the perspective's potential.

Several basic social forms are given special treatment: (*a*) unilateral monopoly, (*b*) division of labor, (*c*) social circles, (*d*) stratification, and along with Karen Cook, (*e*) centrality in networks. Each of these network forms is discussed below.

**Unilateral monopoly.**   In the network outlined below, actor A is a source of valuable resources for actors $B_1$, $B_2$, and $B_3$. Actors $B_1$, $B_2$, and $B_3$ provide rewards for A, but since A has multiple sources for rewards and the Bs only have A as a source for their rewards, the situation is a unilateral monopoly.

**FIGURE 13–1**

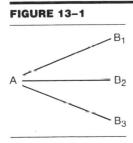

Such a structure often typifies interpersonal as well as intercorporate units. For example, A could be a female date for three different men, $B_1$, $B_2$, and $B_3$. Or A could be a corporation that is the sole supplier of raw resources for three other manufacturing corporations, $B_1$, $B_2$, and $B_3$. Or A could be a governmental body, and Bs dependent agencies. Thus, it is immediately evident that by focusing on the structure of the exchange relationship, many of the micro versus macro problems of exchange analysis, as well as of sociological theory in general, are reduced.

Another important feature of the unilateral monopoly presented above is that, in terms of Emerson's definitions, it is imbalanced and thus its structure is subject to change. Previous propositions and corollaries listed in Table 13–1 provide an initial clue as to what might occur. Corollary

1.3 argues that A will use its power advantage and increase costs for each B. Corollary 1.1 indicates that with each increment in costs for the Bs, their behaviors will vary and they will seek alternative rewards from $A_2$, $A_3$, . . ., $A_n$. If another A can be found, then the structure of the network would change.

Emerson developed additional corollaries and theorems to account for the various ways this unilateral monopoly can become balanced. For instance, if no $A_2$, $A_3$, . . ., $A_n$ exist and Bs cannot communicate with each other, the following corollary would apply (termed by Emerson, *Exploitation Type I*):

> **Corollary 1.3.1:** The more an exchange relation between A and multiple Bs approximates a unilateral monopoly, the more additional resources each B will introduce into the exchange relation, with A's resource utilization remaining constant or decreasing.

Emerson saw this adaptation as short-lived, since the network will become even more unbalanced. Assuming that Bs can survive as an entity without resources from A, then Theorem 8 applies (termed by Emerson, *Exploitation Type II*):

> **Theorem 8:** The more an exchange relation between A and multiple Bs approximates a unilateral monopoly, the less valuable to Bs the resources provided by A across continuing transactions. (From Corollary 1.3, Theorem 4, and Corollary 4.1).

This theorem thus predicts that balancing operation 1—a decrease in the value of the reward for those at a power disadvantage—will operate to balance a unilateral monopoly where no alternative sources of rewards exist and where Bs cannot effectively communicate.

Other balancing operations are possible, if other conditions exist. If Bs can communicate, they might form a coalition (balancing operation 4) and require A to balance exchanges with a united coalition of Bs. If one B can provide a resource not possessed by the other Bs, then a division of labor among Bs (operations 3 and 4) would emerge. Or if another source of resources, $A_2$, can be found (operation 2), then the power advantage of $A_1$ is decreased. Each of these possible changes will occur under varying conditions, but Corollary 1.3.1 and Theorem 8 provide a reason for the initiation of changes—a reason derived from basic principles of operant psychology.

**Division of labor.**     The emergence of a division of labor is one of many ways to balance exchange relations in a unilateral monopoly. If each of the Bs can provide different resources for A, then they are likely to use these in the exchange with A and to specialize in providing A with these resources. This decreases the power of A and establishes a new type

**FIGURE 13–2**

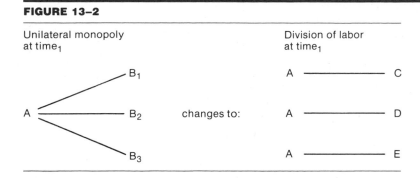

Unilateral monopoly at time$_1$ · changes to: · Division of labor at time$_1$

of network. For example, in Figure 13-2, the unilateral monopoly at the left is transformed to the division of labor form at the right, with $B_1$ becoming a new type of actor, C, with its own resources; with $B_2$ also specializing and becoming a new actor, D; and with $B_3$ doing the same and becoming actor E.

Emerson developed an additional theorem to describe this kind of change, where each B has its unique resources:

> ***Theorem 9:*** The more resources are distributed *non*uniformly across Bs in a unilateral monopoly with A, the more likely is each B to specialize and establish a separate exchange relation with A. (From theorems not discussed here and Corollaries 1.1 and 1.3.1).

Several points should be emphasized. First, the units in this transformation can be individual or collective actors. Second, the change in the structure or form of the network is described in terms of a theorem systematically derived from operant principles, corollaries, and other theorems. The theorem can thus apply to a wide variety of micro and macro contexts. For example, the theorem could apply to workers in an office who specialize and provide A with resources not available from others. It could also apply to a division in a corporation that seeks to balance its relations with the central authority by reorganizing itself in ways that distinguish it, and the services it can provide, from other divisions. Or it could apply to relations between a colonial power (A) and its colonized nations ($B_1$, $B_2$, $B_3$), who specialize (become C, D, and E) in their predominant economic activities in order to establish a less dependent relationship with A.

**Social circles.**   Emerson emphasized that some exchanges are intercategory and others intracategory. An intercategory exchange is one

**FIGURE 13–3**

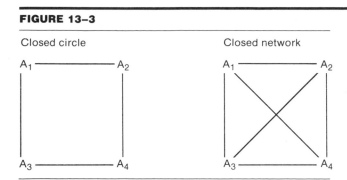

Closed circle

Closed network

**FIGURE 13–4**

where one type of resource is exchanged for another type—money for goods, advice for esteem, tobacco for steel knives, and so on. The networks discussed thus far have involved *inter*category exchanges between actors with different resources (A, B, C, D, E). An *intra*category is one where the same resources are being exchanged—affection for affection, advice for advice, goods for goods, and so on. As I indicated earlier, such exchanges are symbolized by using the same letter—$A_1$, $A_2$, $A_3$, and so forth—to represent actors with similar resources. Emerson then developed another theorem to describe what will occur in these intracategory exchanges.

*Theorem 10:* The more an exchange approximates an intracategory exchange, the more likely are exchange relations to become closed (From Theorem 5, corollaries 1.3 and 1.1).

Emerson defines "closed" as either a circle of relations (diagramed on the left in Figure 13-3) or as a balanced network where all actors exchange with each other (diagramed on the right in Figure 13-3).

Emerson offered the example of tennis networks to illustrate this balancing process. If two tennis players of equal ability, $A_1$ and $A_2$, play together regularly, this is a balanced intracategory exchange—tennis for tennis. However, if $A_3$ enters and plays with $A_2$, then $A_2$ now enjoys a power advantage, as is diagramed in Figure 13-4.

This is a unilateral monopoly, but unlike those discussed earlier, it is an intracategory monopoly. $A_1$ and $A_3$ are dependent upon $A_2$ for tennis. This relation is unbalanced and sets into motion processes of balance. $A_4$ may be found, creating either the circle or balanced network diagramed above. Once this kind of closed and balanced network is achieved, it resists entry by others, $A_5$, $A_6$, $A_7$, . . ., $A_n$, because as each additional actor enters, the network becomes unbalanced. Such a network, of course, is not confined to individuals; it can apply to nations forming a military alliance or common market, or to cartels of corporations, and other collective units.

**Stratified networks.**    The discussion on how intracategory exchanges often achieve balance through closure can help us understand processes of stratification. If, for example, tennis players $A_1$, $A_2$, $A_3$, and $A_4$ are unequal in ability, with $A_1$ and $A_2$ having more ability than $A_3$ and $A_4$, an initial circle may form among $A_1$, $A_2$, $A_3$, and $A_4$; but over time, $A_1$ and $A_2$ will find more gratification in playing each other, and $A_3$ and $A_4$ may have to incur too many costs in initiating invitations to $A_1$ and $A_2$. For an $A_1$ and $A_3$ tennis match is unbalanced; $A_3$ will have to provide additional resources—the tennis balls, praise, esteem, self-deprecation. The result will be for two classes to develop, as is diagramed below:

$$\text{Upper social class } A_1 \text{———} A_2$$
$$\text{Lower social class } A_3 \text{———} A_4$$

Moreover, $A_1$ and $A_2$ may enter into new exchanges with $A_5$ and $A_6$ at their ability level, forming a new social circle or network. Similarly, $A_3$ and $A_4$ may form new tennis relations with $A_7$ and $A_8$, creating social circles and networks with players at their ability level. The result is for stratification to reveal the pattern in Figure 13-5.

Emerson's discussion of stratification processes was tentative, but he developed a theorem to describe these stratifying tendencies:

> *Theorem 11:* The more resources are equally valued and the more resources are unequally distributed across a number of actors, the more likely is the network to stratify in terms of resource magnitudes and the more likely are actors with a given level of resources to form closed exchange networks (From Theorem 5, propositions 1 and 4).

Again, this theorem can apply to corporate units as well as individuals. Nations become stratified and form social circles, such as is the case with the distinctions between the developed and underdeveloped nations and the alliances among countries within these two classes. Or it can apply to traditional sociological definitions of class, since closed networks tend to form among members within, rather than across, social classes.

**The dynamics of centrality.**    An important concept in network analysis is *centrality*. Indeed, it is considered one of the most critical

**FIGURE 13–5**

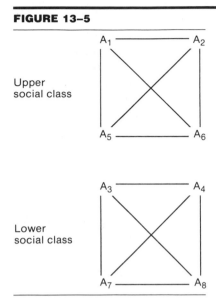

Upper
social class

Lower
social class

properties of a network. Typically, centrality is determined by a variety of measures that locate a point in a network in terms of (*a*) the number of other points with which it is connected, (*b*) the number of points between which it falls, or (*c*) the closeness of a point to others in a network.[8] These measures of centrality are not the same, but the general idea is this: a point (or actor) is central to the extent that it connects with many other points (actors), lies between other points, or is close to other points. In Figure 13-6, for example, actors $A_1$ and $A_2$ are more central in terms of the number of points between which they fall and also the number of points to which they are connected after two steps ($A_1$ and $A_2$ are, after two steps, connected to all other points, whereas it takes three or four steps for the other As to be so connected).

Most network analyses simply describe centrality, but Karen Cook has tried to use Emerson's theoretical ideas to explain the dynamics of it.[9] I will simplify her argument and also rephrase it a bit, but the essential logic is the same. Let me begin by creating a theorem that summarizes her hypothesis.[10]

---

[8]Linton C. Freeman, "Centrality in Social Networks: Conceptual Clarification," *Social Networks* 1 (1979), pp. 241–56.

[9]Karen S. Cook et al., "The Distribution of Power in Exchange Networks."

[10]This is my wording of a more complex argument presented by Cook, Emerson, and others. See ibid.

**FIGURE 13–6**

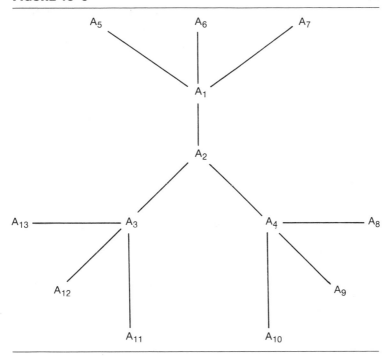

***Theorem 12:*** Over time, the distribution of power in complex net-works decentralizes around those actors (points) who possess the highest relative degree of access to resources (From Corollary 1.3.1 and theorems 4 and 5).

Using the above figure as an illustration of this theorem, Cook would predict that power will become increasingly concentrated in $A_3$, $A_4$, and $A_1$. $A_2$ will become less powerful and, in a more sociological sense, less central. In fact, the entire network will, over time, collapse around $A_3$, $A_4$, and $A_1$. Why should this be so? The basic argument that follows from the dynamics of power and dependence is this: $A_3$, $A_4$, and $A_1$ each have a unilateral monopoly with at least three other As (for example, $A_3$ has a monopoly exchange relation with $A_{11}$, $A_{12}$, and $A_{13}$). Thus, to get re-sources, $A_2$ must bargain with other As—that is, $A_1$, $A_3$, and $A_4$—who can extract more resources from those As over which it possesses a monopoly. And so, $A_1$, $A_3$, and $A_4$ will increase exchanges with their monopolized partners and decrease exchanges with $A_2$, who, in all likelihood, will be-come like the monopolized As. Hence, the network will decentralize around $A_1$, $A_3$, and $A_4$, who possess the highest relative resources (by virtue of their respective unilateral monopolies).

The critical point here is that Cook and her associates are trying to use the basic principles developed by Emerson to address more complex network systems. In so doing, they can explain the process of centrality (and perhaps other network properties) in terms of theoretical deductions. Up to this point, network analysis has typically described centrality using various measures, whereas the Emerson-Cook approach allows these network properties to be explained in terms of an abstract theoretical proposition.

## EXCHANGE NETWORK ANALYSIS: A CONCLUDING COMMENT

Of the current exchange theories, I think that the Emerson-Cook approach offers the most potential.[11] Let me close by simply listing the points that make it superior to those discussed in previous chapters:

1. The Emerson-Cook approach evidences considerably more deductive rigor than Homans's scheme. Emerson and Cook have used operant principles to build a theoretical scheme that executes Homans's assertions about what theory should be. But in contrast to Homans's efforts, their analysis does not define as givens what is of most interest to sociologists: patterns of social structure. The Emerson-Cook scheme uses the principles of operant psychology in ways that allow for *sociological* theorizing, while ignoring the issue of reductionism and avoiding the ad hoc and ex post facto flavor of Homans's polemics.

2. The exchange network approach has retained and expanded upon Blau's and Homans's concern with the dynamics of power. Emerson abandoned, however, the ideologically loaded concept of dialectics and instead sought to derive theorems that describe how dependence, use of power, and balancing operations operate as sources of change in social structures. Moreover, this analysis is free from the polemics of conflict theorizing, while providing a set of principles for explaining why imbalance in exchange relations sets into motion processes of change.

3. This approach also removes much of the vagueness surrounding Homans's and Blau's conceptualizations of social structures as "institutional piles" and "organized collectivities." Social structure in network analysis has a more precise definition as patterns of connections among actors in networks of exchange relations. Furthermore, using digraph notation and other mathematical concepts opens

---

[11]Again, let me emphasize that others are also working with this approach. See, in particular, the references to Willer cited in note 4.

the possibility that social structures can be more precisely defined. At the same time, the Emerson-Cook strategy puts some theory into what has been, I believe, a highly atheoretical approach. Indeed, I think that network sociology has become overly enamored with developing ever more sophisticated mathematical techniques for describing increasingly hypothetical network structures.

4. By concentrating on the forms of relations, analysis of the nature of individual actors is forfeited. Yet, this emphasis allows for theories that are distinctly sociological and that avoid the issue of whether or not they are micro or macro. Much exchange theory, and sociological theory in general, evidences considerable discontinuity between processes and structures among individuals and those among collective units. Network analysis is less prone to such discontinuity since it focuses on the form of the relationship among units.

5. Finally, network analysis bypasses the problem of tautology by taking as a given the existence of actors seeking gratification or reinforcement in social situations. This unit is a fact of social life, and its existence is not the end point—as is the case in operant psychology—but the beginning of analysis. Exchange network theory begins with an exchange relation and then seeks to understand variations and changes in its form in terms of *the properties of the relation* rather than the attributes of the actors.

These are the strong points of the Emerson-Cook approach. To a great extent, the future of exchange theory hinges on how well these apparent advantages obviate the long-standing logical problem of tautology and substantive problems of vagueness and micro-macro discontinuity. It is difficult to know at this point just whether or not Cook's elaboration of Emerson's basic approach can resolve these problems. Yet it does present an alternative to Homans's and Blau's perspectives, which, for all their insight, are rather vague in how they conceptualize social structure. And an exchange theory that cannot analyze the complexities of social structure beyond metaphorical accounts is not likely to be useful in building theory.

## PART FOUR

# Interactionist Theory

## CHAPTER 14

# Early Interactionism and Phenomenology

I think that some of the most intriguing questions in social theory concern the relationships between society and the individual. In what ways does one mirror the other? How does society shape individuals, or how do individuals create and maintain and change society? How are society and the personality of individuals interrelated and yet separate emergent phenomena? Indeed, as I have already emphasized for virtually all theorists in the previous chapters, the issue of micro versus macro sociological analysis boils down to a question of the relationship between the properties of individuals and interaction, on the one side, and those of social structure, on the other.

It was near the close of the 19th century that the grand analytical schemes of Marx, Durkheim, Spencer, and other Europeans were supplemented by a concern for the specific processes that link individuals to one another and to society. Instead of focusing on macrostructures and processes, such as evolution, class conflict, and the nature of the body social, attention shifted to the study of processes of social interaction and their consequences for the individual and the society. And out of this shift in concern came a variety of interactionist theories. For the most part, the theory is American, but we will need to be aware of important European contributions to the emergence of interactionism.

## EARLY AMERICAN INSIGHTS

Modern interactionism draws its inspiration from a number of prominent thinkers in America and Europe, all of whom wrote between 1880 and

1935. Yet, I believe that interactionism is indebted to the genius of one in particular, George Herbert Mead. Much like Darwin's great synthesis of the theory of evolution from his own studies and the speculations of others, so interactionist ideas were codified by George Herbert Mead. Mead borrowed ideas from others and combined them with his own insights to produce a synthesis that still stands as the conceptual core of modern interactionism. And so, I will begin with Mead's synthesis; and then later, I will turn to European thought and indicate some of the ways that it supplemented Mead's great work.

To appreciate Mead's feat, I think it best to review the contributions of three thinkers who most influenced him: William James, John Dewey, and Charles Horton Cooley. Each of these scholars provided a key concept that was to form the basis of Mead's synthesis.

## William James (1842–1910) and the Concept of "Self"

The Harvard psychologist William James was perhaps the first social scientist to develop a clear concept of self. James recognized that humans have the capacity to view themselves as objects and to develop self-feelings and attitudes toward themselves. Just as humans can (*a*) denote symbolically other people and aspects of the world around them, (*b*) develop attitudes and feelings toward these objects, and (*c*) construct typical responses toward objects, so they can denote themselves, develop self-feelings and attitudes, and construct responses toward themselves. James called these capacities *self* and recognized their importance in shaping the way people respond in the world.

James developed a typology of selves: "the material self," which includes those physical objects that humans view as part of their being and as crucial to their identity; the "social self," which involves the self-feelings that individuals derive from associations with other people; and the "spiritual self," which embraces the general cognitive style and capacities typifying an individual.[1] This typology was never adopted by subsequent interactionists, but James's notion of the social self was to become a part of all interactionists' formulations.

James's concept of the social self recognizes that people's feelings about themselves arise out of interaction with others. As he noted, "a man has as many social selves as there are individuals who recognize him."[2] Yet James did not carry this initial insight very far. He was, after all, a psychologist who was more concerned with internal psychological functioning of individuals than with the social processes out of which the capacities of individuals arise.

---

[1] William James, *The Principles of Psychology* (New York: Henry Holt, 1890), pp. 292–99 of vol. 1.

[2] Ibid., p. 294.

## Self and Social Process: Charles Horton Cooley

I believe that Charles Horton Cooley made two significant breakthroughs in the study of self.[3] First, he refined the concept of self, viewing it as the process in which individuals see themselves as objects, along with other objects, in their social environment. Second, he recognized that self emerges out of communication with others. As individuals interact with each other, they interpret each other's gestures and thereby see themselves from the viewpoint of others. They imagine how others evaluate them, and they derive images of themselves or self-feelings and attitudes. Cooley termed this process *the looking glass self*: the gestures of others serve as mirrors in which people see and evaluate themselves, just as they see and evaluate other objects in their social environment.

Cooley also recognized that self arises out of interaction in group contexts. He developed the concept of "primary group" to emphasize that participation in front of the looking glass for some groups is more important in the genesis and maintenance of self than participation in other groups. Those small groups where personal and intimate ties exist are the most important in shaping people's self-feelings and attitudes.

Cooley thus refined and narrowed James's notion of self and forced the recognition that it arises out of symbolic communication with others in group contexts. These insights were to influence profoundly the thought of George Herbert Mead.

## Pragmatism and Thinking: The Contribution of John Dewey (1859–1952)

John Dewey was, for a brief period, a colleague of Cooley's at the University of Michigan. But more important was Dewey's enduring association with George Herbert Mead, whom he brought to the University of Chicago. As the chief exponent of a school of thought known as *pragmatism,* Dewey stressed the process of human adjustment to the world, in which humans constantly seek to master the conditions of their environment. And thus the unique characteristics of humans arise out of the *process* of adjusting to their life conditions.

What is unique to humans, Dewey argued, is their capacity for thinking. Mind is not a structure but a process that emerges out of humans' efforts to adjust to their environment. Moreover, mind is the unique capacity that allows humans to deal with conditions around them.

Dewey thus devoted considerable effort to understanding human consciousness. His basic questions were: How does mind work? And how

---

[3]Charles Horton Cooley, *Human Nature and the Social Order* (New York: Charles Scribner's Sons, 1902) and *Social Organization: A Study of the Larger Mind* (New York: Charles Scribner's Sons, 1916).

does it facilitate adaptation to the environment? Mind for Dewey is the process of denoting objects in the environment, ascertaining potential lines of conduct, imagining the consequences of pursuing each line, inhibiting inappropriate responses, and then, selecting a line of conduct that will facilitate adjustment. Mind is thus the process of thinking, which involves deliberation:

> Deliberation is a dramatic rehearsal (in imagination) of various competing possible lines of action. . . . Deliberation is an experiment in finding out what the various lines of possible action are really like. It is an experiment in making various combinations of selected elements . . . to see what the resultant action would be like if it were entered upon.[4]

Dewey's conception of mind as a process of adjustment, rather than as a thing or entity, was to be critical in shaping Mead's thought. For much as Cooley had done for the concept of self, Dewey had demonstrated that mind emerges and is sustained through interactions in the social world. This line of thought from both Cooley and Dewey was to prove decisive as Mead's great synthesis unfolded.

## Main Currents of Thought in America: Pragmatism, Darwinism, and Behaviorism

At the time that Mead began to formulate his synthesis, I think the convergence of several intellectual traditions was crucial since it appears to have influenced the direction of Mead's thought. Mead considered himself a behaviorist, but not of the mechanical stimulus-response type. In fact, many of his ideas were intended as a refutation of such prominent behaviorists as John B. Watson. Mead accepted the basic premise of behaviorism—that is, the view that reinforcement guides and directs action. He was, however, to use this principle in a novel way. Moreover, he rejected as untenable the methodological presumption of early behaviorism that it was inappropriate to study the internal dynamics of the human mind. James's, Cooley's, and Dewey's influence assured that Mead would rework the principle of reinforcement in ways that allowed for the consideration of mind and self.

Another strain of thought that shaped Mead's synthesis is pragmatism, as it was acquired through exposure with Dewey. As I noted, pragmatism sees organisms as practical creatures who come to terms with the actual conditions of the world. Coupled with behaviorism, pragmatism offered a new way of viewing human life: human beings seek to cope with their actual conditions, but they learn those behavioral patterns that

---

[4]John Dewey, *Human Nature and Human Conduct* (New York: Henry Holt, 1922), p. 190. For an earlier statement of these ideas, see John Dewey, *Psychology* (New York: Harper & Row, 1886).

provide gratification; and the most important type of gratification is adjustment to social contexts.

This line of argument was buttressed in Mead's synthesis by yet another related intellectual tradition, Darwinism. Mead recognized that humans are organisms who seek to find a niche in which they can adapt. Historically, this was true of humans as an evolving species, and more important, it is true of humans as they discover a niche in the social world. Mead's commitment to behaviorism and pragmatism thus allowed him to apply the basic principle of Darwinian theory to each human: that which facilitates survival or adaptation of the organism will be retained.

In this way, behaviorist, pragmatist, and Darwinian principles blended into an image of humans as attempting to adjust to the world around them and as retaining those characteristics—particularly mind and self—that enable them to adapt to their surroundings. Mind, self, and other unique features of humans evolve out of efforts to survive in the social environment. They are thus capacities that arise from the processes of coping, adjusting, adapting, and achieving the ultimate gratification or reinforcement: survival. For this reason, Mead's analysis emphasizes the processes by which the infant organism acquires mind and self as an adaptation to society. But Mead did much more; he showed how society could survive only from the capacities for mind and self among individuals. From Mead's perspective, then, the capacities for mind, self, and society are intimately connected.

## George Herbert Mead's Synthesis

The names of William James, Charles Horton Cooley, and John Dewey figure prominently in the development of interactionism, but George Herbert Mead brought their related concepts together into a coherent theoretical perspective that linked the emergence of the human mind, the social self, and the structure of society to the process of social interaction.[5] As I have emphasized, Mead appears to have begun his synthesis with two basic assumptions: (1) the biological frailty of human organisms force

---

[5]Mead's most important sociological ideas can be found in the published lecture notes of his students. His most important exposition of interactionism is found in his *Mind, Self, and Society*, ed. C. W. Morris (Chicago: University of Chicago Press, 1934). Other useful sources include George Herbert Mead, *Selected Writings* (Indianapolis: Bobbs-Merrill, 1964); and Anselm Strauss, ed., *George Herbert Mead on Social Psychology* (Chicago: University of Chicago Press, 1964). For excellent secondary sources on the thought of Mead, see Tamotsu Shibutani, *Society and Personality: An Interactionist Approach* (Englewood Cliffs, N.J.: Prentice-Hall, 1962); Anselm Strauss, *Mirrors and Masks: The Search for Identity* (Glencoe, Ill.: Free Press, 1959); Bernard N. Meltzer, "Mead's Social Psychology," in *The Social Psychology of George Herbert Mead* (Ann Arbor, Mich.: Center for Sociological Research, 1964), pp. 10–31; Jonathan H. Turner, "Returning to Social Physics: Illustrations from George Herbert Mead," *Perspectives in Social Theory* 2 (1981). Also see Jonathan H. Turner and Leonard Beeghley, *The Emergence of Sociological Theory* (Homewood, Ill.: Dorsey Press, 1981).

their cooperation with each other in group contexts in order to survive; and (2) those actions within and among human organisms that facilitate their cooperation, and hence their survival or adjustment, will be retained. Starting from these assumptions, Mead was able to reorganize the concepts of others so that they denoted how mind, the social self, and society arise and are sustained through interaction.

**Mind.**    Following Dewey's lead, Mead recognized that the unique feature of the human mind is its capacity to (1) use symbols to designate objects in the environment, (2) rehearse covertly alternative lines of action toward these objects, and (3) inhibit inappropriate lines of action and select a proper course of overt action. Mead termed this process of using symbols or language covertly *imaginative rehearsal,* revealing his conception of mind as a *process* rather than a structure. Further, as I will develop more fully later, the existence and persistence of society, or cooperation in organized groups, is viewed by Mead as dependent upon this capacity of humans to imaginatively rehearse lines of action toward each other and thereby select those behaviors that facilitate cooperation.

Much of Mead's analysis focuses not so much on the mind of mature organisms but on how this capacity first develops in individuals. Unless mind emerges in infants, neither society nor self can exist. In accordance with principles of behaviorism, Darwinism, and pragmatism, Mead stressed that mind arises out of a selective process in which an infant's initially wide repertoire of random gestures are narrowed as some gestures bring favorable reactions from those upon whom the infant is dependent for survival. Such selection of gestures facilitating adjustment can occur either through trial and error or through conscious coaching by those with whom the infant must cooperate. Eventually, through either of these processes, gestures come to have common meanings for both the infant and those in its environment. With this development, gestures now denote the same objects and carry similar dispositions for all the parties to an interaction. Gestures that have such common meanings are termed by Mead *conventional gestures.* These conventional gestures have increased efficiency for interaction among individuals because they allow for more precise communication of desires and wants as well as intended courses of action— thereby increasing the capacity of organisms to adjust to one another.

The ability to use and to interpret conventional gestures with common meanings represents a significant step in the development of mind, self, and society. By perceiving and interpreting gestures, humans can now assume the perspective (dispositions, needs, wants, and propensities to act) of those with whom they must cooperate for survival. By reading and then interpreting covertly conventional gestures, individuals are able to imaginatively rehearse alternative lines of action that will facilitate adjustment to others. Thus, by being able to put oneself in another's place, or to "take the role of the other" to use Mead's concept, the covert rehearsal of action can take on a new level of efficiency, since actors can better gauge the consequences of their actions for others and thereby increase the probability of cooperative interaction.

Thus, when an organism develops the capacity (1) to understand conventional gestures, (2) to employ these gestures to take the role of others, and (3) to imaginatively rehearse alternative lines of action, Mead believed such an organism to possess "mind."

**Self.** Drawing from James and Cooley, Mead stressed that just as humans can designate symbolically other actors in the environment, so they can symbolically represent themselves as an object. The interpretation of gestures, then, can not only facilitate human cooperation, but it can also serve as the basis for self-assessment and evaluation. This capacity to derive images of oneself as an object of evaluation in interaction is dependent upon the processes of mind. What Mead saw as significant about this process is that, as organisms mature, the transitory "self-images" derived from specific others in each interactive situation eventually become crystallized into a more or less stabilized "self-conception" of oneself as a certain type of object. With these self-conceptions, individuals' actions take on consistency, since they are now mediated through a coherent and stable set of attitudes, dispositions, or meanings about oneself as a certain type of person.

Mead chose to highlight three stages in the development of self, each stage marking not only a change in the kinds of transitory self-images an individual can derive from role-taking but also an increasing crystallization of a more stabilized self-conception. The initial stage of role-taking in which self-images can be derived is termed *play*. In play, infant organisms are capable of assuming the perspective of only a limited number of others, at first only one or two. Later, by virtue of biological maturation and practice at role-taking, the maturing organism becomes capable of taking the role of several others engaged in organized activity. Mead termed this stage the *game* because it designates the capacity to derive multiple self-images from, and to cooperate with, a group of individuals engaged in some coordinated activity. (Mead typically illustrated this stage by giving the example of a baseball game in which all individuals must symbolically assume the role of all others on the team in order to participate effectively.) The final stage in the development of self occurs when an individual can take the role of the "generalized other" or "community of attitudes" evident in a society. At this stage, individuals are seen as capable of assuming the overall perspective of a community, or general beliefs, values, and norms. This means that humans can both (1) increase the appropriateness of their responses to others with whom they must interact and (2) expand their evaluative self-images from the expectations of specific others to the standards and perspective of the broader community. Thus, it is this ever-increasing capacity to take roles with an ever-expanding body of others that marks the stages in the development of self.

**Society.**    For Mead, society or institutions represent the organized and patterned interactions among diverse individuals.[6] Such organization of interactions is dependent upon mind. Without the capacities of mind to take roles and imaginatively rehearse alternative lines of activity, individuals could not coordinate their activities. Mead emphasized:

> The immediate effect of such role-taking lies in the control which the individual is able to exercise over his own response. The control of the action of the individual in a co-operative process can take place in the conduct of the individual himself if he can take the role of the other. It is this control of the response of the individual himself through taking the role of the other that leads to the value of this type of communication from the point of view of the organization of the conduct in the group.[7]

Society is also dependent upon the capacities of self, especially the process of evaluating oneself from the perspective of the generalized other. Without the ability to see and evaluate oneself as an object from this community of attitudes, social control would rest solely on self-evaluations derived from role-taking with specific and immediately present others—thus making coordination of diverse activities among larger groups extremely difficult.[8]

While Mead was vitally concerned with how society and its institutions are maintained and perpetuated by the capacities of mind and self, these concepts also allowed him to view society as constantly in flux and rife with potential change. The fact that role-taking and imaginative rehearsal are ongoing processes among the participants in any interaction situation reveals the potential these processes give individuals for adjusting and readjusting their responses. Furthermore, the insertion of self as an object into the interactive process underscores the fact that the outcome of interaction will be affected by the ways in which self-conceptions alter the initial reading of gestures and the subsequent rehearsal of alternative lines of behavior. Such a perspective thus emphasizes that social organization is both perpetuated and altered through the adjustive capacities of mind and the mediating impact of self:

> Thus the institutions of society are organized forms of group or social activity—forms so organized that the individual members of society can act adequately and socially by taking the attitudes of others toward these activ-

---

[6]For a more detailed analysis, see Jonathan H. Turner, "A Note on G. H. Mead's Behavioristic Theory of Social Structure," *Journal for the Theory of Social Behavior* 12 (July 1982), pp. 213–22.

[7]Mead, *Mind, Self, and Society*, p. 254.

[8]Ibid., pp. 256–57.

ities. ... [But] there is no necessary or inevitable reason why social institutions should be oppressive or rigidly conservative, or why they should not rather be, as many are, flexible and progressive, fostering individuality rather than discouraging it.[9]

In this passage, I think, is a clue to Mead's abiding distaste for rigid and oppressive patterns of social organization. He viewed society as a *constructed* phenomenon that arises out of the adjustive interactions among individuals. As such, society can be altered or reconstructed through the processes denoted by the concepts of mind and self. However, I believe that Mead went one step further and stressed that change is frequently unpredictable, even by those emitting the change-inducing behavior. To account for this indeterminacy of action, Mead used two concepts first developed by William James, the "I" and the "me".[10] For Mead, the "I" points to the impulsive tendencies of individuals, and the "me" represents the self-image of behavior after it has been emitted. With these concepts, Mead emphasized that the "I," or impulsive behavior, cannot be predicted because the individual can only "know in experience" (the "me") what has actually transpired and what the consequences of the "I" have been.

In sum, then, society for Mead represents those constructed patterns of coordinated activity that are maintained by, and changed through, symbolic interaction among and within actors. Both the maintenance and change of society, therefore, occur through the processes of mind and self. While many of the interactions causing both stability and change in groups are viewed by Mead as predictable, the possibility for spontaneous and unpredictable actions that alter existing patterns of interaction is also likely.

This conceptual legacy had a profound impact on a generation of American sociologists prior to the posthumous publication of Mead's lectures in 1934. Yet, despite the suggestiveness of Mead's concepts, I think that they fail to address some important theoretical issues.

The most important of these issues concerns the vagueness of his concepts in denoting the nature of social organization or society and the precise points of articulation between society and the individual. Mead viewed society as organized activity, regulated by the generalized other, in which individuals make adjustments and cooperate with one another. Such adjustments and the cooperation are seen as possible by virtue of the capacities of mind and self. Whereas mind and self emerged out of existent patterns of social organization, the maintenance or change of such organization is viewed by Mead as a reflection of the processes of mind and self. Although these and related concepts of the Meadian scheme point to the mutual interaction of society and the individual and although

---

[9]Ibid., pp. 261–62.
[10]See James, *Principles of Psychology*, pp. 135–76.

the concepts of mind and self denote crucial processes through which this dependency is maintained, they do not allow for the analysis of variations in patterns of social organization and in the various ways individuals are implicated in these patterns. To note that society is coordinated activity and is maintained or changed through the role-taking and the self-assessment processes of individuals offers only a broad conceptual portrait of the linkages between the individual and society. Indeed, Mead's picture of society does not indicate how variable types of social organization reciprocally interact with variable properties of self and mind. Thus, in the end, Mead's concepts appeared to emphasize that society shapes mind and self, whereas mind and self affect society—a simple but profound observation for the times but one that needed supplementation.

The difficult task of filling in the details of this broad portrait began only four decades ago, as researchers and theorists began to encounter the vague and circular nature of Mead's conceptual perspective. The initial efforts at documenting more precisely the points of articulation between society and the individual led to attempts at formulating a series of concepts that could expose the basic units from which society is constructed. In this way, the linkages between society and the individual could be more adequately conceptualized.

## Conceptualizing Structure and Role

And so although Mead's synthesis provided the initial conceptual breakthrough, it did not satisfactorily resolve the problem of how participation in the *structure* of society shaped individual conduct, and vice versa. In an effort to resolve this vagueness, sociological inquiry began to focus on the concept of role. Individuals were seen as playing roles associated with positions in larger networks of positions. And with this vision, efforts to understand more about social structures and how individuals are implicated in them intensified during the 1920s and 1930s. This line of inquiry was to become known as *role theory*.

## Robert Park and Role Theory

Robert Park, who came to the University of Chicago near the end of Mead's career, was one of the first to extend Mead's ideas through an emphasis on roles. As he observed, "everybody is always and everywhere, more or less consciously, playing a role."[11] But Park stressed that roles are linked to structural positions in society and that self is intimately

---

[11]Robert E. Park, "Behind Our Masks," *Survey Graphic* 56 (May 1926), p. 135. For a convenient summary of the thrust of early research efforts in role theory, see Ralph H. Turner, "Social Roles: Sociological Aspects," *International Encyclopaedia of the Social Sciences* (New York: Macmillan, 1968).

linked to playing roles within the confines of the positions of social structure.

> The conceptions which men form of themselves seem to depend upon their vocations, and in general upon the role they seek to play in communities and social groups in which they live, as well as upon the recognition and status which society accords them in these roles. It is status, i.e., recognition by the community, that confers upon the individual the character of a person, since a person is an individual who has status, not necessarily legal, but social.[12]

Park's analysis stresses the fact that self emerges from the multiple roles that people play.[13] In turn, roles are connected to positions in social structures. I see this kind of analysis as shifting attention to the nature of society and how its structure influences the processes outlined in Mead's synthesis.

## Jacob Moreno and Role Theory

Inspired in part by Mead's concept of role-taking and by his own, earlier studies in Europe, Jacob Moreno was one of the first to develop the concept of role-playing. In *Who Shall Survive* and in many publications in the journals that he founded in America, Moreno began to view social organization as a network of roles that constrained and channeled behavior.[14] In his early works, Moreno distinguished different types of roles: (*a*) "psychosomatic roles," in which behavior is related to basic biological needs, as conditioned by culture, and in which role enactment is typically unconscious; (*b*) "psychodramatic roles," in which individuals behave in accordance with the specific expectations of a particular social context; and (*c*) "social roles," in which individuals conform to the more general expectations of various conventional social categories (for example, worker, Christian, mother, and father).

Despite the suggestiveness of these distinctions, I see their importance as coming not so much from their substantive content, but from their intent: to conceptualize social structures as organized networks of expectations that require varying types of role enactments by individuals. In this way, analysis can move beyond the vague Meadian conceptualization of society as coordinated activity regulated by the generalized other to a conceptualization of social organization as various *types* of interrelated role enactments regulated by varying *types* of expectations.

---

[12]Robert E. Park, *Society* (New York: Free Press, 1955), pp. 285–86.

[13]Indeed, Park studied briefly with Simmel in Berlin and apparently acquired insight into Simmel's study of the individual and the web of group affiliations (see later discussion). Coupled with his exposure to William James at Harvard, who also stressed the multiple sources of self, it is clear that Mead's legacy was supplemented by Simmel and James through the work of Robert Park.

[14]Jacob Moreno, *Who Shall Survive* (Washington, D.C., 1934); rev. ed. (New York: Beacon House, 1953).

## Ralph Linton and Role Theory

Shortly after Moreno's publication of *Who Shall Survive*, the anthropologist Ralph Linton further conceptualized the nature of social organization, and the individual's imbeddedness in it, by distinguishing the concepts of role, status, and individuals from one another:

> A status, as distinct from the individual who may occupy it, is simply a collection of rights and duties. . . . A *role* represents the dynamic aspect of status. The individual is socially assigned to a status and occupies it with relation to other statuses. When he puts the rights and duties which constitute the status into effect, he is performing a role.[15]

In this passage are a number of important conceptual distinctions. Social structure reveals several distinct elements: (*a*) a network of positions, (*b*) a corresponding system of expectations, and (*c*) patterns of behavior that are enacted with regard to the expectations of particular networks of interrelated positions. In retrospect, these distinctions may appear self-evident and trivial, but I feel that they made possible the subsequent elaboration of many interactionist concepts:

1. Linton's distinctions allow for the conceptualization of society in terms of clear-cut variables: the nature and kind of interrelations among positions and the types of expectations attending these positions.
2. The variables Mead denoted by the concepts of mind and self can be analytically distinguished from both social structure (positions and expectations) and behavior (role enactment).
3. By conceptually separating the processes of role-taking and imaginative rehearsal from both social structure and behavior, the points of articulation between society and the individual can be more clearly marked, since role-taking pertains to covert interpretations of the expectations attending networks of statuses and role denotes the enactment of these expectations as mediated by self.

Thus, by offering more conceptual insight into the nature of social organization, Park, Moreno, and Linton provided a needed supplement to Mead's suggestive concepts. For now it would be possible to understand more precisely the interrelations among mind, self, and society.

## EARLY EUROPEAN INSIGHTS

At the same time that American theory turned to the study of interaction and roles, European thinking was making a similar shift in emphasis.

---

[15]Ralph Linton, *The Study of Man* (New York: Appleton-Century-Crofts, 1936), p. 28.

The more macro-oriented work of Max Weber and Émile Durkheim became increasingly concerned with meaning and how society "gets inside" the individual. But neither Weber nor Durkheim were as interactionistic in approach as Georg Simmel. But in the end, the main theoretical contribution to interactionism from Europe comes from philosophical phenomenology. And so, I will briefly summarize Weber's, Durkheim's, and Simmel's interactionist ideas; and then, I will turn to the early phenomenologists Edmund Husserl and Alfred Schutz.

## Georg Simmel and "Sociation"

Georg Simmel was perhaps the first European sociologist to begin a serious exploration of interaction, or "sociability" as he called it. In so doing, he elevated the study of interaction from the taken-for-granted.[16] For Simmel, as for the first generation of American sociologists in Chicago, the macrostructures and processes studied by functional and some conflict theories—class, the state, family, religion, evolution—are ultimately reflections of the specific interactions among people. These interactions result in emergent social phenomena, but considerable insight into the latter can be attained by understanding the basic interactive processes that first give and then sustain their existence.

In Chapter 6, I discussed Simmel's analysis of the forms of conflict; and in Chapter 10, I summarized his exchange theory. But Simmel's study of interaction extends beyond just the analysis of conflict and exchange, for he was concerned with understanding the forms and consequences of many diverse types of interactions. Some of his most important insights, which influenced American interactionists, concern the relationship between the individual and society. In his famous essay on "the web of group affiliations," for example, Simmel emphasized that human personality emerges from, and is shaped by, the particular configuration of a person's group affiliations.[17] What people are—that is, how they think of themselves and are prepared to act—is circumscribed by their group memberships. As he emphasized, "the genesis of the personality [is] the point of intersection for innumerable social influences, as the end-product of heritages derived from the most diverse groups and periods of adjustment."[18]

Although Simmel did not analyze in great detail the emergence of human personality, his "formal sociology" did break away from the macro

---

[16]Georg Simmel, "Sociability," in *The Sociology of Georg Simmel*, ed. K. H. Wolff (New York: Free Press, 1950), pp. 40–57. For an excellent secondary account of Simmel's significance for interactionism, see Randall Collins and Michael Makowsky, *The Discovery of Society* (New York: Random House, 1972), pp. 138–42.

[17]*Conflict and the Web of Group Affiliations*, trans. R. Bendix (Glencoe, Ill.: Free Press, 1955; originally published in 1922).

[18]Ibid., p. 141.

concerns of early German, French, and British sociologists. He began in Europe a mode of analysis that, as I have just summarized, became the prime concern of the first generation of American sociologists. Simmel thus could be considered one of the first European interactionists.

## Émile Durkheim's Metamorphosis

In his *Division of Labor in Society,* Émile Durkheim portrayed social reality as an emergent phenomena, *sui generis,* and as not reducible to the psychic states of individuals. And yet, in his later works, such as *The Elementary Forms of Religious Life,* Durkheim began to ask: How does society rule the individual? How is it that society "gets inside" individuals and guides them from within? Why do people share common orientations and perspectives?[19] Durkheim never answered these questions effectively, for his earlier emphasis on social structures prevented him from seeing the micro reality of interactions among individuals implicated in macro social structures. But I think it significant that the most forceful advocate of the sociologistic position became intrigued with the relationship between the individual and society. I see two critical lines of interactionist thought in *Elementary Forms*: (1) the analysis of ritual and (2) the concern with categories of thought.

  1. The implicit theory of ritual argues that people's sense of solidarity is reinforced by ritual activity. Durkheim emphasized that religious rituals are, in essence, the worship of society. But there are more general implications to his ideas: people's sense of attachment to the social order and to each other is very much dependent upon ritual performances. That is, interpersonal rituals are vital to the maintenance of the macro social order.[20]

  2. The concern with thought in *Elementary Forms* also influenced social theory. Durkheim emphasized that "the collective conscience" is not "entirely outside us" and that people's definitions of, and orientations to, situations are related to the organization of subjective consciousness. The categories of this consciousness, however, reflect the structural arrangements of society. Hence, varying macro structures generate different forms of thought and perception of the world. Such forms feed back and reinforce social structures.

But Durkheim's metamorphosis influenced structural sociology more than interactionism, and so, I will take up these ideas again in later chapters (see 19–21). I mention them here only to stress that a dramatic

---

[19] Émile Durkheim, *The Elementary Forms of Religious Life* (New York: Free Press, 1954; originally published in 1912).

[20] Randall Collins, *Conflict Sociology* (New York: Academic Press, 1975) develops this idea. See Chapter 21.

shift from macro to micro theorizing was occurring, even among the most avowed macrotheorist, Émile Durkheim.

## Max Weber and "Social Action"

Max Weber was also becoming increasingly concerned with the micro social world, although I think that his most important insights are in the area of macro and historical sociology. Yet Weber's definition of sociology was highly compatible with the flourishing American school of interactionism. For Weber, sociology is "that science which aims at the interpretative understanding of social behavior in order to gain an explanation of its causes, its course, and its effects."[21] Moreover, the behavior to be studied by sociology is seen by Weber as social action that includes:

> All human behavior when and insofar as the acting individual attaches a subjective meaning to it. Action in this sense may be overt, purely inward, or subjective; it may consist of positive intervention in a situation, of deliberately refraining from such intervention, or passively acquiescing in the situation. Action is social insofar as by virtue of the subjective meaning attached to it by the acting individual (or individuals), it takes account of the behavior of others and is thereby oriented in its course.[22]

Thus, Weber recognized that the reality behind the macrostructures of society—classes, the state, institutions, and nations—are the meaningful and symbolic interactions among people. Moreover, Weber's methodology stresses the need for understanding macrostructures and processes "at the level of meaning." For in the real world, actors interpret and give meaning to the reality around them and act in terms of these meanings. And yet, despite this key insight, Weber's actual analysis of social structures—class, status, party, change, religion, bureaucracy, and the like—rarely follows his own methodological prescriptions. As with other European thinkers, he tended to focus on social and cultural *structures* and the impact of these structures upon each other. The interacting and interpreting person is often lost amid Weber's elaborate taxonomies of structures and analyses of historical events. And it is just this failing that was to attract the attention of Alfred Schutz, who, more than any other European thinker, was to translate phenomenology into a perspective that could be incorporated into interactionist theory.

## European Phenomenology

Phenomenology began as the project of the German philosopher Edmund Husserl (1859–1938).[23] In his hands, I think, this project showed few signs

---

[21]Max Weber, *Basic Concepts in Sociology* (New York: Citadel Press, 1964), p. 29.

[22]Max Weber, *The Theory of Social and Economic Organization* (New York: Free Press, 1947; originally published after Weber's death), p. 88.

[23]For some readable, general references on phenomenology, see George Psathas, ed.,

of being anything more than an orgy of subjectivism. Yet, as I will emphasize, the German social thinker Alfred Schutz was to take Husserl's concepts and transform them into an interactionist analysis that has exerted considerable influence on modern-day interactionism. I am sure that Schutz's migration to the United States in 1939 facilitated this translation, especially as he came into contact with American interactionism, but my sense is that all of his most important ideas were formulated before he came. His subsequent work while in America involved an elaboration of basic ideas originally developed in Europe. I will first analyze Husserl's original phenomenology and then turn to Schutz's critique of Max Weber and his transformation of Husserl's ideas into an interactionist perspective.

**Edmund Husserl's project.** As the father of phenomenology, there can be little doubt that Edmund Husserl's thought has profoundly influenced contemporary social science. Yet, as I have suggested, his ideas have been transformed, especially by Alfred Schutz. Indeed, Husserl would be upset by what is now attributed to his genius. As Z. Bauman notes: "It took guile, utterly illegitimate as viewed from the Husserlian perspective, to devise a social science which would claim to be the brainchild, or logical consequence of the phenomenological project."[24]

Husserl's ideas, then, have been selectively borrowed and used in ways that he would not condone to develop modern phenomenology and various forms of interactionist thought. In reviewing Husserl's contribution, therefore, I think it best to focus more on what was borrowed than on the details of his complete philosophical scheme. I will therefore highlight several features of his work: (1) the basic philosophical dilemma, (2) the properties of consciousness, (3) the critique of naturalistic empiricism, and (4) the philosophical alternative to social science.[25]

---

*Phenomenological Sociology* (New York: John Wiley & Sons, 1973); Richard M. Zaner, *The Way of Phenomenology: Criticism as a Philosophical Discipline* (New York: Pegasus, 1970); Peter L. Berger and Thomas Luckman, *The Social Construction of Reality* (Garden City, N.Y.: Doubleday Publishing, 1966); Herbert Spiegelberg, *The Phenomenological Movement*, vols. 1 and 2, 2d ed. (The Hague, Holland: Martinus Nijhoff, 1969); Hans P. Neisser, "The Phenomenological Approach in Social Science," *Philosophy and Phenomenological Research* 20 (1959), pp. 198–212; Stephen Strasser, *Phenomenology and the Human Sciences* (Pittsburgh, Pa.: Duquesne University Press, 1963); and Maurice Natanson, ed., *Phenomenology and the Social Sciences* (Evanston, Ill.: Northwestern University Press, 1973); Quentin Lauer, *Phenomenology: Its Genesis and Prospect* (New York: Harper Torchbooks, 1965).

[24]Bauman, "On the Philosophical Status of Ethnomethodology," *The Sociological Review* 21 (February 1973), p. 6.

[25]Husserl's basic ideas are contained in the following: *Phenomenology and the Crisis of Western Philosophy* (New York: Harper & Row, 1965, originally published 1936); *Ideas: General Introduction to Pure Phenomenology* (London: Collier-Macmillan, 1969; originally published in 1913); "Phenomenology," in *The Encyclopedia Britannica,* 14th ed., vol. 17, col. 699–702, 1929. For excellent secondary analyses, see Helmut R. Wagner, "The Scope

1. Basic questions confronting all inquiry are: What is real? What actually exists in the world? How is it possible to know what exists? For the philosopher Husserl, these were central questions that required attention. Husserl reasoned that humans know about the world only through experience. All notions of an external world, "out there," are mediated through the senses and can only be known through mental consciousness. The existence of other people, values, norms, and physical objects is always mediated by experiences as these register on people's conscious awareness. One does not directly have contact with reality; contact is always indirect and mediated through the processes of the human mind.

Since the process of consciousness is so important and central to knowledge, philosophic inquiry must first attempt to understand how this process operates and how it influences human affairs. It is this concern with the process of consciousness—of how experience creates a sense of an external reality—that was to become the central concern of phenomenology.

2. Husserl initially made reference to the "world of the natural attitude." Later, he was to use the phrase *lifeworld*. In either case, with these concepts he emphasized that humans operate in a taken-for-granted world that permeates their mental life. It is the world that humans sense to exist. It is composed of the objects, peoples, places, ideas, and other things that people see and perceive as setting the parameters for their existence, for their activities, and for their pursuits.

This lifeworld or world of the natural attitude *is* reality for humans. I see two features of Husserl's conception of natural attitude as influencing modern interactionist thought:

1. The lifeworld is taken for granted. It is rarely the topic of reflective thought; and yet, it structures and shapes the way people act and think.
2. Humans operate on the presumption that they experience the same world. Since people experience only their own consciousness, they have little capacity to directly determine if this presumption is correct. Yet people act *as if* they experienced a common world.

Human activity, then, is conducted in a lifeworld that is taken for granted and that is presumed to be experienced collectively. This fact

of Phenomenological Sociology," in *Phenomenological Sociology*, ed. G. Psathas, pp. 61–86 and "Husserl and Historicism," *Social Research* 39 (Winter 1972), pp. 696–719; Aron Gurwitsch, "The Common-Sense World as Social Reality," *Social Research* 29 (Spring 1962), pp. 50–72; Robert J. Antonio, "Phenomenological Sociology," in *Sociology: A Multiple Paradigm Science*, ed. G. Ritzer (Boston: Allyn & Bacon, 1975), pp. 109–12; Robert Welsh Jordan, "Husserl's Phenomenology as an 'Historical Science,' " *Social Research* 35 (Summer 1968), pp. 245–59.

brought Husserl back to his original problem: How do humans break out of their lifeworld and ascertain what is real? If people's lifeworld structures their consciousness and their actions, how is an objective science of human behavior and organization possible? These questions led Husserl to criticize what he termed *naturalistic-science,* or the position that I advocated in Chapter 1.

3. As I stressed in Chapter 1, science assumes that a factual world exists out there, independent of, and external to, human senses and consciousness. Through the scientific method, this factual world can be directly known. With successive efforts at its measurement, increasing understanding of its properties can be ascertained. But Husserl challenged this vision of science: if one can only know through consciousness and if consciousness is structured by an implicit lifeworld, then how can objective measurement of some external and real world be possible? How is science able to measure objectively an external world when the only world that individuals experience is the lifeworld of their consciousness?

4. Husserl's solution to this problem is a philosophical one. He advocated what he termed the search for the *essence of consciousness.* To understand social events, the basic process through which these events are mediated—that is, consciousness—must be comprehended. The substantive *content* of consciousness, or the lifeworld, is not what is important, but the abstract processes of consciousness, per se, are to be the topic of philosophic inquiry.

Husserl advocated what he termed *the radical abstraction of the individual* from interpersonal experience. Investigators must suspend their natural attitude and seek to understand the fundamental processes of consciousness, per se. One must discover, in Husserl's words, "Pure Mind." To do this, it is necessary to perform epoch—that is, to see if the substance of one's lifeworld can be suspended. Only when divorced from the substance of the lifeworld can the fundamental and abstract properties of consciousness be exposed and understood. And with understanding of these properties, then real insight into the nature of reality would be possible. For if all that humans know is presented through consciousness, it is necessary to understand the nature of consciousness in abstraction from the specific substance or content of the lifeworld.

I should caution here that Husserl was not advocating Max Weber's method of *verstehen,* or sympathetic introspection into an investigator's own mind. Nor was he suggesting the unstructured and intuitive search for people's definitions of situations. These methods would, he argued, only produce data on the substance of the lifeworld and would be no different than the structured measuring instruments of positivism. Rather, Husserl's goal was to create an abstract theory of consciousness that bracketed out, or suspended, any presumption of "an external social world out there."

Not surprisingly, I think, Husserl's philosophical doctrine failed. He never succeeded in developing an abstract theory of consciousness, radically abstracted from the lifeworld. But his ideas set into motion a new line of thought that was to become the basis for modern phenomenology and for its elaboration into ethnomethodology and other forms of theory. Indeed, recall Jurgen Habermas's critical project where the lifeworld is a prominent concept (Chapter 9). Or, as I will emphasize for ethnomethodology in Chapter 18 and in the work of two microstructuralists in Chapters 21 and 22, Husserl's ideas have endured, although in a dramatically transformed way. This transformation was, I feel, the major accomplishment of Alfred Schutz's early work. Indeed, he converted Husserl's phenomenological project into a type of interactionism.

**The phenomenological-interactionism of Alfred Schutz.**
Alfred Schutz migrated to the United States in 1939 from Austria, after spending a year in Paris. With his interaction in American intellectual circles and the translation of his early works into English over the last decades, Schutz's contribution to sociological theorizing is becoming increasingly recognized.[26] As I have emphasized, his contribution resides in his ability to blend Husserl's radical phenomenology with Max Weber's action theory and American interactionism. This blend was, in turn, to stimulate the further development of phenomenology, the emergence of ethnomethodology, and the refinement of other theoretical perspectives.

Schutz's work begins with a critique of his compatriot Max Weber, who employed the concept of social action in his many and varied inquiries.[27] Social action occurs when actors are consciously aware of each other and attribute meanings to their common situation. For Weber, then, a science of society must seek to understand social reality "at the level of meaning." Sociological inquiry must penetrate people's consciousness and discover how they view, define, and see the world. Weber advocated the method of *verstehen,* or sympathetic introspection. Investigators must become sufficiently involved in situations to be able to get inside the subjective world of actors. Causal and statistical analysis of complex social structures would be incomplete and inaccurate without such verstehen analysis.

Schutz's first major work addressed Weber's conception of action. His analysis is critical and detailed, and I need not summarize it here, except

---

[26]For basic ideas of Alfred Schutz, see his *The Phenomenology of the Social World* (Evanston, Ill.: Northwestern University Press, 1967; originally published in 1932); *Collected Papers*, vols. 1, 2, 3 (The Hague, Holland: Martinus Nijhoff, 1964, 1970, and 1971, respectively). For excellent secondary analyses, see Maurice Natanson, "Alfred Schutz on Social Reality and Social Science," *Social Research* 35 (Summer 1968), pp. 217–44.

[27]Schutz, *The Phenomenology of the Social World*, 1921.

to note that the basic critique turns on Weber's failure to use his verstehen method and to explore *why,* and through what processes, actors come to share common meanings. In Schutz's eye, Weber simply assumes that actors share subjective meanings, leading Schutz to ask: Why and how do actors come to acquire common subjective states in a situation? How do they create a common view of the world? This is the problem of "intersubjectivity," and it is central to Schutz's intellectual scheme. As Richard D. Zaner summarizes:

> How is it possible that although I cannot live in your seeing of things, cannot feel your love and hatred, cannot have an immediate and direct perception of your mental life as it is for you—how is it that I can nevertheless share your thoughts, feelings, and attitudes? For Schutz the "problem" of intersubjectivity is here encountered in its full force.[28]

I should, of course, stress how close this concern with intersubjectivity is to G. H. Mead's analysis of role-taking, which was the process by which actors anticipate each others' dispositions to act.

Schutz was more influenced in his early years by Husserl's phenomenology than by anything Mead had written. And yet, as Mead would have directed, Schutz departs immediately from Husserl's strategy of holding the individual in radical abstraction and of searching for Pure Mind or the abstract laws of consciousness. He accepts Husserl's notion that humans hold a natural attitude and lifeworld that is taken for granted and that shapes who they are and what they will do. He also accepts Husserl's notion that people perceive that they share the same lifeworld and act *as if* they lived in a common world of experiences and sensations. Moreover, Schutz acknowledges the power of Husserl's argument that social scientists cannot know about an external social world out there independently of their own lifeworld.

Having accepted these lines of thought from Husserl, however, Schutz advocates Weber's strategy of sympathetic introspection into people's consciousness. Only by observing people in interaction rather than in radical abstraction can the processes whereby actors come to share the same world be discovered. Social science cannot come to understand how and why actors create a common subjective world independently of watching them do so. This abandonment of Husserl's phenomenological project liberated phenomenology from philosophy and allowed sociologists to study empirically what Schutz considered the most important social reality: the creation and maintenance of intersubjectivity—that is, a common subjective world among pluralities of interacting individuals.

With his immigration to the United States, Schutz's phenomenology came under the influence of early symbolic interactionists, particularly

---

[28]Richard M. Zaner, "Theory of Intersubjectivity: Alfred Schutz," *Social Research* 28 (Spring 1961), p. 76.

G. H. Mead and W. I. Thomas. But I am not sure that Mead and other Chicago School interactionists exerted great influence on Schutz, who did devote some attention to symbolic interactionism.[29] Indeed, their influence may have been subtle, if not subliminal. The early symbolic interactionist's concern with the process of constructing shared meanings was, of course, similar to Schutz's desire to understand intersubjectivity. Schutz thus found immediate affinity with W. I. Thomas's "definition of the situation," since this concept emphasizes that actors construct orientations to, and dispositions to act in, situations. Moreover, Thomas's recognition that definitions of situations are learned from past experiences while being altered in present interactions appears to have influenced Schutz's conceptualization of the process of intersubjectivity. Mead's recognition that mind is a social process, arising out of interaction and yet facilitating interaction, probably had considerable appeal for Schutz. But if there was any direct influence from Chicago, I think it was Mead's concept of role-taking. For Schutz became vitally concerned with the process whereby actors come to know each other's role and to typify each other as likely to behave in certain ways. Additionally, Mead's concept of the generalized other may have influenced Schutz in that actors are seen as sharing a "community of attitudes"—or, in other words, common subjective states. Yet, although there is considerable affinity and perhaps some cross-fertilization between early symbolic interactionists' conceptualizations and Schutz's phenomenology, Schutz was to inspire a line of sociological inquiry that often challenges the interactionism initiated by Mead.

Having reviewed some of the intellectual influences on Schutz, let me now summarize his scheme and indicate some of its implications for sociological theorizing. Unfortunately, Schutz died just as he was beginning a systematic synthesis of his ideas, and as a result, only a somewhat fragmented but suggestive framework is evident in his collective work. But his early analysis of Weber, Husserl, and interactionism led to a concern with a number of key issues: (1) How do actors create a common *action* subjective world? (2) What implications does this creation have for how *order* social order is maintained?

All humans, Schutz asserted, carry in their minds rules, social recipes, conceptions of appropriate conduct, and other information that allows them to act in their social world. Extending Husserl's concept of lifeworld, Schutz views the sum of these rules, recipes, conceptions, and information as the individual's "stock knowledge at hand." Such stock knowledge gives people a frame of reference or orientation with which they can interpret events as they pragmatically act on the world around them.

Several features of this stock knowledge at hand are given particular emphasis by Schutz:

---

[29]See Schutz, *Collected Papers* for references to interactionists.

1. People's reality *is* their stock knowledge. For the members of a society, stock knowledge constitutes a "paramount reality"—a sense of an absolute reality that shapes and guides all social events. Actors use this stock knowledge and sense of reality as they pragmatically seek to deal with others in their environment.

2. The existence of stock knowledge that bestows a sense of reality on events gives the social world, as Schutz agreed with Husserl, a taken-for-granted character. The stock knowledge is rarely the object of conscious reflection but rather an implicit set of assumptions and procedures that are silently used by individuals as they interact.

3. Stock knowledge is learned. It is acquired through socialization within a common social and cultural world, but it becomes *the* reality for actors in this world.

4. People operate under a number of assumptions that allow them to create a sense of a "reciprocity of perspectives." That is, others with whom an actor must deal are considered to share an actor's stock knowledge at hand. And, while these others may have unique components in their stock knowledge because of their particular biographies, these can be ignored by actors.

5. The existence of stock knowledge, its acquisition through socialization, and its capacity to promote reciprocity of perspectives all operate to give actors in a situation a *sense* or *presumption* that the world is the same for all and that it reveals identical properties for all. What often holds society together is this presumption of a common world.

6. The presumption of a common world allows actors to engage in the process of typification. Action in most situations, except the most personal and intimate, can proceed through mutual typification as actors use their stock knowledge to categorize each other and to adjust their responses to these typifications.[30] With typification, actors can effectively deal with their world, since every nuance and characteristic of their situation does not have to be examined. Moreover, typification facilitates entrance into the social world; it simplifies adjustment because it allows for humans to treat each other as categories, or as "typical" objects of a particular kind.

These points of emphasis in Schutz's thought represent, as I noted earlier, a blending of ideas from European phenomenology and American interactionism. The emphasis on stock knowledge is clearly borrowed from Husserl, but it is highly compatible with Mead's notion of the generalized other. The concern with the taken-for-granted character of the

---

[30]Ralph H. Turner's emphasis on role differentiation and accretion is an example of how these ideas have been extended by role theorists. See Chapter 17.

world as it is shaped by stock knowledge is also borrowed from Husserl, but is similar to early interactionists' discussions of habit and routine behaviors. The emphasis on the acquired nature of stock knowledge coincides with early interactionists' discussions of the socialization process. The concern with the reciprocity of perspectives and with the process of typification owes much to Husserl and Weber, but is very compatible with Mead's notion of role-taking by which actors read each other's role and perspective.

But the major departure from interactionism should also be emphasized: actors operate on an unverified *presumption* that they share a common world; and this *sense* of a common world and the practices that produce this sense are crucial in maintaining social order. In other words, social organization may be possible not so much by the substance and content of stock knowledge but by the actual fact of reciprocity of perspectives or by successful typification as actors presume that they share intersubjective states. Schutz did not carry this line of inquiry far, but it was to inspire new avenues of phenomenological inquiry.

In sum, then, I think that Schutz is primarily responsible for liberating Husserl's concern with the basic properties and processes of consciousness from radical abstraction. Schutz brought Husserl's vision of a lifeworld back into the process of interaction. In so doing, he began to ask how actors come to share, or presume that they share, intersubjective states. He made Husserl's ideas more compatible with interactionists' concern with socialization and role-taking as well as with their emphasis on pragmatic actors seeking to cope with their world. But Schutz gave these concerns a new twist: humans act *as if* they see the world in similar ways, and they deal with each other *as if* others could be typified and categorized. This shift in emphasis to the interpersonal processes by which actors create a sense of a shared world was to inspire challenges to traditional interactionism and role theory and, in the process, to correct for some deficiencies in Meadian interactionism.

## MODERN INTERACTIONISM: A REVIEW

The Meadian legacy has directly inspired a theoretical perspective that can best be termed *symbolic interactionism.* This perspective, which I will discuss in the next chapter, focuses on how the symbolic processes of role-taking, imaginative rehearsal, and self-evaluation by individuals attempting to adjust to one another are the basis for social organization. While accepting the analytical importance of these symbolic processes, a more recent theoretical tradition has placed conceptual emphasis on the vision of social structure connoted by Park's, Moreno's, and Linton's concepts. Although not as clearly codified or as unified as the symbolic interactionist position, this theoretical perspective—the subject of Chapter 16—can be labeled *structural role theory,* because it focuses primarily analytical attention on the *structure of status networks and attendant expectations* as they circumscribe the internal symbolic processes of individuals and the eventual enactment of roles. As a reaction to this emphasis on structure, more process versions of role theory have emerged, which are explored in Chapter 17.

In some respects, the distinction between symbolic interactionism and the two role theoretic approaches may initially appear arbitrary, since each perspective relies heavily on the thought of George Herbert Mead and since both are concerned with the relationship between the individual and society. Yet, despite the fact that each represents a variant of interactionism, I think that there are great differences in emphasis between symbolic interactionism and all role theories. However, Ralph H. Turner's process approach comes close to uniting symbolic interactionism and role theory into a unified interactionist perspective (see Chapter 17).

Finally, I will examine in Chapter 18 the major interactionist perspective inspired by phenomenology: ethnomethodology. This perspective challenges much interactionist theory, but as I will emphasize, this challenge has been rather shrill and, at times, silly. It is much wiser, I believe, for ethnomethodology to be seen as an important supplement to traditional interactionist theory.

# CHAPTER 15

# The Symbolic Interactionism of Herbert Blumer and Manford Kuhn

All interactionist theory draws upon the theoretical synthesis provided by G. H. Mead. Yet, various contemporary thinkers have selectively borrowed Mead's ideas, and as a result, interactionist theorizing reveals considerable diversity. Even within a particular interactionist school of thought, there is conceptual controversy. Nowhere is this kind of controversy more evident than within *symbolic interactionism,* the theoretical perspective most closely tied to Mead's ideas.

The poles around which this controversy rages are termed the Iowa and Chicago Schools of symbolic interactionism.[1] These labels are, I feel, somewhat archaic and inappropriate for several reasons. First, the principle exponent of the Chicago School, Herbert Blumer, left Chicago more than 30 years ago; it is true that he took over Mead's social psychology course at Chicago upon the latter's death and that he has defined himself as the principle interpreter of Mead's thought, but the association with Chicago is now so remote as to make the label seem rather contrived. Second, although many who follow Blumer's general approach were trained at the University of Chicago, an equal number who are less sympathetic to Blumer's advocacy were also trained there. Moreover, many of these Chicago-trained interactionists are more in tune with the principle figure

---

[1]Bernard N. Meltzer and Jerome W. Petras, "The Chicago and Iowa Schools of Symbolic Interactionism," in *Human Nature and Collective Behavior,* ed. T. Shibutani (Englewood Cliffs, N.J.: Prentice-Hall, 1970).

of the Iowa School, Manford Kuhn. Third, Kuhn's use of quantitative measures of interactionist ideas while at the State University at Iowa were, in fact, pioneered by members of the Chicago department in the 1930s.[2] And fourth, symbolic interactionists are located all over the country and employ such a diversity of approaches that simple labels are much less relevant than they were a few decades ago.[3]

Yet, having said this, I will use the distinction between the Iowa and Chicago Schools in this chapter. For I think that Kuhn's positivistic approach and Blumer's critique of deductive theory do represent differences. Symbolic interactionists still gravitate toward Kuhn's or Blumer's advocacy. And so, if I am to represent the scope and diversity of views within symbolic interactionism, a detailed review of Blumer's and Kuhn's respective approaches is a reasonable place to begin.

## SYMBOLIC INTERACTIONISM: POINTS OF CONVERGENCE

Before turning to the points of divergence between the Iowa and Chicago Schools, let me review the common legacy of Mead's assumptions that all symbolic interactionists employ. These points of convergence are, I believe, what make symbolic interactionism a distinctive theoretical perspective.

### Humans as Symbol Users

Symbolic interactionists, as their name implies, place enormous emphasis on the capacity of humans to create and use symbols. In contrast to other animals, whose symbolic capacities are limited or nonexistent, the very essence of humans and the world that they create flows from their ability

---

[2]Jonathan H. Turner, "The Rise of Scientific Sociology," *Science* 227 (March 15, 1985); see also, Martin Bulmer, *The Chicago School of Sociology* (Chicago: University of Chicago Press, 1984) and Lester R. Kurtz, *Evaluating Chicago Sociology* (Chicago: University of Chicago Press, 1984).

[3]For examples, consult Jerome G. Manis and Bernard N. Meltzer, eds., *Symbolic Interaction: A Reader in Social Psychology* (Boston: Allyn & Bacon, 1972); J. Cardwell, *Social Psychology: A Symbolic Interactionist Approach* (Philadelphia: F. A. Davis Co., 1971); Alfred Lindesmith and Anselm Strauss, *Social Psychology* (New York: Holt, Rinehart & Winston, 1968); Arnold Rose, ed., *Human Behavior and Social Process* (Boston: Houghton Mifflin, 1962); Tamotsu Shibutani, *Society and Personality* (Englewood Cliffs, N.J.: Prentice-Hall, 1961); C. K. Warriner, *The Emergence of Society* (Homewood, Ill.: Dorsey Press, 1970); Gregory Stone and H. Farberman, eds., *Symbolic Interaction: A Reader in Social Psychology* (Waltham, Mass.: Xerox Learning Systems, 1970); John P. Hewitt, *Self and Society: A Symbolic Interactionist Social Psychology* (Boston: Allyn & Bacon, 1976); Robert H. Lauer and Warren H. Handel, *Social Psychology: The Theory and Application of Symbolic Interactionism* (Boston: Houghton Mifflin, 1977); Sheldon Stryker, *Symbolic Interactionism* (Menlo Park, Calif.: Benjamin-Cummings, 1980); Clark McPhail, "The Problems and Prospects of Behavioral Perspectives," *The American Sociologist* 16 (1981), pp. 172–74.

to symbolically represent each other, objects, ideas, and virtually any phase of their experience. Without the capacity to create symbols and to use them in human affairs, patterns of social organization among humans could not be created, maintained, or changed. Humans have become, to a very great degree, liberated from instinctual and biological programming and thus must rely on their symbol-using powers to adapt and survive in the world.

## Symbolic Communication

Humans use symbols to communicate with each other. By virtue of their capacity to agree upon the meaning of vocal and bodily gestures, humans can effectively communicate. Symbolic communication is, of course, extremely complex, since people use more than word or language symbols in communication. They also use facial gestures, voice tones, body countenance, and other symbolic gestures in which there is common meaning and understanding.

## Interaction and Role-Taking

By reading and interpreting the gestures of others, humans communicate and interact. They become able to mutually read each other, to anticipate each other's responses, and to adjust to each other. Mead termed this basic capacity "taking the role of the other," or role-taking—the ability to see the other's attitudes and dispositions to act. Interactionists still emphasize the process of role-taking as the basic mechanism by which interaction occurs. For example, the late Arnold Rose, who was one of the leaders of contemporary interactionism, indicated that role-taking "means that the individual communicator imagines—evokes within himself—how the recipient understands that communication."[4] Or, as another modern interactionist, Sheldon Stryker, emphasizes, role-taking is "anticipating the responses of others with one in some social act."[5] And as Alfred Lindesmith and Anselm Strauss emphasize, role-taking is "imaginatively assuming the position or point of view of another person."[6]

Without the ability to read gestures and to use these gestures as a basis for putting oneself in the position of others, interaction could not occur. And without interaction, patterns of social organization could not exist.

---

[4]Rose, *Human Behavior*, p. 8.

[5]Sheldon Stryker, "Symbolic Interaction as an Approach to Family Research," *Marriage and Family Living* 2 (May 1959), pp. 111–19. See also his "Role-Taking Accuracy and Adjustment," *Sociometry* 20 (December 1957), pp. 286–96.

[6]Lindesmith and Strauss, *Social Psychology*, p. 282.

## Interaction, Humans, and Society

Just as Mead emphasized that mind, self, and society are intimately connected to each other, so contemporary interactionists analyze the relation between the genesis of "humanness" and patterns of interaction. What makes humans unique as species and what enables each individual to possess distinctive characteristics is the result of interaction in society. Conversely, what makes society possible is the capacities that humans acquire as they grow and mature in society.

I find that current symbolic interactionists tend to emphasize the same human capacities as Mead: the genesis of mind and self. Mind is the capacity to think: to symbolically denote, weigh, assess, anticipate, map, and construct courses of action. Although Mead's term, *mind,* is rarely used today, the processes that this term denotes are given great emphasis. As Rose indicates:

> Thinking is the process by which possible symbolic solutions and other future courses of action are examined, assessed for their relative advantages and disadvantages in terms of the values of the individual, and one of them chosen for action.[7]

Moreover, the concept of mind has been reformulated to embrace what W. I. Thomas termed *the definition of the situation.*[8] With the capacities of mind, actors can name, categorize, and orient themselves to constellations of objects—including themselves as objects—in all situations. In this way, they can assess, weigh, and sort out appropriate lines of conduct.[9]

As the concept of the definition of the situation underscores, self is still a key concept in the interactionist literature. Present emphasis in the interactionist orientation is on (a) the emergence of self-conceptions—relatively stable and enduring conceptions that people have about themselves—and (b) the ability to derive self-images—pictures of oneself as an object in social situations. Self is thus a major object that people inject into their definitions of situations. It shapes much of what they see, feel, and do in the world around them.

Society, or relatively stable patterns of interaction, is seen by interactionists as possible only by virtue of people's capacities to define situations and, most particularly, to view themselves as objects in situations. Society can exist by virtue of human capacities for thinking and defining as well as for self-reflection and evaluation.

---

[7]Rose, *Human Behavior,* p. 12.

[8]W. I. Thomas, "The Definition of the Situation," in *Symbolic Interaction,* ed. J. Manis and B. Meltzer, pp. 331–36.

[9]For clear statements on the concept of "definition of the situation" as it is currently used in interactionist theory, see Lindesmith and Strauss, *Social Psychology,* pp. 280–83.

In sum, these points of emphasis constitute the core of the interactionist approach. Humans create and use symbols. They communicate with symbols. They interact through role-taking, which involves the reading of symbols emitted by others. What makes them unique as a species—the existence of mind and self—arises out of interaction. Conversely, the emergence of these capacities allows for the interactions that form the basis of society.

## AREAS OF DISAGREEMENT AND CONTROVERSY

From this initial starting point, Blumer and Kuhn often diverge, as do more recent advocates of their respective positions.[10] I see the major areas of disagreement as revolving around the following issues: (1) What is the nature of the individual? (2) What is the nature of interaction? (3) What is the nature of social organization? (4) What is the most appropriate method for studying humans and society? And (5) what is the best form of sociological theorizing? Let me now examine each of these five controversial questions in more detail.

### The Nature of the Individual

Both Blumer and Kuhn have emphasized the ability of humans to use symbols and to develop capacities for thinking, defining, and self-reflection. However, there is considerable disagreement over the degree of structure and stability in human personality. Blumer emphasized that humans have the capacity to view themselves as objects and to insert any object into an interaction situation. Therefore, human actors are not pushed and pulled around by social and psychological forces but are *active creators* of the world to which they respond. Interaction and emergent patterns of social organization can only be understood by focusing on these capacities of individuals to create symbolically the world of objects to which they respond. For there is always the potential for spontaneity and

---

[10]The following comparison draws heavily from Meltzer's and Petras's "The Chicago and Iowa Schools" but extends their analysis by drawing from the following works of Blumer and Kuhn. For Blumer, *Symbolic Interactionism: Perspective and Method* (Englewood Cliffs, N.J.: Prentice-Hall, 1969); "Comment on 'Parsons as a Symbolic Interactionist,'" *Sociological Inquiry* 45 (Winter 1975), pp. 59–62. For Kuhn, "Major Trends in Symbolic Interaction Theory in the Past Twenty-Five Years," *Sociological Quarterly* 5 (Winter 1964), pp. 61–84; "The Reference Group Reconsidered," *Sociological Quarterly* 5 (Winter 1964), pp. 6–21; "Factors in Personality: Socio-Cultural Determinants as Seen through the Amish," in *Aspects of Culture and Personality*, ed. F. L. Kittsu (New York: Abelard-Schuman, 1954); "Self-attitudes by Age, Sex, and Professional Training," in *Symbolic Interaction*, ed. G. Stone and H. Farberman, pp. 424–36; T. S. McPartland, "An Empirical Investigation of Self-Attitude," *American Sociological Review* 19 (February 1954), pp. 68–76; "Family Impact on Personality," in *Problems in Social Psychology*, ed. J. E. Hulett and R. Stagner (Urbana, Ill.: University of Illinois, 1953); C. Addison Hickman, *Individuals, Groups, and Economic Behavior* (New York: Dryden Press, 1956).

indeterminacy in human behavior. If humans can invoke any object into a situation, they can radically alter their definitions of that situation, and hence, their behaviors. Self is but one of many objects to be seen in a situation; other objects from the past, present, or anticipated future can also be evoked and provide a basis for action.

In contrast, Kuhn emphasized the importance of people's "core self" as an object. Through socialization, humans acquire a relatively stable set of meanings and attitudes toward themselves. The core self will shape and constrain the way people will define situations by circumscribing the cues that will be seen and the objects that will be injected into social situations. Human personality is thus structured and comparatively stable, giving people's actions a continuity and predictability. And if it is possible to know the expectations of those groups that have shaped a person's core self and that provide a basis for its validation, then human behavior could, in principle, be highly predictable.[11] As Kuhn and Hickman noted:

> As self theory views the individual, he derives his plans of action from the roles he plays and the statuses he occupies in the groups with which he feels identified—his reference groups. His attitudes toward himself as an object are the best indexes to these plans of action, and hence to the action itself, in that they are the anchoring points from which self-evaluations and other-evaluations are made.[12]

## The Nature of Interaction

Both Blumer and Kuhn have stressed the process of role-taking in which humans mutually emit and interpret each other's gestures. From the information gained through this interpretation of gestures, actors are able to rehearse covertly various lines of activity and then emit those behaviors that can allow cooperative and organized activity. As might be expected, however, Blumer and Kuhn disagree over the degree to which interactions are actively constructed. Blumer's scheme, and that of most of the Chicago School, emphasizes the following points:

1. In addition to viewing each other as objects in an interaction situation, actors select and designate symbolically additional objects in any interaction. (a) One of the most important of these objects is the self. On the one hand, self can represent the transitory images that an actor derives from interpreting the gestures of others; on the

---

[11]For an interesting methodological critique of Kuhn's self-theory, see Charles W. Tucker, "Some Methodological Problems of Kuhn's Self Theory," *Sociological Quarterly* 7 (Winter 1966), pp. 345–58.

[12]Hickman and Kuhn, *Individuals, Groups, and Economic Behavior*, pp. 224–25.

other, self can denote the more enduring conceptions of one as an object that an actor brings to and interjects into the interaction. (*b*) Another important class of objects are the varying types of expectation structures—for example, norms and values—that may exist to guide interaction. (*c*) Finally, because of the human organism's capacity to manipulate symbols, almost any other object—whether another person, a set of standards, or a dimension of self—may be inserted into the interaction.

2. It is because of the objects in interaction situations that actors have various dispositions to act. Thus, in order to understand the potentials for action among groups of individuals, it is necessary to understand the world of objects that they have symbolically designated.

3. In terms of the particular cluster of objects and of the dispositions to act that they imply, each actor arrives at a definition of the situation. Such a definition serves as a general frame of reference within which the consequences of specific lines of conduct are assessed. This process is termed *mapping.*

4. The selection of a particular line of behavior involves complex symbolic processes. At a minimum, actors typically evaluate: (*a*) the demands of others immediately present; (*b*) the self-images they derive from role-taking, not only with others in the situation but also with those not actually present; (*c*) the normative expectations they perceive to exist in the situation; and (*d*) the dispositions to act toward any additional objects they may inject symbolically into the interaction.

5. Once behavior is emitted, redefinition of the situation and perhaps remapping of action may occur as the reactions of others are interpreted and as new objects are injected into, and old ones discarded from, the interaction.

Thus, by emphasizing the interpreting, evaluating, defining, and mapping processes, Blumer stressed the creative, constructed, and changeable nature of interaction. Rather than constituting the mere vehicle through which preexisting psychological, social, and cultural structures inexorably shape behavior, the symbolic nature of interaction assures that social, cultural, and psychological structures will be altered and changed through shifting the definitions and behaviors of humans.

In contrast to Blumer's scheme, Kuhn stressed the power of the core self and the group context to constrain interaction. Much interaction is released rather than constructed, as interacting individuals follow the dictates of the self-attitudes and the expectations of their respective roles. Although Kuhn would certainly not have denied the potential for constructing and reconstructing interactions, he tended to view individuals as highly constrained in their behaviors by virtue of their core self and the requirements of their mutual situation.

## The Nature of Social Organization

Symbolic interactionism tends to concentrate on the interactive *processes* by which humans form social relationships rather than the *end products* of interactions. Moreover, both Blumer and Kuhn, as well as other interactionists, have tended to emphasize the microprocesses among individuals within small group contexts. Blumer has consistently advocated a view of social organization as temporary and constantly changing, whereas Kuhn typically focused on the more structured aspects of social situations. Additionally, Blumer argued for a view of social structure as merely one of many objects that actors employ in their definition of a situation.

As Blumer has emphasized:

1. Since behavior is a reflection of the interpretive, evaluational, definitional, and mapping processes of individuals in various interaction contexts, social organization represents an active fitting together of action by those in interaction. Social organization must therefore be viewed as more of a process than a structure.

2. Social structure is an emergent phenomenon that is not reducible to the constituent actions of individuals, but it is difficult to understand patterns of social organization without recognizing that they represent an interlacing of the separate behaviors among individuals.

3. Although much interaction is repetitive and structured by clear-cut expectations and common definitions of the situation, its symbolic nature reveals the potential for new objects to be inserted or old ones altered and abandoned in a situation. The result is that reinterpretation, reevaluation, redefinition, and remapping of behaviors can always occur. Social structure must therefore be viewed as rife with potential for alteration and change.

4. Thus, patterns of social organization represent emergent phenomena that can serve as objects that define situations for actors. However, the very symbolic processes that give rise and sustain these patterns can also operate to change and alter them.

In contrast to this emphasis, Kuhn usually sought to isolate the more structured features of situations. In conformity with what I term *structural role theory* in the next chapter, Kuhn saw social situations as constituting relatively stable networks of positions with attendant expectations or norms. Interactions often create such networks, but once created, people conform to the expectations of those positions in which they have anchored their self-attitudes.

By reviewing different assumptions of Blumer and Kuhn over the nature of individuals, interaction, and social organization, it is clear that Chicago School interactionists view individuals as potentially spontaneous, interaction as constantly in the process of change, and social or-

ganization as fluid and tenuous.[13] Iowa School interactionists are more
prone to see individual personality and social organization as structured,
with interactions being constrained by these structures.[14] These differences in assumptions have resulted in, or perhaps have been a reflection
of, varying conceptions of how to investigate the social world and how
to build theory.

## The Nature of Methods

E. L. Quarantelli and Joseph Cooper have observed that Mead's ideas
provide for contemporary interactionists a "frame of reference within
which an observer can look at behavior rather than a specific set of hypotheses to be tested."[15] There can be little doubt that this statement is
true. Yet there is much literature attempting to test some of the implications of Mead's ideas, especially those about self, with standard research
protocols. This diversity in methodological approaches is underscored by
the contrasting methodologies of Blumer and Kuhn. Indeed, the many
students and students-of-students of these two figures tend to use Mead's
ideas as either a sensitizing framework or as an inspiration for narrow
research hypotheses.

Methodological approaches to studying the social world follow from
thinkers' assumptions about what they can, or will, discover. The divergence of Blumer's and Kuhn's methodologies thus reflects their varying
assumptions about the operation of symbolic processes. Ultimately, I think
that their differences boil down to the question of causality. Whether or
not events are viewed as the result of deterministic causes will influence
the methodologies that are employed. Thus, to appreciate why Blumer
and Kuhn diverge in their methodological approaches, it is necessary to
see how their assumptions about individual interaction and social organization have become translated into a set of causal images that dictates
different methodological approaches.

**Diverging assumptions about causality.** For Blumer, the Meadian legacy challenges the utility of theoretical perspectives that

---

[13]Prominent thinkers leaning toward Blumer's position include Anselm Strauss, Alfred
Lindesmith, Tamotsu Shibutani, and Ralph Turner. For a critique of Blumer's use of Mead,
see Clark McPhail and Cynthia Rexroat, "Mead vs. Blumer," *American Sociological Review*
44 (1979), pp. 449–67.

[14]Prominent Iowa School interactionists include Frank Miyamoto, Sanford Dornbusch,
Simon Dinitz, Harry Dick, Sheldon Stryker, and Theodore Sarbin. For a list of studies by
Kuhn's students, see Harold A. Mulford and Winfield W. Salisbury II, "Self-Conceptions
in a General Population," *Sociological Quarterly* 5 (Winter 1964), pp. 35–46. Again, these
individuals and those in note 12 would resist this classification, since none advocate as
extreme a position as Kuhn or Blumer. Yet, the tendency to follow either Kuhn's or Blumer's
assumptions is evident in their work and in that of many others.

[15]E. L. Quarantelli and Joseph Cooper, "Self-conceptions and Others: A Further Test of
Meadian Hypotheses," *Sociological Quarterly* 7 (Summer 1966), pp. 281–97.

underemphasize the internal symbolic processes of actors attempting to fit together their respective behaviors into an organized pattern.[16] Rather than being the result of system forces, societal needs, and structural mechanisms, social organization is the result of the mutual interpretations, evaluations, definitions, and mappings of individual actors. Thus, the symbolic processes of individuals cannot be viewed as a neutral medium through which social forces operate, but instead these processes must be viewed as shaping the ways social patterns are formed, sustained, and changed.

Similarly, as I emphasized earlier, Blumer's approach challenges theoretical perspectives that view behavior as the mere releasing of propensities built into a structured personality. Just as patterns of social organization must be conceptualized as in a continual state of potential flux through the processes of interpretation, evaluation, definition, and mapping, so the human personality must also be viewed as a constantly unfolding process rather than a rigid structure from which behavior is mechanically released. By virtue of the fact that humans can make varying and changing symbolic indications to themselves, they are capable of altering and shifting behavior. Behavior is not so much released as it is constructed by actors making successive indications to themselves.

For Blumer, social structures and normative expectations are objects that must be interpreted and then used to define a situation and to map out the prospective behaviors that ultimately create and sustain social structures. From this perspective, overt behavior at one point generates self-images that serve as objects for individuals to symbolically map subsequent actions at another point in time. At the same time, existing personality traits, such as self-conceptions, self-esteem, and internalized needs, mediate each successive phase of interpretation of gestures, evaluation of self-images, definition of the situation, and mapping of diverse behaviors.

In such a scheme, causality is difficult to discern. Social structures do not cause behavior since they are only one class of objects inserted into an actor's seemingly unpredictable symbolic thinking. Similarly, self is only another object inserted into the definitional process. Action is thus created out of the potentially large number of objects that actors can insert into situations. In this vision of the social world, then, behavior does not reveal clear causes. Indeed, the variables influencing an individual's definition of the situation and action are of the actor's own choosing and apparently not subject to clear causal analysis.

[16]See particularly Blumer's "Society as Symbolic Interaction," in *Human Behavior and Social Process*, ed. A. Rose, pp. 179–92 (reprinted in Blumer's *Symbolic Interactionism*); "Sociological Implications of the Thought of George Herbert Mead," in *Symbolic Interactionism*; and "The Methodological Position of Symbolic Interactionism," in *Symbolic Interactionism*.

In contrast to this seemingly *in*deterministic view of causality, Kuhn argued that the social world is deterministic. The apparent spontaneity and indeterminacy of human behavior are simply the result of insufficient knowledge about the variables influencing people's definitions and actions. For if the social experiences of individuals can be discerned, it is possible to know what caused the emergence of their core self. With knowledge of the core self, of the expectations that have become internalized as a result of people's experiences, and of the particular expectations of a given situation, it is possible to understand and predict people's definitions of situations and their conduct. Naturally, this level of knowledge is impossible with current methodological techniques, but insight into deterministic causes of behavior and emergent patterns of social organization is possible *in principle*. For Kuhn, then, methodological strategies should therefore be directed at seeking the causes of behaviors.

**Diverging methodological protocols.** These differing assumptions about causality have shaped divergent methodological approaches within symbolic interactionism. The extremes of these diverging approaches are, I feel, best illustrated by Blumer's and Kuhn's respective approaches.

Blumer has mounted a consistent and persistent line of attack on sociological theory and research.[17] His criticism questions the utility of current research procedures for unearthing the symbolic processes from which social structures and personality are built and sustained. Rather than letting the nature of the empirical world dictate the kinds of research strategies used in its study, Blumer and others have argued that present practices allow research strategies to determine what is to be studied:

> Instead of going to the empirical social world in the first and last instances, resort is made instead to a priori theoretical schemes, to sets of unverified concepts, and to canonized protocols of research procedure. These come to be the governing agents in dealing with the empirical social world, forcing research to serve their character and bending the empirical world to their premises.[18]

For Blumer, then, the fads of research protocol blind investigators and theorists to the real character of the social world. Such research and theoretical protocols force analysis away from the direct examination of the empirical world in favor of preconceived notions of what is true and how these truths should be studied. In contrast, the processes of symbolic interaction dictate that research methodologies should respect the character

---

[17]See, in particular, Blumer's "Methodological Position."
[18]Ibid., p. 33.

of empirical reality and adopt methodological procedures that encourage its direct and unbiased examination.[19]

To achieve this end, the research act itself must be viewed as a process of symbolic interaction in which researchers take the role of those individuals whom they are studying. To do such role-taking effectively, researchers must study interaction with a set of concepts that, rather than prematurely structuring the social world for investigators, sensitize them to interactive processes. This approach would enable investigators to maintain the distinction between the concepts of science and those of the interacting individuals under study. In this way, the interpretive and definitional processes of actors adjusting to one another in concrete situations can guide the refinement and eventual incorporation of scientific concepts into theoretical statements on the interactive processes that make up society.

Blumer has advocated a twofold process of research, which first involves "exploration" in which researchers prepare to observe concrete situations and then revise their observations as new impressions of the situation arise. Second, exploration must be followed by a process of "inspection," whereby researchers use their observations to dictate how scientific concepts are to be refined and incorporated into more abstract and generic statements of relationships among concepts. In this dual research process, investigators must understand each actor's definition of the situation, the relationship of this definition to the objects actors perceive in the situation, and the relationship of objects to specific others, groups, and expectations in both the actor's immediate and remote social worlds.[20] In this way, the research used to build the abstract concepts and propositions of sociological theory is connected to the empirical world of actors interpreting, evaluating, defining, and mapping the behaviors that sustain patterns of social organization.

A major area of controversy over Blumer's methodological position concerns the issue of operationalization of concepts. How is it possible to operationalize concepts, such as self and definition of the situation, so that different investigators at different times and in different contexts can study the same phenomena? I see Blumer as defining away the question of how the interpretative, evaluational, definitional, and mapping processes are to be studied in terms of clear-cut operational definitions.

---

[19]For an interesting discussion of the contrasts between these research strategies, see Llewellyn Gross, "Theory Construction in Sociology: A Methodological Inquiry," in *Symposium on Sociological Theory,* ed. L. Gross (New York: Harper & Row, 1959), pp. 531–63.

[20]For an eloquent and reasoned argument in support of Blumer's position, see Norman K. Denzin, *The Research Act: A Theoretical Introduction to Sociological Methods* (Chicago: Aldine Publishing, 1970), pp. 185–218; and Norman K. Denzin, "Symbolic Interactionism and Ethnomethodology," in *Understanding Everyday Life: Toward a Reconstruction of Sociological Knowledge,* ed. J. D. Douglas (Chicago: Aldine Publishing, 1970), pp. 259–84.

For Blumer, however, such questions "show a profound misunderstanding of both scientific inquiry and symbolic interactionism."[21] The concepts and propositions of symbolic interactionism allow for the direct examination of the empirical world; therefore, "their value and their validity are to be determined in that examination and not in seeing how they fare when subjected to the alien criteria of an irrelevant methodology." According to Blumer, these "alien criteria" embrace a false set of assumptions about just how concepts should be attached to events in the empirical world. In general, these "false" assumptions posit that for each abstract concept a set of operational definitions should guide researchers, who then examine the empirical cases denoted by the operational definition.

Blumer has consistently emphasized current deficiencies in the attachment of sociological concepts to actual events in the empirical world:

> This ambiguous nature of concepts is the basic deficiency in social theory. It hinders us in coming to close grips with our empirical world, for we are not sure of what to grip. Our uncertainty as to what we are referring obstructs us from asking pertinent questions and setting relevant problems for research.[22]

Blumer argues that it is only through the methodological processes of exploration and inspection that concepts can be attached to the empirical. Rather than seeking a false sense of scientific security through rigid operational definitions, sociological theory must accept the fact that the attachment of abstract concepts to the empirical world must be an *ongoing process* of investigators exploring and inspecting events in the empirical world.

In sum, then, Blumer's presentation of the methodological position of symbolic interactionism questions the current research protocols. As an alternate, he advocates (a) the more frequent use of the exploration-inspection process, whereby researchers seek to understand the symbolic processes that shape interaction; and (b) the recognition that only through ongoing research activities can concepts remain attached to the fluid interaction processes of the empirical world. In turn, this methodological position has profound implications for the construction of theory in sociology, as we will see shortly.

In contrast to Blumer's position, Kuhn's vision of a deterministic world led him to emphasize the commonality of methods in all the sciences. The key task of methodology is to provide operational definitions of concepts so that their implications can be tested against the actual facts of social life. Most of Kuhn's career was thus devoted to taking the suggestive but vague concepts of Mead's framework and developing measures of them. He sought to find replicable measures of such concepts as

---

[21]Blumer, "Methodological Position," p. 49.

[22]Herbert Blumer, "What Is Wrong with Social Theory?" *American Sociological Review* 19 (August 1954), pp. 146–58.

self, social act, social object, and reference group.[23] His most famous measuring instrument—the Twenty Statements Test (TST)—can serve to illustrate his strategy. With the TST, he sought to measure core self—the more enduring and basic attitudes that people have about themselves—by assessing people's answers to the question, "What kind of person are you?"[24] For example, the most common variant of the TST reads as follows:

> In the spaces below, please give 20 different answers to the question, "Who Am I?" Give these as if you were giving them to yourself, not to somebody else. Write fairly rapidly, for the time is limited.

Answers to such questions can be coded and scaled so that variations in people's self-conceptions can be linked to either prior social experiences or behaviors. Thus, Kuhn sought to find empirical indicators of key concepts. These indicators would allow for viewing recorded variations in one concept, such as self, to be linked to variations in other measurable concepts. In this way, Mead's legacy could be tested and used to build a theory of symbolic interactionism.

## The Nature and Possibilities of Sociological Theory

Blumer's and Kuhn's assumptions about the nature of the individual, interaction, social organization, causality, and methodology are reflected in their different visions of what theory is, should, and can be. Again, Blumer and Kuhn stand at opposite poles, with most interactionists standing between these extremes and yet leaning toward one or the other.

**Blumer's theory-building strategy.** Blumer's assumptions, image of causal processes, and methodological position have all come to dictate a particular conception of sociological theory. The recognition that sociological concepts do not come to grips with the empirical world is seen by Blumer as the result not only of inattention to actual events in the empirical world but also of the kind of world it is. The use of more definitive concepts referring to classes of precisely defined events is perhaps desirable in theory building, but it may be impossible, given the nature of the empirical world. Since this world is composed of constantly shifting processes of symbolic interaction among actors in various contextual situations, the use of concepts that rip only some of the actual ongoing events from this context will fail to capture the contextual nature of the social world. More important, the fact that social reality is ultimately "constructed" from the symbolic processes among individuals as-

---

[23]Meltzer and Petras, "The Chicago and Iowa Schools."

[24]For an important critique of this methodology, see Tucker, "Some Methodological Problems."

sures that the actual instances denoted by concepts will shift and vary, thereby defying easy classification through rigid operational definitions.

These facts, Blumer argued, require the use of "sensitizing concepts," which, although lacking the precise specification of attributes and events of definitive concepts, do provide clues and suggestions about where to look for certain classes of phenomena. As such, sensitizing concepts offer a general sense of what is relevant and thereby allow investigators to approach flexibly a shifting empirical world and feel out and pick one's way in an unknown terrain. The use of this kind of concept does not necessarily reflect a lack of rigor in sociological theory but rather a recognition that if "our empirical world presents itself in the form of distinctive and unique happenings or situations and if we seek through the direct study of this world to establish classes of objects and relations between classes, we are . . . forced to work with sensitizing concepts."[25]

The nature of the empirical world may preclude the development of definitive concepts, but sensitizing concepts can be improved and refined by flexibly approaching empirical situations denoted by sensitizing concepts and then by assessing how actual events stack up against the concepts. Although the lack of fixed bench marks and definitions makes this task more difficult for sensitizing concepts than for definitive ones, the progressive refinement of sensitizing concepts is possible through "careful and imaginative study of the stubborn world to which such concepts are addressed."[26] Furthermore, sensitizing concepts formulated in this way can be communicated and used to build sociological theory; and although formal definitions and rigid classifications are not appropriate, sensitizing concepts can be explicitly communicated through descriptions and illustrations of the events to which they pertain.

In sum, the ongoing refinement, formulation, and communication of sensitizing concepts must inevitably be the building block of sociological theory. With careful formulation, they can be incorporated into provisional theoretical statements that specify the conditions under which various types of interaction are likely to occur. In this way, the concepts of theory will recognize the shifting nature of the social world and thereby provide a more accurate set of statements about social organization.

The nature of the social world and the type of theory it dictates have profound implications for just how such theoretical statements are to be constructed and organized into theoretical formats. Blumer's emphasis on the constructed nature of reality and on the types of concepts that this fact necessitates has led him to emphasize inductive theory construction. In inductive theory, generic propositions are abstracted from observations of concrete interaction situations. This emphasis on induction

---

[25]Blumer, "What's Wrong with Social Theory," p. 150.
[26]Ibid.

is considered desirable, since current attempts at deductive theorizing in sociology usually do not involve rigorous derivations of propositions from each other nor a scrupulous search for the negative empirical cases that would refute propositions.[27] These failings, Blumer contends, assure that deductive sociological theory will remain unconnected to the events of the empirical world and, hence, unable to correct for errors in its theoretical statements. Coupled with the tendency for fads of research protocol to dictate research problems and methods used to investigate them, it appears unlikely that deductive theory and the research it inspires can unearth those processes that would confirm or refute its generic statements. In the wake of this theoretical impasse, then, it is crucial that sociological theorizing refamiliarize itself with the actual events of the empirical world. As Blumer argued: "No theorizing, however ingenious, and no observance of scientific protocol, however meticulous, are substitutes for developing familiarity with what is actually going on in the sphere of life under study."[28] Without such inductive familiarity, sociological theory will remain a self-fulfilling set of theoretical prophecies bearing little relationship to the phenomena it is supposed to explain.

**Kuhn's theory-building strategy.** Kuhn advocated a more deductive format for sociological theorizing than Blumer. Although his own work does not reveal great deductive rigor, he held that subsumption of lower-order propositions under more general principles is the most appropriate way to build theory. He visualized his "self-theory" as one step in the building of theory. By developing general statements on how self-attitudes emerge and shape social action, it would be possible to understand and predict human behavior. Moreover, less general propositions about aspects of self could be subsumed under general propositions about processes of symbolic interaction.

While Kuhn recognized that symbolic interaction theory had become partitioned into many suborientations, including his own self-theory, he held a vision of a unified body of theoretical principles. As he concluded in an assessment of interactionist theory:

> I would see in the next 25 years of symbolic interaction theory an accelerated development of research techniques, on the one hand, and a coalescing of most of the separate subtheories.[29]

Thus, the ultimate goal of theory is consolidation or "coalescing" of testable lower-order theories under a general set of symbolic interactionist principles. Self-theory, as developed by Kuhn, would be but one set of derivations from a more general system of interactionist principles. In

[27]Blumer, "Methodological Position."
[28]Ibid., p. 39.
[29]Kuhn, "Major Trends," p. 80.

contrast to Blumer, then, theory for Kuhn was ultimately to form a unified system from which specific propositions about different aspects or phases of symbolic interactionism could be derived.

## The Chicago and Iowa Schools: An Overview

In Table 15-1, I have summarized the points of convergence and divergence of the Chicago and Iowa Schools, or of Blumer and Kuhn. The two right columns explore a number of issues over which there is disagreement among interactionists. But I think it important to place these disagreements within the context of the points where symbolic interactionists agree, as I have done in the left column.

I should caution again that distinctions between a Chicago and Iowa school are hazardous when examining the work of a particular symbolic interactionist. The distinction denotes only *tendencies* to view humans, interaction, social organization, methods, and theory in a particular way. Few symbolic interactionists follow literally either Blumer's or Kuhn's positions. These positions merely represent the boundaries within which symbolic interactionists work.

## SYMBOLIC INTERACTIONISM: A CONCLUDING COMMENT

Blumer's vision of symbolic interactionism advocates a clear-cut strategy for building sociological theory. The emphasis on the interpretive, evaluative, definitional, and mapping processes of actors has come to dictate that it is only through induction from these processes that sociological theory can be built. Further, the ever-shifting nature of these symbolic processes necessitates that the concepts of sociological theory be sensitizing rather than definitive, with the result that deductive theorizing should be replaced by an inductive approach. Thus, whether as a preferred strategy or as a logical necessity, the Blumer interactionist strategy is to induce generic statements, employing sensitizing concepts, from the ongoing symbolic processes of individuals in concrete interaction situations.

Such a strategy is likely to keep theorizing attuned to the processual nature of the social world. However, I feel that this approach and, to a lesser extent, Kuhn's has not been able to link conceptually the processes of symbolic interaction to the formation of different patterns of social organization. Furthermore, the utility of induction from the symbolic exchanges among individuals for the analysis of interaction among more macro, collective social units has yet to be demonstrated. Unless these problems can be resolved, I do not think it wise to follow exclusively the strategy of Blumer and others of his persuasion. Until symbolic interactionists of all persuasions demonstrate in a more compelling manner than is currently the case that the inductive approach utilizing sensitizing

**TABLE 15–1**    Convergence and Divergence in the Chicago and Iowa Schools of Symbolic Interactionism

| *Theoretical Issues* | *Convergence of Schools* |
| --- | --- |
| The nature of humans | Humans create and use symbols to denote aspects of the world around them. |
| | What makes humans unique are their symbolic capacities. |
| | Humans are capable of symbolically denoting and involving objects, which can then serve to shape their definitions of social situations and, hence, their actions. |
| | Humans are capable of self-reflection and evaluation. They see themselves as objects in most social situations. |
| The nature of interaction | Interaction is dependent upon people's capacities to emit and interpret gestures. |
| | Role-taking is the key mechanism of interaction, for it enables actors to view the other's perspective, as well as that of others and groups not physically present. |
| | Role-taking and mind operate together by allowing actors to use the perspectives of others and groups as a basis for their deliberations, or definitions of situations, before acting. In this way, people can adjust their responses to each other and to social situations. |
| The nature of social organization | Social structure is created, maintained, and changed by processes of symbolic interaction. |
| | It is not possible to understand patterns of social organization—even the most elaborate—without knowledge of the symbolic processes among individuals who ultimately make up this pattern. |
| The nature of sociological methods | Sociological methods must focus on the processes by which people define situations and select courses of action. |
| | Methods must focus on individual persons. |
| The nature of sociological theory | Theory must be about processes of interaction and seek to isolate out the conditions under which general types of behaviors and interactions are likely to occur. |

**TABLE 15–1**  (*concluded*)

| Chicago School | Iowa School |
|---|---|
| Humans with minds can introject any object into a situation. | Humans with minds can define situations, but there tends to be consistency in terms of the objects that they introject into situations. |
| Although self is an important object, it is not the only object. | Self is the most important object in the definition of a situation. |
| Humans weigh, assess, and map courses of action before action, but humans can potentially alter their definitions and actions. | Humans weigh, assess, and map courses of action, but they do so through the prism of their core self and the groups in which this self is anchored. |
| Interaction is a constant process of role-taking with others and groups. | Interaction is dependent upon the process of role-taking. |
| Others and groups thus become objects that are involved in people's definitions of situations. | The expectations of others and norms of the situation are important considerations in arriving at definitions of situations. |
| Self is another important object that enters into people's definitions. | People's core self is the most important consideration and constraint on interaction. |
| People's definitions of situations involve weighing and assessing objects and then mapping courses of action. | |
| Interaction involves constantly shifting definitions and changing patterns of action and interaction. | Interaction most often involves actions that conform to situational expectations as mitigated by the requirements of the core self. |
| Social structure is constructed by actors adjusting their responses to each other. | Social structures are composed of networks of positions with attendant expectations or norms. |
| Social structure is one of many objects that actors introject into their definitions of situations. | While symbolic interactions create and change structures, once these structures are created they operate to constrain interaction. |
| Social structure is subject to constant realignments as actors' definitions and behaviors change, forcing new adjustments from others. | Social structures are thus relatively stable, especially when people's core self is invested in particular networks of positions. |
| Sociological methods must seek to penetrate the actors' mental world and see how they construct courses of action. | Sociological methods must seek to measure with reliable instruments actors' symbolic processes. |
| Researchers must be attuned to the multiple, varied, ever-shifting, and often indeterminate influences on definitions of situations and actions. | Research should be directed toward defining and measuring those variables that causally influence behaviors. |
| Research must therefore use observational, biographical, and unstructured interview techniques if it is to penetrate people's definitional processes and take account of changes in these processes. | Research must therefore use structured measuring instruments, such as questionnaires, to get reliable and valid measures of key variables. |
| Only sensitizing concepts are possible in sociology. | Sociology can develop precisely defined concepts with clear empirical measures. |
| Deductive theory is thus not possible in sociology. | Theory can thus be deductive, with a limited number of general propositions subsuming lower-order propositions and empirical generalizations on specific phases of symbolic interaction. |
| At best, theory can offer general and tentative descriptions and interpretations of behaviors and patterns of interaction. | Theory can offer abstract explanations that can allow for predictions of behavior and interaction. |

concepts can account for more complex forms of social organization, pursuit of its strategy will preclude theorizing about much of the social world.

Yet, I feel that both Blumer's and Kuhn's strategies call attention to some important substantive and theoretical issues that are often ignored in social theory. First, it is necessary that sociological theorizing be more willing to undertake the difficult task of linking conceptually structural categories to classes of social processes that underlie these categories. For this task, symbolic interactionism has provided a wealth of suggestive concepts. Second, macrosociological theorizing has traditionally remained detached from the processes of the social world it attempts to describe. Much of the detachment stems from a failure to define concepts clearly and provide operational clues about what processes in the empirical world they denote. To the extent that symbolic interactionist concepts can supplement such theorizing, they will potentially provide a bridge to actual empirical processes and thereby help attach sociological theory to the events it purports to explain.

Symbolic interactionism has great potential for correcting the past inadequacies of sociological theory, but it has yet to demonstrate exactly *how* this corrective influence is to be exerted. At present, symbolic interactionism seems capable of analyzing micro social patterns (and their impact on personality,) particularly the self. Although interactionism has provided important insights in the study of socialization, deviance, and micro social processes, it has yet to demonstrate any great potential for analyzing complex, macro social patterns. At best, it can provide in its present form a supplement to macroanalysis by giving researchers a framework and measuring instruments to analyze microprocesses within macro social events.

I find that much of symbolic interaction, especially Blumer's advocacy, consists of gallant assertions that "society is symbolic interaction" but without indicating what types of emergent structures are created, sustained, and changed by what types of interaction in what types of contexts. Much like the critics' allegations about Parsons's social system, Dahrendorf's imperatively coordinated association, Homans's institutional piles, or Blau's organized collectivities, social structural phenomena emerge somewhat mysteriously and are then sustained or changed by vague references to interactive processes. The vagueness of the links between the interaction process and its social structural products leaves symbolic interactionism with a legacy of assertions but little in the way of carefully documented statements about how, when, where, and with what probability interaction processes operate to create, sustain, and change varying patterns of social organization.[30] It is to this goal that interactionist theory must redirect its efforts.

---

[30]Probably the most significant effort to overcome this problem is an unfinished manuscript by Tamotsu Shibutani, *Social Processes: An Introduction to Sociology* (Berkeley, Calif.: University of California Press, 1986).

# CHAPTER 16

## Structural Role Theory

One of the most ambiguous concepts in sociology is "role." For example, is a role simply overt behavior? Is it a conception of appropriate behavior? Is it normatively expected behavior? Is it behavior enacted by virtue of incumbency in a status position? Or is it all of these? The lack of a definitive answer to these questions has led some to advocate that sociology abandon the concept.[1] I think that this solution is far too extreme. Instead, we must try to clarify our conceptualization of roles, and so, in this and the next chapter, I will present the range of approaches in the analysis of roles.

My sense is that there is a structural approach to roles at one extreme and a more processual strategy at the other.[2] This diversity mirrors the range of approaches within interactionism in general. We might view this range as a continuum and use the analogy of a play and a game to illustrate its dimensions.[3] At one pole of this continuum, individuals are seen as players in the theater, while at the other end, players are considered to be participants in a pick-up game. When human action is seen as occurring

---

[1]See, for example, Anthony Giddens, *The Constitution of Society* (Berkeley, Calif.: University of California Press, 1984).

[2]For two recent efforts to play down this distinction, see Warren Handel, "Normative Expectations and the Emergence of Meaning as Solutions to Problems: Convergence of Structural and Interactionist Views," *American Journal of Sociology* 84 (1979), pp. 855–81; and Jerold Heiss, "Social Roles," in *Social Psychology: Sociological Perspectives,* ed. M. Rosenberg, and R. H. Turner (New York: Basic Books, 1981), pp. 94–132.

[3]Bernard Farber, "A Research Model: Family Crisis and Games Strategy," in *Kinship and Family Organization,* ed. B. Farber (New York: John Wiley & Sons, 1966), pp. 430–34. Walter Wallace (*Sociological Theory* [Chicago: Aldine Publishing, 1969], pp. 34–35) has more recently chosen this same analogy to describe symbolic interactionism.

in a theater, interaction is likely to be viewed as highly structured by the script, directors, other actors, and the audience. When conceptualized as a game, interaction is more likely to be seen as less structured and as influenced by the wide range of tactics available to participants.

In this chapter, I will examine the more structural approach to role theory.[4] I will not examine any one scholar's work because, in truth, there is no one theoretical approach. Rather, there is a large number of research-oriented scholars who have contributed collectively to a structural conceptualization of roles. Indeed, one of the major problems of the structural approach is the lack of theoretical synthesis. As a result, my efforts in this chapter will revolve around framing the issues that need to be theoretically synthesized.

## THE CONCEPTUAL THRUST OF STRUCTURAL ROLE THEORY

The thrust of the structural role perspective, as it flowed from a mixture of Park's, Simmel's, Moreno's, Linton's, and Mead's insights, has often been captured by quoting a famous passage from Shakespeare's *As You Like It*:

> All the world's a stage
> and all the men and women merely players:
> They have their exits and their entrances;
> And one man in his time plays many parts (Act II, scene vii).

The analogy is then drawn between the players on the stage and the actors of society.[5] Just as players have a clearly defined part to play, so actors in society occupy clear positions; just as players must follow a written script, so actors in society must follow norms; just as players must obey the orders of a director, so actors in society must conform to the dictates of those with power or those of importance; just as players must react to each other's performance on the stage, so members of society must mutually adjust their responses to one another; just as players respond to the audience, so actors in society take the role of various audiences or "generalized others"; and just as players with varying abilities and capacities bring to each role their unique interpretations, so actors with varying self-conceptions and role-playing skills have their own styles of interaction.

---

[4]For the first early analytical statements, see Jacob Moreno, *Who Shall Survive*, rev. ed. (New York: Beacon House, 1953; original ed., 1934); and Ralph Linton, *The Study of Man* (New York: Appleton-Century-Crofts, 1936).

[5]For an example of this form of analogizing, see Bruce J. Biddle and Edwin Thomas, *Role Theory: Concepts and Research* (New York: John Wiley & Sons, 1966), pp. 3–4. For the best-known dramaturgical model, see Erving Goffman, *The Presentation of Self in Everyday Life* (Garden City, N.Y.: Doubleday Publishing, 1959).

Despite its simplicity, I think that the analogy is appropriate. As we will come to appreciate, the role-theoretic perspective supports the thrust of Shakespeare's passage. At the outset, however, I should caution again that despite its pervasiveness in sociology, role analysis is far from being a well-articulated perspective.

## IMAGES OF SOCIETY AND THE INDIVIDUAL

Shakespeare's passage provides, I feel, the general outline of what role theorists assume about the social world. In the concept of *stage* are assumptions about the nature of social organization; in the concept of *players* are implicit assumptions about the nature of the individual; and in the vision of men and women as "merely players" who have "their exits and their entrances" are a series of assumptions about the relationship of individuals to patterns of social organization.

### The Nature of Social Organization

For structural role theorists, the social world is viewed as a network of variously interrelated *positions*, or statuses, within which individuals enact roles.[6] For each position, as well as for groups and classes of positions, various kinds of expectations about how incumbents are to behave can be discerned. Thus, social organization is ultimately composed of various networks of statuses and expectations.[7]

Statuses are typically analyzed in terms of how they are interrelated to one another to form various types of social units. In terms of variables such as size, degree of differentiation, and complexity of interrelatedness, status networks are classified into forms ranging from various types of groups to larger forms of collective organization. There has been some analysis of their formal properties, but status networks are rarely analyzed independently of the types of expectations attendant upon them. Part of the reason for this close relation between form and content is that the types of expectations that typify particular networks of positions represent one of their defining characteristics. It is usually assumed that the behavior emitted by incumbents is not an exclusive function of the structure

---

[6]For a recent effort to bring together structurally oriented conceptions of role, see Bruce Biddle, *Role Theory: Expectations, Identities, and Behaviors* (New York: Academic Press, 1979).

[7]See, for example, Jacob L. Moreno, "Contributions of Sociometry to Research Methodology in Sociology," *American Sociological Review* 12 (June 1947), pp. 287–92; Jacob L. Moreno, ed., *The Sociometry Reader* (Glencoe, Ill.: Free Press, 1960); Oscar A. Oeser and Frank Harary, "Role Structures: A Description in Terms of Graph Theory," *Human Relations* 15 (May 1962), pp. 89–109; and Darwin Cartwright and Frank Harary, "Structural Balance: A Generalization of Heider's Theory," *Psychological Review* 63 (September 1956), pp. 277–93.

of positions, per se, but also of the kinds of expectations that inhere in these positions.

The range of expectations denoted by role-theoretic concepts is diverse. Pursuing the dramaturgical analogy to a play, I see three general classes of expectations as typifying structural role theory's vision of the world: (a) expectations from the "script"; (b) expectations from other "players"; and (c) expectations from the "audience."

**Expectations from the script.**   Much of social reality can be considered to read like a script in that for many positions there are norms specifying just how an individual ought to behave. The degree to which activity is regulated by norms varies under different conditions; thus, one of the questions to be resolved by role theory concerns the conditions under which norms vary in terms of such variables as scope, power, efficacy, specificity, clarity, and degree of conflict with each other.

**Expectations from other players.**   In addition to the normative structuring of behavior and social relations, role theory also focuses on the demands emitted by the other players in an interaction situation. Such demands, interpreted through role-taking of others' gestures, constitute one of the most important forces shaping human conduct.

**Expectations from the audience.**   A final source of expectations comes from the audiences of individuals occupying statuses. These audiences can be real or imagined, constitute an actual group or a social category, involve membership or simply a desire to be a member. It is necessary only that the expectations imputed by individuals to such variously conceived audiences be used to guide conduct. As such, the audiences comprise a frame of reference, or reference group, that circumscribes the behavior of actors in various statuses.[8]

In sum, then, structural role theory views the social world as organized in terms of expectations from a variety of sources, whether the script, other players, or various audiences. Just which types of expectations are attendant upon a given status, or network of positions, is one of the important empirical questions that follows from this assumption.

---

[8]Mead's concept of the generalized other anticipated this analytical concern with reference groups. For some of the important conceptual distinctions in the theory of reference group behavior, see Robert K. Merton, "Continuities in the Theory of Reference Groups and Social Structure," pp. 225–80; Tamotsu Shibutani, "Reference Groups as Perspectives," *American Journal of Sociology* 60 (May 1955), pp. 562–69; Harold H. Kelley, "Two Functions of Reference Groups," in *Readings in Social Psychology,* ed. G. E. Swanson et al. (New York: Henry Holt, 1958); Ralph H. Turner, "Role-Taking, Role Standpoint, and Reference Group Behavior," *American Journal of Sociology* 61 (January 1956), pp. 316–28; and Herbert Hyman and Eleanor Singer, eds., *Readings in Reference Group Behavior* (New York: Free Press, 1968).

Although structural role theory implicitly assumes that virtually the entire social spectrum is structured in terms of statuses and expectations, rarely is this whole spectrum studied. In fact, I find that role analysis usually concentrates on restricted status networks, such as the types of expectations evident in more micro social units like small groups. Such an emphasis can be seen as representing a strategy for analytically coping with the incredible complexity of the entire status network and attendant expectations of a society or of some of its larger units. In this delimitation of inquiry, however, I believe that there is an implicit view of the social order as structured only by certain basic kinds of micro groups and organizations. Larger social phenomena, such as social classes or nation-states and relations among them, are less relevant because there is a presumption that these phenomena can be understood in terms of their constituent groups and organizations.

This emphasis on the microstructures of society is perhaps inevitable in light of the fact that role theory ultimately attempts to account for types of role performances by individuals. Although macro patterns of social organization are viewed as providing much of the "structure" for these performances, society cannot be conceptualized independently of its individual incumbents and their performances.

## The Nature of the Individual

Structural role theorists generally conceptualize the individual in terms of two basic attributes: (a) self-related characteristics and (b) role-playing skills and capacities. The self-related concepts of role theory are diverse, but I see them as concerned with the impact of self-conceptions on people's interpretation of the expectations guiding conduct in a particular status. Role-playing skills denote those capacities of individuals to perceive various types of expectations and then, with varying degrees of competence and with different role-playing styles, to follow a selected set of expectations. These two attributes—self and role-playing skills—are obviously interrelated, since self-conceptions will mediate the perception of expectations and the way roles are enacted, while role-playing skills will determine the kinds of self-images derived from an interaction situation and those involved in the construction of a stable self-conception.

This view of the individual parallels Mead's portrayal of mind and self. For Mead and contemporary role theorists, the capacity to take roles and mediate self-images through a stable self-conception is what distinguishes the human organism. Although this conceptualization of self and role-playing capacities offers the potential for visualizing unique interpretations of expectations and for analyzing spontaneous forms of role-playing, the opposite set of assumptions is more often connoted in structural role theory. That is, emphasis is on the ways that individuals conform to what is expected of them by virtue of occupying a particular status. The degree and form of conformity are usually seen as the result of a variety of internal processes operating on individuals. Depending on the interactive situation, these internal processes are conceptualized in terms of variables such as (1) the degree to which expectations have been internalized as a part of an individual's need structure,[9] (2) the extent to which negative or positive sanctions are perceived by the individual to accompany a particular set of expectations,[10] (3) the degree to which expectations are used as a yardstick for self-evaluation,[11] and (4) the extent to which expectations represent either interpretations of others' actual responses or merely anticipations of their potential responses.[12] Just which combination of these internal processes operates in a particular inter-action situation depends upon the nature of the statuses and attendant expectations. While this complex interactive process has yet to be codified into an inventory of theoretical statements, it remains one of the principal goals of role theory.

From this conceptualization, the individual is assumed to be not so much a creative role entrepreneur who tries to change and alter social structure through varied and unique responses, but rather a pragmatic performer who attempts to cope with and adjust to the variety of expectations inhering in social structure. These implicit assumptions about the nature of the individual are consistent with Mead's concern with the adaptation and adjustment of the human organism to society, but they clearly underemphasize the creative consequences of mind and self for the construction and reconstruction of society. Thus, structural role theory has tended to expand conceptually upon only part of the Meadian legacy. This tendency assures some degree of assumptive one-sidedness, which is understandable in light of the role theorists' concern for sorting out only certain types of dynamic interrelationships between society and the individual.

## The Articulation between the Individual and Society

The point of articulation between society and the individual is denoted by the concept of role and involves individuals who are incumbent in statuses and who employ self and role-playing capacities to adjust to

[9]For example, Talcott Parsons, *The Social System* (New York: Free Press, 1951), pp. 1–94; and William J. Goode, "Norm Commitment and Conformity to Role-Status Obligations," *American Journal of Sociology* 66 (November 1960), pp. 246–58.

[10]For example, B. F. Skinner, *Science and Human Behavior* (New York: Macmillan, 1953), pp. 313–55, 403–19; Biddle and Thomas, *Role Theory*, pp. 27–28; Shaw and Costanzo, *Theories of Social Psychology*, pp. 332–33.

[11]Kelley, "Two Functions of Reference Groups"; Turner, "Role-Taking, Role Standpoint"; and Ralph H. Turner, "Self and Other in Moral Judgement," *American Sociological Review* 19 (June 1954), pp. 254–63.

[12]Turner, "Role-Taking, Role Standpoint."

various types of expectations. Despite agreement over these general features of role, current conceptualizations differ.[13] Depending upon which component of role is emphasized, I see three alternative conceptualizations.[14]

**Prescribed roles.**   When conceptual emphasis is placed upon the expectations on individuals in status positions, then the social world is assumed to be composed of relatively clear-cut prescriptions. The individual's self and role-playing skills are seen as operating to meet such prescriptions, with the result that analytical emphasis is drawn to the degree of conformity to the demands of a particular status.

**Subjective roles.**   Since all expectations are mediated through the prism of self, they are subject to interpretations by individuals in statuses. When conceptual emphasis falls upon the perceptions and interpretations of expectations, the social world is seen as structured in terms of individuals' subjective assessments of the interaction situation. As a consequence, the interpersonal style of individuals who interpret and then adjust to expectations is given primary consideration.

**Enacted roles.**   Ultimately, expectations and the subjective assessment by individuals of these expectations are manifested in behavior. When conceptual priority is given to overt behavior, the social world is viewed as a network of interrelated behaviors. The more stress that is placed upon overt role enactment, the less evident will be analyses of either expectations or individual interpretations of them.

When viewed separately from each other, I think it is clear that these three conceptual notions are inadequate. For overt human behavior obviously involves a subjective assessment of various types of expectations. In fact, a review of the research and theoretical literature on role theory demonstrates that the prescriptive, subjective, or enacted components of roles receive *varying degrees* of emphasis and that theoretical efforts usually deal with the complex causal relationships among these components.

Perhaps more than any conceptual perspective, role theory portrays images of causality rather than an explicit set of causal linkages. Part of

[13]For summaries of the various uses of the concept, see Lionel J. Neiman and James W. Hughes, "The Problem of the Concept of Role—A Re-survey of the Literature," *Social Forces* 60 (December 1981), pp. 141–49; Ragnar Rommetveit, *Social Norms and Roles: Explorations in the Psychology of Enduring Social Pressures* (Minneapolis: University of Minnesota Press, 1955); Biddle and Thomas, *Role Theory*; Marvin E. Shaw and Philip R. Costanzo, *Theories of Social Psychology* (New York: McGraw-Hill, 1970), pp. 334–38; and Morton Deutsch and Robert M. Krauss, *Theories in Social Psychology* (New York: Basic Books), pp. 173–77.

[14]Deutsch and Krauss, *Theories in Social Psychology,* p. 175; Daniel J. Levinson, "Role, Personality, and Social Structure in the Organizational Setting," *Journal of Abnormal and Social Psychology* 58 (March 1959), pp. 170–80.

**FIGURE 16-1**   The Causal Imagery of Role Theory

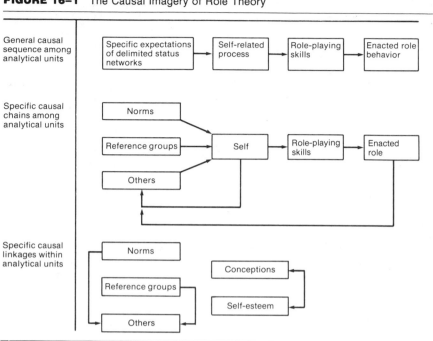

the reason for this vagueness stems from the fact that the label "role theory" embraces a wide number of specific perspectives in a variety of substantive areas. Despite these qualifications, I think that role theorists have tended to develop concepts that denote specific interaction processes without revealing the precise ways these concepts are interrelated. To the extent that I can bring into focus role theory's causal images, they appear to emphasize the deterministic consequences of social structure on interaction. However, rarely are larger, more inclusive units of culture and structure included in this causal analysis. Rather, concern tends to be with the impact of specific norms, others, and reference groups associated with particular clusters of status positions on (a) self-interpretations and evaluations, (b) role-playing capacities, or (c) overt role behavior. While there is considerable variability in the role-theoretic literature, my sense is that self-interpretations and evaluations are usually viewed as having a deterministic impact on role-playing capacities, which then circumscribe overt role behavior. I have depicted these causal images in Figure 16-1.

As I have portrayed in the middle section of Figure 16-1, the specific causal images evident in the literature are more complex than the general portrayal at the top of the figure. Expectations are still viewed as determinative, but role theorists have frequently emphasized the reciprocal nature of causal processes. That is, certain stages in the causal sequence are seen as feeding back and affecting the subsequent causal relations among analytical units, which are portrayed in the middle section of Figure 16–1. Although there are numerous potential interconnections among these units, I find that structural role theory has emphasized only a few of these causal linkages, as is designated by the arrows in the figure. Furthermore, to the extent that specific units of analysis are conceptualized for expectations, self-variables, role-playing skills, and overt behavior, only some of the causal interconnections among these units are explored, as I have indicated at the bottom of Figure 16–1.

With respect to the interrelations among expectations, self, role-playing skills, and overt behavior, I see structural role theory as being primarily concerned with conceptualizing how different types of expectations are mediated by self-interpretations and evaluations and then circumscribed by role-playing skills in a way that a given style of role performance is evident. This style is then typically analyzed in terms of its degree of conformity to expectations.[15] However, at each stage in this sequence, certain feedback processes are also emphasized so that the degree of significance of norms, others, or reference groups for the maintenance of individuals' self-conceptions is considered critical in influencing which expectations are most likely to receive the most attention. For this causal nexus, emphasis is on the degree of imbeddedness of self in certain groups,[16] the degree of intimacy with specific others,[17] and the degree of commitment to, or internalization of, certain norms.[18] Another prominent feedback process that has received considerable attention is the impact of overt behavior at one point in time on the expectations of others as they shape the individual's self-conception and subsequent role behavior at

---

[15]The study of deviance, socialization, and role-playing in complex organizations and small groups has profited from this form of analysis.

[16]For example, see Norman Denzin, "Symbolic Interactionism and Ethnomethodology," in *Understanding Everyday Life: Toward a Reconstruction of Sociological Knowledge,* ed. J. D. Douglas (Chicago: Aldine Publishing, 1970), pp. 259–84. For the most thorough set of such studies in this area, see Sarbin's examinations of the intensity of self-involvement and role-playing behavior: Theodore R. Sarbin, "Role Theory," in *Handbook of Social Psychology,* ed. G. Lindzey, vol. 1 (Reading, Mass.: Addison-Wesley Publishing, 1954), pp. 223–58; Theodore R. Sarbin and Norman L. Farberow, "Contributions to Role-Taking Theory: A Clinical Study of Self and Role," *Journal of Abnormal and Social Psychology* 47 (January 1952), pp. 117–25; and Theodore R. Sarbin and Bernard G. Rosenberg, "Contributions to Role-Taking Theory," *Journal of Social Psychology* 42 (August 1955), pp. 71–81.

[17]See, for example, Tamotsu Shibutani, *Society and Personality* (Englewood Cliffs, N.J.: Prentice-Hall, 1961), pp. 367–403.

[18]John Finley Scott, *Internalization of Norms: A Sociological Theory of Moral Commitment* (Englewood Cliffs, N.J.: Prentice-Hall, 1971), pp. 127–215; William Goode, "Norm Commitment and Conformity"; B. F. Skinner, *Science and Human Behavior.*

another point in time. In this context, the childhood and adult socialization of the individual and the emergence of self have been extensively studied,[19] as has the emergence of deviant behavior.[20]

With respect to interrelations within the analytical units of the overall causal sequence, I think that the arrows at the bottom of Figure 16-1 portray the current theoretical emphasis of the literature. In regard to the interrelations among types of expectations, analytical attention appears to be on how specific others personify group norms or the standards of reference groups. In turn, these significant others are often viewed as deterministically linking the self-interpretations and evaluations of an individual to either the norms of a group or the standards of a reference group.[21] With respect to the relations among the components of self, analysis appears to have followed the lead of William James[22] by focusing on the connections between the self-esteem and the self-conception of an individual.[23] In turn, the interaction between self-esteem and other components of self is viewed as the result of reactions from various others who affect the self-images of the individual. Finally, all these components interact in complex ways to shape the individual's overt behavior.

Thus, looking back at Figure 16-1, it is evident that only some processes have been extensively studied. Relatively little theoretical attention has been drawn, I feel, to the following potential connections indicated in the figure: (a) broader social and cultural structure and specific patterns of interaction, (b) enacted role behaviors and their effect on role-playing capacities, (c) these role-playing capacities and self, and (d) enacted roles and the self-assessments that occur *independently* of role-taking with specific others or groups.[24] Rather, concern has been focused on the re-

---

[19]For example, see Anselm Strauss, *Mirrors and Masks* (Glencoe, Ill.: Free Press, 1959), pp. 100–18; Shibutani, *Society and Personality,* pp. 471–596; Orville G. Brim and Stanton Wheeler, *Socialization after Childhood* (New York: John Wiley & Sons, 1966).

[20]See Edwin Lemert, *Social Pathology* (New York: McGraw-Hill, 1951); Thomas Scheff, "The Role of the Mentally Ill and the Dynamics of Mental Disorder: A Research Framework," *Sociometry* 26 (December 1963), pp. 436–53; Howard Becker, *Outsiders: Studies in the Sociology of Deviance* (New York: Free Press, 1963).

[21]Turner, "Role-Taking, Role Standpoint"; Shibutani, *Society and Personality,* pp. 249–80.

[22]William James, *Principles of Psychology,* 2 vols. (New York: Henry Holt, 1890).

[23]See Shibutani, *Society and Personality,* pp. 433–46.

[24]There is much experimental literature on the impact of various types of "contrived" role-playing on attitudes and other psychological attributes of individuals; as yet, the findings of these studies have not been incorporated into the role-theoretic framework. For some examples of these studies, see Bert T. King and Irving L. Janis, "Comparison of the Effectiveness of Improvised versus Non-Improvised Role-Playing in Producing Opinion Changes," *Human Relations* 9 (May 1956), pp. 177–86; Irving C. Janis and Bert T. King, "The Influence of Role Playing on Opinion Change," *Journal of Abnormal and Social Psychology* 49 (April 1954), pp. 211–18; Paul E. Breer and Edwin A. Locke, *Task Experience as a Source of Attitudes* (Homewood, Ill.: Dorsey Press, 1955); Theodore Sarbin and V. L. Allen, "Role Enactment, Audience Feedback, and Attitude Change," *Sociometry* 27 (June 1964), pp. 183–94.

lations between self and expectations as they affect, and are affected by, enacted roles.

## PROBLEMS AND ISSUES IN BUILDING ROLE THEORY

### Constructing Propositions

To this point, I see role-theoretic concepts as providing only a means for categorizing and classifying expectations, self, role-playing capacities, role enactment, and relationships among these analytical units. The use of concepts is confined primarily to classification of different phenomena, whether attention is drawn to the forms of status networks,[25] types and sources of expectations,[26] relations of self to expectations,[27] or the enactment of roles.[28] In the future, as they begin the difficult task of building interrelated inventories of propositions, structural role theorists, I believe, will confront several theoretical problems.

First, they must fill in the gaps of their causal imagery. To continue emphasizing only some causal links while ignoring others will encourage skewed sets of theoretical statements. Particularly crucial in this context will be the development of propositions that specify the linkages between concepts denoting more inclusive social and cultural variables, on the one hand, and concepts pointing to specific interaction variables, on the other.

Another problem is that the current propositions that do exist in the literature will have to be reformulated so that they specify when certain role processes are likely to occur. For example, in the theory of reference-group behavior, propositions assert that the use of a particular group as a frame of reference is likely to occur when (a) contact with members of a reference group is likely, (b) dissatisfaction with alternative group memberships exists, (c) perception of potential rewards from a group is likely, (d) the perception of that group's standards is possible, and (e) perception of the availability of significant others in the group is possible.[29] Although

---

[25]For example, see Davis, *Human Society*; Merton, *Social Theory and Social Structure*; Benoit, "Status, Status Types"; and Biddle and Thomas, *Role Theory*, pp. 23–41.

[26]Davis, *Human Society*; Richard T. Morris, "A Typology of Norms," *American Sociological Review* 21 (October 1956), pp. 610–13; Alan R. Anderson and Omar K. Moore, "The Formal Analysis of Normative Concepts," *American Sociological Review* 22 (February 1957), pp. 9–16; Williams, *American Society*.

[27]Turner, "Role-Taking, Role Standpoint"; and Sarbin and Allen, "Role Enactment, Audience Feedback."

[28]Goffman, *Presentation of Self*; Sarbin, "Role Theory"; John H. Mann and Carola H. Mann, "The Effect of Role-Playing Experience on Role-Playing Ability," *Sociometry* 22 (March 1959), pp. 69–74; and William J. Goode, "A Theory of Role Strain," *American Sociological Review* 25 (August 1960), pp. 483–96.

[29]Example drawn from summary in Alvin Boskoff, *The Mosaic of Sociological Theory* (New York: Thomas Y. Crowell, 1972), pp. 49–51.

these propositions are suggestive, they offer few clues as to what forms of contact, what levels of dissatisfaction, what types of rewards and costs, which group standards, and what type of significant others serve as conditions for use as a frame of reference by an individual. Furthermore, many relevant variables are not included in these propositions. For instance, in order to improve the theory of reference-group behavior, I think it necessary to incorporate theoretical statements on the intensity of self-involvement, the capacity to assume roles in a group, the nature of group standards, and their compatibility with various facets of an individual's self-conception.

These are the problems that a theoretical perspective attempting to link social-structural and individual personality variables will inevitably encounter. When psychological variables, such as self-concept, self-esteem, and role-playing capacities, are seen as interacting with cultural and structural variables, such as status, norm, reference group, and others, the resulting inventory of theoretical statements will become complex. Such an inventory must not only delve into the internal states of individuals but must also cut across several levels of emergent phenomena—at a minimum, the individual, the immediate interaction situation, and the more inclusive structural and cultural contexts within which the interaction occurs. Yet, despite the difficulties involved, I think that structural role theory is crucial to resolving some of the theoretical gaps in sociology, especially those that concern the micro versus macro debate (see Chapter 1).

## Methodological Implications

The potential utility of role theory derives from its concern with the complex interrelations among the expectations of social structure, the mediation of these expectations through self-conceptions and role-playing capacities of actors in statuses, and the resulting enactment of role behaviors. Measurement of role enactment does not pose a major methodological obstacle, since it is the most observable of the phenomena studied by role theorists. However, to the extent that such overt behavior reflects the impact of expectations and self-related variables, several methodological problems become evident. The complexity of the interrelations between role behavior, on the one hand, and self and expectations, on the other, as well as the difficulty of finding indicators of these interrelations, pose a series of methodological problems that continue to make it difficult to construct bodies of theoretical statements on the relation between society and the individual.

Since one of the assumed links between society and the individual revolves around the expectations that confront individuals, it is theoretically crucial that various types of expectations and the ways they affect individuals be measurable. One method is to infer expectations from observed behavior. The most obvious problem with this approach is that expectations can only be known after the emission of the behavior they are supposed to circumscribe. Therefore, the concept of expectations as inferred from behavior has little theoretical utility, since it cannot be measured independently of behavior. Hence, role behavior cannot be predicted from the content of expectations and their relationship to self. An alternative method involves (a) the accumulation of verbal accounts of individuals prior to a particular interaction sequence,[30] (b) the inference of what types of expectations are guiding conduct, and (c) the prediction of how role behavior will unfold in terms of these expectations. This method has the advantage of making predictions about the impact of expectations, but it suffers from the fact that, much like inferences drawn from role enactment, expectations are not measurable independently of the individual who is to be guided by them.[31] The end result of these methodological dilemmas is for expectations to represent inferences that are difficult to discern independently of the behavior—whether verbal accounts or role enactment—that they are supposed to guide.

A final alternative to this methodological problem is for researchers to become active participants in social settings and from this participation to derive some "intuitive sense" of the kinds of expectations that are operating on actors. From this intuitive sense it is then presumed that more formal conceptual representation of different types of expectations and of their varying impact on selves and behavior can be made. The principal drawback to such an approach is that one researcher's intuitive sense is not another's, and the result may be that the expectation structure observed by different researchers in the same situation is a "negotiated" product as researchers attempt to achieve consensus as to exactly what this structure is to be. However, to the extent that such a negotiated conceptualization has predictive value, it would represent an indicator of the expectation structure that is, in part at least, derived independently of the verbal statements and behavior of those whose conduct it is supposed to guide.

In sum, then, I believe that studying expectations is a difficult enterprise. Since most bodies of sociological theory assume the existence of an expectation structure, it is crucial that these methodological problems be exposed because they have profound implications for theory building. The most important of these implications concerns the possibility of

---

[30]There are many ways to accumulate such accounts, ranging from informal observations and unstructured interviews with subjects to highly structured interviews and questionnaires. All of these have been employed by role theorists, whether in natural settings or the small-group laboratory.

[31]This dilemma anticipates the discussion of ethnomethodology to be undertaken in a later chapter, for, as the ethnomethodologist would argue, these verbal accounts are the "reality" that guides conduct. From this perspective, the assumption of a "really real" world, independent of an actor's mental construction of it, is considered to be unfounded.

building theory with concepts that are not measurable, even in principle. Examining either role behavior or verbal statements and then inferring the existence of expectations tends to make specific propositions tautologous, since variation in behavior is explained by variation in phenomena inferred from such behavior. The use of participant or observational techniques overcomes this problem, but it presents the equally perplexing question of how different researchers are to replicate, and hence potentially refute, each other's findings. If conceptualization of the expectation structure is a negotiated product, the subsequent investigation of similar phenomena by different investigators would require renegotiation. When the nature of phenomena that are incorporated into theoretical statements is not explicitly defined and classified in terms of independently verifiable, clear-cut, and agreed-upon standards but is instead the product of negotiation, then the statements are not refutable, even in principle. As products of negotiation, they have little utility for building a scientific body of knowledge. Ultimately, I imagine that the severity of these problems is a matter of subjective assessment. Some of these problems would appear to be fundamental, whereas others stem from the inadequacies of current research techniques.

Whether problems with conceptualizing expectations are seen as either fundamental or technical, they are compounded by the methodological problems of measuring self-related variables. How is it possible to derive operational indicators of self-conceptions, self-esteem, and intrapsychic assessments of the situation? As the discussion of Blumer and Kuhn in the last chapter stressed, verbal accounts and observational techniques have typically been used to tap these dimensions of interaction. Although they are technically inadequate in that their accuracy can be questioned, verbal and observational accounts do not raise the same fundamental questions as do expectations, since they do seem measurable in principle. The problems arise only when attempts are made to link these self-related variables to expectations that are presumed to have an independent existence that guides the creation and subsequent operation of self-related processes. While the independent existence of norms, others, reference groups, and the like is intuitively pleasing, just how these phenomena are to be conceptualized and measured separately from the self-related processes they are assumed to circumscribe remains a central problem of interactionism in general.

The substantive criticisms of structural role theory revolve around the overly circumscribed vision of human behavior, and presumably of social organization, that it connotes. Although it can be argued that current role theory is too diverse to be vulnerable to this line of criticism, I think that both theory and research in this tradition portray a highly structured view of social reality.

Structural role theory assumes the social world to be organized in terms of status networks and corresponding clusterings of expectations.

While these expectations are viewed as mediated by self- and role-playing capacities (subjective role), the main thrust is on how individuals adjust and adapt to the demands of the "script," other "actors," and the "audiences" of the "play." Undoubtedly, much social action is structured in this way, but my sense is that analysis is loaded in the direction of assuming too much structure and order in the social world.

The conspicuous conceptualization of role conflicts[32] (conflicts among expectations), role strain[33] (the impossibility of meeting all expectations), and anomie[34] (the lack of clear-cut expectations) in role theory would seemingly balance this overly structured conception of reality. Yet frequently, strain, conflict, and anomie are viewed as deviant situations that represent exceptions to the structure of the normal social order. What is critical, then, is that these concepts be elaborated upon and inserted into current theoretical statements. In this way, they can serve to specify the conditions under which the social world is less circumscribed by social structure.

The causal imagery of role theory also contributes to an overly structured vision of social reality. Figure 16–1 emphasizes that the causal thrust of role theory is on the way expectations, as mediated by selves and role-playing capacities, circumscribe role enactment. Although attention is drawn to the feedback consequences of role enactment for expectations, this analysis usually concerns how behaviors of individuals alter the reactions of others in such a way that self-conceptions are reinforced or changed.

The determinative consequences of role enactments for changes and alterations in social structure are, I believe, ignored in this mode of structural analysis. In focusing primarily on how changes of behavior affect self-conceptions, role theory has underemphasized the fact that behavior can also force changes in the organization of status networks, norms, reference groups, the responses of others, and other features of social structure. Until structural role theory stresses the consequences of role enactment, not only for self-related variables but also for the properties of structure, it will continue to conceptualize the social world as excessively ordered.

Some of the logical problems of role-theoretic analysis further contribute to this conception of the social world. The vagueness of just how and under what conditions social structure affects self and role enactment

---

[32]For example, see John W. Getzels and E. C. Guba, "Role, Role Conflict, and Effectiveness," *American Sociological Review* 19 (February 1954), pp. 164–75; Talcott Parsons, *Social System*, pp. 280–93; Merton, *Social Theory and Social Structure*, pp. 369–79; and Robert L. Kahn et al., *Organizational Stress: Studies in Role Conflict and Ambiguity* (New York: John Wiley & Sons, 1974).

[33]Goode, "Theory of Role Strain."

[34]Merton, *Social Theory and Social Structure*, pp. 121–51.

leaves much of role analysis with the empty assertion that society shapes individual conduct. If role-theoretic assumptions are to have theoretical significance, it is essential to specify just when, where, how, and through what processes this circumscription of role behavior occurs. In fact, in the absence of theoretical specificity, I think that a subtle form of functionalism is connoted: the needs of social structure and the individual require that behavior be circumscribed. This functionalism is further sustained by the classificatory nature of role-theoretic concepts. In denoting the types of interrelations among society, self, and behavior without indicating the conditions under which these relationships are likely to exist, these concepts appear to denote what processes must occur without indicating when, where, and how they are to occur.[35]

Finally, the methodological problems of measuring expectations separately from the very processes that they are supposed to circumscribe makes even more mysterious just how and in what ways social structure affects individual conduct. Again, the inability to measure this crucial causal nexus leaves the role theorist with the uninteresting assertion that society shapes and guides individual conduct.

These problems have led others to propose a more processual version of role theory. Yet, it would be foolish, I think, to ignore this more structural orientation. Social structures do exist; they do reveal normative expectations; they do order people's access to reference groups; and they do circumscribe people's options and self-evaluations. It has become very "trendy" in social theory to ignore these facts, especially after the effort to kill off Parsonian functionalism. I think that the more process-oriented theorists had a legitimate criticism but they have often overreacted and posited a social universe in which people are interpersonal entrepreneurs and gadflies. Nonetheless, let us now turn to the more processual approach of Ralph H. Turner, keeping in mind that roles are often enacted in social structures and that theoretical sociology must confront this fact. For although structural role theory has very clear problems, it does attempt to analyze an important dynamic of social reality.

---

[35]Although most structural role theorists would vehemently deny it, they have followed Parsons's strategy for building theory, except on a more micro level. In developing concepts to classify and order role-related phenomena, without also developing clear-cut propositions, they have created a conceptual order without indicating when and how the order denoted by concepts is maintained (or broken down or reconstructed).

# CHAPTER 17

# The Process Role Theory of Ralph H. Turner

Within interactionist theorizing, there is considerable diversity. Most of this diversity, however, revolves around one central question: to what extent do the interactions of individuals represent an enactment of expectations inhering in social structure, or conversely, to what degree are lines of interaction fluid and negotiated anew in each encounter among individuals? Among symbolic interactionists, the Blumer versus Kuhn debate addresses this issue; and among role theorists, this is the central question.[1] In the last chapter, I presented a summary and analysis of more structural versions of role theory; and so, in this chapter, I will concentrate on the more process-oriented role theory of Ralph H. Turner.[2]

## THE CRITIQUE OF STRUCTURAL THEORY

Over the course of several decades, Ralph H. Turner has mounted a consistent line of criticism against role theory.[3] This criticism incorporates several lines of attack: (1) Role theory presents an overly structured vision of the social world, with its emphasis upon norms, status positions, and the enactment of normative expectations. (2) Role theory tends to concentrate an inordinate amount of research and theory-building effort on

---

[1]See Chapter 15.

[2]I am often asked if I am related to Ralph H. Turner. To avoid charges of familial favoritism, let me emphasize that we are not related to each other.

[3]See, for example, Ralph H. Turner, "Role-Taking: Process versus Conformity," in *Human Behavior and Social Processes,* ed. A. Rose (Boston: Houghton Mifflin, 1962), pp. 20–40.

"abnormal" social processes, such as role conflict and role strain, thereby ignoring the normal processes of human interaction. (3) Role theory is not theory but rather a series of disjointed and unconnected propositions. (4) Role theory has not utilized to the degree required Mead's concept of role-taking as its central concept.

It is criticism on the overly structural view of roles that has, I believe, been the main impetus to Turner's alternative approach. Indeed, he has recently emphasized the overly structural bias in role theory, even among those who have tried to reconcile structural and processual accounts of roles.[4] He attacks structural approaches with a series of questions. First, does the structural conception of role add anything that is not covered by the concept of normative expectation? For if roles are merely enactments of expectations, why even introduce the concept of role? Second, can the structural analysis of roles deal with roles that are not lodged in some organizational structure? Most roles, Turner contends, are not attached to a clear structure; and if conceptualization of roles requires that we examine roles with structural positions and expectations, then analysis is dramatically limited. Third, can structural orientations to roles deal with situations where new roles are created or old ones changed by efforts of people to realize certain values or beliefs? For if roles are part of structure, how is it possible to analyze the emergence of new roles, often in defiance of structural dictates?

These questions led Turner to posit a series of unresolved issues in role theory, which, he claims, structural role theory cannot handle. One issue is whether or not roles are acts of conformity to norms or creative constructions of actors. Turner believes that roles involving normative conformity are, in reality, exceptional cases that occur when a repressive structure limits opportunities, when people receive few rewards from their roles, and when people are insecure about their capabilities. But these are relatively rare situations, and so in most social contexts, people negotiate their respective roles.

Another issue is whether or not roles are inventories of specific behaviors or more general gestalts and configurations of meaning about lines of conduct. It is rare, Turner argues, for actors to be able to list precisely the behaviors of a role; more typically, they can communicate only general attitudes, styles, and loosely defined behavioral options associated with a role. Only in rigid and pathological structures are roles so clearly defined as to constitute a list of appropriate behaviors.

---

[4]Ralph H. Turner, "Unanswered Questions in the Convergence between Structuralist and Interactionist Role Theories," in *Perspectives on Sociological Theory,* ed. S. N. Eisenstadt and H. J. Helle (London: Sage Publications, 1985). In particular, he addresses Warren Handel, "Normative Expectations and the Emergence of Meaning as Solutions to Problems: Convergence of Structural and Interactionist Views," *American Journal of Sociology* 84 (1979), pp. 855–81.

Yet another issue is: Are roles fixed and predetermined, or do individuals negotiate which roles they are going to play in a situation? Even in highly structural situations, roles are negotiated. And in most social encounters, individuals must actively make roles for themselves and negotiate with others to their right to play a given role.

What emerges from Turner's questions and presentation of unresolved issues in role theory is a view of roles as general configurations of responses that people negotiate as they form social relations. They are not mere enactments of expectations, and they are not always tied to positions in structures. In light of these considerations, Turner offers a conceptualization of roles that emphasizes the process of interaction over the dictates of social structures.

## INTERACTION AND ROLES

### The Role-Making Process

Turner utilizes and extends Mead's concept of role-taking to describe the nature of social action. Turner assumes that "it is the tendency to shape the phenomenal world into roles which is the key to the role-taking as the core process in interaction."[5] Like Mead and Blumer, Turner stresses the fact that actors emit gestures or cues—words, bodily countenance, voice inflections, dress, facial expressions, and other gestures—as they interact. Actors use these gestures to "put themselves in the other's role" and to adjust their lines of conduct in ways that can facilitate cooperation. This is essentially Mead's definition of taking the role of the other, or role-taking.

Turner then extends Mead's concept. He first argues that cultural definitions of roles are often vague and even contradictory. At best, they provide a general framework within which actors must construct a line of conduct. Thus, actors *make* their roles and communicate to others *what* role they are playing. Turner then argues that humans act *as if* all others in their environment are playing *identifiable roles*.[6] Humans assume others to be playing a role, and this assumption is what gives interaction a common basis. Operating with this folk assumption, people then read gestures and cues in an effort to determine what role others are playing.[7] This effort is facilitated by others creating and asserting their roles, with the result that they actively emit cues as to what roles they are attempting to play.

---

[5]Turner, "Role-Taking: Processes versus Conformity."

[6]Ibid.; "Social Roles: Sociological Aspects," *International Encyclopedia of the Social Sciences* (New York: Macmillan, 1968).

[7]"The Normative Coherence of Folk Concepts," *Research Studies of the State College of Washington* 25 (June 1957).

For Turner, then, role-taking is also "role-making." Humans make roles in three senses: (1) They are often faced with only a loose cultural framework in which they must make a role to play. (2) They assume others are playing a role and thus make an effort to discover the underlying role behind a person's acts. (3) Humans seek to make a role for themselves in all social situations by emitting cues to others that give them claim on a particular role. This role-taking process as it becomes transformed into a role-making process is the underlying basis for all human interaction. It is what ultimately allows people to interact and cooperate with each other.

## The "Folk Norm of Consistency"

As people interact with each other, Turner argues, they assess behavior not in terms of its conformity to imputed norms or positions in a social structure but rather in regard to its consistency. Humans seek to group each other's behavior into coherent wholes or gestalts, and by doing so, they can make sense of each other's actions, anticipate each other's behavior, and adjust to each other's responses. If another's responses are inconsistent and not seen as part of an underlying role, then interaction will prove difficult. Thus, there is an implicit "norm of consistency" in people's interactions with each other. Humans attempt to assess the consistency of others' actions in order to discern the underlying role that is being played.

With the concepts of role-making and the norm of consistency, Turner shifts the analysis of roles toward a position that symbolic interactionists such as Blumer might appreciate. This shift is underscored by a third major assumption with which Turner approaches the analysis of roles: interaction is always a tentative process.

## The Tentative Nature of Interaction

Turner echoes Blumer's position when he states that "interaction is always a tentative process, a process of continuously testing the conception one has of the role of the other."[8] Humans are constantly interpreting additional cues emitted by others and using these new cues to see if they are consistent with those previously emitted and with the imputed roles of others. If they are consistent, then the actor will continue to adjust responses in accordance with the imputed role of the other. But as soon as inconsistent cues are emitted, the identification of the other's role will undergo revision. Thus, a given imputation of a particular role to another person will only persist as long as it provides a stable framework for

---

[8]Turner, "Role-Taking: Processes Versus Conformity," p. 23.

interaction. The tentative nature of the role-making process points to another facet of roles: the process of role verification.

## The Process of Role Verification

Actors seek to verify that behaviors and other cues emitted by people in a situation do indeed constitute a role. Turner argues that such efforts at verification or validation are achieved by the application of external and internal criteria. The most often used internal criterion is the degree to which an actor perceives a role to facilitate interaction. External criteria can vary, but in general, they involve assessment of a role by important others, relevant groups, or commonly agreed-upon standards. When an imputed role is validated or verified in this way, then it can serve as a stable basis for continued interaction among actors.

## Self-Conceptions and Role

All humans reveal self-conceptions of themselves as certain kinds of objects. Humans develop self-attitudes and feelings out of their interactions with others, but as Turner and all role theorists emphasize, actors attempt to present themselves in ways that will reinforce their self-conceptions.[9] Since others will always seek to determine an actor's role, it becomes necessary for an actor to inform others, through cues and gestures, about the degree to which self is anchored in a role. Thus, actors will signal each other about their self identity and the extent to which their role is consistent with their self-conception. For example, roles not consistent with a person's self-conception will likely be played with considerable distance and disdain, whereas those that an individual considers central to self definitions will be played much differently.[10]

Let me now sum up Turner's basic assumptions. An emphasis on the behavioral aspect of role is retained, since it is through behavioral cues that actors impute roles to each other. The notion that roles are conceptions of expected behaviors is also preserved, for the assignment of a role to a person invokes an expectation that a certain type and range of responses will ensue. The view that roles are the norms attendant on status positions is given less emphasis but not ignored, since norms and positions

---

[9]Ralph H. Turner, "The Role and the Person," *American Journal of Sociology* 84 (1978), pp. 1–23.

[10]Turner, "Social Roles: Sociological Aspects." Turner has extensively analyzed this process of self-anchorage in roles. See, for example, Ralph H. Turner, "The Real Self: From Institution to Impulse," *American Journal of Sociology* 81 (1970), pp. 989–1016; Ralph H. Turner and Victoria Billings, "The Social Context of Self-Feeling," working paper; Ralph H. Turner and Steven Gordon, "The Boundaries of the Self: The Relationship of Authenticity to Inauthenticity in the Self-Conception," in *Self-Concept: Advances in Theory and Research,* ed. M. D. Lynch et al. (Cambridge, Mass.: Ballinger Publishing Co., 1981).

can be the basis for assigning and verifying roles.[11] And the conception of roles as parts that people learn to play is preserved, for people are able to denote each other's roles by virtue of their prior socialization into a common role repertoire.

Not only do these assumptions embrace the major points of emphasis in prominent definitions of role, but they also help reconcile the differences between symbolic interactionism and more structural versions of role theory. Turner's assumptions employ the key concepts of Mead's synthesis, while taking cognizance of Blumer's emphasis on the processes that underlie patterns of joint action. These assumptions also point to the normal processes of interaction but are sufficiently general to embrace the possibility of conflictual and stressful interactions. And these assumptions about the role-making process do not preclude the analysis of structured interaction, since formal norms and status positions are often the major cues for ascertaining the roles of people as well as a source of verification for imputed roles.

Assumptions are, however, only as good as the theory that they can generate. I think it particularly significant that Turner delineates an explicit strategy for translating these assumptions into theoretical propositions. My sense is that the execution of this strategy will help interactionism bridge the gap between suggestive assumptions and concepts, on the one hand, and the current plethora of narrow empirical propositions, on the other. Let me now outline the basic elements of this strategy.

## THE STRATEGY FOR BUILDING ROLE THEORY

While Turner accepts the process orientation of Blumer, he is committed to developing interactionism into "something akin to axiomatic theory."[12] He recognizes that, in its present state, role theory is segmented into a series of narrow propositions and hypotheses and that role theorists have been reluctant "to find unifying themes to link various role processes."

Turner's strategy is to use propositions from the large number of research studies to build more formal and abstract theoretical statements. The goal is to maintain a productive dialogue between specific empirical propositions and more abstract theoretical statements.

### The Concepts of Role Theory

Turner argues against rigid definitions of concepts when beginning the theory-building process. It is more useful, he contends, to begin with

---

[11]Ralph H. Turner, "Rule Learning as Role Learning," *International Journal of Critical Sociology* 1 (September 1974).

[12]Ralph H. Turner, "Strategy for Developing an Integrated Role Theory," *Humboldt Journal of Social Relations* 7 (Winter 1980), pp. 123–39 and "Role Theory as Theory," unpublished manuscript.

loosely defined concepts such as "actor," "role," "other," and "situation." The concepts will take on greater clarity as propositions incorporating them are developed. Moreover, early emphasis on concept formation "turns our attention from empirical to definitional concerns, from dynamic to static questions, and many a theory-building enterprise becomes hopelessly diverted into creating an elegant system that neither suggests nor generates new empirical propositions."[13]

Turner adopts Blumer's position that theorists must begin with sensitizing concepts. As I will document shortly, however, he uses these concepts in ways that will allow for the formulation of more precise definitions and propositions.

## Sorting Out Tendencies

Without definitive concepts and with a large body of segmented propositions, an alternative way of linking sensitizing concepts to observe empirical regularities is necessary. Turner advocates the use of what he terms *main tendency* propositions to link concepts to empirical regularities and to consolidate the thrust of these regularities.[14] What Turner seeks is a series of statements that highlight what tends to occur in the normal operation of systems of interaction. These statements are not true propositions because they are not of the form: under $C_1, C_2, C_3, \ldots, C_n$ $x$ varies with $y$. Rather, they are statements of the form: in most normal situations, event $x$ tends to occur. These are not statements of covariance, but statements of what is presumed to typically transpire in the course of interaction.

Turner provides a long list of main tendency propositions with respect to a number of issues: (a) the emergence and character of roles, (b) role as an interactive framework, (c) roles in relation to actors, (d) role in organizational setting, (e) role in societal setting, and (f) role and the person. Let me summarize some of these tendency propositions.

**Emergence and character of roles.**    In these propositions, Turner presents some observations about the nature of the social world as a series of empirical tendencies. I should emphasize, however, that such tendencies are observed through the heavy prism of Turner's assumptions.

1. In any interactive situation, behavior, sentiments, and motives tend to be differentiated into units that can be termed roles; once differentiated, elements of behavior, sentiment, and motives that appear in the same situation tend to be assigned to existing roles. (Tendencies for role differentiation and accretion.)

---

[13]Turner, "Strategy," pp. 123–24.
[14]Turner, "Social Roles: Sociological Aspects."

2. In any interactive situation, the meaning of individual actions for ego (the actor) and for any alter is assigned on the basis of the imputed role. (Tendencies for meaningfulness.)

3. In connection with every role, there is a tendency for certain attributes of actors, aspects of behavior, and features of situations to become salient cues for the identification of roles. (Tendencies for role cues.)

4. The character of a role—that is, its definition—will tend to change if there are persistent changes in either the behaviors of those presumed to be playing the role or the contexts in which the role is played. (Tendencies for behavioral correspondence.)

5. Every role tends to acquire an evaluation in terms of rank and social desirability. (Tendencies for evaluation.)

These propositions both reassert Turner's assumptions about the social world and provide several points of elaboration. People are seen as viewing the world in terms of roles; they are visualized as employing a folk norm to seek consistency of behaviors and to assign behavioral elements to an imputed role (role differentiation and accretion). Actors are viewed as interpreting situations by virtue of imputing roles to each other (meaningfulness tendency). Humans are observed to use cues of other actors' attributes and behaviors, as well as the situation, to identify roles (role cues). When role behaviors or situations are permanently altered, the definition of role will also undergo change (behavioral correspondence). And humans tend to evaluate roles by ranking them in terms of power, prestige, and esteem, while assessing them with regard to their degree of social desirability and worth (tendency for evaluation).

**Role as an interactive framework.**    In these tendency propositions, Turner elaborates his assumption that interaction cannot proceed without the identification and assignment of roles. These propositions specify the ways in which roles provide a means for interaction to occur.

6. The establishment and persistence of interaction tend to depend upon the emergence and identification of ego and alter roles. (Tendency for interaction in terms of roles.)

7. Each role tends to form as a comprehensive way of coping with one or more relevant alter roles. (Tendency for role complementarity.)

8. There is a tendency for stabilized roles to be assigned the character of legitimate expectations and to be seen as the appropriate way to behave in a situation. (Tendency for legitimate expectations.)

In these propositions, interaction is seen as dependent upon the identification of roles. Moreover, roles tend to be complements of others—as is the case with wife-husband, parent-child, boss-employee roles—and thus operate to regularize interaction among complementary roles. Finally, roles that prove useful and that allow for stable and fruitful interaction are translated into expectations that future transactions will and should occur as in the past.

**Role in relation to actor.**  These propositions concern the relationship between actors and the roles that provide the framework for interaction.

9. Once stabilized, the role structure tends to persist, regardless of changes in actors. (Tendency for role persistence.)
10. There is a tendency to identify a given individual with a given role and a complementary tendency for an individual to adopt a given role for the duration of the interaction. (Tendency in role allocation.)
11. To the extent that ego's role is an adaptation to alter's role, it incorporates some conception of alter's role. (Tendency for role-taking.)
12. Role behavior tends to be judged as adequate or inadequate by comparison with a conception of the role in question. (Tendency to assess role adequacy.)
13. The degree of adequacy in role performance of an actor determines the extent to which others will respond and reciprocate an actor's role performance. (Tendency for role reciprocity.)

Thus, once actors identify and assign each other to roles, the roles persist; and new actors will tend to be assigned to those roles that already exist in a situation. Humans also tend to adopt roles for the duration of an interaction, while having knowledge of the roles that others are playing. Additionally, actors carry with them general conceptions of what a role entails and what constitutes adequate performance. Finally, the adequacy of a person's role performance greatly influences the extent to which the role, and the rights, privileges, and complementary behaviors that it deserves, will be acknowledged.

**Role in organizational settings.**  Turner rejects an overly structural view of roles, but he still recognizes that many roles are enacted in structured contexts, necessitating a listing of additional tendencies in the role-making processes.

14. To the extent that roles are incorporated into an organizational setting, organizational goals tend to become crucial criteria for role differentiation, evaluation, complementarity, legitimacy or expectation, consensus, allocation, and judgments of adequacy. (Tendency for organization goal dominance).
15. To the extent that roles are incorporated into an organizational setting, the right to define the legitimate character of roles, to

set the evaluations on roles, to allocate roles, and to judge role adequacy tend to be lodged in particular roles. (Tendency for legitimate role definers.)

16. To the extent that roles are incorporated into an organizational setting, differentiation tends to link roles to statuses in the organization. (Tendency for status.)

17. To the extent that roles are incorporated into an organizational setting, each role tends to develop as a pattern of adaptation to multiple alter roles. (Tendency for role sets.)

18. To the extent that roles are incorporated into an organizational setting, the persistence of roles is intensified through tradition and formalization. (Tendency for formalization.)

When roles are lodged in organizations, then, its goals and key personnel become important in the role-making process. Moreover, it is primarily within organizations that status and role become merged. In this way, Turner incorporates Linton's insight that status and role *can* become highly related, but he does not abandon Mead's and Blumer's emphasis that much interaction occurs in contexts where roles are not circumscribed by networks of clearly defined status positions. Turner also recognizes that roles in structured situations develop as ways of adapting to a number of other roles that are typically assigned by role definers or required by organizational goals. Finally, roles within organizations tend to become formalized in that written agreements and tradition come to have the power to maintain a given role system and to shape normative expectations.

**Role in societal setting.**    Many roles are identified, assumed, and imputed in relation to a broader societal context. And so, in the tendencies listed below, Turner first argues that people tend to group behaviors in different social contexts into as few unifying roles as is possible. Thus, people will identify a role as a way of making sense of disparate behaviors in different contexts. At the societal level, values are the equivalent of goals in organizational settings for identifying, differentiating, allocating, evaluating, and legitimating roles. Finally, all people tend to assume multiple roles in society, but they tend to assume roles that are consistent with each other. Thus:

19. Similar roles in different contexts tend to become merged, so as to be identified as a single role recurring in different relationships. (Tendency for economy or roles.)

20. To the extent that roles refer to more general social contexts and situations, differentiation tends to link roles to social values. (Tendency for value anchorage.)

21. The individual in society tends to be assigned and to assume roles consistent with each other. (Tendency for allocation consistency.)

**Role and the person.** The "person" is a concept employed by Turner to denote "the distinctive repertoire of roles" that an individual enacts in relevant social settings. The concept of person is his means for summarizing the way in which individuals cope with their roles. In the generalizations below, Turner observes that people seek to resolve tensions among roles and to avoid contradictions between self-conceptions and roles. These propositions are, to a very great extent, elaborations of Turner's assumptions about the relationship between self-conceptions and role.

22. Actors tend to act so as to alleviate role strain arising out of role contradiction, role conflict, and role inadequacy and to heighten the gratifications of high role adequacy. (Tendency to resolve role strain.)

23. Individuals in society tend to adopt as a framework for their own behavior and as a perspective for interpretation of the behavior of others a repertoire of role relationships. (Tendency to be socialized into common culture.)

24. Individuals tend to form self-conceptions by selective identification of certain roles from their repertoires as more characteristically "themselves" than other roles. (Tendency to anchor self-conception.)

25. The self-conception tends to stress those roles that supply the basis for effective adaptation to relevant alters. (Adaptation of self-conception tendency.)

26. To the extent that roles must be played in situations that contradict the self conception, those roles will be assigned role distance, and mechanisms for demonstrating lack of personal involvement will be employed. (Tendency for role distance.)

These 26 generalizations represent only the first step in Turner's theoretical strategy. These empirical tendencies incorporate the loosely defined concepts of interactionism, but they link these concepts to actual events presumed to occur in the social world. Naturally, more tendencies might be discerned and recorded. The list of 26 is sufficient, I think, to illustrate what Turner views as the next step in developing a more integrated role theory.

## Generating and Organizing Empirical Propositions

As I have emphasized, the tendency propositions are not true propositions. They do not reveal relations of covariance among variables. However, Turner believes that the tendency propositions can help generate true empirical propositions of the form: $x$ varies with $y$. This is done by attempting to determine the empirical conditions that shape the degree or rate of variation in a tendency proposition. For example, Tendency Proposition 22 becomes the dependent variable in a search for independent variables that can specify the conditions under which actors "tend to act to alleviate role strain." The tendency proposition thus provides an initial set of guidelines for developing true propositions about relationships among variables.

Furthermore, since the tendency propositions are grouped together, as was done in the sections above, the true empirical propositions will be organized around related tendencies. As such, the propositions are less scattered and disparate than would be the case if the search for propositions had not begun with the delineation of certain normal tendencies. Yet, I still find the transition from the tendency propositions to the true empirical propositions rather vague. Nonetheless, Turner's propositions about the person and role can illustrate the potential of his theory-building strategy (the last section in the tendency propositions above).[15]

The person is viewed as the repertoire of roles that he or she plays. And while "people are normally quite different actors in different roles, and even have senses of 'who they are,' " humans also use roles as a means for self-identification and self-validation.[16] Some roles are thus more important to individuals and resist compartmentalization, or separation, from a person's self-concept. Roles that arouse strong self-feelings, which people appear to play across situations, refuse to abandon, and embellish with associated attitudes, are likely to involve considerable merger of the individual's self with the role.

Thus, to generate an empirical proposition from these tendencies, we need to know the conditions under which individuals become identified with roles, using the role for purposes of self-identification and validation. Tendency Propositions 24 and 26 can be dependent variables organizing a search for the conditions under which individuals tend "to form self-conceptions by selective identification of certain roles from their repertoire as more characteristically themselves than other roles" and to show "role distance" and "a lack of personal involvement" in situations that "contradict the self-conception." For all the other tendency propositions listed, a similar search could be initiated in an effort to discover the empirical conditions that influence their rate, degree, and extent of occurrence.[17]

Turner divides his discussion of person and role into two general lines of analysis: (1) how do others in the situation discover a merger of role and person, and (2) how do the individuals come to lodge their selves in

---

[15]Turner, "Role and the Person." See also note 10.

[16]Ibid., p. 2.

[17]In his most recent effort, "Strategy for Developing an Integrated Role Theory," Turner has focused on "role allocation" and "role differentiation" because he views these as the two most critical tendencies. My example of "the person and role" results in the same explanatory principles. Thus, this illustration provides additional examples of Turner's strategy.

**TABLE 17–1**    Others and Role Merger in One Situation

I.   The more inflexible the allocation of actors to a role, the greater the tendency for members of the social circle to identify the role with the person, and the stronger the tendency for the actors to accept that identification for themselves.

II.  The more comprehensively and strictly differentiated the role, the greater the tendency for members of the social circle to identify the role with the person, and the stronger the tendency for actors to accept that identification for themselves.

III. The more conflictual the relationship between roles, the greater the tendency for members of the social circle to identify the role with the person, and the stronger the tendency for the actors to accept that identification for themselves.

IV.  The higher and more consistent the judgments of role adequacy, the greater the tendency for members of the social circle to identify the role with the person, and the stronger the tendency for the actors to accept that identification for themselves.

V.   The more difficult the role is thought to be, the greater the tendency for members of the social circle to identify the role with the person, and the stronger the tendency for actors to accept that identification for themselves.

VI.  The more polar the evaluation of a role as favorable or unfavorable, the greater the tendency for members of the social circle to identify the role with the person, and the stronger the tendency for the actors to accept that identification for themselves.

VII. The more polar the social rank of a role as high or low, the greater the tendency for members of the social circle to identify the role with the person, and the stronger the tendency for the actors to accept that identification for themselves.

VIII. The greater the potential power vested in a role, the greater the tendency for members of the social circle to identify the role with the person, and the stronger the tendency for the actors to accept that identification for themselves.

IX.  The greater the discretion vested in a role, the greater the tendency for members of the social circle to identify the role with the person, and the stronger the tendency for the actors to accept that identification for themselves.

X.   The greater the extent to which members of a social circle are bonded to role incumbents by ties of identification, the greater the tendency for them to identify the role with the person, and the stronger the tendency for the actors to accept that identification for themselves.

XI.  The more intimate the role relationship between an actor's social circle and alter roles, the greater the tendency for them to identify the role with the person, and the stronger the tendency for the actor to accept that identification.

certain roles? Each of these questions organizes the propositions that I have listed, respectively, in Tables 17-1 and 17-2.

In Table 17-1, Turner examines the simplest situation where an actor's interaction with others is confined to one situation. When so confined, others in that situation will identify the role as integral to the person's self-identification; and the person will accept this identification by others under the conditions listed in each of the 11 propositions. For example, if there is little flexibility in assuming a role (Proposition I), then merger of person and role is increased. In Proposition II, the more

**TABLE 17-2**   Others, Person, and Role in Multiple Settings

I. The broader the setting in which a role is lodged, the greater the tendency for others to identify the role with the person, and the stronger the tendency for the actors to accept that identification for themselves.

II. The more a role in one setting determines allocation and performance of roles in other settings, the greater the tendency for others to identify the role with the person, and the stronger the tendency for the actors to accept that identification for themselves.

III. The more conspicuous and widely recognizable the role cues, the greater the tendency for others to identify the role with the person, and the stronger the tendency for the actors to accept that identification for themselves.

IV. The more a role exemplifies the goals and nature of the group or organization in which it is lodged, the greater the tendency for others to identify the role with the person, and the stronger the tendency for the actors to accept that identification for themselves.

V. The more that allocation to a role is understood to be temporary and the role discontinuous in content with respect to preceding and succeeding roles, the greater the tendency for community members not to identify the role with the person, and the stronger the tendency for the actors not to identify role with self.

clearly defined and distinguishable the role, the greater the tendency for person-role merger. In Proposition III, the more that roles among person and others are in conflict, the greater the role-person merger—and so on for the remaining propositions. What is critical in these and other propositions is that they reveal covariance between variables and thus constitute true propositions.

The social settings of actors often overlap. People see each other in different settings, but as they interact, they seek to discover which role is part of a person's self-identification. The five propositions in Table 17-2 are examples of some of the considerations that Turner views as operating in multiple social settings to influence role-person merger. People in multiple settings will be likely to identify the role with the person, and the person will likely accept this identification when the role cuts across many social settings (I), the role influences the other roles that a person can play and/or how they are played (II), the role is highly conspicuous (III), the role exemplifies, or personifies, the nature of the social unit in which it is lodged (IV). Proposition V is an example of a condition under which roles will not merge with the person. When a role is short-lived and inconsistent with other roles played by a person, then the individual will not identify with the role.

The propositions in Tables 17-1 and 17-2 address the question of how others in situations discover a person-role merger. However, people are rarely passive, accepting the labels of others. People actively seek to dictate the merger of their self with a role. This fact is stressed with the concept of role-making, thus requiring still more propositions on self and role merger.

**TABLE 17-3** Individual Efforts at Role Merger

I. The more highly evaluated a role, the greater the tendency to locate self in that role.

II. The more adequately a role can be performed, the greater the tendency to locate self in that role.

III. The higher the evaluation of roles among a repertoire of roles that can be played adequately, the greater the tendency to locate self in the roles of highest evaluation.

IV. The more visible and readily appraisable role performance, the greater the tendency to locate self in highly evaluated roles will be modified by the tendency to locate self in roles that can be played with high degrees of adequacy.

V. The more the scope of an individual's social world exceeds the boundaries of the social circle of a given role, the greater the tendency to use evaluations of the larger community rather than those of a specific social circle to locate self in a role.

VI. The more intrinsic (as opposed to extrinsic) the benefits derived from enacting a role, the greater the tendency to locate self in that role.

VII. The greater the investment of time and effort in gaining or maintaining the opportunity to claim a role or in learning to play a role, the greater the tendency to locate self in that role.

VIII. The greater the sacrifice made in gaining or maintaining the opportunity to claim a role or in learning to play a role, the greater the tendency to locate self in that role.

IX. The more publicly a role is played and the more actors must explain and justify a role, the greater the tendency to locate self in that role.

X. The more unresolved role strain encountered in a role has been prolonged, the greater the tendency to locate self in that role.

Turner expands upon Mead's insight that the emergence of self-conceptions in individuals facilitates interaction and the functioning of society. Self provides individuals with a way to discriminate among roles and to partition them in terms of their importance and significance. If individuals could not do this, they would emotionally exhaust themselves. They could disrupt the flow of society by trying to play all roles equally well and with the same degree of intensity. Additionally, self allows actors to maintain an identity across roles and to resist sanctions that would force them to act in contradictory ways. And, finally, self gives action consistency and coherence across roles, which allows others to anticipate that an actor will behave in a given way, thereby enabling others to adjust their response to the actor.

The propositions in Table 17-3 offer some insight into these processes. People are likely to locate their self in roles that are highly evaluated, that they can perform well, that are both highly evaluated *and* played well (actors will, by implication, avoid roles of high evaluation that they cannot play well), that are visible and more readily subject to evaluation by others, that are comprehensive and cut across social contexts, that provide personal and subjectively defined benefits, that involve the expenditure of time and effort, that involve sacrifice in reaching, that are publicly played and in need of public justification, and that involve prolonged role strain and effort to eliminate strain.

These propositions on the person and role listed in Tables 17–1, 17–2, and 17–3 are only tentative. Similar empirical propositions need to be developed for Turner's other tendency statements. Yet, even clearly articulated empirical propositions represent only crude groupings of statements and tendencies. Such propositions are the result of speculation, and they can, no doubt, suggest additional propositions. But these empirical propositions are not organized *deductively*—that is, in a way that would allow them to be deduced from a small number of abstract propositions or "axioms." The next step in Turner's strategy, therefore, involves an effort to generate explanatory propositions.

## Developing Explanatory Propositions

Turner has applied a number of different labels to what are termed here *explanatory propositions.* Turner's avowed strategy is to ask the questions: Why should a series of empirical propositions cohere around a main tendency? Is there some common principle that would explain why the tendency should occur and why the empirical propositions with the tendency as the dependent variable should hold true?

Once a number of potential explanatory propositions have been discovered, Turner suggests that efforts be made to determine if some have more explanatory power than others and if those with less power can be seen as derivatives of the more powerful propositions. In this way, explanatory propositions are consolidated into a small number of abstract statements from which lower-level explanatory propositions, empirical propositions, and main tendency propositions can be deduced.

Turner has only partially followed his avowed strategy. I think that he narrows too quickly his search for explanatory propositions to just two: (1) a proposition about "functionality" and (2) another about "tenability."[18]

**The functionality proposition.**    Turner discusses this explanatory proposition in the context of the tendency for roles to become differentiated (Tendency Proposition I), to use role cues (Tendency 3), and to be assigned or allocated for the duration of an interaction (Tendency 10). However, he views this proposition as a potential explanation of many more tendencies. He concentrates on these tendencies because he considers them to be the most important.[19]

---

[18]Ibid.

[19]Ibid. He does this also because he feels these are perhaps the most generic dimensions of roles.

What is the functionality proposition? Functionality is "the processes whereby roles are used to achieve ends or goals in an effective and efficient manner." I should note here that these functionality considerations are not stated as true propositions with at least two variables. To me, functionality simply states another tendency proposition: people often use roles as a way to efficiently and effectively reach goals, and this fact will "explain" many tendency and empirical propositions.

Applying this functionality proposition to the tendency for role differentiation yields the following deductive explanation: "the nature and degree of role differentiation tend to vary according to functional requirements of effectiveness and efficiency." For Turner, such a statement begins to explain role differentiation in a deductive sense.

**The tenability proposition.** Tenability exists when "the conditions surrounding performance of that role make it possible to play it with some personal reward." Thus, people must receive reinforcement, whether this be confirmation of self, bolstering of self-esteem, an equitable ratio of rights to duties, or some other consideration. Similarly, for me, this proposition seems to be yet another tendency proposition, although it does converge with behaviorism and exchange theory (see Chapters 10–13). Applying this explanatory proposition to the tendency for role differentiation results in the following deduction: "the nature and degree of role differentiation vary according to the requirements of tenability."

Fortunately, Turner's search for explanatory propositions does not end here. He then asks: when are functionality or tenability considerations more likely to prevail? In his exploration for these conditions, Turner develops what I see as more interesting propositions:[20]

1. The more goal-oriented interaction among individuals, the more operative are considerations of functionality, and the less operative considerations of tenability.
2. The more individuals bring to an interaction external power and other salient attributes, the more operative are considerations of viability, and the less operative are considerations of functionality.

Each of these two propositions now possesses at least two variables and thus can serve as a more powerful explanatory proposition. Considerations of tenability and functionality are now dependent variables that vary under the impact, respectively, of the external attributes of actors, such as power, and the degree of instrumentality of interaction.

Returning to the tendency proposition of role differentiation, I can convert Turner's argument into a more precise deductive format:

---

[20] I have phrased these differently than Turner would, but the meaning is the same. See Turner, "Strategy."

1. The more goal-oriented interaction among individuals, the more operative considerations of functionality, and the less operative considerations of tenability.
2. Plurality of actors, $A$, in situations, $S$, are seeking to reach a specific goal, $G$.
3. Therefore, the more $A$ interacts in $S$ in pursuit of $G$, the more considerations of functionality and the less considerations of tenability operate in the differentiation of roles among $A$ in $S$.

In this way, the form of deductive theory is achieved with a specific prediction about what should occur when deduced from a true abstract proposition.

Thus far, I have applied Turner's explanatory propositions only to tendency propositions. But he also intends that explanatory propositions be used to interpret empirical ones. The empirical propositions on the person and role that I summarized in Tables 17–1, 17–2, and 17–3 cannot all be examined here, and so I will focus on only one so as to assess the usefulness of Turner's explanatory propositions. What is said about the utility of Turner's strategy for this one proposition also pertains to the others. Below is the empirical proposition to be explained:

> The greater the investment of time and effort in gaining or maintaining the opportunity to claim a role, the greater the tendency to locate self in that role.

This empirical proposition should, in principle, be deducible from the two explanatory propositions. Let me construct a crude deductive explanation:

1. The more goal-oriented interaction among individuals, the more operative considerations of functionality, and the less operative considerations of tenability.
2. The more individuals bring to interaction external power and other salient attributes, the more operative are considerations of tenability, and the less operative are considerations of functionality.
3. Investment of time and effort in claiming and maintaining a role usually means that an actor will bring to that role special attributes.
4. Therefore, by 2 above, the more individuals bring salient attributes to a role, the more operative are considerations of tenability, and hence, the greater the tendency to locate self in that role.

I think that such efforts to deduce the empirical propositions yield considerable insight as to *why* people are willing to locate their selves in roles. By working hard to claim and maintain a role, actors set up expectations that they should receive rewards proportionate to their investments. In other words, tenability considerations become important. And when these become more important than functionality considerations, people are more willing to locate their selves in, and identify with, roles.

The insertion of the concept of tenability also provides, as Turner intended, an explanation for *why* the independent variables in the other person and role propositions should increase the likelihood of self-location in roles. For example, to the extent that "role adequacy," "role evaluation," "role visibility," "scope of social world," "intrinsic benefits," and the other independent variables of Turner's empirical propositions on "individual efforts at role merger" (see earlier listings in Table 17-3) can be seen as specific types or forms of the tenability principle, he has provided a common explanation of *why* people should locate self in a role.

## PROCESS ROLE THEORY: A BRIEF ASSESSMENT OF TURNER'S APPROACH

In assessing Turner's strategy, let me return to some of the issues of substance, method, and theory that have plagued interactionism in general. With regard to substantive issues, Turner's assumptions emphasize the fluid nature of interactive processes, but in contrast to Blumer he holds a deterministic view of causality. Moreover, unlike Blumer, he does not make exaggerated claims about the range and scope of his theoretical efforts, which are about individuals and the microprocesses by which they come to terms with each other in varying types of social contexts. There is no claim that all social events can be understood by his role theory. Rather, to the extent that attention to the interactive processes of individuals is considered important, Turner argues that his approach is the most appropriate.

With respect to method, Turner's empirical work on a variety of topics attests to his recognition that operationalization of concepts is critical.[21] Observation techniques are an important research tool, but survey and experimental techniques that utilize structured measuring instruments are also deemed appropriate.

---

[21]For representative examples of the variety of empirical research conducted by Turner, see "The Navy Disbursing Officer as a Bureaucrat," *American Sociological Review* 12 (June 1947), pp. 342-48; "Moral Judgement: A Study in Roles," *American Sociological Review* 17 (January 1952), pp. 70-77; "Occupational Patterns of Inequality," *American Journal of Sociology* 50 (March 1954), pp. 437-47; "Zoot-Suiters and Mexicans: Symbols in Crowd Behavior" (with S. J. Surace), *American Journal of Sociology* 62 (July 1956), pp. 14-20; "The Changing Ideology of Success: A Study of Aspirations of High School Men in Los Angeles," *Transactions of the Third World Congress of Sociology* 5 (1956), pp. 35-44; "An Experiment in Modification of the Role Conceptions," *Yearbook of the American Philosophical Society* (1959), pp. 329-32; "Some Family Determinists of Ambition," *Sociology and Social Research* 46 (July 1962), pp. 397-411; *The Social Context of Ambition* (San Francisco: Chandler & Sharp Publishing, Inc., 1964); and "Ambiguity and Interchangeability in Role Attribution" (with Norma Shosid), *American Sociological Review* 41 (December 1976); "The True Self Method for Studying Self-Conception," *Symbolic Interaction* 4 (1981), pp. 1-20.

Finally, more than most interactionists, Turner has been concerned with building theory. He recognizes that it is necessary to move beyond sensitizing frameworks to propositions and that interactionism must begin to explore strategies for developing deductive relations among propositions. Although I think that his functionality and tenability propositions will require revision and supplementation, he has at least developed a strategy that may yield more powerful propositions.

In sum, then, I feel Turner's role theory is one of the best efforts to incorporate all varieties of symbolic interactionism and role theory into a conceptual framework and strategy that stresses theory building and theory testing. The general direction and thrust of his approach should, I feel, be emulated if interactionism is to remain a viable theoretical perspective.

# CHAPTER 18

# The Ethnomethodological Challenge

In recent years, a more phenomenological form of interactionism has emerged. This alternative interactionism goes by a number of labels, but I see *ethnomethodology* as the most descriptive. As this label underscores, ethnomethodology examines the "folk" (ethno) "methods" that people use in dealing with each other. I should emphasize at the outset, however, that ethnomethodologists would resent being discussed as interactionists,[1] Indeed, they see themselves as proposing a radical new paradigm that challenges existing conceptions of social reality, from functionalism to symbolic interactionism. Yet, as I will argue, this challenge is more bluster than substance. In fact, I do not see ethnomethodology as a challenge; rather, it represents an important supplement to current interactionist theorizing.

But why do ethnomethodologists so often see themselves as paradigmatic messiahs? The answer resides in ethnomethodologists' contention that they have discovered an alternative reality that cannot be conceptualized by existing theoretical perspectives. And they raise a question that owes its inspiration to Husserl and Schutz: how do sociologists and other groups of humans create and sustain for each other the *presumption* that the social world has a real character? A "more real" phenomenon for those who propose this question revolves around the complex ways people (laypersons and sociologists alike) go about consciously and

---

[1]See, for example, Thomas P. Wilson, "Normative and Interpretative Paradigms in Sociology," in *Understanding Everyday Life*, ed. J. Douglas (London: Routledge & Kegan Paul, 1970).

unconsciously constructing, maintaining, and altering their "sense" of an external social reality. In fact, the cement that holds society together may not be the values, norms, common definitions, exchange payoffs, role bargains, interest coalitions, and the like of current social theory, but people's explicit and implicit "methods" for creating the presumption of a social order.

Such is the general profile of their challenge. In viewing it, I think that ethnomethodology has uncovered some important social processes. But they have also been a bit pretentious, if not preposterous, in their claims about the "new reality" that they have uncovered. But let me not judge ethnomethodology too severely before I have discussed it in more detail. I will begin with a brief overview of its origins and then turn to a sampling of its major figures and other claims.

## THE ORIGINS OF ETHNOMETHODOLOGY

Ethnomethodology borrows and extends ideas from phenomenology and, despite disclaimers to the contrary, from Meadian-inspired symbolic interactionism. In extending the ideas of these schools of thought, however, ethnomethodology claims to posit a different view of the world. And so, to appreciate just how ethnomethodology differs from more traditional forms of sociological theory, I will assess it in relation to those perspectives from which it tries to disassociate itself, but from which it still has drawn considerable inspiration.

### Blumer's Interactionism and Ethnomethodology

As I emphasized in Chapter 15, Herbert Blumer's interactionism emphasizes the constructed and fluid nature of interaction. Because actors possess extensive symbolic capacities, they are capable of: (a) introjecting new objects into situations, (b) redefining situations, and (c) realigning their joint actions. As Blumer emphasizes, "it would be wise to recognize that any given [act] is mediated by acting units interpreting the situations with which they are confronted."[2] While these situations consist of norms, values, roles, beliefs, and social structures, they are merely types of many "objects" that can be symbolically introjected and reshuffled to produce new definitions of situations.

These ideas advocate a concern with how meanings, or definitions, are created by actors interacting in situations. The emphasis is on the *process* of interaction and on how actors create common meanings in dealing with each other. This line of inquiry is also pursued by ethnomethodologists. The ethnomethodologist also focuses on interaction and

---

[2]Herbert Blumer, "Society as Symbolic Interaction," in *Human Behavior and Social Process,* ed. A. Rose (Boston: Houghton Mifflin, 1962).

on the creation of meanings in situations. But there is an important shift in emphasis that corresponds to Alfred Schutz's analysis of the lifeworld: In what ways do people create a *sense* that they share a common view of the world? And how do people arrive at the *presumption* that there is an objective, external world? Blumer's interactionism stresses the process of creating meaning, but it acknowledges the existence of an external social order. Ethnomethodology suspends, or "brackets" in Edmund Husserl's terms, the issue of whether or not there is an external world of norms, roles, values, and beliefs. Instead, it concentrates on how interaction creates among actors a *sense* of a factual world "out there."

## Goffman's Dramaturgical Analysis and Ethnomethodology

To the dismay of many ethnomethodologists, Paul Attewell has argued that the work of the symbolic interactionist Erving Goffman represents a significant source of inspiration for ethnomethodology.[3] Goffman's work has often been termed the *dramaturgical school* of interactionism because it focuses on the ways that actors manipulate gestures to create an impression in a particular social scene. Goffman tends to emphasize the process of impression management, per se, and not the purposes or goals toward which action is directed. Much of Goffman's analysis thus concentrates on the form of interaction itself rather than on the structures it creates, sustains, or changes.[4] For example, Goffman has insightfully analyzed how actors validate self-conceptions, how they justify their actions through gestures, how they demonstrate their membership in groups, how they display social distance, how they adjust to physical stigmas, and how they interpersonally manipulate many other situations.

This concern with the management of social scenes is also prominent in ethnomethodological analysis. Ethnomethodologists share Goffman's concern with the techniques by which actors create impressions in social situations, but their interest is not with individuals' impression-management, but with how actors create a *sense of a common reality*. Ethnomethodologists thus concentrate on interactional techniques, but they ask a somewhat different question than Goffman: How do such interpersonal techniques sustain a sense of social reality?

---

[3]Paul Attewell, "Ethnomethodology Since Garfinkel," *Theory and Society* 1 (1974), pp. 179–210.

[4]This is not always true, especially in some of his more institutional works, such as *Asylums* (Garden City, N. Y.: Anchor Books, 1961). Other representative works by Goffman include *The Presentation of Self in Everyday Life* (Garden City, N. Y.: Doubleday Publishing, 1959); *Interaction Ritual* (Garden City, N. Y.: Anchor Books, 1967); *Encounters* (Indianapolis, Ind.: Bobbs-Merrill, 1961); *Stigma* (Englewood Cliffs, N.J.: Prentice-Hall, 1963).

## Alfred Schutz, Phenomenology, and Ethnomethodology

Schutz's phenomenology, as I noted in Chapter 14, liberated phenomenology from Husserl's philosophical project.[5] Schutz asserted the importance of studying how interaction creates and maintains a "paramount reality." He was also concerned with how actors achieve reciprocity of perspectives and how they construct a taken-for-granted world that gives order to social life.

This emphasis on the taken-for-granted nature of the world and the importance of this lifeworld for maintaining an actor's sense of reality becomes a prime concern of ethnomethodologists. Indeed, many ethnomethodological concepts are borrowed or adapted from Husserl's and Schutz's phenomenology. Yet, ethnomethodologists adapt phenomenological analysis to the issue of how social order is maintained by the practices that actors use to create a sense that they share the same lifeworld.

Let me now summarize my argument thus far. Ethnomethodology draws from and extends the concerns of interactionists such as Blumer and Goffman and the phenomenological projects of Husserl and Schutz. It emphasizes the process of interaction, the use of interpersonal techniques to create situational impressions, and the importance of perceptions of consensus among actors. In extending interactionism and phenomenology, ethnomethodologists often think that they posit a different vision of the social world and an alternative orientation for understanding the question of how social organization is created, maintained, and changed. As Mehan and Wood note, ethnomethodologists "have chosen to ask not how order is possible, but rather to ask *how a sense of order is possible.*" (I have added the emphasis here.)[6]

## THE NATURE OF ETHNOMETHODOLOGY

### Metaphysics or Methodology?

Ethnomethodology has often been misunderstood. Part of the reason for this misunderstanding stems from the vagueness of the prose of some

---

[5]See, in particular, Alfred Schutz, *Collected Papers I: The Problem of Social Reality,* ed. Maurice Natanson (The Hague, Holland: Martinus Nijhoff, 1962); Alfred Schutz, *Collected Papers II: Studies in Social Theory,* ed. Arvid Broderson (The Hague, Holland: Martinus Nijhoff, 1964); and Alfred Schutz, *Collected Papers III: Studies in Phenomenological Philosophy* (The Hague, Holland: Martinus Nijhoff, 1966). For adaptations of these ideas to interactionism and ethnomethodology, see Alfred Schutz and Thomas Luckmann, *The Structure of the Lifeworld* (Evanston, Ill.: Northwestern University Press, 1973) as well as Thomas Luckmann, ed., *Phenomenology and Sociology* (New York: Penguin Books, 1978). See also Robert C. Freeman, "Phenomenological Sociology and Ethnomethodology," in *Introduction to the Sociologies of Everyday Life,* eds. J. Douglas et al. (Boston: Allyn & Bacon, 1980).

[6]Hugh Mehan and Houston Wood, *The Reality of Ethnomethodology* (New York: John Wiley & Sons, 1975), p. 190. This is an excellent statement of the ethnomethodological perspective.

ethnomethodologists.[7] One form of such misinterpretation asserts that ethnomethodology represents a "corrective" to current sociological theorizing because it points to sources of bias among scientific investigators. From this position, it is assumed that ethnomethodology can serve to check the reliability and validity of investigators' observations by exposing not only their biases, but those of the scientific community accepting their observations. Although ethnomethodology might be used for this purpose, if one were so inclined, those who advocate this use have failed, I think, to grasp the main thrust of the ethnomethodological position. For the ethnomethodologist, emphasis is not on questions about the reliability and validity of investigators' observations, but on the methods used by scientific investigators and laypersons alike to construct, maintain, and perhaps alter what each considers and believes to be a valid and reliable set of statements about order in the world. The methodology in the ethnomethodological perspective does not address questions about the proper, unbiased, or truly scientific search for knowledge; rather, ethnomethodology is concerned with the common methods people employ—whether scientists, housewives, insurance salespersons, or laborers—to create a sense of order about the situations in which they interact. I think that the best clue to this conceptual emphasis can be found in the word ethnomethodology—*ology*, "study of"; *method*, "the methods [used by]"; and *ethno*, "folk or people."

Another related source of misunderstanding in commentaries on ethnomethodology comes from those who assume that this perspective simply uses "soft" research methods, such as participant observation, to uncover some of the taken-for-granted rules, assumptions, and rituals of members in groups.[8] This interpretation would appear to transform ethnomethodology into a research-oriented variant of the symbolic interactionist

---

[7]See, for example, Harold Garfinkel, *Studies in Ethnomethodology* (Englewood Cliffs, N.J.: Prentice-Hall, 1967). However, recent portrayals of the ethnomethodological position have done much to clarify this initial vagueness. See, for example, Mehan and Wood, *The Reality of Ethnomethodology*; D. Lawrence Wieder, *Language and Social Reality* (The Hague, Holland: Mouton Publishers, 1973); Don H. Zimmerman and Melvin Pollner, "The Everyday World as Phenomenon," in *Understanding Everyday Life,* ed. J. D. Douglas (Chicago: Aldine Publishing, 1970), pp. 80–103; Don H. Zimmerman and D. Lawrence Wieder, "Ethnomethodology and the Problem of Order: Comment on Denzin," in *Understanding Everyday Life,* pp. 285–95; Randall Collins and Michael Makowsky, *The Discovery of Society* (New York: Random House, 1972), pp. 209–13; George Psathas, "Ethnomethods and Phenomenology," *Social Research* 35 (September 1968), pp. 500–520; Roy Turner, ed., *Ethnomethodology* (Baltimore: Penguin Books, 1974); Thomas P. Wilson and Don H. Zimmerman, "Ethnomethodology, Sociology and Theory," *Humboldt Journal of Social Relations* 7 (Fall-Winter 1979–80), pp. 52–88; Warren Handel, *Ethnomethodology: How People Make Sense* (Englewood Cliffs, N.J.: Prentice-Hall, 1982); and George Psathas, ed., *Everyday Language: Studies in Ethnomethodology* (New York: Irvington Publishers, 1979).

[8]For example, see Norman K. Denzin, "Symbolic Interactionism and Ethnomethodology," *American Sociological Review* 34 (December 1969), pp. 922–34.

perspective.[9] Such a variant of ethnomethods would now represent a more conscientious effort to get at actors' interpretative processes and the resulting definitions of the situation. By employing various techniques for observation of, and participation in, the symbolic world of those interacting individuals under study, a more accurate reading of how situations are defined, how norms emerge, and how social action is controlled could be achieved. Although ethnomethodologists do employ observation and participant methods to study interacting individuals, their concerns are not the same as those of symbolic interactionists. Like all dominant forms of sociological theorizing, interactionists posit that common definitions, values, and norms emerge from interaction and serve to regulate how people perceive the world and interact with each other. For the interactionist, concern is with the conditions under which various types of explicit and implicit definitions, norms, and values emerge and thereby resolve the problem of how social organization is possible. In contrast, ethnomethodologists are interested in *how* members come to agree upon an *impression* that there are such things as rules, definitions, and values. Just what types of rules and definitions emerge is not a central concern of the ethnomethodologist, since there are more fundamental questions: Through *what types of methods* do people go about seeing, describing, and asserting that rules and definitions exist? How do people use their beliefs that definitions and rules exist to describe for each other the social order?

Again, the methods of ethnomethodology do not refer to a new and improved technique on the part of scientific sociology for deriving a more accurate picture of people's definitions of the situation and of the norms of social structure (as is the case with interactionists). For the ethnomethodologist, emphasis is on the *methods employed by those under study* in creating, maintaining, and altering their presumption that a social order actually exists out there in the real world.

## Concepts and Principles of Ethnomethodology

Alfred Schutz postulated one basic reality—the paramount—in which people's conduct of their everyday affairs occurs. Most contemporary ethnomethodologists, however, are less interested in whether or not there is one or multiple realities, lifeworlds, or natural attitudes. Far more important in ethnomethodological analysis is the development of concepts and principles that can help explain how people's sense of reality is constructed, maintained, and changed. Although ethnomethodology has yet to develop a unified body of concepts or propositions, I see a conceptual

---

[9]For another example of this interpretation, see Walter L. Wallace, *Sociological Theory* (Chicago: Aldine Publishing, 1969), pp. 34–36.

core in the ethnomethodological perspective. Let me review some of its key elements.

**Reflexive action and interaction.**[10]    Much interaction operates to sustain a particular vision of reality. For example, ritual activity directed toward the gods sustains the belief that gods influence everyday affairs. Such ritual activity is an example of reflexive action; it operates to maintain a certain vision of reality. Even when the facts would seem to contradict a belief, human interaction upholds the contradicted belief. For instance, should intense prayer and ritual activity not bring forth the desired intervention from the gods, rather than reject beliefs the devout proclaim that they did not pray hard enough, that their cause was not just, or that the gods in their wisdom have a greater plan. Such behavior is reflexive; it upholds or reinforces a belief, even in the face of evidence that the belief may be incorrect.

Much human interaction is reflexive. Humans interpret cues, gestures, words, and other information from each other in a way that sustains a particular vision of reality. Even contradictory evidence is reflexively interpreted to maintain a body of belief and knowledge. The concept of reflexivity thus focuses attention on how people in interaction go about maintaining the presumption that they are guided by a particular reality. Much of ethnomethodological inquiry addresses this question of how reflexive interaction occurs. That is, what concepts and principles can be developed to explain the conditions under which different reflexive actions among interacting parties are likely to occur.

**The indexicality of meaning.**    The gestures, cues, words, and other information sent and received by interacting parties have meaning in a *particular context*. Without some knowledge of the context (the biographies of the interacting parties, their avowed purpose, their past interactive experiences, and so forth—it would easily be possible to misinterpret the symbolic communication among interacting individuals. This fact of interactive life is denoted by the concept of *indexicality*.[11] To say that an expression is indexical is to emphasize that the meaning of that expression is tied to a particular context.

This phenomenon of indexicality draws attention to the problem of how actors in a context construct a vision of reality in that context. They develop expressions that invoke their common vision about what is real

[10]For an early discussion of this phenomenon, see Garfinkel, *Studies in Ethnomethodology*. A more readable discussion can be found in Mehan and Wood, *The Reality of Ethnomethodology*, pp. 137–78.

[11]Garfinkel, *Studies in Ethnomethodology*; Garfinkel and Sacks, "The Formal Properties of Practical Actions," in *Theoretical Sociology*, ed. J. C. McKinney and E. A. Tiryakian (New York: Appleton-Century-Crofts, 1970).

in their situation. The concept of indexicality thus directs an investigator's attention to actual interactive contexts in order to see how actors go about creating indexical expressions—words, facial and body gestures, and other cues—to create and sustain the presumption that a particular reality governs their affairs.

With these two key concepts, reflexivity and indexicality, I think that the interactionists' concern with the process of symbolic communication is retained, while much of the phenomenological legacy of Schutz is rejuvenated. Concern is with how actors use gestures to create and sustain a lifeworld, body of knowledge, or natural attitude about what is real. The emphasis is not on the content of the lifeworld, but on the methods or techniques that actors use to create, maintain, or even alter a vision of reality. As Mehan and Wood note, "the ethnomethodological theory of the reality constructor is about the *procedures* that accomplish reality. It is not about any specific reality."[12] This emphasis has led ethnomethodologists to isolate the general types of methods employed by interacting actors.

**Some general interactive methods.**    When analytical attention focuses on the methods that people use to construct a sense of reality, the task of the theorist is to isolate the general types of interpersonal techniques that people employ in interaction. Aaron Cicourel, for example, has summarized a number of such techniques or methods isolated by ethnomethodologists: (1) searching for the normal form, (2) doing reciprocity of perspectives, and (3) using the et cetera principle.[13]

*Searching for the normal form.*    If interacting parties sense that ambiguity exists over what is real and that their interaction is strained, they will emit gestures to tell each other to return to what is "normal" in their contextual situation. Actors are presumed to hold a vision of a normal form for situations or to be motivated to create one; and hence much of their action is designed to reach this form.

*Doing a reciprocity of perspectives.*    Borrowing from Schutz's formulation, ethnomethodologists have emphasized that actors operate under the presumption, and actively seek to communicate the fact, that they would have the same experiences were they to switch places. Furthermore, until they are so informed by specific gestures, actors can ignore differences in perspectives that might arise from their unique biographies. Thus, much interaction will be consumed with gestures that seek to assure others that a reciprocity of perspectives does indeed exist.

[12]Mehan and Wood, *The Reality of Ethnomethodology*, p. 114.

[13]Aaron V. Cicourel, *Cognitive Sociology* (London: Macmillan, 1973), pp. 85–88. It should be noted that these principles are implicit in Garfinkel's *Studies in Ethnomethodology*.

***Using the et cetera principle.*** In examining an actual interaction, much is left unsaid. Actors must constantly "fill in" or "wait for" information necessary to "make sense" of another's words or deeds. When actors do so, they are using the et cetera principle. They are agreeing not to disrupt the interaction by asking for the needed information; they are willing to wait or to fill in. For example, the common phrase, "you know," which usually appears after an utterance, is often an assertion by one actor to another invoking the et cetera principle. The other is thus informed not to disrupt the interaction and the sense of reality in the situation with a counter utterance, such as, "No, I do not know."

These three general types of folk methods are but examples of what ethnomethodologists seek to discover. There are certainly more folk methods. For some ethnomethodologists, the ultimate goal of theory is to determine the conditions under which these and other interpersonal techniques will be used to construct, maintain, or change a sense of reality. Yet, I have found few such propositions in the ethnomethodological literature. But let me try to imagine the nature of propositions, should they ever be developed.

**Two general ethnomethodological propositions.** I see ethnomethodological propositions as following several assumptions: (1) Social order is maintained by the use of techniques that give actors a sense that they share a common reality. (2) The substance of the common reality is less important in maintaining social order than the actors' acceptance of a common set of techniques. With these assumptions, I offer two examples of what ethnomethodological propositions might look like if ethnomethodologists ever got around to generating them.

1. The more actors fail to agree on the use of interactive techniques, such as the et cetera principle, the search for the normal form, and doing the reciprocity of perspectives, the more likely is interaction to be disrupted, and hence, the less likely is social order to be maintained.
2. The more interaction proceeds on the basis of different, taken-for-granted visions of reality, the more likely is interaction to be disrupted, and hence, the less likely is social order to be maintained.

These propositions can perhaps be visualized as general laws from which more specific propositions on how actors go about constructing, maintaining, or changing their sense of reality could be developed. What is needed in ethnomethodology is to discover the *specific conditions* under which particular folk techniques are likely to be used to create a sense of a common world among interacting individuals. Indeed, I think that ethnomethodologists should worry less about whether or not they have discovered a radically new reality and instead direct their efforts to developing some general propositions about the conditions under which actors will use various "folk methods."

## Varieties of Ethnomethodological Inquiry

**Garfinkel's pioneering inquiries.**   Harold Garfinkel's *Studies in Ethnomethodology* firmly established ethnomethodology as a distinctive theoretical perspective.[14] Although the book is not a formal theoretical statement, the studies and the commentary in it established the domain of ethnomethodological inquiry. Subsequent ethnomethodological research and theory begins with Garfinkel's insights and takes them in a variety of directions.

Garfinkel's work established ethnomethodology as a field of inquiry that seeks to understand the methods people employ to make sense out of their world. He places considerable emphasis on language as the vehicle by which this reality construction is done. Indeed, for Garfinkel, interacting individuals' efforts to account for their actions—that is, to represent them verbally to others—is the primary method by which the world is constructed. In Garfinkel's terms, *to do* interaction is *to tell* interaction; or in other words, the primary folk technique used by actors is verbal description. In this way, people use their accounts to construct a sense of reality.

Garfinkel places enormous emphasis on indexicality—that is, on the fact that members' accounts are tied to particular contexts and situations. An utterance, Garfinkel notes, indexes much more than it actually says; it also evokes connotations that can only be understood in the context of a situation. Garfinkel's work was thus the first to stress the indexical nature of interpersonal cues and to emphasize that individuals seek to use accounts to create a sense of reality.

In addition to laying much of the groundwork for current ethnomethodology, Garfinkel and his associates conducted a number of interesting empirical studies in an effort to validate their assumptions about what is real. One line of empirical inquiry is known as the *breeching experiment,* in which the normal course of interaction is deliberately interrupted. For example, Garfinkel reports a series of conversations in which student experimenters challenged every statement of selected subjects. The end result was a series of conversations revealing the following pattern:

*Subject:* I had a flat tire.

*Experimenter:* What do you mean, you had a flat tire?

*Subject:* (appears momentarily stunned and then replies in a hostile
manner): What do you mean, "What do you mean?" A flat tire is

---

[14]Garfinkel, *Studies in Ethnomethodology.*

a flat tire. That is what I meant. Nothing special. What a crazy question![15]

In this situation, the experimenter was apparently violating an implicit rule for this type of interaction and thereby aroused not only the hostility of the subject but also a negative sanction, "What a crazy question!" Seemingly, in any interaction there are certain background features that everyone should understand and that should not be questioned in order for all parties to be able to "conduct their common conversational affairs without interference."[16] Such implicit methods appear to guide a considerable amount of everyday affairs and are critical for the construction of at least the perception among interacting humans that an external social order exists. In this conversation, for example, the et cetera principle and the search for the normal form are invoked by the subject. Through breeching, Garfinkel hoped to discover implicit ethnomethods by forcing actors to *actively* engage in the process of reality reconstruction after the situation had been disrupted.

Other research strategies also yielded insights into the methods parties use in an interaction for constructing a sense of reality. Garfinkel and his associates summarized the "decision rules" jurors employed in reaching a verdict.[17] By examining a group such as a jury, which must by the nature of its task develop an interpretation of what really happened, the ethnomethodologist might achieve some insight into the generic properties of the processes of constructing *a sense of social reality*. From the investigators' observations of jurors, it appeared that "a person is 95 percent juror before [coming] near the court," indicating that through their participation in other social settings and through instructions from the court, they had accepted the "official" rules for reaching a verdict. However, these rules were altered somewhat as participants came together in an actual jury setting and began the "work of assembling the 'corpus' which serves as grounds for inferring the correctness of a verdict."[18] Because the inevitable ambiguities of the cases before them made it difficult for strict conformity to the official rules of jury deliberation, new decision rules were invoked in order to allow jurors to achieve a "correct" view of "what actually happened." But in their retrospective reporting to interviewers of how they reached the verdicts, jurors typically invoked the "official line" to justify the correctness of their decisions. When interviewers drew attention to discrepancies between the jurors' ideal accounts and actual practices, jurors became anxious, indicating that somewhat

---

[15]Ibid., p. 42.
[16]Ibid.
[17]Ibid., pp. 104–15.
[18]Ibid., p. 110.

different rules had been used to construct the corpus of what really happened.

In sum, I think that these two examples of Garfinkel's research strategy illustrate the general intent of much ethnomethodological inquiry: to penetrate natural social settings or create social settings in which the investigator can observe humans attempting to assert, create, maintain, or change the rules for constructing the appearance of consensus over the structure of the real world. By focusing on the process or methods for constructing a reality rather than on the substance or content of the reality itself, research from the ethnomethodological point of view can potentially provide a more interesting and relevant answer to the question of "how and why society is possible." Garfinkel's studies have stimulated a variety of research and theoretical strategies. Several of the most prominent strategies are briefly discussed below.

**Harvey Sacks's linguistic analysis.**   Until his untimely death in 1976, Harvey Sacks exerted considerable influence within ethnomethodology. Although his work is not well known outside ethnomethodological circles, it represents an attempt to extend Garfinkel's concern with verbal accounts while eliminating some of the problems posed by indexicality.

Sacks was one of the first ethnomethodologists to articulate the phenomenological critique of sociology and to use this critique to build what he thought was an alternative form of theorizing.[19] The basic thrust of Sacks's critique can be stated as follows: Sociologists assume that language is a resource used in generating concepts and theories of the social world. In point of fact, however, sociologists are confusing resource and topic. In using language, sociologists are creating a reality; their words are not a neutral vehicle but *the* topic of inquiry for true sociological analysis.[20]

Sacks's solution to this problem in sociology is typical of phenomenologists. If the pure properties of language can be understood, then it would be possible to have an objective social science without confusing resource with subject matter. Sacks's research tended to concentrate on the formal properties of language-in-use. Typically, Sacks would take verbatim transcripts of actors in interaction and seek to understand the formal properties of the conversation, while ignoring its substance. Such a tactic resolved the problem of indexicality, since Sacks simply ignored the substance and context of conversation and focused on its form. For example, "sequences of talk" among actors might occupy his attention.[21]

---

[19]Harvey Sacks, "Sociological Description," *Berkeley Journal of Sociology* 8 (1963), pp. 1–17.

[20]Harvey Sacks, "An Initial Investigation of the Usability of Conversational Data for Doing Sociology" in *Studies in Interaction,* ed. D. Sudnow (New York: Free Press, 1972).

[21]His best-known study, for example, is the coauthored article with Emmanuel Schegloff and Gail Jefferson, "A Simplest Systematics for the Analysis of Turn Taking in Conversation," *Language* 50 (1974), pp. 696–735.

Sacks thus began to take ethnomethodology into formal linguistics, a trend that has continued and, in fact, seems to dominate current ethnomethodology. More importantly, he sought to discover universal forms of interaction—that is, abstracted patterns of talk—that might apply to all conversations. In this way, he began to search for the laws of reality construction among interacting individuals.

**Aaron Cicourel's cognitive approach.**    In his *Method and Measurement in Sociology*, Aaron Cicourel launched a line of attack on sociology similar to Sacks's.[22] The use of mathematics, he argues, will not remove the problems associated with language, because mathematics is a language that does not necessarily correspond to the phenomena that it describes. Instead, it "distorts and obliterates, acts as a filter or grid for that which will pass as knowledge in a given era."[23] The use of statistics similarly distorts: events cannot be counted, averaged, and otherwise manipulated. Such statistical manipulations soon make sociological descriptions inaccurate and mold sociological analysis to the dictates of statistical logic.

In a less severe tone, Cicourel also questions Garfinkel's assertion that interaction and verbal accounts are the same process.[24] Cicourel notes that humans see, sense, and feel much that they cannot communicate with words. Humans use "multiple-modalities" for communicating in situations. Verbal accounts represent crude and incomplete translations of what is actually communicated in interaction. This recognition has led Cicourel to rename his brand of ethnomethodology, *cognitive sociology*.

The details of his analysis are, I think, less important than the general intent of his effort to transform sociological research and theory. Basically, he has sought to uncover the universal "interpretive procedures" by which humans organize their cognitions and give meaning to situations.[25] It is through these interpretive procedures that people develop a sense of social structure and are able to organize their actions. These interpretive procedures are universal and invariant in humans; and their discovery would allow for understanding of how humans create a sense of social structure in the world around them.

**Zimmerman's, Pollner's, and Wieder's situational approach.**
Sacks and Cicourel have focused on the universal properties, respectively,

---

[22]Aaron V. Cicourel, *Method and Measurement in Sociology* (New York: Free Press, 1964).

[23]Ibid., p. 35.

[24]Aaron V. Cicourel, "Cross Modal Communication," in *Linguistics and Language Science, Monograph 25,* ed. R. Shuy (Washington, D.C.: Georgetown University Press, 1973).

[25]See, for example, his *Cognitive Sociology* and "Basic and Normative Rules in the Negotiation of Status and Role," in *Recent Sociology No. 2,* ed. H. P. Dreitzel (New York: Macmillan, 1970).

of language use and cognitive perception/representation. This concern with invariance, or universal folk methods, has become increasingly prominent in ethnomethodological inquiry. In a number of essays, for example, Don Zimmerman, D. Lawrence Wieder, and Melvin Pollner have developed an approach that seeks to uncover the universal procedures people employ to construct a sense of reality.[26] Their position is perhaps the most clearly stated of all ethnomethodologies, drawing inspiration from Garfinkel but extending his ideas. Let me summarize their argument:

1. In all interaction situations, humans attempt to construct the appearance of consensus over relevant features of the interaction setting.
2. These setting features can include attitudes, opinions, beliefs, and other cognitions about the nature of the social setting in which they interact.
3. Humans engage in a variety of explicit and implicit interpersonal practices and methods to construct, maintain, and perhaps alter *the appearance* of consensus over these setting features.
4. Such interpersonal practices and methods result in the assembling and disassembling of what can be termed an *occasional corpus*— that is, the *perception* by interacting humans that the current setting has an orderly and understandable structure.
5. This appearance of consensus is not only the result of agreement on the substance and content of the occasioned corpus but also a reflection of each participant's compliance with the rules and procedures for assemblage and disassemblage of this consensus. In communicating, in however subtle a manner, that parties accept the implicit rules for constructing an occasioned corpus, they go a long way in establishing consensus over what is out there in the interaction setting.
6. In each interaction situation, the rules for constructing the occasioned corpus will be unique in some respects and hence not completely generalizable to other settings—thus requiring that humans in each and every interaction situation use interpersonal methods in search for agreement on the implicit rules for the assemblage of an occasioned corpus.
7. Thus, by constructing, reaffirming, or altering the rules for constructing an occasioned corpus, members in a setting are able to offer each other the appearance of an orderly and connected world out there, which compels certain perceptions and actions on their part.

---

[26]See, for example, Zimmerman and Pollner, "The World as a Phenomenon"; Zimmerman and Wieder, "Ethnomethodology and the Problem of Order"; Wieder, *Language and Social Reality.*

It is from these kinds of assumptions about human interaction that Zimmerman's, Pollner's, and Wieder's ethnomethodology takes its subject matter. Rather than focusing on the actual content and substance of the occasioned corpus and on the ways members believe it to force certain perceptions and actions, attention is drawn primarily to the *methods humans use* to construct, maintain, and change the *appearance* of an orderly and connected social world. These methods are directly observable and constitute a major portion of people's actions in everyday life. In contrast, the actual substance and content of the occasioned corpus is not directly observable and can only be inferred. Furthermore, in concentrating on the *process* of creating, sustaining, and changing the occasioned corpus, it can be asked: Is not the process of creating for each other the appearance of a stable social order more critical to understand how society is possible than the actual substance and content of the occasioned corpus? Is there anything more to society than members' beliefs that it is out there forcing them to do and see certain things? If this fact is true, order is not the result of the particular structure of the corpus but of the human capacity to continually assemble and disassemble the corpus in each and every interaction situation. This perspective suggests to ethnomethodologists like Zimmerman, Pollner, Wieder, and many others that theoretical attention should therefore be placed on the ongoing process of assembling and disassembling the appearance of social order and to the particular methods people employ in doing so.

## NEW PARADIGM OR IMPORTANT SUPPLEMENT?

I think that ethnomethodology has uncovered a series of interpersonal processes that traditional interactionists have failed to conceptualize. The implicit methods that people use to communicate a sense of social order are, I believe, a very crucial dimension of social interaction and organization. The theoretical goal is to specify the generic conditions under which various folk methods are used by individuals.

The rather extreme polemics about the "new reality" exposed by ethnomethodologists are, I feel, best forgotten.[27] The few findings of ethnomethodologists do not sustain their metaphysical vision of the world any more than they support interactionist formulations. Indeed, the findings of ethnomethodologists blend very nicely with those of symbolic interactionists, role theorists, and other theoretical traditions. Ethnomethodologists have, therefore, rather overstated their case. I do not doubt that people's sense of sharing a common world is an important property

---

[27]For an interesting discussion of this assumption that challenges the ethnomethodological perspective, see Bill Harrell, "Symbols, Perception, and Meaning," in *Sociological Theory: Inquiries and Paradigms,* ed. L. Gross (New York: Harper & Row, 1967), pp. 104–27.

of interaction and organization, but it is not the only interactive dynamic. And to the degree that ethnomethodologists assert that their domain of inquiry is *the only* reality, they make themselves look foolish.[28]

It is time, I think, for ethnomethodologists to get off their high horse and begin to integrate their ideas into social theory. For too much effort has been spent challenging and attacking "normal sociology"; the goals of theoretical cumulation would be better served if there was a conscious and concerted attempt by ethnomethodologists to integrate their ideas with those of mainstream interactionism.[29]

---

[28]I agree with Lewis Coser on this issue. See his "Two Methods in Search of a Substance," *American Sociological Review* 40 (1975), pp. 691–700. I also agree with him about the "other method" discussed in this article.

[29]Actually, many nonethnomethodologists, such as Jurgen Habermas (see Chapter 9), Randall Collins (see Chapter 21), and Anthony Giddens (see Chapter 22), have used the ideas of ethnomethodologists to build interesting theory—far more interesting than that produced by the ethnomethodologists themselves.

## PART FIVE

# Structural Theory

# CHAPTER 19

# The Origins of Structural Theorizing

## THE IDEA OF SOCIAL STRUCTURE

Despite sociologists' frequent use of the concept *social structure,* its meaning remains unclear. My sense is that notions of structure are employed as metaphors for describing social interaction and relations that endure over time, but beyond this, structure is not conceptualized precisely. Through previous chapters, we have come across labels to denote structure—labels like "social system," "imperatively coordinated associations," "institutions," "strains toward integration," "networks," and so on. All of these and other concepts emphasize that human social relations become patterned and comparatively stable over time; and most theoretical perspectives in sociology try to understand how and why this is so. But curiously, even as theorists make these efforts, their conceptualization of social structure remains vague. In this last group of chapters, I will examine several representative approaches that seek to conceptualize social structure more explicitly.

Each of these approaches is eclectic, borrowing from those perspectives that I have already summarized; and each owes its inspiration to a number of early thinkers who framed the general problems of structural analysis and who provided many of the critical concepts. These early thinkers are by now familiar, because I have examined them in other contexts. But in this chapter, I want to focus more precisely on how they each conceptualized social structure and how their respective views have stimulated more modern structural theorizing.[1] As I do so, it will be evident that many of the basic issues that trouble sociological theorizing become highly visible in structural theories. For example, can sociology be a science, or is there something different and unique about human structures? Can social structure be conceptualized independently of the microprocesses from which it is constituted, or must it be analyzed in terms of these microprocesses? And can the basic dimensions—both macro and micro—of structure be isolated and analyzed by theory, or is structure merely a reification?[2] As is evident, structural theorizing forces us to deal with sociology's more difficult questions. Let me now trace the origins of these questions in the structural thought of sociology's early masters.

## KARL MARX AND STRUCTURAL ANALYSIS

There have been explicit efforts to reinterpret Marx by French structuralists, who, I should emphasize, are not discussed in the following chapters.[3] Despite the failure of such reinterpretations of Marx in structuralist terms, Marx's ideas have nonetheless been influenced by the development of less mystical analysis of social structure.[4] This influence revolves around Marx's conceptions of (1) system reproduction and (2) system contradiction.[5] I have imposed more modern terminology on Marx here, but the ideas are his. Let me briefly review each.

1. Marx was concerned with how patterns of inequality "reproduce" themselves. That is, how is inequality in power and wealth sustained? And how are social relations structured to sustain these inequalities? This metaphor of social reproduction has been picked

---

[1]For one recent effort to clarify the "structuralisms" that pervade social theory, see Bruce H. Mayhew, "Structuralism versus Individualism: Part 1, Shadowboxing in the Dark" and "Structuralism versus Individualism: Part II, Ideological and Other Obfuscations," *Social Forces* 59 (2 and 3, 1981), pp. 335-75 and 627-48, respectively. See also a volume edited by Ino Rossi, *Structural Sociology* (New York: Columbia University Press, 1982) for representative analyses.

[2]For example, see Douglas W. Maynard and Thomas P. Wilson, "On the Reification of Social Structure," *Current Perspectives in Social Theory* 1 (1980), pp. 287-322.

[3]Such is the case because I do not think that they have generated any theory, even if we include meta-theory as part of sociological theorizing. Structuralism is, of course, a broad intellectual movement, and its most Marxist exponent was Louis Althusser, *For Marx* (New York: Penguin Books, 1969) and *Politics and History* (London: NLB, 1977). For an interesting secondary review, see also Alison Assiter, "Althusser and Structuralism," *The British Journal of Sociology* 35 (2, 1984), pp. 272-94.

[4]See appendix for my review of Lévi-Strauss, the most prominent of these French structuralists.

[5]See Karl Marx, *A Contribution to the Critique of Political Economy* (New York: International Publishers, 1970); *The Economic and Philosophic Manuscripts of 1844* (New York: International Publishers, 1964; and *Capital: A Critical Analysis of Capitalist Production* (New York: International Publishers, 1967).

up by many structural theorists who like to view social structures as "reproduced" by the repetitive social encounters among individuals.

From this metaphorical use of Marx's ideas comes a vision of social structure as the distribution of resources among actors who use their respective resources in social encounters and, in the process, reproduce social structure and its attendant distribution of resources. Thus, structure *is* the symbolic, material, and political resources that actors have in their encounters; and as they employ these resources to their advantage, they reproduce the structure of their social relations because they sustain their respective shares of resources. For example, those who can control where others are physically located, who have access to coercion, who control communication channels, and who can manipulate the flow of information can "structure" successive encounters with others who have fewer resources in ways that reproduce inequalities. In so doing, they reproduce structure, but structure is tied to the interactive encounters among individuals using their resources. It is not something "out there" beyond actors and their interactions in concrete situations.

2. Marx was, of course, interested in changing capitalist society; and so, he needed to introduce a concept that could break the vicious cycle of system reproduction. His analysis of Hegel's dialectics gave him the critical idea of "contradiction." Material social arrangements contain, he argued, patterns of social relations that are self-transforming. For example, capitalists must concentrate large pools of labor around machines in urban areas, which allow workers to communicate their grievances and to organize politically to change the very nature of capitalism. Thus, private expropriation of profits by capitalists stands in contradiction to the socially organized production process; and over time, this underlying contradiction will produce conflictual social relations—i.e., a revolution by workers—that change and transform the nature of social relations and, hence, social structure.[6]

Again, my sense is that this notion of contradiction is borrowed in a metaphorical way. It is used to introduce conflict and change into structural analysis. It posits, in essence, that the distribution of resources that sustains or reproduces social relations is inherently subject to redistribution, under certain conditions. The main condition is inequality. That is, structures reproduced through unequal distribution of symbolic, material, and political resources will exhibit underlying contradictions that will, in turn, generate pressures for interactions that *do not* reproduce the structure but instead transform it in some way through redistribution of resources.

---

[6]Karl Marx and Friedrich Engels, *The Communist Manifesto* (New York: International Publishers, 1971).

There is, I think, an implicit exchange theory in these notions of structure. In some works, such as those by Randall Collins (Chapter 21), these exchange ideas in Marx's analysis and in the metaphorical extension of his ideas become more explicit. In other structural analyses, such as Anthony Giddens's "structuration theory" (see Chapter 22), they are left recessive. And in still other approaches, such as that of Peter Blau, whose early work was an explicit exchange perspective (see Chapter 12), the exchange basis of social structure is no longer conceptualized and is abandoned altogether. Among those who still use Marx's ideas, I think that they dramatically distort them in an effort to address the microfoundations of macrostructures. Yet, these distortions are, as we will see shortly, rather creative and, from any point of view, not something over which we should unduly agonize. Indeed, I think it best to use the ideas of early scholars, transforming them as we see necessary in order to explain social phenomena.

## THE STRUCTURAL ANALYSIS OF HERBERT SPENCER

### Spencer's Macrostructuralism

Herbert Spencer's work is most commonly identified with functional theorizing. But in actual fact, Spencer's work is far less functional than is commonly recognized.[7] I think that a much more accurate label is *macrostructural,* which violates, of course, our other misinterpretation of Spencer as the staunch individualist who coined the phrase "survival of the fittest." For contrary to our stereotypes, Spencer's main theoretical problem was the relationship among (a) the size of a population, (b) the rates of contact and interaction among its members, (c) the level of differentiation of activities and subgroupings in a population, and finally, (d) the pattern of its integration. I see this emphasis as macrostructural because there is not much concern with how individuals build and sustain structure; rather, emphasis is on the form of structures and how they constrain individual actions.[8] Let me recapitulate Spencer's macrostructural theory.[9]

For Spencer, increases in population size generate pressures for transformation in the ways that activities of its members are organized. One pressure for change comes from the fact that rates of face-to-face contact decline with increases in size; people simply cannot all interact with each other. As a result, informal social control is disrupted, forcing the elab-

---

[7]See Jonathan H. Turner, *Herbert Spencer: Toward a Renewed Appreciation* (Beverly Hills, Calif. and London: Sage Publications, 1985).

[8]But as I will stress shortly, he did develop such a microsociological approach.

[9]Herbert Spencer, *The Principles of Sociology* (New York: D. Appleton, 1885).

oration of specialized agencies of political control. Moreover, once such concentration of power increases, so do inequalities; and thus, large populations are more likely to evidence social classes and strata than smaller ones.

A related pressure comes from the fact that as populations grow, they extend their geographical territories. As people live and interact in different places, they develop somewhat distinctive outlooks and patterns of behavior. They become culturally differentiated; and if these differences are to be controlled and relations among culturally differentiated subpopulations are to be regularized, concentrations of power are necessary—thus increasing the level of differentiation along political as well as cultural dimensions.

Another pressure for change in structure comes from the increased pressures on resources that a larger population exerts. This kind of pressure exerts itself in several ways. First, under resource scarcity, there is increased competition, which leads to specialization as some are more fit to survive in some social niches than others. Second, as the size of a population increases relative to its resources, production and distribution of resources becomes increasingly problematic. As a result, specialization of individuals and organizations in order to expand production and facilitate distribution becomes necessary. And third, competition and growing specialization generate problems of coordination and control, thereby encouraging further elaboration of political power to regulate and coordinate activity.

Thus, for Spencer, increases in size generate pressures for increased social differentiation of activities and for expanded concentration of power. Inherent in differentiation, per se, is inequality since some individuals and groups will usurp resources. But as differentiation requires ever more concentrations of power, then inequalities are escalated.

Differentiating populations reveal problems of integration—that is, difficulties coordinating activities. This is the result of the following processes: (a) informal controls are reduced as people can no longer interact face-to-face; (b) cultural and regional distinctions emerge as people spread out in space; (c) common sentiments, or values and beliefs, cannot be sustained among people who cannot interact frequently and who are spread out in space; and (d) concentrated power becomes a double-edged sword, for its use is necessary for coordination and control, but it also generates inequalities and resentments, which escalate integrative problems.

These problems of integration are endemic to differentiating populations. And for Spencer, they contain an inherent dialectic: as political centralization and control are extended, inequalities and resentments about political control increase, and as these resentments escalate, there are pressures for decentralization of power. Yet, decentralized power increases freedom at the cost of escalated competition and decreased coordination; and as problems of coordination mount and as people resent competitive abuses, then there are pressures for centralization of power to regulate affairs. There is, therefore, an inherent cycle between more centralized and decentralized systems.

Such is Spencer's macrostructural sociology; and I think that it can be found in most contemporary structural themes. But Spencer also tried to develop a more micro approach, which, although not greatly developed, anticipates many present-day efforts to theorize about the microfoundations of macrostructural processes. Let me briefly summarize this microstructural approach.

## Spencer's Microstructuralism

Spencer argued that ultimately all macrostructures are built from "ceremonial practices"—that is, rituals, forms of address, bodily movements, dress, badges and emblems, and other stereotyped presentations of self and sequences of behavior. Moreover, macrostructures are sustained through ceremonies, or interaction rituals. He argued that too often these more micro processes are ignored because next to the macrostructures—the state, classes, and religion, for example—"ceremonial control" seems "of no significance." Yet, Spencer did emphasize that growing size and complexity at the macrostructural level undermine the extent to which ceremonial control can be effective. But his major concern was with how ritualized interaction varies under conditions of inequality. His guiding proposition is that the greater is the degree of political centralization in a population, the greater is the level of inequality, and hence, the more pronounced are interaction rituals and the more they will be used to mark ranks.

Spencer's analysis of ceremony or interaction rituals is, I think, one of the first efforts in sociology to analyze the connection between macroprocesses of size, differentiation, spatial distribution, political centralization, and class inequalities with more micro processes that produce and reproduce these macro properties of society. His work was very much in the spirit of contemporary structural approaches, but tragically, his ideas have been ignored, as evidenced by Talcott Parsons's remark in 1937, "who now reads Spencer?" Yet, as I think will be evident in the following chapters, contemporary theorists have rediscovered many of Spencer's insights.

One reason for our ignorance of Spencer is our misunderstanding of his work. Sociologists frequently equate his ideas with what is now called a right wing ideology. Such a conclusion is too simple a portrayal and has kept sociologists from fully appreciating Spencer's genius. Another reason for our misconception of Spencer is that we have allowed Émile Durkheim's biased evaluation of Spencer to color our view.[10] Indeed,

---

[10]Émile Durkheim, *The Division of Labor in Society* (New York: Free Press, 1947).

Durkheim did a most unreasonable thing: he borrowed many ideas from Spencer, but at the same time, he was so critical of him that it was easy to lose sight of the fact that most of Durkheim's basic macrostructural ideas were anticipated 20 to 40 years earlier in Spencer's work. Thus, I think that much of the Spencerian influence on contemporary structural theory comes via Durkheim's "borrowing" of Spencer's structural analysis.

## THE STRUCTURALISM OF ÉMILE DURKHEIM

As with Spencer, I examined the work of Émile Durkheim in Chapter 2 on the emergence of functionalism. But unlike Spencer, Durkheim's work has directly influenced nonfunctional structural analysis in contemporary social theory. Indeed, he is one of the main intellectual inspirations for what can be loosely termed *French structuralism,* whose major proponent, Claude Lévi-Strauss, is summarized in the appendix to this chapter.[11] More important than this brand of structuralism is the influence of Durkheim's ideas on more explicitly sociological analyses of structures. In this area, his influence has been threefold: (1) the concern with social-structural differentiation, (2) the emphasis on cognitive processes, and (3) the analysis of ritual activities and social solidarity. Let me examine each of these in turn.

1. Durkheim's analysis of structural differentiation is very similar to Spencer's.[12] The increasing size of a population, especially when concentrated, escalates competition, which, in turn, leads to differentiation. However, Durkheim sees his approach as different from that of Spencer, who is accused of underemphasizing the significance of common sentiments in social systems. Durkheim made this charge stick, but it is patently false, as a reading of Book I of Spencer's *The Principles of Sociology* would indicate.[13] More significant than his obfuscation of Spencer's work is the basic proposition that Durkheim advanced: the "volume," "intensity," and "determinateness" of the "collective conscience" decrease with structural differentiation.[14] The idea here is that as systems differentiate, people perform different activities and are attached to diverse groups. As a result, their concrete actions can no longer be regulated by common ideas and sentiments; at best, they can hold in common only the most "general," "abstracted," and "enfeebled" ideas. This situation produces the basic dilemma of all large, complex systems: If common ideas—values, beliefs, ideologies, and dogmas, for instance—cannot regulate and

---

[11]Again, I do not think that this approach has led anywhere, and hence, I am not going to analyze it in any detail.

[12]Durkheim, *The Division of Labor.*

[13]Spencer, *The Principles of Sociology.*

[14]See Jonathan H. Turner and Leonard Beeghley, *The Emergence of Sociological Theory* (Homewood, Ill.: Dorsey Press, 1981), pp. 334–41 for a detailed analysis.

coordinate activities, what is to hold a society together? What is to integrate the differentiated units?[15]

Durkheim's answer is similar to Spencer's in several respects. First, he recognized that increasing concentrations of power and political authority become necessary, although, just like Spencer, he saw this as a necessary evil. Second, he viewed relations of exchange and their normative regulation as increasing. And third, he emphasized that differentiation involves the creation of subcultures where common sentiments emerge among subgroupings who are located in similar regions and places in the division of labor.

Thus, much like Spencer, Durkheim emphasized the macrostructural processes of size, spatial distribution, differentiation, and resolution of integrative problems. But he also stressed the importance of ideas as an integrating force. And this emphasis increasingly drew him toward a more cognitive approach to structural analysis.

2. As early as 1900, Durkheim had recognized that common ideas "rule us from within." And by the second decade of this century,[16] he was arguing that at the roots of all our judgments there are a "certain number of essential ideas . . . of space, class, number, cause, substance . . . (that) correspond to the most universal properties of things . . . (and that) are like the solid frame which encloses all thought."[17] But what determines the content of these "essential ideas?" Durkheim's answer was "the structure of society." That is, the categories by which we perceive the world are determined by the structure and pattern of our social relations, and it is in this way that human categories of thought reinforce the structure of society.

This line of argument was to become the main ingredient of French structuralism, which, as I indicated earlier, is summarized in the appendix. Most modern structuralists tend to turn "Durkheim on his head" in their insistence that "deep structures" of thought, lodged in human biology, determine the structure of social relations. Durkheim argued just the opposite: structures of thought reflect social structural arrangements, and in so doing, they reinforce and reproduce those arrangements.[18] The particulars of Durkheim's analysis are not, I feel, very illuminating,[19] but the

---

[15]This is, I should stress, the basic dilemma that Adam Smith proposed much earlier in his treatise.

[16]Émile Durkheim, *The Elementary Forms of Religious Life* (New York: Free Press, 1947; originally published in 1912).

[17]Ibid., p. 9.

[18]So did some of the early linguists who borrowed from Durkheim. But modern linguistics has turned Durkheim, and those early French thinkers who borrowed from him, "on their heads."

[19]Indeed, at times they are embarrassingly bad. For example, see Émile Durkheim and Marcel Mauss, *Primitive Classification* (Chicago: University of Chicago Press, 1963; originally published in 1903).

general approach can be found in much contemporary structural analysis. But this modern analysis takes a slightly different tack: social structure is, to a very great extent, the mental categories that actors have about their social relations. People use their ideas about how to approach and organize social relations, and in so doing, they reproduce these relations and give them continuity across time. Moreover, they reinforce their ideas about these relations, which then become the cognitive resources and guidelines for subsequent interactions.

Thus, ideas are not floating around freely detached from people; cognitions about social structures are part of individuals' stocks of knowledge. Similarly, social structure is not some ex cathedra entity wholly external to individuals that pushes them around; it is embodied in actors' cognitions and then used as an interactive resource in social relations to produce, reproduce, and potentially change patterns of social relations.

This line of argument, which strikes me as a bit vague but which is asserted with sincerity and seriousness by many modern thinkers, shifts attention away from macrostructure toward microstructural analysis of what individuals in specific encounters actually *think and do* with their stocks of knowledge about social relations. As analysis shifts to the micro foundations of the macro order, Durkheim's ideas on ritual often serve as a conceptual springboard.

3. Durkheim made a simple observation about religious rituals: society is personified in the sacred forces of religions, and so, the worship of these forces is, in fact, the worship of society.[20] Rituals addressed toward gods and supernatural forces are thus an affirmation of the power of society; and as people enact these rituals, they legitimate existing social relations.

In his more discursive statements about the Arunta aborigines in *The Elementary Forms of Religious Life,* Durkheim expanded these ideas somewhat.[21] Rituals among individuals who are gathered together promote a sense of solidarity, a convergence of outlooks, and an increase in social attachments. Using rather distorted accounts of Arunta aborigines, Durkheim believed that data on the periodic gatherings among traditional peoples offered a window on the past; they were, in a sense, "living fossils" about the nature of the first human societies. As a result, Durkheim concluded that society is built from religious rituals that promote social attachments and solidarity as well as a convergence of outlooks.

Contemporary structural theories often extend these ideas further. It is argued that the micro basis of social structure revolves around the daily interaction rituals that people perform in all social encounters. These rituals are essential, it is asserted, for maintaining continuity across social encounters and for giving people a sense of psychological security. Social

---

[20]Durkheim, *The Elementary Forms.*
[21]Ibid.

structure is thus built up from chains of interaction rituals that connect successive encounters together and give individuals psychological security as well as a sense of attachment to a larger social order.

In sum, I think that the major works in Durkheim's career anticipate the various positions in structural analysis today. The early work on size, differentiation, and integration is clearly macrostructural in that social structure is an emergent reality, *sui generis*, and is understandable in terms of its own dynamics.[22] The later works begin to recognize that "the collective force is not entirely outside of us; it does not act upon us wholly from without; but rather, since society cannot exist except in and through individual consciousness, this force must also penetrate us and organize itself within us."[23] And as a result of this recognition, the microfoundations of structure—mental stocks of knowledge and interaction rituals—are increasingly emphasized. Durkheim's first works are thus representative of contemporary macrostructural theory, whereas the later works on religion are incorporated into present-day microstructural theory. And just as Durkheim could never reconcile the two, so contemporary structural theorists grapple unsuccessfully with the relation between micro and macro dimensions of social structure.

## MAX WEBER AND STRUCTURAL ANALYSIS

Max Weber defined sociology as "a science concerning itself with the interpretive understanding of a social action and thereby with a causal explanation of its course and consequences."[24] In actual practice, however, Weber's sociology is decidedly macro in emphasis, although he often attempted to discern what social structural arrangements "mean" to participants in these arrangements. But Weber did confront the micro-macro issues in the beginning portions of his *Economy and Society,* which, though they appear early, were written later in his career as he began to ponder the connection between micro and macro reality.[25]

As I noted in Chapters 2 and 3, Weber's analysis of structure has been more influential on the functional approach of Talcott Parsons than contemporary structuralism. Yet, he addressed the question of how structure is built from action and interaction; and this has increasingly become a concern of structural theorizing. Moreover, his tendency to classify processes with typologies is, I feel, still a prominent mode of analysis in

---

[22]Durkheim, *The Division of Labor.*

[23]Durkheim, *The Elementary Forms*, p. 9.

[24]Max Weber, *Economy and Society* (New York: Bedminister Press, 1968), p. 4.

[25]See Jonathan H. Turner, "The Concept of Action in Sociological Analysis," in *Analytical and Sociological Theories of Action,* ed. G. Seeba and R. Toumea (Dordrecht, Holland: Reidel Publishers, 1985).

structural theorizing, especially that of Anthony Giddens (see Chapter 22).

Weber's conceptual approach led him to visualize "institutional orders" as constructed from social interactions among actors. But Weber never really said *how* this is done. Instead, he generated a series of definitions and typologies. There are types of social actions that lead to types of interaction that, in turn, cause the creation and maintenance of types of institutional orders, or structures. Conversely, types of institutional orders circumscribe the kinds of actions and interactions that can occur. I have not filled in the details of these typologies here, because they are not so relevant as the general approach: visualize types of structure as constructed from types of action and interaction among subjectively oriented actors. But Weber's analysis is highly static because all he really did was classify types of orientations, actions, interactions, and structures. For example, an "economic order" is constructed from actions and interactions among "instrumentally oriented" actors. Such rough correlations among typologies do not tell us very much about *how and through what processes* macrostructures are created, sustained, and changed by microinteractions. Thus, I see Weber's contributions to modern structural thinking as rather minimal. He framed the issue, but his methodology did not allow him to resolve it.

## GEORG SIMMEL'S STRUCTURAL APPROACH

Georg Simmel's influence on modern structural analysis is very direct in the sense that Peter Blau acknowledges his debt to Simmel's analysis of numbers, size, and interaction. In one of his many provocative essays, Simmel observed the effects of increasing numbers on interaction patterns.[26] The form of social relations must, Simmel argued, change with varying numbers of interactants. For example, the nature of interaction changes dramatically when a dyad becomes a triad, since the addition of a third party introduces the possibility of coalitions of two against one. More important for modern macrostructural analysis is Simmel's related observation that as the number of people introduced into an encounter or a group increases, the potential number of ties or relations among them increases exponentially. For example, two people can have only 2 ties, but three can have 6, four can have 12, and so on. The basic insight here is that size affects the kinds of social ties and rates of interaction among individuals and, hence, the form of social structure.[27] Thus, numbers of people become an important macrostructural force because they affect

---

[26]See essays in Kurt Wolff's edited volume on *The Sociology of Georg Simmel* (New York: Free Press, 1950).

[27]This is, in reality, a more precise way of stating Spencer's and Durkheim's analysis of size and differentiation.

rates of interaction; and conversely, the rates of possible interaction among individuals determine the kinds of relations that can be built among them and, thereby, the forms of macrostructure that are possible.

As I stressed in Chapter 6, Simmel also developed an exchange perspective that was directly critical of Marx's approach.[28] He recognized more than Marx did that social interaction involves exchanges of resources among individuals and that the nature of the resources as well as their respective values determine the patterns of social differentiation among actors. The form of differentiation at the macrostructural level is thus produced by the microexchanges among individuals, but once this form is produced, it affects the distribution of actors' respective resources. The result is that it reproduces itself by loading the dice in favor of some actors over others. Yet, as more generalized media, such as money, are used in exchanges, then actors can have more options in their exchanges (since a generalized media can be used in a greater variety of situations). And so, there is more possibility of micro-level exchanges changing an existing structural pattern.

However, I do not think that these exchange ideas have exerted much direct influence on modern structural analysis. They have had to be rediscovered by microstructural theorists, such as Collins (see Chapter 21), who use an implicit exchange theory to analyze the microdynamics of macrostructures. Thus, Simmel cannot be counted among the main progenitors of contemporary structural analysis, even though his ideas have clear relevance for many structural theories.

## INTERACTIONISM AND MICROSTRUCTURALISM

As structural analyses have become more concerned with the interactive processes by which structure is produced and reproduced, they have turned to interactionist theory—primarily ethnomethodology, phenomenology, Chicago School symbolic interactionism, and the work of Erving Goffman.[29] All of these interactionist traditions are built from the conceptual base laid by George Herbert Mead[30] and, to a lesser extent, Alfred Schutz.[31] Let me first examine Mead's ideas that reappear in contemporary structural analysis and then turn to Schutz's approach.

---

[28]Georg Simmel, *The Philosophy of Money* (Boston: Routledge & Kegan Paul, 1978).

[29]See, for example, Erving Goffman, *The Presentation of Self in Everyday Life* (Garden City, N.Y.: Doubleday Publishing, 1959); *Behavior in Public Places* (New York: Free Press, 1963); *Forms of Talk* (Boston: Blackwell Scientific Publications, Inc., 1981).

[30]George Herbert Mead, *Mind, Self, and Society* (Chicago: University of Chicago Press, 1934).

[31]Alfred Schutz, *The Phenomenology of the Social World* (Evanston, Ill.: Northwestern University Press, 1967; originally published in 1932).

## G. H. Mead's Behavioristic Structuralism

As I noted in Chapter 14, Mead was a social behaviorist. By this, he meant that those behavioral capacities that facilitate adjustment to the social environment will be retained by a maturing individual. They are retained because they are reinforced by virtue of the fact that they facilitate adjustment to ongoing patterns of social organization. What, then, are these behavioral capacities that facilitate adjustment to social structures? For Mead, they are (1) the capacity to assume the perspective of a variety of others (role-taking); (2) to see oneself as an object in situations and to adjust response in accordance with self-perceptions and evaluations (self); and (3) to engage in the process of "imaginative rehearsal" of alternative lines of conduct and their potential outcomes (mind).

For Mead, existing social structures—that is, organized and coordinated activities among individuals—exert "selection pressures" for the development of capacities for role-taking, self, and mind. Once these capacities exist, they allow individuals to adjust their conduct to others, thereby making coordinated activities or social structures possible.[32]

With these basic elements, Mead presents a general image of social organization as constructed and actively sustained through the mutual reading of gestures (role-taking), the evaluation of oneself from the perspective of generalized others (self) or "communities of attitudes," and the reflexive weighing of alternatives (mind). These ideas are, today, very much a part of most microstructural approaches. For it is through capacities for role-taking, self-reflection, and minded thought that social structure is produced and reproduced. Yet, most micro approaches tend to underemphasize Mead's view that social structure—that is, existing ways of coordinating activities—constrain and circumscribe the options of individuals. In particular, Mead stressed role-taking with the generalized other and self-evaluation in terms of communities of attitudes. That is, structure is reproduced by people's use of general attitudes (values, beliefs, and norms in modern terms) as well as by spontaneous interpersonal practices. For most microstructuralists, however, this emphasis on "cultural" and "normative" constraints smacks of Parsonian functionalism, and so they steer away from it. Moreover, microstructuralists tend to ignore Mead's conception of self as relatively stable across situations and as providing a compass by which acts are ordered and structured in a given direction and with a consistent interpersonal style.

Microstructuralists thus take only part of Mead's legacy, where emphasis is on situational interpersonal practices. They tend to ignore Mead's emphasis on conformity to generalized others and on acts sustaining a

---

[32]For more detail, see Jonathan H. Turner, "A Note on G. H. Mead's Behavioristic Theory of Social Structure," *Journal for the Theory of Social Behavior* 12 (July 1984), pp. 213–22.

stable self-conception. And when they do address this question of symbolic constraints, microstructuralists more frequently turn to Alfred Schutz.

## Alfred Schutz

Microstructuralists seem to prefer Schutz's conceptualization of <u>stock knowledge</u> at hand to Mead's notion of generalized others and to modern conceptions of roles, values, beliefs, and norms. I assume that this preference comes from the metaphorical idea of stocks that can be used selectively as the actor wants and desires. Schutz's conception would appear to de-emphasize explicit normative constraints and roles. But does it? Let me quote Schutz:

> Now, to the natural man all his past experiences are present as *ordered* (italics in original), as knowledge or as awareness of what to expect, just as the whole external world is present to him as ordered. Ordinarily, and unless he is forced to solve a special kind of problem, he does not ask questions about how this ordered world was constituted. The particular patterns of order we are now considering are synthetic meaning—configurations of already lived experience.[33]

For me, Schutz's view emphasizes constraint. Norms, values, beliefs, roles are indeed highly salient parts of one's implicit and, if need be, explicit interpretation of a situation. They "order" experiences and lines of conduct. But for microstructuralists, the concept of stock knowledge is meant to connote something much less ordered and structured. For them, it is a series of vaguely held cognitions that are used to construct lines of conduct in strategic conduct. Thus, while some structuralists take Schutz's label, I do not think that they use it in the way that he intended.

Just as is done for Mead's concept of the generalized other, microstructuralists de-emphasize the *imposition* of cultural ideas—norms, values, beliefs, roles—on individuals. They want to stress the active process of reproduction of social relations rather than the reactive process of conformity to norms and roles. In this way, they can distinguish their efforts from those of functionalists like Talcott Parsons.

## MODERN STRUCTURAL ANALYSIS

As this brief review of Marx's, Spencer's, Durkheim's, Weber's, Simmel's, Mead's, and Schutz's ideas would indicate, modern structural theory goes in two directions within sociology. First, there is a macrostructural approach concerned with structural properties—size, differentiation, heterogeneity, inequality, and the like—and their consequences for the

---

[33]Schutz, *The Phenomenology of the Social World,* p. 81.

integration of social structures. When interaction is examined, it is conceptualized in terms of rates or even as random process.[34] Second, there is a more microstructural approach that views structure as constructed from interaction. Such microapproaches typically attempt to integrate macro and micro levels of analysis, whereas macroapproaches do not.

There is a third line of structural argument, which might be termed *structuralism.* As I have mentioned, I do not think that this strategy has much to offer sociological theory because it becomes excessively mentalistic and often reductionistic, seeing social structures as expressions of genetic mental codes. I do not want to give this mentalistic structuralism much emphasis because it is not very theoretical, but in the appendix, I offer a quick review of its most prominent advocate, Claude Lévi-Strauss.

Much more significant, I think, are the more sociological efforts of (1) Peter Blau, whose recent work is a good example of a macrostructural approach, (2) Randall Collins, whose work is increasingly microstructural (although there is an effort to redefine macro and integrate it with micro-level analysis), and (3) Anthony Giddens, whose "structuration theory" explicitly attempts to synthesize macro- and microanalysis (although I think it is essentially a microtheory). These authors are performing highly creative structural analyses. And hence, I will emphasize their work in the next three chapters. But for those who want a glimpse of a more mentalistic structural approach, I offer this appendix.

# APPENDIX: THE STRUCTURALISM OF CLAUDE LÉVI-STRAUSS

In recent decades, Claude Lévi-Strauss has become a dominant figure in anthropology, and in the last few years, sociologists with a mentalistic and reductionist bias have been attracted to his work. In Chapter 10 on the emergence of exchange theory, I briefly examined Lévi-Strauss's analysis of bridal exchanges. In *The Elementary Structure of Kinship,*[35] Lévi-Strauss only hints at the more philosophical view of the world that his analysis of kinship implies.[36] Most of his book examines the varying levels of social solidarity that emerge from direct and indirect bridal exchanges among kin groups. Yet, in many ways, *The Elementary Structure of Kinship* is a transitional work between his intellectual debt to Émile

---

[34]See, for example, the "baseline approach" of Bruce H. Mayhew and various collaborators. In particular, consult his argument in a special issue of *The Journal of Mathematical Sociology* 9 (4, 1984).

[35]Claude Lévi-Strauss, *The Elementary Structures of Kinship* (Paris: University of France, 1949).

[36]Actually, an earlier work, "The Analysis of Structure in Linguistics and in Anthropology," *Word* 1 (1945), pp. 1–21, provided a better clue as to the form of Lévi-Strauss's structuralism.

Durkheim[37] and Marcel Mauss.[38] There are, however, also clear departures from Durkheim and Mauss, which signal that Lévi-Strauss was to "turn Durkheim on his head" in much the same way that Marx was to revise Hegel. For as Durkheim and Mauss had argued in *Primitive Classification*, human cognitive categories reflect the structure of society.[39] In contrast, Lévi-Strauss's structuralism came to the opposite conclusion: the structure of society is but a surface manifestation of fundamental mental processes.

Lévi-Strauss came to this position under the influence of structural linguistics, as initially chartered by Ferdinand de Saussure[40] and Roman Jakobson. Ferdinand de Saussure is typically considered both the father of structural linguistics[41] and of Lévi-Strauss's structuralism. In reality, as a contemporary of Durkheim, de Saussure was far more committed to Durkheim's vision of reality than is typically acknowledged. Yet, he made a critical breakthrough in linguistic analysis of the 19th century: speech is but a surface manifestation of more fundamental mental processes.[42] Language is not speech nor the written word; but rather, it is a particular way of thinking, which, in true Durkheimian fashion, de Saussure viewed as a product of the general patterns of social and cultural organization among people. This distinction of speech as a mere surface manifestation of underlying mental processes was to increasingly be used as a metaphor for Lévi-Strauss's structuralism. Of course, this metaphor is as old as Plato's view of reality as a mere reflection of universal essences and as recent as Marx's dictum that cultural values and beliefs, as well as institutional arrangements, are reflections of an underlying substructure.

Lévi-Strauss also borrows from the early 20th-century linguist Roman Jakobson the notion that the mental thought underlying language occurs in terms of *binary contrasts,* such as good-bad, male-female, yes-no, black-white, and human-nonhuman. Moreover, drawing from Jakobson and others, Lévi-Strauss views the underlying mental reality of binary opposites as organized, or mediated, by a series of "innate codes" or rules that can be used to generate many different social forms: language, art,

---

[37]See notes 10 and 16.

[38]Marcel Mauss, *The Gift* (New York: Free Press, 1954; originally published in 1924) is given particular credit. It must be remembered, of course, that Mauss was Durkheim's student and son-in-law.

[39]Émile Durkheim and Marcel Mauss, *Primitive Classification.* Originally published in 1903, this is a rather extreme and unsuccessful effort to show how mental categories directly reflect the spatial and structural organization of a population. It is a horribly flawed work, but it is the most extreme statement of Durkheim's sociologistic position.

[40]Ferdinand de Saussure, *Course in General Linguistics* (New York: McGraw-Hill, 1966); originally compiled posthumously by his students from their lecture notes in 1915.

[41]I suspect that this is a retrospectively bestowed title by those looking for their intellectual roots.

[42]Such analysis had focused on the written languages of Europe, seeking their evolutionary origins.

music, social structure, myths, values, beliefs, and so on.[43] Thus, over the last decades, Lévi-Strauss's structuralism has become concerned with understanding cultural and social patterns in terms of the universal mental processes that are rooted in the biochemistry of the human brain.[44] It is in this sense that Lévi-Strauss's structuralism is mentalistic and reductionistic. And for this reason, I do not think that it is sociologically very useful.[45] Indeed, it is more philosophy than science. Yet, since it now generates so much intellectual interest, even in sociology, let me at least summarize its basic line of argument.[46]

Without enumerating the full complexity (and vagueness) of his approach, I see the following as the critical steps and built-in assumptions of Lévi-Strauss's theoretical (philosophical) strategy:

1. The empirically observable must be viewed as a *system* of relationships among components—whether these components be elements of myths and folktales or positions in a kinship system.
2. It is appropriate to construct "statistical models" of these observable systems to summarize the empirically observable relationships among components.
3. Such models, however, are only a surface manifestation of more fundamental forms of reality. These forms are the result of using various codes or rules to organize different binary opposites. Such forms can be visualized through the construction of "mechanical models," which articulate the logical results of using various rules to organize different binary oppositions.
4. The tendencies of statistical models will reflect, imperfectly, the properties of the mechanical model. But it is the latter that is "more real."
5. The mechanical model is built from rules and binary oppositions that are innate to humans and rooted in the biochemistry and neurology of the brain.

---

[43]Actually, Jakobson simply argued that children's phonological development occurs as a system in which contrasts are critical—for example, "papa versus mama" or the contrasts that children learn between vowels and consonants. Lévi-Strauss appears to have added the jargon of information theory and computer technology.

[44]See, for example, Claude Lévi-Strauss, "Social Structure," in *Anthropology Today,* ed. A. Kroeber (Chicago: University of Chicago Press, 1953), pp. 524–53; *Structural Anthropology* (Paris: Plon, 1958; trans. 1963 by Basic Books); and *Mythologiques: le cru et le cuit* (Paris: Plon, 1964).

[45]For relevant critiques, see Marvin Harris, *The Rise of Anthropological Theory* (New York: Thomas Y. Crowell, 1968), pp. 464–513, and Eugene A. Hammel, "The Myth of Structural Analysis" (Addison-Wesley Module, no. 25, 1972).

[46]See, for example, Mirian Glucksmann, *Structuralist Analysis in Contemporary Social Thought* (London: Routledge & Kegan Paul, 1974). A more sympathetic review of Lévi-Strauss, as well as a more general review of structuralist thought, can be found in Tom Bottomore and Robert Nisbet, "Structuralism," in their *A History of Sociological Analysis* (New York: Basic Books, 1978).

Steps 1 and 2 are about as far as Lévi-Strauss went in the first publication of *The Elementary Forms of Kinship*. Subsequent work on kinship and on myths has invoked at least the rhetoric of Steps 3, 4, and 5. What makes structuralism distinctive, therefore, is the commitment to the assumptions and strategy implied in these last steps. The major problem with this strategy is that it is untestable, for if mechanical models are never perfectly reflected in the empirical world, how is it possible to confirm or disconfirm the application of rules to binary opposites? As Marshall Sahlins sarcastically remarked, "What is apparent is false and what is hidden from perception and contradicts it is true."[47] I think that there are more profitable ways to analyze social structure, and so, let me now turn to them in the next three chapters.

---

[47]Marshall D. Sahlins, "On the Delphic Writings of Claude Lévi-Strauss," *Scientific American* 214 (1966), p. 134.

# CHAPTER 20

# The Macrostructuralism of Peter M. Blau

In Chapter 12, I examined Peter Blau's exchange structuralism. In this review of Blau's exchange theory, the tension among processes of differentiation, integration, and conflict figured prominently. In recent years, Blau has examined these basic processes with an alternative theory, which he labels *macrostructural*.[1] Although his earlier theory can still prove useful to those working within the exchange theoretic perspective, Blau's macrostructuralism is clearly intended to replace and supplant his exchange theory. In this recent effort, Blau attempts to develop a more rigorous theory that follows from a more clearly articulated view of theory construction than was evident in his earlier exchange theory.[2] In my analysis to follow, I will concentrate, respectively, on the strategy, substance, and theoretical format of Blau's new theory.

## BLAU'S THEORETICAL STRATEGY

Blau's new work is explicitly deductive and advocates a "covering law" vision of theory (see Chapter 1). In Blau's view, a scientific theory is a

---

[1]See Peter M. Blau, *Inequality and Heterogeneity: A Primitive Theory of Social Structure* (New York: Free Press, 1977); "A Macrosociological Theory of Social Structure," *American Journal of Sociology* 83 (July 1977), pp. 26–54; see also "Contrasting Theoretical Perspectives," in *The Micro-Macro Link,* ed. J. C. Alexander, B. Gisen, R. Munch, and N. J. Smelser (Berkeley, Calif.: University of California Press, in press).

[2]Indeed, he views his work on exchange as a prolegomenon—a kind of pretheory, which, by its nature, would be unsystematic. Indeed, in Chapter 12, I had to extract the theoretical principles.

"hierarchical system of propositions of increasing levels of generality. All lower order propositions follow in strict logic from higher order ones alone."[3] In developing such a theory, a number of steps are critical, and their successful implementation is what typifies good theory.

First, theory must begin with a conception of the basic subject matter—that is, what is to be explained? In deductive theory, the phenomenon to be explained by a theory is termed the *explicandum.* For Blau, the explicandum is the "pattern of relations between people in society, particularly those of their social relations that integrate society's diverse groups and strata into a distinct coherent social structure."[4]

In addressing this range of phenomena, Blau offers a narrow definition of macrostructure. Discussions of social structure, Blau notes, typically recognize "that there are differences in social positions, that there are social relations among these positions, and that people's positions and corresponding roles influence their social relations."[5] But most theoretical efforts extend the conceptual inventory, adding such notions as psychological needs, cultural values and beliefs, norms, technological forces, class antagonisms, dialectics, and functions, In contrast to these tendencies, Blau prefers to postulate a narrow view of social structure as consisting of the distributions of people among different social positions and their associations.

> To speak of social structure is to speak of differentiation among people. For social structures, as conceptualized, are rooted in the social distinctions people make in their role relations and social associations.[6]

Yet, when one examines an entire society, a community, or any macrostructure, analysis becomes more complicated. The number of people and positions to be analyzed is great. Moreover, people occupy many different positions simultaneously—religious, familial, neighborhood, work, recreational, political, educational, and the like. Thus, for each type of position, there is a separate distribution of the population, making a macrostructure a "multidimensional space of social positions among which people are distributed and which affect their social relations."[7] But how are all these relations among large numbers of people occupying simultaneously many different positions to be analyzed? In Blau's portrayal, microstructural analysis would seek to analyze each and every relation among all people in all positions, but when the numbers of people, po-

---

[3]Peter M. Blau, "Elements of Sociological Theorizing," *Humboldt Journal of Social Relations* 7 (Fall-Winter, 1979–80), p. 105. This article contains Blau's statement of his theoretical strategy that is outlined in this section.

[4]Ibid., p. 112.

[5]"A Macrosociological Theory of Social Structure," p. 27.

[6]Ibid., p. 28.

[7]Ibid.

sitions, and relations become large, macrostructural analysis must be concerned with the general "patterns of social relations among different social positions occupied by many persons, not with the networks of all relations between individuals."[8] This is done by defining social positions in terms of common attributes of people—age, sex, race, occupation, religion—and then by examining their overall rates of association. Note that not every person nor every association is examined—only general categories of people and overall rates of association among people in these categories. In this way, macrostructural theory is distinguished from the microstructural approaches, sociometry, and network analysis.[9]

Thus, Blau's "concept of the basic subject matter" to be examined is similar to many previous theoretical approaches in that it is concerned with how different groups and social strata come to form integrated or conflictual social wholes. But in contrast to most efforts on this topic, I see Blau as taking a very narrow view of social structure that excludes many variables, such as the cultural and psychological, that are typically included in traditional orientations. Yet, this narrow definition of structure is macro in focus, for unlike microanalysis of groups where each and every position and relation is plotted, concern is with the general attributes that distinguish types of people and that influence their overall rates of association.

A second critical element in building theory is "familiarity with relevant empirical knowledge." The often rigid line between deduction and induction is artificial, Blau argues, since deduction rarely occurs in an empirical vacuum. Indeed, the very questions to be answered by a deductive theory are typically the result of interesting empirical findings. Thus, to know what it is that a theory should explain requires familiarity with existing empirical generalizations.[10]

A third element in a theory is the "creative insight" that is typically embodied in a "central theoretical term" or "operator." An operator "supplies the organizing principle for the major theoretical propositions."[11] In Blau's theory, the central concept is the *intersection of parameters*. A parameter in Blau's theory is simply the criterion by which a position is distinguished—such as age, sex, race, income, wealth, education, or any basis that people use to distinguish one another and that consequently affects their rates of association. The intersection of parameters denotes the fact that parameters are variously correlated with each other. When

---

[8]Ibid.

[9]Actually, as network analysis begins to deal with larger populations, they do as Blau advocates. See, for example, Harrison C. White, Scott A. Boorman, and Ronald L. Breiger, "Social Structure from Multiple Networks I," *American Journal of Sociology* 81 (January 1976), pp. 730–80.

[10]Blau's empirical work on organizations and socioeconomic status preceded his theoretical efforts. He has thus followed his own advice.

[11]Blau, "Elements of Sociological Theorizing," p. 107.

parameters intersect, occupancy in one position is not likely to be correlated with, or to predict, occupancy in another. For example, race in some societies may not be associated with income; nor is prestige associated with education. Conversely, when parameters consolidate, they reveal high correlations—race and income as well as education and prestige are highly correlated in that being of a particular racial group predicts income or level of education, which, in turn, assign a person a corresponding level of prestige. Intersecting parameters reduce divisions in a society because, under this condition, people associate with a diversity of others in at least some of their positions. In contrast, *consolidation of parameters* tends to create divisions in a society since positions cluster together in ways that reduce associations with others outside a particular circle of associations. For instance, the wealthy in most societies live in certain neighborhoods, attend private schools, engage in recreation only with each other, and hold other consolidated positions. The result is that they are separated from others who are not wealthy in society. Thus, for Blau, "the degree to which parameters intersect, or alternatively consolidate differences in social positions through their strong correlations, reflects the most important structural conditions in a society, which have crucial consequences for conflict and for social integration."[12]

A fourth central element of theory building is conceptual clarification of key terms, especially of the operator. For Blau, such clarification involves distinguishing patterns of differentiation in terms of two basic types of parameters. One basic type is a "nominal parameter," which divides people into different groups that are not rank ordered. The other type is the "graduated parameter," which differentiates people in terms of hierarchical status rankings. Thus, all macrostructures reveal varying degrees of differentiation in terms of nominal and graduated parameters. When people are differentiated into many groups in terms of numerous nominal parameters, then a high degree of "heterogeneity" exists. That is, when two randomly chosen people are unlikely to belong to the same group, heterogeneity is high. When people are differentiated into widely different status positions on the basis of graduated parameters, then "inequality" is high. That is, when the differences in relative standing among people distinguished by a graduated parameter are great, inequality is high. Thus, differentiation varies along two axes, heterogeneity and inequality.[13] The specific dynamics of such differentiation are to be understood with additional concepts, which I will discuss shortly when the theory itself is examined, but the notion of intersecting parameters is still the key operator, since it increases heterogeneity and decreases inequality.

A fifth important element in theory construction is the development of a deductive system—that is, the incorporation of concepts into prop-

---

[12]Blau, "A Macrosociological Theory of Social Structure," p. 32.
[13]Blau, *Inequality and Heterogeneity*, p. 281.

ositions and then the hierarchical ordering of them. Although Blau uses the vocabulary of axiomatic theory, his system of propositions is what I termed *formal theorizing* in Chapter 1, because it does not evidence the rigor of true axiomatic theory (for as I emphasized, very little theory in the social sciences can meet the criteria of axiomatic theory). In Blau's view, the ordering of propositions involves (a) the articulation of a number of simple assumptions as axioms and (b) the development of theorems that apply these assumptions to generic types of social relations. For example, Blau's most basic assumption is that social associations are more prevalent among persons in proximate positions than among those in distant social positions. Thus, people at similar ranks or in the same group are more likely to interact than those in divergent ranks or different groups. With this and other assumptions to be discussed shortly and with the central operator and additional concepts, Blau can then generate a number of theorems that explain why events in the empirical world should occur. The essence of Blau's theory thus involves the articulation of some simple axioms or assumptions and the incorporation of these into theorems that state relations among carefully defined concepts that have empirical referents.

The final element of theory construction involves "confronting the theory with empirical data." There are two types of data to be used in such confrontations. One is the existing data, which can be interpreted and understood in terms of the theory. Another is the rigorous deduction of hypotheses from the theorems, which serve to organize the collection of new data.[14]

In sum, then, the creative act of theory construction involves (1) a conception of what is to be explained, (2) familiarity with relevant knowledge, (3) a central term or operator, (4) conceptual elaboration and clarification, (5) a deductive system of propositions, and (6) confrontation of the theory with empirical data. This vision has clearly guided the substantive formulation of Blau's theory of macrostructure.

## BLAU'S THEORY OF MACROSTRUCTURE

Blau argues that in some theories the primitive assumptions represent brilliant insights and mark the real contribution of the theory. In contrast, other theories state obvious and simplistic assumptions that are viewed as givens and are taken for granted. In such theories, "the contribution of the theory rests on the new knowledge derived from the systematic analysis of the implications of combinations of simple assumptions and definitions."[15] Blau views his theory as belonging to this second type.

---

[14]Blau has attempted to do so. For example, see his and Joseph E. Schwartz's, *Crosscutting Social Circles* (Orlando, Fla.: Academic Press, 1984).

[15]Ibid., p. 245.

Simple assumptions, or axioms, serve as premises for theorems, with the result that the power of the theory to explain events resides in its theorems and in subsequent deductions from these theorems to specific empirical cases.

One problem with axiomatic theory in general and with Blau's execution of this strategy is the proliferation of propositions. Blau articulates 21 assumptions, 34 major theorems, and more than 150 subtheorems (corollaries) in many different "sets of theorems." In its present form, then, I find the theory unmanageable. Much of this problem resides, I believe, in the fact that the major theorems are stated at different levels of abstraction and, as a result, they overlap a great deal. Indeed, I find some to be little more than empirical generalizations that illustrate a relationship stated in a more abstract theorem. Another problem is Blau's insistence that axioms must represent simple assumptions and that 21 such assumptions are necessary to generate all of the theorems.[16] Moreover, Blau argues each axiom must represent a primitive assumption that is not derivable from another assumption. Thus, any theory that begins with more than 20 assumptions can generate 34 theorems rather easily and many more corollaries besides. But such a theory branches out in so many directions that it loses the elegance and coherence of powerful theories.

Most of these problems can be overcome, I think, if Blau's narrow and restrictive view of axiomatic theory is relaxed. Thus, in presenting the theory, I will remove some of Blau's restrictions. In particular, I will shorten the list of assumptions and include only the most critical ones. Moreover, I will eliminate the redundancy among the theorems. In Table 20–1, I have listed Blau's "axioms" after this necessary surgery.[17] From these axiomatic premises, there are four basic theorems in Blau's theory. I have listed these in Table 20–2. All other theorems in Blau's scheme can, I believe, be derived from these and, hence, constitute corollaries of these four major theorems listed.

In Table 20–2, Theorem I asserts that if people occupy different positions in many groups and ranks and that if these positions are not highly correlated, then diverse and varied associations are likely to ensue. Conversely, if occupancy in one group or rank is highly correlated with positions in other groups or ranks, then opportunities for associations with other people are more limited, and associations will be with the same persons. The effects of such intersection and consolidation become amplified, as is stated in Theorem II. Consolidation will become amplified because, as Axioms III and IV stress, people usually come to know and like friends of their friends, and once such relations are established, they

---

[16]See Blau, "Elements of Sociological Theorizing," p. 10.

[17]See my earlier effort along these lines: Jonathan H. Turner, "A Theory of Social Structure: An Assessment of Blau's Strategy," *Contemporary Sociology* 7 (November 1978), pp. 698–705.

**TABLE 20–1** A Revised List of Blau's "Axioms"

I. People in a society associate with others not in their group or status rank.

II. Social associations among people in proximate positions are more prevalent than those in distant positions.
   A. In-group associations are more prevalent than out-group associations.
   B. The prevalence of associations declines with increasing status distance.

III. Established relations are resistant to disruption.

IV. Strangers who have common associates become, over time, associates.

V. Associates in other groups or strata often facilitate mobility to these groups or strata.

VI. The distribution of status positions is skewed so that there are always fewer high-ranking positions than middle- and low-ranking positions.

VII. Social associations depend upon opportunities for social contact.

VIII. The influences of various parameters on social associations are partly additive and not always contingent on each other.

**TABLE 20–2** A Revised List of Blau's Basic Theorems

I. The more multiple parameters intersect and remain unconsolidated, the greater is the degree of heterogeneity and the less is the level of inequality, and hence, the more likely are social associations among people (from Axioms I, II, and VII).

II. The more multiple parameters intersect or consolidate, the more likely is their effect on social associations to exceed the additive effects of the parameters alone (from Axioms I, III, IV, and VIII).

III. The more parameters intersect, the greater is the rate of mobility, and the more likely are social associations (from Axioms I, II, V, and VII).

IV. The greater is the size differences between two groups or status ranks distinguished by a parameter, the more likely are social associations among members in the smaller group or rank with members of the larger group to exceed those of members in the larger group with those in the smaller (from Axioms I, II, VI, and VII).

resist disruption. Intersection tends to become amplified for the same reasons, but this process continually expands. This is because, in contrast to consolidation, which creates closed circles of associations, intersection constantly creates new opportunities for additional social association. Theorem III states that intersection creates opportunities for mobility, since as Axiom V posits, people tend to help each other be mobile. And once people are mobile, their opportunities for social association increase, but additionally, as Axiom III argues, they tend to maintain their old social relations that they had before mobility. Theorem IV states a mathematical truism, or the law of proportion. If there are reciprocal relations between groups or ranks of different size, then these reciprocal relations must constitute a larger proportion of the total relations in the smaller group. That is, it has fewer people who can potentially generate relations, whereas the larger group has more people who can have a greater number of total relations; therefore, the same number of reciprocal relations must represent a greater portion of the smaller than the larger groups' total relations.

From these four theorems, then, I believe that most other theorems in Blau's many "theorem sets" can be derived.[18] Probably the most interesting of the many examples that I could offer concern those that can be derived from Theorem I on intersecting parameters and Theorem IV on proportions. For example, Blau's Theorem 26 postulates that "the further society's differentiation penetrates into successive subunits of its structural components, the more it promotes the integration of groups by increasing intergroup relations."[19] This theorem is directly derivable from the notion of intersection versus consolidation of parameters (Theorem I above). If a pattern of differentiation—for example, inequality of wealth—repeats itself in every community in a society (this is successive penetration), then the wealthy and not so wealthy people are more likely to interact than if all wealthy people live in one community and all poor people in another (this would be consolidation of wealth with community). Since societies or any social system vary in terms of degrees of such successive penetration, their integration will also vary.

Let me take another example. In Table 20–2, Blau's Theorem IV states that members of smaller groups or strata have more relations as a proportion of their total with larger groups or strata than do members of larger groups or strata with those in smaller groups.[20] Thus, since the distribution of people in status ranks will reveal a pyramid form, at least from the middle ranks upward,[21] high-ranking people are more likely to have relations with lower-ranking persons than are lower-ranking with higher-ranking persons. Such a simple artifact of mathematical proportions can help explain, perhaps, the hostility of lower ranks toward higher ranks, with whom they have little contact. Race and ethnic relations can similarly be analyzed in this way, since majority members, who are the larger group, are less likely to have relations with the minority than is the minority with the majority. As a result, stereotypes and prejudice can be more readily maintained when there is little contact by the majority, especially when the processes described by this proportion principle are exacerbated by the processes described in the intersection of parameters principle (since minority status is often highly correlated with other positions that the majority does not occupy).

Blau's basic theorems suggest many ways to analyze concrete empirical cases, as Blau seeks to do throughout his work with various theorems

---

[18]I suspect that Blau would disagree with this.

[19]See Blau, *Inequality and Heterogeneity,* p. 183.

[20]See Ibid., pp. 42 and 73.

[21]Sometimes the lowest ranks are small, thereby creating a diamond-shaped distribution.

and as he has done in his research.[22] As he emphasizes, these efforts all address the basic issue of social integration. For he assumes that social contact and association among differentiated positions promote cooperation and accommodation. Integration is thus viewed as the result of high rates of interaction among people in different groups and strata. But, differentiation poses barriers to interaction and association. As can be seen by the theorems listed above, or by a review of Blau's numerous propositions, the theorems state structural conditions that promote or retard social associations and, hence, integration. But unlike many other analyses of this basic topic, Blau's propositions are purely structural and pertain to the number of positions, their degree of intersection or consolidation or their degree of inequality and heterogeneity, and the distribution of people in these positions.

The theory is, of course, much more complex than my presentation here, but the general profile and intent of his approach is clear. Such a structural approach, cast into a formal format, offers considerable promise, but it is not without problems. Let me close, therefore, by offering a brief assessment of this theoretical approach.

## MACROSTRUCTURALISM: AN ASSESSMENT

Blau has isolated what he defines as two basic properties of the social universe—heterogeneity and inequality as they are determined by the consolidation or intersection of parameters. He has also developed some abstract principles about the dynamics inherent in these. This is, I believe, the best way to develop theory; and as I have said elsewhere, I consider this effort one of the most significant of this century.[23] Having said this, however, I will mention what I see as two limitations.

First, I think that the theory is too functional. In Figure 20–1, I have diagramed Blau's basic model to highlight this implicit functionalism. In a subtle way, Blau assumes a functional need for integration of society and views high rates of interactions as the way to meet this need. The theoretical question then becomes one of determining what macrostructural forces affect rates of interaction. His answer: intersection and consolidation of parameters as they determine the respective levels of heterogeneity and inequality in a population. Many objections to this kind of functional reasoning are immediately obviated by the fact that Blau translates his ideas into propositions where the dependent variable is "social association" and "rates of interaction" without any functional trimmings (about "needs," "requisites," and the like). Nonetheless, I raise the issue because it limits the range of phenomena about which Blau is

[22]Blau and Schwartz, *Crosscutting Social Circles.*
[23]Turner, "A Theory of Social Structure," p. 705.

**FIGURE 20–1**   Blau's Functional Imagery

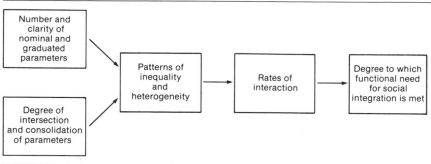

willing to theorize. If the need for integration is the implicit theoretical question, then only those properties of the universe that are relevant to this issue will be present in a theory—in Blau's case, rates of interaction and parameters.

A second and related objection to Blau's theory is that it excludes so much. Interaction is conceptualized as a rate rather than as a process; roles are relegated to their effects on parameters; values, beliefs, norms, and other idea systems are eliminated or only viewed as relevant to the extent that they help people define parameters; and the social-psychological properties of the universe, such as self-conceptions and other cognitions of humans, are simply eliminated. Moreover, the theory cannot tell us why a given set of parameters exists in the first place; instead, we are only told about their functional consequences. Thus, I think that Blau's theory achieves parsimony by eliminating many critical dynamics of the social universe, including those responsible for variations in his own theoretical variable (nominal and graduated parameters).

Thus, in the end, Blau offers an interesting set of abstract propositions on "rates of interaction" among populations of individuals. This is not, however, a trivial issue, because I believe that many of the dynamics of social structure are affected by such rates of interaction. But at the same time, much is excluded. And so, I view Blau's theory as an important contribution to only one dimension of macrostructure, rates of interaction as these are affected by two very critical properties of social structure, inequality and heterogeneity. But this is not all there is to human organization, even when viewed in macrostructural terms; and approaches that claim otherwise will, for all their insight, be too limiting.

# CHAPTER 21

# The Microstructuralism of Randall Collins

## THE MICRO AND MACRO REALMS

In contrast to the macrostructuralism of Peter Blau stands the microstructuralism of Randall Collins. For Blau and other macrostructuralists, "structures" can be conceptualized as emergent phenomena that influence rates of interaction, whereas for Collins "structures" can best be understood in terms of the microprocesses that are aggregated in space and across time to produce and sustain them.

I have termed Collins's approach *microstructural* because of his assertion that most sociological conceptions of structure are reifications and metaphors. He does not deny the existence of social structures and macro reality; rather, he argues that macro theories often disconnect structures from the very processes by which they are constituted. For Collins asks: what is structure and what does it really look like? His answer in early works is, itself, somewhat metaphorical:

> Imagine the view of human society from the vantage point of an airplane. What we can observe are buildings, roads, vehicles, and—if our senses were keen enough—people moving back and forth and talking to each other. Quite literally, this is all there is; all of our explanations and all of our subjects to be explained must be grounded in such observations. "Social structure" could be brought into such a picture if we understand that men live by anticipating future encounters and remembering past ones. Structure is recurring sorts of encounters. An imaginary aerial time-lapse photograph, then, would render social structure as a set of light streaks showing the heaviness of social traffic. If we go on to imagine different colored streaks corresponding to the emotional quality of contacts—perhaps gray for purely formal relations, brown for

organizational relations infused with more personal commitments, yellow for social relations, and red for close personal friendships—we would have an even more significant map.[1]

Recent work has been more explicit.[2] Social structure is conceptualized as "chains of interaction rituals" that are stretched out in time through their repetition by individuals in concrete settings. That is, if encounters among individuals are repeated again and again over time, then there is a structure to their interaction. Social structure becomes ever more macro when there is an increasing number of persons involved in social encounters and an extension of the physical space in which these encounters occur.[3] Thus, for Collins macrostructure consists of only three dimensions: (1) the sheer numbers of persons and encounters involved; (2) the amount of time consumed by an encounter and the degree to which it is connected to previous encounters; and (3) the amount and pattern of physical space used to emit the interaction rituals that typify an encounter. The more encounters are repeated across time, the more people that are involved; and the more space that is consumed, then the more macro is a social structure.

This is, I think, a very extreme line of argument, for macrostructure is defined simply by space, number, and time. In Figure 21-1, I have simplified a figure used by Collins to illustrate this point.[4] Across the top of the figure is listed a crude time scale, ranging from seconds to centuries. And down the left side I have indicated the number of people involved and the space utilized in encounters. Within the body of the figure, illustrative structures are mentioned. As one moves from the upper left to lower right portions of the figure, one also goes from micro- to macroanalysis.

With respect to the time dimension, one critical issue is the length of time consumed by an encounter in which interaction occurs; and another more important issue is the degree to which each encounter is a link in a chain of encounters. Thus, a one-time interaction that lasts only a few seconds or minutes is sociologically much less interesting than encounters involving various interactive rituals that are repeated again and again. In Collins's eyes, then, sociological theory should be most

---

[1]Randall Collins, *Conflict Sociology: Toward an Explanatory Science* (New York: Academic Press, 1975), p. 56.

[2]Randall Collins, "On the Micro-Foundations of Macro-Sociology," *American Journal of Sociology* 86 (March 1981), pp. 984–1014; "Micro-translation as a Theory Building Strategy," in *Advances in Social Theory and Methodology: Toward an Integration of Micro- and Macro-Sociology*, ed. K. Knorr-Cetina and A. V. Cicourel (London: Routledge & Kegan Paul, 1981); and "Interaction Ritual Chains, Power and Property: The Micro-Macro Connection as an Empirically-Based Theoretical Problem," in *The Micro-Macro Problem*, ed. J. C. Alexander et al. (Berkeley, Calif.: University of California Press, in press).

[3]Collins, "Interaction Ritual Chains."

[4]Collins, "On the Micro-Foundations of Macro-Sociology."

**FIGURE 21–1**  Micro and Macro: Time, Space, and Number

| Square feet | Number of persons | Time | | | | | |
|---|---|---|---|---|---|---|---|
| | | Seconds | Minutes | Hours | Days | Years | Centuries |
| 1-3 | Person | MICRO | | | | Life-history | Genealogy |
| $3-10^2$ | Several persons | Fleeting encounters | | Small groups | | | |
| $10^3-10^6$ | Several hundred to thousands | | | | Crowds, organizations, communities, social movements, | | |
| $10^7-10^{14}$ | Thousands to millions | | | | | Societies | |
| | | | | | | Empires | |
| | | | | | | | MACRO |

interested in "chains of interaction rituals" that extend across time. Such chains represent a life history for an individual when enacted over years; and if over generations, then they are part of a genealogy. More interesting sociologically, however, are chains of interaction among several people in an encounter, especially if interaction rituals are repeated over relatively long time periods. And if there are many individuals linked together, directly and indirectly, through chains of interaction rituals and who use ever larger amounts of space, then social structures become increasingly macro. Micro and macro in reality are, therefore, on a continuum that, at the extreme micro end, involves few people using little space in short-term interactions and that, at the macro end, involves very complex and long-term chains of direct and indirect interaction among large numbers of people extended across physical space.

As is evident, Collins does not reject macro reality as a phenomena worth studying. But there is an important implication in his position: the macro world is constructed from chains of interaction. There can be variation with respect to the number of people involved, the length of time consumed, and the amount of space utilized, but the one invariant property of structure is interaction among people. Social structure is ultimately chains of interaction rituals, and so, sociological theory must emphasize what individuals actually do, for "structures never do anything; it is only persons in real situations who act."[5] Thus, a theory of social structure must seek the "energizing processes" of social structure in the interactions of individuals. Theory must explain macrostructures in terms of principles that help us understand how micro interactions are stretched over time, expanded in number, and extended across space.

Unlike other theorists who have made similar assertions, Collins does not advocate a micro reduction of macroprocesses. Explanation of macrostructural processes is not simply a matter of asserting that the only reality is the individual in interaction. We cannot, Collins would argue, merely outline how people interact and leave the matter settled. Instead, theory must provide principles that inform us about how and through what processes interactions are stretched across time in chains of encounters and aggregated in space among increasing numbers of individuals. Thus, a theory of social structure must address the macro variables of time, space, and number if it is to say anything about those structures of most interest to sociologists—groups, organizations, crowds, social classes, societies, empires, and the like.

I think that this attention to macrostructural processes makes Collins's approach unique among those who stress the interactive foundations of structure. Moreover, he emphasizes that many interactive encounters occur within an existing macrostructure (built, of course, from past chains of interaction) that determines the number of people present, their respective resources, how long they will interact, and where they will position themselves in space. As they interact, they reproduce the macrostructure or potentially change it. And so, there is almost always a reciprocity between the purely micro, interactive dimensions of social reality and the macro context in which these microprocesses occur.

Yet, the "energizer" behind social reality is the interaction ritual. Macrostructures are created, sustained, and changed at the level of what people in interaction do in their encounters. And thus, the central task of sociological theory is to develop some principles about interaction rituals. Surprisingly, Collins's early work left many of these interaction processes somewhat implicit, moving rather quickly away from microanalysis of interaction to macrostructural concerns about organizations, the state, geopolitics, and the like. It is only recently that he has sought to explicate in more detail a theory of "interaction ritual chains."[6] Let me review the tentative and provisional outlines of this latest theory and then return to Collins's earlier work, which still, I think, represents his most significant contribution to sociological theory.

---

[5]Collins, "Interaction Ritual Chains."
[6]Ibid.

# INTERACTION RITUAL CHAINS

I see Collins's conceptualization of "interaction ritual chains" as a mixture of exchange theory, portions of interactionism, and perhaps elements of psychoanalytic theory. His perspective is clearly an exchange theory because he visualizes social life as a constant negotiation among individuals with resources trying to strike bargains with each other in social markets. It is interactionist with an ethnomethodological twist in that there is heavy emphasis on conversation and talk as key resources in social markets. And it is psychoanalytic since emotion is viewed as the underlying motivational force behind interaction and social structure. Yet, as Collins mixes these three traditions together, he becomes an intellectual alchemist, blending them with the ideas of Marx, Weber, and Durkheim to produce a new and highly original theoretical approach.

For Collins, the basic micro unit of analysis is the "encounter" of at least two people who confront each other and interact. The encounter is, in Collins's words, a "shared conversational reality" and will involve negotiations among individuals who possess varying resources and motivations to participate in the interaction.[7] That is, people will have resources, such as stored memories of previous conversations, vocal styles, special knowledge, access to wider communication networks, the capacity to call upon others to support their position or to coerce, the right to determine the physical location of parties, and so on. These resources can be defined as an individual's "cultural capital." People will also bring a given level of motivation, or "emotional energy," to participate in the conversation in a particular manner. Just how people feel about an encounter will, to a very great extent, influence what transpires in the present and in future encounters.

As people negotiate their shared conversational reality by using their cultural capital and expending their emotional energy, they are, in essence, negotiating over their respective membership in groups.[8] Indeed, the more issues of inclusion or exclusion from group membership are involved in an encounter, the more intense will be the negotiation among individuals, and the more will individuals spend their cultural capital and expend their emotional energies.

When individuals' levels of cultural capital are equal and their motivations are similar—for example, in a conversation among friends—the parties can all increase their cultural capital (memories, vocal styles) and their emotional energy (their "good feelings" about the encounter). However, many social encounters are among unequals in that some have more cultural capital and motivational energy to expend than others. Those with more capital and emotion can control the conversation, dictating

---

[7]Ibid.

[8]Ibid.

topics, content, and even where people stand and what they are allowed to say. For example, an authoritative boss in an office speaking to a subordinate has more cultural capital—the ability, for instance, to control pay, dictate where people work—and more emotional energy to mobilize in the conversation (since it will be more rewarding for the superordinate than subordinate). Thus, the boss will increase both his or her cultural capital (affirmation of dominance) and emotional energy (feelings of control) from the conversation, whereas the employee will lose capital and energy (memories of being told what to do and bad feelings about subordination). Such encounters will, if repeated and stretched across time, become highly formal and ritualized with the subordinate expending as little energy and capital as possible at each meeting.

Most encounters are, of course, less extreme than this example. There is usually room for more negotiation in a conversational encounter. Moreover, most encounters are structured in terms of previous encounters, in several senses. First, parties know what to expect in terms of their memories and previous feelings about the conversation, and hence, they can take care to use their resources wisely and appropriate the correct amount of emotional energy. Second, many encounters are circumscribed by the macro system as it has been constructed from chains of past encounters. There is usually a physical place where talk occurs; there is usually a typical number of others in the situation; and there is a normal duration for a conversation in a situation. Thus, an encounter in a grocery store, in a school classroom, and in other well-known contexts where the macrostructure delimits place, number, and duration and where people already have a sense for the right mixture of cultural capital and emotional energy will proceed with relative ease and with a high degree of ritual (stereotyped sequences of talk).

The repetition of such encounters—for example, each day at home, the office, and school—is what builds and sustains structures. And as these ritualized chains of interaction embrace increasingly larger numbers of people and are extended in space in various configurations, they produce and reproduce macrostructures.

There is an important methodological corollary to this line of theoretical argument.[9] If macrostructures are produced and sustained by chains of interaction rituals among individuals using cultural capital and expending emotional energy, then one should study structure by sampling encounters across time. By sampling encounters over time, it becomes possible to have a sense for what people are doing—how they talk, gesture, position themselves as well as how they feel about what is occurring. Such a strategy for studying social structure involves what Collins calls *micro*

---

[9]Collins, "Micro-translation as a Theory-building Strategy" as well as "Micro-methods as a Basis for Macro-sociology," *Urban Life* 12 (1983), pp. 184–202.

*translation* of macrostructures. That is, if macrostructures are nothing more than complex chains of interaction rituals stretched across time and space among large numbers of people, then to understand such structures, we need to "translate" them into those interactive processes from which they are constituted—interaction rituals chains. Research projects should not, therefore, sample at one point in time with questionnaires, but rather, they should select encounters over time where people can be observed talking to each other.

Much of Collins's substantive and methodological arguments are in their formative stages. The analysis of interaction ritual chains is still preliminary and evolving. For this reason, I find the line of argument often vague and imprecise, but I think that the essentials have been summarized.

With the more recent approach in mind, I now want to return to Collins's earlier work, which he entitled *conflict sociology*.[10] There is no great incompatibility between this recent and earlier work, but there is a shift in vocabulary. Conversation, ritual, and negotiation are prominent in Collins's early work, although the introduction of emotion as the coinage of interaction rituals is given more emphasis in recent works. But the emphasis on inequality of resources and how people deal with this fact is prominent in both the earlier and later conceptual work. And the willingness to move back and forth between the micro reality of conversations to the macro dynamics of world geopolitics (see Figure 21-1) is also evident in both the older and newer work.[11] As I proceed to review Collins's conflict sociology, which is in reality an exchange perspective, I will try to reconcile the vocabularies of the earlier conflict approach with the more recent emphasis on chains of interaction rituals.

## CONFLICT SOCIOLOGY

Collins's general argument about the interactive foundations of social structure and the effects of the macro dimensions of space, time, and size on interaction were anticipated in earlier works. In *Conflict Sociology*, Collins proposed the following steps for building social theory.[12] First, examine typical real-life situations where people encounter each other. Second, focus on the material arrangements that affect interaction—the physical layout of situations, the means and modes of communication, the available tools, weapons, and goods. Third, assess the relative resources

---

[10]It really should have been "exchange sociology," but I guess that "conflict sociology" sounded better and appealed more to the bias of sociology. See his *Conflict Sociology*.

[11]See, for example, Randall Collins, "Long-term Social Change and the Territorial Power of States" in his *Sociology Since Midcentury: Essays in Theory Cumulation* (New York: Academic Press, 1981).

[12]Collins, *Conflict Sociology*, pp. 60–61.

that people bring to, use in, or extract from encounters. Fourth, entertain the general hypotheses that those with resources press their advantage, that those without resources seek the best deal they can get under the circumstances, and that stability and change are to be explained in terms of the lineups and shifts in the distribution of resources. Fifth, assume that cultural symbols—ideas, beliefs, norms, values, and the like—are used to represent the interests of those parties who have the resources to make their views prevail. Sixth, look for the general and generic features of particular cases so that more abstract propositions can be extracted from the empirical particulars of a situation.

Thus, as with his recent work on interaction rituals, there is a concern with the encounter, with the distribution of individuals in physical space, with their respective capital or resources to use in exchanges, and with inequalities in resources. As with his recent work, the respective resources of individuals are critical: "power" is the capacity to coerce or to have others do so on one's behalf; "material resources" are wealth and the control of money as well as property or the capacity to control the physical setting and people's place in it; and "symbolic resources" are the respective levels of linguistic and conversational resources as well as the capacity to use cultural ideas, such as ideologies, values, and beliefs, for one's purposes.

A central consideration in all of Collins's propositions is "social density," or the number of people co-present in a situation where an encounter takes place. Social density is, of course, part of the macrostructure since it is typically the result of past chains of interaction. But it can also be a "material resource" that some individuals can use to their advantage. Thus, the interaction in an encounter will be most affected by the participants' relative resources and the density or number of individuals co-present. These variables influence the two underlying micro dynamics in Collins's scheme, talk, and ritual.

## Talk and Ritual

For Collins, talk is the emission of verbal and nonverbal gestures that carry meaning and that are used to communicate with others and to sustain (or create) a common sense of reality. Collins classifies conversations among people in terms of the type of talk employed, including "practical conversations" (used to accomplish ends or goals), "ideological conversations" (used to arouse emotions to legitimate certain actions and situations), "intellectual conversation" (discussions of ideas and issues), "entertainment talk" (conversation for its own enjoyment), "gossip" (discussions and evaluations of acquaintances), and "personal talk" (discussions of oneself).[13] Since talk is one of the key symbolic resources of

---

[13]Ibid., pp. 114–31.

---

**TABLE 21–1**  Key Propositions on the Conditions Producing Talk and Conversation

I. The likelihood of talk and conversational exchanges among individuals is a positive and additive function of (a) the degree of their physical co-presence; (b) the emotional gratifications retained from their previous conversational exchanges; (c) the perceived attractiveness of their respective resources; and (d) their level of previous ritual activity.

II. The greater is the degree of equality and similarity in the resources of individuals, the more likely are conversational exchanges to be (a) personal; (b) flexible; and (c) long-term.

III. The greater is the level of inequality in the resources of individuals, the more likely are conversational exchanges to be (a) impersonal; (b) highly ritualized; and (c) short-term.

IV. The greater is the amount of talk among individuals, especially among equals, the more likely are (a) strong, positive emotions; (b) sentiments of liking; (c) common agreements, moods, outlooks, and beliefs; and (d) strong social attachments sustained by rituals.

---

individuals in encounters, much of what transpires among interacting individuals is talk and the use of this cultural capital to develop their respective lines of conduct. In Table 21-1, I have listed some of Collins's propositions on conversations, which, I should add, have been altered somewhat in order to make them more parsimonious and to reconcile them with his more recent terminology. As can be seen from Proposition I in Table 21-1, the likelihood that people will talk is related to their sheer co-presence, for if others are near, one is likely to strike up a conversation. More important sociologically are conversations that are part of a "chain" of previous encounters. If people felt good about a past conversation, they will usually make efforts to have another; and if they perceive each others' resources, especially symbolic or cultural but also material ones, as desirable, then they will seek to talk again. And if they have developed ritualized interaction that affirms their common group membership, they will be likely to enact those rituals again. As Proposition II indicates, conversations among equals who share common levels of resources will be more personal, flexible, and long-term because people feel comfortable with such conversations. As a result, the encounter raises their levels of emotional energy and increases their cultural capital. That is, they are anxious to talk again and to pick up where they left off. However, the nature of talk in an encounter changes dramatically when there is inequality in the resources of the participants. As Proposition III emphasizes, subordinates will try to avoid wasting or losing emotional energy and spending their cultural capital by keeping the interaction brief, formal, and highly ritualized with trite and inexpensive words. Yet, as Proposition IV argues, even under conditions of inequality and even more when equality exists, people who interact and talk in repeated encounters will tend, over time, to develop positive sentiments and will have positive emotional feelings. Moreover, they will also converge in their definitions of situations and develop common moods, outlooks, beliefs, and ideas. And finally, they will be likely to develop strong attachments and a sense of group solidarity, which is sustained through rituals.

As can be seen from the above propositions, rituals are a central element of any encounter. Following Durkheim[14] and extending the analysis of ritual to include Erving Goffman's[15] vision of "everyday" interaction, Collins views rituals as comparatively stereotyped sequences of gestures that people emit to create and sustain a particular type of social relation. Thus, rituals are not just confined to formal actions confirming the sacred or the body politic; they are the essence of normal encounters among people in each of their life spheres: home, work, recreation, neighborhood, and the like. Understanding the conditions under which varying rituals are generated is thus central to an analysis of microsocial processes or, for that matter, any macro pattern. Thus, much of what is actually observable about societies and social systems is ordinary people talking to each other and engaging in a variety of interaction rituals that allow them to create, sustain, and alter a sense of reality.

Unfortunately, Collins's articulation of theoretical principles in this area is somewhat disjointed. He formalizes—most insightfully I should add—Durkheim's theory of ritual and social solidarity from *Elementary Forms of the Religious Life* (see Chapter 2), and he supplements this analysis with insights from Malinowski's and Radcliffe-Brown's work.[16] The end result is the propositions listed in Table 21-2. As can be seen from Proposition I, ritual activity increases with the presence of others, with the duration of their presence, and with the degree to which they are pursuing common issues and questions. And as rituals increase, so do people's common attachments and outlooks, as I have indicated in Proposition II. That is, as people in situations talk and develop ritual ways of addressing each other, they begin to develop emotional attachments, and they accumulate an investment of cultural capital over successive encounters. As their levels of emotional and cultural investment in the chain of encounters increase, they develop a sense of group solidarity, which is sustained by the very rituals that produced it (see Principle V in Table 21-2). Moreover, as a group's sense of boundedness increases,

---

[14]Émile Durkheim, *The Elementary Forms of the Religious Life* (New York: Free Press, 1948; originally published in 1912).

[15]See, for example, *The Presentation of Self in Everyday Life* and other works by Erving Goffman, including: *Encounters* (Indianapolis, Ind.: Bobbs-Merrill, 1961); *Interaction Ritual* (New York: Anchor Books, 1967); and *Behavior in Public Places* (Glencoe, Ill.: Free Press, 1963).

[16]See A. R. Radcliffe-Brown, *The Andaman Islanders* (New York: Free Press, 1948; originally published in 1922); Bronislaw Malinowski, *Magic, Science and Religion* (Garden City, N. Y.: Doubleday Publishing, 1948).

**TABLE 21–2**   Key Propositions on the Conditions Producing Ritual Activity

*Durkheim's Principles*

I. The degree of ritual activity among individuals is a positive and additive function of (*a*) the extent of actors' physical co-presence; (*b*) the length of actors' physical co-presence; (*c*) the number of actors physically co-present; and (*d*) the degree of common focus among actors.

II. The degree of social attachment and common outlook among individuals is a positive function of their degree of ritual activity.

III. The greater is the degree of ritual activity sustaining social attachments and common outlook among individuals, the more likely will deviations from established rituals be negatively and severely sanctioned.

*Malinowski's Principle*

IV. The greater is the physical danger of activities among individuals, the greater is their likelihood of invoking rituals that previously promoted social attachments and a common outlook.

*Radcliffe-Brown's Principle*

V. The greater is the level of social attachment and common outlook among individuals in a group, the greater will be ritual activity during (*a*) movements of individuals into or out of the group; and (*b*) movement of individuals to new positions within the group.

movement into or out of the group will be marked by rituals (ranging, for example, from greetings of welcome to a tear-filled farewell party).

Thus, the essence of interaction is talk and ritual; and as chains of encounters are linked together over time, conversations take on a more personal and also a ritualized character that results from and, at the same time, reinforces the growing sense of group solidarity among individuals. Such is the case because the individuals have "invested" their cultural capital (conversational resources) and have derived positive feelings from being defined as group members. I do not think that Collins has developed these ideas to any great extent, but we can see his intent: to view social structure as the linking together of encounters through talk and ritual. This basic view of the micro reality of social life pervades all of Collins's sociology, especially as he begins to move to the analysis of inequalities in social life.

## Deference and Demeanor

Inequality and stratification are structures only in the sense of being temporal chains of interaction rituals among varying numbers of people with different levels of resources. Thus, to understand these structures, it is necessary to examine what people actually do across time and in space. One thing that they do in interaction is exhibit deference and demeanor. Collins and his coauthor Joan Annett define *deference* as the process of manipulating gestures to show respect to others; or if one is in a position to command respect, the process of manipulation of gestures is to elicit respect from others.[17] The actual manipulation of gestures is termed *demeanor.* Deference and demeanor are, therefore, intimately connected to each other. They are also tied to talk and rituals, since talk involves the use of gestures and since deference and demeanor tend to become ritualized. Hence, deference and demeanor can be visualized as one form of talk and ritual activity—a form that is most evident in those interactions that create and sustain inequalities among people.

Collins visualizes several variables as central to understanding deference and demeanor:

1. Inequality in resources, particularly wealth and power.
2. Social density variables revolving around the degree to which behaviors are under the "surveillance of others" in a situation.
3. Social density variables revolving around the degree to which communications networks are "cosmopolitan" (i.e., unrestricted to others who are co-present in a situation).

In Table 21–3, these variables are incorporated into a few abstract propositions that capture the essence of Collins's and Annett's numerous propositions and descriptions of the history of deference and demeanor.[18] In these propositions, Collins and Annett argue that rituals and talk revealing deference and demeanor are most pronounced between people of unequal status, especially when their actions are observable and when communication outside the situation is restricted. Such density and surveillance are, of course, properties of the macrostructure as it distributes varying numbers of people in space. As surveillance decreases, however, unequals avoid contact or perform deference and demeanor rituals in a perfunctory manner. For example, military protocol will be much more pronounced among an officer and enlisted personnel in public on a military base than in situations where surveillance is lacking (e.g., off the base). Moreover, Collins and Annett stress that inequalities and low mobility between unequal groups create pressures for intragroup deference and demeanor rituals, especially when communications outside the group are low (for example, among new army recruits and their officers or among prison inmates and guards). But as communication outside the group increases and/or as surveillance by group members decreases, then deference and demeanor will decrease.

## Class Cultures

These microprocesses of talk, ritual, deference, and demeanor explain what are often seen as more macroprocesses in societies. One such process

---

[17]Randall Collins and Joan Annett, "A Short History of Deference and Demeanor," in *Conflict Sociology*, pp. 161–224.

[18]Ibid., pp. 216–19.

---

**TABLE 21–3**  Key Propositions on Deference and Demeanor

---

I. The visibility, explicitness, and predictability of deference and demeanor rituals and talk among individuals is a positive and additive function of:

  A. The degree of inequality in resources among individuals, especially with respect to:

   1. Material wealth.
   2. Power.

  B. The degree of surveillance by others of behaviors emitted by individuals, with surveillance being a positive function of:

   1. The extent to which others are co-present.
   2. The degree of homogeneity in outlook of others.

  C. The restrictiveness of communication networks (low cosmopolitanism), with restrictiveness being a negative function of:

   1. The degree of complexity in communications technologies.
   2. The degree of mobility of individuals.

II. The greater is the degree of inequality among individuals and the lower is the level of surveillance, the more likely are behaviors to be directed toward:

  A. Avoidance of contact and emission of deference and demeanor by individuals.
  B. Perfunctory performance of deference and demeanor by individuals when avoidance is not possible.

III. The greater is the degree of inequality among individuals and the lower is the level of cosmopolitanism among individuals, the more likely are behaviors to be directed toward simplified but highly visible deference and demeanor.

IV. The greater is the degree of inequality among individuals, and the less is the degree of mobility among groups with varying levels of resources, the more visible, explicit, and predictable are deference and demeanor rituals and talk within these groups.

V. The greater is the equality among individuals, and the greater is the degree of cosmopolitanism and/or the less is the level of surveillance, the less compelling are deference and demeanor talk and rituals.

---

is variation in the class cultures. That is, people in different social classes tend to exhibit diverging behaviors, outlooks, and interpersonal styles. These differences are accountable in terms of two main variables:

1. The degree to which one possesses and uses the capacity to coerce, to materially bestow, and to symbolically manipulate others so that one can give orders in an encounter and have these orders followed.
2. The degree to which communication is confined to others who are physically co-present in a situation, or conversely, the degree to which communication is diverse, involving the use of multiple modes of contact with many others in different situations.

Utilizing these two general classes of variables, which are part of the macrostructure that has been built up in past chains of interaction as well as several less central ones such as wealth and physical exertion on the job, Collins describes the class cultures of American society. More

**TABLE 21–4**   Key Propositions on Class Cultures

I. Giving orders to others in a situation is a positive and additive function of the capacity to mobilize and use coercive, material, and symbolic resources.

II. The behavioral attributes of self-assuredness, the initiation of talk, positive self-feelings, and identification with the goals of a situation are a positive function of the capacity to give orders to others in that situation.

III. The behavioral attributes of toughness, courage, and action in a situation are a positive function of the degree of physical exertion and danger in that situation.

IV. The degree of behavioral conformity exhibited in a situation is a positive function of the degree to which people can communicate only with others who are physically co-present in that situation and is a negative function of the degree to which people can communicate with a diversity of others who are not physically co-present.

V. The outlook and behavioral tendencies of an individual are an additive function of those spheres of life—work, politics, home, recreation, community—where varying degrees of giving-receiving orders, physical exertion, danger, and communication occur.

significantly for theory building, he also offers several abstract propositions that stipulate certain important relationships among power, order-giving, communication networks, and behavioral tendencies among individuals. I have restated these relationships in somewhat altered form in Table 21-4.[19] With these principles, Collins explains variations in the behaviors, outlooks, and interpersonal styles of individuals in different occupations and status groups. For example, those occupations that require order-giving, that reveal high co-presence of others, and that involve little physical exertion will generate behaviors that are distinctive and that circumscribe other activities, such as whom one marries, where one lives, what one values, and what activities one pursues in various spheres of life. Different weights to these variables would cause varying behavioral tendencies in individuals. Thus, it is from the processes delineated in the propositions of Table 21-4 that understanding of such variables as class culture, ethnic cultures, lifestyles, and other concerns of investigators of stratification is to be achieved. But such understanding is anchored in the recognition that these class cultures are built up and sustained by interaction chains where deference and demeanor rituals have figured prominently. Thus, a class culture is not mere internalization of values and beliefs as well as simple socialization (although this is no doubt involved), but rather, it is the result of repeated encounters among unequals under varying conditions imposed by the macrostructure as it has been built up from past chains of interaction.

---

[19]Collins, *Conflict Sociology*, pp. 49–88.

---

**TABLE 21–5**  Key Propositions on Sex Stratification

---

I. Control over sexual activities between males and females as well as talk and ritual activities is a positive and additive function of:

  A. The degree of one sex's control over the means of coercion, which is a negative function of:

   1. The existence of coercive powers outside sexual partners and family groupings (such as the state).
   2. The presence of relatives of the subordinate sex.

  B. The degree to which one sex controls material resources, which is a positive and additive function of:

   1. The level of economic surplus in a population.
   2. The degree to which key economic activities are performed by one sex.
   3. The degree to which resources are inherited rather than earned.

II. The greater is the degree of control of sexual relations and related activities by one sex, the more likely are sexual relations to be defined as property relations, and the more likely are they to be normatively regulated by rules of incest, exogamy, and endogamy.

III. The greater is the degree of control of sexual relations and related activities by one sex, the greater will be the efforts of the other sex to:

  A. Reduce sexual encounters.
  B. Regulate them through ritual.

---

## Sexual Stratification

The propositions in Tables 21–1 through 21–4 represent, I think, Collins's theoretical approach to the analysis of stratification. The propositions in these tables provide the basic principles for the analysis of specific forms of stratification, such as those created by age and sexual categories. For as is clearly evident, stratification for Collins is a process that occurs in types of encounters among individuals in diverse spheres of life. One such sphere is encounters between males and females that become organized into family relations and elaborated into kinship systems. In Table 21–5, I have summarized some of Collins's propositions on sexual stratification. Deductions from these, Collins implicitly argues, can help explain the nature of talk and ritual between the sexes as well as the structuring of male-female encounters in kinship systems. These latter deductions are not produced in the table, but Collins provides numerous additional propositions[20] and discursive text[21] to illustrate the properties and dynamics of sexual stratification.

These propositions can, in Collins's eyes, explain the diversity in chains of sexual encounters and the resulting structure of family systems. For example, in societies where females perform much of the economic

---

[20]Ibid., pp. 281–84.

[21]Ibid., pp. 225–59; see also the relevant chapters in his *Family Sociology* (Chicago: Nelson-Hall Publishers, 1985).

---

**TABLE 21–6**   Key Propositions on Age Stratification

---

I. The degree of age stratification among individuals is a positive and additive function of the degree to which individuals in one age group control (a) the means of coercion; (b) material resources; (c) symbolic resources (e.g., capacity to evaluate actions in terms of moral values); and (d) sociability (e.g., access to peers, recreation, and related activities).

II. The form of control exercised by individuals in one age group over individuals in another age group is a direct function of the types of resources that are most controlled by the dominant groups (see I(a), (b), (c), (d) above).

III. The greater is the degree of age stratification, the greater is the level of ritual interaction between individuals in different age groups, and conversely, the more equally balanced are the resources between age groups, the less is the level of ritual activity between individuals in different age groups.

IV. The greater are the efforts by individuals of one age group to control individuals in another age group but the greater the level of resources available to individuals of subordinate age groups, the greater is the level of conflict between individuals of different age groups.

---

labor and where wealth is passed through the female line (as is the case in matrilineal kinship systems), male dominance is greatly mitigated. Or in American society, females who enter the labor force possess resources to counter the males' control of the means of coercion, thereby reducing male dominance (especially since the state rather than kin groups is the ultimate source of coercive power in the society). Conversely, women who do not work are often forced to counter the economic and coercive power of males by limiting sexual encounters and by ritualizing such encounters when they do occur. Many other specific forms of male-female stratification can, in Collins's view, be explained by making deductions from these abstract propositions to specific empirical cases. But such explanations do not rely upon concepts of norms, values, and roles. Rather, they emphasize the respective resources that people have and how these determine what happens in an encounter as well as how structures are built up from chains of encounters among individuals with varying resources.

## Age Stratification

Another universal form of stratification is by age, which, like sexual relations, involves control of resources by individuals in one age group and efforts by individuals in subordinate age groups to mitigate their situation in daily encounters. I have listed several of Collins's key propositions on this in Table 21–6. These propositions can, I think, explain variations in age stratification.[22] For example, among poor families in America, parents often possess only physical coercion in abundance (not having money,

---

[22]Collins, *Conflict Sociology*, pp. 259–81.

much leisure, or capacity to provide recreation), whereas youth often possess counterresources of their own, such as extensive peer relations and moral codes of peer evaluation that are built up from chains of encounters among themselves. The result is often high levels of conflict between parents and children. In contrast, affluent parents possess many resources, such as money, the capacity to schedule recreation, and the time to impose and sanction moral standards. As a result, they typically resort to coercion as a punishment of last resort, only after material incentives, moral shaming, or withholding of leisure-time privileges fail to generate conformity to parental dictates. Interaction in such families will, despite its seeming informality, involve the use of ritual and talk in clear deference and demeanor activities. Similar kinds of analyses can, I believe, be made of other societies using these principles as premises from which deductions to specific empirical cases can be made.

## Organizational Processes

After examining stratification processes, Collins turns to an extensive analysis of organizations and develops a rather long inventory of propositions on their properties and dynamics.[23] These propositions overlap, to some degree, with those on stratification, since an organization is typically a stratified system with a comparatively clear hierarchy of authority. In Table 21-7, I have extracted only three groups of propositions from Collins's analysis. These revolve around processes of organizational control, the administration of control, and the general organizational structure. Other topic areas in Collins's inventory are either incorporated into these propositions or omitted. Moreover, I have rephrased considerably the propositions and have also stated them at a higher level of abstraction than in Collins's text. By placing the propositions at a high level of abstraction, I think that they can explain political control in more than complex organizations; in my view, they would seem relevant to understanding other patterns of social organization, such as entire societies.

Even as Collins begins to examine more macrostructures, like bureaucratic organizations, it is evident that the conceptual emphasis is on microprocesses. Organization control, its administration, and the general structure of an organization are all created and sustained by people using resources in encounters. As these encounters are repeated, the chains of interactions develop a structure, whose profile depends on the respective levels and types of resources possessed by participants.

## The State and Economy

Collins develops propositions on many topics in *Conflict Sociology,* but I will close with an illustration of his more purely macroanalysis of the

---

[23]Ibid., pp. 286–347.

**TABLE 21–7** Key Propositions on Organizations

### Processes of Organizational Control

 I. The degree of control in patterns of social organization is a positive and additive function of the concentration among individuals of (a) coercive resources; (b) material resources; and (c) symbolic resources.

 II. The form of control in patterns of social organization is a function of the type of resource that is concentrated in the hands of those individuals seeking to control others.

 III. The more control is sought through the use of coercive resources, the more likely are those subject to the application of these resources to (a) seek escape; (b) fight back, if escape is impossible; (c) comply if the above are impossible and if material incentives exist; and (d) sluggishly comply if the above do not apply.

 IV. The more control is sought through the use of material resources, the more likely are those subject to the manipulation of material incentives to (a) develop acquisitive orientations; and (b) develop a strategy of self-interested manipulation.

 V. The more control is sought through the use of symbolic resources, the more likely are those subject to the application of such resources to (a) experience indoctrination into values and beliefs; (b) be members of homogeneous cohorts of recruits; (c) be subject to efforts to encourage intraorganizational contact; (d) be subject to efforts to discourage extraorganizational contact; (e) participate in ritual activities, especially those involving rites de passage; and (f) be rewarded for conformity with upward mobility.

### Administration of Control

 VI. The more those in authority employ coercive and material incentives to control others, the greater is the reliance on surveillance as an administrative device to control.

 VII. The more those in authority use surveillance to control, the greater is (a) the level of alienation by those subject to surveillance; (b) the level of conformity in only highly visible behaviors; and (c) the ratio of supervisory to nonsupervisory individuals.

 VIII. The more those in authority employ symbolic resources to control others, the greater is their reliance on systems of standardized rules to achieve control.

 IX. The greater is the reliance on systems of standardized rules, the greater is (a) the impersonality of interactions; (b) standardization of behaviors; and (c) the dispersion of authority.

### Organizational Structure

 X. Centralization of authority is a positive and additive function of (a) the concentration of resources; (b) the capacity to mobilize the administration of control through surveillance, material incentives, and systems of rules; (c) the capacity to control the flow of information; (d) the capacity to control contingencies of the environment; and (e) the degree to which the tasks to be performed are routine.

 XI. The bureaucratization of authority and social relations is a positive and additive function of (a) record-keeping technologies; (b) nonkinship agents of socialization of potential incumbents; (c) money markets; (d) transportation facilities; (e) nonpersonal centers of power; and (f) diverse centers of power and authority.

---

**TABLE 21–8**  Key Propositions on the State, Economy, and Ideology

I.  The size and scale of political organization is a positive function of the productive capacity of the economy.

II.  The productive capacity of the economy is a positive and additive function of (*a*) level of technology; (*b*) level of natural resources; (*c*) population size; and (*d*) efficiency in the organization of labor.

III.  The form of political organization is related to the levels of and interactive effects among (*a*) size of territories to be governed; (*b*) the absolute numbers of people to be governed; (*c*) the distribution and diversity of people in a territory; (*d*) the organization of coercive force (armies); (*e*) the distribution (dispersion or concentration) of power and other resources among a population; and (*f*) the degree of symbolic unification within and among social units.

IV.  The stability of the state is a negative and additive function of:

　A.  The capacity for political mobilization by other groups, which is a positive function of:

　　1.  The level of wealth.
　　2.  The capacity for organization as a status group (see I–V in Table 21–2; I, III, and VI in Table 21–3).

　B.  The incapacity of the state to resolve periodic crises.

---

state and economy.[24] A cursory look at Table 21–8 reveals, I think, few references to individuals at the micro level. One might, as Collins would insist, make micro translations of the processes incorporated into the propositions, but it is clear that Collins abandons discussions of micro-interactional ritual chains when he begins to talk about large-scale social processes. And even his insistence that the macro is no more than size, number, and time seems somewhat strained, although population size and extent of territory are crucial variables in the propositions.

## MICROSTRUCTURALISM: AN ASSESSMENT

I think that Collins's work is among the most creative in social theory today. Its great strength resides in the effort to develop abstract propositions about fundamental properties of the universe. For unlike so many in social theory today, Collins is not so antipositivist that he must retreat into an excessive relativism and solipsism.

A related strength in Collins's approach is his willingness to theorize. Meta-theoretical pontification is minimal; and he gets right down to the business of developing propositions about the social universe. Moreover, he is willing to theorize about a wide range of phenomena in terms of just a few fundamental ideas. He thus achieves breadth of substantive analysis without an overly elaborate conceptual scheme. Instead, he makes deductions from a limited number of basic propositions.

---

[24]Ibid., pp. 348–413.

Equally significant, I think, is that Collins's work is filled with creative insights. He takes ideas from diverse intellectual traditions and combines them with his own ideas to produce works that are stimulating. For in the end, theory is not just mechanical induction or deduction; it involves creative leaps of imagination, and Collins's work is filled with them.

The substantiveness of Collins's theoretical approach reflects this creativity. He has sought to conceptualize the basic nature of interaction and how it produces and reproduces more macrostructures, and vice versa. At times, I think that he argues too polemically as to the micro basis of reality, but his conceptualization of the micro realm in terms of inter-action ritual chains among actors using resources to their advantage and the macro realm in terms of chains of encounters that are strung out in time and stretched in space among various numbers of individuals is, I believe, a useful way to look at the social world. Simply stated in these terms, however, Collins's work would not be so interesting. But as he translates these metaphorical ideas into abstract propositions, the approach begins to come to life.

But there are, I think, some major problems with the approach. First, despite his assertion that much existing social theory is metaphorical in its conception of structure, I find his own formulations rather vague and metaphorical. He rarely defines concepts precisely; and he shifts his vocabulary in ways that often make it difficult to get a clear grasp of even such central concepts as resources, power, coercion, property, wealth, negotiations, encounters, rituals, and structures. Indeed, as I have presented his ideas in this chapter, I have had to make many inferences about his meaning. I think that Collins gets away with this vagueness in concept formation because he writes so well. Indeed, he is probably the best writer in academic sociology today, and because he can be so engaging, he can also be conceptually very slippery and vague.

A second problem is that in Collins's *Conflict Sociology* and elsewhere, there is a lack of deductive rigor in the propositions. There are simply too many propositions that overlap each other and that do not follow from well-articulated axioms, corollaries, and theorems. Naturally, it can be argued that at the more preliminary stages of theory building such deductive precision is not possible nor even desirable. To lose richness of insight in the name of theoretical elegance and precision is obviously not desirable in an immature science like sociology. Yet, with more than 400 propositions in *Conflict Sociology*, Collins's inventory becomes unmanageable. In many ways, my reformulations of Collins's propositions represent an attempt to make them more manageable. But in the end, Collins will need to articulate some basic theorems if his theoretical strategy is to realize its full potential.

If this latter effort is made, one suspects that the "axioms" or highest-order propositions would look very much like those of exchange theory (see chapters 10–13). For in the final analysis, Collins's propositions typically deal with (1) the respective resources of individuals, (2) the effort to use resources to advantage and to avoid heavy costs in the process, (3) the differentiation of individuals in terms of their respective resources, and (4) the processes by which such differentiation is regularized, on the one hand, and is the source of conflict and change, on the other. Collins's ideas on "interaction ritual chains" do this to some extent, but only in a most imprecise and metaphorical sense. I believe that considerably more attention should be devoted to rigorous definitions of concepts and explicit formulation of his implicit exchange theoretic propositions. In this way, the full potential of this microstructural approach can be realized.

# CHAPTER 22

# The Structuration Theory
## of Anthony Giddens

Among the recent efforts to redirect sociological theorizing is Anthony Giddens's work on what he terms *the theory of structuration*.[1] In a critical fashion, Giddens has mounted a consistent line of attack against existing forms of theorizing, particularly functionalism, Marxism, structuralism, phenomenology, portions of traditional symbolic interactionism, and role theory.[2] In their place, he has attempted to create a theoretical approach that eliminates the shortcomings of these perspectives and that, at the same time, tries to blend interactionist concepts with those allowing for an understanding of the structural properties of societies.

To appreciate Giddens's strategy, I think that it is wise to begin by outlining his critique of social theory. In this way, I can place the strategy and substance of "structuration theory" into its critical context.

## THE CRITIQUE OF SOCIAL THEORY

### Rejecting Naturalism and Positivism

At the core of Giddens's effort to redirect social theory is the rejection of a "covering law" view of sociological explanation (see Chapter 1). In

---

[1]The basic theory is presented in numerous places, but the two most comprehensive statements are Anthony Giddens, *The Constitution of Society: Outline of the Theory of Structuration* (Oxford: Polity Press, 1984) and *Central Problems in Social Theory* (London: Macmillan Press, LTD, 1979). The University of California Press also has editions of these two books.

[2]See, in particular, Anthony Giddens, *Profiles and Critiques in Social Theory* (London: Macmillan Press LTD, 1982) and *New Rules of Sociological Method: A Positive Critique of Interpretative Sociologies* (London: Hutchinson Ross Publishing Co., 1976).

what I feel is a shortsighted view, he flatly dismisses the idea that sociology can be like the natural sciences. For Giddens, there can be no enduring abstract laws about social processes. In asserting this view, he echoes Herbert Blumer's charge that social organization is changeable by the acts of individuals, and thus, there can be no laws about the invariant properties of social organization.[3] And much like Blumer, he visualizes "the concepts of theory . . . should for many research purposes be regarded as sensitizing devices, nothing more."[4] I should emphasize, however, that the reasons for this assertion are different than those traditionally advocated by Chicago School symbolic interactionism.

First, Giddens asserts that social theorizing involves a "double hermeneutic" that, stripped of this jargon, asserts that the concepts and generalizations used by social scientists to understand social processes can be employed by agents to alter these processes, thereby potentially obviating the generalizations of "science." We must recognize, Giddens contends, that lay actors are also "social theorists who alter their theories in the light of their experience and are receptive to incoming information."[5] And thus, social science theories are not often "news" to lay actors, and when they are, such theories can be used to transform the very order they describe. For within the capacity of humans to be reflexive—that is, to think about their situation—is the ability to change it.[6]

Second, social theory is by its nature social criticism. Social theory often contradicts "the reasons that people give for doing things" and is, therefore, a critique of these reasons and the social arrangements that people construct in the name of these reasons. Sociology does not, therefore, need to develop a separate body of critical theory, as others have argued (see Chapter 9); it *is* critical theory by its very nature and by virtue of the effects it can have on social processes.

The implications of these facts, Giddens believes, are profound. We need to stop imitating the natural sciences. We must cease evaluating our success as an intellectual activity in terms of whether or not we have discovered "timeless laws." We must recognize that social theory does not exist "outside" our universe. We should accept the fact that what sociologists and lay actors do is, in a fundamental sense, very much the same. And, we must redirect our efforts at developing "sensitizing concepts" that allow us to understand the active processes of interaction among individuals as they produce and reproduce social structures while being guided by these structures.

---

[3]See Chapter 15.

[4]Giddens, *The Constitution of Society,* p. 326.

[5]Ibid., p. 335.

[6]Giddens lists conditions under which social science will not have "transformational implications" for social organization; see ibid., pp. 341–43.

## Obviating Sociological Dualisms

I think that one of the most useful criticisms mounted by Giddens is the rejection of dualisms in social theory—micro versus macro theory, subject (people) versus object (structure), individual versus society, subjectivism versus objectivism, and similar dichotomies around which great debate rages. At the heart of his approach is the assertion that "so-called 'microsociological' study does not deal with a reality that is somehow more substantial than that with which 'macrosociological' analysis is concerned. But neither, on the contrary, is interaction in situations of co-presence simply ephemeral, as contrasted to the solidity of large-scale or long-established institutions."[7] The process of "structur*ation*" is intended to emphasize that the individual-society, subject-object, and micro-macro dichotomies do not constitute a dualism, but a "duality." That is, people in interaction use the rules and resources that constitute social structure in their day-to-day routines in contexts of co-presence, and in so doing, they reproduce these rules and resources of structure. Thus, individual action, interaction, and social structure are all implicated in each other. They do not constitute separate realities, but a duality within the same reality, for "the structural properties of social systems are both the medium and the outcome of the practices that constitute those systems."[8] One cannot understand action and interaction without reference to the rules and resources of social structure, whereas one cannot fully understand large-scale, long-term institutional structures without knowledge of how actors use the rules and resources of these institutional structures in concrete interaction.

At times, Giddens recognizes, it is necessary to "bracket out" consideration of either individuals in interaction or institutional structures. But this is a methodological procedure rather than an ontological assertion. I think that Giddens is correct in his conclusion that too much social theory converts this methodological procedure of bracketing with ontological statements about what is really real in the social universe.

## The Critique of Functionalism and Evolutionism

In what I think can be viewed as the merciless flogging of two dying horses, Giddens has consistently attacked (1) functionalism, or the analysis of social phenomena in terms of the needs that structures meet; and (2) evolutionism, or the description of the inexorable stages that societies must pass through on the road to modernity. Functionalist theories are almost all evolutionary (see Chapters 2–5); and thus Giddens rejects them as an appropriate approach to understanding society. Similarly—and here

---

[7] Ibid., p. 26.

[8] Giddens, *Central Problems in Social Theory*, p. 69.

Giddens is more creative—he attacks Marx's work and much contemporary Marxism as both functional and evolutionary and, hence, not very useful.[9]

I think that Giddens's list of criticisms is fairly standard, and we need not review them here. However, I see the general argument as very important: functional analysis tends to ignore the active processes of agents in interaction and to overemphasize social structure as an "external constraint" on actors, whereas evolutionary analysis tends to stress the inexorable movement of societies in response to some causal factor, such as size, war, and means of production. For Giddens, the "duality of structure" is lost in all of this analysis of functional needs, the constraints of structure, the stages of development, and the "prime causes" of change. That is, agents in situations of interaction are not seen as doing very much; and structure is seen to march along disembodied from the actors who are involved in its reproduction or transformation.

## The Limits of Interactionism

Giddens draws upon interactionist theory, especially that developed by Erving Goffman. Yet, he is critical of Goffman and other interactionist theories in several respects. First, they tend to perpetuate the dualism (as opposed to duality) of individual versus structure. Rarely do interactionists discuss social structure in a way that allows for an understanding of how it is reproduced through the processes of interaction. Moreover, some interactionists are openly chauvinistic, dismissing institutional processes as somehow less "real" than face-to-face symbolic interaction.

Second, interactionist theories tend to ignore motivation. In other words, what drives actors to do what they do? There is an implicit view of actors, especially in Goffman's dramaturgy, as cynical manipulators of gestures in staging areas. But rarely are the questions asked: why do actors engage in certain gesturing practices?; why enter or exit a stage or region?; or why use a "folk method"? Thus, interactionist theory needs a revision in terms of a theory of motivation that avoids the imprecision and mysticism of psychoanalytic theory while moving beyond a view of actors as cynical and self-centered orchestrators of gestures.

Third, more structurally oriented forms of interactionism, such as structural role theory, begin to visualize roles as the constitutive basis of structure. In Giddens's view, it is actual practices of people or collective units, not roles, that are the point of articulation between the individual and society. While these practices may be influenced by an agent's position, "social systems . . . are regularized social practices, sustained in encounters." Too often, the concept of role has been used as a substitute

---

[9]See, in particular, Anthony Giddens, *A Contemporary Critique of Historical Materialism: Volume 1, Power, Property and the State* (London: Macmillan Press LTD, 1981).

for normative constraints on individuals who passively perform their assigned roles. As a result, the typification of structure as a system of roles
tends to remove the active, reflexive, creative, and potentially transformative behaviors of agents.

## The Critique of Structuralism

Giddens has been very critical of Claude Lévi-Strauss's structuralism (see
appendix to Chapter 19), because it simply ignores human agency or the
capacity of people to reflect, monitor, define, and decide. In such structuralist approaches, actors are pushed, if not compelled, to act in accordance with immanent systems of codes. Other forms of structural theorizing, such as Peter Blau's macrostructuralism, are chauvinistic and simply
define away as relevant to sociology the reflexive capacities of human
agents.[10] In such macrostructuralism, social structure simply requires actors to do its bidding.

In all of these and other structural theories, then, there is a failure
to recognize that structure is actively reproduced (or altered) by agents
in interaction. For Giddens, structure is not some ex cathedra, external,
and constraining force that makes humans into robots and dupes. Rather,
structure is implicated in, and reproduced by, the day-to-day routines of
people in interaction. It is, in Giddens's words, "both constraining and
enabling." One cannot, therefore, define away people in interaction as
peripheral to the task of sociological explanation.

Let me now summarize. Giddens criticizes sociological theory for its
unwarranted belief that universal laws can be developed, for its unnecessary dualisms, for its functionalism and evolutionism, for its failure to
implicate motives and structure in the process of interaction, and for its
tendency to view structure and symbols as somehow alien to the actors
who produce, reproduce, and transform these structures and symbols.
Unlike many critics, Giddens does not dismount his soap box at this point
and go home. To his credit, he then tries to develop an alternative mode
of theoretical analysis that, he believes, overcomes these deficiencies.

## THE "THEORY OF STRUCTURATION"

Since Giddens does not believe that abstract laws of social action, interaction, and organization exist, his "theory of structuration" is not a series
of propositions. Instead, I see the theory as a cluster of sensitizing concepts linked together discursively. Giddens's work is thus what I called a
*sensitizing conceptual scheme* in Chapter 1. The key concept is "structuration," which is intended to communicate the "duality of structure."

---

[10]See *The Constitution of Society,* pp. 207–13.

That is, social structure is used by active agents; and in so using the properties of structure, they transform or reproduce this structure. Thus, the process of structuration requires a conceptualization of the nature of structure, of the agents who use structure, and of the ways that these are mutually implicated in each other to produce varying patterns of human organization.

## Reconceptualizing Structure and Social System

For Giddens, structure can be conceptualized as the "rules" and "resources" that actors use in "interaction contexts" that extend across "space" and over "time." In so using these rules and resources, actors sustain or reproduce structures in space and time.

Rules are "generalizable procedures" that actors understand and use in various circumstances. For Giddens, a rule is a methodology or technique that actors know about, often only implicitly, and that provides a relevant formula for action.[11] From a sociological perspective, the most important rules are those which agents use in the reproduction of social relations over significant lengths of time and across space. These rules reveal certain characteristics: (1) they are frequently used in (a) conversations, (b) interaction rituals, and (c) the daily routines of individuals; (2) they are tacitly grasped and understood and are part of the "stock knowledge" of competent actors; (3) they are informal, remaining unwritten and unarticulated; and (4) they are weakly sanctioned through interpersonal techniques.[12]

With this conceptualization, Giddens subsumes (a) the functionalist's emphasis on institutional norms and cultural values, (b) the ethnomethodologist's emphasis on folk methods, (c) the structuralist's concern with the generative nature of symbols and codes, and (d) just about all other conceptualizations in between. The thrust of Giddens's argument is that rules are part of actors' "knowledgeability." Some may be normative in that actors can articulate and explicitly make reference to them, but many other rules are more implicitly understood and used to guide the flow of interaction in ways that are not easily expressed or verbalized. Moreover, actors can transform rules into new combinations as they confront and deal with each other and the contextual particulars of their interaction.

As the other critical property of structure, resources are facilities that actors use to get things done. For even if there are well-understood methodologies and formulas—that is, rules—to guide action, there must also be the capacity to perform tasks. Such capacity requires resources, or the material equipment and the organizational ability to act in situations.

---

[11]Ibid., pp. 20–21.
[12]Ibid., p. 22.

Giddens visualizes resources as what generates power.[13] Power is not a resource, as much social theory argues. Rather, the mobilization of other resources is what gives actors power to get things done. Thus, power is integral to the very existence of structure, for as actors interact, they use resources; and as they use resources, they mobilize power to shape the actions of others.

Giddens visualizes rules and resources as "transformational" and as "mediating."[14] What he means by these terms is that rules and resources can be transformed into many different patterns and profiles. Resources can be mobilized in various ways to perform activities and achieve ends through the exercise of different forms and degrees of power; rules can generate many diverse combinations of methodologies and formulas to guide how people communicate, interact, and adjust to each other. Rules and resources are mediating in that they are what tie social relations together. They are what actors use to create, sustain, or transform relations across time and in space. And because rules and resources are inherently transformational—that is, generative of diverse combinations—they can lace together many different patterns of social relations in time and space.

Giddens develops a typology of rules and resources that I think is rather vague and imprecise.[15] He sees the three concepts in this typology—domination, legitimation, and signification—as "theoretical primitives," which, I suspect, is an excuse for defining them imprecisely. The basic idea is that resources are the stuff of domination because they involve the mobilization of material and organizational facilities to do things. Some rules are transformed into instruments of legitimation because they make things seem correct and appropriate. Other rules are used to create signification, or meaningful symbolic systems, because they provide people with ways to see and interpret events. Actually, I think that the scheme makes more sense if the concepts of domination, legitimation, and signification are given less emphasis and the elements of his discussion are selectively extracted to create the typology presented in Figure 22-1.

In the left column of Figure 22-1, structure is viewed by Giddens as composed of rules and resources. Rules are transformed into two basic types of mediating processes: (1) normative, or the creation of rights and obligations in a context; and (2) interpretative, or the generation of schemes and stocks of taken-for-granted knowledge in a context. Resources are transformed into two major types of facilities that can mediate social relations: (1) authoritative resources, or the organizational capacity to control and direct the patterns of interactions in a context; and (2) al-

---

[13]Ibid., pp. 14–16.

[14]Here Giddens seems to be taking what is useful from "structuralism" and reworking these ideas into a more sociological approach.

[15]*The Constitution of Society,* p. 29 and *Central Problems in Social Theory,* pp. 97–107.

**FIGURE 22-1**  Social Structure, Social System, and the Modalities of Connection

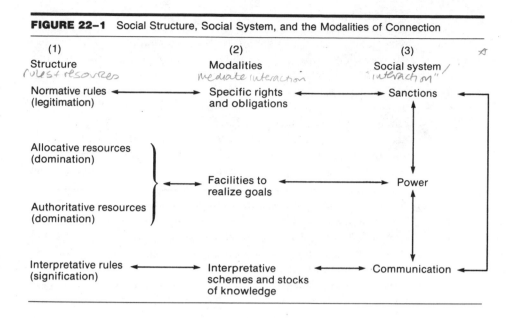

| (1)<br>Structure<br>*rules + resources* | (2)<br>Modalities<br>*mediate interaction* | (3)<br>Social system /<br>*"interaction"* |
|---|---|---|
| Normative rules ←→<br>(legitimation) | Specific rights ←→<br>and obligations | Sanctions |
| Allocative resources<br>(domination) } ←→<br>Authoritative resources<br>(domination) } | Facilities to ←→<br>realize goals | Power |
| Interpretative rules ←→<br>(signification) | Interpretative<br>schemes and stocks<br>of knowledge ←→ | Communication |

locative resources, or the use of material features, artifacts, and goods to control and direct patterns of interaction in a context.

Giddens sees these types of rules and resources as mediating interaction via three modalities, as is portrayed in column 2 of Figure 22-1: norms, facilities, and interpretative schemes. I have deviated somewhat from Giddens's discussion, but the same idea is that rules and resources are attached to interaction, or "social system" in Giddens's terms, via these three modalities. These modalities are then used to (a) generate the power that enables some actors to control others, (b) affirm the norms that, in turn, allow actors to be sanctioned for their conformity or nonconformity, and (c) create and use the interpretative schemes that make it possible for actors to communicate with each other.

Giddens also stresses that rules and resources are interrelated. In a discussion that I see as very similar to many by Talcott Parsons (see Chapter 3), Giddens emphasizes that the modalities and their use in interaction are only separated analytically. In the actual flow of interaction in the real empirical world, they exist simultaneously, thereby making their separation merely an exercise of analytical decomposition. Thus, the use of power, sanctions, and media of communication are interconnected, as are the rules and resources of social structure. In social systems, where people are co-present and interact, power is used to secure a particular set of rights and obligations as well as a system of communication; and conversely, power can be exercised only through communication and sanctioning.

I think it reasonable to ask: why does Giddens create this analytic scheme of social structure and social system, especially since it is very vague? I suspect that the answer resides in Giddens's desire to visualize structure in entirely different terms than either functional or structuralist theory. For Giddens, social structure is to be seen as something used by actors, not as some external reality that pushes and shoves actors around. Thus, social structure is defined as the rules and resources that can be transformed as actors use them in concrete settings. But then, the question arises: how is structure to be connected to what people actually do in interaction settings, or what Giddens terms "social systems"? The answer is the awkward notion of modalities, whereby rules and resources are transformed into power, sanctions, and communication. Thus, structure is not a mysterious system of codes, as Lévi-Strauss and other structural idealists imply, nor is it a set of determinative parameters and external constraints on actors, as Peter Blau and other macrostructuralists contend. In Giddens's conceptualization, social structure is transformative and flexible; it is "part of" actors in concrete situations; and it is used by them to create patterns of social relations across space and through time.

Moreover, I think that this typology allows Giddens to emphasize that as agents interact in social systems, they can reproduce rules and resources (via the modalities) or they can transform them. Thus, social interaction and social structure are reciprocally implicated. Structuration is, therefore, the dual processes in which rules and resources are used to organize interaction across time and in space and, by virtue of this use, to reproduce or transform these rules and resources.

## Reconceptualizing Institutions

For Giddens, institutions are systems of interaction in societies that endure over time and that distribute people in space. Giddens uses what I see as rather vague phrases like "deeply sedimented across time and in space in societies" to express the idea that when rules and resources are reproduced over long periods of time and in explicit regions of space, then institutions can be said to exist in a society. Giddens offers a typology of institutions in terms of the weights and combinations of rules and resources that are implicated in interaction.[16] If signification (interpretative rules) is primary, followed respectively by domination (allocative and authoritative resources) and then by legitimation (normative rules), a "symbolic order" exists. If authoritative domination, signification, and legitimation are successively combined, political institutionalization occurs. If allocative dominance, signification, and legitimation are ordered, eco-

---

[16]*Central Problems in Social Theory,* p. 107; and *The Constitution of Society,* p. 31.

**TABLE 22–1**  The Typology of Institutions

| Type of Institution | | Rank Order of Emphasis on Rules and Resources |
| --- | --- | --- |
| 1. Symbolic orders, or modes of discourse, and patterns of communication | are produced and reproduced by | the use of interpretative rules (signification) in conjunction with normative rules (legitimation) and allocative as well as authoritative resources (domination). |
| 2. Political institutions | are produced and reproduced by | the use of authoritative resources (domination) in conjunction with interpretative rules (signification) and normative rules (legitimation). |
| 3. Economic institutions | are produced and reproduced by | the use of allocative resources (domination) in conjunction with interpretative rules (signification) and normative rules (legitimation). |
| 4. Legal institutions | are produced and reproduced by | the use of normative rules (legitimation) in conjunction with authoritative and allocative resources (domination) and interpretative rules (signification). |

nomic institutionalization prevails. And if legitimation, dominance, and signification are rank ordered, institutionalization of law occurs. Table 22-1 summarizes Giddens's argument.

In so many ways, I see this typology as imprecise, and thankfully, it is not used very much in his subsequent analysis of structuralism. But once again I think it reasonable to ask: why generate it in the first place, especially since it smacks of the same kind of concept mongering found in much functional analysis? One reason appears to be Giddens's desire to reject functional modes of institutional analysis by presenting his alternative. Most functional theories analyze the process of institutional differentiation among, for example, economy, law, polity, education, and kinship (see Chapters 2-5). Such differentiation is typically seen to occur in an evolutionary framework, with each stage of evolution marked by increased separation and autonomy of institutions from each other. Giddens wishes to avoid this mechanical view of institutionalization, in several senses. First, systems of interaction in empirical contexts are a mixture of institutional processes. Economic, political, legal, and symbolic orders are not easily separated; there is usually an element of each in any social system context. Second, institutions are tied to the rules and resources that agents employ and thereby reproduce; they are not external to individuals because they are formed by the use of varying rules and resources in actual social relations. Third, the most basic dimensions of all rules and resources—signification, domination, and legitimation—are all involved in institutionalization; it is only their relative salience for actors that gives the stabilization of relations across time and in space its distinctive institutional character.

To his credit, Giddens is unlike many interactionists because he wants to acknowledge the importance of analyzing stabilized social relations—that is, institutionalization. But as with all interactionist theory, he wishes to stress that institutionalized social relations are actively reproduced in terms of the creative transformations of rules and resources that are employed by agents in actual interaction. Thus, one of the most important structural features of social relations is their institutionalization in space and across time. Such institutionalization moves along four dimensions—law, economy, political, and symbolic—which are distinguished from each other in terms of the relative use of various rules and resources. I am not sure that he needed the typology in Table 22-1 to make this important point, but it is the vehicle by which he chose to make his argument, and so, I have discussed it here.

## Structural Principles, Sets, and Properties

The extent and form of institutionalization in societies is related to what Giddens terms *structural principles*.[17] These are the most general principles that guide the organization of societal totalities. These are what "stretch systems across time and space," and they allow for "system integration" or the maintenance of reciprocal relations among units in a society. For Giddens, "structural principles can thus be understood as the principles of organization which allow recognizably consistent forms of time-space distanciation on the basis of definite mechanisms of societal integration."[18] I find such definitions rather vague, to say the least, but the basic idea seems to be that rules and resources are used by active agents in accordance with fundamental principles of organization. Such principles guide just how rules and resources are transformed and employed to mediate social relations.

On the basis of their underlying structural principles, three basic types of societies have existed: (1) "Tribal societies," which are organized in terms of structural principles that emphasize kinship and tradition as the mediating force behind social relations across time and in space; (2) "class-divided societies," which are organized in terms of an urban-rural differentiation, with urban areas revealing distinctive political institutions that can be separated from economic institutions, formal codes of law or legal institutions, and modes of symbolic coordination or ordering through written texts and testaments; and (3) "class societies," which involve

---

[17]*The Constitution of Society*, pp. 179–93.
[18]Ibid., p. 181.

structural principles that separate and yet interconnect all four institutional spheres, especially the economic and political.[19]

Structural principles are implicated in the production and reproduction of "structure*s*" or "structural sets." These structural sets are rule/resource bundles, or combinations and configurations of rules and resources, which are used to produce and reproduce certain types and forms of social relations across time and space. Giddens offers the example of how the structural principles of class societies (differentiation and clear separation of economy and polity) guide the use of the following structural set: *private property-money-capital-labor-contract-profit*. The details of his analysis are less important than the general idea that the general structural principles of class societies are transformed into more specific sets of rules and resources that agents use to mediate social relations. The above structural set is used in capitalist societies and, as a consequence, is reproduced. In turn, such reproduction of the structural set reaffirms the more abstract structural principles of class societies.

As these and other structural sets are used by agents and as they are thereby reproduced, societies develop "structural properties," which are "institutionalized features of social systems, stretching across time and space."[20] That is, social relations become patterned in certain typical ways. Thus, the structural set of private property-money-capital-labor contract-profit can mediate only certain patterns of relations; that is, if this is the rule/resource bundle with which agents must work, then only certain forms of relations can be produced and reproduced in the economic sphere. Hence, the institutionalization of relations in time and space reveals a particular form, or in Giddens's terms, structural property.

## Structural Contradiction

Giddens always wants to emphasize the inherent "transformative" potential of rules and resources. Structural principles, he argues, "operate in terms of one another but yet also contravene each other."[21] In other words, they reveal contradictions that can be either primary or secondary. A "primary contradiction" is one between structural principles that are formative and constitute a society, whereas a "secondary contradiction" is one that is "brought into being by primary contradictions."[22] For example, there is a contradiction between structural principles that mediate the institutionalization of private profits, on the one hand, and those that mediate socialized production, on the other. If workers pool their labor

---

[19]For an extensive discussion of this typology, see Giddens's *A Contemporary Critique of Historical Materialism.*

[20]*The Constitution of Society*, p. 185.

[21]Ibid., p. 193.

[22]Ibid.

to produce goods and services, it is contradictory to allow only some to enjoy profits of such socialized labor.

Contradictions are not, Giddens emphasizes, the same as conflicts. Contradiction is a "disjunction of structural principles of system organization," whereas conflict is the actual struggle between actors in "definite social practices."[23] Thus, the contradiction between private profits and socialized labor is not, itself, a conflict. It can create situations of conflict, such as struggles between management and labor in a specific time and place, but such conflicts are not the same as contradiction.

I must confess to being somewhat confused by Giddens's discussion of these topics. It is a most imprecise analysis. Yet, beneath all of the jargon is, I feel, an important insight: the institutional patterns of a society represent the creation and use by agents of very generalized and abstract principles; these principles represent the development of particular rules and the mobilization of certain resources; such principles generate more concrete "bundles" or "sets" of rules and resources that agents actively use to produce and reproduce social relations in concrete settings; and many of these principles and sets contain contradictory elements that can encourage actual conflicts among actors. In this way, structure "constrains" but is not something disembodied from agents. Rather, the "properties" of total societies are not external to individuals and collectivities but are persistently reproduced through the use of structural principles and sets by agents who act. Let me now turn to Giddens's discussion of these active agents.

## Agents, Agency, and Action

As is evident, Giddens visualizes structure as a duality, as something that is part of the actions of agents. And so in Giddens's approach, it is essential to understand the dynamics of human agency. He proposes a "stratification model," which I see as an effort to synthesize psychoanalytic theory, phenomenology, ethnomethodology, and elements of action theory. This model is depicted in the lower portions of Figure 22–2. For Giddens, "agency" denotes the events that an actor perpetrates rather than "intentions," "purposes," "ends," or other states. Agency is what an actor actually does in a situation that has visible consequences (not necessarily intended consequences). To understand the dynamics of agency requires analysis of each element on the model.

As I have drawn the model in Figure 22–2, it actually combines two overlapping models in Giddens's discussion, but his intent is reasonably clear: humans "reflexively monitor" their own conduct and that of others;

---

[23]Ibid., p. 198.

**FIGURE 22–2**  The Dynamics of Agency

Institutionalized
patterns
    (a)   Regionalized contexts
    (b)   Routinized contexts

Interaction with others in
contexts (social system)

Reflexive monitoring of actions

Rationalization through
discursive consciousness

Interpretation through
practical consciousness

Unconscious pressures

Unconscious motives to sustain
ontological security
(achieving trust with others
and reducing anxiety)

in other words, they pay attention, note, calculate, and assess the consequences of actions.[24] Monitoring is influenced by two levels of consciousness.[25] One is "discursive consciousness," which involves the capacity to give reasons for or rationalize what one does (and presumably to do the same for others' behavior). "Practical consciousness" is the stock of knowledge that one implicitly uses to act in situations and to interpret the actions of others. It is this knowledgeability that is constantly used, but rarely articulated, to interpret events—one's own and those of others. Almost all acts are indexical, to use Garfinkel's term, in that they must be interpreted by their context; and it is this implicit stock

---

[24]Ibid., pp. 5–7; see also *Central Problems in Social Theory*, pp. 56–59.

[25]His debt to Schutz and phenomenology is evident here, but he has liberated it from its subjectivism. See Chapter 14 on the emergence of interactionism.

of knowledge that provides these contextual interpretations and frameworks.[26]

There are also unconscious dimensions to human agency. There are many pressures to act in certain ways, which an actor does not perceive. Indeed, Giddens argues that much motivation is unconscious. Moreover, motivation is often much more diffuse than action theories portray. That is, there is no one-to-one relation between *an* act and *a* motive. Actors may be able to rationalize through their capacity for discursive consciousness in ways that make this one-to-one relationship seem to be what directs action. But in fact, much of what propels action lies below consciousness and, at best, provides very general and diffuse pressures to act. Moreover, much action may not be motivated at all; an actor simply monitors and responds to the environment.

In trying to reintroduce the *unconscious* into social theory, Giddens adopts Erik Erickson's psychoanalytic ideas.[27] The basic "force" behind much action is an unconscious set of processes to gain a "sense of trust" in interaction with others. Giddens terms this set of processes the *ontological security system* of an agent. That is, one of the driving but highly diffuse forces behind action is the desire to sustain ontological security or the sense of trust that comes from being able to reduce anxiety in social relations. Actors need to have this sense of trust. How they go about reducing anxiety to secure this sense is often unconscious because the mechanisms involved are developed before linguistic skills emerge in the young and because there may also be psychodynamics, such as repression, that keep these fundamental feelings and their resolution from becoming conscious. In general, Giddens argues that ontological security is maintained through the routinization of encounters with others, through the successful interpretation of acts in terms of practical or stock knowledge, and through the capacity for rationalization that comes with discursive consciousness.

As the top portions of Figure 22-2 emphasize, institutionalized patterns have an effect on, while being a consequence of, the dynamics of agency. As we will see shortly, unconscious motives for ontological security require routinized interactions (predictable, stable over time) that are regionalized (ordered in space). Such regionalization and routinization is the product of past interactions of agents, while being sustained or reproduced through the present (and future) actions of agents. To sustain routines and regions, actors must monitor their actions, while drawing upon their stock knowledge and discursive capacities. In this way, Giddens visualizes institutionalized patterns implicated in the very nature of agency. Institutions and agents cannot exist without each other, for institutions

---

[26]Here Giddens is using ideas of phenomenology and ethnomethodology without all the ontological and metaphorical rhetoric.

[27]*The Constitution of Society*, pp. 45–59.

are reproduced practices by agents, whereas the conscious and unconscious dynamics of agency depend upon the routines and regions provided by institutionalized patterns.

## Routinization and Regionalization of Interaction

Both the ontological security of agents and the institutionalization of structures in time and space depend upon routinized and regionalized interaction among actors. Routinization of interaction patterns is what gives them continuity across time, thereby reproducing structure (rules and resources) and structures (institutions). At the same time, routinization gives predictability to actions and, in so doing, provides for a sense of ontological security. Thus, routines become critical for the most basic aspects of structure and human agency. Similarly, regionalization orders action in space by positioning actors in places vis-à-vis one another and by circumscribing how they are to present themselves and act. As with routines, the regionalization of interaction is essential to the sustenance of broader structural patterns and ontological security of actors, because it orders people's interactions in space and time, which, in turn, reproduces structures and meets an agent's need for ontological security. Let me now elaborate on these general ideas because I think they mark an important contribution to social theory.

**Routines.** In discussing routines, Giddens sees them as the key link between the episodic character of interactions (they start, proceed, and end), on the one hand, and basic trust and security, on the other.[28] Moreover, "the routinization of encounters is of major significance in binding the fleeting encounter to social reproduction and thus to the seeming 'fixity' of institutions."[29] In a very interesting discussion in which he borrows heavily from Erving Goffman but with a phenomenological twist, Giddens proposes several procedures, or mechanisms, that humans use to sustain routines: (1) opening and closing rituals, (2) turn taking, (3) tact, (4) positioning, and (5) framing. These are not necessarily exclusive,[30] and I must confess that I am guessing here as to Giddens's actual intent; but the general idea is that people employ these mechanisms to sustain routines and, thereby, reproduce social structures while maintaining ontological security. Let me elaborate briefly on these five routines.

1. Since interaction is serial—that is, it occurs sequentially—there must be symbolic markers of opening and closing. Such markers are essential to the maintenance of routines because they indicate when

---

[28]Ibid., pp. 60–109.
[29]Ibid., p. 72.
[30]I have created this list from what is a much more rambling discussion.

in the flow of time the elements of routine interaction are to begin and end. There are many such interpersonal markers—words, facial gestures, positions of bodies—and there are physical markers, such as rooms, buildings, roads, and equipment that also signal when certain routinized interactions are to begin and end (note, for example, the interpersonal and physical markers for a lecture, which is a highly routinized interaction that sustains the ontological security of agents and perpetuates institutional patterns).

2. Turn taking in a conversation is another process that sustains a routine. All competent actors contain in their practical consciousness, or implicit stock of knowledge, a sense of how conversations are to proceed sequentially. There are "folk methods" that people rely on to construct sequences of talk, and in so doing, they sustain a routine and, hence, their psychological sense of security and the larger institutional context (think, for example, about a conversation that did not proceed smoothly in terms of conversational turn taking; and recall how disruptive this was for one's sense of order and routine).

3. Tact is, in Giddens's view, "the main mechanism that sustains 'trust' or 'ontological security' over long time-space spans." By tact, Giddens means "a latent conceptual agreement among participants in interaction" about just how each party is to gesture and respond and about what is appropriate and inappropriate.[31] People carry with them implicit stocks of knowledge that signal to them what would be "tactful" and what would be "rude" and "intrusive." And they use this sense of tact to regulate their emission of gestures, their talking, and their relative positioning in situations in order "to remain tactful," thereby sustaining their sense of trust and the larger social order. (Imagine interactions where tact is not exercised and how they disrupt routines, our sense of comfort, and our perceptions of an orderly situation.)

4. Giddens rejects the idea of "role" as very useful and substitutes the notion of "position." People bring to situations a position or "social identity that carries with it a certain range of prerogatives and obligations," and they emit gestures in a process of mutual positioning, such as locating their bodies in certain points, asserting their prerogatives, and signaling their obligations. In so doing, interactions can be routinized, and people can sustain their sense of mutual trust as well as the larger social structures in which their interaction occurs. (For example, examine a student-student or professor-student interaction in terms of positioning and determine how it sustains a sense of trust and the institutional structure.)

---

[31]*The Constitution of Society*, p. 75. Surprisingly, Giddens never really defines "tact," assuming we know what it means. I had to infer this definition.

5. Much of the coherence of positioning activities is made possible by "frames" that provide formulas for interpreting a context. Interactions tend to be framed in the sense that there are rules that apply to them, but these are not purely normative in the sense of precise instructions for participants. Equally important, frames are more implicitly held, and they operate as markers that assert when certain behaviors and demeanors should be activated. (For example, compare your sense of how to comport yourself at a funeral, cocktail party, class, and other contexts that are "framed.")

In sum, social structure is extended across time by these techniques that produce and reproduce routines. In so stretching interaction across time in an orderly and predictable manner, people realize their need for a sense of trust in others. In this way, then, Giddens connects the most basic properties of structure (rules and resources) to the most fundamental features of human agents (unconscious motives).

**Regionalization.** Structuration theory is concerned with the reproduction of relations not only across time but also in space. With the concept of regionalization of interaction, Giddens addresses the intersection of space and time.[32] For interaction is not just serial, moving in time; it is also located in space. Again borrowing from Goffman and also time-geography, Giddens introduces the concept of "locale" to account for the physical space in which interaction occurs as well as the contextual knowledge about what is to occur in this space. In a locale, actors are not only establishing their presence with respect to each other but they are also using their stocks of practical knowledge to interpret the context of the locale. Such interpretations provide them with the relevant frames, the appropriate procedures for tact, and the salient forms for sequencing gestures and talk.

Giddens classifies locales in terms of their "modes." Locales vary in terms of (1) their physical and symbolic boundaries, (2) their duration across time, (3) their span or extension in physical space, and (4) their character or the ways they connect to other locales and to broader institutional patterns. Locales also vary in terms of the degree to which they force people to sustain high public presence (what Goffman termed *front stage*) or to allow retreats to back regions where public presence is reduced (Goffman's *back stage*).[33] They also vary in regard to how much disclosure of self (feelings, attitudes, and emotions) that they require, some allowing "enclosure" or the withholding of self and other locales requiring "disclosure" of at least some aspects of self.

---

[32]Ibid., pp. 110–44.

[33]See Erving Goffman, *The Presentation of Self in Everyday Life* (Garden City, N.Y.: Doubleday Publishing, 1959).

**FIGURE 22–3**    Key Elements of "Structuration Theory"

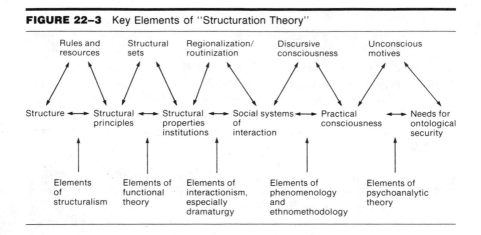

Regionalization of interaction through the creation of locales facilitates the maintenance of routines. In turn, the maintenance of routines across time and space sustains institutional structures. Thus, it is through routinized and regionalized systems of interaction that the reflexive capacities of agents operate to reproduce institutional patterns.

## THE THEORY OF STRUCTURATION: A SUMMARY AND ASSESSMENT

The most important part of Giddens's theoretical effort is the synthesis of diverse theoretical traditions. Figure 22–3 summarizes the main elements of his theory and indicates the theoretical tradition incorporated into each element. Giddens's conceptualization of structure as rules and resources that are inherently generative of many diverse combinations and his vision that societies reveal general structural principles and sets borrows from French structuralism (see appendix to Chapter 19) but, in a very real sense, turns this structuralism on its head. Structure is not something that is lodged in human biology, nor is it a free-floating system of ideas and ideals. Rather, it is actively produced, reproduced, and transformed by the capacities of agents. Structural analysis is thus reattached to the ongoing process of interaction.

The analysis of modalities through which rules and resources influence interaction and the typology of institutions conceptualizes the useful portions of functional analysis: the processes of institutionalization or the creation and maintenance of relatively stable social relations. This emphasis on institutions and institutionalization corrects for deficiencies in most forms of structuralism and interactionism. Some modes of structural analysis, such as the structural idealism of Lévi-Strauss, deny the ontological status of institutions, seeing them as merely derivative of more fundamental codes. Other forms of structural analysis, such as that by Peter Blau (see Chapter 20) or Bruce Mayhew,[34] analyze structure without reference to either the processes behind human agency and interaction or the symbolic rules and resources created and used by actors. At the other extreme, interactionists fail to address the topic of structure, typically viewing it as an "object," "frame," or some other given within which the interpersonal process unfolds. In contrast to the deficiencies of these approaches, Giddens's theory is vitally concerned with the way in which interaction becomes "deeply sedimented in time and space." But unlike much functional theorizing, institutions do not constitute an "external constraint" but a process of reproduction by actors in situations of co-presence.

The discussion of regionalization and routinization is an important theoretical contribution because it attaches institutional analysis to the interactions of actors in situations of co-presence. By inserting Goffman's dramaturgical concepts, coupled with time-space geography, Giddens anchors the rather vague typology of institutions and their imprecise portrayal as "deeply sedimented in time and space" to something less slippery: actors orienting their bodies and self in regionalized and routinized situations of co-presence. But because the staging regions of interaction exist within broader time-space regions as these are shaped by structural principles, sets, and institutions, the processes of interactive dramaturgy are connected to the broader structures of societal totalities. In this way, the limitations of most interactionist theory are overcome.

The analysis of discursive and practical consciousness draws from both phenomenology and ethnomethodology, but it connects them conceptually to interactionism, on the one side, and psychoanalytic theory, on the other. Giddens corrects for the extremes of ethnomethodology, which have tended to deny the ontological reality of social structures and phenomenology, which has frequently become an orgy of subjectivism. He does so by emphasizing the reflexive monitoring of action in situations of co-presence, with such monitoring involving layers of conscience and unconscious activity. Actors use rules and resources that are part of both discursive consciousness and practical stocks of knowledge; and this discursive and practical consciousness involves the subtle application of folk or ethno methods in regions of co-presence. And unlike phenomenology, ethnomethodology, and interactionism, which do not devote much effort to conceptualizing motivation, or unlike functionalism and its intellectual companion, "action theory," which are prone to develop rather mechanical views of motivation (e.g., for each act, there is a causative motive), Giddens reworks the psychoanalytic concept of anxiety and unconscious

---

[34]See, for example, Bruce Mayhew, "Hierarchical Differentiation in Imperatively Co-ordinated Associations," *Research in the Sociology of Organizations* 2 (1983), pp. 153–229.

motivation. The result is a perspective that ties diffuse and largely unconscious needs for "ontological security" into actors' reflexive monitoring, use of ethno methods, and participation in routinized interaction.

Such are the strong points of Giddens's theory, as I see them. He has performed, I feel, a remarkable synthesis that demonstrates how very diverse theoretical perspectives can be pulled together into a reasonably coherent theoretical scheme. I do see many problems with his approach, however. Let me now turn to these, cautioning that my perception is guided by my theoretical bias, which Giddens and many others in sociology do not share.

One major problem is that while Giddens's writing is crisp and eloquent, it is also vague. There is a great deal of jargon, metaphor, and just plain imprecision. It is often difficult to understand in more than a general way what is being said. I sense that "structuration theory" is very much like Parsonian functionalism in at least one sense: one has to "internalize" the perspective with all its imprecision in order to use it. One must become an intellectual convert to Giddens's cause and, in the best tradition of the ethnomethodologists' et cetera principle, accept what he has to say, even though you cannot quite understand some of it. One must feel, as opposed to verbalize, elements of structuration theory; and this is not, I feel, the way to build social theory.

The above is a remarkable conclusion, I admit, in light of the fact that the theory has been articulated several times in major works, has received considerable and deserved attention,[35] has always offered many definitions of concepts and graphic portrayals of their relations, and has even presented us with a glossary of theoretical terms in its latest incarnation.[36] Thus, it might be seriously asked: how can I reach the conclusion that the theory is vague? It just is, for several reasons. First, the theory is actually a series of definitions. The linkages among concepts are always rather vaguely stated, despite their suggestiveness. Second, Giddens often argues by example rather than analytically. It is extremely difficult to interpret an analytical discussion that is presented by example. (For example, Giddens offers the same example in several works to illustrate the concepts of structural principles and structural sets; and yet, the definitions of these ideas and the conceptual discussion of them are decidedly unclear.)

Another problem is that Giddens's theory is, in reality, only a system of concepts. It is very much like Talcott Parsons's strategy of "analytical realism," although I find Giddens's scheme far more interesting and in-

---

[35]For recent commentaries, see the special volumes of the following journals devoted to Giddens's work: *Theory, Culture, and Society*, vol. 1 (no. 2, 1982) and *Journal for the Theory of Social Behavior*, vol. 13 (no. 1, 1983). See also John B. Thompson, *Studies in the Theory of Ideology* (Berkeley, Calif.: University of California Press, 1984).

[36]*The Constitution of Society*, pp. 373–77.

triguing than Parsons's. Giddens's theory is a series of definitions that are not precisely linked together. Moreover, the scheme tends to become concerned with its own architecture—that is, with the elaboration of additional concepts in a vain effort to "complete" the edifice that, like all conceptual schemes, just keeps growing.

As Giddens admits, this conceptual scheme offers "sensitizing concepts" for the researcher. He does not believe that a natural science view of explanation is appropriate for the social sciences, and he consistently associates functionalism, naturalism, and objectivism—the unholy alliance or "orthodox consensus" that he and others are breaking down. The irony is that he produces a scheme that in its form looks very much like Parsons's. The substantive thrust is, of course, vastly different and superior to Parsons's. But it looks like Parsons's scheme in its overconcern with conceptual definitions, in its typological character, and in its need to be intellectually internalized when using it to analyze a particular problem. (I should add, however, that both Giddens's and Parsons's interpretation of empirical events is highly stimulating[37]; and thus as others internalize and use Giddens's scheme, I am sure interesting interpretations of empirical events will result.)

These problems, which many would not see as problems at all, stem from what I believe is the major deficiency of Giddens's approach: the rejection of positivism and naturalism. Much of this rejection is made plausible by associating a search for natural laws with functionalism, evolutionism, and other highly deficient forms of theorizing. But guilt by association is not a sufficient reason to reject the search for abstract principles. If one does not believe that there are invariant properties of the social universe that can be articulated in abstract principles, then what is a theorist to do? The answer is: construct conceptual schemes that sensitize us to empirical processes and that allow us to describe rather than explain these processes. In fact, descriptions of events are what Giddens and many others mean by explanation.

His view of explanation is misguided, although I must confess that Giddens has produced an important contribution with it (I can only imagine how much better it would be if he dropped this extreme antiscience viewpoint). There are several reasons for this assertion, which, I should emphasize again, many others do not share. First, Giddens's work contradicts his belief that there are no invariant properties of the social world. If there are not basic and fundamental processes, what good is his conceptual scheme? Will it not be outdated as soon as lay actors incorporate it? My answer is no; and so is Giddens's, at least implicitly. Giddens has isolated some of the basic properties and processes of the universe; and

---

[37]And in Chapter 6 of ibid., he uses the scheme to re-interpret insightfully several empirical studies.

just because lay actors know about them and lock them into their discursive and practical consciousness, these properties will not change. Second, and this is related to the above point, Giddens has a very narrow view of what a law is. For Giddens, a law is an empirical generalization—a statement of covariance among empirical events. If this is your vision of law, then it is easy to assert that there are no universal laws, since indeed empirical events change (in accord, I should add, with many of the invariant processes in Giddens's conceptual scheme). Third, I think there are several examples of laws in Giddens's scheme, and it is at just these points where he articulates a law that the scheme takes on more clarity and, for me at least, more interest. Here is one example of a law that Giddens articulates but that he would deny as universal: "The level of anxiety experienced at the level of discursive and practical levels of consciousness is a positive function of the degree of disruption in the daily routines for an actor." There is also a similar proposition about anxiety and unconscious trust and ontological security, but I will for the present ignore this. There are many propositions like this one in Giddens's scheme; and these are universal. If they were not, then his scheme would not make any sense. And most importantly, the law is not obviated by our knowledge of it, for an actor will not feel less anxiety if day-to-day routines are disrupted. One might even use the law to diagnose the problem and create new, or restore the old, routines, but in the process, the law has not been obviated. For, when one's routines are disrupted, the individual will experience anxiety.

I have not extracted these and many propositions from Giddens, since it would violate the essence of his approach. But here resides the great flaw; and I hope that others working with Giddens's concept are not so antipositivistic as he. For there is too much insight into the basic properties and dynamics of human action, interaction, and organization to use the scheme as a mere "sensitizing device." It has far more potential than Giddens would admit for helping develop a natural science of society—that is, for developing abstract laws of the social universe.

# Name Index

i

# Subject Index

## ABOUT THE AUTHOR

**Jonathan H. Turner** is professor of Sociology at the University of California at Riverside. He received his Bachelor of Arts degree from the University of California in 1965 and his Ph.D. from Cornell University in 1968. He is the author of fourteen books on a variety of topics, including sociological theory, American society, social organization, and ethnic relations. He is currently writing two books on theoretical sociology, one dealing with the process of social interaction and the other on macrostructural processes in societies.

A NOTE ON THE TYPE

The text of this book is set in 10/12 Century Schoolbook, a typeface
based on a design drawn in 1894 by L. B. Benton and T. L. DeVinne
for the *Century* magazine. Century Schoolbook is an excellent example
of a refined Egyptian typeface. The Egyptian family of faces is
characterized by thick slab serifs and little contrast between thick and
thin strokes. The large x-height and simple letter forms of Century
Schoolbook make it very legible.

Composed by Impressions, Inc., Madison, Wisconsin.

Printed and bound by R. R. Donnelley & Sons, Crawfordsville, Indiana.